To

M. L. SEIDMAN
F. E. SEIDMAN
P. K. SEIDMAN

My Brothers, Partners, and Collaborators

Seidman's Legislative History of Excess Profits Tax Laws

SEIDMAN'S
LEGISLATIVE HISTORY
of
EXCESS PROFITS TAX LAWS

1946-1917

by

J. S. SEIDMAN

*Member, the New York Bar; Partner,
Seidman & Seidman, Certified Public Accountants;
Author, Seidman's Legislative History
of Federal Income Tax Laws*

NEW YORK
PRENTICE-HALL, INC.
1947

COPYRIGHT, 1947, BY
PRENTICE-HALL, INC.

All Rights Reserved.

PREFACE

OUR FEDERAL excess profits tax laws are far from clear. One way—and frequently the only way—to find out what they mean is to determine, through their legislative history, what Congress intended them to mean.

The aim of this book is to reveal that intent through the mouth of Congress. Specifically, this book seeks to place under the thumb of all those interested in the meaning of the federal excess profits tax laws everything of interpretive significance said to or by Congress and passed or rejected by it, from the beginning of excess profits tax legislation (1917) to date.

It should now be possible to run up and down the ladder of time and in short order ascertain precisely what Congress said and intended on any particular subject in excess profits taxes ever since it began legislating on that subject.

All tax services and texts start *with* the law and work out *from* it to the rulings, adjudications, and commentary. None of them builds up *to* the law. There is a great void regarding the law's formative stages. Occasionally, a committee report is mentioned, but nowhere is the full story given.

Why this void? That there is a practical need for familiarity with Congressional intent has long been recognized. The sole or clinching argument in many a tax case and the sustaining basis for many a ruling have been provided by an explanation of the law made during its course through Congress. What is more, I am convinced that many a decision or ruling would have gone along different channels, or controversy might never have arisen in the first place, had the Congressional intent, as manifested by the entire legislative history of the particular provision in question, been brought to the notice of the judicial or administrative bodies.

Investigations into legislative history are, as a rule, woefully inadequate. Running down legislative history has probably meant little more to most of us than looking for applicable committee reports. Reference to Congressional discussion is rare, and hearings before the respective committees have been almost entirely neglected.

Furthermore, the search is generally confined to material arising under the particular act involved. The history and significance of analogous provisions in other acts are generally overlooked or ignored. This may be fatal. For example, the relief provisions in the 1942 Act are not new to that act. They have a long trail of antecedents in prior acts. What was said about them in the formulation of the prior acts is just as vital as what was said while the 1942 Act was under consideration

by Congress. In point of fact, some features may not have been discussed in the development of the 1942 Act for the reason that all there
was to say had already been said in the course of passage of the prior
acts. If, therefore, our search stops with the 1942 Act, we erroneously
conclude that Congress never did explain what it intended by those
features of the relief provisions.

Another bad omission in the ordinary examination into legislative
history is the *unenacted* bill. This is especially true of the type of bill
that is ultimately merged into the basic revenue act or is the prototype
of a later enactment. Frequently, in the course of development of a
basic revenue act, floor amendments are made at the last minute without any explanation. Often these floor amendments are merely provisions that have been nursed along in a separate bill. These provisions
may have been amply explained in the committee reports, Congressional
discussion, or hearings on the separate bill. If, therefore, a review of
legislative history is confined only to material directly under the basic
revenue act, a conclusion that Congress has not explained the provision
is erroneous.

In short, the probabilities are that the average investigation is a hit-
or-miss affair, with the omissions predominating. This is a very natural
condition. Time and patience are required. Moreover, the inaccessi-
bility of the necessary material is a formidable barrier. Consider merely
the basic material needed: all the bill prints in the different legislative
stages of all bills, enacted and unenacted, pertaining to excess profits
taxes from the present time back to 1917; all the committee reports,
Congressional Records, and reports of hearings. Although at any one
time, only one particular provision may be under investigation, the
entire body of material must be examined to locate the segment applicable to the one provision. This exhaustive examination becomes
necessary since the material, with the exception of the bill prints, is
generally not specifically marked or arranged in any particular order.

Through this book, it is hoped that it shall no longer be necessary for
any of us to grapple with such a task, but that instead, we shall now
have, readily available, a complete legislative history of excess profits
tax provisions.

*   *   *

The foregoing may explain why, in spite of the practical need for a
compilation of legislative history on excess profits taxes, no such work
has previously appeared. What seemed at first to be a mere "scissors-
and-paste" job developed, in my case, into a long, arduous task. Even
then, I needed and received extensive assistance.

My brothers and partners, M. L. Seidman, F. E. Seidman, and P. K.
Seidman are really co-authors. To them this work is dedicated.

The needed material would not have been completely accessible to
me but for the good offices of Senator James A. Meade of New York,
his military aide, Lt. Commander J. J. McTigue, and the cooperation
of Elmer A. Lewis (House Document Room), as well as members of

the staff of the Ways and Means Committee, Senate Finance Committee, and Joint Committee on Internal Revenue Taxation.

The burden of the extensive secretarial work was carried by Harry Levine and Margaret Macaulay. I frequently consulted Benjamin Grund, my partner and chief of the firm's Tax Department.

J. S. SEIDMAN

OCTOBER, 1947

TABLE OF CONTENTS

GUIDES TO THE USE OF THIS BOOK

AS IN the case of *Seidman's Legislative History of Federal Income Tax Laws*, a compact yet comprehensive one-volume treatment has been made possible through several simplifying and time-saving features.

Provisions having no legislative history have not been set forth at all. By a careful process of selection (as later detailed), the statutory provisions have been confined to essential, substantive items, and the wording of even those items has been set forth only to the extent required by their legislative history. Provisions similar in language or scope and with a common legislative history have been treated jointly, thereby avoiding a tremendous amount of duplication.

To the same end, where a report of the Senate Finance Committee in respect to a particular provision was lengthy, and was the same or substantially the same as the Ways and Means Committee report, a simple statement to that effect has been made without duplicating the report.

All discussion on the floor of Congress has been combed to eliminate mere parliamentary formalities or other irrelevancies and mere repetition of the contents of committee reports. Discussion on matters not deemed particularly weighty or illuminating from an interpretive standpoint has been either omitted entirely or set forth by digest or general reference.

Hearings in all cases have been set forth by descriptive digest. Express reference has been made to witnesses from the Treasury Department or other official sources because of the interpretive significance of such testimony.

In the case of unenacted but related provisions, the gist rather than the complete text has been set forth where the substance and not the language was the material factor.

General order of arrangement.—The order of arrangement is by Code sections. For each Code section, the material has been arranged act by act, with the latest act first. The 1917 and 1918 material has been set forth separately, in order of section number, and tied in by cross reference to the respective Code sections.

The respective items of legislative history applicable to a provision have been set forth in the order approximating their relative weight for interpretive purposes. In this regard, a provision is considered to have a legislative history in a particular act if: (a) a language change occurred on its way through Congress; (b) a committee reported on it; (c) floor discussion took place on it; (d) hearings were held on it; or

(e) there was an unenacted provision related to it which had a legislative history.

Hearings of the various committees included.—The material includes reference not only to the hearings of the Ways and Means Committee and Senate Finance Committee, but also the special hearings of the Joint Committee on Internal Revenue Taxation in 1946 on section 722.

The hearings on the Second Revenue Act of 1940 originated with joint hearings by the Ways and Means Committee and Senate Finance Committee. These hearings have been labelled in this book as Ways and Means Committee hearings in view of subsequent hearings held independently by the Senate Finance Committee.

Importance of prior and subsequent acts.—It is at all times necessary to review the legislative history of analogous provisions in both prior and subsequent acts for the light they may cast on the provision of the particular act under investigation. What Congress said about a provision in one act is vital in the interpretation of a corresponding provision in another act. Furthermore, legislative history of a provision does not necessarily begin with the act in which the provision is first adopted or end with the act in which it last appears. Not infrequently earlier acts contain a rejected proposal for the enactment of a similar provision, or later acts contain a rejected proposal for its restoration. The legislative history of these proposals may be highly informative.

Exclusion of subjects of limited significance.—Provisions deemed to have no substantial interpretive significance have been excluded. As a result, provisions having to do with rates or exemptions, and those dealing with administrative detail such as returns and tax payments, penalties, publicity of figures, and the like, have not been treated. Substantive provisions of the Code, outmoded because retroactively repealed to the beginning of excess profits taxes in 1940, like the provision for highest bracket amount, or the binding election of the income or invested capital credit, have all been excluded.

Exclusion of provisions with insubstantial or no legislative history.—Provisions having no legislative history in the 1940 or subsequent Revenue Acts have not been set forth at all. In the case of the 1918 and prior acts, such provisions have been set forth only because copies of these acts may not be readily available.

Changes of a mere clerical nature, like spelling, capitalization, or ending punctuation, have not been considered sufficiently important to cause a provision to be set forth if such changes were the only items in the legislative history.

Even as to provisions included, if part of the legislative history material branched off into inconsequential subjects, that part was omitted. Thus, there have been omitted reports or discussion as to whether relief claims must be filed in six months, one year, etc. Then again, where a report merely declared that a given provision is the same as the existing act, and where that report constituted the sole item of legislative history, it has been omitted. The same practice has been followed in the case of Conference Committee reports that merely set forth the language changes made in conference without explanation.

Whether an omission of a provision has been made because of subject matter or because of lack of legislative history can readily be determined from the section index. If the provision has not been listed at all in the section index, the omission was made because of subject matter. All other provisions have been listed in the section index even though they may have no legislative history.

Scope of inclusion of Congressional discussion.—Consistent with the policy of confining material to what is meaningful from an interpretive standpoint, all discussion on the floor of Congress appertaining to general economic and political aspects has been omitted. Furthermore, only discussion arising in the regular course of debate on the bill or act involved has been set forth. Inserts in the *Congressional Record* of radio talks, articles of outsiders, memorials, and the like, have been excluded.

In conformity with the principle that items having no legislative history were to be omitted, amendments ordered to lie on the table and amendments acted upon without discussion have been omitted.

Units of statutory subdivision.—The statutory parts have been set forth on the basis of the smallest structural unit (section, subsection, paragraph, or subparagraph, as the case may be) which, from the nature of the legislative history, lends itself to individual treatment. In most instances, this has meant the paragraph.

The section as a whole has been considered the unit with respect to material applicable in common to all subdivisions of a section. Such material has been labelled as being general in character and has been crossreferenced as well as indexed under each of the respective subdivisions of the section. For example, for section 718(a)(6), of the Code there appears in a center heading "Sec. 718(a)(6) In General". This has been crossreferenced under every subdivision of sec. 718(a)(6) as well as in the index.

In all cases, the setting of the particular provision in terms of its section or other subdivision heading has been shown. For example, sec. 710(c)(2) of the Second Revenue Act of 1940 has been set up as follows:

[SEC. 710. IMPOSITION OF TAX.]

[(c) Unused Excess Profits Credit Adjustment.—]

(2) Definition of unused excess profits credit.—

(Section headings that underwent language changes in their course through Congress have been explained only in connection with the first provision in the book involving the heading. The explanation has not been repeated where the heading is thereafter used in bracketed form merely to provide the setting for some subdivision.)

In some provisions in the statute there is an introductory sentence or clause that serves as a lead-off for all subdivisions that follow. For example, sec. 727 in the Second Revenue Act of 1940 starts as follows: "The following corporations shall be exempt from the tax imposed by this subchapter:" This introductory part may have a legislative history of its own, and for reference purposes, has been considered as part of the first ensuing subdivision. Here it would be sec. 727(a).

Incidentally, the Second Revenue Act of 1940 has been referred to merely as the Revenue Act of 1940 or the 1940 Act. Any reference to the first Revenue Act of 1940 has been specifically described as such.

Provisions treated jointly.—Joint treatment has been accorded different parts of the statute that are basically alike in language or scope, and whose legislative history is of common applicability. An illustration of this is provided in secs. 711(a)(1)(E) and 711(a)(2)(H) of the Code. The language of both is virtually the same. The one deals with an adjustment for the income credit; the other, with the same adjustment for the invested capital credit. The joint treatment avoids a tremendous amount of duplication.

There are instances where two Code provisions have been treated jointly, but the legislative history in a particular act affects only one of them. For example, sec. 722(a) and sec. 720(d) have been treated jointly. However, in the 1942 Act, the legislative history affects only sec. 720(d). A notation in the margin sets this forth so that those interested in sec. 722(a) will automatically know that sec. 722(a) is not involved at that particular point.

Order of arrangement in special situations.—Where, in addition to reports, discussion, or hearings on the particular act, *material from other acts* has been set forth under the same provision, the material of the particular act has been shown first, followed, under the respective report, discussion, and hearings captions, by the material from the other acts, with the most recent act first. For example, if under a provision of the Revenue Act of 1940 reference has been made to reports, not only on that Act, but also on the Revenue Acts of 1941 and 1942, there has been shown first, the 1940 Act reports, and then, appropriately identified, the 1942 and 1941 Act reports in the order mentioned.

Where references to hearings are the only items of legislative history of a provision in a particular act, they have not been set forth under that act but under the analogous provision in the nearest act (in point of time) having a more extensive legislative history. In this way it has been possible to avoid setting up statutory provisions solely as a background for references to hearings.

Unenacted provisions and their history have been set off by horizontal lines, as the last item in the history of the particular Code section. The legislative history of unenacted provisions has been treated as part of the legislative history of enacted provisions to which they are most nearly related in subject matter.

Amendments made by special acts have been set forth under their own label in their proper chronology. Thus, immediately before sec. 722(d) in the Revenue Act of 1942, there has been set forth, and so described in the margin, the amendment to it made by the Act of Dec. 17, 1943.

Minor errors in official material.—In the early acts particularly, there are minor differences—primarily in punctuation, capitalization, and so forth—between the acts as they appear in the final bill prints and as they appear in the statutes-at-large. Unless it was obvious which one was correct, the Conference Committee bill print or report has been followed. Where there was no such print or report, the statutes-at-large have been followed.

Errors of spelling, grammar, and the like, in reports and in the *Congressional Record* have been permitted to stand exactly as they appear in these official documents. Errors in section reference have been called to attention by footnote.

Seidman's Legislative History of Excess Profits Tax Laws

CODE SECTIONS AND THEIR LEGISLATIVE HISTORY

[SEC. 710.   IMPOSITION OF TAX.]

[(a)   **Imposition.—**]

[(1)   **General Rule**—There shall be levied * * * a tax equal to * * *]

(B)   an amount which * * * equals 80 per centum of the corporation surtax net income * * * *without regard to 80 per centum of the credit provided in section 26 (h) (relating to credit for dividends paid on certain preferred stock).*

Committee Reports

Report—Senate Finance Committee (78th Cong., 1st Sess., S. Rept. 627).— Subsection (b), which was not in the House bill, amends section 710 (a) (1) (B) of the code to provide that in computing corporation surtax net income, for purpose of applying the 80 percent limitation provided in such section, 80 percent of the credit provided in section 26 (h), relating to credit for dividends paid on the preferred stock of public utilities, shall be disregarded. This amendment is to correct a technical error in drafting whereby a public utility subject to the 80 percent limitation would have its total income and excess profits tax liability reduced by an amount equal to 80 percent of the dividends which it paid on its preferred stock during the taxable year. The credit provided in section 26 (h) was intended, however, as a credit only for purposes of the surtax. By providing that corporation surtax net income shall be computed for purposes of the 80 percent limitation without regard to 80 percent of the credit provided in section 26 (h), your committee has made the necessary correction, and at the same time has provided that a public utility which is subject to the 80 percent limitation shall receive the same tax advantage as a result of paying dividends on its preferred stock as a public utility which is

not subject to such limitation.   (p. 71)

Report—Conference Committee (78th Cong., 2d Sess., H. Rept. 1079).— Amendment No. 86: This amendment, for which there is no corresponding provision in the House bill, is designed to correct a technical drafting error made in section 710 (a) (1) (B) of the code, as added by section 202 of the Revenue Act of 1942, whereby a public utility would become subject to the 80-percent income and excess-profits tax limitation and would have its excess-profits tax liability reduced by virtue of the credit for dividends paid on its preferred stock during the taxable year. The credit for dividends paid provided in section 26 (h) of the code, however, was intended as a credit only for purposes of the surtax. The amendment provides that for purposes of the 80-percent tax limitation corporation surtax net income shall be computed without regard to 80 percent of the credit for dividends paid provided in section 26 (h). This not only corrects the error but also provides that a public utility subject to the 80-percent tax limitation obtains the same benefit from the payment of dividends on its preferred stock as a public utility which is not subject to the 80-percent limitation. The House recedes.   (p. 59)

2   SECTION 710(a)(1)(B) [See inside back cover

Congressional Discussion

Discussion—Senate (Cong. Rec. Vol. 90).—MR. TAFT. It never was intended by the Congress last year when it exempted preferred stock that it was in any way to decrease the excess-profits tax. It was only intended to affect the super-taxes on corporations. The Treasury Department says that it did affect the excess-profits tax merely because of a mistake in drafting and that immediately after the bill was passed they advised everyone it was a mistake and that they would endeavor to have it corrected retroactively. I do not think there was any intention when we permitted the deduction of preferred-stock dividends in any way to modify or decrease the excess-profits tax.

* * *

MR. LA FOLLETTE. Mr. President, this matter has been brought to my attention since the committee acted upon the bill. It appears that in drafting the original provision, language was employed which I think clearly was subject to the interpretation that companies could pay dividends on their preferred stocks and get credit for them. The Treasury Department later, after the bill was enacted, realized that a mistake had been made in drafting, and issued a bulletin, if that is the proper term, the date of which, as I recall, was April 29, 1943, stating that an error had been made, that it was solely intended as a relief provision, and that they would seek to have the language corrected in the next tax bill. (p. 109)

Sec. 710(a)(3)

1943
203(b)

[SEC. 710. IMPOSITION OF TAX.]

[(a) Imposition.—]

(3) **Taxable Years Beginning in 1941 and Ending after June 30, 1942.**—In the case of a taxable year beginning in 1941 and ending after June 30, 1942, the tax shall be an amount equal to the sum of—

(A) that portion of a tentative tax under this subchapter, computed as if the law applicable to taxable years beginning on January 1, 1941, were applicable to such taxable year, which the number of days in such taxable year before July 1, 1942, bears to the total number of days in such taxable year, plus

(B) that portion of a tentative tax under this subchapter, computed as if the law applicable to taxable years beginning on January 1, 1941, were applicable to such taxable year, but as if the amendments made by sections 105 (a), (b) (other than those relating to dividends on the preferred stock of public utilities), (c), (d), and (e) (1), 202, and 206 of the Revenue Act of 1942 were applicable to such taxable year, which the number of days in such taxable year after June 30, 1942, bears to the total number of days in such taxable year.

Committee Reports

Report—Ways and Means Committee (78th Cong., 1st Sess., H. Rept. 871).—Section 710 (a) (3), as added by section 203 of the Revenue Act of 1942, contains special rules for the computation of the excess profits tax under subchapter E of chapter 2 in the case of taxable years beginning in 1941 and ending after June 30, 1942. This tax is the sum of the pro-rated portions of two tentative taxes.

The first tentative tax is computed under the law applicable to the taxable year beginning in 1941 and at the rates (or in the amounts of tax) specified for such a taxable year but without regard to the provisions of section 710 (a) (3). The second tentative tax is computed under the law applicable to the taxable year beginning in 1941, but with certain modifications relating to certain deductions and credits in the base for computing the tax, and at the rates (or in the amounts of tax) specified for a taxable year beginning in 1942. The second tentative tax is to be computed without regard to the provisions of section 710 (a) (3), except insofar as certain provisions of the code are made applicable by such section.

In computing the second tentative excess profits tax under section 710 (a) (3) (B) the 80 percent limitation provided by section 710 (a) (1) (B) might be applicable. Under this limitation the excess profits tax cannot exceed an amount which when added to the tax imposed under chapter 1 equals 80 percent of the corporation surtax net income (computed without regard to the credit provided in section 26 (e) relating to income subject to excess profits tax imposed by subchapter E of chapter 2). If such limitation is applicable, it becomes necessary to ascertain the amount of the tax under chapter 1 for the taxable year. It was the intention that in computing the second tentative excess profits tax under section 710 (a) (3) (B) the amount of the tax under chapter 1 to be used in computing the 80 percent limitation should be the second tentative normal and surtax computed under subparagraph (B) of section 108 (a) (1). That section provides for a tax computation similar to that of section 710 (a) (3) in computing normal tax and surtax. However, because of a technical inadvertence, no specific provision was inserted in section 710 (a) (3) providing that the total tax computed under section 108 (a) (1) should be disregarded, and that only the second tentative tax computed under

section 108 (a) (1) (B) should be used in the computation of the 80 percent limitation. Moreover, this technical omission might give rise to a circular computation in cases in which the 80 percent limitation is applicable since the first tentative normal and surtax to be used in computing the total normal tax and surtax under section 108 (a) (1) (A) is based upon the allowance of the excess profits tax as a deduction in computing net income, and since the portion of such excess profits tax under the 80 percent limitation could not be ascertained until the total normal tax and surtax had been first computed under 108 (a) (1) (A).

The regulations promulgated by the Commissioner under section 710 (a) (3) give expression to the computation intended to be prescribed by section 710 (a) (3) which would require a parallel computation of the first tentative excess profits tax under section 710 (a) (3) (A) and the first tentative normal tax and surtax under section 108 (a) (1) (A), and a parallel computation of the second tentative excess profits tax under section 710 (a) (3) (B) and the second tentative normal tax and surtax under section 108 (a) (1) (B). Inasmuch as an amendment to section 710 to relate to taxable years beginning in 1943 and ending in 1944 was required in any event, your committee has made an exception to the decision to postpone to next year clarifying changes required as a result of the provisions added by the Revenue Act of 1942, and has therefore amended section 710 (a) (3) and section 108 (a) (1), retroactively, so as to remove any technical ambiguity which might have inhered in such sections as added by the Revenue Act of 1942, to clarify their provisions, and to give express statutory approval to the regulations issued by the Commissioner. (p. 55-57)

Report—Senate Finance Committee (78th Cong., 1st Sess., S. Rept. 627).— Same as Ways and Means Committee Report. (p. 72-73)

Committee Hearings

Hearings—Senate Finance Committee.—Objections to fiscal year computation. (J. W. Hooper, p. 728; W. A. Cooper, p. 1101-05)

| Sec. 710(b)(3) |

1940
201

[SEC. 710. IMPOSITION OF TAX.]

[(b) **Definition of Adjusted Excess Profits Net Income.**— * * * means the excess profits net income * * * minus the sum of:]

(3) **Unused Excess Profits Credit.**—IN THE CASE OF A TAXPAYER THE NORMAL-TAX NET INCOME OF WHICH FOR THE TAXABLE YEAR IS NOT MORE THAN $25,000, THE AMOUNT BY WHICH THE EXCESS PROFITS CREDIT FOR THE PRECEDING TAXABLE YEAR (IF BEGINNING AFTER DECEMBER 31, 1939) EXCEEDS THE EXCESS PROFITS NET INCOME FOR SUCH PRECEDING TAXABLE YEAR.

Committee Reports

Report—Conference Committee (76th Cong., 3d Sess., H. Rept. 3002).—An additional credit is also allowed, in computing such adjusted excess-profits net income, to corporations whose normal-tax net income for the taxable year is not in excess of $25,000, such additional credit to consist of the amount if any, by which the excess profits credit for the preceding taxable year exceeded the excess-profits net income for such year. It is understood that the Treasury and members of the staff of the Joint Committee on Internal Revenue Taxation will study the operation of this limited carry-over, with a view to its possible extension or modification, and will report to the appropriate committees on the subject as soon as possible. (p. 44)

Congressional Discussion

Discussion—Senate; on Report of Conference Committee (Cong. Rec. Vol. 86).—Mr. Harrison. * * * In the Senate bill we allowed a 2-year carry-over of the unused exemption with respect to the canning and mining industries. We finally compromised, after a long discussion, by providing a 1-year carry-over of the unused exemption to be applied to all corporations whose income did not exceed $25,000 for the taxable year. (p. 12919)

| Sec. 710(c)(1) |

1942
204(b)

[SEC. 710. IMPOSITION OF TAX.]

(c) **Unused Excess Profits Credit Adjustment.**—

(1) **Computation of Unused Excess Profits Credit Adjustment.**—*The unused excess profits credit adjustment for any taxable year shall be the aggregate of the unused excess profits credit carry-overs and unused excess profits credit carry-backs to such taxable year.*

Committee Reports

Report—Senate Finance Committee (77th Cong., 2d Sess., S. Rept. 1631).— The sum of the carry-backs and carry-overs to any taxable year, which may be credited against the excess profits net income for such taxable year to determine the adjusted excess profits net income, is the "unused excess profits credit adjustment" for such taxable year. (p. 183)

Sec. 710(c)(2)

[SEC. 710. IMPOSITION OF TAX.]

1942
204(b)

[(c) Unused Excess Profits Credit Adjustment.—]

(2) Definition of Unused Excess Profits Credit.— ~~(c) Excess Profits Credit Carry-over. Section 710~~ <(a)> ~~(c) (1) (defining the unused excess-profits credit)~~ is amended by inserting at the end thereof the following new sentence: ~~"For such purpose, in the case of taxable years beginning after December 31, 1941, the excess-profits credit and the excess-profits net income for any taxable year beginning in 1940 or in 1941 shall be computed under the law applicable to taxable years beginning in 1942."~~ *The term "unused excess profits credit" means the excess, if any, of the excess profits credit for any taxable year beginning after December 31, 1939, over the excess profits net income for such taxable year, computed on the basis of the excess profits credit applicable to such taxable year. For such purpose the excess profits credit and the excess profits net income for any taxable year beginning in 1940 shall be computed under the law applicable to taxable years beginning in 1941. The unused excess profits credit for a taxable year of less than twelve months shall be an amount which is such part of the unused excess profits credit determined under the first sentence of this paragraph as the number of days in the taxable year is of the number of days in the twelve months ending with the close of the taxable year.*

Committee Reports

Report—Ways and Means Committee (77th Cong., 2d Sess., H. Rept. 2333). —Provision is also made that in computing the excess profits credit carry-over, the excess profits credit and excess profits net income for taxable years beginning in 1940 and 1941 shall be computed under the law applicable to taxable years beginning in 1942. (p. 139)

Report—Senate Finance Committee (77th Cong., 2d Sess., S. Rept. 1631).— This section also amends section 710 (c) to provide that the unused excess profits credit for a taxable year of less than 12 months shall be reduced to an amount which is such part thereof as the number of days in the taxable year is of the number of days in the 12 months ending with the close of the taxable year. The excess profits credit is designed to apply against the excess profits net income for a 12-month period, and gross distortion results from treating the part not used in a short taxable year the same as the unused credit for a 12-month taxable year. Under existing law, the excess profits net income is placed on an annual basis by reference to the period of time involved in the short taxable year, and the excess over this amount of the excess profits credit is treated as an unused excess profits credit which may be carried over to succeeding taxable years. In effect, this places on an annual basis the excess of the excess profits credit allocable to the short period over the excess profits net income for such period, and permits this distorted amount to be carried over as a credit in succeeding years. For example, the taxpayer, with a $91,250 excess profits credit, changes from the calendar year basis to the fiscal year basis ending January 31. It files a return for the short period, January 1–31, 1942, in which period it has an excess profits net income of $6,200. This excess profits net income, placed on an annual basis under section 711 (a) (3), is $73,000, and the $91,250 excess profits credit for such taxable year exceeds this amount by $18,250. This $18,250 is an unused excess profits credit for the short taxable year under existing law. Since the $91,250 excess profits credit is designed to apply to a year of 365 days, only $7,750 of the excess profits credit is properly allocable to the 31 day period, and only the $1,550 excess of this amount

over the $6,200 excess profits net income should be treated as an unused excess profits credit for the short taxable year. Under the amendment made by this section, therefore, the $18,250 unused excess profits credit determined on an annual basis would be reduced by reference to the period of time included in the short taxable year (that is, $1,550, or $\frac{31}{365}$ of $18,250). (p. 183–184)

The only change made by your committee in this section of the bill is the elimination from the bill of the provision requiring computation of the excess profits credit carry-over from taxable years beginning in 1940 and 1941 under the law applicable to taxable years beginning in 1942. (p. 185)

Report—Conference Committee (77th Cong., 2d Sess., H. Rept. 2586).— Amendment No. 275: This amendment eliminates the provision in the House bill requiring computation of the excess profits credit carry-over from taxable years beginning in 1940 and 1941 under the law applicable to taxable years beginning in 1942. The House recedes. (p. 59)

Committee Hearings

Hearings—Ways and Means Committee.—Computing credit on basis of law in year from which credit arises. (R. N. Miller, p. 172–173, 180)

Hearings—Senate Finance Committee.—Explanation of provision. (J.

O'Brien—H. Legis. Counsel—p. 103)

Computing credit on basis of law in year from which credit arises. (R. N. Miller, p. 357–358; A. L. Hopkins, p. 1754; E. C. Alvord, p. 1799–1800; H. J. Rudick, p. 2347–48)

1941
202(e)

[SEC. 710. IMPOSITION OF TAX.]

[(c) **Excess Profits Credit Carry-over.—**]

* * * For such purpose the excess-profits credit and the excess-profits net income for any taxable year beginning in 1940 shall be computed under the law applicable to taxable years beginning in 1941.

Committee Reports

Report—Ways and Means Committee (77th Cong., 1st Sess., H. Rept. 1040).— It is also provided that, in computing the excess-profits credit carry-over, the excess-profits credit and excess-profits net income for taxable years beginning in 1940 shall be computed as if the amend-

ments made by this bill were applicable. (p. 47)

Report—Senate Finance Committee (77th Cong., 1st Sess., S. Rept. 673).— Same as Ways and Means Committee Report. (p. 38)

Committee Hearings

Hearings—Senate Finance Committee.—Determining carry-over on basis of law applicable in year carry-over arises.

(E. C. Alvord, p. 637-638; H. B. Fernald, p. 882; W. A. M. Cooper, p. 1195-96; C. R. Hook, p. 1325-40)

UNENACTED RELATED PROVISIONS

1940 Act

[Sec. 201 of Senate Finance Committee bill]

[SEC. 721.   ABNORMALITIES IN INCOME IN TAXABLE PERIOD.]

(c)   **Excess Profits Credit Carry-over.**—

〖*(1)   Definition of unused excess-profits credit.—The term "unused excess-profits credit" means the excess, if any of the excess-profits credit for any taxable year beginning after December 31, 1939, over the excess-profits net income for such taxable year, computed on the basis of the excess-profits credit applicable to such taxable year.*〗

Sec. 710(c)(3)

[SEC. 122.   REPEAL OF EXCESS PROFITS TAX IN 1946.]

1945
122(b)
122(d)

(b)   **Carry-backs from Years After 1945, Etc.**—*Despite the provisions of subsection (a) of this section the provisions of subchapter E of chapter 2 shall remain in force for the purposes of the determination of the taxes imposed by such subchapter for taxable years beginning before January 1, 1946, such determination to be made as if subsection (a) had not been enacted but with the application of the amendments made by subsection (c) of this section and section 131 of this Act.*

(d)   **Affiliated Groups.**—*Subsection (b) shall be applied in the case of corporations making or required to make a consolidated return under chapter 1 for any taxable year beginning after December 31, 1945, and in the case of a corporation making a separate return for any such taxable year which was a member of a group which made or was required to make a consolidated return for any prior taxable year, in such manner as may be prescribed in regulations prescribed by the Commissioner with the approval of the Secretary prior to the last day prescribed by law for the making of the return for the year beginning after December 31, 1945.*

Committee Reports

Report—Ways and Means Committee (79th Cong., 1st Sess., H. Rept. 1106).— Your committee also decided that the need of railroads and certain other industries for an extension of the unused excess-profits credit carry-back 1 year beyond the repeal of the excess-profits tax presents a problem of sufficient importance to merit special consideration in the next tax bill. (p. 10)

Report—Senate Finance Committee (79th Cong., 1st Sess., S. Rept. 655).— However, it is recognized that this carry-back is subject to abuse and inequity.

Therefore your committee is studying ways of removing the abuses of this provision and expects to propose retroactive legislation on this subject in the near future. (p. 19)

Your committee, however, has provided in section 122 (b) of the bill that the provisions of subchapter E of chapter 2, which relate to the excess-profits tax, shall remain in force for purposes of the determination of excess-profits taxes for taxable years beginning prior to January 1, 1946. The determination of such taxes is to be made with the application of the amendments made by sections 122 (c) and 131 of the bill. Section 131 relates to fiscal-year taxpayers. * * * Thus, even though no excess-profits tax will be imposed for a taxable year beginning in 1946, there may be an unused excess-profits credit for such taxable year, and such unused excess-profits credit may be carried back and may affect the excess-profits tax otherwise imposed for taxable years beginning in 1944 or 1945. All provisions of law necessary to compute the excess-profits credit, the excess-profits net income, and the unused excess-profits credit for a taxable year beginning in 1946, and the unused excess-profits credit carry-back from such taxable year, shall be taken into account in determining the unused excess-profits credit and the resulting carry-back in the same manner as if an excess-profits tax were imposed for such taxable year. In determining the unused excess-profits credit adjustment for taxable years beginning prior to January 1, 1946, the unused excess-profits credit for a taxable year beginning in 1946 may be computed by taking into account a constructive average base period net income determined under section 722 of the code. A taxable year beginning in 1946 for purposes of the excess-profits tax shall be the same taxable year as that for purposes of the tax imposed by chapter 1 of the code.

There is danger that the operation of the unused excess-profits credit carry-back provision, particularly in 1946, may make possible certain abuses. These potential abuses might arise through various devices or transactions entered into wholly or in large part for the purpose of obtaining refunds of wartime excess-profits taxes through unused credit carry-backs, or through transactions having the apparent effect of creating carry-back refunds in situations unrelated to the purpose and intent of the provisions allowing carry-backs. While various tax-avoidance schemes are already dealt with either by express provision in the internal-revenue laws or through court decisions, your committee will give further consideration to the necessity or desirability of retroactive legislation in this connection.

Subsection (d) of section 122 applies with respect to an affiliated group of corporations making consolidated returns. Unused excess-profits credit carry-backs from taxable years subsequent to 1945 may become a factor in the case of such corporations. The consolidated return involved may be a consolidated income-tax return made for a taxable year beginning in 1946; or it may be a consolidated income- or excess-profits-tax return made for the taxable year 1944 or 1945; or consolidated returns may be made for the several taxable years involved. Section 122 (d) provides that, in all such cases, the carry-backs from a subsequent taxable year, whether or not a consolidated return is made for such year, shall be given effect in such manner as the Commissioner, with the approval of the Secretary, shall have prescribed by regulations prior to the last day prescribed by law for the making of the return for such year, which date includes the last day of any extension of time granted by the Commissioner. (p. 29-30)

Report—Conference Committee (79th Cong., 1st Sess., H. Rept. 1165).— Senate amendment 29 also provides that, despite the repeal of the excess-profits tax for 1946, the provisions of the excess-profits-tax law shall remain in force so as to permit carry-back of the unused excess-profits credit from 1946 to 1944 and 1945, and so as to assure the making of the necessary adjustments in the net operating loss carry-backs. The amendment provides that there shall be no carry-back of unused excess-profits credits from taxable years beginning after December 31, 1946. The amendment also makes provision for the application of the carry-back in the case of affiliated groups of corporations. (p. 7)

Congressional Discussion

Discussion—Senate (Cong. Rec. Vol. 91).—MR. GEORGE. Mr. President, if the Senator will permit me, let me say that the loss carry-back provision applicable to the excess-profits tax does permit a carry-back of a loss against the taxes actually paid during a profit year. The theory of the loss carry-back is simply that in a war period, with rapidly fluctuating prices and with rapidly fluctuating inventories, it is not quite possible for any taxpayer to be said to have made a profit unless more than 1 year is considered. In an ordinary, normal period in many cases it is difficult enough to determine whether profits have actually been made. But particularly is that true in a war period. So there are two types of loss carry-back. One is the loss carry-back of losses sustained. That is not affected by this bill, and of course that continues. Then there is the loss carry-back of the unused excess-profits credit. If a corporation has an unused excess-profits credit in any year, it may carry it back as against taxes actually paid in the two preceding years. That is the general or ordinary principle.

The Secretary of the Treasury recognized that it would not be equitable or fair to cut off the excess-profits taxpayers without some advantage accruing from the unused excess-profits credit available to them. But he did say that he did not think the unused excess-profits credit should be continued for more than 1 year after the repeal of the tax.

MR. O'MAHONEY. Well, will this credit which may be carried back against the accrued taxes of previous years be a credit accruing under this bill, that is to say, a credit which accrues in the future?

MR. GEORGE. If the taxpayer has an unused excess-profits credit arising in 1946, it may be carried back to 1945 or 1944.

MR. O'MAHONEY. Well, we are now in 1945.

MR. GEORGE. Yes.

MR. O'MAHONEY. Therefore, it would seem to me that this proposal has the effect of making it possible for a corporation which has made an excess profit and has become liable for an excess-profits tax during the war years to apply against that war tax a credit which will be earned in a peace year.

MR. GEORGE. That is true. That is what the provision is intended to do. * * *

There was suggested on the part of the railroads and various other corporations that they be allowed to set up a deferred maintenance reserve. They could not make the improvements during the war. They said, "Therefore, let us have a reserve which we can now set up, which we can use after the war to do the things we should have been doing during the war." Then there was a larger group of corporations which said, "We want and we must have, if we are to be saved from bankruptcy, a depreciation reserve or an inventory reserve to meet our problems."

What happened was that we did not grant the relief which either group asked for, or even the relief which other types asked for. We provided for a carry-back provision. Subsequently, because of great inequities which we found developing, we provided for an unused excess-profits credit carry-back.

I should like to say further to the Senator that we recognized that there were some corporations which were in a position to take advantage and which might take great advantage of even this 1-year carry-back of unused excess-profits credit.

* * *

I think a typical example would be in the case of a corporation which, through 1946, had merely maintained a skeleton organization, very largely hoping to realize profits out of the application of this very principle, and therefore the necessity of a further study and further legislation in order to meet the abuses if, as, and when they may arise.

MR. O'MAHONEY. I appreciate the Senator's reference to that aspect of the situation, because I was about to raise that question, having read the sentence from the report on page 19. However, it is recognized in the report that this carry-back is subject to abuse. The recognition by the committee of the fact that it is subject to abuse and inequities, and the declaration which the Senator just read from page 30 of the report, constitute, in the Senator's opinion, I take it, as well as in the opinion of other members of his committee, sufficient notice to taxpayers that abuses will not be tolerated.

MR. GEORGE. They will not be tolerated. The Senator is entirely correct. That fact undoubtedly was in the mind of the Secretary of the Treasury when he asked for a reduction of the period from 2 years to 1 year.

MR. O'MAHONEY. Of course, we are all familiar with the fact that advantage is always taken of the letter of any tax law in order to create losses which may be deducted from taxes due. That, of course, is something which should be avoided, particularly when having emerged from the war we create a system by which, apparently, losses which might be voluntarily incurred during peacetime could be set aside as deductions against profits which had been properly a subject of high taxation during the war.

MR. GEORGE. The Senator is quite correct. We incorporated this provision at two places in the bill in order to serve as a warning. (Daily, p. 10107-08)

1942
204(b)

[SEC. 710. IMPOSITION OF TAX.]

[(c)   Unused Excess Profits Credit Adjustment.—]

(3)   Amount of Unused Excess Profits Credit Carry-back and Carry-over.—

(A)   Unused Excess Profits Credit Carry-back.—*If for any taxable year beginning after December 31, 1941, the taxpayer has an unused excess profits credit, such unused excess profits credit shall be an unused excess profits credit carry-back for each of the two preceding taxable years, except that the carry-back in the case of the first preceding taxable year shall be the excess, if any, of the amount of such unused excess profits credit over the adjusted excess profits net income for the second preceding taxable year computed for such taxable year (i) by determining the unused excess profits credit adjustment without regard to such unused excess profits credit, and (ii) without the deduction of the specific exemption provided in subsection (b) (1).*

(B)   Unused Excess Profits Credit Carry-over.—*If for any taxable year beginning after December 31, 1939, the taxpayer has an unused excess profits credit, such unused excess profits credit shall be an unused excess profits credit carry-over for each of the two succeeding taxable years, except that the carry-over in the case of the second succeeding taxable year shall be the excess, if any, of the amount of such unused excess profits credit over the adjusted excess profits net income for the intervening taxable year computed for such intervening taxable year (i) by determining the unused excess profits credit adjustment without regard to such unused excess profits credit or to any unused excess profits credit carry-back, and (ii) without the deduction of the specific exemption provided in subsection (b) (1). For the purposes of the preceding sentence, the unused excess profits credit for any taxable year beginning after December 31, 1941, shall first be reduced by the sum of the adjusted excess profits net income for each of the two preceding taxable years (computed for each such preceding taxable year (i) by determining the unused excess profits credit adjustment without regard to such unused excess profits credit or to the unused excess profits credit for the succeeding taxable year, and (ii) without the deduction of the specific exemption provided in subsection (b) (1)).*

is computed by reducing the $70,000 unused excess profits credit by the sum of the adjusted excess profits net income for 1944 and 1945, computed for each such year without the deduction of any $5,000 specific exemption or of any carry-back from 1946 or from any year subsequent to 1946. (For 1944, the adjusted excess profits net income so computed is $0, that is, the $55,000 excess profits net income for such year less the $100,000 excess profits credit and the $10,000 carry-back from 1945. For 1945, the adjusted excess profits net income so computed is $0, that is, the $25,000 excess profits net income for 1945 less the $100,000 excess profits credit.)

(d) For 1948, the carry-over is $20,000, computed by reducing the $70,000 carry-over to 1947 by the adjusted excess profits net income for 1947 computed without the deduction of the $5,000 specific exemption or of the carry-over from 1946 or of any carry-over or carry-back from a year subsequent to 1946 (that is, the $160,000 excess profits net income for 1947 less the $100,000 excess profits credit and the $10,000 carry-over from 1945).

The sum of the carry-backs and carry-overs to any taxable year, which may be credited against the excess profits net income for such taxable year to determine the adjusted excess profits net income, is the "unused excess profits credit adjustment" for such taxable year. Thus, in the above illustration, the "unused excess profits credit adjustment" for 1943 is $95,000, the sum of the $20,000 carry-back from 1944 and the $75,000 carry-back from 1945. (p. 180-183)

Report—Conference Committee (77th Cong., 2d Sess., H. Rept. 2586).— Amendment No. 262: This amendment adds to the bill a new section to permit unused excess profits credit for any taxable year beginning on or after January 1, 1942, to be carried back and credited against excess profits net income for each of the two preceding years (but not for any taxable year beginning before January 1, 1941). That portion of the unused excess profits credit for any taxable year which is not used as a carryback may be carried forward, as under existing law, to the two succeeding taxable years. The House recedes. (p. 56)

Congressional Discussion

Discussion—House; on Report of Conference Committee (Cong. Rec. Vol. 88).—Mr. Treadway. * * * Another Senate amendment adopted by the conference was the 2-year carry-back of net losses and unused excess-profits credits.

This change is intended largely to take care of companies who are obliged by existing restrictions to defer upkeep and maintenance expenditures, which would otherwise be an allowable deduction in the current year. (p. 8470)

Committee Hearings
1943 Act

Hearings—Ways and Means Committee.—Making unused credit available to successor corporations. (E. C. Alvord, p. 684-685)

Hearings—Senate Finance Committee.—Making unused credit available to successor corporations. (E. C. Alvord, p. 614-615)

[SEC. 710. IMPOSITION OF TAX.]

[(c) Excess Profits Credit Carry-over.—]

EPTA
2(b)

(2) Computation of Excess Profits Credit Carry-over.—The excess profits credit carry-over for any taxable year shall be the sum of the following:

(A) The unused excess profits credit for the first preceding taxable year; and

(B)   The unused excess profits credit for the second preceding taxable year * * *

Committee Reports

Report—Ways and Means Committee (77th Cong., 1st Sess., H. Rept. 146).— The bill affords relief in the following situations:

1. It relieves the hardships which may be caused by the sharply fluctuating earnings of many types of companies, the activities of which are dependent upon business cycles, by allowing unused excess-profits credits to be carried over into the two succeeding taxable years, thereby tending to level off the unusual effects due to rise and fall of income. In addition, the allowance of such an excess profits credit carry-over will be of substantial benefit to new corporations, and to old corporations undergoing a period of expansion. (p. 2)

This amendment removes the restriction of the carry-over privilege to corporations with normal-tax net incomes of not more than $25,000, making it applicable to all corporations, and provides for a 2-year carry-over instead of a 1-year carry-over. (p. 4)

Report—Senate Finance Committee (77th Cong., 1st Sess., S. Rept. 75).— Same as Ways and Means Committee Report. (p. 3, 5, respectively)

Congressional Discussion

Discussion—Senate (Cong. Rec. Vol. 87).—Mr. Harrison. * * * Section 2: The bill provides for a 2-year carry-over of the unused excess-profits credit. The unused excess-profits credit for any taxable year is the amount by which the excess-profits credit for such taxable year exceeds the excess-profits net income for such year. This provision will be extremely helpful to new corporations and to old corporations undergoing a period of expansion. It will be recalled that the Senate last year adopted a provision for a 2-year carry-over of the unused excess-profits credit for any taxable year beginning after December 31, 1939, in the case of a corporation, 80 percent or more of whose gross income is derived from mining or processing minerals or from processing or otherwise preparing for market any seasonable fruit or vegetable, or any fish or other marine animal life. In the conference, this provision was eliminated and a substitute provided which allowed a 1-year carry-over in the case of a corporation, the normal tax net income for the year did not exceed $25,000. It was requested in the conference report that the Treasury and the staff of the Joint Committee on Internal Revenue Taxation were to study this limited carry-over with a view to its possible extension. As a result of this study, the bill now provides for a 2-year carry-over for all corporations, regardless of the size of their net income. (p. 1637)

Mr. George. Let me point out the fact that it is very helpful to mining companies in that it provides for a 2-year carry-over of any unused credit that a taxpayer may have, whether he is on the prior-earning basis or the invested-capital basis. That is very helpful. Suppose that during that 2 years a corporation has had a loss or did not earn anything. It had a base, however, which would have given it a certain exemption from the excess-profits tax. Suppose, then, that in the third or fourth year of its operation it had a large profit. In the taxable year the amendment would give it the right to carry over 2 years of its unearned credit as against the profits of the year in which it had an abnormally large profit.

Mr. Adams. Does the bill give the taxpayer the right to do that, rather than leaving it discretionary with the Commissioner of Internal Revenue?

Mr. George. It gives him that right also, and gives him the right to elect either the prior-earnings base or the invested-capital base, or to change it, as the Senator from Missouri has pointed out. The taxpayer is not irrevocably bound. (p. 1687)

UNENACTED RELATED PROVISIONS

1943 Act

[Sec. 120½ of Senate bill]

[SEC. 710. IMPOSITION OF TAX.]

  [(c) Unused Excess Profits Credit Adjustment.—]

  [(3) Amount of Unused Excess Profits Credit Carry-back and Carry-over.—]

  [*(C) Certain reorganized railroad corporations and predecessor corporations' deemed to be same taxpayer.—For the purposes of this subsection, if the basis of the property of a railroad corporation, as defined in section 77m of the National Bankruptcy Act, as amended, is prescribed by section 113 (a) (20), the acquiring corporation and the corporation whose property was acquired, within the meaning of section 113 (a) (20), shall be deemed to be the same taxpayer.*]

Committee Reports

Report—Conference Committee (77th Cong., 2d Sess., H. Rept. 2586).— Amendment No. 56: This amendment, for which there is no corresponding provision in the House bill, adds a new subparagraph to section 710 (c) (3) to provide that if the basis of the property of a railroad corporation (as defined in section 77m of the National Bankruptcy Act, as amended) is prescribed by section 113 (a) (20), the acquiring corporation and the corporation whose property was acquired, within the meaning of section 113 (a) (20), shall be deemed to be the same taxpayer for the purposes of the unused excess profits credit adjustment. The Senate recedes. (p. 52)

Congressional Discussion

Discussion—Senate (Cong. Rec. Vol. 90).—MR. CLARK of Missouri. Mr. President, the purpose of the amendment is to correct an obvious and, I am very certain, an unintentional discrimination in the law as it now exists. In the present state of the law, a very material difference is made between railroad corporations which have reorganized and maintained their theretofore existing corporate structure, and railroads in connection with the reorganization of which, by reason of the local law, it has been necessary to form a new corporation. I do not think that was ever the intention of the Congress, in the first place. I think it should be corrected. I do not think there is any basis of distinction as to the carry-over—and that is all the amendment applies to—as between corporations which are organized in States where they are permitted to reorganize with the old corporation in existence and corporations located in States where the local law is different, and where they are required to form a new corporation. (p. 374-375)

1940 Act

[Sec. 201 of Senate Finance Committee bill]

[SEC. 721.   ABNORMALITIES IN INCOME IN TAXABLE PERIOD.]

[(b) *Corporations engaged in processing certain commodities.—* In the case of a taxpayer 80 per centum or more of the gross income of which for the taxable year is derived <u>from mining or processing minerals,</u> or from processing or otherwise preparing for market any seasonal fruit or vegetable, or any fish or other marine life, the adjusted excess profits net income computed under section 710 (b) for such taxable year shall be further reduced by the amount of the excess profits credit carry-over computed under subsection (c) of this section.]

[(c)   **Excess Profits Credit Carry-over.**—]

[(2) *Computation of excess-profits credit carry-over.*—The excess-profits credit carry-over for any taxable year shall be the sum of the following:

[(A)   The unused excess-profits credit for the first preceding taxable year; and

[(B)   The unused excess-profits credit for the second preceding taxable year reduced by the amount, if any, by which the excess-profits net income for the first preceding taxable year exceeds the sum of—

[(i)   The excess-profits credit for such first preceding taxable year, plus

[(ii)   The unused excess-profits credit for the third preceding taxable year.]

Congressional Discussion

Discussion—Senate (Cong. Rec. Vol. 86).—MR. O'MAHONEY. I desire to ask the chairman of the Finance Committee to what extent the bill, as it has been reported, affects the carry-over provisions of the pending law with respect to corporations which are engaged, let us say, in agricultural pursuits—livestock corporations, for example.

MR. HARRISON. The only part of the bill where the carryover provision is effective is in the provision which applies to the seasonal canning business, the vegetable, fruit, and fish businesses. Quite a strong argument was made before the committee by a representative of those interests. We sought to take care of it through the general relief provisions which we have written into the law, but

the experts said the provision could not be drafted quickly to apply in the general relief provisions. Then they said they thought the provision we made would correct the situation, and we have sought to help them through giving them a 1-year carry-over.

MR. O'MAHONEY. That deals with what particular industry?

MR. HARRISON. That deals with the seasonal canning business, and pertains to vegetables, fruits, and fish, and that one exception, a provision covering that industry, was put in the bill. We would much rather have preferred to put it in under the general relief provisions where so many other items are carried.

MR. O'MAHONEY. May I ask the Senator whether the bill makes any change in the present law with respect to carry-overs? Does the bill as it has been reported by the committee make any change in the present law with respect to carry-overs upon normal income?

Mr. Harrison. It does not.

Mr. O'Mahoney. So that the carry-over provisions of this measure refer exclusively to excess profits?

Mr. Harrison. Absolutely, and only for 2 years. That pertains only to this one industry.

Mr. O'Mahoney. Of course, it is obvious that if we are bringing to pass an excess-profits tax we are dealing with abnormal profits under abnormal provisions, but I wanted to be sure that there was nothing in the bill which would adversely affect the normal activities of normal businesses which are not likely to gain any excess profits because of the condition in which the country finds itself.

Mr. Harrison. The Senator has that assurance. (p. 12183-184)

Discussion—Senate; on Report of Conference Committee (Cong. Rec. Vol. 86).—Mr. Harrison. * * * In the Senate bill we allowed a 2-year carry-over of the unused exemption with respect to the canning and mining industries. We finally compromised, after a long discussion, by providing a 1-year carry-over of the unused exemption to be applied to all corporations whose income did not exceed $25,000 for the taxable year. (p. 12919)

Committee Hearings

Hearings—Ways and Means Committee.—Allowing unused credit carry-over. (J. L. Sullivan—Treas. Dept.—p. 90-91; W. H. Cooper, p. 317)

Hearings—Senate Finance Committee.—Allowing unused credit carry-over. (W. A. Cooper, p. 47, 52-53; A. B. Chapman, p. 394; C. W. Dudley, p. 402, 405)

> Sec. 711(a)(1)(A)
> Sec. 711(a)(2)(C)
> Sec. 711(b)(1)(A)

SEC. 711. EXCESS PROFITS NET INCOME.

(a) **Taxable Years Beginning After December 31, 1939.**— * * *

(1) Excess profits credit computed under income credit.— * * * the adjustments shall be as follows:

(A) **Income Subject to Excess Profits Tax.**—In computing such normal-tax net income the credit provided in section 26(e) (relating to income subject to the tax imposed by this subchapter) shall not be allowed;

Sec. 711(a)(2)(C) is the corresponding provision for the invested capital credit, and is the same as Sec. 711(a)(1)(A).

1942
206(a)(1)
[711(a)(1)(A)]
206(a)(2)
[711(a)(2)(C)]

Committee Reports

Report—Ways and Means Committee (77th Cong., 2d Sess., H. Rept. 2333).—The change made by section 105 of the bill in the base of the income tax imposed by chapter 1 of the Code through the allowance of adjusted excess profits net income as a credit in computing normal tax net income requires certain technical amendments in computing excess profits net income under section 711(a)(1) and (2) of the Code, which is based upon normal tax net income. This section of the bill disallows such credit in computing normal tax net income for purposes of both the excess profits net income computed under the income credit

and the excess profits net income computed under the invested-capital credit. (p. 139)

Committee Hearings

Hearings—Senate Finance Committee.—Explanation of provision. (J.

O'Brien—H. Legis. Counsel—p. 103)

1941
202(c)
[711(a)
(1)(A)]
[711(a)
(2)(C)]
[711(b)
(1)(A)]

SEC. 711. EXCESS PROFITS NET INCOME.

(a) **Taxable Years Beginning After December 31, 1939.**— * * *

    (1) Excess profits credit computed under income credit.— * * * the adjustments shall be as follows:

        (A) Income Taxes.—In computing such normal-tax net income the deduction for the tax imposed by this subchapter shall not be allowed;

Sec. 711(a)(2)(C) is the corresponding provision for the invested capital credit, and is the same as Sec. 711(a)(1)(A).

Section 711 (b) (1) (A) (relating to adjustment for income taxes for taxable years in the base period) is repealed.

Committee Reports

Report—**Ways and Means Committee** (77th Cong., 1st Sess., H. Rept. 1040).— (1) *Reversal of the deduction for income and excess-profits taxes.*—Under existing law, the income tax is allowed as a deduction in the computation of the excess-profits tax. It seems unfair to allow that part of the income tax which is computed on income which is not subject to the excess-profits tax to reduce the excess-profits net income. Canada allows only that part of the income tax which is computed upon income subject to the excess-profits tax. Under the World War Act, the excess-profits tax was allowed as a deduction in computing the normal tax but the normal tax was not allowed as a deduction in computing the excess-profits tax. This is also the rule which is now applied by the British. The tax result in Canada is practically the same as the British rule and our 1918 rule. However, it is believed that the World War rule is much simpler in its application. Your committee has, therefore, deemed it advisable to return to the 1918 rule, and has disallowed the deduction of income taxes, both in the base

period and in the taxable year, in computing the excess-profits tax. The deduction is allowed in computing both the normal tax and the surtax. The effect of the reversal of the deduction is that the 8 percent credit on invested capital provided in the bill is equivalent to a credit on invested capital of 5.6 percent after deduction of the normal tax and surtax, and the 7-percent credit on invested capital is equivalent to a credit on invested capital of 4.9 percent after deduction of the normal tax and surtax. (p. 24)

This section provides that the income tax imposed by chapter 1 of the Internal Revenue Code and by corresponding provisions of prior revenue acts shall not constitute an adjustment in determining excess-profits net income for current and base period taxable years. Section 23 (c) (2) is amended to provide for the deduction of the excess-profits tax in determining income subject to chapter 1 tax. Furthermore, the taxpayer, if using the average-earnings method, has its excess-profits credit increased by the corresponding nondeduction of income taxes in determining its average base period net income.

It is provided that the deduction shall be allowed only in computing the income tax imposed for the taxable year for which the excess-profits tax is levied. By providing that any excess-profits tax paid after the taxable year shall be deemed to have been paid within the taxable year, the same treatment is accorded to taxpayers on the cash basis as is accorded to taxpayers on the accrual basis. It is also provided that the excess-profits tax shall be computed, for the purposes of this deduction, without reduction by the foreign tax credit, and

without regard to the adjustments provided for in section 734.

Since the excess-profits net income for a taxable year is primarily the normal-tax net income with certain adjustments, it is necessary to amend section 711 (a) to require an adjustment to normal-tax net income in the form of a disallowance of the deduction of the excess-profits tax. (p. 46-47)

Report—Senate Finance Committee (77th Cong., 1st Sess., S. Rept. 673).— Substantially same as Ways and Means Committee Report. (p. 14, 37-38, respectively)

Congressional Discussion

Discussion—Senate (Cong. Rec. Vol. 87).—On reversal of credit, in general.

(p. 7268)

Committee Hearings

Hearings—Ways and Means Committee.—Allowing income tax as a deduction. (Controllers Institute of America, p. 1717)

Hearings—Senate Finance Committee.—Not allowing income tax as a de-

duction. (J. L. Sullivan—Treas. Dept. —p. 38)

Allowing income tax as a deduction. (J. W. Hooper, p. 699; H. B. Fernald, p. 880; P. W. Adams, p. 1013; L. H. Parker, p. 1462)

SEC. 711. EXCESS PROFITS NET INCOME.

(a) **Taxable Years Beginning After December 31, 1939.**— * * *

   (1) **Excess profits credit computed under income credit.**— * * * the adjustments shall be as follows:

      (A) **Income Taxes.**—The deduction for taxes shall be increased by an amount equal to the tax *(not including the tax under section 102)* under Chapter 1 for such taxable year;

> Sec. 711(a)(2)(C) is the corresponding provision for the invested capital credit, and is the same as sec. 711 (a)(1)(A).
> Sec. 711(b)(1)(A) is the corresponding provision for base period income, and is substantially the same as sec. 711 (a)(1)(A).

1940
201
[711(a)
(1)(A)]
[711(a)
(2)(C)]
[711(b)
(1)(A)]

Committee Reports

Report—Ways and Means Subcommittee (76th Cong., 3d Sess., H. Rept. Aug. 8, 1940).—(3) A deduction is allowed equal to the normal corporate income tax payable for such year. (p. 6)

(1) The deduction for taxes paid or accrued is to be increased by an amount

equal to the income tax payable for such taxable year. (p. 13)

Report—Ways and Means Committee (76th Cong., 3d Sess., H. Rept. 2894).— (1) The deduction for taxes paid or accrued under the law applicable to the taxable year is to be increased by an amount equal to the amount of the tax under chapter 1 payable for such taxable year. (p. 19)

Report—Conference Committee (76th Cong., 3d Sess., H. Rept. 3002).—*Senate amendment.*—In addition to certain technical amendments, the Senate amendment made the following changes in and additions to the adjustments contained in the House bill:

(1) The additional deduction on ac-

count of corporate income taxes was modified so as to exclude the section 102 tax imposed on corporations improperly accumulating surplus. Under both the House and Senate bills, however, the normal corporate income tax (after the allowance of the foreign tax credit) for the taxable year for which the excess-profits net income is being computed is allowable as an additional deduction. (p. 44)

Congressional Discussion

Discussion—Senate (Cong. Rec. Vol. 86).—The Chief Clerk. In the amendment of the committee on page 86, line 20, after the word "tax", it is proposed to insert in parentheses the words "not including the tax under section 102."

Mr. HARRISON. These three amendments I have to present were prepared by the legislative draftsmen. They are merely technical in character. They carry no substance. Did the Senator ask me why I was asking that the amend-

ment be inserted?

*   *   *

Mr. DANAHER. What would the amendment do, I ask the Senator from Mississippi?

Mr. HARRISON. Under these amendments in computing the tax both under the income and invested-capital methods, and for the purposes of the base period, the surtax on corporations improperly accumulating a surplus does not increase the deduction for taxes. (p. 12173)

Committee Hearings

Hearings—Ways and Means Committee.—Allowing deduction for foreign

earnings or taxes. (C. H. Brook, p. 243-244; H. B. Fernald, p. 285)

1918
320

[Set forth on pages 329, 330]

1917
206

[Set forth on page 358]

3/3/17
200

[Set forth on page 370]

Sec. 711(a)(1)(B)
Sec. 711(a)(2)(D)
Sec. 711(b)(1)(B)

1942
207(a)
207(c)
207(e)

[SEC. 711. EXCESS PROFITS NET INCOME.]

[(a) **Taxable Years Beginning After December 31, 1939.**— * * *]

[(1) **Excess profits credit computed under income credit.**— * * * the adjustments shall be as follows:]

(B) **Gains and Losses From Sales or Exchanges of Capital Assets.**—There shall be excluded gains and losses from sales or exchanges of capital assets held for more than ~~15~~ *6* months.

Secs. 711(a)(2)(D) and 711(b)(1)(B) are the corresponding provisions for the invested capital credit and base period income respectively, and are the same as sec. 711(a)(1)(B).

Committee Reports

Report—Senate Finance Committee (77th Cong., 2d Sess., S. Rept. 1631.— Both the House bill and this section strike out the special excess profits tax provision excluding from excess profits net income the excess of gains over losses from the sale or exchange of property subject to an allowance for depreciation, since such gains and losses will be excluded if they are treated as capital gains and losses under section 117 (j), added to the Code by section 153.[1]   (p. 185)

[1] Sec. 151 of the Act.

Committee Hearings

Hearings—Senate Finance Committee.—Allowing deduction for short term losses.   (A. L. Hopkins, p. 1754, 1760)

[SEC. 711. EXCESS PROFITS NET INCOME.]

[(a) **Taxable Years Beginning After December 31, 1939.— * * *]**

[(1) **Excess profits credit computed under income credit.—** * * * the adjustments shall be as follows:]

[(B) **Long-term Gains and Losses.— * * *]** *There shall be excluded the excess of the recognized gains from the sale, exchange, or involuntary conversion (as a result of destruction in whole or in part, theft or seizure, or an exercise of the power of requisition or condemnation or the threat or imminence thereof) of property held for more than eighteen months which is of a character which is subject to the allowance for depreciation provided in section 23 (1) over the recognized losses from the sale, exchange, or involuntary conversion of such property. For the purposes of this subparagraph, section 117 (h) (1) and (2) shall apply in determining the period for which the taxpayer has held property which is of a character which is subject to the allowance for depreciation provided in section 23 (l).*

Secs. 711(a)(2)(D) and 711(b)(1)(B) are the corresponding provisions for the invested capital credit and base period income respectively, and are the same as sec. 711(a)(1)(B).

Committee Reports

Report—Senate Finance Committee (77th Cong., 2d Sess., S. Rept. 1631).— This section, for which there is no corresponding provision in the House bill, provides that gains and losses on the involuntary conversion of property of a character subject to the allowance or depreciation provided in section 23 (l), held for more than 6 months, shall be treated for excess profits tax purposes the same as gains and losses from the sale or exchange of such property. Under this amendment the excess of gains from such sales, exchanges, and involuntary conversions over the losses therefrom is excluded from excess profits net income. For the purposes of this section, property is involuntarily converted if it is destroyed in whole or in part, stolen, seized, requisitioned, or condemned. For ex-

1942
208

ample if a taxpayer has a gain of $1,000 from the sale of property of a character subject to the allowance for depreciation provided in section 23 (1), held for more than 6 months, a gain of $800 from insurance on such property which was destroyed by fire, or $1,800 of gain, and a loss of $600 from the total destruction by fire of such property which was not insured, the excess of $1,800 over $600 is excluded from excess profits net income. This section also provides that the determination of the period for which such property has been held shall be made under the same provisions as are applicable in determining the holding period of capital assets under section 117.

This amendment is applicable only to taxable years beginning after December 31, 1939, and not beginning after December 31, 1941. The amendments made by sections 153[1] and 207 of the bill, applicable to taxable years beginning after December 31, 1941, make it unnecessary

to enact similar provisions with respect to taxable years beginning after December 31, 1941.   (p. 186)

[1] Sec. 151 of the Act.

Report—Conference Committee (77th Cong., 2d Sess., H. Rept. 2586).— Amendment No. 289: This amendment, which is applicable only to taxable years beginning after December 31, 1939, and not beginning after December 31, 1941, provides that gains or losses on the involuntary conversion of property of a character subject to the allowance for depreciation provided in section 23 (l), held for more than 18 months, shall be treated for excess profits tax purposes the same as gains or losses from the sale or exchange of such property. In the determination of the period for which such property has been held, the provisions of section 117 for determining the holding period of capital assets shall apply.   The House recedes.   (p. 59)

1940

201

[SEC. 711. EXCESS PROFITS NET INCOME.]

[(a)   Taxable Years Beginning After December 31, 1939.— * * *]

   [(1)   Excess profits credit computed under income credit.— * * * the adjustments shall be as follows:]

      (B)   Long-term[1] Gains and Losses.—There shall be excluded long-term capital gains and losses. ~~For the purposes of this subparagraph, property otherwise constituting a capital asset shall not be deemed to be excluded from the definition of such term because it was of a character which is subject to the allowance for depreciation provided in section 23 (1) of Chapter 1; and~~ *There shall be excluded the excess of gains from the sale or exchange of property held for more than eighteen months which is of a character which is subject to the allowance for depreciation provided in section 23 (l) over the losses from the sale or exchange of such property;*

   [1] The word "Capital" preceded the word "Gains" in the Ways and Means Committee heading, but it was stricken by the Senate Finance Committee.

   Secs. 711 (a)(2)(D) and 711 (b)(1)(B) are the corresponding provisions for the invested capital credit and base period income respectively, and are the same as sec. 711 (a)(1)(B).

Committee Reports

Report—Ways and Means Subcommittee (76th Cong., 3d Sess., H. Rept. Aug. 8, 1940).—(4) Gains or losses from the sale or exchange of assets (depreciable or nondepreciable) held for more than 18 months are disregarded for the purpose of the excess-profits tax. (p. 6)

(2)   The amount of any gain or loss

realized upon the sale or exchange of any asset (depreciable or nondepreciable held for more than 18 months is to be excluded from the computation. (p. 13)

Report—Ways and Means Committee (76th Cong., 3d Sess., H. Rept. 2894).— Your committee has recommended certain special relief provisions, which are as follows:

* * *

(3) The elimination of gains or losses from the sale or exchange of assets (depreciable or nondepreciable) held over 18 months, for the purpose of the base period as well as the taxable year. (p. 13, 14)

(2) The amount of any gain or loss realized upon the sale or exchange of a capital asset held for more than 18 months shall be excluded. For the purpose of this adjustment, capital asset means a capital asset as defined in section 117 of the Internal Revenue Code but without any exception with respect to an asset of a character which is subject to the allowance for depreciation if such asset otherwise constitutes a capital asset within the meaning of the definition. (p. 19)

Report—Senate Finance Committee (76th Cong., 3d Sess., S. Rept. 2114).— (1) The treatment of gains and losses on depreciable assets held for more than 18 months as long-term capital gains and losses has been eliminated. In lieu thereof a provision has been inserted providing that only the excess of gains arising from the sale or exchange of such assets over any losses arising from the sale or exchange of such assets shall be excluded from the computation. The effect of this provision is to allow losses from the sale or exchange of depreciable assets held for more than 18 months to be deducted from ordinary income to the extent such losses exceed the gains from similar transactions. (p. 11)

Report—Conference Committee (76th Cong., 3d Sess., H. Rept. 3002).—*Senate amendment.*—In addition to certain technical amendments, the Senate amendment made the following changes in and additions to the adjustments contained in the House bill:

* * *

(2) The treatment of gains and losses on depreciable assets held for more than 18 months as long-term capital gains and losses and their consequent exclusion from the computation was eliminated. In lieu thereof a provision was inserted providing that only the excess of gains arising from the sale or exchange of such assets over any losses arising therefrom should be excluded from the computation. The effect of this provision is to allow losses from the sale or exchange of depreciable assets held for more than 18 months to be deducted from ordinary income to the extent such losses exceed the gains from similar transactions. (p. 44)

Congressional Discussion

Discussion—Senate; on Report of Conference Committee (Cong. Rec. Vol. 86).—MR. HARRISON. * * * In this report, the conference agreed to relieve what we termed hard cases, such as the following:

First. Under the Senate bill, for instance, losses from the sale of depreciable assets were allowed to be deducted in computing the income for the taxable year. This was agreed to. (p. 12918)

Committee Hearings

Hearings—Ways and Means Committee.—Allowing deduction for short term capital losses. (P. D. Seghers, p. 159)

Not excluding gains or losses on sales of depreciable assets. (W. H. Cooper, p. 317)

Allowing a deduction for post-war inventory losses. (A. B. Chapman, p. 384)

Hearings—Senate Finance Commit- tee.—Eliminating gains or losses on capital assets held less than 18 months. (F. P. Byerly, p. 363; D. E. Casey, p. 428)

Determining depreciation deduction in base period in same manner as current period. (W. A. Cooper, p. 63)

Eliminating gains or losses on capital assets held less than 18 months. (K. Carroad, p. 35; A. B. Trudgian, p. 83)

Not excluding gains or losses on sales of depreciable assets. (W. A. Cooper, p. 55)

Allowing losses on sale of depreciable assets. (W. S. Mack Jr., p. 232-234, 237)

Allowing a deduction for post-war inventory losses. (A. B. Chapman, p. 395)

> Sec. 711(a)(1)(C)
> Sec. 711(a)(2)(E)
> Sec. 711(b)(1)(C)

[SEC. 711. EXCESS PROFITS NET INCOME.]

[(a) Taxable Years Beginning After December 31, 1939.— * * *]

[(1) Excess profits credit computed under income credit.— * * * the adjustments shall be as follows:]

(C) Income From Retirement or Discharge of Bonds, and So Forth.—There shall be excluded, in the case of any ~~corporation, income derived from the retirement or discharge of any of its bonds, debentures, notes, or certificates or other evidences of indebtedness, which have been outstanding for more than eighteen months.~~ *taxpayer, income [(including amounts includible in income for the taxable year in which retirement or discharge occurs, on account of premium received upon issuance)] derived from the retirement or discharge by the taxpayer of any bond, debenture, note, or certificate or other evidence of indebtedness, if the obligation of the taxpayer has been outstanding for more than eighteen months;* INCLUDING, IN CASE THE ISSUANCE WAS AT A PREMIUM, THE AMOUNT INCLUDIBLE IN INCOME FOR SUCH YEAR SOLELY BECAUSE OF SUCH RETIREMENT OR DISCHARGE;

> Secs. 711 (b)(1)(C) and 711 (a)(2)(E) are the corresponding provisions for the invested capital credit and base period income respectively, and are the same as sec. 711 (a)(1)(C).

Committee Reports

Report—Ways and Means Committee (76th Cong., 3d Sess., H. Rept. 2894).— Your committee has recommended certain special relief provisions, which are as follows:

* * *

(4) The exclusion of income derived from the retirement or discharge of any bonds, debentures, notes, or certificates or other evidences of indebtedness which have been outstanding for more than 18 months. (p. 13, 14)

(3) There shall be excluded the amount of any income derived from the retirement or discharge by the corporation of any of its bonds, debentures, notes, or certificates of indebtedness, or any indebtedness evidenced by a writing which (including renewed obligations) were outstanding for more than 18 months prior to the date of such retirement or discharge. (p. 19)

Report—Senate Finance Committee (76th Cong., 3d Sess., S. Rept. 2114).— (2) The adjustment on account of income derived from the retirement or discharge of bonds, etc., has been rewritten to make certain that amounts which would be otherwise includible upon such retirement or discharge on account of any premium received upon issuance shall be left out of the computation, and that the adjustment shall apply although the indebtedness retired or discharged is indebtedness which has been assumed by the taxpayer and, although it is evidenced, so far as the taxpayer is concerned, only by a contract with the person whose liabilities have been assumed.

(3) A new adjustment has been added, applicable whether the excess-profits credit is computed under the income or invested capital plan and to taxable years in the base period as well as to taxable years under the excess-profits tax, requiring that any deductions otherwise allowable on account of the retirement or discharge of indebtedness shall be disallowed if the taxpayer's obligation has been outstanding for more than 18 months. The amounts so to be disallowed include the deduction otherwise allowable under section 23 (a) for expenses paid or incurred in connection with such retirement or discharge (including any premium paid upon any such retirement or discharge), the deduction for losses otherwise allowable in such connection, and the deduction otherwise allowable on account of the issuance of the bonds or other evidence of indebtedness at a discount. (p. 11-12)

Report—Conference Committee (76th Cong., 3d Sess., H. Rept. 3002).—*Senate amendment.*—In addition to certain technical amendments, the Senate amendment made the following changes in and additions to the adjustments contained in the House bill:

* * *

(3) The adjustment on account of income derived from the retirement or discharge of bonds, etc., was rewritten to make certain that amounts which would be otherwise includible upon such retirement or discharge on account of any premium received upon issuance should be left out of the computation, and that the adjustment should apply although the indebtedness retired or discharged is indebtedness which has been assumed by the taxpayer and although it is evidenced, so far as the taxpayer is concerned, only by a contract with the person whose liabilities have been assumed.

(4) A corresponding adjustment was added requiring that certain deductions otherwise allowable on account of the retirement or discharge of bonds, etc., should be excluded from the computation. (p. 44)

Conference agreement.—With the exceptions and modifications described below, the Senate provision is adopted:

(1) The adjustment relative to income realized upon the retirement or discharge of bonds, etc., has been further redrafted so as to make certain that the excluded income on account of the issuance of the bonds at a premium relates only to premium unamortized on the date of retirement or discharge. There is not to be excluded from income the accrued amortization of bond premium for that portion of the taxable year preceding such retirement or discharge.

(2) The adjustment requiring that certain deductions otherwise allowable on account of the retirement or discharge of bonds, etc., should be excluded from the computation has been eliminated for taxable years after the base period. As retained relative to taxable years in the base period, it has been redrafted so as to make certain that the excluded deduction on account of the issuance of bonds, etc., at a discount relates only to discount unamortized on the date of the retirement or discharge. The ordinary deduction for amortization of bond discount accrued for that portion of the taxable year preceding the retirement or discharge is not to be excluded from the computation. (p. 45-46)

Congressional Discussion

Discussion—Senate; on Report of Conference Committee (Cong. Rec. Vol. 86).—MR. HARRISON. * * * In this report, the conference agreed to relieve what we termed hard cases, such as the following:

* * *

Sixth. The Senate bill prevented income in the base period from being reduced by deductions on account of retirement or discharge of bonds. This was agreed to. (p. 12918)

Committee Hearings

Hearings—Ways and Means Committee.—Allowing a deduction for income on discharge of bonds. (P. D. Seghers, p. 159)

Hearings—Senate Finance Committee.—Eliminating income from retirement of bonds outstanding less than 18 months. (A. B. Trudgian, p. 83)

Explanation of provision. (C. F. Stam—Jt. Com. on Int. Rev. Taxn.—p. 191-192)

> Sec. 711(a)(1)(D)
> Sec. 711(a)(2)(F)

1940
201

[SEC. 711. EXCESS PROFITS NET INCOME.]

[(a) Taxable Years Beginning After December 31, 1939.— * * *]

[(1) Excess profits credit computed under income credit.— * * * the adjustments shall be as follows:]

(D) Refunds and Interest on Agricultural Adjustment Act Taxes.—*There shall be excluded income attributable to refund of tax paid under the Agricultural Adjustment Act of 1933, as amended, and interest upon any such refund;*

Sec. 711 (a)(2)(F) is the corresponding provision for the invested capital credit, and is the same as sec. 711 (a)(1)(D).

Committee Reports

Report—Senate Finance Committee (76th Cong., 3d Sess., S. Rept. 2114).—(3) Refunds of processing taxes, including interest thereon. This adjustment applies to the taxable years after the base period, whichever method of computing the excess-profits credit is used, and reduces gross income by the amount of such refunds and interest. (p. 5)

(4) A new adjustment has been added applicable only to taxable years under the excess-profits tax requiring the exclusion of income attributable to refunds of Agricultural Adjustment Act taxes and interest upon such refunds. (p. 12)

Report—Conference Committee (76th Cong., 3d Sess., H. Rept. 3002).—Same, except for clerical changes, as p. 12 of Senate Finance Committee report. (p. 44)

Congressional Discussion

Discussion—Senate; on Report of Conference Committee (Cong. Rec. Vol. 86).—MR. HARRISON. * * * In this report, the conference agreed to relieve what we termed hard cases, such as the following:

*   *   *

Second. The Senate bill did not require refunds and interest on Agricultural Adjustment Act taxes to be included in income for the purposes of the excess-profits tax. That was agreed to in conference. (p. 12918)

Committee Hearings

Hearings—Senate Finance Committee.—Eliminating income from AAA refunds. (E. C. Alvord, p. 273-274; S. C. Williams, p. 361)

1942 Act

Hearings—Senate Finance Committee.—Explanation of provision. (J.   O'Brien—H. Legis. Counsel—p. 104)

> ### Sec. 711(a)(1)(E)
> ### Sec. 711(a)(2)(H)

[SEC. 711. EXCESS PROFITS NET INCOME.]

[(a) **Taxable Years Beginning After December 31, 1939.**— * * *]

[(1) **Excess profits credit computed under income credit.**— * * * the adjustments shall be as follows:]

(E) **Recoveries of Bad Debts.**—*There shall be excluded income attributable to the recovery of a bad debt if a deduction with reference to such debt was allowable from gross income for any taxable year* BEGINNING *prior to January 1, 1940;*

Sec. 711 (a)(2)(H) is the corresponding provision for the invested capital credit, and is the same as sec. 711 (a)(1)(E).

Committee Reports

Report—Conference Committee (76th Cong., 3d Sess., H. Rept. 3002).—*Senate amendment.*—In addition to certain technical amendments, the Senate amendment made the following changes in and additions to the adjustments contained in the House bill:

* * *

(9) Income attributable to the recovery of a bad debt, if a deduction from gross income was allowed with reference to such debt was allowed from gross income for a taxable year beginning prior to January 1, 1940, is excluded in the case of taxable years after the base period. (p. 44, 45)

Congressional Discussion

Discussion—Senate; on Report of Conference Committee (Cong. Rec. Vol. 86).—Mr. Harrison. * * * In this report, the conference agreed to relieve what we termed hard cases, such as the following:

* * *

Fifth. The Senate bill exempted from the excess profits tax income attributable to the recovery of a bad debt if such debt was deductible from gross income for any taxable year prior to January 1, 1940. This was agreed to. (p. 12918)

Committee Hearings

Hearings—Senate Finance Committee.—Allowing credit for payment of   debts. (R. Little, p. 379-381)

1942 Act

Hearings—Ways and Means Committee.—Allowing credit for payment of debts. (W. P. Hobby, p. 2077-88)

Hearings—Senate Finance Committee.—Allowing credit for payment of   debts. (B. B. Priest, p. 405-412; M. H. Robineau, p. 443-446; T. F. Patton, p. 911; W. B. Stokely, Jr., p. 1024-26; G. M. Gadsby, p. 1193; J. R. Whiting, p. 1815; P. Arkwright, p. 1845)

1941 Act

Hearings—Senate Finance Committee.—Allowing as a deduction amount paid to retire debt of reorganized companies. (G. M. Ungaro, p. 1086, 1087-92)

1918
320(a)

[Set forth on page 329]

1917
206

[Set forth on page 358]

Sec. 711(a)(1)(F)
Sec. 711(a)(2)(A)
Sec. 711(b)(1)(G)

1942
211(a)
[711(a)
(2)(A)]

[SEC. 711. EXCESS PROFITS NET INCOME.]

[(a) Taxable Years Beginning After December 31, 1939.— * * *]

[(2) Excess profits credit computed under invested capital credit.— * * * the adjustments shall be as follows:]

(A) Dividends Received.—*The credit for dividends received shall apply, without limitation, to all dividends on stock of all corporations, except that no credit for dividends received shall be allowed with respect to dividends (actual or constructive) on stock of foreign personal holding companies or dividends on stock which is not a capital asset.*

Committee Reports

Report—Senate Finance Committee (77th Cong., 2d Sess., S. Rept. 1631).— This section, which is not contained in the House bill, amends existing law by providing that dividends on stock which is not a capital asset shall be included in full in the computation of excess profits net income of a taxpayer using the excess profits credit based on invested capital.

Under existing law stock is generally treated as an inadmissible asset and subtracted from invested capital. At the same time the dividends are excluded from excess profits net income. Stock which is not a capital asset, however, is treated as an admissible asset. But dividends on such stock are included only to the extent that they exceed the dividends received credit.

Since stock which is not a capital asset is an admissible asset, and is not subtracted from invested capital through the inadmissible-asset adjustment, the entire amount of dividends upon such stock, and not merely the 15 percent included because of section 26 (b), should be subject to excess profits tax. The amendment made by this section accomplishes this result by providing that, in the case of a taxpayer using the excess profits credit based on invested capital, the credit for dividends received shall not be allowed with respect to dividends on stock which is not a capital asset. Since the result reached under the present law is clearly an oversight, this amendment is made applicable to all excess profits tax taxable years beginning after December 31, 1939. (p. 189-190)

Report—Conference Committee (77th Cong., 2d Sess., H. Rept. 2586).— Amendment No. 292: This amendment incorporates a new section to amend existing law by providing that dividends on stock which is not a capital asset shall be included in full in the computation of excess profits net income of a taxpayer using the excess profits credit based on invested capital. * * * The House recedes. (p. 60)

[SEC. 711. EXCESS PROFITS NET INCOME.]

[(a) Taxable Years Beginning After December 31, 1939.— * * *]

[(2) Excess profits credit computed under invested capital credit.— * * * the adjustments shall be as follows:]

(A) Dividends Received. * * * This subparagraph shall not apply to dividends on stock which is not a capital asset.

Committee Reports

Report—Ways and Means Committee (77th Cong., 1st Sess., H. Rept. 146).— For corporations using the invested capital credit dividends, except dividends (actual or constructive) on the stock of foreign personal holding companies, are excluded from the excess profits net income. Likewise, stock in corporations, except stock in a foreign personal holding company, is made an inadmissible asset by section 720 (a) (1) of the present law. Corporate stocks held by dealers, not as investments for themselves but for sale to their customers, are, in reality, no different from any other article held for sale by a dealer.

Section 12 of the bill amends section 720 (a) (1) of the present law so as to allow corporate stocks held by a dealer for sale to customers to be treated as admissible assets. However, dividends on stocks so treated are subjected to the excess-profits tax to the extent that they exceed the credit for dividends received provided in section 26 (b) of the Internal Revenue Code. Such stocks held by dealers for investment would continue to be treated as inadmissible assets. (p. 20)
Report—Senate Finance Committee (77th Cong., 1st Sess., S. Rept. 75).— Same as Ways and Means Committee Report. (p. 20-21)

Congressional Discussion

Discussion—Senate (Cong. Rec. Vol. 87).—Mr. Harrison. * * * Section 12: This section permits a dealer in securities to treat stocks which it holds for sale to customers as admissible assets in computing invested capital. As the gains from such sales are subject to the excess-

profits tax, it is believed only proper not to require the taxpayer to reduce his invested capital through investments in such stocks. Any dividends received on such stocks while they are held by the dealer are subject to excess-profits tax in his hands. (p. 1638)

[SEC. 711. EXCESS PROFITS NET INCOME.]

[(a) Taxable Years Beginning After December 31, 1939.— * * *]

[(1) Excess profits credit computed under income credit.— * * * the adjustments shall be as follows:]

(F) Dividends Received.—*The credit for dividends received shall apply, without limitation, to dividends on stock of [all] DOMESTIC corporations, [except dividends (actual or constructive) on stock of foreign personal-holding companies;]*

Secs. 711 (a)(2)(A) and 711 (b)(1)(G) are the corresponding provisions for the invested capital credit and base period income. Sec. 711 (b)(1)(G) is the same as sec. 711 (a)(1)(F). Sec. 711 (a)(2)(A) is the same as sec. 711 (a)(1)(F) of the Senate Bill.

Committee Reports

Report—Ways and Means Subcommittee (76th Cong., 3d Sess., H. Rept. Aug. 8, 1940).—(1) Dividends received: The credit for dividends received will be 100 percent and will apply to dividends on the stock of all corporations, whether domestic or foreign, except dividends (actual or constructive) on stock of foreign personal holding companies. (p 6)

(4) Instead of the limited credit for dividends received allowed by section 26 (b), a credit is to be allowed of the full amount of all dividends received from another corporation, whether foreign or domestic (except foreign personal holding companies). (p. 13)

Report—Ways and Means Committee (76th Cong., 3d Sess., H. Rept. 2894).—Where the second method of measuring excess-profits is used, the normal-tax net income for both the taxable years and the years in the base period is further adjusted by increasing the credit for dividends received to 100 percent and making it applicable to dividends on the stock of all corporations, whether domestic or foreign, except dividends (actual or constructive) on stock of foreign personal holding companies. (p. 8)

(5) Instead of the limited credit for dividends received, allowed in computing the normal tax net income, a credit is to be allowed in the full amount of all dividends received (without regard to the limitation as to the amount of the adjusted net income) from another corporation, whether foreign or domestic, except dividends (actual or constructive) on stock of foreign personal holding companies. (p. 19)

Report—Conference Committee (76th Cong., 3d Sess., H. Rept. 3002).—*Senate amendment.*—In addition to certain technical amendments, the Senate amendment made the following changes in and additions to the adjustments contained in the House bill:

*   *   *

(11) Corporations computing their excess-profits credit under the income plan are given the same dividends received credit, both for taxable years in the base period and for taxable years after the base period, as is given to corporations computing their excess-profits credit on the invested capital plan, i. e., the full amount of all dividends received, except dividends on stock of a foreign personal holding company. (p. 44, 45)

Conference agreement.—With the exceptions and modifications described below, the Senate provision is adopted.

*   *   *

(5) Corporations computing their excess-profits credit on the income plan are allowed a dividends-received credit of 100 percent of the dividends received from a domestic corporation, but, unlike corporations on the invested-capital plan, are given no credit for dividends received from a foreign corporation. Such dividends, however, if their receipt constitutes an abnormality, are entitled to the treatment provided by section 721. (p. 45, 46)

Congressional Discussion

Discussion—Senate (Cong. Rec. Vol. 86).—Mr. George. * * * Both the House bill and the committee amendment provide that taxpayers who choose the invested-capital method of computing their tax will not be taxed on any part of the dividends they receive from other corporations.

This provision seems eminently fair, since dividends from domestic corporations represent earnings which have been subjected to tax in the hands of the paying corporation, and dividends from foreign corporations represent earnings which have been subjected to tax in the country in which they are earned.

However, both the House bill and the committee amendment impose the excess-profits tax on 15 percent of domestic dividends and 100 percent of foreign dividends received by taxpayers who choose the average-earnings method. This is obviously an unfair discrimination, for which there is no justification whatever.

The proposed amendment, while it is in three parts, and should be inserted in three separate sections of the bill, excludes all dividends from the computation of income, both in the base period and in the taxable year, in cases where the average-earning method is selected. (p. 12253)

Discussion—Senate; on Report of Conference Committee (Cong. Rec. Vol. 86).—Mr. Harrison. * * * In this report, the conference agreed to relieve what we termed hard cases, such as the following:

*   *   *

Third. The Senate bill allowed corporations electing the average-earnings method to deduct in full dividends re-ceived from other corporations, whether domestic or foreign. A similar deduction was allowed under the House bill to corporations electing the average-earnings method. Under the conference agreement, the Senate provision was retained as to domestic dividends. In the case of foreign dividends, relief was granted under the abnormality or general relief section.   (p. 12918)

1940 (1st) Act

Discussion—Senate (Cong. Rec. Vol. 86).—Mr. LaFollette. * * * Since the stock owned by one corporation in another corporation is excluded from the invested capital of the first corporation, dividends received from such subsidiary by the parent corporation are not included in income for the purpose of computing the excess-profits tax.   (p. 8598)

Committee Hearings

Hearings—Ways and Means Committee.—Allowing deduction for divi-dends.   (P. D. Seghers, p. 159)

[Set forth on page 358] $\frac{1917}{206}$

[Set forth on page 374] $\frac{3/3/17}{203}$

> Sec. 711(a)(1)(G)
> Sec. 711(a)(2)(I)

Section 711 (a) (1) (G) (relating to the deduction for charitable contributions, etc., in computing excess profits net income under the income credit) is repealed. $\frac{1942}{206(b)}$

Section 711 (a) (2) (I) (relating to the deduction for charitable contributions, etc., in computing excess profits net income under the invested capital method) is repealed.

Committee Reports

Report—Ways and Means Committee (77th Cong., 2d Sess., H. Rept. 2333).— This section also repeals the provisions of existing law (section 711 (a) (1) (G) and (2) (I) of the Code) disallowing the deduction of the excess profits tax from gross income in determining other deductions which are based upon a percentage of the taxpayer's net income or net income from property. Such provisions of existing law are unnecessary in view of the general disallowance of the excess-profits tax as a deduction, as provided by amendments made by section 105 (c) of the bill.   (p. 139)

1941
202(d)

[SEC. 711. EXCESS PROFITS NET INCOME.]

[(a) **Taxable Years Beginning After December 31, 1939.—** * * *]

[(1) **Excess profits credit computed under income credit.—**
* * * the adjustments shall be as follows:]

(G) **Computation of Charitable, Etc., Deductions.—**In determining any deduction the amount of which is limited to a percentage of the taxpayer's net income (or net income from the property), such net income (or net income from the property) shall be computed without regard to the deduction on account of the tax imposed by this subchapter.

Sec. 711 (a)(2)(I) is the corresponding provision for the invested capital credit, and is the same as sec. 711 (a)(1)(G).

Committee Reports

Report—Ways and Means Committee (77th Cong., 1st Sess., H. Rept. 1040).— A further adjustment is added to this section in the form of a provision stating that, for the purpose of computing any deduction or credit which is limited to a certain percentage of the taxpayer's net income—e. g., the deduction for charitable contributions or for percentage depletion—such net income (or, in the case of percentage depletion, such net income from the property) shall be computed without regard to the deduction on account of the excess-profits tax. (p. 47)

Report—Senate Finance Committee (77th Cong., 1st Sess., S. Rept. 673).— Same as Ways and Means Committee Report. (p. 38)

Committee Hearings

Hearings—Senate Finance Committee.—Objections to the provision. (H. B. Fernald, p. 881-882)

Sec. 711(a)(1)(H)

1942
205(b)

[SEC. 711. EXCESS PROFITS NET INCOME.]

[(a) **Taxable Years Beginning After December 31, 1939.—** * * *]

[(1) **Excess profits credit computed under income credit.—**
* * * the adjustments shall be as follows:]

(H) **Life Insurance Companies.—** * * * and, in the case of a life insurance company, for any taxable year beginning after December 31, 1941, the adjusted normal tax net income, as defined in section 202 (a), minus 3¼ per centum of the unearned premiums and unpaid losses on cancellable health and accident insurance contracts, *In the case of a life insurance company, there shall be deducted from the normal tax net income, the excess of (1) the product of (i) the figure determined and proclaimed under section 202 (b) and (ii) the excess profits net income computed without regard to this subparagraph, over (2) the adjustment for certain reserves provided in section 202 (c).*

Committee Reports

Report—Ways and Means Committee (77th Cong., 2d Sess., H. Rept. 2333).— Subsection (a)[1] of this section amends section 711 (a) of the code, by providing that the excess profits net income subject to specified adjustments in the case of a life insurance company, for any taxable year beginning after December 31, 1941, shall be the adjusted normal-tax net income, as defined in section 202 (a), minus 3¼ percent of the unearned premiums and unpaid losses on cancelable health and accident insurance contracts. (p. 138)

[1] Subsection (b) of the Act.

Report—Senate Finance Committee (77th Cong., 2d Sess., S. Rept. 1631).— Subsection (b) is new and amends section 711 (a) (1) of the Code, by adding a new subparagraph providing a deduction from the normal tax net income of a life insurance company of the excess of the product of the figure determined and proclaimed under section 202 (b) and the excess profits net income computed without regard to the provisions of the new subparagraph over the adjustment for certain reserves provided in section 202 (c).　(p. 184)

Report—Conference Committee (77th Cong., 2d Sess., H. Rept. 2586).—In computing the adjusted excess profits net income of a life insurance company under the income credit, the House bill is amended to allow a deduction from normal tax net income of the excess of the product of the figure determined and proclaimed by the Secretary under section 202 (b) and the excess profits net income computed without regard to this provision, over the adjustment for certain reserves. * * * The House recedes. (p. 58)

Sec. 711(a)(1)(I)
Sec. 711(a)(2)(K)

[SEC. 711.　EXCESS PROFITS NET INCOME.]

[(a)　Taxable Years Beginning After December 31, 1939.— * * *]

1943
208(d)
208(e)

[(1)　Excess profits credit computed under income credit.— * * * the adjustments shall be as follows:]

(I)　Nontaxable Income of Certain Industries With Depletable Resources.—In the case of a producer of minerals, or a producer of logs or lumber from a timber block, or a lessor of mineral property, or a timber block, as defined in section 735, there shall be excluded nontaxable income from exempt excess output of mines and timber blocks provided in section 735; in the case of a natural gas company, as defined in section 735, there shall be excluded nontaxable income from exempt excess output provided in section 735; and in the case of a producer of minerals, or a producer of logs or lumber from a timber block, there shall be excluded nontaxable bonus income provided in section 735.　In respect of nontaxable bonus income provided in section 735 (c), a corporation described in section 735 (c) (2) shall be deemed a producer of minerals for the purposes of this subparagraph.

Sec. 711(a)(2)(K) is the corresponding provision for the invested capital credit, and is the same as sec. 711(a)(1)(I).

Committee Reports

Report—Ways and Means Committee (78th Cong., 1st Sess., H. Rept. 871) — The present excess-profits tax treatment given certain excess output and bonus income for mineral and timber property is extended to lessors of mineral property or a timber block, new coal and iron mines and timber blocks not in operation during the base period, and certain natural gas companies. (p. 33)

This section amends sections 711 (a) (1) (I), 711 (a) (2) (K), and various paragraphs of section 735 so as to exempt from excess profits tax a certain portion of the income of a lessor of mineral property or a timber block, of new coal and iron mines and timber blocks not in operation during the base period, and of certain natural gas companies.

Under existing law a lessor is not included within the definition of a producer of minerals or a producer of logs or lumber from a timber block which is entitled to exclude from its excess profits net income the amount of nontaxable income from exempt excess output. Sections 711 (a) (1) (I), 711 (a) (2) (K), and 735 (a) (1) are amended by this section to permit a lessor to exclude from excess profits net income nontaxable income from exempt excess output as defined in section 735 (b). (p. 58)

Section 711 (a) (1) (I) and (a) (2) (K) are amended so as not to authorize a lessor to exclude from excess profits net income any amounts of royalties which could be claimed to represent a distribution by the lessee producer of nontaxable bonus income derived from bonus payments made by any agency of the United States Government pursuant to section 735 (c). (p. 58)

Therefore section 711 (a) (1) (I) and (a) (2) (K) is amended to include natural gas companies within the scope of those corporations entitled to exclude nontaxable income from exempt excess output in the computation of excess profits net income. (p. 59)

Report—Senate Finance Committee (78th Cong., 1st Sess., S. Rept. 627).— Same as p. 58, 59 of Ways and Means Committee Report. (p. 75, 76, respectively).

Report—Conference Committee (78th Cong., 2d Sess., H. Rept. 1079).— Amendment No. 109: Section 727 (h) of the code provides that a corporation subject to the provisions of title IV of the Civil Aeronautics Act of 1938 shall be exempt from the excess profits tax, if, after excluding from its gross income compensation received from the United States for the transportation of mail by aircraft, its adjusted excess profits net income for such year is zero or less. This amendment, for which there is no corresponding provision in the House bill, provides that the exclusion of air-mail compensation shall also be made in determining the amount of the unused excess profits credit for such year available under section 710 (c) as an offset to adjusted excess profits net income in other taxable years. To the extent, however, that the unused excess profits credit adjustment is attributable to the exclusion of mail pay, such credit is available to the taxpayer solely for the purposes of applying section 727 (h); i. e., only if such unused excess profits credit adjustment coupled with the exclusion required for the current year, again produces a zero adjusted excess profits net income. * * * The House recedes with technical amendments serving to clarify the language of the provision. * * * (p. 61-62)

Committee Hearings

Hearings—Ways and Means Committee.—Extending same relief to lessors as to owners. (J. M. B. Lewis, Jr., p. 238-243; G. T. Howard, p. 243-247)

Extending relief to natural gas industry. (I. J. Underwood, p. 717-741)

Hearings—Senate Finance Committee.—Extending same relief to lessors as to owners. (R. Paul—Treas. Dept.— p. 68-69; H. B. Fernald, p. 932)

Extending relief to natural gas industry. (I. J. Underwood, p. 181-201)

[SEC. 711.   EXCESS PROFITS NET INCOME.]

[(a)   Taxable Years Beginning After December 31, 1939.— * * *]

1942
209(a)
209(b)

[(1)   Excess profits credit computed under income credit.— * * * the adjustments shall be as follows:]

(I)   Nontaxable Income of Certain Industries With Depletable Resources.—*In the case of a producer of minerals,* OR A PRODUCER OF LOGS OR LUMBER FROM A TIMBER BLOCK, *as defined in section 735, there shall be excluded nontaxable income from exempt excess output of mines* AND TIMBER BLOCKS *and nontaxable bonus income provided in section 735.*

Sec. 711(a)(2)(K) is the corresponding provision for the invested capital credit, and is the same as sec. 711(a)(1)(I).

Committee Reports

Report—Senate Finance Committee (77th Cong., 2d Sess., S. Rept. 1631).— This section is new, no corresponding section having appeared in the House bill.   Your committee has added a new section 735 and new subsections to section 711 (a) (1) and section 711 (a) (2) (relating to the computation of excess profits net income when the excess profits credit is computed under the income credit and under the invested capital credit, respectively) to provide for the exclusion in the computation of excess profits net income of a producer of minerals as defined in section 735, of nontaxable income from exempt excess output of mineral property and nontaxable bonus income provided in section 735. (p. 186)

Sec. 711(a)(1)(J)
Sec. 711(a)(2)(L)

[SEC. 711.   EXCESS PROFITS NET INCOME.]

[(a)   Taxable Years Beginning After December 31, 1939.— * * *]

1942
210(a)
210(b)

[(1)   Excess profits credit computed under income credit.— * * * the adjustments shall be as follows:]

(J)   Net Operating Loss Deduction Adjustment.—*The net operating loss deduction shall be adjusted as follows:*

(i)   In computing the net operating loss for any taxable year under section 122 (a), and the net income for any taxable year under section 122 (b), no deduction shall be allowed for any excess profits tax imposed by this subchapter; and IF THE EXCESS PROFITS CREDIT FOR SUCH TAXABLE YEAR WAS COMPUTED UNDER SECTION 714, THE DEDUCTION FOR INTEREST SHALL BE REDUCED BY THE AMOUNT OF ANY REDUCTION UNDER PARAGRAPH (2) (B) FOR SUCH TAXABLE YEAR; AND

(ii) In lieu of the reduction provided in section 122 (c), such reduction shall be in the amount by which the excess profits net income computed with the exceptions and limitations specified in section 122 (d) (1), (2), (3) and (4) AND COMPUTED WITHOUT REGARD TO SUBPARAGRAPH (B), WITHOUT REGARD TO ANY CREDIT FOR DIVIDENDS RECEIVED, AND WITHOUT REGARD TO ANY CREDIT FOR INTEREST RECEIVED PROVIDED IN SECTION *26 (a) exceeds the excess profits net income (computed without the net operating loss deduction).*

Sec. 711(a)(2)(L) is the corresponding provision for the invested capital credit. It is substantially the same as sec. 711(a)(1)(J) except that at the end of sec. 711(a)(2)(L)(i) the Senate bill contained the following which was stricken by the Conference Committee:

[*and the gross income shall be increased by the amount of the adjustment specified by subparagraph (G) of this paragraph to the extent that such adjustment includes interest other than interest described in section 122 (d) (2)*]

Committee Reports

Report—Conference Committee (77th Cong., 2d Sess., H. Rept. 2586).— Amendment No. 291: This amendment inserted a new section in the bill to provide for the adjustment of the net operating loss deduction in computing excess profits net income. Under existing law, this deduction is designed for use in determining net income, and the adjustments required by this amendment are necessary to coordinate this deduction with the provisions for the computation of excess profits net income. The House recedes with amendments providing that the adjustments to the computations made for any taxable year in determining the net operating loss deduction are determined with respect to the excess profits tax adjustments for the year for which such computations are made. For example, if section 711 (a) (2) (B) (reducing the deduction for interest in certain cases) is applicable to the taxpayer in the taxable year in which a net operating loss is sustained, an adjustment corresponding to that required by section 711 (a) (2) (B) is made in determining the net operating loss, even though section 711 (a) (2) (B) is not applicable in the taxable year in which the net operating loss deduction, determined on the basis of such net operating loss, is claimed. (p. 60)

Congressional Discussion

Discussion—Senate (Cong. Rec. Vol. 88).—Mr. GEORGE. Mr. President, I send to the desk and ask to have stated a new amendment to be inserted at the proper place in the bill. Let me state that the Treasury has no objection to the amendment. It is solely for the purpose of eliminating duplications and other imperfections in the net-operating-loss carry-over provisions as they apply to the computations of net excess-profits income. (p. 8015)

Mr. DANAHER. Mr. President, I should like to ask the Senator from Georgia to explain, if he will do so, the type of cases which the proposed amendment is designed to cover.

Mr. GEORGE. The amendment would apply to the excess-profits carry-over provision. The amendment has been submitted to the Treasury. It is intended to eliminate duplications in the section as it was written, and to clarify certain provisions of the section.

MR. DANAHER. Does it follow the lines which we have hitherto agreed upon as a matter of policy with reference to the section?

MR. GEORGE. Oh, yes; I can assure the Senator that it does. That is my understanding of it, and it is offered on the basis of Treasury approval.

MR. DANAHER. I understand further that it is suggested by our own legislative drafting staff to correct some technicalities in previous provisions; is that correct?

MR. GEORGE. Yes. (p. 8015)

Sec. 711(a)(2)(A)

[Set forth with sec. 711(a)(1)(F), page 28]

Sec. 711(a)(2)(B)

[SEC. 711. EXCESS PROFITS NET INCOME.]

[(a) **Taxable Years Beginning After December 31, 1939.—** * * *]

[(2) **Excess profits credit computed under invested capital credit.—** * * * the adjustments shall be as follows:]

(B) **Interest.—**The deduction for interest shall be reduced by an amount ~~which is the same percentage~~ *equal to 50 per centum* of so much of such interest as represents interest on the indebtedness included in the daily amounts of borrowed capital (determined under section 719 (a)) ~~as the percentage which the sum of the daily amounts of borrowed invested capital (determined under section 719 (b)) is of the sum of the daily amounts of the borrowed capital;~~

Committee Reports

Report—Ways and Means Subcommittee (76th Cong., 3d Sess., H. Rept. Aug. 8, 1940).—(2) Interest: The deduction allowable for interest paid or accrued during the taxable year shall be reduced by an amount which is the same percentage of so much of such interest as represents interest on borrowed capital as the borrowed invested capital is of the total borrowed capital. (p. 6)

(3) The deduction for interest on indebtedness which represents borrowed capital is to be reduced by an amount which is the same percentage of such interest as the amount of borrowed capital included in invested capital is of the total borrowed capital. (p. 13)

Report—Ways and Means Committee (76th Cong., 3d Sess., H. Rept. 2894).—Same as p. 6 of the Ways and Means Subcommittee Report (p. 19). In addition, there is the following:

In addition, the deduction for interest paid or accrued is reduced by an amount which is the same percentage of so much of such interest as represents interest on borrowed capital (as defined in the bill) as the borrowed invested capital (as defined in the bill) is of the total borrowed capital. (p. 8)

Report—Senate Finance Committee (76th Cong., 3d Sess., S. Rept. 2114).—(5) The adjustment applicable to the invested capital method on account of interest has been simplified on account of the substitution of a flat 50-percent rule for the inclusion of borrowed capital in invested capital in lieu of the varying percentages contained in the House bill. (p. 12)

Committee Hearings

Hearings—Ways and Means Committee.—Adjusting for interest already disallowed because incurred to carry tax exempt securities. (W. H. Cooper, p. 317)

Hearings—Senate Finance Committee.—Limiting interest adjustment to interest on borrowed capital. (A. B. Trudgian, p. 83)

Sec. 711(a)(2)(C)

[Set forth with sec. 711(a)(1)(A), page 17]

Sec. 711(a)(2)(D)

[Set forth with sec. 711(a)(1)(B), page 20]

Sec. 711(a)(2)(E)

[Set forth with sec. 711(a)(1)(C), page 24]

Sec. 711(a)(2)(F)

[Set forth with sec. 711(a)(1)(D), page 26]

Sec. 711(a)(2)(G)

1940
201

[SEC. 711. EXCESS PROFITS NET INCOME.]

[(a) **Taxable Years Beginning After December 31, 1939.**— * * *]

[(2) **Excess profits credit computed under invested capital credit.**— * * * the adjustments shall be as follows:]

(G) **Interest on Certain Government Obligations.**—*The normal-tax net income shall be increased by an amount equal to [(i) the interest on such obligations of the United States or of corporations organized under Act of Congress as, under their terms, is not exempt from excess profits taxes, and (ii) if the taxpayer has elected under section 720 (d) to treat for the taxable year as admissible assets other obligations of the character described under section 22 (b) (4), the interest on such*

other obligations;] THE AMOUNT OF THE INTEREST ON OB-
LIGATIONS HELD DURING THE TAXABLE YEAR WHICH
ARE DESCRIBED IN SECTION 22 (b) (4) ANY PART OF THE
INTEREST FROM WHICH IS EXCLUDIBLE FROM GROSS
INCOME OR ALLOWABLE AS A CREDIT AGAINST NET
INCOME, IF THE TAXPAYER HAS SO ELECTED UNDER
SECTION 720 (d); AND

Committee Reports

**Report—Senate Finance Committee
(76th Cong., 3d Sess., S. Rept. 2114).—**
(4) Interest on tax-exempt securities.
Interest on Federal securities subject to
excess-profits tax is included in gross income and such securities are treated as
admissible assets. If the taxpayer elects
to treat other tax-exempt securities as
admissible assets, he must include the
interest therefrom in his gross income.
This adjustment is applicable only to
taxable years after the base period and to
cases where the excess-profits credit is
computed under the invested capital
method. (p. 5)

(6) It is provided that, if the excess-
profits credit is computed under the invested capital plan, the normal-tax net
income shall be increased by an amount
equal to the interest on Federal obligations not specifically exempted from
excess-profits taxes and in addition
thereto, the interest on all other Federal,
State, or local obligations, if the taxpayer
elects, under section 720 (d), to treat all
such other obligations as admissible
assets for the taxable year. (p. 12)

**Report—Conference Committee (76th
Cong., 3d Sess., H. Rept. 3002).—***Senate
amendment.*—In addition to certain technical amendments, the Senate amendment made the following changes in and
additions to the adjustments contained
in the House bill:

* * *

(6) It was also provided that, if the
excess-profits credit is computed under
the invested-capital plan, the normal-tax
net income should be increased by an
amount equal to the interest on United
States obligations and the obligations of
Federal instrumentalities not specifically
exempted from excess-profits taxes and,
in addition thereto, the interest on all
other Federal, State, or local obligations,
if the taxpayer elects, under section
720 (d) (added by the Senate amendment), to treat all such other obligations
as admissible assets for the taxable year.
(p. 44, 44-45)

Conference agreement.—With the exceptions and modifications described below, the Senate provision is adopted.

* * *

(3) The adjustment relative to interest on Federal, State, and local obligations has been revised as follows: The
distinction between certain United States
obligations and obligations of Federal
instrumentalities, on the one hand, and
all other Federal, State, or local obligations, on the other, has been eliminated,
and the treatment of all such obligations
has been made optional with the taxpayer. Instead of requiring the taxpayer to elect to treat such obligations
as admissible assets and having the taxation of the interest derived therefrom
follow as a consequence, however, the
conference agreement provides that the
taxpayer's election shall be with respect
to the inclusion of the interest in income
and that, if such an election is made, the
obligations from which such interest was
derived shall be treated as admissible
assets for the taxable year. See discussion under section 720. A taxpayer
must elect as to all such interest and may
not elect as to only a portion thereof.
(p. 45, 46)

Sec. 711(a)(2)(H)

[Set forth with sec. 711(a)(1)(E), page 27]

Sec. 711(a)(2)(I)

[Set forth with sec. 711(a)(1)(G), page 31]

Sec. 711(a)(2)(J)

1942
205(c)

[SEC. 711. EXCESS PROFITS NET INCOME.]

[(a) **Taxable Years Beginning After December 31, 1939.—** * * *]

[(2) **Excess profits credit computed under invested capital credit.—** * * * the adjustments shall be as follows:]

(J) ~~In the case of a life insurance company, the reserve and other policy liability credit shall be reduced by 50 per centum thereof.~~ *In the case of a life insurance company, there shall be deducted from the normal tax net income, 50 per centum of the excess of (1) the product of (i) the figure determined and proclaimed under section 202 (b) and (ii) the excess profits net income computed without regard to this subparagraph, over (2) the adjustment for certain reserves provided in section 202 (c).*

Committee Reports

Report—Ways and Means Committee (77th Cong., 2d Sess., H. Rept. 2333).— Subsection (b)[1] amends section 711 (a) (2) of the code, relating to the excess profits credit computed under invested capital, by providing that in the case of a life insurance company the reserve and other policy liability credit shall be reduced by 50 percent thereof. (p. 138)

[1] Subsection (c) of the Act.

Report—Senate Finance Committee (77th Cong., 2d Sess., S. Rept. 1631).— Subsection (c) revises the proposed amendment to section 711 (a) (2) of the Code, contained in the House bill, relating to the excess profits credit computed under invested capital by providing that in the case of a life insurance company there shall be deducted from the normal tax net income 50 percent of the excess of the product of the figure determined and proclaimed under section 202 (b) and the excess profits net income computed without regard to the subparagraph over the adjustment for certain reserves provided in section 202 (c). (p. 184)

Report—Conference Committee (77th Cong., 2d Sess., H. Rept. 2586).— In computing the adjusted excess profits net income of a life insurance company under the income credit, the House bill is amended to allow a deduction from normal tax net income of the excess of the product of the figure determined and proclaimed by the Secretary under section 202 (b) and the excess profits net income computed without regard to this provision, over the adjustment for certain reserves. Under the invested capital credit this deduction is 50 percent of such excess. The House recedes. (p. 58)

Sec. 711(a)(2)(K)

[Set forth with sec. 711(a)(1)(I), page 33]

Sec. 711(a)(2)(L)

[Set forth with sec. 711(a)(1)(J), page 35]

Sec. 711(a)(3)

[SEC. 711. EXCESS PROFITS NET INCOME.]

1942
213(a)

[(a) Taxable Years Beginning After December 31, 1939.— * * *]

(3) Taxable Year Less Than Twelve Months.— * * *

(B) Exception.—If the taxpayer establishes its adjusted excess profits net income for the period of twelve months beginning with the first day of the short taxable year, computed as if such twelve-month period were a taxable year, under the law applicable to the short taxable year, and using the credits applicable in determining the adjusted excess profits net income for such short taxable year, then the tax for the short taxable year shall be reduced to an amount which is such part of the tax computed on such adjusted excess profits net income so established as the excess profits net income for the short taxable year is of the excess profits net income for such twelve-month period. * * *

Committee Reports

Report—Ways and Means Committee (77th Cong., 2d Sess., H. Rept. 2333).— A corporation filing an excess profits tax return for a taxable year of less than 12 months is required under section 711 (a) (3) of existing law to place its excess profits net income on an annual basis by multiplying it by the number of days in a full year and dividing by the number of days in the short taxable year.

This section of the bill amends section 711 (a) (3) of the Code to provide that a taxpayer having a short taxable year may compute its excess-profits tax for the short period with reference to its actual adjusted excess-profits net income for a 12-month period. This provision affords relief similar to that granted by the amendments contained in section 126[1] of the bill with respect to the income tax. In the case of a short taxable year caused by the taxpayer becoming affiliated, or breaking affiliation, with a group filing a consolidated return for the period during which the corporation was affiliated, the regulations with respect to consolidated returns may, of course, make other provision for establishing the adjusted excess-profits net income for a 12-month period, such as by requiring the corporation to use as the 12-month period the annual accounting period in which the short taxable year falls.   (p. 139-140)

[1] Sec. 135 of the Act.

Committee Hearings

Hearings—Senate Finance Committee.—Explanation of provision. (J. O'Brien—H. Legis. Counsel—p. 103)

[Set forth on page 326]

Sec. 711(b)(1)(A)

[Set forth with sec. 711(a)(1)(A), page 17]

Sec. 711(b)(1)(B)

[Set forth with sec. 711(a)(1)(B), page 20]

Sec. 711(b)(1)(C)

[Set forth with sec. 711(a)(1)(C), page 24]

Sec. 711(b)(1)(D)

[SEC. 711.   EXCESS PROFITS NET INCOME.]

[(b)   Taxable Years in Base Period.—]

[(1)   General rule and adjustments.— * * *]

(D)   Deductions on Account of Retirement or Discharge of Bonds, and So Forth.—*If during the taxable year the taxpayer retires or discharges any bond, debenture, note, or certificate or other evidence of indebtedness, if the obligation of the taxpayer has been outstanding for more than eighteen months, the following deductions for such taxable year shall not be allowed:*

(i)   The deduction allowable under section 23 (a) for expenses paid or incurred in connection with such retirement or discharge;

(ii)   The deduction for losses allowable by reason of such retirement or discharge; and

(iii) [*The deduction allowable on account of the issuance at a discount of the bond, debenture, note, or certificate, or other evidence of indebtedness retired or discharged*] IN CASE THE ISSUANCE WAS AT A DISCOUNT, THE AMOUNT DEDUCTIBLE FOR SUCH YEAR SOLELY BECAUSE OF SUCH RETIREMENT OR DISCHARGE;

The Senate Finance Committee bill included the same provision for the income and invested capital credits, but they were stricken by the Conference Committee.

Committee Reports

Report—Senate Finance Committee (76th Cong., 3d Sess., S. Rept. 2114).— To the adjustments provided in the House bill for the purpose of determining excess profits net income, your committee has added the following: * * *

(2) Losses and expenses resulting from the retirement or discharge by the taxpayer certain indebtedness outstanding for more than 18 months. This adjustment is applicable with respect to both the base period and taxable years thereafter, whichever method of computing the excess-profits credit is used, and has the effect of restoring these losses and expenses to net income. (p. 5)

Committee Hearings

Hearings—Ways and Means Committee.—Eliminating costs incident to redemption of bonds at premium, including unamortized discount. (F. P. Byerly, p. 363)

Hearings—Senate Finance Committee.—Eliminating costs incident to redemption of bonds at premium, including unamortized discount. (W. A. Cooper, p. 55; E. D. Evans, p. 67-68; W. G. Woolfolk, p. 239-240; E. Clark, p. 241-244; E. C. Alvord, p. 263, 272; J. W. Hooper, p. 353; A. B. Chapman, p. 388-395)

UNENACTED RELATED PROVISION

1940 Act
[Sec. 201 of Senate bill]

[SEC. 711. EXCESS PROFITS NET INCOME.]

[(b) **Taxable Years in Base Period.**—]

[(1) **General rule and adjustments.** * * *]

[*(J)*   *Bad debt deductions.—The deduction under 23 (K) for any taxable year for bad debts shall be decreased by an amount representing unrecovered loans made by a parent corporation to its subsidiary.*]

Committee Reports

Report—Conference Committee (76th Cong., 3d Sess., H. Rept. 3002).—*Senate amendment.*—In addition to certain technical amendments, the Senate amendment made the following changes in and additions to the adjustments contained in the House bill:

* * *

(13) In case of taxable years in the base period, the deduction under section 23 (k) for bad debts is decreased by an amount representing unrecovered loans made by a parent corporation to its subsidiary, in so far as such deduction includes an amount representing such unrecovered loans. (p. 44, 45)

Conference agreement.—With the exceptions and modifications described below, the Senate provision is adopted.

* * *

(7) The adjustment in the base period on account of bad debts representing unrecovered loans made by a parent corporation to a subsidiary has been eliminated. (p. 45, 47)

Congressional Discussion

Discussion—Senate (Cong. Rec. Vol. 86).—Mr. Barkley. Mr. President, the amendment would simply permit another category of deductions in normal income to apply to the excess-profits tax, so that where the parent company——(p. 12305)

Discussion—Senate; on Report of Conference Committee (Cong. Rec. Vol. 86).—MR. HARRISON. I know of only one special relief provision which was not so incorporated. That was the one which was offered by the Senator from Kentucky [Mr. BARKLEY], to give relief rela-

tive to an unrecovered debt in connection with a loan made by a parent corporation to its subsidiary; and the House conferees would not accept that amendment.

MR. BARKLEY. Mr. President, I understand that that provision went out on the insistence of the Treasury Department.

MR. HARRISON. The Senator is right. (p. 12918)

Committee Hearings

Hearings—Senate Finance Committee.—Eliminating losses from bad debts and worthless securities. (E. R. Clark, p. 429-430)

Sec. 711(b)(1)(E)

[SEC. 711. EXCESS PROFITS NET INCOME.]

[(b) Taxable Years in Base Period.—]

[(1) General rule and adjustments.— * * *]

(E) Casualty,[1] Demolition, and Similar Losses.—Deductions *under section 23 (f)* for losses arising from fires, storms, shipwreck, or other casualty, or from theft, *or arising from the demolition, abandonment, or loss of useful value of property,* not compensated for by insurance or otherwise, shall not be allowed.

[1] The words "Demolition, and Similar" were added by the Senate Finance Committee.

Committee Reports

Report—Ways and Means Committee (76th Cong., 3d Sess., H. Rept. 2894).—For the years in the base period only, where either method of measuring excess profits is used, the normal-tax net income is adjusted further by the addition thereto of the amount of losses, not compensated for by insurance or otherwise, arising from fires, storms, shipwreck, or other casualty, or from theft. (p. 8)

Your committee has recommended certain special relief provisions, which are as follows:

   * * *

(2) A corporation which suffered losses during the base period because of fire, storm, shipwreck, or other casualty or from theft, not compensated for by insurance or otherwise, is afforded relief by having such deductions disallowed for

the purpose of the excess-profits tax computation of the base-period income. This has the effect of increasing the base-period income. (p. 13, 14)

Additional adjustments with respect to the base period are that deductions for losses arising from fires, storms, shipwreck, or other casualty, or from theft, not compensated for by insurance or otherwise are not included. * * * (p. 20)

Report—Senate Finance Committee (76th Cong., 3d Sess., S. Rept. 2114).—To the adjustments provided in the House bill for the purpose of determining excess profits net income, your committee has added the following:

(1) Uninsured losses resulting from the demolition, abandonment, or loss of useful value of property. This adjustment applies only to years in the base

period and the effect of it is to increase net income by the amount then allowed as a deduction from gross income. (p. 5)

(7) The adjustment on account of casualty losses has been expanded so as to exclude from the computation of excess-profits net income for taxable years in the base period, losses arising from the demolition, abandonment, and loss of useful value of property. (p. 12)

Report—Conference Committee (76th Cong., 3d Sess., H. Rept. 3002).—*Senate*

amendment.—In addition to certain technical amendments, the Senate amendment made the following changes in and additions to the adjustments contained in the House bill:

* * *

(7) Losses arising from the demolition, abandonment, and loss of useful value of property are excluded from the computation of excess-profits net income for taxable years in the base period. (p. 44, 45)

Congressional Discussion

Discussion—Senate; on Report of Conference Committee (Cong. Rec. Vol. 86).—Mr. Harrison. * * * In this report, the conference agreed to relieve what we termed hard cases, such as the following:

* * *

Seventh. The Senate bill prevented income in the base period from being reduced by losses arising from demolition, abandonment, or loss of useful value of property not compensated for by insurance. This was agreed to. (p. 12918)

Committee Hearings

Hearings—Ways and Means Committee.—Eliminating loss on abandonment or destruction of property. (F. P. Byerly, p. 363)

Hearings—Senate Finance Committee.—Eliminating loss on abandonment

or destruction of property. (K. Carroad, p. 35)

Explanation of provision. (C. F. Stam—Jt. Com. on Int. Rev. Taxn.—p. 192)

Sec. 711(b)(1)(F)

[SEC. 711. EXCESS PROFITS NET INCOME.]

[(b) Taxable Years in Base Period.—]

[(1) General rule and adjustments.— * * *]

(F)[1] **Repayment of Processing Tax to Vendee.**—The deduction under section 23 (a), for any taxable year, for expenses shall be decreased by an amount ~~equal to~~ *which bears the same ratio to* the amount deductible on account of any repayment or credit by the corporation to its vendee of any amount attributable to any tax under the Agricultural Adjustment Act of 1933, as amended, ~~For the purposes of this clause, the adjustment for the first taxable year in the base period shall be the excess of the amount so deductible for such year over the amount includible in gross income for such year by reason of the tax under such Act which was not paid, and the adjustment for any succeeding taxable year in the base period shall be the excess of the amount so deductible for such year and all previous years in the~~

~~base period over the amounts so includible in gross income for such year and all previous taxable years in the base period.~~ *as the excess of the aggregate of the amounts so deductible in the base period over the aggregate of the amounts attributable to taxes under such Act collected from its vendees which were includible in the corporation's gross income in the base period and which were not paid, bears to the aggregate of the amounts so deductible in the base period;*

[1] The heading is as worded by the Senate Finance Committee. The Ways and Means Committee heading read "Repayment to Vendees of Processing Tax".

Committee Reports

Report—Ways and Means Committee (76th Cong., 3d Sess., H. Rept. 2894).— In addition, there is added back, for the years in the base period, the amounts which were deductible on account of any repayment or credit by a corporation to its vendee of any amount attributable to any tax under the Agricultural Adjustment Act. (p. 8)

Your committee has recommended certain special relief provisions, which are as follows:

(1) Special treatment is allowed for corporations which were required to refund to their vendees amounts attributable to any tax which was not paid under the Agricultural Adjustment Act of 1933, as amended. These amounts were allowed as deductions for business expenses in computing income subject to the corporation normal tax for the taxable years in the base period. This resulted in a distortion of the income in the base period. Your committee has provided that any deduction for business expenses in the base period may be decreased by the amount of the excess of such repayments over the amount required to be included in gross income by reason of such taxes for the purpose of the excess-profits tax. (p. 13-14)

Additional adjustments with respect to the base period are that * * * the deduction for expenses is diminished by payments or credits to vendees of reimbursements to them of processing and other taxes under the Agricultural Adjustment Act of 1933. (p. 20)

Report—Senate Finance Committee (76th Cong., 3d Sess., S. Rept. 2114).— (8) The adjustment on account of repayment of Agricultural Adjustment Act taxes to vendees has been rewritten to remedy certain technical defects contained in the House bill. (p. 12)

Congressional Discussion

Discussion—Senate (Cong. Rec. Vol. 86).—MR. VANDENBERG. * * * Third. To accomplish our hasty objective, by needlessly commingling these unrelated matters we present the taxpayer with so dense a puzzle that only a Philadelphia lawyer, a certified public accountant, and an extraordinarily clever crystal gazer in combined effort can chart the answer; and even then the courts will finally have to find out precisely what we thought we were doing when we wrote the law.

One can test that statement, Mr. President, by taking up this bill and opening it anywhere he pleases. I do not intend to labor the subject, but let us open the bill at random and see what we find, on page 93, describing the repayment of the processing tax to vendees. * * *

MR. HARRISON. Was not that provision offered by the Senator from Michigan?

MR. VANDENBERG. No, indeed.

MR. HARRISON. He was insisting upon such an amendment going into the relief provisions of the law.

MR. VANDENBERG. The Senator from Michigan was never insisting upon any amendment in any such language as that. The Senator from Michigan was insisting that there should be a complete exemption in respect to processing taxes;

but whether this is what I was talking about or not I leave to the Senator. If he says it is, I am grateful and happy; but I doubt whether even he would dare give me that assurance.

MR. HARRISON. I was delighted when the committee accepted the insistence of the Senator from Michigan upon incorporating such a provision in the bill.

MR. VANDENBERG. I think the purpose which the Senator describes is excellent. I am just wondering whether we have reached the purpose. I cannot recognize in this meandering language anything I ever talked about. It certainly cinches my point if the father of an idea cannot even recognize his own child. (p. 12061)

Committee Hearings

Hearings—Senate Finance Committee.—Explanation of provision. (J. L.   Sullivan—Treas. Dept.—p. 120)

Sec. 711(b)(1)(G)

[Set forth with sec. 711(a)(1)(F), page 28]

Sec. 711(b)(1)(H)

[SEC. 711. EXCESS PROFITS NET INCOME.]

   [(b)   Taxable Years in Base Period.—]

      [(1)   General rule and adjustments.— * * *]

         (H)   Payment of Judgments, and So Forth.—Deductions attributable to any claim, award, judgment, or decree against the taxpayer, * * * if normal for the taxpayer, but in excess of 125 per centum of the average amount of such deductions in the four previous taxable years, shall be disallowed in an amount equal to such excess;

EPTA
3

Committee Reports

Report—Ways and Means Committee (77th Cong., 1st Sess., H. Rept. 146).— The 125-percent rule, which, in the interests of certainty, is a substitute for the "grossly disproportionate" test in existing law, is also made applicable to subsection (H) (old subsection (G)), adjusting deductions for the payment of claims, awards, judgments, and decrees against the taxpayer, and to subsection (I) (old subsection (H)), adjusting deductions attributable to intangible drilling and development costs with respect to oil and gas wells or mines. (p. 5)

Report—Senate Finance Committee (77th Cong., 1st Sess., S. Rept. 75).— Same as Ways and Means Committee Report. (p. 5)

[SEC. 711. EXCESS PROFITS NET INCOME.]

   [(b)   Taxable Years in Base Period.—]

      [(1)   General rule and adjustments.— * * *]

1940
201

(G) Payment of Judgments, and So Forth.—*Deductions attributable to any claim, award, judgment, or decree against the taxpayer, or interest on any of the foregoing, shall not be allowed if in the light of the taxpayer's business it* [*is*] WAS *abnormal for the taxpayer to incur a liability of such character or, if the taxpayer normally* [*incurs*] INCURRED *such liability, the amount of such liability in the taxable year* [*is*] WAS *grossly disproportionate to the amount of such liability in the four previous taxable years.*

Committee Reports

Report—Senate Finance Committee (76th Cong., 3d Sess., S. Rept. 2114).—(5) Unusual and nonrecurring claims, judgments, awards, and decrees. Unusual or abnormal amounts paid out because of claims, judgments, awards, and decrees are not deducted from the gross income of years in the base period. (p. 5)

(9) An additional adjustment is provided, applicable only to taxable years. in the base period, to the effect that deductions attributable to any claim, award, judgment, or decree against the taxpayer, or interest thereon, will not be required to be taken into account if, in the light of the taxpayer's business, it is abnormal for the taxpayer to incur a liability of such character or, if the taxpayer normally incurs liabilities of such character, the amount of the particular liabilities of such character in the taxable year is grossly disproportionate to the average amount of liabilities of such character in each of the 4 previous taxable years. (p. 12)

Report—Conference Committee (76th Cong., 3d Sess., H. Rept. 3002).—*Senate amendment.*—In addition to certain technical amendments, the Senate amendment made the following changes in and additions to the adjustments contained in the House bill:

*   *   *

(8) An additional adjustment was provided, applicable only to taxable years in the base period, to the effect that deductions attributable to any claim, award, judgment, or decree against the taxpayer, or interest thereon, would not be required to be taken into account if, in the light of the taxpayer's business, it is abnormal for the taxpayer to incur a liability of such character or, if the taxpayer normally incurs liabilities of such character, the amount of the particular liabilities of such character in the taxable year is grossly disproportionate to the average amount of liabilities of such character in each of the four previous taxable years. (p. 44, 45)

Sec. 711(b)(1)(I)

[SEC. 711. EXCESS PROFITS NET INCOME.]

[(b) Taxable Years in Base Period.—]

[(1) General rule and adjustments.— * * *]

(I) Intangible Drilling and Development Costs.—Deductions attributable to intangible drilling and development costs paid or incurred in or for the drilling of wells or the preparation of wells for the production of oil or gas, and for development costs in the case of mines, if abnormal for the taxpayer, shall not be allowed, and if normal for the taxpayer, but in excess of 125 per centum of the average amount of such deductions in the four previous taxable years, shall be disallowed in an amount equal to such excess; and

Committee Reports

Report—Ways and Means Committee (77th Cong., 1st Sess., H. Rept. 146).— The 125-percent rule, which, in the interests of certainty, is a substitute for the "grossly disproportionate" test in existing law, is also made applicable to subsection (H) (old subsection (G)), adjusting deductions for the payment of claims, awards, judgments, and decrees against the taxpayer, and to subsection (I) (old subsection (H)), adjusting deductions attributable to intangible drilling and development costs with respect to oil and gas wells or mines. (p. 5)

Report—Senate Finance Committee (77th Cong., 1st Sess., S. Rept. 75).— Same as Ways and Means Committee Report. (p. 5)

[SEC. 711. EXCESS PROFITS NET INCOME.]

[(b)   Taxable Years in Base Period.—]

[(1)   General rule and adjustments.— * * *]

(H)   All expenditures for intangible drilling and development costs paid or incurred in or for the drilling of wells or the preparation of wells for the production of oil or gas, or expenditures for development costs in the case of mines, which the taxpayer has deducted from gross income as an expense, shall not be allowed to the extent that in the light of the taxpayer's business it was abnormal for the taxpayer to incurr a liability of such character or, if the taxpayer normally incurred such liability, to the extent that the amount of such liability in the taxable year was grossly disproportionate to the amount of such liability in the four previous taxable years; and

This paragraph was added by the Conference Committee.

Committee Reports

Report—Conference Committee (76th Cong., 3d Sess., H. Rept. 3002).—As retained relative to taxable years in the base period, the adjustment has been limited to deductions allowed in respect of expenditures for intangible drilling and development costs paid or incurred in or for the drilling of wells or the preparation of wells for the production of oil or gas, or for development costs in the case of mines. Such deductions are excluded only if and to the extent that in the light of the taxpayer's business it is abnormal for the taxpayer to incur a liability of such character or, if the taxpayer normally incurs such liability, only to the extent that the amount of such liability in the taxable year in question was grossly disproportionate to the amount of such liability in the 4 previous taxable years. (p. 45-46)

UNENACTED RELATED PROVISION
1940 Act
[Sec. 201 of Senate bill]

[SEC. 711. EXCESS PROFITS NET INCOME.]

[(a)   Taxable Years Beginning After December 31, 1939.— * * *]

[(1)   Excess profits credit computed under income credit.— * * *]

[(G) *Deductions in connection with exploration.—Deductions allowed in connection with exploration, discovery, prospecting, research, or development of tangible property, patents, formulae, or processes, or any combination of the foregoing;]*

Sec. 711 (b)(1)(H) is the corresponding provision for base period income, and is the same as sec. 711 (a)(1)(G).

Committee Reports

Report—Conference Committee (76th Cong., 3d Sess., H. Rept. 3002).—*Senate amendment.*—In addition to certain technical amendments, the Senate amendment made the following changes in and additions to the adjustments contained in the House bill:

*   *   *

(10) A new adjustment, applicable to both the taxable years in the base period and taxable years after the base period in the case of corporations computing their excess-profits credit under the income plan, was added requiring the exclusion of any deductions in connection with exploration, discovery, prospecting, research, or development of tangible property, patents, formulae or processes, or any combination of the foregoing. * * *

Conference agreement.—With the exceptions and modifications described below, the Senate provision is adopted.

*   *   *

(4) The adjustment requiring the exclusion of any deduction in connection with exploration, etc., has been eliminated as to taxable years after the base period. (p. 44, 45, 46)

Committee Hearings

Hearings—Ways and Means Committee.—Eliminating expenditures for research and development. (P. E. Shorb, p. 115-117)

Sec. 711(b)(1)(J)

[SEC. 711. EXCESS PROFITS NET INCOME.]

[(b) Taxable Years in Base Period.—]

[(1) General rule and adjustments.— * * *]

(J) **Abnormal Deductions.**—Under regulations prescribed by the Commissioner, with the approval of the Secretary, for the determination, for the purposes of this subparagraph, of the classification of deductions—

(i) Deductions of any class shall not be allowed if deductions of such class were abnormal for the taxpayer, and

(ii) If the class of deductions was normal for the taxpayer, but the deductions of such class were in excess of 125 per centum of the average amount of deductions of such class for the four previous taxable years, they shall be disallowed in an amount equal to such excess.

Committee Reports

Report—Ways and Means Committee (77th Cong., 1st Sess., H. Rept. 146).— The bill affords relief in the following situations:

* * *

2. It adds to the list of adjustments for specific items of abnormal deductions, set out in section 711 (b) of the existing law, a further adjustment for abnormal deductions of any class during the years in the base period. (p. 2, 3)

To ascertain the excess-profits credit based on income, it is necessary to determine the excess-profits net income for the taxable years in the base period. For the purposes of computing the excess-profits net income for such years, section 711 (b) (1) of the present law provides for adjustments to the normal-tax or special-class net income, with respect to a number of specific items of both income and deductions. In addition to the adjustments for the deductions specified by the present law, the amendments made by this section provide that any deduction will be disallowed for the base period if it was of a class abnormal for the taxpayer. If such deduction was of a class normal for the taxpayer, then to the extent that it exceeds 125 percent of the average amount of the deductions of such class for the 4 previous taxable years, such excess will be disallowed. (p. 4-5)

Report—Senate Finance Committee (77th Cong., 1st Sess., S. Rept. 75).— Same as Ways and Means Committee Report. (p. 3; 5, respectively)

Congressional Discussion

Discussion—Senate (Cong. Rec. Vol. 87).—Mr. Harrison. * * * Section 3: Under existing law, there were certain deductions disallowed in computing the base-period credit because of their abnormal character. These consisted of expenses in connection with payments of judgments and expenditures for intangible drilling and development costs in connection with oil and gas wells or expenditures for development costs in the case of mines. These deductions were disallowed if it was abnormal for the taxpayer to incur such expenditures or if the taxpayer normally incurred such liability to the extent that the amount of such liability in the taxable year was grossly disproportionate to the amount of such liability in the four previous years. The bill broadens the class of abnormal deductions. It provides that deductions of any class shall be disallowed if deductions of such class were abnormal for the taxpayer, and if they were normal but in excess of 125 percent of the average amount of deductions of such class for the 4 previous taxable years. The 125-percent rule is substituted for the grossly disproportionate test of existing law. This would mean that the taxpayer's deductions of an abnormal class in the taxable year would have to exceed by more than 25 percent the average of the deductions for the same class in the 4 preceding taxable years. If the taxpayer was not in existence in the 4 previous taxable years, it may use certain succeeding taxable years. (p. 1637-38)

Committee Hearings
1943 Act

Hearings—Senate Finance Committee.—Eliminating from base period deductions past service payments in pension trusts. (E. C. Alvord, p. 615; A. B. Chapman, p. 832)

1942 Act

Hearings—Senate Finance Committee.—Including in base period income amounts allocated to it under section 721.

(G. V. Pach, p. 369; E. C. Alvord, p. 1797; A. B. Chapman, p. 2079, 2086)

1941 Act

Hearings—Ways and Means Committee.—Difficulties of applying term "class." (R. N. Miller, p. 473; F. A. Godchaux, Jr., p. 1752)

Including in base period income amounts allocated to it under section 721. (H. B. Fernald, p. 1570, 1574; Control-

lers Institute of America, p. 1716)

Hearings—Senate Finance Committee.—Including in base period income amounts allocated to it under section 721. (E. C. Alvord, p. 640, 642; A. B. Chapman, p. 754, 764; H. B. Fernald, p. 883)

Sec. 711(b)(1)(K)

[SEC. 711. EXCESS PROFITS NET INCOME.]

[(b)   Taxable Years in Base Period.—]

[(1)   General rule and adjustments.— * * *]

(K)   Rules for Application of Subparagraphs (H), (I), and (J).—For the purposes of subparagraphs (H), (I), and (J)—

(i)   If the taxpayer was not in existence for four previous taxable years, then such average amount specified in such subparagraphs shall be determined for the previous taxable years it was in existence and the succeeding taxable years which begin before the beginning of the taxpayer's second taxable year under this subchapter. If the number of such succeeding years is greater than the number necessary to obtain an aggregate of four taxable years there shall be omitted so many of such succeeding years, beginning with the last, as are necessary to reduce the aggregate to four.

(ii)   Deductions shall not be disallowed under such subparagraphs unless the taxpayer establishes that the abnormality or excess is not a consequence of an increase in the gross income of the taxpayer in its base period or a decrease in the amount of some other deduction in its base period, and is not a consequence of a change at any time in the type, manner of operation, size, or condition of the business engaged in by the taxpayer.

(iii)   The amount of deductions of any class to be disallowed under such subparagraphs with respect to any taxable year shall not exceed the amount by which the deductions of such class for such taxable year exceed the deductions of such class for the taxable year for which the tax under this subchapter is being computed.

Committee Reports

Report—Ways and Means Committee (77th Cong., 1st Sess., H. Rept. 146).—New subsection (K) permits the adjustments provided in new subsections (H), (I), and (J) to be made also where the taxpayer was not in existence for 4 previous taxable years. In such case it will use such previous taxable years during which it was in existence, plus the succeeding taxable years which began before the beginning of its second taxable year subject to the excess-profits tax, but in no case to aggregate more than 4 taxable years. For example, corporation A came into existence on July 1, 1938. For the purpose of measuring abnormalities or excesses of deductions for the taxable year beginning July 1, 1938, it may use the taxable years beginning July 1, 1939, and July 1, 1940. Since the taxable year beginning July 1, 1941, would be the taxpayer's second taxable year subject to the excess-profits tax, that year may not be used. This subsection also restricts the benefits of new subsections (H), (I), and (J) by placing upon the taxpayer the burden of establishing that the abnormalities or excesses in the deductions treated by those subsections are not the consequences of an increased gross income or a decrease in the size of other deductions in the base period or of changes in the type, manner of operation, size, or condition of the business conducted by the taxpayer.

Nor will deductions of any class be disallowed for any taxable year unless they exceed the amount by which the deductions of the same class for such year exceed the deductions of such class for the taxable year for which the excess-profits tax is being computed. For ex-

ample, for the taxable year in the base period, 1938, a corporation had a deduction of $200,000, although its average deduction of the same class for all of the years in the test period were only $100,000. If in 1940 it had deductions of that class totaling $100,000, for the purpose of determining its average earnings credit to be used in computing its excess-profits tax for 1940, $75,000 of the deduction in 1938 would be disallowed, thereby increasing the excess-profits credit. This would be true since to the extent that the deductions of this class in 1938 exceed 125 percent of the average deductions of the same class during the test period, they are disallowed. If in 1941, however, this taxpayer had deductions of this class totaling $150,000, only $50,000, of the $200,000 for 1938 would be disallowed in determining the average-earnings credit for use against the excess-profits net income for 1941. (p. 5)

Report—Senate Finance Committee (77th Cong., 1st Sess., S. Rept. 75).— Same as Ways and Means Committee Report. (p. 5-6)

Committee Hearings
1941 Act

Hearings—Senate Finance Committee.—Adjusting base period earnings for increased income due to decreased expense. (L. J. Hoban, p. 972-973)

Sec. 711(b)(2)

[SEC. 711. EXCESS PROFITS NET INCOME.]

[(b) Taxable Years in Base Period.—]

1942
207(g)

(2) Capital Gains and Losses.—For the purposes of this subsection the normal-tax net income and the special-class net income referred to in paragraph (1) shall be computed as if section 23 (g) (2), section 23 (k) (2), and section 117 were part of the revenue law applicable to the taxable year the excess profits net income of which is being computed, with the exception that the capital loss carry-over provided in subsection (e) (1) of section 117 shall be applicable to net capital losses for taxable years beginning after December 31, 1934. * * *

Committee Reports

Report—Senate Finance Committee (77th Cong., 2d Sess., S. Rept. 1631).— In conformity with the changes made by section 152[1] of the bill, a technical amendment is made to the provisions of section 711 (b) (2) which permit a net short-term capital loss carry-over in computing base period net income.   (p. 185-186)

[1] Sec. 150 of the Act.

[SEC. 711.   EXCESS PROFITS NET INCOME.]

[(b)   Taxable Years in Base Period.—]

(2)   Capital Gains and Losses.—For the purposes of this subsection the normal-tax net income and the special-class net income referred to in paragraph (1) shall be computed as if section *23 (g) (2)*, *section 23 (k) (2), and section* 117 were part of the revenue law applicable to the taxable year the excess profits net income of which is being computed, with the ~~exceptions (A)~~ *exception* ~~that property otherwise constituting a capital asset shall not, if held for more than eighteen months, be deemed to be excluded from the definition of such term because it was of a character which is subject to the allowance for depreciation provided for in section 23 (l), and (B)~~ that the net short-term capital loss carry-over provided in subsection (e) of ~~such~~ section *117* shall be applicable to net short-term capital losses for taxable years beginning after December 31, 1934.   ~~The exception provided in clause (B)~~ *Such exception* shall not apply for the purposes of computing the tax under this subchapter for any taxable year beginning before January 1, 1941.

Committee Reports

Report—Ways and Means Committee (76th Cong., 3d Sess., H. Rept. 2894).— The normal tax net income or the special class net income for taxable years in the base period is to be computed as if section 117 of the Internal Revenue Code were a part of the revenue law applicable to the taxable year for which such income is being determined, with the exceptions hereinafter noted.   In the application of section 117, the definition of capital assets is to be applied in the case of property held for more than 18 months as if depreciable assets were not excluded; that is, depreciable assets would be treated as capital assets if they are otherwise qualified as capital assets under the definition.   If the computation of the excess-profits net income for a taxable year in the base period is being made in connection with the determination of the excess-profits tax liability for a taxable year beginning after December 31, 1940, then the net short-term capital loss carry-over provided in section 117 (e) shall be applicable to net short-term capital losses for taxable years beginning after December 31, 1934. Section 117 (e) is not applicable if the base period computation is being made for the purpose of determining the excess-profits tax liability for a taxable year beginning before January 1, 1941. (p. 19-20)

Report—Senate Finance Committee (76th Cong., 3d Sess., S. Rept. 2114).— If the excess-profits credit was computed on the invested-capital plan, the normal-tax net income was further adjusted by increasing the credit for dividends received to 100 percent and making it applicable to dividends on the stock of all corporations, whether domestic or foreign, except dividends (actual or constructive) on stock of foreign personal holding companies; and by reducing the deduction for interest paid or accrued by an amount which was the same percentage of the interest on borrowed capital as the borrowed invested capital was of the total borrowed capital. (p. 11)

The House provision applying section 117 of the Internal Revenue Code (relative to capital gains and losses) to taxable years in the base period has been retained. Certain changes have been made therein in view of the revised treatment above described in the case of depreciable assets. In addition, section 23 (g) and (k) of the Internal Revenue Code have been made applicable to taxable years in the base period, in order that long-term losses due to securities (stocks and bonds) having become worthless shall be disallowed in computing excess profits net income for taxable years in which such losses were not treated as capital losses under the income-tax law applicable to such years.

(p. 12)

Report—Conference Committee (76th Cong., 3d Sess., H. Rept. 3002).—*Senate amendment.*—In addition to certain technical amendments, the Senate amendment made the following changes in and additions to the adjustments contained in the House bill: * * *

In addition to applying section 117 of the Internal Revenue Code (relative to capital gains and losses) to taxable years in the base period, which was done in the House bill, the Senate amendment applies section 23 (g) and (k) to such taxable years in order that long-term losses due to securities (stocks and bonds) having become worthless would be disallowed in computing excess-profits net income for taxable years in which such losses were not treated as capital losses under the income-tax law applicable to such years. (p. 44, 45)

> Sec. 712(a)
> Sec. 712(b)*
> Sec. 741(a)*
> * In Part

SEC. 712. EXCESS PROFITS CREDIT—ALLOWANCE.

(a) Domestic Corporations.—*In the case of a domestic corporation which was in existence before January 1, 1940, the excess profits credit for any taxable year shall be an amount computed under section 713 or section 714, whichever amount results in the lesser tax under this subchapter for the taxable year for which the tax under this subchapter is being computed. In the case of all other domestic corporations the excess profits credit for any taxable year shall be an amount computed under section 714. * * **

EPTA
13
[712(a)]
[712(b)]
14
[741(a)]

Secs. 712 (b) and 741 (a) are the corresponding provisions for foreign corporations and acquiring corporations, respectively, and are substantially the same as sec. 712 (a) insofar as here material.

Committee Reports

Report—Senate Finance Committee (77th Cong., 1st Sess., S. Rept. 75).— Under existing law a corporation entitled to use either the income credit or the invested capital credit is required irrevocably to choose between such credits for each taxable year. The amendments adopted by your committee relieve the taxpayer of the hardship of having to make such an election and provide instead that the credit shall be the one resulting in the lesser tax. (p. 1)

Under existing law a domestic corporation which was in existence before

January 1, 1940, is required to elect in its return between the credit based upon invested capital and the credit based upon base-period income. The committee bill relieves the taxpayer of the necessity of making such an election and instead provides that the credit shall be an amount computed under either section 713 (the credit based upon base-period income) or section 714 (the credit based upon invested capital), whichever amount results in the lesser tax for the taxable year for which the tax is being computed. (p. 21)

Congressional Discussion

Discussion—Senate (Cong. Rec. Vol. 87).—MR. GEORGE. * * * The bill as now amended gives him the right to change that election, and to use as the basis whichever method will require him to pay the smaller tax. That alone, in the whole field of corporate taxpayers, is an inestimable advantage to him, because there are so many borderline cases in which the corporation cannot early and easily determine whether it should take its invested capital or its prior earnings as the basis.

This bill, in some of its provisions, gives a chance to build up a better base, a more accurate base, and it also gives to the corporation the option—not at the time it makes its return, but at the time the taxes finally are to be paid or the liability is determined—to take either average earnings or invested capital as the base, which would be of very great benefit particularly to companies which are rapidly growing, companies which are more or less speculative in their operations.

MR. ADAMS. I was thinking not alone of mining companies. The bill applies equally to an inventor.

MR. GEORGE. It applies to all.

MR. ADAMS. It applies to a man who was working on an invention over a period of years, spending his resources, and finally accomplishing his purpose.

MR. GEORGE. The Senator is correct. It applies to all equally. It applies to every corporation, regardless of the kind of business it is doing. (p. 1636-37)

MR. HARRISON. * * * Sections 13, 14, 15, and 16: These sections of the bill deal with the right of a corporation to elect either the average-earnings credit or the invested-capital credit. Under the present law, a taxpayer who elects one or the other of the credits is required to be bound by such election for the taxable year for which the credit was made. Since it is very difficult for many tax-payers to determine accurately what their invested capital is, it will result in a serious hardship to force them to be bound by an election made at this time. The amendments which were inserted by your committee will permit the taxpayer to adopt that credit which results in the lesser tax. (p. 1638-39)

Discussion—House, after Bill passed Senate (Cong. Rec. Vol. 87).—MR. DOUGHTON. * * * As the bill passed the House it gave the corporations, the tax-payers, the option to elect or take either the average earning plan or the invested-capital plan in making out its return. The amendment gives to the taxpayer the option of taking both the average-earning plan and the invested-capital plan in making the returns. * * * But if he makes it out under both the average earning plan and the invested-capital plan, under the Senate amendment automatically he pays the lesser tax. In other words, the tax is paid on whichever plan makes his tax the least. (p. 1692)

MR. COOPER. * * * The other amendment is one which contains some real substance and is an additional advantage to the taxpayer. In other words, under the Senate amendment a corporation may file its return under both plans, the average-earning plan and the invested-capital plan, and then whichever is to the advantage of the corporation it may be used.

MR. CARLSON. Does a taxpayer have an opportunity to choose whichever method he wants to use in alternate years or does he have to stay with the method he chooses under this plan?

MR. COOPER. No. If the gentleman will indulge me I can explain that a little further. The gentleman will recall the two plans embraced in the excess-profits-tax bill passed last year. The tax-payer corporation had to elect one plan or the other. All this Senate provision means is that the corporation may file the return under both plans and whichever is found to its best interest it can take advantage of that. To illustrate, assume that a corporation claimed the benefit of one of these specific relief provisions contained in the pending bill. If that relief it has claimed is granted, it would be to its interest to use the average-earning plan. But assuming that the Treasury Department may deny the relief it has requested, it might then find it would have been to its best interests to use the invested-capital plan. This

makes it possible for it to file the return under both plans and then whichever is found to be to its best interest it may take advantage of it.

MR. DOUGHTON. He automatically gets the advantage of it?

MR. COOPER. Yes.

·MR. VOORHIS of California. What happens the next year? Can he do the same thing the next year?

MR. COOPER. He has the same opportunity the next year and in succeeding years. (p. 1692)

[SEC. 712. EXCESS PROFITS CREDIT—ALLOWANCE.]

1940

201
[712(a)]

(a) **Domestic Corporations.**—In the case of a domestic corporation, ~~the first taxable year of which~~ ~~under this subchapter begins on any date in 1940,~~ which was in existence ~~during the entire forty-eight months prior to such date,~~ *before January 1, 1940* the excess profits credit for any taxable year shall, at the election of the taxpayer * * * be an amount computed under section 713 or section 714. * * * In the case of all other domestic corporations the excess profits credit for any taxable year shall be an amount computed under section 714. * * *

Committee Reports

Report—Ways and Means Subcommittee (76th Cong., 3d Sess., H. Rept. Aug. 8, 1940).—Your subcommittee recommends that the excess-profits credit be computed under two alternative methods. It is further recommended that a taxpayer in existence during the whole of the base period (the years 1936 to 1939, inclusive) be permitted to elect for each taxable year whichever method it chooses. A taxpayer which was not in existence during the whole of such base period would be required to compute the credit under the second[1] of the following alternative methods: (p. 10)

[1] Relating to invested capital method.

Report—Ways and Means Committee (76th Cong., 3d Sess., H. Rept. 2894).— (a) *Corporations in existence during entire base period.*—In determining the portion of the earnings to be considered as excess profits, the taxpayer, if in existence actually or constructively during the entire base period, may choose either of two standards of measurement. (p. 3)

The choice is available to the following classes of corporations:

(1) A domestic corporation, the first taxable year of which begins in 1940, if it was in existence for at least 48 months prior to the beginning of such taxable year. (p. 4)

(c) *Corporations not in existence in the base period.*—Corporations which come into existence after the close of the base period (other than those companies which are allowed the use of a substituted base-period experience because of certain tax-free exchanges and reorganizations) must measure their excess profits under the second method. (p. 5)

Section 712 provides that a domestic corporation, the first excess-profits tax taxable year of which begins on any date in 1940, and which was in existence during the entire 48 months prior to such date, shall be permitted to elect for each taxable year the credit under section 713 or section 714. * * * In the case of all other domestic corporations, the excess-profits credit for any taxable year must be computed in accordance with the invested capital method provided in section 714. (p. 20)

Report—Senate Finance Committee

(76th Cong., 3d Sess., S. Rept. 2114).— *Corporations which may elect.*—Under the House bill the privilege of electing the average earnings in the base period as the standard of measurement of excess profits was restricted to corporations actually or constructively in existence during the entire base period. (p. 4)

Domestic corporations.—Under the House bill a domestic corporation was permitted to choose between the income credit and the invested capital credit only if it had been in existence during the entire 48 months prior to the beginning of its first taxable year which began in 1940. All other domestic corporations were required to compute their excess-profits credit on the invested capital plan.

Under the bill as reported by your committee any domestic corporation which was in existence before January 1, 1940, may choose between the income credit and the invested capital credit. (p. 13)

Report—Conference Committee (76th Cong., 3d Sess., H. Rept. 3002).—*House bill.*—Under the House bill a domestic corporation was permitted to choose between the income credit and the invested capital credit only if it had been in existence during the entire 48 months prior to the beginning of its first taxable year which began in 1940. * * *

All other domestic * * * corporations subject to excess-profits tax were required to compute their excess-profits credit on the invested-capital plan.

Senate amendment.—Under the Senate amendment all domestic corporations which have been in existence prior to January 1, 1940, * * * are permitted to choose between the income and the invested capital plan. All other corporations * * * must compute their excess-profits credit on the invested capital plan.

Conference agreement.—The Senate provision is adopted. (p. 47)

Congressional Discussion

Discussion—Senate (Cong. Rec. Vol. 86).—Rejected amendment to determine credit on basis of lesser tax. (p. 12184-185)

Committee Hearings
1942 Act

Hearings—Senate Finance Committee.—Measuring corporate existence by actual transaction of business. (E. C. Alvord, p. 1797-98)

1917
203

[Set forth on page 350]

Sec. 712(b)

1942
212(a)

Section 712 (b) (relating to the excess profits credit of foreign corporations) * * * are amended by striking out "or having an office or place of business therein", wherever occurring therein and section 712 (b) is amended by striking out "or had an office or place of business therein".

Committee Hearings

Hearings—Senate Finance Committee.—Explanation of provision. (J. O'Brien—H. Legis. Counsel—p. 103)

[Set forth with sec. 712(a), page 55]

SEC. 712. EXCESS PROFITS CREDIT—ALLOWANCE.

(b) Foreign Corporations.—In the case of a foreign corporation engaged in trade or business within the United States or having an office or place of business therein, the first taxable year of which under this subchapter begins on any date in 1940, which was in existence on the day forty-eight months prior to such date and which at any time during each of the taxable years in such forty-eight months was engaged in trade or business within the United States or had an office or place of business therein, the excess profits credit for any taxable year shall, *at the election of the taxpayer * * ** be an amount computed under section 713 *or section 714*. In the case of all other such foreign corporations the excess profits credit for any taxable year shall be an amount computed under section 714. * * *

Committee Reports

Report—Ways and Means Subcommittee (76th Cong., 3d Sess., H. Rept. Aug. 8, 1940).—In the case of a foreign corporation in existence during the entire base period and engaged in trade or business in the United States or having an office or place of business therein, your subcommittee recommends that its excess profits credit consist of the excess of its excess profits net income for the taxable year over its average excess profits net income for the base period, with no adjustments for additions to or reductions in capital. (p. 8)

Report—Ways and Means Committee (76th Cong., 3d Sess., H. Rept. 2894).—In the case of a foreign corporation in existence during the entire base period and engaged in trade or business in the United States or having an office or place of business therein, its excess-profits credit consists of the excess of its excess-profits net income for the taxable year over its average excess-profits net income for the base period, with no adjustments for additions to or reductions in capital. (p. 12)

In the case of a foreign corporation engaged in trade or business within the United States or having an office or place of business therein, if its first excess-profits tax taxable year begins on any date in 1940 and it was in existence during the entire 48 months prior to such date and was engaged in trade or business within the United States or had an office or place of business therein at any time during each of the taxable years in the 48 months prior to such date, it must compute its excess-profits credit by the method provided in section 713. All other foreign corporations engaged in trade or business within the United States or having an office or place of business therein are required to compute their excess-profits credit in accordance with the method provided in section 714. (p. 20)

Report—Senate Finance Committee (76th Cong., 3d Sess., S. Rept. 2114).—Those foreign corporations, further, which under the House bill were confined to the use of the income credit are, under your committee bill, permitted to use the income or the invested capital credit. (p. 4)

The election privilege has also been extended to foreign corporations engaged in trade or business within the United States at some time during each of the years in the base period. (p. 4)

Your committee has extended to foreign corporations engaged in trade or business within the United States at some time in all the years in the base period the same right of election of the method of computing excess-profits credit as is allowed domestic corporations. (p. 6)

Foreign corporations.—Under the

House bill a foreign corporation subject to excess-profits tax was required to compute its excess-profits credit on the average-earnings plan if it was in existence during the entire 48 months prior to the beginning of its first excess-profits tax taxable year beginning in 1940 and was engaged in trade or business within the United States or had an office or place of business therein at any time during each of the taxable years in the 48 months prior to such date. All other foreign corporations subject to excess-profits tax were required to compute their excess-profits credit on the invested capital plan.

Under the bill as reported by your committee the first class of foreign corporations is entitled to choose between the income credit and the invested-capital credit. * * * The treatment of other foreign corporations subject to tax is the same under this section as it was under the House bill. (p. 13)

Report—Conference Committee (76th Cong., 3d Sess., H. Rept. 3002).—*House bill.* * * * Foreign corporations subject to excess-profits tax were required to compute their excess-profits credit on the

income plan if they were in existence during the entire 48 months prior to the beginning of their first excess-profits tax taxable year beginning in 1940 and were engaged in trade or business within the United States or had an office or place of business therein at any time during each of the taxable years in the 48 months prior to such date. All other domestic and foreign corporations subject to excess-profits tax were required to compute their excess-profits credit on the invested-capital plan.

Senate amendment.—Under the Senate amendment all domestic corporations which have been in existence prior to January 1, 1940, and all foreign corporations which, under the House bill, were required to compute their excess-profits credit on the income plan, are permitted to choose between the income and the invested capital plan. All other corporations including corporations which for any taxable year do not file returns, must compute their excess-profits credit on the invested capital plan.

Conference agreement.—The Senate provision is adopted. (p. 47)

Committee Hearings

Hearings—Senate Finance Committee.—Allowing election of income or invested capital methods to foreign corporation. (W. A. Cooper, p. 63-64)

1917
203(c)

[Set forth on page 350]

3/3/17
200

[Set forth on page 370]

Sec. 713(a)

1940
201

SEC. 713. EXCESS PROFITS CREDIT—BASED ON INCOME.

(a) **Amount of Excess Profits Credit.**—The excess profits credit for any taxable year, computed under this section, shall be—

(1) **Domestic corporations.**—In the case of a domestic corporation—

(A) 95 PER CENTUM OF the average base period net income, as defined in subsection (b),

(B)   PLUS [increased by] 8 per centum of the net capital addition, as defined in subsection (c), or

(C)   MINUS [decreased by] 6 per centum of the net capital reduction, as defined in subsection (c).

(2)   **Foreign corporations.**—In the case of a foreign corporation, 95 PER CENTUM OF the average base period net income.

Committee Reports

Report—**Ways and Means Subcommittee** (76th Cong., 3d Sess., H. Rept. Aug. 8, 1940).—(a)   It may take as a credit against its net income for the taxable year its average earnings for the base period.   The amount so arrived at shall be increased by 8 percent of the additions to capital occurring after the beginning of the taxpayer's first taxable year under the excess-profits tax and decreased by 6 percent of reductions in capital during the same period: or (p. 3)

Credit based on average base period income.—Your subcommittee recommends that the credit computed under the first alternative be based upon a comparison of net income for the taxable year with the average net income for the base period.   The credit is to consist of the average net income for the base period increased by 8 percent of money or property (taken at its basis for tax purposes) paid into the corporation for stock or as paid-in surplus or as a contribution to capital after the beginning of the taxpayer's first taxable year under the excess-profits tax.   The credit is to be decreased by 6 percent of distributions other than distributions of earnings or profits, made after the beginning of such year.   (p. 10)

If the corporation acquires new capital after the beginning of its first taxable year under the excess-profits tax, its credit, as arrived at in the above example, will be increased by 8 percent of such new capital.   For example, if a corporation on a calendar-year basis acquired $100,000 of new capital on January 1, 1940, its excess-profits credit of $100,000 as shown in the above example would be increased by $8,000 (8 percent of the $100,000 addition to capital).

If the corporation reduces its capital after the beginning of its first taxable year under the excess-profits tax its excess-profits credit will be reduced by 6 percent of the reduction in capital.

Thus, in the above case, if a reduction in capital of $100,000, instead of an increase of such amount, had occurred, the excess-profits credit of $100,000 would be reduced to $94,000.   (p. 7)

Report—**Ways and Means Committee** (76th Cong., 3d Sess., H. Rept. 2894).—If this method is chosen, the taxpayer measures its excess profits by a comparison of its earnings for the taxable year with its average earnings for the base period.   For the purposes of the comparison, the average earnings for the base period are increased by 8 percent of the net additions to capital occurring after the beginning of the taxpayer's first taxable year under the bill, or decreased by 6 percent of the net reductions in capital during the same period.   The amount so arrived at constitutes the taxpayer's excess-profits credit which, when deducted from the earnings for the taxable year, determines the excess profits, or the portion of the income which after the deduction of the specific exemption of $5,000 is subjected to excess-profits tax. (p. 4)

The credit provided under section 713 is based upon a comparison of income for the taxable year with the average income for the base period.   Such credit consists of the average base period net income reduction in capital after the beginning of such taxable year.   (p. 20)

If the excess-profits credit of a foreign corporation is required to be computed under section 713, no adjustments are allowed for additions to or reductions in capital.   (p. 20)

If a domestic corporation computes its excess-profits credit on the basis of the average earnings for the base period, such credit is adjusted for any changes in capital occurring after the beginning of its first taxable year under the excess-profits tax.   The excess-profits credit will be increased by 8 percent of the net capital addition for the taxable year or decreased by 6 percent of the net capital reduction for the taxable year. (p. 21)

Report—Conference Committee (76th Cong., 3d Sess., H. Rept. 3002).—In addition, it is provided that, in computing the income credit, the amount thereof, prior to adjustment on account of capital additions or capital reductions, shall be 95 percent of the average base period net income instead of 100 percent of such average base-period net income.

This 5-percent reduction of the average base period net income is in lieu of the House provision which included an additional $4\frac{1}{10}$ percent of the normal-tax net income in the excess profits tax of corporations electing the income plan and provided a 5-percent differential in the graduated rate schedule applicable to such corporations. (p. 48)

Congressional Discussion

Discussion—House; on Report of Conference Committee (Cong. Rec. Vol. 86).—On use of 95 percent instead of 100 percent of base period income, in general. (p. 12966-967)

MR. CASE of South Dakota. As I understand it, there are two main methods, either earnings over a basic period, or the invested capital, that can be used?

MR. COOPER. That is true. The conference report provides for an alternative plan that the corporation may elect.

MR. CASE of South Dakota. What about the case of a corporation that may have an earnings-period history and changes its capital structure materially, either increases it or reduces it, during the taxable period?

MR. COOPER. It then has a right to elect whichever plan it wants to; and, of course, will elect the plan that results in the less tax.

MR. CASE of South Dakota. But is there not any provision in the bill that would take care of greatly increased earnings, because of the increased capital invested?

MR. COOPER. Well, it is allowed 8 percent on its invested capital for the taxable year.

MR. CASE of South Dakota. In other words, there is a sort of combination plan?

MR. COOPER. I mean 8 percent of its income for the taxable year on the invested capital.

MR. CASE of South Dakota. There is a provision which takes care of changes in capital structure and still permitting the corporation to use its earnings-period history?

MR. COOPER. Yes; that is correct. (p. 12967-968)

1918
———
311(a)

[Set forth on page 326]

1917
———
203

[Set forth on page 350]

```
Sec. 713(b)(1)
Sec. 713(c)
Sec. 713(d)(1)
Sec. 713(d)(3)
Sec. 713(e)
Sec. 742(b)*
* In Part
```

[Set forth on following page]

[SEC. 713. EXCESS PROFITS CREDIT—BASED ON INCOME.]

(c) **Deficit in Excess Profits Net Income.**—For the purposes of this section the term "deficit in excess profits net income" with respect to any taxable year means the amount by which the deductions plus the credit for dividends received and the credit provided in section 26 (a) (relating to interest on certain obligations of the United States and its instrumentalities) exceeded the gross income. * * *

1942
214(a)
[713(c)]

Committee Reports

Report—Ways and Means Committee (77th Cong., 2d Sess., H. Rept. 2333).— This section provides in effect that in the case of corporations employing the income credit in determining their excess profits tax, the credit for tax free interest on certain obligations of the United States and its instrumentalities provided in section 26 (a) shall be taken into ac-count, along with the deductions and the credit for dividends received, in computing deficits in the base period income under section 713 of the Internal Revenue Code. (p. 140)

Report—Senate Finance Committee (77th Cong., 2d Sess., S. Rept. 1631).— Substantially the same as the Ways and Means Committee Report. (p. 190)

Committee Hearings

Hearings—Senate Finance Committee.—Explanation of provision. (J. O'Brien—H. Legis. Counsel—p. 104)

[SEC. 713. EXCESS PROFITS CREDIT—BASED ON INCOME.]

[(e) **Average Base Period Net Income—General Average.**—The average base period net income determined under this subsection shall be determined as follows:]

1942
215
[713(e)
(1)]

(1) *By computing the aggregate of the excess profits net income for each of the taxable years of the taxpayer in the base period, reduced by the sum of the deficits in excess profits net income for each of such years. If the excess profits net income (or deficit in excess profits net income) for one taxable year in the base period divided by the number of months in such taxable year is less than 75 per centum of the aggregate of the excess profits net income (reduced by deficits in excess profits net income) for the other taxable years in the taxpayer's base period divided by the number of months in such other taxable years (herein called "average monthly amount") the amount used for such one year under this paragraph shall be 75 per centum of the average monthly amount multiplied by the number of months in such one year, and the year increased under this sentence shall be the year the increase in which will produce the highest average base period net income;*

Committee Reports

Report—Senate Finance Committee (77th Cong., 2d Sess., S. Rept. 1631).— Section 713 (e) of the Code, which provides for the determination of the general average base period net income, authorizes the exclusion of the largest deficit for any taxable year in the base period in such computation. Your committee has amended this section to provide however, that in case the excess profits net income or deficit in excess profits net income for a taxable year in the base period divided by the number of months in such year is less than 75 percent of the aggregate of the excess profits net income (reduced by deficits in excess profits net income) for the remaining years divided by the number of months in such remaining years (called average monthly amount), the base period net income for such year shall be an amount equal to 75 percent of the average monthly amount multiplied by the number of months in such year.

The increase in excess profits net income authorized by this amendment shall be applicable only in the case of 1 year in the base period, and to that year for which the increase in the income will produce the highest base period net income. The benefits afforded by this amendment extend to taxable years of less than 12 months as well as to taxable years of 12 months, and are available to taxpayers which were in existence only for a portion of the base period. However, taxpayers computing the excess profits credit based on income under section 713 (f) of the Code, relating to average base period net income in case of increased earnings in last half of base period, are not entitled as well, to the increase in base period net income provided by this amendment. (p. 191)

Report—Conference Committee (77th Cong., 2d Sess., H. Rept. 2586).— Amendment No. 297: This amendment adds a new section to the bill to amend section 713 (e) of the Code to provide that, in case the average monthly excess profits net income or deficit in excess profits net income for a taxable year in the base period is less than 75 percent of the aggregate of the excess profits net income (reduced by deficits in excess profits net income) for the remaining years, divided by the number of months in such remaining years (called average monthly amount), the base period net income for such year shall be an amount equal to 75 percent of the average monthly amount multiplied by the number of months in such year.

This adjustment is applicable only in the case of one year in the base period, and to that year for which the increase in excess profits net income will produce the highest base period net income. The House recedes. (p. 60-61)

1940
201
[713(b)
(1)]
[713(c)]
[713(d)
(1)]
[713(d)
(3)]
[713(e)]
[742(b)]

[SEC. 713. EXCESS PROFITS CREDIT—BASED ON INCOME.]

(b) **Average Base Period Net Income.**—For the purposes of this section the average base period net income of the taxpayer shall be determined as follows:

(1) By computing the aggregate of the excess profits net income for each of the taxable years of the taxpayer beginning after December 31, 1935, and before January 1, 1940, reduced, in the case of each such taxable year in which the deductions plus the credit for dividends received exceeded the gross income, by the amount ~~attributable to~~ [*of*] ATTRIBUTABLE TO such excess ~~under~~ [*determined as provided in*] UNDER paragraph (4); [*but there shall be excluded from such computation the excess profits net income or excess of deductions plus the credit for dividends received over gross income for one of such taxable years, as the taxpayer may select.*]

(2) By dividing the amount ascertained under paragraph (1) by the total number of months in all such taxable years; [*less the number of months in the taxable year selected by the taxpayer for exclusion under paragraph (1)*]; and

(3) By multiplying the amount ascertained under paragraph (2) by twelve.

(4) For the purposes of paragraph (1)—

(A) In determining whether, for any taxable year, the deductions plus the credit for dividends received exceeded the gross income, and in determining the amount of such excess, the adjustments provided in section 711 (b) ~~(2)~~ ~~(A)~~ *(1)* shall be made; and

(B)[1] The amount attributable to any taxable year in which there is such an excess shall be the amount of such excess, except that such amount shall be zero if there is only one such year, or, if more than one, shall be zero for the year in which such excess is the greatest.

(6) In no case shall the average base period net income be less than zero.

[1] Paragraph (B) was stricken by the Senate, but restored by the Conference Committee.

[SEC. 742. AVERAGE BASE PERIOD NET INCOME.]

[In the case of a taxpayer which is an acquiring corporation * * * its average base period net income * * * shall be computed as follows, in lieu of the method provided in section 713:]

(b) By adding the plus amounts ascertained under subsection (a) (3) for each year of the base period;* and by subtracting from such sum, if for two or more years of the base period there was a minus amount, the sum of such minus amounts, excluding the greatest.* [*and subtracting from such sum the sum of the minus amounts, excluding, however, one of such plus amounts, or one of such minus amounts, as the taxpayer may select.*]

The part between the asterisks was stricken by the Senate, and the part in underlined italics substituted. The Conference Committee restored the Ways and Means Committee provision and struck the Senate substitute.

Committee Reports

Report—Ways and Means Subcommittee (76th Cong., 3d Sess., H. Rept. Aug. 8, 1940).—For the purpose of ascertaining the previous earning experience of corporations which is to be used as a comparative measure of their earnings for the taxable year, it is recommended that the years 1936 to 1939, inclusive, constitute the base period. (p. 3)

Report—Ways and Means Committee (76th Cong., 3d Sess., H. Rept. 2894).— For the purpose of ascertaining the previous earning experience to be used as a comparative measure of earnings for the taxable years under the bill, the years 1936 to 1939, inclusive, are selected to constitute a base period. (p. 3)

Under this method the excess-profits credit for the taxable year is the aggregate of earnings for all of its taxable years in the base period divided by the total number of those years. In the event of a deficit for 1 year in the base period, the aggregate earnings for the other years are not reduced thereby. If there are deficits in more than one year in the base period, the aggregate earnings for the other years are reduced by all such deficits except the one for the year in which the greatest deficit occurred. But in all cases the aggregate so determined is divided by the total number of years in the base period.

For example, corporation X had earnings of $300,000 in 1936, and $200,000 in 1937. In 1938 it had a deficit (that is, an excess of deductions and net income credits over gross income) of $150,000 and in 1939 another of $100,000. Its aggregate earnings for the base period are $400,000; that is $300,000 plus $200,000 minus $100,000; the greatest deficit, the $150,000 deficit, being disregarded. The average earnings for the base period are, therefore, $100,000, or $400,000 divided by the number of years in the period. (p. 5)

The term "base period" means the taxable years beginning after December 31, 1935, and before January 1, 1940.

The base period net income consists of the aggregate of the excess-profits net income for each of the taxable years of the taxpayer included in the base period less, in the case of taxable years included in such base period in which the deductions plus the credit for dividends received exceed the gross income, the amount of such excess, except as pointed out in the following paragraph of this report. In determining such excess, the adjustments required by section 711 (b) (in respect of long-term capital gains and losses, the deduction for taxes, casualty losses, processing tax repayments, and the exclusion of income derived from the retirement or discharge of indebtedness of the corporation) for the purpose of computing the excess-profits net income shall be made. The average base period net income is determined by dividing the base period net income by the total number of months in the taxable years included in the base period and multiplying the quotient thus obtained by 12.

With respect to taxable years in which the deductions plus the credit for dividends received exceed the gross income the following rules are applicable to the treatment of such excess: If the deductions plus the credit for dividends received exceeded the gross income in only 1 year, the amount of the excess to be taken into account in computing the average base period net income shall be zero. If the deductions plus the credit for dividends received exceed the gross income in more than 1 of the taxable years included in such base period, the amount to be taken into account in computing the average base period net income shall be zero for the year in which such excess is the greatest and for the other year or years shall be the amount of the excess determined in respect of such year or years.

For the purpose of the excess-profits credit, the average base period net income shall not in any case be less than zero. (p. 20-21)

Report—Senate Finance Committee (76th Cong., 3d Sess., S. Rept. 2114).— The base period under the House bill, the years 1936 to 1939, inclusive, is retained for the purposes of the income method of computing the excess-profits credit. (p. 4)

Report—Conference Committee (76th Cong., 3d Sess., H. Rept. 3002).—*House bill.*—Under the House bill all taxable years in the base period, including taxable years for which there were deficits, were taken into account in computing the average base period net income, except that the loss for one deficit year (the largest, if the taxpayer had more than one) was not to be applied in reduction of the aggregate income for other years. In ascertaining the average, however, the period covered by such taxable year was taken into account, i. e., the aggregate for the other years was divided by the total number of years in the base period, not by such total number less one.

Senate amendment.—In lieu of the treatment relative to deficits contained in the House bill, the Senate amendment provides that a taxpayer may entirely exclude one base period taxable year in computing its average earnings. Not only may the excess-profits net income or the deficit for such year be excluded from the computation, but the period embraced by such taxable year is excluded in ascertaining the average base period net income for the base period. Thus, if the base period includes 4 calendar years and the taxpayer chooses to drop one of such years out of the computation, the aggregate income for the remaining 3 years is divided by three, and not by four, in ascertaining the base-period average. (p. 47-48)

Conference agreement.—The Senate provision permitting the complete exclusion of 1 year in the computation of average base-period net income has been eliminated, and the House provision relative to the treatment of deficit years has been restored. (p. 48)

Senate amendment. * * * A change, corresponding to that made in section 713, was made in section 742, authorizing the omission of one taxable year in the computation of average base period net income.

Conference agreement.—The Senate provisions are adopted, except to the extent they authorize the complete exclusion of one taxable year in computing average base-period net income. (See sec. 713.)   (p. 57)

Congressional Discussion

Discussion—House (Cong. Rec. Vol. 86).—On average method in general. (p. 11248, 11250, 11260)

Discussion—Senate (Cong. Rec. Vol. 86).—Mr. PITTMAN. Mr. President, I wish to apologize for the language. The language was taken from the bill itself. As I understand, it is a repetition of the language in the bill, with the exception of one paragraph. The one paragraph is paragraph (2), which says:

By dividing the amount ascertained under paragraph (1) by the total number of months in all such taxable years, less the number of months in the taxable year selected by the taxpayer for exclusion under paragraph (1).

All it means is simply this: Instead of having 4 years, and being allowed to set aside 1 of the 4 years, and dividing the 3 remaining years by 4, the amendment provides for dividing the 3 years by 3. The absurdity of thinking that anyone is receiving a benefit by being allowed to deduct an abnormally low year, and then divide the profit for the other 3 years by 4, should be apparent. If there were a profit of $100 a year for 3 years, and for the 4th year there were a profit of $80, if the $380 were divided by 4 the result would be $95, which is below the normal profit for 3 years. If there were no profit for 1 year, if 1 year should represent a total loss, and the profit for the 3 years selected were divided by 4, the result would be $75.

In other words, any way on earth it is figured, you are $25 below the normal average.

If you are going to have a normal proposition, have it normal; but it is absurd to say that you will get an average normal when you divide 3 by 4.

MR. HARRISON. Mr. President, I would have no objection to the amendment going to conference striking out "4" and inserting "3." That is what the Senator seeks, as I understand.

MR. PITTMAN. I seek to have the 3 years divided by 3 instead of 4.

MR. HARRISON. The only trouble is that the Senator's amendment would strike from the bill one or two amendments which the Senate Finance Committee put in which we thought would be very helpful, and which we wanted to have go to conference. As the amendment is drawn, those parts which are stricken out, which are in the bill, would not be in conference, and they ought to be in conference.

As to taking 3 out of 4 years to reach the average earning, the Treasury and the House Ways and Means Committee have practically come to an accord; but at the last moment they found that there would be such a loss of revenue by virtue of this amendment that they adopted another method of dealing with these deficit years. There was strong sentiment in the Finance Committee to give corporations the advantage of 3 out of 4 years in selecting the average-earning base method; but when we struck out the 4.1 percent and put the 3.1 percent tax on all corporations we felt that the bill could not stand it. There would be too much loss of revenue. (p. 12349)

Discussion—House; on Report of Conference Committee (Cong. Rec. Vol. 86).—Mr. MURDOCK of Arizona. I understand there was a Senate amendment which provided for taking any 3 of the last 4 years as the base. Was that Senate amendment agreed to?

MR. COOPER. No. We did not agree to that amendment. We retained the House provision of allowing the corporation to count any one deficit year of the 4 years of the base period at zero, but we did not accept the amendment to take any 3 out of the 4 years, for the very obvious reason that we were told it would lose about $60,000,000 of revenue. (p. 12968)

Discussion—Senate; on Report of Conference Committee (Cong. Rec. Vol. 86).—Mr. HARRISON. * * * The Senator from Nevada (Mr. Pittman) offered another amendment which would have committed a corporation to take 3 out of the 4 base years in computing its tax under the average earnings method, but because of changes in other parts of the bill, and because of the large loss in revenue which would result from such an amend-

ment the conferees were unwilling to accept it. (p. 12920)

Committee Hearings

Hearings—Ways and Means Committee.—Adjusting base period to fiscal years. (E. A. Conniff, p. 63, 64)
Hearings—Senate Finance Commit-

tee.—Explanation of provision. (C. F. Stam—Jt. Com. on Int. Rev. Taxn.— p. 187, 204)

1918
310
[713(b)
(1)]

[Set forth on page 326]

1918
320(b)
[713(e)]

[Set forth on page 330]

1917
200
[713(b)
(1)]

[Set forth on page 348]

1917
204
[713(b)
(1)]

[Set forth on page 352]

Sec. 713(d)(2)

1940
201

[SEC. 713. EXCESS PROFITS CREDIT—BASED ON INCOME.]

[(b)   Average Base Period Net Income— * * *]

(5) *For the purposes of paragraph (1), if the taxpayer was in existence during only part of the 48 months preceding the beginning of its first taxable year under this subchapter (hereinafter in this paragraph called "base period"), its excess profits net income—*

(A)   for each taxable year of twelve months (beginning with the beginning of such base period) during which it was not in existence, shall be an amount equal to 8 per centum of the excess of—

(i)   the daily invested capital for the first day of the taxpayer's first taxable year beginning after December 31, 1939, over

(ii)   an amount equal to the same percentage of such daily invested capital as is applicable under section 720 in reduction of the average invested capital of the preceding taxable year;

(B)   for the taxable year of less than twelve months consisting of that part of the remainder of the base period during which it was not in existence, shall be the amount ascertained for a full year under subparagraph (A), multiplied by the number of days in such taxable year of less than twelve months and divided by the number of days in the twelve months ending with the close of such taxable year.

Committee Reports

Report—Ways and Means Subcommittee (76th Cong., 3d Sess., H. Rept. Aug. 8, 1940).—As to corporations which were in existence during only part of the base period, it is recommended that for any part of the base period during which they were not in existence they be deemed to have had an invested capital equal to their actual invested capital as of the first day of its taxable year 1940 upon which base they are deemed to have received earnings of 10 percent on the first $500,000 and 8 percent on the balance. (p. 4)

Report—Ways and Means Committee (76th Cong., 3d Sess., H. Rept. 2894).—
(b) *Corporations in existence during only part of the base period.*—Corporations in existence for only a part of the base period must measure their excess profits by the second method.

For this purpose they are supplied an invested capital for the period during which they were not in existence equal to their invested capital at the beginning of their 1940 taxable year, and upon that hypothetical invested capital they are deemed to have earned 10 percent of the first $500,000 of such invested capital and 8 percent of the amount in excess of $500,000.

For example, corporation A came into existence on January 1, 1938. It had an invested capital as of January 1, 1940, of $800,000 and keeps its books and accounts on a calendar-year basis. It had an average invested capital and excess-profits net income for the portion of the base period during which it was actually in existence as indicated. These factors for the portion of the base period during which it was not in existence are supplied as follows:

Year	Invested capital	Excess profits net income	Base-period percentage
1936	*$800,000	*$74,000	....
1937	*$800,000	*$74,000	....
1938	650,000	45,500	....
1939	700,000	63,000	....
Total	2,950,000	256,500	8.7
1940	800,000	....	....

The amounts marked by an asterisk (*) do not represent the actual experience of the corporation but have been supplied by the invested capital for 1940, upon which a yield of 10 percent for the first $500,000 and 8 percent on the balance is assumed.

Thus, the portion of the earnings for the taxable year in excess of an amount equal to 8.7 percent of the invested capital for the taxable year is considered excess profits and, after being reduced by the specific exemption of $5,000, is subject to tax. (p. 4-5)

Report—Senate Finance Committee (76th Cong., 3d Sess., S. Rept. 2114).—Your committee bill also extends this privilege to corporations in existence during any part of the base period. Such a corporation is deemed to have had, in that portion of the base period when it was not in existence, earnings equal in amount to 8 percent of its invested capital at the beginning of its first taxable year in 1940. (p. 4)

First method—Based on income.—Under the bill reported by your committee, corporations in existence during any part of the base period may use this method and for that purpose are allowed, for the part of the base period during which they were not in existence, a hypothetical income equal to 8 percent of their invested capital at the beginning of their first taxable year in 1940. (p. 4)

Owing to the fact that section 712 has been changed so as to allow a domestic corporation which was not in existence during the entire base period to choose the income credit, section 713 has been changed by the insertion of additional provisions giving corporations which were not in existence during the entire base period an excess-profits net income for that portion of the base period during which they were not in existence. For each 12 months of such period the excess-profits net income is deemed to be 8 percent of the corporation's daily invested capital for the first day of its first taxable year subject to the excess-profits tax reduced on account of inadmissibles by the same ratio as is applicable under section 720 in reduction of the average invested capital of the preceding taxable year. Thus if the ratio of inadmissibles to total assets in the last taxable year of the base period were as 1 to 3, the daily invested capital as of the day following the close of such taxable year would be reduced by one-third thereof, and 8 percent of such reduced amount would constitute the corporation's excess-profits net income for each period of 12 months in the base period during which it was not in existence. The excess-profits net income for a period of less than 12 months during which it was not so in existence is a proportionate part of such amount. (p. 13)

Report—Conference Committee (76th Cong., 3d Sess., H. Rept. 3002).—*Senate amendment.* * * * Since under the Senate amendment all domestic corporations which have been in existence prior to January 1, 1940, are permitted to choose between the income and the invested capital plan, even though they may not have been in existence during the entire base period, the Senate amendment also provides for a constructive excess-profits net income in the case of corporations electing the income plan for such portion of the base period as the corporation was not in existence. Such excess-profits net income is to be computed in the same manner as the House bill provided in the case of corporations electing the invested-capital plan, i. e., 8 percent of the invested capital for the day following the close of the base period, reduced by the same ratio of inadmissibles as is applicable to the last year of the base period. (p. 48)

Conference agreement. * * * In view of the conference agreement on sections 711 and 712, the Senate provision relative to a constructive excess profits net income in the case of corporations in existence during part, but not all, of the base period has been retained. (p. 48)

Committee Hearings

Hearings—Senate Finance Committee.—Explanation of provision. (C. F. Stam—Jt. Com. on Int. Rev. Taxn.—p. 196, 207)

Sec. 713(d)(3)

[Set forth with sec. 713(b)(1), page 62]

Sec. 713(e)

[Set forth with sec. 713(b)(1), page 62]

Sec. 713(f)(1)-(6)

EPTA
4(b)

[SEC. 713. EXCESS PROFITS CREDIT—BASED ON INCOME.]

(f) **Average Base Period Net Income—Increased Earnings in Last Half of Base Period.**—The average base period net income determined under this subsection shall be determined as follows:

(1) By computing, for each of the taxable years of the taxpayer in its base period, the excess profits net income for such year, or the deficit in excess profits net income for such year;

(2) By computing for each half of the base period the aggregate of the excess profits net income for each of the taxable years in such half, reduced, if for one or more of such years there was a deficit in excess profits net income, by the sum of such deficits. For the purposes of such computation, if any taxable year is partly within each half of the

base period there shall be allocated to the first half an amount of the excess profits net income or deficit in excess profits net income, as the case may be, for such taxable year, which bears the same ratio thereto as the number of months falling within such half bears to the entire number of months in such taxable year; and the remainder shall be allocated to the second half;

(3)   If the amount ascertained under paragraph (2) for the second half is greater than the amount ascertained for the first half, by dividing the difference by two;

(4)   By adding the amount ascertained under paragraph (3) to the amount ascertained under paragraph (2) for the second half of the base period;

(5)   By dividing the amount found under paragraph (4) by the number of months in the second half of the base period and by multiplying the result by twelve;

(6)   The amount ascertained under paragraph (5) shall be the average base period net income determined under this subsection, except that the average base period net income determined under this subsection shall in no case be greater than the highest excess profits net income for any taxable year in the base period. * * *

Committee Reports

Report—Ways and Means Committee (77th Cong., 1st Sess., H. Rept. 146).—The bill affords relief in the following situations:

*   *   *

3.   Relief is provided for corporations that experienced rapid growth during the base period. Under existing law, only the average experience during those years can be counted in determining the excess-profits credit based on income. Corporations whose facilities and production capacities were substantially increased during this period would thus be penalized as compared to corporations which had already achieved and maintained a high and constant level of production. The bill will give effect to the ratio of increase during these years. This treatment will afford a substantial advantage to these expanding companies as compared with the use of the level average now required. (p. 2, 3)

The amendments made by this section are designed for the relief of corporations that experienced rapid growth during the base period. In determining the excess profits credit based on income the present law requires the use of the average earning experience of the corporation during the years in the base period. Trends of growth during this period are

given no weight. Thus, corporations which have materially expanded in the base period and have for the last year in such period a business capacity and an income much larger than that for the first year, are restricted under existing law to the use of a level average of such years. The inequities of this treatment may be illustrated by a comparison of two corporations, both of which have average base period earnings of $250,000 and, under the present law, the same credit based on income. One of these corporations has shown substantial growth during these base period years while the other has maintained a constant level.

Tax year	Excess profits net income	
	Corporation A	Corporation B
1936.........	$250,000	$100,000
1937.........	250,000	200,000
1938.........	250,000	300,000
1939.........	250,000	400,000
Total...	1,000,000	1,000,000
Average	250,000	250,000

To give these two corporations the same excess-profits credit based on income as does the existing law, operates inequitably in the case of corporation B, whose earnings have steadily increased during the base period. A credit of $250,000 does not properly reflect its earning power as of the time the excess-profits tax became applicable.

Section 4 of the bill provides an optional method whereby the factor of growth will be taken into account in ascertaining the base-period average.

The method provided for by this section is operative only where the earnings for the second half of the base period are in excess of the earnings for the first half of such period. For this purpose, the base period is divided into halves, each of an equal number of months. The aggregate of the excess-profits net income for each half is first determined. The excess of the aggregate for the second half over the aggregate for the first half is then ascertained and divided by two. The amount so found is then added to the excess-profits net income for the second half and the sum resulting from such addition is divided by the number of months in the second half and multiplied by 12. The resulting figure will be the average base period net income (95 percent of which is to be used in ascertaining the credit), except that the average base period net income so computed cannot exceed the highest excess-profits net income for any taxable year in the base period.

An example of the operation of this section is as follows: Suppose a taxpayer reporting on the calendar-year basis has the following amounts of excess-profits net income for the base period years:

1936, $100,000; 1937, $200,000; 1938, $300,000; and 1939, $400,000. Under the present provisions its average base period net income would be $250,000. Under the proposed amendment its average base period income would be computed as follows:

Sum of excess-profits net income for second half of base period..........	$700,000
Sum of excess-profits net income for first half.........................	300,000
Difference....................	400,000
Difference divided by 2..............	200,000
Second half excess-profits net income..	700,000
Total of last 2 amounts........	900,000
Total placed upon an annual basis (divided by number of months in second half of base period, 24, and multiplied by 12)...........................	450,000
Highest excess-profits net income for any taxable year..................	400,000
Average base period net income......	400,000

This method in the case of growing corporations will thus provide a credit which is closely related to the earnings of the second half of the base period, so that the factor of growth is thus taken into account in the computation of the credit. (p. 6-7)

Provision is made in the amendment for the manner of computation where the taxpayer, because of changes in its accounting period or for other reasons, has more or less than 4 taxable year, and where part of 1 taxable year is in the first half of the base period and the other part is in the second half. To illustrate this division of a taxable year lying partly in the first half and partly in the second, the following example is given:

Years in the base period		Number of months	Excess profits, net income
Beginning—	Ending—		
Sept. 1, 1936........................	Aug. 31, 1937........................	12	$30,000
Sept. 1, 1937........................	Dec. 31, 1937........................	4	20,000
Jan. 1, 1938........................	Dec. 31, 1938........................	12	60,000
Jan. 1, 1939........................	Dec. 31, 1939........................	12	100,000
Total..		40	210,000
FIRST HALF			
The taxable year beginning Sept. 1, 1936, and ending Aug. 31, 1937...........		12	30,000
The taxable year beginning Sept. 1, 1937, and ending Dec. 31, 1937...........		4	20,000
One-third of the taxable year beginning Jan. 1, 1938, and ending Dec. 31, 1938		4	20,000
Total..		20	70,000
SECOND HALF			
Two-thirds of the taxable year beginning Jan. 1, 1938, and ending Dec. 31, 1938		8	40,000
The taxable year beginning Jan. 1, 1939, and ending Dec. 31, 1939............		12	100,000
Total..		20	140,000

In making the computations under this alternative a deficit in excess-profits net income (or in the case of more than one deficit, the greatest deficit) is not counted as zero as in the case of the computation on the straight average basis.   (p. 9)

Report—Senate Finance Committee (77th Cong., 1st Sess., S. Rept. 75).— Same as Ways and Means Committee Report.   (p. 3, 6-7, 9, respectively)

Congressional Discussion

Discussion—House (Cong. Rec. Vol. 87).—Mr. Cooper. * * * This bill provides a new or a third formula to take care of growing corporations, and in this connection I invite attention to page 6 of the bill, section 4, "Computation of average base period net income." To take care of growing corporations the base period, which you will remember, is the calendar years 1936, 1937, 1938, and 1939, is divided into two parts, the first two years, 1936 and 1937, in one part, and the years 1938 and 1939 in the second part. Now, you take the average for each part, the average for the first 2 years and then the average for the second 2 years, then you subtract the average of the first 2 years from the average of the second 2 years, you divide that by two and then you add that to the average for the second 2 years.

If I may be permitted, I will give you an illustration. Assume that the excess-profits tax net income was as follows: In 1936 the corporation had $100, in 1937 $200, in 1938 $300, and in 1939 $400, which makes a total of $1,000. The average of the first 2 years is $150 and the average for the second 2 years is $350. You subtract the average of the first 2 years from the average of the second 2 years and that gives you a difference of $200, and you divide this by two and that gives you $100. This $100 is added to the average of the last 2 years, which was $350, which would make $450. However, it is provided that this credit shall not exceed the amount of the excess-profits tax net income of any one year, and it will be recalled that the highest amount was $400 for the year 1939. Therefore, instead of getting a credit of $450 as this formula would produce, the corporation would get $400, which is the maximum amount for any one year during the base period. Under present law this would be $250; under this bill it would be $400. This illustration will give some idea of the advantages that are afforded by the provisions of this bill for the growing corporation.   (p. 1379-80)

Discussion—Senate (Cong. Rec. Vol. 87).—Mr. Harrison. * * * Section 4: Growing corporations: The bill provides special relief for growing corporations. This relief is applicable only where the excess profits net income for the second half of the base period is in excess of the excess profits net income for the first half. For this purpose, the base period is divided into 2 halves. For example, in the case of a calendar year corporation, the first half will consist of the calendar years 1936 and 1937. The second half will consist of the calendar years 1938 and 1939. The average for the first half is subtracted from the average for the second half. The amount so found is divided by two and then added to the average for the second half. This is the average base period income, if it does not exceed the highest excess-profits tax net income for any taxable year in the base period.

*   *   *

It will be noted that this taxpayer's average base period income has been increased from $250,000 to $400,000. Because corporations with the last fiscal years in 1940 will acquire a growth in their late base period 1940 years which might not be normal, the bill applies a different rule to those corporations whose last fiscal year in the base periods ends after May 31, 1940. To accomplish this, the excess-profits net income for any taxable year in the base period ending after May 31, 1940, is reduced by the ratio which the number of months in such years after May 31, 1940, bears to the entire months in such year. To such income so reduced is then added an amount which bears the same ratio to the excess-profits net income of the preceding year as the number of months after May 31, 1940, bears to the number of months in such preceding taxable pear.[1]   (p. 1638)

---

[1] [year].

Committee Hearings
1942 Act

Hearings—Ways and Means Committee.—Extending scope of growth provisions. (R. Paul—Treas. Dept.—p. 109-110)

Hearings—Senate Finance Committee.—Eliminating restriction as to maximum inclusion of any one year. (E. C. Alvord, p. 1781-82, 1790-91)

1941 Act

Hearings—Senate Finance Committee.—Explanation and shortcomings of provision. (E. C. Alvord, p. 638-639)

Committee Hearings
1940 Act

Hearings—Ways and Means Committee.—Allowing extra credit for growth in earnings within base period. (C. David-son, p. 127-129; F. L. Crawford, p. 146-147)

1918
311
(b)-(d)

[Set forth on page 327]

Sec. 713(f)(7)

EPTA
4(b)

[SEC. 713. EXCESS PROFITS CREDIT—BASED ON INCOME.]

[(f) **Average Base Period Net Income—Increased Earnings in Last Half of Base Period.**—The average base period net income determined under this subsection shall be determined as follows:]

(7) For the purposes of this subsection, the excess profits net income for any taxable year ending after May 31, 1940, shall not be greater than an amount computed as follows:

(A) By reducing the excess profits net income by an amount which bears the same ratio thereto as the number of months after May 31, 1940, bears to the total number of months in such taxable year; and

(B) By adding to the amount ascertained under subparagraph (A) an amount which bears the same ratio to the excess profits net income for the last preceding taxable year as such number of months after May 31, 1940, bears to the number of months in such preceding year. The amount added under this subparagraph shall not exceed the amount of the excess profits net income for such last preceding taxable year.

(C) If the number of months in such preceding taxable year is less than such number of months after May 31, 1940, by adding to the amount ascertained under subparagraph (B) an amount which bears the same ratio to the excess profits net income for the second preceding taxable year as the excess of such number of months after May 31, 1940, over the number of months in such preceding taxable year bears to the number of months in such second preceding taxable year.

Committee Reports

Report—Ways and Means Committee (77th Cong., 1st Sess., H. Rept. 146).— The 1st of June 1940 marks generally the beginning of the industrial expansion under the National Defense Program. It was because of this that the amortization allowance in the Second Revenue Act of 1940 was confined to construction and acquisition after June 10, 1940. Corporations whose last taxable years in the base period extend beyond May 31, 1940, may have greatly expanded their facilities of production and, consequently, their income after that date. In giving effect to the factor of growth during the base period, equitable demands do not indicate that growth after May 31, 1940, should not be taken into account.

For this reason, section 713 (f) (7), as set out in section 4 of the bill, limits the benefits to be accorded to the growth factor to increases occurring prior to June 1, 1940. In order to achieve this result in the determination of the growth factor, the excess-profits net income for any taxable year in the base period ending after May 31, 1940, is reduced by the ratio which the number of months in such year after May 31, 1940, bears to the entire number of months in such year. To such income so reduced is then added an amount which bears the same ratio to the excess-profits net income of the preceding year as the number of months after May 31, 1940, bears to the number of months in such preceding taxable year.

For example, a corporation accounts on the basis of fiscal years beginning October 1 and ending September 30. It had an excess-profits net income of $300,000 for the year ending September 30, 1939, and $600,000 for the year ending September 30, 1940. Both of these taxable years are in the base period but 4 months of the fiscal year 1940 are after May 31, 1940. As applied to this corporation, this provision would operate as follows:

Taxable Year	Period		Number of months	Excess-profits net income
	Beginning—	Ending—		
1939...................................	Oct. 1, 1938	Sept. 30, 1939	12	$400,000
1940...................................	Oct. 1, 1939 June 1, 1940	May 31, 1940 Sept. 30, 1940	8 4	} 600,000
Under subpar. (A) of sec. 713 (f) (7) the excess profits net income for 1940 is reduced by 4/12 or ⅓ of $600,000, equals...				200,000
Total.......				400,000
Under subpar. (B) this sum is increased by 4/12 of the excess profits net income for 1939 or ⅓ of $400,000, equals..				133,333
Total...........				533,000

Thus, for the purposes of this method of computing the excess profits credit, $533,333 would become the excess profits net income for 1940 in lieu of $600,000, the actual figure for that year.

If, in the above example, the number of months in the preceding taxable year had been less than the number of months in the fiscal year 1940 after May 31, 1940, then recourse must be had to the second preceding taxable year to find the income to be attributed to the excess of such months. For example, a corporation has for its last three taxable years in the base period the following taxable periods and excess profits net incomes:

Taxable years		Number of months	Excess profits net income
Beginning	Ending		
July 1, 1938...................	June 30, 1939...............	12	$400,000
July 1, 1939...................	Sept. 30, 1939...............	3	75,000
Oct. 1, 1939...................	Sept. 30, 1940...............	12	600,000

Instead of the treatment set out in the previous example, subparagraphs (B) and (C) prescribe the following:

Taxable years	Period		Number of months	Excess profits net income
	Beginning—	Ending—		
1939, first..............................	July 1, 1938	June 30, 1939	12	$400,000
1939, second.............................	July 1, 1939	Sept. 30, 1939	3	75,000
1940.....................................	{Oct. 1, 1939	May 31, 1940	8	} 600,000
	June 1, 1940	Sept. 30, 1940	4	
As in the previous example, subparagraph (A) would reduce the excess profits net income for 1940 by 4/12 or ⅓ of $600,000 equals...................................				200,000
Total........				400,000
Under subparagraph (B) there would be added to the sum so obtained the entire excess profits net income for the 3 months constituting the second 1939 fiscal year..........				75,000
For the 1 month still not taken into account, subparagraph (C) has recourse to the first 1939 fiscal year and attributes to such month 1/12 of $400,000 equals..............				33,333
Total..				508,333

Thus, for the purpose of the computation under subsection (f), the corporation would have an excess profits net income for its fiscal year 1940, the last year in its base period, of $508,333 instead of the actual amount of $600,000. (p. 7-9)

Report—Senate Finance Committee (77th Cong., 1st Sess., S. Rept. 75).— Same as Ways and Means Committee Report. (p. 7-9)

Sec. 713(g)(1)

1940
201

[SEC. 713. EXCESS PROFITS CREDIT—BASED ON INCOME.]

(c) Adjustments in Excess Profits Credit on Account of Capital Changes.—For the purposes of this section—

(1) The net capital addition for the taxable year shall be the excess, divided by the number of days in the taxable year, of the aggregate of the daily capital addition for each day of the taxable year over the aggregate of the daily capital reduction for each day of the taxable year.

Committee Reports

Report—Ways and Means Committee (76th Cong., 3d Sess., H. Rept. 2894).— The net capital addition for the taxable year is computed by taking the aggregate of the daily capital addition for each day of the taxable year and subtracting therefrom the aggregate of the daily capital reduction for each day of the taxable year. The difference thus obtained is divided by the number of days in the taxable year. (p. 21)

Sec. 713(g)(2)

1940
201

[SEC. 713. EXCESS PROFITS CREDIT—BASED ON INCOME.]

[(c) Adjustments in Excess Profits Credit on Account of Capital Changes.—For the purposes of this section—]

(2) The net capital reduction for the taxable year shall be the excess, divided by the number of days in the taxable year, of the aggregate of the daily capital reduction for each day of the taxable year over the aggregate of the daily capital addition for each day of the taxable year.

Committee Reports

Report—Ways and Means Committee (76th Cong., 3d Sess., H. Rept. 2894).— If the aggregate of the daily capital reductions exceeds the aggregate of the daily capital additions, the excess divided by the number of days in the taxable year represents the net capital reduction for the taxable year. (p. 21)

Sec. 713(g)(3)

[SEC. 713. EXCESS PROFITS CREDIT—BASED ON INCOME.]

1940
201

[(c) Adjustments in Excess Profits Credit on Account of Capital Changes.—For the purposes of this section—]

(3) The daily capital addition for any day of the taxable year shall be the aggregate of the amounts of money and property paid in for stock, or as paid-in surplus, or as a contribution to capital, after the beginning of the taxpayer's first taxable year under this subchapter and prior to such day. In determining the amount of any property paid in, such property shall be included in an amount determined in the manner provided in section 718 (a) (2). A distribution by the taxpayer to its shareholders in its stock or rights to acquire its stock shall not be regarded as money or property paid in for stock, or as paid-in surplus, or as a contribution to capital. The amount ascertained under this paragraph shall be reduced by the excess, if any, of the excluded capital for such day over the excluded capital for the first day of the taxpayer's first taxable year under this subchapter. For the purposes of this paragraph the excluded capital for any day shall be an amount equal to the sum of the following:

(A) The aggregate of the adjusted basis (for determining loss upon sale or exchange) as of the beginning of such day, of obligations held by the taxpayer at the beginning of such day, which are described in section 22 (b) (4) (A), (B), or (C) any part of the interest from which is excludible from gross income or allowable as a credit against net income; and

(B) ⟨85 per centum of the⟩ *The* aggregate of the adjusted basis (for determining loss upon sale or exchange) as of the beginning of such day, of stock *of* [*all*] DOMESTIC *corporations* held by the taxpayer at the beginning of such day, with respect to dividends upon which the credit provided in section 26 (b) is allowable. [*except stock of foreign personal-holding companies*]. The daily capital addition shall in no case be less than zero. * * *

Committee Reports

Report—Ways and Means Committee (76th Cong., 3d Sess., H. Rept. 2894).— The daily capital addition for any day of the taxable year is the aggregate of the amount of money and property paid in for stock, or as paid-in surplus, or as a contribution to capital, after the beginning of the taxpayer's first taxable year under the excess-profits tax and prior to the day for which the computation is made. Property paid in is included in an amount equal to its unadjusted basis for determining loss upon sale or exchange. If such unadjusted basis is a substituted basis, it is adjusted with respect to the period before the property was paid in, in the manner provided in section 113 (b) (2). For the purpose of determining the amount of the daily capital addition a distribution by the taxpayer to its shareholders in its stock or right to acquire its stock shall not be regarded as money or property paid in for stock, or as paid-in surplus, or as a contribution to capital.

The amount of the daily capital addition as above computed shall be reduced by the excess, if any, of the excluded capital for such day over the excluded capital for the first day of the taxpayer's first taxable year under the excess-profits tax. Excluded capital consists of (1) obligations described in section 22 (b) (4) (A), (B), or (C), any part of the interest upon which is excludible from gross income or allowable as a credit against net income, and (2) stock held by the taxpayer the dividends upon which are allowed as a credit under section 26 (b). The excluded capital for any day is an amount equal to the sum of the following:

(1) The aggregate of the adjusted basis (for determining loss upon sale or exchange) as of the beginning of such day of the above-described obligations held by the taxpayer at the beginning of such day; and

(2) Eighty-five percent of the aggregate of the adjusted basis (for determining loss upon sale or exchange) as of the beginning of such day of the above-described stock held by the taxpayer at the beginning of such day.

The capital so excluded for the purpose of determining the additions to invested capital represents capital the income from which is not subjected to tax. (p. 21-22)

Report—Conference Committee (76th Cong., 3d Sess., H. Rept. 3002).—*Senate amendment.* * * * The adjustment on account of capital additions and reductions was amended so as to treat 100 percent of the stock of another corporation owned by the taxpayer as excluded capital. This conforms with the change made in the dividends received credit of corporations computing their excess-profits credit on the income plan. (p. 48)

Conference agreement. * * * In view of the conference agreement on sections 711 and 712, the Senate provision relative to a constructive excess profits net income in the case of corporations in existence during part, but not all, of the base period has been retained, and the treatment of corporate stock as excluded capital has been limited to the stock of domestic corporations. (p. 48)

Committee Hearings

Hearings—Ways and Means Committee.—Including non-taxable stock dividends in increase in capital. (C. W. Dudley, p. 275)

Hearings—Senate Finance Committee.—Including non-taxable stock dividends in increase in capital. (W. A. Cooper, p. 56)

Adjusting capital reductions for decreases in inadmissible assets. (W. A. Cooper, p. 56)

Treating taxable stock dividends as additions to capital. (E. C. Alvord, p. 273)

Sec. 713(g)(4)

[Set forth on following page]

[SEC. 713. EXCESS PROFITS CREDIT—BASED ON INCOME.] $\frac{1940}{201}$

[(c) **Adjustments in Excess Profits Credit on Account of Capital Changes.**—For the purposes of this section—]

(4) The daily capital reduction for any day of the taxable year shall be the aggregate of the amounts of distributions to shareholders, not out of earnings and profits, after the beginning of the taxpayer's first taxable year under this subchapter and prior to such day.

Committee Reports

Report—Ways and Means Committee (76th Cong., 3d Sess., H. Rept. 2894).— The daily capital reduction for any day of the taxable year is the aggregate of the amounts of distributions to shareholders after the beginning of the taxpayer's first taxable year under the excess-profits tax and prior to such day, which distributions are not out of earnings and profits. (p. 22)

$$\boxed{\text{Sec. } 713(g)(5)}$$

[SEC. 713. EXCESS PROFITS CREDIT—BASED ON INCOME.] $\frac{1942}{216}$

[(g) **Adjustments in Excess Profits Credit on Account of Capital Changes.**—For the purposes of this section—]

(5) If, on any day of the taxable year, the taxpayer and any one or more other corporations are members of the same controlled group, then the daily capital reduction of the taxpayer for such day shall be increased by whichever of the following amounts is the lesser:

(A) The aggregate of the adjusted basis (for determining loss upon sale or exchange) of stock in such other corporation (or if more than one, in such other corporations) acquired by the taxpayer after the beginning of the taxpayer's first taxable year under this subchapter, minus the aggregate of the adjusted basis (for determining loss upon sale or exchange) of stock in such other corporation (or if more than one, in such other corporations) disposed of by the taxpayer prior to such day and after the beginning of the taxpayer's first taxable year under this subchapter; or

(B) The excess of the aggregate of the adjusted basis (for determining loss upon sale or exchange) of stock in all domestic corporations and of obligations described in section 22 (b) (4), held by the taxpayer at the beginning of such day over the aggregate of the adjusted basis (for determining loss upon sale or exchange) of stock in all domestic corporations and of obligations described in section 22 (b) (4), held by the taxpayer at the beginning of its first taxable year under this subchapter.

If any stock or obligations described in subparagraph (A) or (B) was disposed of prior to such day, its basis shall be determined under the law applicable to the year in which so disposed of. The excluded capital of the taxpayer for such day shall be reduced by the amount by which the taxpayer's daily capital reduction for such day is increased under this paragraph. * * *

Committee Reports

Report—Ways and Means Committee (77th Cong., 2d Sess., H. Rept. 2333).— This section is applicable to taxable years beginning after December 31, 1941, and applies to any taxpayer which is a member of a controlled group and which owns stock in one or more corporations in such controlled group acquired after the beginning of the taxpayer's first taxable year under the excess profits tax. In general, it provides that such stock owned by the taxpayer on any day of the taxable year shall be a daily capital reduction for such day.

Two rules are provided by this section for the determination of the amount of the daily capital reduction on account of such stock for any day of a taxable year beginning after December 31, 1941. The first rule is to the effect that the daily capital reduction for such day shall be the aggregate of the adjusted basis (for determining loss upon sale or exchange) of the stock acquired by the taxpayer after the beginning of the taxpayer's first taxable year under the excess profits tax, minus the aggregate of the adjusted basis (for determining loss upon sale or exchange) of the stock disposed of by the taxpayer prior to such day and after the beginning of the taxpayer's first taxable year under the excess profits tax.

The second rule limits the amount of such daily capital reduction to the excess of the aggregate of the adjusted basis (for determining loss upon sale or exchange) of excluded capital, held by the taxpayer at the beginning of such day, over the aggregate of the adjusted basis (for determining loss upon sale or exchange) of excluded capital, held by the taxpayer at the beginning of its first taxable year under the excess profits tax. The daily capital reduction for any such day shall be an amount equal to the lesser of the amounts determined by the application of the foregoing rules.

In case any stock or obligation referred to in section 210[1] is disposed of prior to the day for which the computation is being made, its basis shall be determined under the law applicable to the year in which so disposed of. The excluded capital of the taxpayer for any such day shall be reduced by the amount by which the taxpayer's daily capital reduction for such day is increased under this section. (p. 140-141)

[1] Sec. 216 of the Act.

Report—Senate Finance Committee (77th Cong., 2d Sess., S. Rept. 1631).— Substantially the same as the Ways and Means Committee Report. (p. 191-192)

Committee Hearings

Hearings—Senate Finance Committee.—Explanation of provision. (J. O'Brien—H. Legis. Counsel—p.104, 105)

Allowing increase in credit for decrease in inadmissibles. (A. L. Hopkins, p. 1754, 1760; E. C. Alvord, p. 1796)

Sec. 715

SEC. 715. DEFINITION OF INVESTED CAPITAL.

For the purposes of this subchapter the invested capital for any taxable year (including the taxable years in the base period) shall be the average invested capital for such year, determined under section 716, reduced by an amount computed under section 720 (relating to inadmissible assets).

⟦*The Commissioner may, under regulations prescribed by him with the approval of the Secretary, permit, in the computation of invested capital, the use of averages or ratios on a monthly, annual, or other appropriate basis, where in his opinion the circumstances do not require daily computations.*⟧ IF THE COMMISSIONER FINDS THAT IN ANY CASE THE DETERMINATION OF INVESTED CAPITAL, ON A BASIS OTHER THAN A DAILY BASIS, WILL PRODUCE AN INVESTED CAPITAL DIFFERING BY NOT MORE THAN $1,000 FROM AN INVESTED CAPITAL DETERMINED ON A DAILY BASIS, HE MAY, UNDER REGULATIONS PRESCRIBED BY HIM WITH THE APPROVAL OF THE SECRETARY, PROVIDE FOR SUCH DETERMINATION ON SUCH OTHER BASIS. * * *

Committee Reports

Report—Ways and Means Committee (76th Cong., 3d Sess., H. Rept. 2894).— Invested capital for any taxable year, including the taxable years in the base period, is defined in section 715 as the average invested capital for such year and is based on the invested capital for each day of the taxable year. (p. 24)

Report—Senate Finance Committee (76th Cong., 3d Sess., S. Rept. 2114).— These sections are the same as in the House bill except that the references to the taxable years in the base period have been eliminated owing to the fact that base-period experience is not taken into account in computing the excess-profits credit based on invested capital. (p. 14)

Report—Conference Committee (76th Cong., 3d Sess., H. Rept. 3002).—The only change, other than clerical and technical changes, made by the Senate amendment in these sections of the House bill was the insertion of a new sentence in section 715 authorizing the Commissioner of Internal Revenue, pursuant to regulations, to permit, in the computation of invested capital, the use of averages or ratios on a monthly, annual, or other appropriate basis, where in his opinion the circumstances do not require daily computation.

Under the conference agreement, the authorization to compute invested capital on some basis other than a daily basis is limited to cases where such other method will not cause the invested capital to vary by more than $1,000 from the invested capital computed on a daily basis. (p. 49)

Committee Hearings
1942 Act

Hearings—Ways and Means Committee.—Allowing Commissioner power to modify requirements as to daily computation of invested capital. (E. C. Alvord, p. 2771)

Hearings—Senate Finance Committee.—Allowing Commissioner power to modify requirements as to daily computation of invested capital. (H. B. Fernald, p. 979)

1941 Act

Hearings—Ways and Means Committee.—Allowing commissioner power to modify requirements as to daily computation of invested capital. (H. B. Fernald, p. 1569, 1572)

Hearings—Senate Finance Committee.—Allowing commissioner power to modify requirements as to daily computation of invested capital. (E. C. Alvord, p. 677; A. B. Chapman, p. 763-764; H. B. Fernald, p. 886)

1918
─────
325
[Set forth on pages 330, 331]

1917
─────
207
[Set forth on page 359]

3/3/17
─────
202
[Set forth on page 371]

Sec. 716

1940
─────
201

SEC. 716. AVERAGE INVESTED CAPITAL.

[1]The average invested capital for any taxable year ~~for which the tax under this subchapter is being computed~~ shall be the aggregate of the daily invested capital for each day of such taxable year, divided by the number of days in such taxable year.

[1] The Ways and Means Committee heading "Taxable Years in the Taxable Period" was stricken by the Senate Finance Committee.

Committee Reports

Report—Ways and Means Subcommittee (76th Cong., 3d Sess., H. Rept. Aug. 8, 1940).—It is recommended that the invested capital for any taxable year (including the years in the base period) be the average invested capital for such year based on the invested capital for each day of the taxable year. (p. 11)

Report—Ways and Means Committee (76th Cong., 3d Sess., H. Rept. 2894).—

Average invested capital is the aggregate of the daily invested capital for each day of the taxable year divided by the number of days in such taxable year or, for a taxable year in the base period, the aggregate of the daily invested capital for each day of such taxable year divided by the number of days in the 12 months ending with the close of the taxable year. (p. 24)

Committee Hearings

Hearings—Senate Finance Committee.—Eliminating computation on daily basis. (H. B. Fernald, p. 276-277, 280-281)

1918
─────
326(d)
[Set forth on page 337]

Sec. 717

1940
─────
201

SEC. 717. DAILY INVESTED CAPITAL.

The daily invested capital for any day of the taxable year shall be the sum of the equity invested capital for such day plus the borrowed invested capital for such day determined under section 719.

Committee Reports

Report—Ways and Means Subcommittee (76th Cong., 3d Sess., H. Rept. Aug. 8, 1940).—Your subcommittee recommends that the invested capital of the taxpayer should consist of equity invested capital and borrowed invested capital. (p. 5)

Report—Ways and Means Committee (76th Cong., 3d Sess., H. Rept. 2894).—The invested capital for a taxable year consists of two component parts: (a) Equity invested capital; and (b) borrowed invested capital. (p. 24)

Sec. 718(a)(1)

SEC. 718. EQUITY INVESTED CAPITAL.

1940
201

(a) **Definition.**—The equity invested capital for any day of any taxable year shall be determined as of the beginning of such day and shall be the sum of the following amounts, reduced as provided in subsection (b)—

(1) **Money Paid In.**—Money previously paid in for stock, or as paid-in surplus, or as a contribution to capital;

Committee Reports

Report—Ways and Means Subcommittee (76th Cong., 3d Sess., H. Rept. Aug. 8, 1940).—Equity invested capital for any day of the taxable year is to be the sum of the following amounts:
(1) Money previously paid in for stock, or as paid-in surplus, or as a contribution to capital; (p. 11)
Report—Ways and Means Committee (76th Cong., 3d Sess., H. Rept. 2894).—(a) *Equity invested capital.*—Equity invested capital is the sum of the following items:
(1) Money paid in for stock or as paid-in surplus or as a contribution to capital; (p. 10)
(a) *Equity invested capital.*—The equity invested capital for any day of the taxable year is determined under section 718, which provides that it shall be determined as of the beginning of such day and shall be the sum of the following amounts— (p. 24)

Committee Hearings

Hearings—Ways and Means Committee.—Problems of money paid in for bonds later converted to stock. (E. C. Alvord, p. 311)
Hearings—Senate Finance Committee.—Including debts forgiven by stockholders. (J. L. Sullivan—Treas. Dept. —p. 133-134)
Including stock issued for services, at value of stock. (R. S. McIver, p. 435)

[Set forth on page 331]

1918
325(b)

[Set forth on page 331]

1918
326(a)

[Set forth on page 359]

[Set forth on page 371]

Sec. 718(a)(2)

[SEC. 718. EQUITY INVESTED CAPITAL.]

[(a) **Definition.**—The equity invested capital for any day * * * shall be the sum of the following amounts * * *]

[(2) **Property paid in.**— * * *] If the property was disposed of before such taxable year, such basis shall be determined under the law applicable to the year of disposition, but without regard to the value of the property as of March 1, 1913. If the property was disposed of before March 1, 1913, its basis shall be considered to be its fair market value at the time paid in. If the unadjusted basis of the property is a substituted basis, such basis shall be adjusted, with respect to the period before the property was paid in, by an amount equal to the adjustments proper under section 115 (l) for determining earnings and profits.

Committee Reports

Report—Ways and Means Committee (77th Cong., 2d Sess., H. Rept. 2333).— This section is designed to correct certain inconsistencies with respect to the basis of property paid in for stock, or as paid-in surplus, or as a contribution to capital.

Section 718 (a) (2) is amended to provide that if property paid in was disposed of before the taxable year, its basis shall be the basis for determining loss applicable to the year of disposition, but without regard to the value of the property as of March 1, 1913. This change coordinates the provision dealing with property paid in for stock with the provision dealing with the effect of the disposition of the property upon earnings and profits. Under section 115 (1), which governs the effect upon earnings and profits of the disposition of property for both income and excess profits tax purposes, the effect of the disposition of property upon such earnings and profits is determined by the law applicable to the year of disposition.

The second sentence to be inserted in the code by this section amends section 718 (a) (2) to take care of the situation in which the property was disposed of prior to March 1, 1913, and provides that in such a case the basis of the property shall be considered to be its fair market value at the time paid in. This is the rule now applied where the taxpayer's basis is cost.

This section also provides that, if the unadjusted basis for determining loss of property paid in (which is the figure at which property paid in is included in equity invested capital) is a substituted basis, such basis shall be adjusted, with respect to the period before the property was paid in, by an amount equal to the adjustments proper under section 115 (l) for the purpose of determining earnings and profits. The change is designed to coordinate the adjustments to be made under section 718 (a) (2) with those entering into the computations under subsection (a) (4) and related provisions of section 718 pursuant to the provisions of section 115 (1). (p. 141-142)

Report—Senate Finance Committee (77th Cong., 2d Sess., S. Rept. 1631).— Substantially the same as the Ways and Means Committee Report. (p. 192-193)

Congressional Discussion

Discussion—House (Cong. Rec. Vol. 88).—MR. DISNEY. * * * 1. For the purpose of determining the amount of invested capital of a corporation attributable to property paid in for stock, or paid in surplus, or as a contribution to capital, the present law counts such property at its unadjusted basis for determining loss. For this purpose, even though the property has already been disposed of, its basis is determined as if the property were still held by the taxpayer. The reason for this treatment is to apply the basis provisions of current law uniformly to all property paid in, regardless of when the property was disposed of.

It is now apparent that the present law reaches a wrong result for the reason that the earnings and profits account of the corporation, which also goes in to make up its invested capital, reflects gain or loss measured by the basis rules in effect in the year in which the property was disposed of. Thus, one portion of the invested capital, namely, that part attributable to property paid in, is computed under current basis rules, while another part, namely, the portion attributable to earnings and profits, is determined under the basis rules applying to the year of the disposition of the property. This treatment results in a serious distortion of the invested-capital picture.

The bill corrects this distortion by providing that the basis of property paid in shall be determined by the rules in effect in the year in which the property was disposed of, except where the disposition occurred prior to March 1, 1913, then its basis is fixed at its fair market value at the time it was paid in to the corporation. (p. 6378-79)

Committee Hearings

Hearings—Ways and Means Committee.—Determining invested capital by reference to basis of assets for gains not losses. (J. W. Hooper, p. 498)

Determining invested capital by reference to predecessor's basis where company reorganized other than through bankruptcy. (E. C. McCobb, p. 539-545; R. V. Fletcher, p. 1815-28; W. J. MacIntosh, p. 1859-77)

Determining invested capital by reference to actual cost, not basis. (A. B. Chapman, p. 877; E. C. Alvord, p. 2766-70, 2777-79)

Hearings—Senate Finance Committee.—Explanation of provision. (J. O'Brien—H. Legis. Counsel—p. 108)

Determining invested capital by reference to predecessor's basis where company reorganized other than through bankruptcy. (R. V. Fletcher, p. 853-881; E. C. Alvord, p. 1796; E. C. McCobb, p. 2111-17; C. W. Lewis, p. 2207-12; R. B. Ralls, p. 2350-51)

Determining invested capital by reference to basis of assets for gains not losses. (H. B. Fernald, p. 979; J. W. Hooper, p. 1175)

Clarifying includibility of stock issued for debts or services. (J. W. Hooper, p. 1175)

Determining invested capital by reference to actual cost, not basis. (A. L. Hopkins, p. 1755, 1760; E. C. Alvord, p. 1778-80, 1795-96; A. B. Chapman, p. 2078)

1943 Act

Hearings—Ways and Means Committee.—Determining invested capital by reference to predecessor's basis where company reorganized other than through bankruptcy. (E. C. McCobb, p. 891-896)

1941 Act

Hearings—Ways and Means Committee.—Determining invested capital by reference to basis of accounting for gains, not losses. (H. B. Fernald, p. 1567-68, 1570)

Determining basis by reference to law controlling at time assets paid in. (Controllers Institute of America, p. 1714-15)

Hearings—Senate Finance Commit-

tee.—Determining basis by reference to law controlling at time assets paid in. (E. C. Alvord, p. 642, 672-676, 682; A. B. Chapman, p. 754, 759-760, 762; H. B. Fernald, p. 883-884; F. Ulmer, p. 1201;

A. Lowenhaupt, p. 1240-41)

Determining invested capital by reference to basis of assets for gains not losses (H. B Fernald, p. 883, 884)

[SEC. 718. EQUITY INVESTED CAPITAL.]

[(a) **Definition.**—The equity invested capital for any day * * * shall be the sum of the following amounts * * *]

(2) **Property Paid In.**—Property (other than money) previously paid in (regardless of the time paid in) for stock, or as paid-in surplus, or as a contribution to capital. Such property shall be included in an amount equal to its basis (unadjusted) for determining loss upon sale or exchange. If the property was disposed of before such taxable year, such basis shall be determined in the same manner as if the property were still held at the beginning of such taxable year. If such unadjusted basis is a substituted basis it shall be adjusted, with respect to the period before the property was paid in, in the manner provided in section 113 (b) (2);

Committee Reports

Report—Ways and Means Subcommittee (76th Cong., 3d Sess., H. Rept. Aug. 8, 1940).—(2) The unadjusted basis (for determining loss) of property other than money previously paid in for stock, or as paid-in surplus, or as a contribution to capital. Property so admitted is taken at its unadjusted basis for determining loss upon the sale or exchange. The use of the unadjusted basis is dictated by the fact that adjustments to basis, notably for depreciation, are reflected in earnings and profits. Where the property so paid in was disposed of before the beginning of the taxable year, the basis is determined just as if the property were still in the taxpayer's hands. The result is uniformity of basis treatment, regardless of the law in effect at the time of the disposition of the property; (p. 11)

Report—Ways and Means Committee (76th Cong., 3d Sess., H. Rept. 2894).— (2) *Property paid in.*—Property other than money previously paid in for stock, or as paid-in surplus, or as a contribution to capital, regardless of the time paid in. Such property shall be included at an amount equal to its unadjusted basis for determining loss upon sale or exchange. If the unadjusted basis of such property is a substituted basis it shall be adjusted,

with respect to the period before the property was paid in, in the manner provided in section 113 (b) (2). The use of the unadjusted basis is dictated by the fact that adjustments of basis, notably for depreciation, are reflected in earnings and profits. If the property so paid in was disposed of before the beginning of the taxable year, such basis is determined in the same manner as if the property were still held by the taxpayer at the beginning of the taxable year. The result is uniformity of basis treatment, regardless of the law in effect at the time of the disposition of the property. (p. 24)

Report (Minority)—Senate Finance Committee (76th Cong., 3d Sess., S. Rept. 2114).—The invested capital of a corporation under my amendment does not depend upon the value at which the corporation's property is carried on its books. Consequently, the corporation which issued its stock for the properties of other corporations and which placed those properties on its books at an excessive valuation will not obtain any tax benefit from such excessive valuation since the valuation is immaterial for the computation of invested capital for tax purposes. As stated above, the controlling figure for excess-profits purposes is the tax cost of property paid in for stock and not its value on the books of the corporation which acquired the property. Moreover, it must be observed that the only property which figures in the computation of invested capital for tax purposes is property received in return for corporate stock issued to acquire such property.

The purchase or sale of property by a corporation has no effect upon its invested capital for tax purposes, so that if a corporation buys property at an inflated price its invested capital will not be increased thereby. The following illustrates the dependence of invested capital upon the tax cost of property paid in for stock rather than its value: Corporation A issues 500,000 shares of stock for the properties of corporation B. It values these shares and these properties at $5,000,000. Actually, the stockholders of corporation B had invested only $2,000,000 of capital and earnings in corporation B. The increase in corporation A's invested capital by reason of this acquisition of property will be $2,000,000 and not $5,000,000.

The invested capital method of computing excess profits thus seeks to determine as fairly as possible the actual dollars invested by the shareholders in the business and remaining at risk in the business. It is only on actual money actually risked that invested capital is based.   (p. 11-12)

Committee Hearings

Hearings—Ways and Means Committee.—Advantages of current invested capital provisions over those in 1918. (J. L. Sullivan—Treas. Dept.—p. 94-95)

Including property issued for stock on basis of market value, not par value of stock.   (P. D. Seghers, p. 160-161)

Problems arising from use of "basis." (E. C. Alvord, p. 311)

Problems arising from bankruptcy reorganizations.   (R. V. Fletcher, p. 354-355)

Hearings—Senate Finance Committee.—Problems arising in connection with treasury stock and invested capital. (K. Carroad, p. 37)

Problems arising from use of "basis." (A. B. Trudgian, p. 78, 82; E. C. Alvord, p. 272; H. B. Fernald, p. 278, 283; A. B. Chapman, p. 392-393)

Explanation of provision. (C. F. Stam—Jt. Com. on Int. Rev. Taxn.— p. 208)

Problems arising from bankruptcy reorganizations.   (R. V. Fletcher, p. 356)

[Set forth on page 331]	**1918** 325(b)
[Set forth on page 331]	**1918** 326(a)
[Set forth on page 359]	**1917** 207
[Set forth on page 371]	**3/3/17** 202

```
Sec. 718(a)(3)
```

[SEC. 718. EQUITY INVESTED CAPITAL.]   **1940** 201

[(a) **Definition.**—The equity invested capital for any day * * * shall be the sum of the following amounts * * *

(3)   ¹Distributions in stock.—Distributions in stock—

(A)   Made prior to such taxable year to the extent to which they are considered distributions of earnings and profits; and

(B)   Previously made during such taxable year to the extent to which they are considered distributions of earnings and profits other than earnings and profits of such taxable year; and

¹ The heading is as worded by the Conference Committee.   The Ways and Means Committee heading read "Taxable Stock Dividends".

Committee Reports

Report—Ways and Means Subcommittee (76th Cong., 3d Sess., H. Rept. Aug. 8, 1940).—(a) *Equity invested capital.*—In computing equity invested capital for any taxable year, the taxpayer would add the sum of the following four items: * * *

(3) Taxable stock dividends: Taxable stock dividends are included in invested capital because they represent in effect a reinvestment of earnings in the business.   (p. 5)

(3) Taxable stock dividends to the extent they constituted a distribution of earnings and profits other than earnings and profits of the taxable year.   To the extent that distributions in stock have reduced the earnings and profits of the corporation, such distributions are included in invested capital.   Conversely, if the dividend was not considered taxable to the distributee under the applicable revenue law, it is not deemed to reduce the earnings and profits account and is, therefore, already reflected in the accumulated earnings and profits: and (p. 11)

Report—Ways and Means Committee (76th Cong., 3d Sess., H. Rept. 2894).— (3) *Taxable stock dividends.*—Distributions in stock of the corporation, or in rights to acquire its stock, to the extent to which they constituted a distribution of earnings and profits other than earnings and profits of the taxable year. Taxable stock dividends are included in invested capital because they represent, in effect, a reinvestment of earnings in the business.   Conversely, if a stock dividend was not subject to tax in the hands of the distributee because it did not constitute income to him within the meaning of the sixteenth amendment to the Constitution or was not taxable to him under the applicable revenue law, it is not deemed to reduce the earnings and profits account and is therefore already reflected in the accumulated earnings and profits.   (p. 24)

Committee Hearings

Hearings—Ways and Means Committee.—Explanation of provision.   (E. C. Alvord, p. 311)

Hearings—Senate Finance Committee.—Explanation of provision.   (C. F. Stam—Jt. Com. on Int. Rev. Taxn.— p. 208)

Sec. 718(a)(4)

[SEC. 718.   EQUITY INVESTED CAPITAL.]

[(a)   Definition.—The equity invested capital for any day * * * shall be the sum of the following amounts * * *]

(4)   Earnings and Profits at Beginning of Year.—The accumulated earnings and profits as of the beginning of such taxable year; AND

Committee Reports

Report—Ways and Means Subcommittee (76th Cong., 3d Sess., H. Rept. Aug. 8, 1940).—Thus, the fluctuations of earnings and profits for the taxable year have no effect upon the invested capital for such year. (p. 5)

Equity invested capital for any day of the taxable year is to be the sum of the following amounts: * * * less the sum of the following amounts: * * *

(2) Any deficit in accumulated earnings and profits as of the beginning of the taxable year; (p. 11, 12)

Report—Ways and Means Committee (76th Cong., 3d Sess., H. Rept. 2894).—Fluctuations in the earnings and profits account for the taxable year have no effect upon the invested capital for the taxable year. Deficits in the earnings and profits account, moreover, do not reduce the invested capital. Nevertheless, deficits in the earnings and profits account must be made good out of earnings and profits before any increase in invested capital results from the earnings and profits account. (p. 10)

Your committee has recommended certain special relief provisions, which are as follows:

*   *   *

(5) Many corporations which had operating deficits would sustain severe hardships if their invested capital was reduced by such deficits. Your committee provided that operating deficits should reduce invested capital only to the extent of the earned surplus. (p. 13, 14)

(4) *Earnings and profits at beginning of year.*—The accumulated earnings and profits as of the beginning of the taxable year. If there is a deficit in the accumulated earnings and profits as of the beginning of the taxable year, such deficit shall not be taken into account and in such cases the earnings and profits as of the beginning of the taxable year shall be considered as zero, for the purpose of computing the invested capital for such year. (p. 25)

1943 Act

Report—Ways and Means Committee (78th Cong., 1st Sess., H. Rept. 871).—Under the invested capital method, corporations are permitted to increase their invested capital by plowing back into the business, earnings which have not been subject to taxation in the hands of the individual shareholder. However, corporations using the average earnings method are not permitted to increase their earnings base by plowing back into the corporation profits which have not been subject to taxation in the hands of the shareholders.

Earnings after January 1, 1939, are

not permitted under the Canadian law to increase the invested capital of the corporation until they have been capitalized by being subject to taxation in the hands of the individual shareholder.

The reason for such a rule was very obvious, for otherwise a company would stop paying dividends and leave its profits in the business in order to obtain the additional invested capital credit. Moreover, the Government would lose not only excess-profits taxes but also individual income taxes from the individual shareholder. (p. 23)

Congressional Discussion

Discussion—House (Cong. Rec. Vol. 86).—MR. DISNEY. The gentleman may be coming to it, but it seems this is an opportune time to call attention to the fact that a benefit particularly to the small corporations is their deficits are not deducted when their invested capital is being considered.

MR. COOPER. That is correct. (p. 11248)

MR. JOHNS. What would be the situation of a corporation which was capitalized we will say at $3,000,000 in 1932, which had losses in 1932, 1933, and 1934; that as a result of these losses its capital was impaired we will say to the extent of $1,000,000, so that its capital was reduced to $2,000,000; that its earnings during the remainder of the time were approximately the same as they were prior to the reduction in capital: Would not this bill be pretty hard on such corporation?

*   *   *

Mr. Cooper. * * * Answering the

gentleman from Wisconsin, I am unable, of course, to give the gentleman a definite answer without having all the factors before me, but my impression is that it would not. (p. 11249)

Committee Hearings

Hearings—Ways and Means Committee.—Advantages of current invested capital provisions over those in 1918. (J. L. Sullivan—Treas. Dept.—p. 94-95)

Including in earnings unrealized profit on installment sales. (P. D. Seghers, p. 152-155)

Making no deduction from invested capital for operating deficits. (C. W. Dudley, p. 275; H. B. Fernald, p. 282-283; E. C. Alvord, p. 311-312; Welles, Kelsey, Cobourn & Harrington, p. 451)

Including reinsurance reserves in

earnings and profits. (National Board of Fire Underwriters, p. 436-437)

Hearings—Senate Finance Committee.—Making no deduction from invested capital for operating deficits. (K. Carroad, p. 34)

Explanation of provision. (C. F. Stam—Jt. Com. on Int. Rev. Taxn.—p. 208)

Including in earnings unrealized profit on installment sales. (B. L. Knowles, p. 221-223; E. C. Alvord, p. 272-273; G. Rogers, p. 471-475)

1943 Act

Hearings—Ways and Means Committee.—Not adjusting railroad earnings and profits on change from retirement to depreciation accounting. (R. V. Fletcher, p. 565-569)

Hearings—Senate Finance Committee.—Not adjusting railroad earnings and profits on change from retirement to depreciation accounting. (R. V. Fletcher, p. 151-152)

1941 Act

Hearings—Senate Finance Committee.—Adjusting invested capital for in-

come taxes only at time of payment. (J. Hooper, p. 619)

UNENACTED RELATED PROVISION

1940 Act

[Sec. 201 of Ways and Means Committee bill]

[SEC. 718. EQUITY INVESTED CAPITAL.]

(d) Computation of accumulated earnings and profits. For the purposes of this section, accumulated earnings and profits shall be determined without regard to whether the accumulation was before, on, or after March 1, 1913. Nothing in section 401 of the Second Revenue Act of 1940 shall affect the extent to which accumulated earnings and profits are increased by reason of increase in value of property accrued before March 1, 1913.

Committee Reports

Report—Senate Finance Committee (76th Cong., 3d Sess., S. Rept. 2114).— (2) Section 718 (d) of the House bill

has been omitted because of the treatment of this matter under section 501 (sec. 401 of the House bill). (p. 14)

Congressional Discussion

Discussion—House: on Report of Conference Committee (Cong. Rec. Vol. 86).—MR. KNUTSON. I have just one more question. Does section 401 entitled "Earnings and Profits of Corporations," as amended in the Senate and rewritten in conference permit the inclusion of pre-March 1, 1913, appreciation, realized since that date, in equity invested capital?

MR. COOPER. Yes. (p. 12965)

Sec. 718(a)(5)
Sec. 718(b)(4)

[SEC. 718. EQUITY INVESTED CAPITAL.]

1940
201

[(a) **Definition.**—The equity invested capital for any day * * * shall be the sum of the following amounts * * *]

(5) Increase on Account of Gain on Tax-free Liquidation. — * * *

[(b) **Reduction in Equity Invested Capital.**—The amount by which the equity invested capital for any day shall be reduced * * * shall be the sum of the following amounts—]

(4) Reduction on Account of Loss on Tax-free Liquidation. — * * *

Committee Reports

Report—Conference Committee (76th Cong., 3d Sess., H. Rept. 3002).—The conference agreement also makes further technical changes in order to eliminate duplications in the computation of equity invested capital. Provisions have been inserted governing the extent to which the equity invested capital of a parent corporation is to be increased or decreased following a liquidation under section 112 (b) (6). This provision enables the provisions of section 718 (b) (3) to be expanded so as to cover all situations in which, under the doctrine of *Commissioner* v. *Sansome* (60 F. (2d) 931), the earnings and profits of one corporation become the earnings and profits of another. (p. 49)

Committee Hearings

Hearings—Ways and Means Committee.—Adjustment for gain or loss on tax-free liquidations. (F. P. Byerly, p. 364-365)

Hearings—Senate Finance Committee.—Adjustment for gain or loss on tax-free liquidations. (K. Carroad, p. 39)

1941 Act

Hearings—Senate Finance Committee.—Limiting provision to cases where predecessor's property is sold. (E. C. Alvord, p. 682-683; A. B. Chapman, p. 761-762)

```
┌─────────────────────┐
│  Sec. 718(a)(6)     │
│  In General         │
└─────────────────────┘
```

[SEC. 718.   EQUITY INVESTED CAPITAL.]

[(a) **Definition.**—The equity invested capital for any day * * * shall be the sum of the following amounts * * *]

(6) **New capital.**—An amount equal to 25 per centum of the new capital for such day.   The term "new capital" for any day means so much of the amounts of money or property includible for such day under paragraphs (1) and (2) as was previously paid in during a taxable year beginning after December 31, 1940, and so much of the distributions in stock includible for such day under paragraph (3) as was previously made during a taxable year beginning after December 31, 1940, subject to the following limitations:

Committee Reports

Report—**Ways and Means Committee** (77th Cong., 1st Sess., H. Rept. 1040).—
(e) *New capital.*—In order to encourage the investment of new capital in corporate enterprise, your committee is impressed with the desirability of offering a special inducement in the form of a more liberal credit where new capital is present.   To achieve this result, new capital is counted at 125 percent.   Thus for every $100 of new capital paid in to a corporation, the invested capital of such corporation is increased by $125.   This method is the equivalent of allowing an invested capital credit on new capital of 10 percent, where 8 percent is allowed on old capital, and 8¾ percent where 7 percent is allowed on old capital.

New capital is limited to money or property paid in for stock during taxable years beginning after December 31, 1940, and taxable stock dividends made during the same period. * * *

Earnings and profits retained in the business are not considered new capital. (p. 26)

This section amends section 718 (a) of the Internal Revenue Code, defining equity invested capital, by adding a new paragraph designated as (6).   The effect of the amendment is to increase by 25 percent the amount includible in equity invested capital on account of new capital.   The term "new capital" is defined to mean the aggregate of the amount of money and property paid in for stock or as paid-in surplus, or as a contribution to capital, and the amount of taxable stock dividends made, during a taxable year beginning after December 31, 1940, subject to certain limitations.   These limitations are intended, in general, to prevent a taxpayer from treating as new capital amounts resulting from mere adjustments in the existing capital, including borrowed capital, of the taxpayer, or of a controlled group of corporations. (p. 47)

Report—**Senate Finance Committee** (77th Cong., 1st Sess., S. Rept. 673).—Same as p. 47 of Ways and Means Committee Report.   (p. 38)

Congressional Discussion

Discussion—**House** (Cong. Rec. Vol. 87).—MR. DOUGHTON. * * * It is felt that there should be some inducement to the investment of new capital in corporate enterprise.   The reluctance of investors to risk their money in corporations engaged in defense industries must be met with governmental funds.   In order to encourage venture capital, your committee has granted an additional allowance of credit with respect to new capital paid in.   For every $100 of money or property paid in for stock, the corporation's invested capital will be increased by $125.   It is hoped that this provision will have a salutary effect upon companies engaged in producing defense materials.   (p. 6471)

Committee Hearings

Hearings—Senate Finance Committee.—Defining new capital. (J. L. Sullivan—Treas. Dept.—p. 39)

Extending new capital provision to those on income credit. (W. A. M.

Cooper, p. 1196; F. Ulmer, p. 1202)

Giving effect to dividends after December 31, 1940. (W. A. M. Cooper, p. 1197)

1940 Act

Hearings—Ways and Means Committee.—Allowing higher credit for new

capital. (B. Dewey, p. 199-200)

Sec. 718(a)(6)(A)

Section 718(a)(6)(A) *is amended by striking out "112 (b) (3), (4), or (5), or so much of section 112 (c), (d), or (e) as refers to section 112 (b) (3), (4), or (5)" and inserting in lieu thereof "112 (b) (3), (4), (5), or (10), or so much of section 112 (c), (d), or (e) as refers to section 112 (b) (3), (4), (5), or (10)".*

1943
121(d)
(6)

Committee Reports

Report—Conference Committee (78th Cong., 2d Sess., H. Rept. 1079).—Under this amendment it is contemplated that where the excess profits credit is determined under the invested capital method, the rule set forth in section 760 of the code will apply to the transferee corporation. In order that the transferee corporation should not be allowed the additional credit for new capital where the reorganization occurs after December 31, 1940, the amendment contains a provision which adds section 112 (b) (10) to the enumerated sections to which the new capital provisions do not apply. (p. 47)

Congressional Discussion

Discussion—Senate (Cong. Rec. Vol. 90).—Mr. George. Mr. President, I now offer the clerical amendments. * * *

they are all purely clerical and technical in nature, (p. 177)

[SEC. 718. EQUITY INVESTED CAPITAL.]

1941
203

[(a) Definition.—The equity invested capital for any day * * * shall be the sum of the following amounts * * *]

(6) New capital.— * * *

(A) There shall not be included money or property paid in by a corporation in an exchange to which section 112 (b) (3), (4), or (5), or so much of section 112 (c), (d), or (e) as refers to section 112 (b) (3), (4), or (5) is applicable (51) *(or would be applicable except for section 371 (g))*, or would have been applicable if the term "control" had been defined in section 112 (h) to mean the ownership of stock possessing more than 50 per centum of the total combined voting power of all classes of stock entitled to vote or more than 50 per centum of the total value of shares of all classes of stock.

Committee Reports

Report—Ways and Means Committee (77th Cong., 1st Sess., H. Rept. 1040).— Borrowed capital does not constitute new capital nor can transactions in certain tax-free exchanges or between corporations which are members of an affiliated group in which more than 50 percent control is present, create new capital. (p. 26)

The limitations provided by subparagraphs (A), (B), and (C) bar from the concept of new capital the amount of any equity invested capital acquired in an exchange occurring during a taxable year beginning after December 31, 1940, to which section 112 (b) (3), (4), or (5), or so much of section 112 (c), (d), or (e) as refers to section 112 (b) (3), (4), or (5) is applicable, or would be applicable if the term "control" had been defined in section 112 (h) to mean the ownership of stock possessing more than 50 percent of the total combined voting power of all classes of stock entitled to vote or more than 50 percent of the total value of all classes of stock. (p. 47-48)

Corporation A issues stock during a taxable year beginning after December 31, 1940, to corporation B in exchange for the transfer of certain property by corporation B. Immediately after the transfer the stock acquired by corporation B has a value of $10,000, the total value of all classes of stock of corporation A then outstanding amounting to $18,000. Corporation A obtains no new capital since the property for which the new stock was issued was obtained in an exchange to which section 112 (b) (5) would be applicable if the term "control" had been defined in section 112 (h) so as to include either the ownership of stock possessing more than 50 percent of the total combined voting power of all classes of stock entitled to vote or more than 50 percent of the total value of all classes of stock outstanding. (p. 48)

Report—Senate Finance Committee

(77th Cong., 1st Sess., S. Rept. 673).— Same as p. 47, 47-48 of Ways and Means Committee Report. (p. 39, 40 respectively) In addition, there is the following:

This section is the same as section 205[1] in the House bill except for certain changes of a technical nature made in subparagraph (A) intended to carry out more completely the provisions of the House bill. (p. 38)

[1] Sec. 203 of the Act.

In order to take care of exchanges under Supplement R of the Internal Revenue Code, which relates to exchanges and distributions in obedience to orders of the Securities and Exchange Commission, and to which section 112 (b), (3), (4), or (5) is made inapplicable by section 371 (g), that portion of subparagraph (A) of the House bill reading:

There shall not be included money or property paid in by a corporation in an exchange to which section 112 (b) (3), (4), or (5), or so much of section 112 (c), (d), or (e) as refers to section 112 (b) (3), (4), or (5) is applicable—

has been changed to read:

There shall not be included money or property paid in by a corporation in an exchange to which section 112 (b) (3), (4), or (5), or so much of section 112 (c), (d), or (e) as refers to section 112 (b) (3), (4), or (5) is applicable (or would be applicable except for section 371 (g)). (p. 39)

Report—Conference Committee (77th Cong., 1st Sess., H. Rept. 1203).— Amendment No. 51: This is a technical amendment designed to make the limitations of section 718 (a) (6) (A) of the Internal Revenue Code, added by section 205 of the House bill, applicable to certain exchanges of the same character as those described in the House bill but which were technically not within such provision because they are governed by Supplement R of the Code rather than section 112 (b) (3), (4) or (5). The House recedes. (p. 12)

[Set forth on page 92]

Sec. 718(a)(6)(B)

[SEC. 718. EQUITY INVESTED CAPITAL.]

[(a) **Definition.**—The equity invested capital for any day * * * shall be the sum of the following amounts * * *]

[(6) **New capital.**— * * *]

   (B) There shall not be included money or property paid in to the taxpayer by a transferor corporation if immediately after such transaction the transferor and the taxpayer are members of the same controlled group. As used in this subparagraph and subparagraph (C), a controlled group means one or more chains of corporations connected through stock ownership with a common parent corporation if (i) more than 50 per centum of the total combined voting power of all classes of stock entitled to vote, or more than 50 per centum of the total value of shares of all classes of stock, of each of the corporations (except the common parent corporation) is owned directly by one or more of the other corporations, and (ii) the common parent corporation owns directly more than 50 per centum of the total combined voting power of all classes of stock entitled to vote, or more than 50 per centum of the total value of shares of all classes of stock, of at least one of the other corporations.

Committee Reports

Report—Ways and Means Committee (77th Cong., 1st Sess., H. Rept. 1040).—Borrowed capital does not constitute new capital nor can transactions in certain tax-free exchanges or between corporations which are members of an affiliated group in which more than 50 percent control is present, create new capital. (p. 26)

These limitations also bar from the concept of new capital any equity invested capital acquired in a transaction between members of a controlled group of corporations as that term is defined in subparagraph (B). (p. 47)

Corporation A owns stock in corporation B, and corporation B owns stock in corporation C. Corporation A transfers property to corporation C in exchange for stock of corporation C. Immediately after the transfer the stock owned by corporation A in corporation B possesses more than 50 percent of the total combined voting power of all classes of stock entitled to vote. Also immediately after such transfer the stock owned by corporation B in corporation C has a value equal to more than 50 percent of the total value of all classes of stock of corporation C.

Corporation C obtains no new capital through the acquisition of the property from corporation A in exchange for its stock, since immediately after the transfer corporation A, the transferor, and corporation C, the transferee, are members of the same controlled group. (p. 48-49)

Report—Senate Finance Committee (77th Cong., 1st Sess., S. Rept. 673).—Same as p. 47, 48-49 of Ways and Means Committee Report. (p. 39, 40, respectively)

1941
203
[718(a)
(6)]
in gen'l

[Set forth on page 92]

Sec. 718(a)(6)(C)

1941
203

[SEC. 718. EQUITY INVESTED CAPITAL.]

[(a) **Definition.**—The equity invested capital for any day * * * shall be the sum of the following amounts * * *]

[(6) **New capital.**— * * *]

(C) There shall not be included a distribution in stock described in paragraph (3) made to another corporation, if immediately after the distribution the taxpayer and the distributee are members of the same controlled group.

Committee Reports

Report—Ways and Means Committee (77th Cong., 1st Sess., H. Rept. 1040).—Corporation A makes a distribution in taxable stock dividends to corporations B and C during a taxable year beginning after December 31, 1940. Immediately after the distribution corporations B and C own stock in corporation A which has a voting power of more than 50 percent of the combined voting power of all classes of stock entitled to vote. Also immediately after the transfer corporation B owns stock in corporation C which has a value of more than 50 percent of the total value of all classes of stock of corporation A. The distribution made by corporation A in the taxable stock dividend does not constitute new capital to corporation A. (p. 49)

Report—Senate Finance Committee (77th Cong., 1st Sess., S. Rept. 673).—Same as Ways and Means Committee Report. (p. 40)

1941
203
[718(a)
(6)]
in gen'l

[Set forth on page 92]

Sec. 718(a)(6)(D)

1941
203

[SEC. 718. EQUITY INVESTED CAPITAL.]

[(a) **Definition.**—The equity invested capital for any day * * * shall be the sum of the following amounts * * *]

[(6) **New capital.**— * * *]

(D) **Increase in Inadmissible Assets.**—The new capital for any day of the taxable year, computed without the application of subparagraph (E), shall be reduced by the excess, if any, of the amount computed under section 720 (b) with respect to inadmissible assets held on such day, over the amount computed under section 720 (b) with re-

spect to inadmissible assets held on the first day of the taxpayer's first
taxable year beginning after December 31, 1940. * * *

Committee Reports

**Report—Ways and Means Committee
(77th Cong., 1st Sess., H. Rept. 1040).—**
Furthermore, capital that would otherwise receive new capital treatment, is
denied such treatment to the extent that
there is a net increase in inadmissible
assets. (p. 26)

The limitations provided by subparagraph (D) have the effect of reducing the amount of new capital as of
any day by the excess of the amount of
inadmissible assets held on that day
over the amount of such assets held on
the first day of the taxpayer's first taxable year beginning after December 31,
1940. This treatment is comparable to
the treatment of excluded assets in the
computation of daily capital additions
under section 713 (g) of the existing law.
(p. 48)

Corporation X makes its excess-profits
tax return on the calendar year basis.
On July 1, 1941, cash in the amount of

$100,000 is paid in for stock. There are
no other changes made in either the
amount of equity invested capital or
borrowed capital at any time during the
year 1941. The adjusted basis of inadmissible assets as of January 1, 1941,
amounts to $5,000. The adjusted basis
of such assets as of July 2, 1941, is increased to $15,000. The new capital of
$100,000 is reduced to $90,000 as of
July 2, 1941, by subparagraph (D), as
shown by the following computation:

> $100,000, new capital, minus ($15,000,
> amount of inadmissibles as of July 2,
> 1941, minus $5,000, amount of inad-
> missibles as of July 1, 1941) =
> $90,000. (p. 49)

**Report—Senate Finance Committee
(77th Cong., 1st Sess., S. Rept. 673).—**
Same as p. 48, 49 of Ways and Means
Committee Report. (p. 39, 40-41 respectively)

Committee Hearings

**Hearings—Senate Finance Commit-
tee.—**Eliminating from increase in inadmissibles, new investments not recognized as new capital. (W. A. M.
Cooper, p. 1197)

[Set forth on page 92]

1941
———
203
[718(a)
(6)]
in gen'l

Sec. 718(a)(6)(E)

[SEC. 718. EQUITY INVESTED CAPITAL.]

1941
———
203

[(a) **Definition.**—The equity invested capital for any day * * *
shall be the sum of the following amounts * * *]

[(6) **New capital.**— * * *]

(E) **Maximum New Capital Allowable.**—The new capital for
any day of the taxable year shall not be more than the amount, if any,
by which—

(i)   the sum of the equity invested capital (computed without
regard to this paragraph) and the borrowed capital (as defined in section
719 (a)) of the taxpayer as of such day, reduced by the amount of

money or property paid in which is excluded by reason of the limitation of subparagraph (A) or (B) of this paragraph, exceeds

     (ii)   the sum of such equity invested capital and borrowed capital as of the beginning of the first day of such taxpayer's first taxable year beginning after December 31, 1940, reduced by the amount, if any, by which the accumulated earnings and profits as of such first day of such first taxable year exceed the accumulated earnings and profits (computed without regard to distributions made in taxable years beginning after December 31, 1940) as of the beginning of the first day of the taxable year for which the tax under this subchapter is being computed.

Committee Reports

Report—Ways and Means Committee (77th Cong., 1st Sess., H. Rept. 1040).— To prevent corporations from turning old capital into new by paying it out to shareholders and then having it reinvested, and to prevent borrowed capital from being transformed into new equity capital, a net capital increase concept is used. For the purposes of measuring such net increases in capital, reference is had to the capital as of the beginning of the first taxable year beginning in 1941. (p. 26)

The limitations under subparagraph (E) prevent new capital as of any day from exceeding the amount by which the total equity invested capital and borrowed capital as of such day, computed without including the 25-percent increase, exceeds the sum of the equity invested capital and borrowed capital as of the first day of the taxpayer's first taxable year beginning after December 31, 1940. Any increase in new capital is thus prevented where the amount of borrowed capital is reduced by the same amount as that by which the equity invested capital is increased, and no increase in new capital will result from a distribution by a stock dividend of earnings and profits accumulated prior to the first day of a taxable year beginning after December 31, 1940. Subparagraph (E), however, is so worded that there is no reduction to the extent that the sum of the equity invested capital and borrowed capital as of any day is less than the sum of the equity invested capital and borrowed capital as of the first day of a taxable year beginning after December 31, 1940, due to an operating deficit occurring in any taxable year during the intervening period. (p. 48)

Corporation Y makes its return on the calendar year basis. Its equity invested capital as of January 1, 1941, amounts to $30,000, consisting of money paid in for stock, $20,000, and accumulated earnings and profits, $10,000. Its borrowed capital as of January 1, 1941, consists of bonds outstanding amounting to $15,000, making the total of its equity invested capital and borrowed capital as of January 1, 1941, $45,000. The corporation has no inadmissible assets at any time during the year 1941. On January 2, 1941, the corporation makes a distribution in taxable stock dividends amounting to $5,000. On July 1, 1941, money is paid in for stock amounting to $15,000, and on July 2, 1941, bonds are retired in the amount of $10,000.

The new capital of $20,000 acquired during the year 1941 represented by a distribution in a taxable stock dividend amounting to $5,000 and by money paid in for stock amounting to $15,000 is reduced to $5,000 on July 3, 1941, due to the retirement of $10,000 of bonds on July 2, 1941, and the fact that the stock dividend is paid out of earnings accumulated before January 1, 1941, under the application of subparagraph (E), shown as follows:

The sum of the equity invested capital and borrowed capital on July 3, 1941 (computed without regard to the 25-percent increase for new capital), amounts to $50,000. This sum exceeds the total equity invested capital and borrowed capital on January 1, 1941, amounting to $45,000, by $5,000. Under subparagraph (E) the new capital shall not be more than such excess. The new capital is thus reduced from $20,000 to $5,000.

If the accumulated earnings and profits of corporation Y as of January 1, 1942, are reduced to zero due to the stock dividend distribution of $5,000 made on January 2, 1941, and an operating deficit of $5,000 during the taxable year 1941, the new capital includible in equity invested capital as of January 1, 1942, would be $10,000 instead of $5,000 under the application of subparagraph (E), as shown by the following computation:

New capital as of January 1, 1942, before application of subparagraph (E), $20,000, shall not be more than the excess of $50,000 (total capital on January 1, 1942, before adding 25 percent under section 718 (a) (6)) over $45,000 (total capital on January 1, 1941) less $5,000 (amount by which the accumulated earnings and profits as of January 1, 1941, exceed the accumulated earnings and profits (computed without regard to distributions as of January 1, 1942), or the new capital cannot exceed $50,000 minus ($45,000 minus $5,000), or $10,000. (p. 49-50)

Report—Senate Finance Committee (77th Cong., 1st Sess., S. Rept. 673).— Same as p. 48, 49-50 of Ways and Means Committee Report.   (p. 39, 41, respectively)

[Set forth on page 92]

1941
203
[718(a)
(6)]
in gen'l

Sec. 718(a)(6)(F)

[SEC. 718.   EQUITY INVESTED CAPITAL.]

1941
203

[(a)   Definition.—The equity invested capital for any day * * * shall be the sum of the following amounts * * *]

[(6)   New capital.— * * *]

(F)   Reduction on Account of Distributions Out of Pre-1941 Accumulated Earnings and Profits.—*The new capital for any day of the taxable year, computed without the application of subparagraph (E), shall be reduced by the amount which, after the beginning of the first taxable year which begins after December 31, 1940, has been distributed out of earnings and profits accumulated prior to the beginning of such first taxable year.*

Committee Reports

Report—Conference Committee (77th Cong., 1st Sess., H. Rept. 1203).— Amendment No. 53: This amendment has the effect of preventing a distribution of taxable stock dividends out of pre-1941 accumulated earnings and profits from constituting new capital solely because of subsequent operating losses or because of subsequently accumulated but undistributed earnings and profits, and also has the effect of preventing money or property paid in from constituting new capital if such money or property merely takes the place of pre-1941 accumulated earnings and profits previously distributed after the beginning of the first taxable year which begins after December 31, 1940.   The House recedes.   (p. 12)

Congressional Discussion

Discussion—Senate (Cong. Rec. Vol. 87).—MR. GEORGE. * * * This amendment is designed first to prevent the distribution of taxable stock dividends out of pre-1941 accumulated earnings and profits from constituting new capital solely because of subsequent operating losses or because of subsequently accumulated but undistributed earnings and profits, and, second, to prevent money or property paid in from constituting new capital if such money or property merely takes the place of pre-1941 accumulated earnings and profits previously distributed after the beginning of the first taxable year which begins after December 31, 1940.

It will be remembered that a liberalizing provision has been made in the bill allowing a credit to those corporations operating on the invested capital basis of $1.25 for each dollar of new capital invested. This is an amendment which is made necessary in order to safeguard and protect the Treasury. (p. 7363)

1941
203
[718(a)
(6)]
in gen'l

[Set forth on page 92]

> ## Sec. 718(b)(1)

1940
201

[SEC. 718. EQUITY INVESTED CAPITAL.]

(b) Reduction in Equity Invested Capital.—The amount by which the equity invested capital for any day shall be reduced as provided in subsection (a) shall be the sum of the following amounts—

(1) Distributions in previous years.—Distributions made prior to such taxable year which were not out of accumulated earnings and profits; and

Committee Reports

Report—Ways and Means Subcommittee (76th Cong., 3d Sess., H. Rept. Aug. 8, 1940).—(4) Earnings and profits at the beginning of the taxable year, * * * less the sum of the following amounts:

(1) Distributions in prior taxable years which were not out of accumulated earnings and profits; * * *

(3) Distributions previously made during the taxable year which were not out of earnings and profits of the taxable year. (p. 11-12)

Report—Ways and Means Committee (76th Cong., 3d Sess., H. Rept. 2894).—

(a) *Equity invested capital.*—Equity invested capital is the sum of the following items: * * * reduced by the sum of the following items:

(1) Distributions out of capital during prior taxable years; (p. 10)

Committee Hearings
1941 Act

Hearings—Senate Finance Committee.—Eliminating the word "accumulated." (H. B. Fernald, p. 884-885)

Sec. 718(b)(2)

[SEC. 718. EQUITY INVESTED CAPITAL.]

[(b) Reduction in Equity Invested Capital.—The amount by which the equity invested capital for any day shall be reduced * * * shall be the sum of the following amounts—]

(2) Distributions During the Year.—Distributions previously made during such taxable year which are not out of the earnings and profits of such taxable year;

1940
201

Committee Reports

Report—Ways and Means Subcommittee (76th Cong., 3d Sess., H. Rept. Aug. 8, 1940).—(4) Earnings and profits at the beginning of the taxable year, * * *

(3) Distributions previously made during the taxable year which were not out of earnings and profits of the taxable year. (p. 11-12)
Report—Ways and Means Committee

(76th Cong., 3d Sess., H. Rept. 2894).—(a) *Equity invested capital.*—Equity invested capital is the sum of the following items: * * * reduced by the sum of the following items: * * *
(2) Distributions previously made during the taxable year out of capital or out of the accumulated earnings and profits as of the beginning of the taxable year. (p. 10)

Committee Hearings

Hearings—Ways and Means Committee.—Inequities where distribution out of unrealized appreciation. (E. C Alvord, p. 311)

Sec. 718(b)(3)

[SEC. 718. EQUITY INVESTED CAPITAL.]

[(b) Reduction in Equity Invested Capital.—The amount by which the equity invested capital for any day shall be reduced * * * shall be the sum of the following amounts—]

1940
201

(3) Earnings and Profits of ¹Another Corporation.—For the purposes of subsection (a) (4) the accumulated earnings and profits of the corporation shall be determined without the inclusion of any of the earnings and profits of a transferor corporation which would otherwise be included by reason of property of such transferor having been paid in for shares of, or as a contribution to the capital of, or as paid-in surplus of, the transferee corporation. *The earnings and profits of [a transferor] ANOTHER corporation which previously at any time were included in accumulated earnings and profits by reason of [property of such transferor having been paid in for shares of, or as a* *contribution to the capital of, or as paid-in surplus of, the transferee corporation.]* a transaction described in section 112 (b) to (e), both inclusive, or in the corresponding provision of a prior revenue law, or by reason of the transfer by such other corporation to the taxpayer of property the basis of which in the hands of the taxpayer is or was determined with reference to its basis in the hands of such other corporation, or would have been so determined if the property had been other than money; and

[1] The word "Another" was substituted by the Conference Committee for the word "Transferor".

Committee Reports

Report—Ways and Means Committee (76th Cong., 3d Sess., H. Rept. 2894).— Under various provisions of the Internal Revenue Code dealing with exchanges and liquidations, the transfer of the property by a corporation to another corporation results in the nonrecognition, in whole or in part, of the gain or loss realized by the transferor upon such transfer. In such cases well established principles of income tax law require that the earnings and profits of the transferor shall go over to the transferee and shall be considered to be earnings and profits of the transferee for tax purposes. Subsection (c) (4) of section 718 provides that such transferred earnings and profits shall not be taken into account in computing the earnings and profits as of the beginning of the taxable year for the purpose of determining the equity invested capital. Inasmuch as the prop-

erty received by the transferee upon such a transfer is included in such cases in the equity invested capital at its adjusted basis in the hands of the transferor, it is necessary to exclude the earnings and profits acquired by the transferee by reason of such transfer in order to avoid duplication. (p. 25)

Report—Senate Finance Committee (76th Cong., 3d Sess., S. Rept. 2114).— Your committee has made no change in the determination of equity invested capital except to clarify the provisions which were designed to avoid any overstatement of invested capital as the result of duplicating amounts in the items of earnings and profits and property paid in. Such a duplication might otherwise arise in the computation of invested capital in cases of reorganization and other tax-free exchanges. (p. 6)

Committee Hearings

Hearings—Ways and Means Committee.—Advantages of current invested capital provisions over those in 1918. (J. L. Sullivan—Treas. Dept.—p. 94-95)

1941 Act

Hearings—Ways and Means Committee.—Excluding instead of deducting earnings of predecessors from invested capital. (H. B. Fernald, p. 1568, 1571)

Hearings—Senate Finance Committee.—Limiting provision to cases where

predecessor's property is sold. (E. C. Alvord, p. 682-683; A. B. Chapman, p. 761-762)

Excluding instead of deducting earnings of predecessors from invested capital. (H. B. Fernald, p. 884)

Sec. 718(b)(4)

[Set forth with sec. 718(a)(5), page 91]

Sec. 718(c)(2)

[SEC. 718. EQUITY INVESTED CAPITAL.]

1940
201

[(c) Rules for Application of Subsections (a) and (b).—For the purposes of subsections (a) and (b)—]

(2) Distributions in First Sixty Days of Taxable Year.—In the application of such ~~subsection~~ *subsections* to any taxable year beginning after December 31, 1940, so much of the distributions (taken in the order of time) made during the first sixty days thereof as does not exceed the accumulated earnings and profits as of the beginning thereof (computed without regard to this paragraph) shall be considered to have been made on the last day of the preceding taxable year.

Committee Reports

Report—Ways and Means Subcommittee (76th Cong., 3d Sess., H. Rept. Aug. 8, 1940).—(4) Earnings and profits at the beginning of the taxable year, and in computing such earnings and profits, distributions made during the first 60 days of the taxable year are considered, to the extent they do not exceed the accumulated earnings and profits as of the beginning of the taxable year, to have been made on the last day of the preceding taxable year, * * * (p. 11-12)

Report—Ways and Means Committee (76th Cong., 3d Sess., H. Rept. 2894).—In computing such earnings and profits for taxable years beginning after December 31, 1940, distributions made during the first 60 days of the taxable year are deemed, to the extent they do not exceed the accumulated earnings and profits as of the beginning of the taxable year, to have been made on the last day of the preceding taxable year. (p. 25)

(2) *Distributions during the year.*—Distributions previously made during the taxable year which are not out of the earnings and profits of such taxable year. Distributions made during the first 60 days of the taxable year, to the extent they do not exceed the accumulated earnings and profits as of the beginning of the taxable year, are deemed to have been made on the last day of the preceding taxable year.

* * *

For the purpose of the conclusive presumption respecting dividends out of earnings and profits paid during the first 60 days of the taxable year, such distributions shall be considered in the order of time and the accumulated earnings and profits as of the beginning of the taxable year shall be computed without regard to the presumption. The presumption applies only with respect to taxable years beginning after December 31, 1940. (p. 25-26)

Committee Hearings

Hearings—Ways and Means Committee.—Eliminating sixty day rule. (H. B. Fernald, p. 283; E. C. Alvord, p. 311; W. H. Cooper, p. 318; A. B. Chapman, p. 380, 382; R. H. Miner, p. 422)

Hearings—Senate Finance Committee.—Eliminating sixty day rule. (W. A. Cooper, p. 56; E. C. Alvord, p. 273; H. B. Fernald, p. 285-286; J. W. Hooper, p. 353; A. B. Chapman, p. 388, 395; E. P. Thomas, p. 492)

104.   SECTION   718(c)(2)   [See inside back cover

1942 Act

Hearings—Ways and Means Committee.—Eliminating sixty day rule. (J.   W. Hooper, p. 498; E. C. Alvord, p. 2777)

1941 Act

Hearings—Senate Finance Committee.—Eliminating sixty day rule. (E.   C. Alvord, p. 682; H. B. Fernald, p. 884)

Sec. 718(c)(3)

1941
202(f)

Section 718 (c) (3) (relating to the computation of earnings and profits for invested capital purposes) is amended by adding after the word "subchapter" the words "or Chapter 1".

Committee Reports

Report—Ways and Means Committee (77th Cong., 1st Sess., H. Rept. 1040).— It is also provided under section 718 (c) (3) with reference to taxpayers on the invested-capital basis, that in determining whether distributions were out of earnings and profits of any excess-profits- tax taxable year, the income tax shall be disregarded in the computation.   (p. 47)

Report—Senate Finance Committee (77th Cong., 1st Sess., S. Rept. 673).— Same as Ways and Means Committee Report. (p. 38)

1940
201

[SEC. 718. EQUITY INVESTED CAPITAL.]

[(c)   **Rules for Application of Subsections (a) and (b).**—For the purposes of subsections (a) and (b)—]

(3) · **Computation of Earnings and Profits of Taxable Year.**—For the purposes of subsections (a) (3) (B) and (b) <(3)> (2) in determining whether a distribution is out of the earnings and profits of any taxable year, such earnings and profits shall be computed as of the close of such taxable year without diminution by reason of any distribution made during such taxable year or by reason of the tax under this subchapter for such year and the determination shall be made without regard to the amount of earnings and profits at the time the distribution was made.

Committee Reports

Report—Ways and Means Committee (76th Cong., 3d Sess., H. Rept. 2894).— In determining whether a taxable stock dividend is out of the earnings and profits of the taxable year, such earnings and profits are computed as of the close of such taxable year without diminution by reason of any distribution made during such taxable year or by reason of the excess-profits tax for such year, and the determination is to be made without regard to the amount of earnings and profits at the time the distribution was made. This rule avoids the necessity of adjusting the earnings and profits of the taxable year by reason of the excess-profits tax imposed with respect to such earnings or by reason of any distribution made during such taxable year for the purpose of determining the amount of earnings and profits available as of the date of distribution.   (p. 24-25)

Moreover, in determining whether a distribution is out of the earnings and profits of any taxable year, such earnings and profits are computed as of the close of such taxable year without diminution by reason of any distribution

made during such taxable year or by reason of the excess-profits tax for such year, and the determination is to be made without regard to the amount of the earnings and profits at the time the distribution was made.   The purpose of this latter rule is the same as indicated in the paragraph dealing with taxable stock dividends.   (p. 25)

Congressional Discussion

Discussion—House (Cong. Rec. Vol. 86).—Mr. Cooper. Mr. Chairman, I ask unanimous consent that, on page 29, line 1, "(3)", where it appears the second time in such line, be stricken out and

that there be inserted in lieu thereof "(2)."

This simply corrects a typographical error.   (p. 11265)

Committee Hearings
1942 Act

Hearings—Senate Finance Committee.—Eliminating sixty day rule. (J.

W. Hooper, p. 1175)

Sec. 718(c)(4)

[SEC. 718.   EQUITY INVESTED CAPITAL.]

1940
201

[(c)   **Rules for Application of Subsections (a) and (b).**—For the purposes of subsection (a) and (b)—]

(4)   **Stock in Case of Merger or Consolidation.**—If a corporation owns stock in another corporation, and—

(A)   such corporations are merged or consolidated in a statutory merger or consolidation, or

(B)   such corporations are parties to a transaction which results in the elimination of such stock in a manner similar to that resulting from a statutory merger or consolidation, then such stock shall not be considered as property paid in for stock of, or as paid-in surplus of, or as a contribution to capital of, the corporation resulting from the transaction referred to in subparagraph (A) or (B).

This subsection was added by the Conference Committee.

Committee Reports

Report—Conference Committee (76th Cong., 3d Sess., H. Rept. 3002).—A proper application of the provisions of section 718 prevents, it is believed, improper duplications in the case of the merger or consolidation of two or more

corporations, one of which owns stock in the other; for the sake of clarity, however, subsection (c) (4) has been inserted dealing with the merger or consolidation of two or more corporations, one of which owns stock in the other.   In case the corporation whose stock is owned by the other, is merged into the other, no corresponding provision is necessary, since the property transferred in the merger represented by such stock is not within any provision of section 718 (a). (p. 49)

1918
330   [Set forth on page 344]

1918
331   [Set forth on page 347]

1917
204   [Set forth on page 352]

1917
208   [Set forth on page 367]

Sec. 718(c)(5)

1942
219(c)

[SEC. 718. EQUITY INVESTED CAPITAL.]

[(c) **Rules for Application of Subsections (a) and (b).**—For the purposes of subsections (a) and (b)—]

(5) **Deficit in Earnings and Profits—Earnings and Profits of Transferor and Transferee.**—*If a corporation (hereinafter called "transferor") transfers substantially all its property to another corporation formed to acquire such property (hereinafter called "transferee"), if—*

(A) the sole consideration for the transfer of such property is the transfer to the transferor or its shareholders of all the stock of all classes (except qualifying shares) of the transferee. (In determining whether the transfer is solely for stock, the assumption by the transferee of a liability of the transferor or the fact that the property acquired is subject to a liability shall be disregarded);

(B) the basis of the property, in the hands of the transferee, for the purposes of this subsection, is determined by reference to the basis of the property in the hands of the transferor;

(C) the transferor is forthwith completely liquidated in pursuance of the plan under which the acquisition of the property is made; and

(D) immediately after the liquidation the shareholders of the transferor own all such stock; for the purposes of this subchapter, in computing the equity invested capital for any day after the date of the acquisition of the property, the earnings and profits or deficit in earnings and profits of the transferee and the transferor shall be computed as if, immediately before the beginning of the taxable year in which such transfer occurs, the transferee had been in existence and sustained a recognized loss, and the transferor had realized a recognized gain, equal to the portion of the deficit in earnings and profits of the transferor attributable to such property.

Committee Reports

Report—Senate Finance Committee (77th Cong., 2d Sess., S. Rept. 1631).— This section is new, no corresponding section having appeared in the House bill. Under existing law an operating loss of a corporation can reduce its invested capital through its accumulated earnings and profits but cannot reduce invested capital, if there are no earnings and profits, by being deducted from the money or property paid in to such corporation. Thus, although earnings and profits increase invested capital, deficits in earnings and profits do not decrease invested capital. Under section 751 of existing law, and under section 760 which has been inserted by this bill to amend section 751, for years beginning after December 31, 1941 (relating to invested capital in case of certain tax-free exchanges), invested capital of a "transferee," as defined in such sections, is computed by taking into account the adjusted basis for determining loss in the hands of the transferee of property received from the transferor. Any loss sustained by the transferor will be reflected in the invested capital of the transferee either in a reduced basis of assets received from the transferor or in a reduced amount of property which will be deemed to have been paid in for stock in case the transferor used borrowed funds to pay its losses, since such sections provide for a reduction in the amount of property deemed to be paid in for stock by the amount of indebtedness of the transferor. Thus, the so-called deficit rule is not applicable in the case of such tax-free exchanges and reorganizations.

Your committee has amended section 718 to provide that in certain cases the invested capital of a transferee, which otherwise would reflect a deficit of the transferor, will be increased by the amount of such deficit and that the invested capital of the transferor will be correspondingly reduced. The rule increasing the invested capital of a corporation by the deficit of its transferor will apply only if a corporation, called the transferor, transfers substantially all its property to another corporation called the transferee, which is formed especially to acquire such property, if (a) the sole consideration for the transfer of such property is the transfer to the

transferor or its shareholders of all the stock of all classes (except qualifying shares) of the transferee; the assumption by the transferee of a liability of the transferor for the acquisition of property subject to such a liability shall be disregarded in determining whether the transfer is solely for stock; (b) the basis of the property in the hands of the transferee, for the purposes of this provision, is determined by reference to the basis of such property in the hands of the transferor; (c) the transferor is forthwith completely liquidated in pursuance of the plan under which the acquisition of the property is made; and (d) immediately after the liquidation, the stockholders of the transferor own all the stock of the transferee. If these factors are present, the invested capital of the transferee otherwise computed shall be increased, and the invested capital of the transferor shall be decreased by the deficit in earnings and profits of the transferor which is attributable to the property so transferred. It is necessary to insure, however, that the transferee shall be deemed to have a deficit in earnings and profits so that subsequent earnings shall first be reduced by the amount of such deficit before any earnings and profits can be determined to have been accumulated and to increase invested capital, and to insure that the deficit of the transferor (which has been transferred to the transferee) shall not continue at the old amount, but should be reduced by the amount so transferred. Your committee has therefore provided that in computing the equity invested capital for any day after the date of acquisition of the property, the earnings and profits or deficit in earnings and profits of the transferee and the transferor shall be computed as if, immediately before beginning of the taxable year in which such transfer occurs, the transferee had been in existence and sustained a recognized loss, and the transferor had realized a recognized gain, equal to that portion of the deficit in earnings and profits of the transferor which is attributable to the property so transferred. (p. 193-194)

Report—Conference Committee (77th Cong., 2d Sess., H. Rept. 2586).— Amendment No. 301: This amendment incorporates a new section to amend section 718 of the Code by providing that, under certain very limited circumstances, the equity invested capital of a "transferee" corporation which receives property from another corporation pursuant to a tax-free exchange or reorganization shall be increased, and the invested capital of the transferor shall be decreased, by the deficit in earnings and profits of the transferor which is attributable to the property so transferred. Subsequent earnings of the transferee shall first be applied to reduce the amount of such deficit before any earnings and profits can be determined to have been accumulated and to increase invested capital. * * * The House recedes. (p. 61)

Committee Hearings

Hearings—Ways and Means Committee.—Including deficits of transferor corporation in invested capital. (H. Satterlee, p. 2253-54, 2255-56)

Hearings—Senate Finance Committee.—Including deficits of transferor corporation in invested capital. (H. Satterlee, p. 388-392, 394-397)

Confining transferee adjustments only to those that eliminate duplication of invested capital. (E. C. Alvord, p. 1797)

1943 Act

Hearings—Ways and Means Committee.—Extending provision to reorganizations generally. (E. C. Alvord, p. 685; Controllers Institute of America, p. 1332)

Hearings—Senate Finance Committee.—Extending provision to reorganizations generally. (E. C. Alvord, p. 615; A. B. Chapman, p. 831)

1918 330	[Set forth on page 344]
1918 331	[Set forth on page 347]
1917 204	[Set forth on page 352]
1917 208	[Set forth on page 367]

Sec. 718(f)

1942
205(d)

[SEC. 718. EQUITY INVESTED CAPITAL.]

(f) The reserves of an insurance company shall not be included in computing equity invested capital under this section but shall be treated as borrowed capital as provided in section 719.

Committee Reports

Report—Ways and Means Committee (77th Cong., 2d Sess., H. Rept. 2333).—

Subsection (c)[1] amends section 718 of the code to provide that the reserves of an insurance company shall not be included in computing equity invested capital under such section but shall be treated as borrowed capital as provided in section 719 of the code.   (p. 139)

[1] Subsection (d) of the Act.

Report—Senate Finance Committee (77th Cong., 2d Sess., S. Rept. 1631).— The treatment of life insurance reserves for the purpose of computing invested capital has been objected to by insurers on the ground that, even though it should result in no excess profits tax liability, it would prejudice their position that policies in the hands of the insured are not appropriate subjects of taxation under State or local property tax laws. While agreeing with the policy of the House bill in treating such reserves in the same manner as borrowed capital for

excess profits tax purposes, your committee desires its action to be interpreted as implying no such prejudice.   (p. 32)

Subsections (d) and (e) except for technical changes are the same as subsections (c) and (d) of the House bill. Subsection (d) amends section 718 of the Code to provide that the reserves of an insurance company shall not be included in computing equity invested capital under such section but shall be treated as borrowed capital as provided in section 719 of the Code.   (p. 184)

The treatment of insurance reserves as borrowed capital in section 205 is for the purpose of determining invested capital and does not mean that your committee regards these funds as in fact borrowed from the policyholders or believes that the policy contracts are in fact evidences of indebtedness.   (p. 185)

Committee Hearings
1941 Act

Hearings—Senate Finance Committee.— Including insurance reserves as invested capital or borrowed capital.   (J. Farley, p. 1307-23)

Sec. 719(a)(1)

Section 719 (a) (1) is amended by striking out ", and not including indebtedness described in section 751 (b) relating to certain exchanges."

1942
230(b)
(2)

Committee Reports

Report—Ways and Means Committee (77th Cong., 2d Sess., H. Rept. 2333).— Section 719 (a) (1) is amended so as to include in borrowed capital the liabilities arising upon an exchange to which section 760 is applicable, and which under existing law are excluded from borrowed capital. Existing rules are ap-

plicable with respect to the interest deduction and computation of borrowed invested capital with respect to such liabilities.   (p. 157)

Report—Senate Finance Committee (77th Cong., 2d Sess., S. Rept. 1631).— Same as Ways and Means Committee Report. (p. 223)

SEC. 719. BORROWED INVESTED CAPITAL.

1940
201

(a) **Borrowed Capital.**—The borrowed capital for any day of any taxable year shall be determined as of the beginning of such day and shall be the SUM OF THE FOLLOWING:

(1) The amount of the outstanding indebtedness (not including interest, and not including indebtedness described in section 751 (b) relating to certain exchanges) of the taxpayer which is evidenced by a

bond, note, bill of exchange, debenture, certificate of indebtedness, mortgage, or deed of trust.

Committee Reports

Report—Ways and Means Subcommittee (76th Cong., 3d Sess., H. Rept. Aug. 8, 1940).—Borrowed invested capital for any day of the taxable year is to be based on the borrowed capital at the beginning of such day, consisting of indebtedness of the taxpayer evidenced by a bond, note, bill of exchange, debenture, certificate of indebtedness, mortgage, or deed of trust, * * * (p. 12)

Report—Ways and Means Committee (76th Cong., 3d Sess., H. Rept. 2894).—

(b) *Borrowed invested Capital.*—Borrowed invested capital for any day of the taxable year is to be based on the borrowed capital at the beginning of such day. Borrowed capital consists of the outstanding indebtedness of the taxpayer (exclusive of interest) which is evidenced by bond, note, debenture, bill of exchange, certificate of indebtedness, mortgage, or deed of trust, or any other written evidence of indebtedness. (p. 26)

1918

325(a)

[Set forth on page 330]

Sec. 719(a)(2)

1940

201

[SEC. 719. BORROWED INVESTED CAPITAL.]

[(a) **Borrowed Capital.**—The borrowed capital for any day * * * shall be the sum of the following:]

(2) *In the case of a taxpayer having a contract (made before the expiration of 30 days after the date of the enactment of the Second Revenue Act of 1940) with a foreign government to furnish articles, materials, or supplies to such foreign government, if such contract provides for advance payment and for repayment by the vender of any part of such advance payment upon cancellation of the contract by such foreign government, the amount which would be required to be so repaid if cancellation occurred at the beginning of such day,* BUT NO AMOUNT SHALL BE CONSIDERED AS BORROWED CAPITAL UNDER THIS PARAGRAPH WHICH HAS BEEN INCLUDIBLE IN GROSS INCOME.

Committee Reports

Report—Conference Committee (76th Cong., 3d Sess., H. Rept. 3002).—*Senate amendment.*— * * * Borrowed capital is defined to mean, in addition to the types of indebtedness described in the House bill, certain amounts received as advance payment in connection with a contract with a foreign government to furnish articles, materials, or supplies, to the extent such amounts would be repayable, pursuant to the terms of the contract, if cancelation by such foreign government occurred at the beginning of the day for which the borrowed capital is being ascertained. Such contract must have been made before the expiration of 30 days after the date of enactment of the bill.

Conference agreement.—The Senate provision has been adopted except that the clause relative to amounts repayable to a foreign government has been redrafted so as to make certain that the amounts included as borrowed capital thereunder do not include amounts treated as income and therefore reflected in equity invested capital through the accumulated earnings and profits account. (p. 49-50)

Congressional Discussion

Discussion—House (Cong. Rec. Vol. 86).—MR. MILLER. Assuming a corporation received $1,000,000 from a foreign government for plant expansion, I take it they would not be entitled to amortization. My question is: Would that be considered the same as borrowed capital, or where would it come into the tax structure?

MR. COOPER. That would not come under the amortization provision. The question there is one of whether the amount paid by the foreign government was an addition to income or an addition to capital. That depends upon the nature of the transaction.

MR. MILLER. Would it be considered borrowed capital? I am trying to figure where that would come into the tax structure. There are cases like that.

MR. COOPER. I would have to have more details to be able intelligently to answer the gentleman, but certainly it would not come under the amortization provision.

MR. MILLER. I had in mind cases where foreign countries have fully paid for plant expansions.

MR. COOPER. They are not included under the amortization provision. (p. 11249)

Committee Hearings

Hearings—Ways and Means Committee.—Eliminating tax advantage of borrowing money. (P. D. Seghers, p. 160)

Treating government furnished plant as borrowed invested capital. (P. W. Adams, p. 258-260)

Including deposit liabilities as borrowed invested capital. (C. H. Mylander, p. 359-362)

Hearings—Senate Finance Committee.—Treating government furnished plant as borrowed invested capital. (J. L. Connolly, p. 105)

1942 Act

Hearings—Ways and Means Committee.—Including all government contract advances without limitation. (E. C. Alvord, p. 2770-71)

Hearings—Senate Finance Committee.—Including obligations under conditional purchase agreements as borrowed invested capital. (F. G. Dorety, p. 881-883)

1941 Act

Hearings—Ways and Means Committee.—Including open accounts payable as borrowed invested capital. (H. C. Greer, p. 1458-59; H. B. Fernald, p. 1568, 1571, 1573)

Including all government contract advances without limitation. (Controllers Institute of America, p. 1717)

Hearings—Senate Finance Committee.—Including all government contract advances without limitation. (E. C. Alvord, p. 676-677; A. B. Chapman, p. 768)

[Set forth on page 330]

┌─────────────────────┐
│ Sec. 719(a)(3)   │
│ Sec. 719(a)(4)   │
└─────────────────────┘

[SEC. 719. BORROWED INVESTED CAPITAL.]

[(a) **Borrowed Capital.**—The borrowed capital for any day * * * shall be the sum of the following:]

(3) In the case of an insurance company, the mean of the amount of the pro rata unearned premiums determined at the beginning and end of the taxable year, plus,

(4) In the case of a life insurance company, the mean of the amount of the (269)life insurance *adjusted* reserves, and the mean of the amount of the reserves on insurance (270)*or annuity* contracts (or contracts arising out of insurance (271)*or annuity* contracts) which do not involve, at the time with reference to which the computation was made, life, health, or accident contingencies, determined at the beginning and end of the taxable year.

Committee Reports

Report—Ways and Means Committee (77th Cong., 2d Sess., H. Rept. 2333).—The treatment of life insurance reserves for the purpose of computing invested capital has been objected to by insurers on the ground that, even though it should result in no excess profits tax liability, it would prejudice their position that policies in the hands of the insured are not appropriate subjects of taxation under State or local property tax laws. While agreeing with the policy of the House bill in treating such reserves in the same manner as borrowed capital for excess profits tax purposes, your committee desires its action to be interpreted as implying no such prejudice. (p. 32)

The latter section[1] is amended to provide that in the case of an insurance company borrowed capital shall include the mean of the amount of the pro rata unearned premiums determined at the beginning and end of the taxable year, and that in the case of a life insurance company borrowed capital shall include the mean of the amount of the life insurance reserves, and the mean of the amount of the reserves on insurance contracts (or contracts arising out of insurance contracts) which do not involve, at the time with reference to which the computation was made, life, health, or accident contingencies, determined at the beginning and end of the taxable year. (p. 139)

[1] Relating to sec. 719.

Report—Senate Finance Committee (77th Cong., 2d Sess., S. Rept. 1631).—Subsections (d) and (e) except for technical changes are the same as subsections (c) and (d) of the House bill. * * * The latter section is amended to provide that in the case of an insurance company borrowed capital shall include the mean of the amount of the pro rata unearned premiums determined at the beginning and end of the taxable year, and that in the case of a life insurance company borrowed capital shall include the mean of the amount of the adjusted reserves, and the mean of the amount of the reserves on insurance or annuity contracts (or contracts arising out of insurance or annuity contracts) which do not involve, at the time with reference to which the computation was made, life, health, or accident contingencies, determined at the beginning and end of the taxable year. The treatment of insurance reserves as borrowed capital in section 205 is for the purpose of determining invested capital and does not mean that your committee regards these funds as in fact borrowed from the policyholders or believes that the policy contracts are in fact evidences of indebtedness. (p. 184-185)

Report—Conference Committee (77th

Cong., 2d Sess., H. Rept. 2586).— Amendments Nos. 269, 270, and 271: These amendments correct technical imperfections in the House bill. The House recedes. (p. 58)

Committee Hearings

Hearings—Senate Finance Committee.—Explanation of provision. (J.

O'Brien—H. Legis. Counsel—p. 103)

1941 Act

Hearings—Senate Finance Committee.—Including insurance reserves as in-

vested capital or borrowed capital. (J. Farley, p. 1307-23)

Sec. 720(a)
Sec. 720(d)

[SEC. 720. ADMISSIBLE AND INADMISSIBLE ASSETS.]

1942
220
[720(d)]

(d) *Treatment of Government Obligations as Admissible Assets.*— *If the excess profits credit for any taxable year is computed under section 714, the taxpayer may in its return for such year elect to increase its normal-tax net income for such taxable year by an amount equal to the amount of the interest on, reduced by the amount of the amortizable bond premium under section 125 attributable to, all obligations held during the taxable year which are described in section 22 (b) (4) any part of the interest from which is excludible from gross income or allowable as a credit against net income.*

Committee Reports

Report—Senate Finance Committee (77th Cong., 2d Sess., S. Rept. 1631).— This section, which did not appear in the bill as passed by the House, makes a technical amendment to section 720 (d), relating to the treatment of Government obligations as admissible assets. It is designed to give effect to the rules under new section 125 of the Code, as added by section 126 of the bill, for deduction of amortizable bond premium in cases in which interest on bonds is included in income.   Under the amendment to section 720 (d), the amount of interest on Government obligations, described in section 22 (b) (4), by which the taxpayer elects to increase its normal tax net income for excess profits tax purposes is to

be reduced by the amount of the amortizable bond premium under section 125 attributable to such obligations. (p. 194)

Report—Conference Committee (77th Cong., 2d Sess., H. Rept. 2586).— Amendment No. 302: This is a technical amendment which amends section 720 (d) of the Code to provide that the amount of interest on Government obligations, described in section 22 (b) (4), by which the taxpayer elects to increase its normal tax net income for excess profits purposes is to be reduced by the amount of the amortizable bond premium attributable to such obligations. The House recedes. (p. 61)

SEC. 720. ADMISSIBLE AND INADMISSIBLE ASSETS.

EPTA
12(a)
[720(a)
(1)]

   (a) **Definitions.**—For the purposes of this subchapter—

     (1) The term "inadmissible assets" means—

      (A) Stock in corporations except stock in a foreign personal-holding company, and except stock which is not a capital asset; and

Committee Reports

Report—Ways and Means Committee (77th Cong., 1st Sess., H. Rept. 146).— For corporations using the invested capital credit dividends, except dividends (actual or constructive) on the stock of foreign personal holding companies, are excluded from the excess profits net income. Likewise, stock in corporations, except stock in a foreign personal holding company, is made an inadmissible asset by section 720 (a) (1) of the present law. Corporate stocks held by dealers, not as investments for themselves but for sale to their customers, are, in reality, no different from any other article held for sale by a dealer. Section 12 of the bill amends section 720 (a) (1) of the present law so as to allow corporate stocks held by a dealer for sale to customers to be treated as admissible assets. However, dividends on stocks so treated are subjected to the excess-profits tax to the extent that they exceed the credit for dividends received provided in section 26 (b) of the Internal Revenue Code. Such stocks held by dealers for investment would continue to be treated as inadmissible assets. (p. 20)

Report—Senate Finance Committee (77th Cong., 1st Sess., S. Rept. 75).— Same as Ways and Means Committee Report. (p. 20-21)

Congressional Discussion

Discussion—Senate (Cong. Rec. Vol. 87).—MR. HARRISON. * * * Section 12: This section permits a dealer in securities to treat stocks which it holds for sale to customers as admissible assets in computing invested capital. As the gains from such sales are subject to the excess-profits tax, it is believed only proper not to require the taxpayer to reduce his invested capital through investments in such stocks. Any dividends received on such stocks while they are held by the dealer are subject to excess-profits tax in his hands. (p. 1638)

1940
201
[720(a)]
[720(d)]

SEC. 720. ADMISSIBLE AND INADMISSIBLE ASSETS.

   (a) **Definitions.**—~~Except~~ ~~as~~ ~~provided~~ ~~in~~ ~~section~~ ~~753~~ ~~(relating~~ ~~to certain exchanges),~~ ~~for~~ *For* the purposes of this subchapter—

     (1) The term "inadmissible assets" means—

      (A) Stock in corporations except stock in a foreign personal-holding company; and

      (B) ~~Obligations~~ *Except as provided in subsection (d), obligations* described in section 22 (b) (4) [(A), (B), or (C)] any part of the interest from which is excludible from gross income or allowable as a credit against net income.

     (2) The term "admissible assets" means all assets other than inadmissible assets.

   (d) [1]*Treatment of Government Obligations as Admissible Assets.*— [*If the excess profits credit for any taxable year is computed under section 714, the following obligations shall be considered, for the purposes of this section, as admissible assets and shall not be considered inadmissible assets:*

(1)   *All obligations of the United States or of corporations organized under Act of Congress held during the taxable year the interest on which is includible in computing excess profits net income for the taxable year under section 711 (a) (2) (H); and*

(2)   *All obligations (other than obligations described in paragraph (1)) of the character described in section 22 (b) (4), if the taxpayer elects in its return for such year to treat all such obligations as admissible assets.]* IF THE EXCESS PROFITS CREDIT FOR ANY TAXABLE YEAR IS COMPUTED UNDER SECTION 714, THE TAXPAYER MAY IN ITS RETURN FOR SUCH YEAR ELECT TO INCREASE ITS NORMAL-TAX NET INCOME FOR SUCH TAXABLE YEAR BY AN AMOUNT EQUAL TO THE AMOUNT OF THE INTEREST ON ALL OBLIGATIONS HELD DURING THE TAXABLE YEAR WHICH ARE DESCRIBED IN SECTION 22 (b) (4) ANY PART OF THE INTEREST FROM WHICH IS EXCLUDIBLE FROM GROSS INCOME OR ALLOWABLE AS A CREDIT AGAINST NET INCOME. IN SUCH CASE, FOR THE PURPOSES OF THIS SECTION, THE TERM "ADMISSIBLE ASSETS" INCLUDES SUCH OBLIGATIONS, AND THE TERM "INADMISSIBLE ASSETS" DOES NOT INCLUDE SUCH OBLIGATIONS.

[1] The heading is as worded by the Conference Committee. The Senate Finance Committee heading read "Certain Government Obligations Treated as Admissible Assets."

Committee Reports

Report—Ways and Means Subcommittee (76th Cong., 3d Sess., H. Rept. Aug. 8, 1940).—"Inadmissible assets" are (1) corporate stocks (except stock in a foreign personal holding company), and (2) State and local securities, obligations of corporate agencies, and obligations of the United States or its possessions. All other assets are "admissible assets." (p. 6)

Inadmissible assets are to consist of stock in other corporations (except foreign personal holding companies) and wholly or partly tax-free obligations. (p. 12)

Report—Ways and Means Committee (76th Cong., 3d Sess., H. Rept. 2894).—"Inadmissible assets" are (1) corporate stocks (except stock in a foreign personal holding company), and (2) State and local securities, obligations of corporate agencies of the United States, and obligations of the United States or its possessions. All other assets are "admissible assets". (p. 11)

Inadmissible assets are:

(1) Stock in a corporation except stock in a foreign personal holding company, and

(2) Obligation described in section 22 (b) (4) (A), (B), or (C) any part of the interest from which is excludible from gross income or allowable as a credit against net income. Such obligations include State and local securities, obligations of corporate agencies organized under an act of Congress, and obligations of the United States or its possessions.

Admissible assets are all assets other than inadmissible assets, except as provided in section 753. (p. 26)

Report—Senate Finance Committee (76th Cong., 3d Sess., S. Rept. 2114).—Under the House bill all State and local securities, obligations of corporate agencies of the United States, and obligations of the United States or its possessions were "inadmissible assets." The committee bill provides that such assets which, under their terms, are not exempt from excess-profits tax shall be classed as "admissible assets." With respect to such securities which are exempt from excess-profits tax, the taxpayer may, if he so elects, treat them as "admissible assets," in which case the interest thereon is included in gross income. (p. 6)

Except for technical changes, section 720 of the House bill has been changed in only one respect, as follows: If the excess-profits credit for any taxable year is computed on the invested-capital plan, the following obligations are to be considered as admissible and not as inadmissible assets for such taxable year:

(1) United States obligations and obligations of Federal instrumentalities the interest from which is not exempt from excess-profits taxation; and

(2) All other Federal, State, and local obligations, if the taxpayer so elects in its return for such year. A taxpayer may not make such an election relative to only a portion of such obligations. The election must be made relative to all such obligations, or none of such obligations may be treated as admissible assets.

Under section 711 (a) (2) (H) (i) the interest described in paragraph (1) above increases the normal tax net income for excess-profits tax purposes. Under section 711 (a) (2) (H) (ii), if the election described in paragraph (2) is made, then all the interest on all such obligations increases the normal-tax net income. (p. 14-15)

Report—Conference Committee (76th Cong., 3d Sess., H. Rept. 3002).—*House bill.*—Under the House bill, in addition to the taxable year. (p. 50)

to corporate stock, all Federal, State, and local obligations were treated as inadmissible assets for the taxable year, and the interest derived therefrom was not included in normal-tax net income, upon the basis of which the excess-profits net income was computed.

Senate amendment.—Under the Senate amendment all United States obligations and obligations of Federal instrumentalities, the interest from which is not exempt from excess-profits taxation, are treated as admissible assets and the interest derived therefrom is subject to tax. In addition, the taxpayer may elect to treat all other Federal, State, and local obligations as admissible assets for the taxable year. If such an election is made, the normal tax net income is increased by the amount of interest derived from such obligations. The taxpayer is required to make a single election relative to all such obligations and may not elect as to only a portion thereof.

Conference agreement.—Under the conference agreement the distinction between certain United States obligations and obligations of Federal instrumentalities, on the one hand, and of other Federal, State, and local obligations, on the other, is eliminated. The taxpayer's election, instead of being an election to treat the obligations in question as admissible assets, is an election to include the interest derived therefrom in normal tax net income. It is provided that, if such an election is made, the obligations from which such included interest is derived are treated as admissible assets for the taxable year. (p. 50)

Committee Hearings

Hearings—Ways and Means Committee.—Eliminating non-dividend paying stocks from inadmissibles. (A. B. Chapman, p. 380, 383)

Hearings—Senate Finance Committee.—Eliminating non-dividend paying

stocks from inadmissibles. (A. B. Trudgian, p. 79, 84-85; A. B. Chapman, p. 387, 393)

Exempting banks from inadmissible asset provision. (C. F. Kuehnle, p. 87, 89-90)

1941 Act

Hearings—Senate Finance Committee.—Allowing option to treat stock as

admissible and tax dividends. (R. V. Fletcher, p. 273-274)

Sec. 720(b)

[SEC. 720.　ADMISSIBLE AND INADMISSIBLE ASSETS.]

(b)　Ratio of Inadmissibles to Total Assets.—The amount by which the average invested capital for any taxable year shall be reduced as provided in section 715 shall be an amount which is the same percentage of such average invested capital as the percentage which the total of the inadmissible assets is of the total of admissible and inadmissible assets.　For such purposes, the amount attributable to each asset held at any time during such taxable year shall be determined by ascertaining the adjusted basis thereof (or, in the case of money, the amount thereof) for each day of such taxable year so held and adding such daily amounts.　The determination of such daily amounts shall be made under regulations prescribed by the Commissioner with the approval of the Secretary.　~~In the case of the taxable year for which the tax under this subchapter is being determined,~~ the The adjusted basis shall be the adjusted basis for determining loss upon sale or exchange as determined under section 113.　~~and in the case of a taxable year in the base period the adjusted basis shall be the adjusted basis for determining loss upon sale or exchange as determined under the income tax law applicable to such taxable year.~~

Committee Reports

Report—Ways and Means Subcommittee (76th Cong., 3d Sess., H. Rept. Aug. 8, 1940).—The average invested capital as computed above is reduced by a percentage which is the ratio of the inadmissible assets of the corporation for the year to the total of admissible and inadmissible assets for such year.　(p. 6)

The invested capital is so reduced for the reason that since the income from inadmissible assets is not taxable to the corporation, the assets from which such income arose should be excluded from invested capital.

Inadmissible assets are not deducted directly from the invested capital for the reason that the total of admissible and inadmissible assets is not ordinarily equal to the invested capital.　(p. 6)

It is recommended that the invested capital be reduced by an amount which is the same percentage of the invested capital as the inadmissible assets of the taxpayer are of its total assets, with an adjustment for short-term capital gains realized upon the sale or other disposition of such inadmissible assets.　(p. 12)

Report—Ways and Means Committee (76th Cong., 3d Sess., H. Rept. 2894).—The average invested capital as computed above is reduced by a percentage which is the ratio of the inadmissible assets of the corporation for the year to the total of admissible and inadmissible assets for such year.　(p. 11)

The invested capital is so reduced for the reason that since the income from inadmissible assets is not taxable to the corporation, the assets from which such income arose should be excluded from invested capital.

Inadmissible assets are not deducted directly from the invested capital for the reason that the total of admissible and inadmissible assets is not ordinarily equal to the invested capital.　(p. 11)

Sections 715 and 720 of the bill provide that the average invested capital of the taxable year shall be reduced by an amount which is the same percentage of invested capital as the inadmissible assets are of the total of admissible and inadmissible assets, with an adjustment for short-term capital gain realized upon the sale or other disposition of such inadmissible assets. The terms "admissible" and "inadmissible assets" are defined in section 720, and the computation to determine the percentage of reduction is made in accordance with the provisions of such section. (p. 26)

The invested capital is so reduced because the income from inadmissible assets is not includible in the excess profits net income of the corporation and, therefore, the assets from which such income arose should be excluded from invested capital. The inadmissible assets are not deducted directly from the invested capital for the reason that the total of admissible and inadmissible assets is not ordinarily equal to the invested capital.

For the purpose of determining the

ratio of inadmissibles to the total of admissibles and inadmissibles, section 720 (b) of the bill provides that the amount attributable to each asset shall be determined, under regulations prescribed by the Commissioner with the approval of the Secretary, by ascertaining the adjusted basis thereof for each day of the taxable year and adding such daily amounts. In the case of a taxable year for which the excess-profits tax is being determined, the adjusted basis shall be the adjusted basis for determining loss upon sale or exchange under section 113, and in the case of a taxable year in the base period the adjusted basis shall be the adjusted basis for determining loss upon sale or exchange as determined under the law applicable to such taxable year. (p. 26-27)

Committee Hearings

Hearings—Senate Finance Committee.—Explanation of provision. (C. F.

Stam—Jt. Com. on Int. Rev. Taxn.—p. 209)

1943 Act

Hearings—Ways and Means Committee.—Applying same basis adjustments to computation of inadmissibles as for earnings and profits. (E. C. Alvord, p. 685; Controllers Institute of America, p. 1332)

Hearings—Senate Finance Committee.—Applying same basis adjustments to computation of inadmissibles as for earnings and profits. (E. C. Alvord, p. 615; G. G. Crowder, p. 786; A. B. Chapman, p. 831; H. B. Fernald, p. 931-932)

1942 Act

Hearings—Ways and Means Committee.—Applying same basis adjustments to computation of inadmissibles as for earnings and profits. (E. C. Alvord, p. 2779)

Hearings—Senate Finance Committee.—Applying same basis adjustments to computation of inadmissible assets as for earnings and profits. (H. B. Fernald, p. 978)

1918
326(c)

[Set forth on page 336]

Sec. 720(c)

1940
201

[SEC. 720. ADMISSIBLE AND INADMISSIBLE ASSETS.]

(c) **Computation if Short-Term Capital Gain.**—If during the taxable year there has been a short-term capital gain with respect to an inadmissible asset, then so much of the amount attributable to such inadmissible asset under subsection (b) as bears the same ratio thereto as such gain bears to the sum of such gain plus the dividends and interest on such asset for such year, shall, for the purpose of determining the ratio of inadmissible assets to the total of admissible and inadmissible assets, be added to the total of admissible assets and subtracted from the total of inadmissible assets.

Committee Reports

Report—Ways and Means Committee (76th Cong., 3d Sess., H. Rept. 2894).— Section 720 (c) of the bill provides that if during the taxable year there has been a short-term capital gain with respect to an inadmissible asset, an adjustment shall be made for the purpose of determining the inadmissible ratio. Under this provision there is added to the total of admissible assets and subtracted from the total of inadmissible assets that proportion of the amount attributable to any inadmissible asset upon which a short-term capital gain was realized which such gain bears to the sum of such gain plus the dividends and interest on such asset for such year. For the purpose of this provision, short-term capital gain means a short-term capital gain as defined in section 117 of the Internal Revenue Code. The effect of this adjustment is to include as an admissible asset that proportion of the amount attributable to the inadmissible asset which the earnings on such asset included in taxable income bear to the total of the earnings on such asset during the taxable year. (p. 27)

Committee Hearings

Hearings—Senate Finance Committee.—Explanation of provision. (C. F. Stam—Jt. Com. on Int. Rev. Taxn.— p. 209-210)

$$\boxed{\text{Sec. 720(d)}}$$

[Set forth with sec. 720(a), page 113]

$$\boxed{\begin{array}{c}\text{Sec. 721(a)(1)}\\ \text{Sec. 721(a)(2)}\end{array}}$$

SEC. 721. ABNORMALITIES IN INCOME IN TAXABLE PERIOD.

EPTA
5

(a) **Definitions.**—For the purposes of this section—

(1) **Abnormal Income.**—The term "abnormal income" means income of any class includible in the gross income of the taxpayer for any taxable year under this subchapter if it is abnormal for the taxpayer to derive income of such class, or, if the taxpayer normally derives income of such class but the amount of such income of such class includible in the gross income of the taxable year is in excess of 125 per centum of the average amount of the gross income of the same

class for the four previous taxable years, or, if the taxpayer was not in existence for four previous taxable years, the taxable years during which the taxpayer was in existence.

(2) **Separate Classes of Income.**—Each of the following subparagraphs shall be held to describe a separate class of income: * * *

Committee Reports

Report—Ways and Means Committee (77th Cong., 1st Sess., H. Rept. 146).— The bill affords relief in the following situations:

* * *

4. Existing law provides for adjustments with respect to six specific classes of abnormal income received during the taxable years subject to the excess-profits tax. These specific items were allowed to be spread over the years to which they are actually attributable. Your committee feel that the relief afforded by this provision should not be limited to these specific items but should be available also with respect to any item of abnormal income as such income is defined in the bill. (p. 2, 3)

Section 721 of the present law provides relief with respect to certain abnormalities in income in the taxable period. These abnormalities, six in number, are specifically described. If abnormal income falling within any one of these six described classes is received by the taxpayer it is provided that such income should be allocated to the taxable years to which it is attributable and the tax for the current year may not exceed the tax for that year without the inclusion of the portions of the item attributable to prior years plus the increases in tax that would have resulted in such prior years from the addition to gross income of the portions of the item attributable to those years. It is believed advisable to extend the principle of this section to any abnormal item of income. As the types of ab-

normal income that may occur cannot be predicted in advance, adequate relief can only be granted by thus extending the scope of this section.

The test of whether an item is abnormal is clarified to provide expressly that if the item includible in the gross income of the taxable year is in excess of 125 percent of the average amount of the gross income of the same class for the 4 previous years it shall be considered abnormal. If the taxpayer was not in existence for the 4 previous taxable years, the test period is the period during which it was in existence. An item will also be considered abnormal if it is of a class which the taxpayer normally does not receive. The mere fact that an item includible in the gross income of the taxpayer is abnormal, or is in excess of 125 percent of the average amount of the gross income of the same class for the test period, does not result in the exclusion of such item from excess-profits net income. It is necessary that the item be found attributable to other taxable years. Consequently, if an increase in business renders an item of income in excess of 125 percent of the income for the test period, the increase in business will not result in such increased income being excluded from excess-profits net income. (p. 9-10)

Report—Senate Finance Committee (77th Cong., 1st Sess., S. Rept. 75).— Same as Ways and Means Committee Report. (p. 3, 10, respectively)

Congressional Discussion

Discussion—House (Cong. Rec. Vol. 87).—Mr. Cooper. * * * Section 721 of the present law includes specific relief provisions for corporations, and under this bill they are left as they are in existing law and a general relief provision is included as to abnormalities in income in the taxable period. (p. 1380)

Discussion—Senate (Cong. Rec. Vol. 87).—Mr. Adams. * * * The Senator will recall that certain provisions for the protection of the mining industry were put in the bill[1] then before us, and those amendments in part failed to survive the conference committee. I wonder whether or not this provision is as favorable to the mining industry as were the amendments which the Senate put in the bill upon the former occasion.

MR. HARRISON. Mr. President, I will say to the Senator from Colorado that the amendments go as far as any legislation we even dreamed we could have enacted. We think the mining interests are greatly helped by virtue of the amendments we have put in, and they are in no way in the world jeopardized.

MR. ADAMS. To what extent are they benefited? The Senator will recall—the matter is hazy in my mind—that it was provided in the bill which passed the Senate on the former occasion that when a mine or other property was developed over a course of years, and money was spent in its development for 1, 2, 3, 4, or 5 years, and at the end of the period those making the development were fortunate enough to make a substantial return—the return which they were seeking in the period of development—the profits of the last year should be distributed back over the period of the development, not to exceed 5 years.

MR. HARRISON. I may say that that matter was very important. In addition to allowing mining interests the right to spread the income over the development period, the bill allows a 2-year carry-over for unused credits, special relief for growing corporations, and other relief for changes in the character of the business.

MR. ADAMS. I know it was in the former bill.

MR. HARRISON. It is in no way affected by what we have done here— that is, the question of allocating the income over the development period.

*   *   *

MR. HARRISON. I may say to the Senator that of course he recalls the discussion we had with reference to the general relief provision of the bill when there were abnormalities, when we gave to the Commission of Internal Revenue, the right to pass on these matters and to show some discretion, and provided that they might go even to the Board of Tax Appeals. We have taken care of that matter as much as it was possible for us to take care of it.

*   *   *

MR. ADAMS. I am asking the Senator

what is the method of relief adopted in the proposed amendment as to the mining industry, and how far does it conform to, and to what extent does it differ from what the Senate tried to do on the former occasion?

MR. HARRISON. We did not change that at all. As explained in the excess-profits tax bill, the Commissioner is required to allocate the income over the period of development, and his action is subject to review by the Board of Tax Appeals.

MR. ADAMS. You did not change what?

MR. HARRISON. We did not change that from the formula which was expressly provided for in the former bill as it passed.

MR. ADAMS. Where is the added benefit in this bill, then, to the mining industry?

MR. GEORGE. Under this bill, which is entirely remedial, it is permissible to go back 10 years, or even further than that. It is permissible to go back through the whole period of development; and in that way the bill is helpful to the mining industry. It is not helpful to the mining industry alone. It is helpful to any type of corporation; but it does result in very great benefit to the particular lines of industry that have a development reaching back over a period of time.

Another thing the amendment does is that various hardship cases are relieved. Many of them would be mining companies as well as other companies; but particularly the period through which the cost of development may be spread goes back further than the amendment which was carried to conference. It may go back through the whole period of development. (p. 1636)

¹ Relating to Code sec. 721(c) in the 1940 Act.

MR. HARRISON. * * * Section 5: Abnormal income in taxable year: Present law provides for six types of abnormal income accruing in the taxable year. These are as follows:

Income arising from claims, judgments, and so forth.

Income arising from long-term contracts.

Income resulting from exploration, prospecting, patents, and so forth, extending over a period of 12 months.

Income due to change of accounting period.

Amounts included in gross income by reason of termination of lease.

Dividends on stock of foreign corporations, except foreign personal-holding companies.

The new bill retains these six types and also includes a general provision covering income of any class of an abnormal character. Under the old law, the test of whether such income was abnormal was whether it was abnormal in the light of the taxpayer's business to derive income of such class, or if the taxpayer

normally derived income of such class, whether the item includible in gross income was grossly disproportionate to the gross income of the same class in the 4 previous taxable years. The new law substitutes for the old test the test as to whether it is abnormal for the taxpayer to derive income of such class, or if the taxpayer normally derives income of such class whether the amount of such income is includible in the gross income of the taxable year is in excess of 125 percent of the average amount of the gross income of the same class, for 4 previous taxable years. (p. 1638)

Committee Hearings
1941 Act

Hearings—Ways and Means Committee.—Adjusting for abnormalities though not attributable to income of another year. (R. N. Miller, p. 472-473)

Difficulties of applying term "class." (R. N. Miller, p. 473; F. A. Godchaux, Jr., p. 1752)

1940
201
Also
[721]
in gen'l

SEC. 721. ABNORMALITIES IN INCOME IN TAXABLE PERIOD.

[1]*If there is includible in the gross income of the taxpayer for any taxable year an item of income of any one or more of the following classes:*

    (a) *Arising out of a claim, award, judgment, or decree, or interest on any of the foregoing; or*

    (b) *Constituting an amount payable under a contract the performance of which required more than 12 months; or*

    (c) *Resulting from exploration, discovery, prospecting, research, or development of tangible property, patents, formulae, or processes, or any combination of the foregoing [by the taxpayer or any of its predecessors,] extending over a period of more than 12 months; or*

    (d) *Includible in gross income for the taxable year rather than for a different taxable year by reason of a change in the taxpayer's accounting period or method of accounting; or*

    (e) *In the case of a lessor of real property, amounts included in gross income for the taxable year by reason of the termination of the lease[, and attributable to improvements on the property]; OR*

    (f) DIVIDENDS ON STOCK OF FOREIGN CORPORATIONS, EXCEPT FOREIGN PERSONAL HOLDING COMPANIES;

and, in the light of the taxpayer's business, it is abnormal for the taxpayer to derive income of such class, or, if the taxpayer normally derives income of such class, the item includible in the gross income of the taxable year is grossly disproportionate to the gross income of the same class in the [4] FOUR previous taxable years, then: [(A)] (1) the amount of such item attributable to any previous taxable year or years shall be determined under rules and regulations prescribed by the Com-

missioner with the approval of the Secretary; [*Provided, That the amount*
of such abnormal income under subsection (3) of this section shall be
attributed equally among the preceding years (not exceeding five years)
during which such research, development, prospecting, or exploration was
being conducted; and (B) the tax under this subchapter for the taxable
year attributable to such item shall not exceed the aggregate of the taxes
under this subchapter attributable to such item had it been received in
the taxable years to which attributable and in the amounts attributable to
each such year, including the taxable year the tax for which under this
subchapter is being computed.] (2) THE AMOUNT OF SUCH ITEM
ATTRIBUTABLE TO ANY FUTURE TAXABLE YEAR OR
YEARS SHALL BE DETERMINED UNDER RULES AND REG-
ULATIONS PRESCRIBED BY THE COMMISSIONER WITH
THE APPROVAL OF THE SECRETARY AND SHALL, FOR
THE PURPOSES OF THIS SUBCHAPTER, BE INCLUDED IN
THE GROSS INCOME FOR THE FUTURE YEAR OR YEARS
TO WHICH ATTRIBUTABLE; AND (3) THE TAX UNDER
THIS SUBCHAPTER FOR THE TAXABLE YEAR (IN WHICH
THE WHOLE OF SUCH ITEM WOULD, WITHOUT REGARD
TO THIS SECTION, BE INCLUDIBLE) SHALL NOT EXCEED
THE SUM OF:

(A) THE TAX UNDER THIS SUBCHAPTER FOR
SUCH TAXABLE YEAR COMPUTED WITHOUT THE INCLU-
SION IN GROSS INCOME OF THE PORTION OF SUCH ITEM
WHICH IS ATTRIBUTABLE TO ANY OTHER TAXABLE
YEAR, AND

(B) THE AGGREGATE OF THE INCREASE IN THE
TAX UNDER THIS SUBCHAPTER WHICH WOULD HAVE
RESULTED FOR EACH PREVIOUS TAXABLE YEAR TO
WHICH ANY PORTION OF SUCH ITEM IS ATTRIBUTABLE,
COMPUTED AS IF AN AMOUNT EQUAL TO SUCH PORTION
HAD BEEN INCLUDED IN GROSS INCOME FOR SUCH PRE-
VIOUSLY TAXABLE YEAR.

[1] The Senate Finance Committee heading "General Provision" was
stricken by the Conference Committee.

Committee Reports

**Report—Senate Finance Committee
(76th Cong., 3d Sess., S. Rept. 2114).—**
The House bill contained a number of
special relief provisions, generally in the
form of adjustments in arriving at the
excess-profits net income. To these,
your committee has added further adjustments to take care of some unusual
cases of hardship. These further adjustments are described in the discussion of
excess-profits net income.

In addition, your committee has provided a relief provision of much wider
and more general application. This provision allows relief in the taxable period
where abnormalities in income occur because of amounts of income (*a*) arising
out of claims and judgments; (*b*) resulting on long-term contracts; (*c*) resulting
from long-term exploration, discovery,
prospecting, research, or development of
property, patents, or processes; (*d*) fall-

ing into one taxable year rather than another because of a change in accounting periods or methods; or (*e*) arising upon the termination of a lease from improvements on the leased property.

To be entitled to relief in such cases, the type of income must be abnormal in the case of the particular taxpayer, in the light of its business, or if of a type normally received by it, must be grossly disproportionate to its income of the same class in the 4 preceding taxable years.

Where, with respect to any particular item of income the taxpayer is entitled to relief under this provision, such item of income will be allocated to the years in which it is properly attributable and the taxpayer's income for the taxable year in which such item would otherwise fall is correspondingly reduced.

In addition, taxpayers, 80 percent or more of whose gross income is derived from processing, canning, or otherwise preparing for market any seasonal fruit or vegetable or any fish or other marine life, are allowed to carry over for 2 years the unused excess-profits credit for any taxable year subject to the excess-profits tax. (p. 7)

Section 721 of the committee amendment is a new section, no comparable provisions having been included in the House bill. Subsection (a) of this section is designed to provide relief in enumerated cases in which the taxpayer's income in any taxable year is abnormally large because of certain special circumstances. The special types of income with respect to which relief may be accorded by this section are as follows:

(1) Income arising out of a claim, award, judgment, or decree, or out of interest on any of the foregoing;

(2) Income received with respect to a contract whose performance required more than 1 year;

(3) Income resulting from the exploration, discovery, prospecting, research, or development of tangible property, patents, formulas, or processes, providing that such exploration, etc., extended over a period of more than 1 year;

(4) Income which is required to be included for the taxable year as a result of a change in the taxpayer's accounting period or method of accounting;

(5) Income received by the lessor of

real property on the termination of the lease as a result of improvements on the property during the lease.

If the taxpayer receives income of any of the above classes, the section provides that relief shall be accorded if either (1) in the light of the taxpayer's business it is abnormal for it to receive such income or (2) although the receipt of such income may be normal, the income so received for the taxable year is grossly disproportionate to the amounts of such income received by the taxpayer in the 4 previous taxable years. If either of these conditions is satisfied with respect to income falling in an enumerated class, the relief accorded by the section is as follows: There is first determined the amount of such income received in the taxable year which is attributable to any previous taxable year or years and the amounts so attributable to such years. Such determination is to be made under rules and regulations prescribed by the Commissioner with the approval of the Secretary. It is expected that such regulations will provide general rules prescribing the method by which the taxable years to which the income is to be attributed and the amounts to be attributed may be ascertained. There is then computed the aggregate of the excess-profits taxes which would have been placed on such income had it been received in the taxable years to which it is thus attributed, as described above, including the taxable year in which the income was in fact received. For the taxable year in which the income was received, the excess-profits tax attributable to such income cannot exceed the aggregate of the taxes so computed. If it is determined that the income received in the taxable year is attributable to years in the base period, the amount of such income so attributable to such years will have the effect of increasing the base period net income and thus the credit under the average-earnings method.

Subsection (b) provides in limited cases a 2-year carry-over of any excess of the excess-profits credit for any taxable year beginning after December 31, 1939, over the excess-profits net income. Such carry-over constitutes an additional subtraction from excess-profits net income in arriving at the adjusted excess-profits net income. Such carry-over is available only to corporations 80 percent or more of the gross income of which for the taxable year is derived from processing or otherwise preparing for market any seasonable fruit or vegetable, or any fish or other marine life.   (p. 15-16)

Report—Conference Committee (76th Cong., 3d Sess., H. Rept. 3002).—*House bill.*—There were no comparable provisions in the House bill.

Senate amendment.—Section 721 (a) of the Senate amendment was designed to provide relief in the case of—

(1) Income arising out of a claim, award, judgment, or decree, or out of interest on any of the foregoing;

(2) Income received with respect to a contract whose performance required more than 1 year;

(3) Income resulting from the exploration, discovery, prospecting, research, or development of tangible property, patents, formulas, or processes, or any combination thereof, by the taxpayer or any of its predecessors, providing that such exploration, etc., extended over a period of more than 1 year;

(4) Income which is required to be included for the taxable year as a result of a change in the taxpayer's accounting period or method of accounting;

(5) Income received by the lessor of real property on the termination of the lease as a result of improvements on the property during the lease.

Any of the above types of income which is abnormal in kind, or which, in the light of the taxpayer's experience in the 4 previous taxable years, is abnormal in amount, is entitled to the following treatment:

The amount thereof attributable to any previous taxable year or years is to be determined under rules and regulations prescribed by the Commissioner with the approval of the Secretary. In the case of income from exploration, etc., the Commissioner is required to allocate in equal amounts so much of such income as is not attributed to the taxable year to each of the preceding years (not exceeding 5) during which the exploration, etc., was conducted. The excess-profits tax for the taxable year shall not exceed the excess-profits tax for such taxable year computed without including such income in gross income, plus the aggregate of the additional excess-profits taxes which

would have been payable in each of the preceding taxable years (including the current taxable year) to which a portion of such income is attributed if such portion had been included in income in such year.

Section 721 (b) provides a 2-year carry-over of the unused excess-profits credit for any taxable year beginning after December 31, 1939, in the case of corporations 80 percent or more of whose gross income is derived from mining or processing minerals or from processing or otherwise preparing for market any seasonal fruit or vegetable, or any fish or other marine life. The unused excess-profits credit for any taxable year is the amount by which the excess-profits credit for such taxable year exceeds the excess-profits net income for such taxable year.

Conference agreement.—The conference agreement retains section 721 with the following modifications:

(1) The item relative to income resulting from explorations, etc., has been rewritten. The exploration, etc., from which the income is derived must be the taxpayer's own exploration. Income resulting from activities of such a character carried on by a predecessor corporation is not entitled to the treatment provided in section 721.

(2) The item relative to income arising from the termination of a lease has been broadened so as to include all income arising from such source and not merely income occasioned by improvements on the property during the term of the lease.

(3) A new category of potentially abnormal income has been added, consisting of dividends on stock of foreign corporations, except foreign personal holding companies. This is part of the conference agreement relative to the dividends received credit of corporations computing their excess-profits credit on the income plan. See section 710.

(4) The fixed rule of allocation applicable to income resulting from exploration, etc., has been eliminated.

(5) A new provision is inserted making certain that income attributed to any future year or years will be included in excess-profits net income for such future year or years and subjected to excess-profits tax.

(6) Subsections (b) and (c), provid-

ing for a special 2-year carry-over of the unused excess-profits credit in the case of certain businesses, are eliminated. (p. 50-51)

Congressional Discussion

Discussion—House (Cong. Rec. Vol. 86).—MR. COFFEE of Washington. In the case of the Boeing Airplane Works of Seattle, I have been advised by its president that during the years immediately preceding the emergency they expended a large amount of money seeking information and making laboratory tests on a heavy bomber, the flying fortress.

* * *

MR. COOPER. The gentleman will find that that is taken care of in the bill. (p. 11250)

Discussion—Senate (Cong. Rec. Vol. 86).—MR. TYDINGS. In the case of a cause of action in law which accrued prior to January 1, 1940, in which there had been a dispute over whether one corporation or another was entitled to receive money in 1938, and in which the suit is not determined until this year, although the money was actually earned and in dispute for a year like 1938, it would be manifestly unfair to tax the 1938 earnings, which have been a matter of litigation, in a year like 1940. I call that matter to the attention of the committee. I ask the Senator whether or not any provision was made to take care of it.

MR. HARRISON. That would come under the relief provision of the bill.

MR. TYDINGS. It is taken care of?

MR. HARRISON. That is one of the things taken care of in the general relief provision.

MR. TYDINGS. I should like to ask the Senator another question. I have in mind a concern which for 15 years has earned no money and paid no dividends. In order to perfect its product it conducted research which cost a tremendous amount of money. It so happens that this year will be the first time it will make any profit, after 15 years of barren returns. I was wondering whether or not the 4- or 5-year average of earnings would apply to a corporation which has had no profit for a period of time such as I have indicated.

MR. HARRISON. That matter is taken care of by the relief provision.

MR. TYDINGS. So all the profit would not be taxed as of this year, but it would be taxed on the basis of recent years?

MR. HARRISON. That is correct on the basis of the years to which the income was attributable.

* * *

MR. DANAHER. Will the Senator take the very case to which the Senator from Maryland has referred and indicate how it is taken care of in the relief provision? Does he mean that there will be special action by the Department?

MR. HARRISON. The general provision for relief cases would take care of that specific case. The general provision is found on page 109.[1]

* * *

MR. KING. The word "abnormalities" is used. In the case of abnormalities in income in the taxable period, a commission is set up which is fully authorized to deal with abnormal cases and work out justice so far as possible. Of course, a great amount of discretion is left to the organization.

MR. DANAHER. It should be. I thank the Senator. (p. 12059-060)

[1] Relating to sec. 721.

MR. BROWN. Mr. President, I should like to make an inquiry of the chairman of the Committee on Finance as to the matters contained on page 109, which is the so-called hardship section. The Senator will recall that we had considerable discussion in the Finance Committee regarding subsection (3) of section 721, on page 109. The Senator will recall also that that is the so-called hardship section by which it is provided that in the calculation of the excess-profits tax attention may be given to prior experience of the corporation or a taxpayer who has been engaged in mining, or research, or development. I raised the question in the committee whether or not in the type of case where an individual or partnership have formed a corporation the taxpayer would be entitled to the relief provided in section 3.[1] That is highly important to many mining corporations. It is highly important to some development corporations in my State of Michigan. The Senator from Mississippi will recall that the committee voted to instruct the experts to draft a provision which would cover the situation. I understand it has not been done. The problem presents considerable difficulty. * * *

MR. HARRISON. I recall the discussion we had in the committee. The committee was in sympathy with the view of the Senator from Michigan [Mr. BROWN], the Senator from Utah [Mr. KING], the Senator from Colorado [Mr. JOHNSON], and others who presented the idea. As I recall, the committee was asked to draft an amendment to the relief provision carrying out this general idea. I understand from the draftsmen that they have tried to do so, but some time will be required to write the provision. That is the information which comes to me. * * *

MR. KING. Let me say to the Senator that the understanding in the committee was that a comprehensive relief provision should be adopted. In my opinion we have not carried out our intentions.

MR. BROWN. According to my understanding, the Finance Committee voted on precisely that question, and asked that such a provision be drafted.

MR. ADAMS. I wonder if the Senator from Utah and the Senator from Mississippi can enlighten me in my ignorance as to how far this section goes in protecting those in the mining industry, who, as Senators know, engage in a development process for years and invest their money without any return. Then in 1 year they happen to derive some profit, the accumulated profit resulting from their efforts for 4 or 5 years past. How far is such a development protected by positive provisions; how far is opportunity afforded for protection merely under rules and regulations; and how far is it left unprotected?

MR. HARRISON. Protection is afforded under the relief provisions of the bill, which permit promoters, developers, or inventors to go back and apportion over several years what they have accumulated in earnings.

MR. ADAMS. Is that a positive right, or is it merely a privilege which may be given by the Commissioner?

MR. HARRISON. That is a specified, particular opportunity permitted them, and does not come under the general pro-

visions, which would buttress that special right.

MR. BROWN. The right of appeal to the Board of Tax Appeals is also granted.

MR. ADAMS. That would also follow. My inquiry is whether or not there is protection by positive declaration, or whether leeway is simply left to the Commissioner, with the approval of the Secretary, to make rules and regulations which might protect or which might not protect.

MR. BROWN. I think the Commissioner is required to grant the opportunity.

MR. HARRISON. Oh, yes; it is specified, and if there is complaint there may be appeal to the courts. This provision was adopted as a relief provision in special cases. It seems to me it cannot be ignored by the Commissioner under any circumstances. The Senator from Colorado [Mr. JOHNSON] was on the committee, and I think he will bear me out in the statement that that was the interpretation placed upon it. We all seemed pretty well satisfied with it.

MR. JOHNSON of Colorado. That was the understanding we had in the committee, and we instructed the drafting division to draft an amendment to bring about the result. This is the language which was brought to us. From the interpretation given by the draftsmen to their own language I am quite satisfied that it does the very thing we want to accomplish.

* * *

MR. CONNALLY. As I understand the effect of this provision, in cases of exploration in the mining, oil, coal, or gas industries, if a concern makes an inordinate profit in 1 year as compared with what it usually makes in a year, it is then allowed to prorate that large amount back over a period of years and divide it up.

Let us assume that a concern makes $1,000,000 in some particular year, and that for the 4 preceding years it has not made anything. It allocates $200,000 of the $1,000,000 to each of the 5 years, and estimates what it would have paid on a normal tax basis for each of the 5 years, and pays the tax on that basis. However, for the purposes of the excess-profits tax it pays only on $200,000 in the taxable year, which would be 1940.

* * *

MR. BROWN. I think the statement of the Senator is accurate, except with regard to the remarks he made about paying the normal tax. The normal tax is paid on the entire amount earned in the calendar year, or $1,000,000.

MR. CONNALLY. That is true; but let me say to the Senator from Michigan that under the practice of the Treasury, in prior years the concern would have been permitted to deduct from its net income the expenses of operation, and all that sort of thing, upon which it had not realized. When it finally obtains a return on the money invested, if it is allowed to capitalize it and use it without paying a tax, it escapes paying any normal tax upon that part of its income. Take the case of a concern which makes nothing for 4 years: Of course, it pays no tax. Then, in the fifth year, it makes $1,000,000. It is proposed that the concern shall have the privilege of prorating the $1,000,000 back over a period of 5 years; and upon the constructive theory that $200,000 of that amount was earned in 1936, we will say, the concern pays the normal tax for that year on $200,000, and so on.

MR. BROWN. I must differ with the Senator. I think he is in error with regard to the normal tax. I asked this precise question of the experts. The normal tax is assessed entirely in the year in which the income is earned, which would be 1940.

MR. CONNALLY. That is correct.

MR. BROWN. There is no levying of a tax back over the previous period. The only purpose of using the previous period is as a basis for calculation of the excess-profits tax, which does not relate to the normal tax at all.

MR. CONNALLY. In any event, the concern is not penalized, except on a pro rata basis, with the excess-profits tax in the year in which the income was earned.

MR. BROWN. The Senator is correct.

MR. JOHNSON of Colorado. I do not happen to be an attorney. My colleague asked a technical legal question, and I have been informed by the experts that this provision does not give the Commissioner discretionary power. It lays down a legal rule, and the Commissioner does not have power to reject it

or otherwise. He must be guided by it.

MR. HARRISON. The Senator is correct.

MR. ADAMS. Mr. President, I am not in touch with these things, and I know little about taxation. However, I am hopeful that that is an entirely correct answer. The language of the general provision is:

If there is includible in the gross income of the taxpayer for any taxable year an item of income of any one or more of the following classes—

And the classes are set out—

and, in the light of the taxpayer's business, it is abnormal for the taxpayer to derive income of such class, or, if the taxpayer normally derives income of such class, the item includible in the gross income of the taxable year is grossly disproportionate to the gross income of the same class in the 4 previous taxable years—

If we are dealing with mines, I suppose that means the average of a group of mines, or mines generally, rather than a particular mine.

MR. HARRISON. That is correct.

MR. ADAMS. The provision continues:

Then: (A) The amount of such item attributable to any previous taxable year or years shall be determined under rules and regulations prescribed by the Commissioner with the approval of the Secretary.

MR. HARRISON. The amount attributable to the previous years is to be fixed by the Commissioner and the Secretary of the Treasury.

MR. ADAMS. But it is left entirely to their judgment and discretion. The Senator from Texas [Mr. CONNALLY] gave an illustration, saying that if there were an income of $1,000,000, the only income over a period of 5 years' development, it would be divided and allocated over a period of 5 years. He used the illustration of $200,000 a year. That is not the requirement. It would be left to the Commissioner, with the approval of the Secretary, to decide how much should be allocated to prior years. The Commissioner might set back one amount for one year, another amount for another year, and a different amount for a third year. Is not that correct?

MR. HARRISON. The Senator is correct, except that there may be an appeal to the courts or to the Board of Tax Appeals from the Commissioner's decision on the question.

* * *

MR. JOHNSON of Colorado. The discretionary features do not pertain to the rule at all; but they do pertain, of course, to calculations involved in the whole matter. Somebody has to attribute the amount to certain years. The rule itself, however, is a matter of definition.

MR. ADAMS. May I ask the Senator, then, what is the rule?

MR. JOHNSON of Colorado. The rule is that a taxpayer having had development work over a period of time, more than 12 months, can go back and take that period of time into consideration.

MR. ADAMS. But it is the Commissioner, not the taxpayer, who decides the question and who attributes the income. Take a man owning a patent on which he has been working for 5 years, he has been putting in his money and his time and all he could borrow from his friends, and suddenly, at the end of 5 years, is able to sell his patent for, say, a million dollars. The bill does not say that the million dollars shall be prorated back evenly over the period of 5 years; it does not lay down any rule; but merely says that if the amount which he received is abnormal and excessive or disproportionate to the gross income of the same class in the 4 preceding taxable years, then "the amount of such item attributable to any previous taxable year or years shall be determined under rules and regulations to be prescribed by the Commissioner with the approval of the Secretary."

If the Commissioner were to decide that nothing should be prorated the first 3 years, and should divide the million dollars into the last 2 years, as a matter of discretion, the owner of the patent would be bound by it, as I read the provision. I am trying to get the information because of its vast importance to the section of the country in which I live.

MR. JOHNSON of Colorado. As I understand the proposal, that only pertains to the arithmetic of the matter, and not to the right of the taxpayer at all.

MR. ADAMS. I wish I could concur with the Senator. The Senator is on the committee, and I will accept his judgment, but he will have to pardon my ignorance.

* * *

MR. HARRISON. I may say to the senior Senator from Colorado that Mr. Stam, who is chief of our staff, and who has had long experience and help in writing this, thinks and so states in a report which I have in my hand that the colleague of the Senator from Colorado is exactly right in his construction of the provision.

MR. ADAMS. Will the Senator, then, translate to me from the expert what is the rule? It is, I am told, a matter of arithmetic.

MR. HARRISON. Very well. I will read:

This section grants certain relief to taxpayers in the following cases:

Where the gross income of the taxpayer for the taxable year includes income of the following classes:

(1) Income from claims, judgments, or interests thereon;

(2) Amounts payable in 1 year from long-term contracts;

(3) Income resulting from exploration, discovery, prospecting, research, or development of tangible property extending over a period of more than 12 months;

(4) Income which is abnormal due to a change in the taxpayer's accounting method or accounting period; and

(5) Buildings taken over by a lessor upon termination of the lease.

In this class of cases, if it is abnormal for the taxpayer to derive income of such class, relief is granted. Relief is also granted where even though the taxpayer normally derives income from such class, the income is grossly disproportionate to the gross income in the same class in the 4 previous taxable years.

In such cases, the excess-profits tax cannot exceed the aggregate taxes if it had been received in the taxable years to which it had been attributable if received ratably over the period.

For example, if a taxpayer receives income from a judgment in 1940, for which claim was pending for a period of 5 years of $1,000, only $200 is reportable as income for 1940 subject to excess-profits tax. The balance is attributable to the base period years, and since no excess-profits tax is imposed for such years, the remaining $800 is not subject to excess-profits tax.

An oil company might derive income from an oil well in 1940, which is much greater than it received in the 4 preceding taxable years for oil wells. If such income is attributable to a 5-year period, only one-fifth would be reportable as income subject to the excess-profits tax for 1940.

I hope that explanation will help somewhat to explain this particular question.

MR. ADAMS. I wish the explanation were in the bill.

MR. HARRISON. It is in the report, I may say to the Senator.

MR. CONNALLY. I wish to correct one thing I said a moment ago. I said that in making out the income for tax purposes and spreading it over a 5-year period the normal tax was estimated as of the year when it was constructively earned; but that was inaccurate. The normal tax is payable in the taxable year 1940, but, for the purpose of the excess-profits tax, it is prorated back over a 5-year period, and only one-fifth of it in the taxable year is assessable under the excess-profits tax. It would have been better for the miners and oil producers had the suggestion I first made been correct.

I made the suggestion in the Finance Committee, and was under the impression that the amendment had been drawn in such fashion as to carry out my original thought, but I see I am in error in that respect. Otherwise I think my statement was accurate. I thank the Senator.

* * *

MR. KING. As I understood the Senator from Texas, I interpreted his observation to mean, if a mining corporation has been working for a number of years—say, 10 years—and a windfall comes on the tenth year, there would be no exception with respect to the normal income tax, but, for the purposes of the excess-profits tax, the amount would be considered to cover 5 years, and the windfall would be allocated to a number of years rather than to the year in which it was paid.

MR. CONNALLY. I will say to the Senator that, if this bill were not passed at all, that is exactly what would happen, but, under existing law, if they get the money in 1940, they would pay the normal tax on all of it.

MR. KING. That is true.

MR. CONNALLY. This does not change that.

MR. KING. It does not change it with respect to the normal tax.

MR. BROWN. Mr. President, I understand the Senator from Delaware has an amendment to offer. I assure him that it will take me only a moment to clear up the matter I have in mind. Referring to subsection 3[1] on page 109, the experts from the Treasury and the Finance Committee tell me that this matter could be perfected in conference if we added the language which I am about to read:

In line 15, after the word "foregoing", to insert the words "by the taxpayer or any of its predecessors."

I therefore ask that the committee amendment be amended as I have suggested. (p. 12174-177)

[1] Relating to sec. 721 (c).

MR. GEORGE. I desire to offer an amendment for the purpose of keeping open for conference the rather restricted terms and provisions of section 721 on page 109. I offer the amendment for that purpose.

* * *

THE CHIEF CLERK. After line 24, page 109, it is proposed to add the following:

or (6) any other abnormality of income or capital. (p. 12182)

MR. GEORGE. While this is covered in the general relief provision found on page 109 of the bill, section 721, I believe it is, nevertheless certain Senators * * * desire to have this amendment inserted in the bill. Since we have inserted one other specific amendment or relief provision[1] very similar to it, there would seem to be no objection to the amendment.

MR. HARRISON. I may say that it was my belief that the matter referred to by the Senator from Georgia [Mr. GEORGE] was amply covered by the relief section of the bill. (p. 12253)

[1] Relating to sec. 722.

MR. ADAMS. I wish to call the attention of the Senator from Mississippi to a suggested amendment which would put in the bill provisions which I am told are in the present statute. I was going to ask that there be added, after the word "Secretary" in line 8, on page 110, the following:

Provided, That the amount of such abnormal income under subsection (3) of this section shall be attributed equally among the preceding years (not exceeding 5 years) during which such research, development, prospecting, or exploration was being conducted.

In other words, instead of leaving it solely to the discretion of the Secretary, that is a specific provision that the abnormal income shall be divided over the preceding years.

MR. HARRISON. I have no objection to the amendment going to conference, but I wish to say——

MR. ADAMS. I accept the warning in advance.

MR. HARRISON. The Senator restricts

his amendment to 5 years when he could have provided a period of 10 years.

MR. ADAMS. I shall be glad to change my amendment from 5 years to 10 years.

MR. HARRISON. Or 20 years.

MR. ADAMS. We will say 10 years. (p. 12183)

MR. ADAMS. Mr. President, a day or two ago, in an effort to protect the mining industry and certain other industries in which a period of research and development precedes the reward, I offered an amendment to the committee amendment, which was inserted in line 8 on page 110, which provided that the abnormal profit or income derived as a result of some periods of research should be attributed to a period of not to exceed 5 years. The chairman of the Finance Committee, with amiable generosity, suggested to me that perhaps 10 years would be all right; and, rather overwhelmed by the generosity, I agreed to it. I should like to reinstate my original amendment, and substitute "five" for "ten." Therefore, I move, in the amendment I offered, that the word "ten" be stricken out and the word "five" inserted. (p. 12350)

Discussion—Senate; on Report of Conference Committee (Cong. Rec. Vol. 86).—MR. HARRISON. * * * In this report, the conference agreed to relieve what we termed hard cases, such as the following:

* * *

Eighth. The Senate bill prevented income in the base period from being reduced by deductions attributable to claims, awards, or judgments against the taxpayer, or interest thereon, if, in the light of the taxpayer's business, it was abnormal for the taxpayer to incur a liability of such character, or if the amount of such liability in the tax period was grossly disproportionate to the amount of such liability in the 4 previous years. This was agreed to. (p. 12918)

MR. ADAMS. I am interested, as are all those from the mining sections, in the provision in reference to abnormal incomes, incomes which appear as a result of a process of development and research carried on over a period of years which result in a substantial profit in 1 year because of the activities of the preceding year or years. That matter was before

the Finance Committee, of course, and before the conference committee.

As the bill came from the Senate committee it contained relief provisions, and gave authority to the Commissioner of Internal Revenue, with the approval of the Secretary, to make adjustments. On the floor an effort was made by an amendment to not only give the authority to make such adjustments, but to make it compulsory, and to establish a mathematical method by which they should be applied. In other words, it provided that if a process of development, say in a mine, had been carried on for 5 years, and there had been loss for 4 years, and if, at the end of the fifth year, if a fortunate mineral discovery were made, the profit should be distributed back over the period of 5 years. That has been taken out. The conference committee recommends the elimination of this mathematical formula for the distribution. As the bill comes from the conference committee power is given the Commissioner, with the approval of the Secretary, to make adjustments, but, as I read it, there is absolutely no compulsion upon the Commissioner to make any such adjustments. We are left absolutely at the mercy of the judgment and decision of the Commissioner and the Secretary of the Treasury.

MR. HARRISON. That has relation to the amendment the Senator offered, the 5-year amendment?

MR. ADAMS. Yes.

MR. HARRISON. We believe that the bill as now written absolutely requires the Commissioner to make the allocation of the income to the proper year.

MR. ADAMS. Will the Senator be good enough to satisfy my mind a little, to ease it, by telling me where the provision is?

MR. HARRISON. Under section 21[1] of the bill as agreed to in conference, the amount attributable to any previous taxable year or years is to be determined under rules and regulations prescribed by the Commissioner with the approval of the Secretary. In the case of income from exploration, and so forth, the Commissioner is required under the language of this section to allocate so much of such income as is not attributed to the taxable year to each of the preceding years.

MR. ADAMS. The Senator is reading

the statement as to the Senate amendment, but not a statement as to the conference report.

MR. HARRISON. I am referring to the section of the law itself and the interpretation placed upon it by both the Treasury and our own experts.

It was the viewpoint of every expert in our conference—those representing our joint committee and those representing the Treasury—that we had taken care of the very situation the Senator pointed out in his amendment; that explorations might not run back just 5 years, but might run back 20 years, and that the Commissioner would be required to make the adjustments.

MR. ADAMS. The Senator is quite correct that the authority exists in the Treasury Department to make the adjustments, but in the conference report there is no compulsion upon the Treasury Department to make the adjustments. It is all within their discretion.

The amount to be attributed to previous years is to be determined by the Commissioner or the Treasury Department. Then the subsections which follow deal with the amount to be attributed to previous years; but the amount to be attributed comes from the exercise of the discretion of the Treasury Department. In other words, there is not a particle of compulsion upon the Treasury Department to meet the problem. Of course, I am hopeful that the Treasury Department will recognize the implications of the language rather than the unrestricted discretion.

MR. HARRISON. If anyone was misled and there could be the interpretation the Senator fears, we were the ones who were misled, because, as I have stated, we were told by every representative of the Treasury Department, and it was as well the belief of our own staff, that the situation was taken care of.

I give the Senator this assurance, that, so far as I am concerned, if, when the question arises, it should be held that what I have stated is not the correct interpretation and construction of the law, we will certainly make every effort to amend the law in order to take care of the situation.

MR. ADAMS. I am very hopeful that the Senator's views in the matter will be carried out. Of course, the Treasury Department naturally, as is true of every other great department, likes to have the power vested in it to make decisions. I am not saying they would not do as the Senator expects, but I am saying that they are not compelled to, under the proposed law, and out of the bill has gone the provision which would have compelled them.

MR. HARRISON. Because we were all very sympathetic with what the Senator had in his mind, when he restricted the matter to 5 years, we thought we were giving him more than his own amendment was giving him by eliminating the 5-year limitation. There may be a difference between the construction on the part of the conferees and the Senator's construction, but I give him every assurance that if there should be any doubt about the construction the Treasury puts on this provision, when the question arises, we will join hands with the Senator in remedying the situation.

MR. ADAMS. I am very happy to have the Senator's assurance. I hope he will not have any occasion to act upon it.

MR. HARRISON. I hope so, too. (p. 12919)

¹ [721].

Committee Hearings

Hearings—Senate Finance Committee.—Treating income from bad debt recoveries. (K. Carroad, p. 35)

Treating income from tax refunds as abnormal. (K. Carroad, p. 35)

Determining tax for short period on basis of pro-rata for actual 12 month period. (W. A. Cooper, p. 47-49, 53-54, 59-60)

Adjusting for interest on prior years tax refund. (P. G. Blazer, p. 223-224)

Special problems resulting from change from installment to accrual basis. (G. Rogers, p. 471-475; R. P. Smith, p. 479-481; E. P. Thomas, p. 491-492)

UNENACTED RELATED PROVISIONS
1942 Act
[Sec. 213(c) of the Ways and Means Committee bill]

[SEC. 721. ABNORMALITIES IN INCOME IN TAXABLE PERIOD.]

[(a) Definitions.—For the purposes of this section—]

[(1) Abnormal Income.— * * *]

~~Income of a class derived from any activity of the business which is taken into account in the determination of a constructive average base period net income under section 722 shall not constitute "abnormal income" for the purposes of this section.~~

Report—Senate Finance Committee (77th Cong., 2d Sess., S. Rept. 1631).— Your committee has deleted the provisions of section 213 (c) of the House bill relating to the treatment under section 721 of the Code of current abnormal income in cases where a constructive average base period net income is determined under section 722 of the Code. Provisions with respect to such cases have been provided by your committee in subsections (d) and (f) of this section and in section 220 (a),[1] adding subsection (1) to section 721. (p. 206)

[1] Sec. 221(a) of the Act.

Report—Conference Committee (77th Cong., 2d Sess., H. Rept. 2586).—The Senate deleted the provisions of the House bill relating to the treatment under section 721 of the Code of current abnormal income in cases where a constructive average base period net income is determined under section 722. Substitute provisions with respect to such cases have been inserted elsewhere by the Senate. (p. 62)

1940 Act
[Sec. 201 of Senate bill]

[SEC. 711. EXCESS PROFITS NET INCOME.]

[(a) Taxable Years Beginning After December 31, 1939.— * * *]

[(1) Excess profits credit computed under income credit.— * * *]

[*(I) Awards of the mixed claims commission, United States and Germany.*—*There shall be excluded amounts received pursuant to an award of the Mixed Claims Commission, United States and Germany, in respect of claims for loss or damage to persons or property sustained prior to November 11, 1918.*]

Committee Reports

Report—Conference Committee (76th Cong., 3d Sess., H. Rept. 3002).—*Senate amendment.*—In addition to certain technical amendments, the Senate amendment made the following changes in and additions to the adjustments contained in the House bill:

*   *   *

(12) Amounts received pursuant to an award of the Mixed Claims Commission, United States and Germany, are excluded from income for taxable years after the base period in the case of corporations computing their excess-profits credit under the income plan. (p. 44, 45)

Conference agreement.—With the exceptions and modifications described below, the Senate provision is adopted.

* * *

(6) The specific adjustment excluding from income awards of the Mixed Claims Commission has been eliminated, since it is already covered by the general provisions of section 721. Such income would be abnormal in kind, and, to the extent it constituted compensation for past losses, would be attributable to the years such losses occurred. Most of these awards of the Mixed Claims Commission were paid many years ago. However, a number of awards to American nationals were rendered by the Commission only recently and have not yet been paid. The conferees were unanimous that such awards when paid, to the extent they do not include current interest, should not and would not be subject to the excess-profits tax. Section 711 (a) (1) (I) of Senate amendment has been omitted from the bill as agreed to in conference by reason of the fact that the conferees are convinced (and have the assurances of the Treasury) that section 721 of the bill accomplishes the same result, since the very nature of the award makes any resulting income abnormal, and none of the amounts paid pursuant to such awards will be attributable to any taxable year beginning after December 31, 1939, within the meaning of such section. Insofar as such amounts are properly includible in the normal tax net income of the recipients, they will, of course, be subject to the normal tax in the year in which they are accrued or (in the case of recipients upon the cash receipts basis) are actually received. (p. 45, 47)

Congressional Discussion

Discussion—Senate; on Report of Conference Committee (Cong. Rec. Vol. 86).—Mr. Harrison. * * * In this report, the conference agreed to relieve what we termed hard cases, such as the following:

* * *

Fourth. With respect to awards of the Mixed Claims Commission, United States and Germany, the Senate bill provided that such awards should not be subject to the excess-profits tax. It was pointed out that these awards were already covered by the general relief provision of the bill with respect to abnormalities in income, and that under that provision they would not be subject to the excess-profits tax. With this in mind, and an agreement to put in the conference report a specific statement to that effect, the specific provision of the Senate bill dealing with the subject was eliminated. (p. 12918)

Mr. George. Mr. President, just a final word with reference to an amendment adopted by the Senate which was specifically omitted in the conference; that is to say, an amendment dealing with the awards of the German-American Mixed Claims Commission, and exempting those awards from the excess profits tax provisions of the bill.

I had the honor to offer that amendment in the Senate, at the request of some Senators who necessarily had to be absent. We were assured—and I think beyond all doubt it is a correct statement —that section 721 (a) (1) of the bill as reported by the conference committee clearly covered the case in hand, and that these awards, when paid and to the extent that they do not include current interest, should not and would not be subject to the excess-profits tax. I take it from the discussion which was had in conference, and the report which has been submitted, that it is important now to note that all such payments made upon these awards—specifically, the German-American awards—except for interest accruing during the taxable year 1940 or thereafter, will be exempt from the excess-profits tax. (p. 12924)

Sec. 721(a)(3)

EPTA
5

[SEC. 721.   ABNORMALITIES IN INCOME IN TAXABLE PERIOD.]

[(a) Definitions.—For the purposes of this section—]

(3) Net Abnormal Income.—The term "net abnormal income" means the amount of the abnormal income less, under regulations prescribed by the Commissioner with the approval of the Secretary, (A) 125 per centum of the average amount of the gross income of the same class determined under paragraph (1), and (B) an amount which bears the same ratio to the amount of any direct costs or expenses, deductible in determining the normal-tax net income of the taxable year, through the expenditure of which such abnormal income was in whole or in part derived as the excess of the amount of such abnormal income over 125 per centum of such average amount bears to the amount of such abnormal income.

Committee Reports

Report—Ways and Means Committee (77th Cong., 1st Sess., H. Rept. 146).— It is provided further that if an item of gross income is found to be abnormal such item shall be reduced by 125 percent of the average amount of the gross income of the same class for the four or less previous taxable years constituting the test period.

Such abnormal item is further reduced by a proportionate part of the direct costs or expenses attributable thereto. The item so reduced is then allocated to the previous or future taxable years to which it is attributable.   (p. 10)

Report—Senate Finance Committee (77th Cong., 1st Sess., S. Rept. 75).— Same as Ways and Means Committee Report.   (p. 10)

Sec. 721(b)

[Set forth on page 122]

1940
201
[721]
in gen'l

Sec. 721(c)

[SEC. 721.   ABNORMALITIES IN INCOME IN TAXABLE PERIOD.]

1942
221(a)

(c) Computation of Tax for Current Taxable Year.—*The tax under this subchapter for the taxable year, in which the whole of such abnormal income would without regard to this section be includible, shall not exceed the sum of:*

(1) *The tax under this subchapter for such taxable year computed without the inclusion in gross income of the portion of the net abnormal income which is attributable to any other taxable year, and*

(2) *The aggregate of the increase in the tax under this subchapter for the taxable year (computed under paragraph (1)) and for each previous taxable year which would have resulted if, for each previous taxable year to which any portion of such net abnormal income is attributable, an amount equal to such portion had been included in the gross income for such previous taxable year.*

Committee Reports

Report—Senate Finance Committee (77th Cong., 2d Sess., S. Rept. 1631).— This section, for which there is no corresponding provision in the House bill, makes technical amendments necessary for the proper computation of tax under section 721, relating to abnormalities in income in the taxable period. Section 721 (c) of existing law provides that if any net abnormal income for a taxable year is attributable to a previous taxable year, the tax for the taxable year shall be the tax computed by excluding such portion of the net abnormal income from gross income for such year, plus the increase in tax for the previous taxable year which would have resulted if such portion had been included in the gross income for such previous year. These provisions do not take into account the fact that, due to a carry-over of net operating loss or of unused excess profits credit from the previous taxable year to another taxable year, the increase in tax as the result of attributing the net abnormal income to the previous taxable year may occur not in the previous taxable year but in a taxable year subsequent thereto. This section amends section 721 (c) to provide that, upon net abnormal income being attributed to a previous taxable year, the increase in tax which would result for any year subsequent to such previous taxable year (including the increase in tax for the current taxable year computed without including the net abnormal income in gross income for such current taxable year) shall be also included in the tax.

Example 1: The taxpayer has in 1940 an unused excess profits credit of $50, which is the basis for an excess profits credit carry-over in 1941. In 1944 the taxpayer has $80 net abnormal income

attributable to 1940. The tax for 1944, computed under section 721 (c), is the tax for 1944 determined without including the $80 in gross income for that year, plus the increase in tax which would result if the $80 were included in gross income for 1940, that is, the increase in tax in 1940 which would result from the inclusion of such amount in gross income, and the increase in tax in 1941 which would result from there being no excess profits credit carry-over from 1940 because of the increase in the gross income for 1940 (the $80 attributed to 1940 offsets the $50 unused excess profits credit for such year).

Example 2: The taxpayer has a net operating loss of $200 in 1939 which forms the basis for a $200 net operating loss carry-over to 1940. In 1940 it has $150 net abnormal income which is attributable to 1939. The tax for 1940, computed under section 721 (c), is the tax for such year determined without including the $150 in gross income, plus the increase in tax which would result from the inclusion of $150 in gross income for 1939. Since the excess profits tax is not applicable to the taxable year 1939, there is no increase in excess profits tax for such year as a result of such inclusion. However, an increase in tax in 1940 would result from the $150, included in gross income in 1939, reducing the net operating loss for 1939, and accordingly reducing the carry-over to 1940. The increase in the tax for 1940 as a result of this decrease in the carry-over is included in computing the tax for 1940 under section 721 (c), that is, under that section the tax for 1940 is the tax determined without including the $150 net abnormal income in gross income, plus the increase in the tax so determined which would result from the carry-over from 1939 being reduced by including the $150 net abnormal income in gross income for 1939.   (p. 194-195)

Report—Conference Committee (77th Cong., 2d Sess., H. Rept. 2586).—

Amendment No. 303: This amendment inserts a new section into the bill to make certain technical changes necessary in the computation of tax under section 721 of the Code, relating to abnormalities in income in the taxable period.   (p. 61)

[Set forth on page 122]

1940
201
[721]
in gen'l

Sec. 721(d)

[SEC. 721. ABNORMALITIES IN INCOME IN TAXABLE PERIOD.]

1942
221(a)

(d) **Computation of Tax for Future Taxable Year.**—*The amount of the net abnormal income attributable to any future taxable year shall, for the purposes of this subchapter, be included in the gross income for such taxable year.*

(1) *The tax under this subchapter for such future taxable year shall not exceed the sum of—*

(A) *the tax under this subchapter for such future taxable year computed without the inclusion in gross income of the portion of such net abnormal income which is attributable to such year, and*

(B) *the decrease in the tax under this subchapter for the previous taxable year in which the whole of such abnormal income would, without regard to this section, be includible which resulted by reason of the computation of such tax for such previous taxable year under the provisions of subsection (c); but the amount of such decrease shall be diminished by the aggregate of the increases in the tax under this subchapter for the future taxable year as computed under subparagraph (A) and for the taxable years intervening between such previous taxable year and such future taxable year which have resulted because of the inclusion of the portions of such net abnormal income attributable to such intervening years in the gross income for such intervening years.*

(2) *If, in the application of subsection (c), net abnormal income from more than one taxable year is attributable to any future taxable year, paragraph (1) of this subsection shall be applied with respect to such future taxable year in the order of the taxable years from which the net abnormal income is attributable beginning with the earliest, as if the portion of the net abnormal income from each such year was the only amount so attributable to such future taxable year, and (except in the case of the portion for the earliest previous taxable year) as if the tax under this subchapter for the future taxable year was the tax determined under paragraph (1) with respect to the portion for the next earlier previous taxable year.*

(3) *If in the application of paragraph (1) to any future taxable year it is determined that the decrease in tax computed under paragraph (1) (B) with respect to the net abnormal income, a portion of which is included*

in the gross income for the future taxable year, does not exceed the aggregate of the increases in tax computed under paragraph (1) (B) with respect to such net abnormal income, then the portions of such net abnormal income attributable to taxable years subsequent to such future taxable year shall not be included in the gross income for such subsequent taxable years. For the purpose of computing the tax under this subchapter for a taxable year subsequent to the future taxable year, the portion of net abnormal income attributable to the future taxable year shall not be included in the gross income for such future taxable year to the extent that the inclusion of such portion of net abnormal income in the gross income for such future taxable year did not result in an increase in tax for such future taxable year by reason of the provisions of paragraph (1).

Committee Reports

Report—Senate Finance Committee (77th Cong., 2d Sess., S. Rept. 1631).— This section, for which there is no corresponding provision in the House bill, makes technical amendments necessary for the proper computation of tax under section 721, relating to abnormalities in income in the taxable period.

*   *   *

Section 721 (d) also provides for the computation of the tax for future taxable years to which net abnormal income from previous taxable years has been attributed. The portion of the net abnormal income attributable to the future taxable year is included in gross income for such taxable year, but the tax resulting from this inclusion cannot exceed the savings in tax caused by the application of section 721 (c) to the taxable year in which the net abnormal income would be includible were it not for section 721, reduced by the aggregate of the increases in tax in the intervening taxable years caused by including portions of the net abnormal income in gross income for such taxable years. This section amends section 721 (d) in a manner similar to the amendments made to section 721 (c) so that the effects of carry-overs will be taken into account in determining the increases in tax in the intervening taxable years. This section also amends section 721 (d) to provide that, for the purpose of computing the carry-over from a future taxable year to any other taxable year, the net abnormal income attributable to the future taxable year shall not be included in the gross income for such future taxable year if it does not, due to the limitations of section 721, result in any tax for such future taxable

year. This change prevents the carry-over from a future taxable year being reduced by those amounts, included in income, which have no tax effect.

This section also provides that in cases in which income from several previous taxable years is attributable to the same future taxable year, the limitations of section 721 (d) will be applied in the case of the portion attributable from the earliest previous taxable year as if that were the only amount attributable to such future taxable year under section 721, and similarly the amounts from other previous taxable years would be treated in chronological order giving effect to the computations with respect to previous amounts. Thus, for example, if $1,000 was attributed from 1940 to 1944, and $2,000 from 1941 to 1944, the limitations of section 721 (d) would be applied to 1944 as if the only net abnormal income attributable to that year was the $1,000 from 1940, the $2,000 from 1941 being treated as ordinary income for 1944. After making the computations under section 721 (d), the limitations of that section would then be applied with respect to the $2,000 from 1941. The tax, before the application of such limitations, would be considered to be the tax determined after applying such limitations with respect to the $1,000 from 1940, and the gross income and other amounts necessary to determine the adjusted excess profits net income are, for the purpose of applying the limitations to the $2,000, considered to be such amounts as would result in the adjusted excess profits net income which would produce such tax. (p. 194, 196)

[SEC. 721. ABNORMALITIES IN INCOME IN TAXABLE PERIOD.]

(d) Computation of Tax for Future Taxable Year.— * * * The tax under this subchapter for such future taxable year shall not exceed— * * *

(2) the decrease in the tax under this subchapter for the previous taxable year in which the whole of such abnormal income would without regard to this section be includible, * * *

Committee Reports

Report—Ways and Means Committee (77th Cong., 1st Sess., H. Rept. 146).— The computation of the tax follows the method presently provided for in section 721, except that a limitation is provided on the amount of tax that may be incurred where the item is attributable in whole or in part to future years. Under this limitation the tax on income at-tributable to future years in no case can exceed the tax that would be payable if the entire income were subject to tax in the year of receipt. (p. 10)

Report—Senate Finance Committee (77th Cong., 1st Sess., S. Rept. 75).— Same as Ways and Means Committee Report. (p. 10)

[Set forth on page 122]

Sec. 721(e)

[SEC. 721. ABNORMALITIES IN INCOME IN TAXABLE PERIOD.]

(e) Application of Section.—*This section shall be applied only for the purpose of computing the tax under this subchapter as provided in subsections (c) and (d), and shall have no effect upon the computation of base period net income. For the purposes of subsections (c) and (d)—*

(1) *Net abnormal income means the aggregate of the net abnormal income of all classes for one taxable year.*

(2) *Under regulations prescribed by the Commissioner with the approval of the Secretary, the tax under this subchapter for previous taxable years shall be computed as if the portions of net abnormal income for each previous taxable year for which the tax was computed under this section were included in the gross income for the other previous taxable years to which such portions were attributable.*

(3) *If both subsections (c) and (d) are applicable to any current taxable year, subsection (d) shall be applied without regard to subsection (c), and subsection (c) shall be applied as if the tax under this subchapter, except for subsection (c), was the tax computed under subsection (d) and as if the gross income and the other amounts necessary to determine the adjusted excess profits net income were those amounts which would result in the tax computed under subsection (d).*

Committee Reports

Report—Senate Finance Committee (77th Cong., 2d Sess., S. Rept. 1631).—Furthermore, this section provides that if net abnormal income is attributed to a previous taxable year from one taxable year, and then an additional amount of net abnormal income is attributed to the same previous taxable year from a second taxable year, the increase in tax upon attributing the net abnormal income to the previous taxable year from the second taxable year shall be determined as if the net abnormal income attributed to the previous taxable year from the first taxable year remained in the gross income for such previous taxable year. Thus, if the taxpayer has a $100 loss in 1940, and has $100 net abnormal income in 1941 attributable to 1940, and $100 net abnormal income in 1942 attributable to 1940, upon attributing the $100 from 1942 to 1940 the gross income for 1940 will be determined as if the $100 attributed to that year from 1941 remained in gross income for that year. Since the $100 attributable from 1941 would offset the $100 loss for 1940,

the inclusion of the $100 from 1942 in gross income for 1940 results in a net income of $100 for that year. (p. 195-196)

This section also provides that if in any taxable year net abnormal income from a previous taxable year is attributable to such year, and portions of the income for such year constitute net abnormal income attributable to previous taxable years, so that both section 721 (c) and section 721 (d) apply to the taxable year, the tax for such taxable year shall be determined by applying the limitations of section 721 (d) first, and then applying the limitations of section 721 (c). This section also makes clear that any amount attributed to a base period taxable year has no effect upon the computation of base period net income, inasmuch as income is attributed to other taxable years only for the purpose of determining increases and decreases in tax which are taken into account in determining the tax under this section. Various other clarifying amendments are made to section 721. (p. 196-197)

Sec. 721(f)

1942
221(a)

[SEC. 721. ABNORMALITIES IN INCOME IN TAXABLE PERIOD.]

(f) *Abnormal Income From Exploration, Etc.—If by reason of taking into account, in determining constructive average base period net income under section 722, exploration, discovery, prospecting, research, or development of tangible property, patents, formulae, or processes, or any combination of the foregoing, extending over a period of more than 12 months, such constructive average base period net income is higher than it would be without such taking into account, only such portion of the income in the taxable year resulting from such activity which is of a class described in subsection (a) (2) (C) as is attributable to another taxable year under this subchapter shall be deemed attributable to a year other than the taxable year.*

Committee Reports

Report—Senate Finance Committee (77th Cong., 2d Sess., S. Rept. 1631).—In addition to the foregoing technical amendments, this section adds subsection (f) to section 721 so as to provide

that if by reason of taking into account exploration, discovery, prospecting, research, or development of tangible property, patents, formulas, or processes, or any combination thereof extending over a period of more than 12 months, the constructive average base period net income as a result of the application of the relief provisions of section 722 is higher than if such activities had not been taken into account, no net abnormal income resulting from such activities which are of a class described in section 721 (a) (2) (C) shall be attributable to the base period, or to any year other than a taxable year under this subchapter. (p. 197)

Report—Conference Committee (77th Cong., 2d Sess., H. Rept. 2586).—Subsection (f) is added to section 721 to provide that, if by reason of taking into account exploration, discovery, prospecting, research, or development of tangible property, patents, formulae, or processes, extending over a period of more than 12 months, the constructive average base period net income as a result of the application of the relief provisions of section 722 is higher than if such activities had not been taken into account, no net abnormal income resulting from such activities which are of a class described in section 721 (a) (2) (C) shall be attributable to the base period, or to any year other than a taxable year under Subchapter E of Chapter 2. * * * The House recedes. (p. 61)

Sec. 722(a)

SEC. 722. GENERAL RELIEF—CONSTRUCTIVE AVERAGE BASE PERIOD NET INCOME.

1942
222(a)

(a) **General Rule.**—In any case in which the taxpayer establishes that the tax computed under this subchapter (without the benefit of this section) results in an excessive and discriminatory tax and establishes what would be a fair and just amount representing normal earnings to be used as a constructive average base period net income for the purposes of an excess profits tax based upon a comparison of normal earnings and earnings during an excess profits tax period, the tax shall be determined by using such constructive average base period net income in lieu of the average base period net income otherwise determined under this subchapter. In determining such constructive average base period net income, no regard shall be had to events or conditions affecting the taxpayer, the industry of which it is a member, or taxpayers generally occurring or existing after December 31, 1939, *except that, in the cases described in the last sentence of section 722 (b) (4) and in section 722 (c), regard shall be had to the change in the character of the business under section 722 (b) (4) or the nature of the taxpayer and the character of its business under section 722 (c) to the extent necessary to establish the normal earnings to be used as the constructive average base period net income.*

Committee Reports

Report—Ways and Means Committee (77th Cong., 2d Sess., H. Rept. 2333).— Section 213[1] of the bill amends the relief provisions of existing law, section 722, broadening its application to cases which do not fall within the specific provisions of existing law, thereby removing certain inequities and alleviating hardships for which relief cannot be obtained at the present time.

The need for this legislation was recognized when the excess-profits tax was enacted in 1940, and in the excess-profits-tax amendments of 1941, as pointed out in the committee reports on those acts. (H. Rept. No. 146, S. Rept. No. 75, on H. R. 3531, 77th Cong., 1st sess.)

It was there stated that equitable considerations demand that every reasonable precaution should be taken to prevent unfair application of the excess-profits tax in abnormal cases; that high rates on excess profits are thoroughly justifiable if the income subject to tax is clearly of the type intended to be reached. The rates now proposed increase the need for expanding the application of the relief section to cases that do not fall under the specific provisions in order to remove inequities and alleviate certain hardships. The amending provisions expanding the operation of the present section 722 are based on experience gained since its enactment and on previous experience with excess-profits taxes in the United States and abroad. Such experience demonstrates that abnormal and unusual cases arise, diverse in character and unforeseeable, for which special legislation is necessary if the purpose of the law is to be carried out.

Taxpayers may obtain relief by meeting one of the specific tests contained in section 722, but the inability to meet the specific tests will not necessarily exclude the taxpayer from the benefits of the section if it can satisfy the Commissioner or the Relief Court that its claim is consistent with the principles underlying the specific tests. If these are met, the tax will be determined on the basis of a constructive base period net income in lieu of the average base period net income determined under the specific provisions of subchapter E. In general, it will be necessary that the taxpayer establish:

1. That the tax computed under the specific provisions of subchapter E results in an excessive and discriminatory tax.

2. What would be a fair and just amount representing normal earnings to be used as a constructive base period net income for an excess-profits tax based upon a comparison of normal earnings and earnings during an excess-profits tax period.

In determining the constructive average base period net income there may not be taken into consideration any event or condition affecting the taxpayer, or the industry of which it is a member, or tax-

payers generally, if the event or condition occurred or existed after December 31, 1939, the end of the base period. (p. 21)

[1] Sec. 222 of the Act.

In the light of the greatly increased excess-profits tax rate, it is believed desirable to afford relief in meritorious cases to corporations which bear an excessive tax burden because of an abnormally low excess profits credit. Therefore section 722 which currently extends relief only in a limited class of cases is revised and broadened so as to remove existing inequities and to alleviate hardship in cases where relief cannot now be obtained. Under this revision, corporations satisfactorily establishing eligibility for relief will have their excess profits tax recomputed on the basis of the excess profits credit based on income. This credit will be predicated upon an amount which is a fair and just reflection of the normal earning capacity of the business and which it is entitled to retain before the imposition of an excess profits tax. Such amount will be used as a constructive average base period net income, replacing the actual average base period net income in the recomputation of the tax under this section. In the case of eligible taxpayers not now entitled to use the excess profits credit based on income, provision is made for the use of such credit computed upon the constructive average base period net income. In order to eliminate consideration of the effects of the war, it is provided that, in determining the constructive average base period net income, no regard shall be had to events or conditions affecting the taxpayer, an industry of which it is a member, or taxpayers generally, occurring or existing after December 31, 1939. Thus high war prices, swollen demand, and other factors which would not be normal prior to the imposition of the excess profits tax shall be eliminated in the computation of the normal or average earning capacity of the taxpayer.

Relief under section 722 is available to two classes of corporations. First, to those entitled to use the excess-profits credit based on income under section 713 if such credit does not represent normal earnings because, for certain reasons, the level of business during the base period was unusually low. If the aver-

age base period net income of a corporation is computed under Supplement A
such corporation shall be treated as if the
business of any person, for the period for
which the income of such person is included in the computation of the average
base period net income of the corporation, were a part of the business of the
corporation. Second, to those corporations not entitled to use the excess profits
credit based on income if the invested
capital credit of such corporations is abnormally low. (p. 142)

**Report—Senate Finance Committee
(77th Cong., 2d Sess., S. Rept. 1631).—**
Substantially the same as p. 142 of the
Ways and Means Committee Report.
In addition, there is the following:

Your committee has provided, however, that in those cases described in the
last sentence of section 722 (b) (4), relating to taxpayers the change in the
character of the business of which accrued after December 31, 1939, and in
section 722 (c), relating to taxpayers
which came into existence after December 31, 1939, regard shall be had to the
change in the character of the business
under section 722 (b) (4) or the nature of
the taxpayer and the character of its
business under section 722 (c) to the
extent necessary to establish the normal
earnings to be used as the constructive
average base period net income. (p. 198)

Your committee has adopted the provisions of the House bill relating to general relief for excess-profits tax purposes
with certain modifications. It is recognized that specific legislation cannot take
care of all of the harsh cases which may
arise under a high excess-profits tax and
that legislation of a general nature is
necessary to provide relief for many unforeseen hardships which may arise under the excess-profits tax law.

Under the House bill, taxpayers who
are entitled to use the average-earnings
basis are permitted to have their base
period earnings reconstructed in cases
of abnormalities or hardships. In order
to secure the benefit of this provision,
taxpayers must meet certain specific
tests to establish that their actual earnings during the base period are abnormal.
This relief is granted to all taxpayers in
existence during the base period, even
though they computed their excess
profits on the invested-capital basis.

Taxpayers who did not come into existence until after the base period, are permitted to have their income constructed
for the base period on a basis comparable
with other taxpayers similarly situated.

To come within the general relief provisions, the taxpayer, in existence during
the base period, must show that the excess profits tax (computed without the
benefit of this section) was excessive and
discriminatory and that the average base
period net income was not a fair measure
of normal earnings. (p. 35-36)

Your committee has made the following changes in the House bill:

 *   *   *

4. Under the House bill, it was provided that in determining the constructive average base-period net income of
the taxpayer no regard shall be had to
events or conditions affecting the taxpayer, the industry of which it is a member, or taxpayers generally, occurring
or existing after December 31, 1939.
There was some doubt as to whether or
not this provision limits other provisions
of this section. Your committee has
amended this provision to make it clear
that it does not preclude an examination
of a taxpayer coming into existence after
December 31, 1939, or of a taxpayer, the
changes in the character of the business
of which properly matured after such
date. (p. 36, 37)

**Report—Conference Committee (77th
Cong., 2d Sess., H. Rept. 2586).—**
Section 213 of the House bill revises and
broadens section 722 of the Code, relating to adjustments in the base period
net income of corporations, to remove
existing inequities and to alleviate hardship in cases where relief cannot now
be obtained. The Senate amendments
clarify the changes made by the House
bill, broaden the relief granted in certain
respects, and alter the administration of
the relief provisions.

In those cases described in the last
sentence of section 722 (b) (4) (relating
to taxpayers the change in the character
of the business of which accrued after
December 31, 1939) and in section 722
(c) (relating to taxpayers which came
into existence after December 31, 1939)
regard shall be had, under the amendments of the Senate, to such changes to
the extent necessary to establish the
normal earnings to be used as the con-

structure average base period net income, despite the general rule that events occurring after December 31, 1939, are to be disregarded. (p. 61-62)

Congressional Discussion

Discussion—House (Cong. Rec. Vol. 88).—MR. DOUGHTON. * * * In previous legislation regarding excess-profits taxes, we have endeavored to allow for hardship cases by a series of specific relief provisions. These provisions have been found inadequate to take care of the many inequities which arise, most of which are unforeseeable. The bill contains a general relief provision to relieve cases of real hardship.

In other words, it is impossible to pass a law and formulate rates and excess-profits-tax provisions that will apply equitably in every case; so we placed in the bill some relief or general provision that will take care of special hardship cases. It is not fair, and it is not in the best interests of the country, to crucify legitimate corporations, so we have endeavored to write a general relief provision broad enough in scope to allow equitable treatment in unusual cases. (p. 6263)

Discussion—Senate (Cong. Rec. Vol. 88).—MR. GEORGE. * * * Our committee gave considerable attention to the general relief provisions in connection with the excess-profits tax. With a rate as high as 90 percent, it is necessary that care be taken to prevent unforeseen hardships. The House provision on general relief was very broad and goes a long way toward accomplishing this objec-

tive. However, your committee made certain changes which it is believed will considerably improve the situation. In the first place, the general relief provision is made retroactive so as to apply to the taxable years 1940 and 1941. The committee has also made it clear that once the taxpayer's credit has been determined under the relief provision such credit may be used for all future years.

* * *

Under the House bill there was a provision that in determining the constructive average base period net income of the taxpayer no regard should be had to events or conditions affecting the taxpayer, the industry of which it is a member or taxpayer generally, occurring or existing after December 31, 1939.

Your committee has amended this provision so as to make it clear that it does not preclude an examination of a taxpayer coming into existence after December 31, 1939, or of a taxpayer the changes in the character of the business of which properly matured after such date. (p. 7795-96)

Discussion—Senate; on Report of Conference Committee (Cong. Rec. Vol. 88).—MR. GEORGE. * * * The Senate relief provisions further broadening the splendid work of the House on section 722 were agreed to. (p. 8410)

Committee Hearings

Hearings—Ways and Means Committee.—Need for broad relief provisions. (R. Paul—Treas. Dept.—p. 82-83, 109; M. L. Seidman, p. 136; R. N. Miller, p. 180, 187-191; P. D. Seghers, p. 1961-62; E. C. Alvord, p. 2779-82)

Measuring relief by reference to competitors' figures. (L. C. Ward, p. 288-293)

Allowing special relief for canning industry. (H. P. Taylor, p. 652-663; W. B. Stokely, Jr., p. 663-682)

Restoring provisions of 1918 Act. (J. G. Jackson, p. 1316; H. Satterlee, p. 2264-65)

Hearings—Senate Finance Committee.—Restoring provisions of 1918 or

1940 Acts. (R. N. Miller, p. 516-520, 522-525; E. C. Alvord, p. 640-641, 683-687; A. B. Chapman, p. 754, 765-766; H. B. Fernald, p. 885)

Allowing special relief for canning industry. (W. B. Stokely, Jr., p. 1443-58)

Hearings—Joint Committee on Internal Revenue Taxation (Feb.-May 1946).—Administrative problems. (J. D. Nunan, Jr.—Comm'r. of Int. Rev.—p. 2-14, 24-30, 46-65, 396-397, 398-399, 450-456)

Difficulties in determining normal earnings. (J. D. Nunan, Jr.—Comm'r. of Int. Rev.—p. 14-16; E. H. McDermott, p. 235)

Difficulties where corporation has diversity of products. (J. D. Nunan, Jr.,—Comm'r. of Int. Rev.—p. 23-24)

Criticism of administration. (P. W. Phillips, p. 66-72, 73-75, 76-79, 80-82; S. B. Gambill, p. 82-91, 93-98; E. A. Converse, Jr., p. 98-102; E. C. Alvord, p. 102-108, 124-125, 133-135; T. Tarleau, p. 146-155; M. Austin, p. 156-159, 162-167; P. D. Seghers, p. 173-175; J. B. Weed, p. 178-179, 184-185; G. S. Eaton, p. 185-190, 193-201; H. Satterlee, p. 204, 206-208; C. M. Edelmann, p. 226; E. H. McDermott, p. 232-234, 239-243; K. W. Gemmill, p. 244-250; H. P. Cochran, p. 250-252; D. W. Huber, p. 253-255; K. S. Wherry, p. 257-259; D. F. Cole, p. 259-266; W. Rogers, p. 266-268; E. McFarland, p. 271-274, 275-276; G. Farr, p. 291-293; R. B. Barker, p. 295-306; J. Carlson, p. 306-310; J. V. Lynskey, p. 317-319; C. N. Goodwin, p. 338-341; W. H. Harrison, p. 342-350; E. Groseclose, p. 357-358; G. M. Brush, p. 359-360; T. N. Beckman, p. 364-367; M. B. Angell, p. 367-371; A. H. Paul, p. 388; L. E. Manuel, p. 392-393; F. P. Battle, p. 393-394)

Problems in determining relationship between secs. 713 (e) and 722. (E. C. Alvord, p. 109-110)

Problems in determining relationship between secs. 713 (f) and 722. (E. C. Alvord, p. 110; M. Austin, p. 161-162;

J. B. Weed, p. 183-184; H. Satterlee, p. 203; G. Rogers, p. 286)

Problems in determining abnormal deductions to be eliminated in reconstruction of base period earnings. (E. C. Alvord, p. 110-112)

Objections to eliminating abnormally high income during base period. (E. C. Alvord, p. 116-117)

Giving effect to post 1939 experience. (E. C. Alvord, p. 117-118, 140; M. Austin, p. 159-160, 168-169; J. B. Weed, p. 181-182; H. Satterlee, p. 202-203, 205; G. Simons, p. 208-209, 211-215; G. Rogers, p. 280-285; J. V. Lynskey, p. 319-320; E. Groseclose, p. 357; C. E. Miller, p. 362-364; C. W. Johnson, p. 380-382; A. H. Paul, p. 385-387)

Defining normal earnings. (M. Austin, p. 160-161)

Modifying requirement that taxpayer "establish" basis for relief. (R. Leigh, p. 277-280; G. Rogers, p. 285-286; G. Farr, p. 293; R. Magill, p. 376; T. B. Benson, p. 382-383; J. D. Nunan, Jr.—Comm'r. of Int. Rev.—p. 397)

Restoring provisions of 1918 Act. (R. J. Welti, p. 288)

Applying to base period any reduced depreciation rate of war years. (J. Carlson, p. 314-315)

Applying broader concept of normal earnings. (J. V. Lynskey, p. 321-326, 327-333; J. E. Brown, p. 374-375)

1943 Act

Hearings—Ways and Means Committee.—Need for broad relief provisions. (B. Botwinick, p. 431-435)

Not confining relief to events occurring prior to 1940. (E. C. Alvord, p. 685; Controllers Institute of America, p. 1333)

Using percentages of cost of goods sold as basis for computing relief. (N. W. Hagelberg, p. 1576-77)

Hearings—Senate Finance Committee.—Not confining relief to events occurring prior to 1940. (E. C. Alvord, p. 615; A. B. Chapman, p. 831-832)

Need for special relief for public utility industry. (W. J. McCoy, p. 704-707)

Need for broad relief provisions. (A. B. Chapman, p. 833-839)

1941 Act

Hearings—Ways and Means Committee.—Restoring provisions of 1918 or 1940 acts. (R. N. Miller, p. 461-466, 473-474; G. M. Morris, p. 468-471; Controllers Institute of America, p. 1718; F. A. Godchaux, Jr., p. 1749-52)

Allowing relief for new types of business in current year. (A. C. Nielsen, p. 1227-32)

Allowing relief for new business. (C. N. Monson, p. 1304-12)

Hearings—Senate Finance Committee.—Explanation of provision. (J. O'Brien—H. Legis. Counsel—p. 108)

Need for broad relief provisions. (W. Citron, p. 155-157; C. M. Tower, p. 157-159; R. N. Miller, p. 352-357, 358-361; J. W. Brooks, p. 425-428; P. D. Seghers,

p. 695-696; L. A. Tanzer, p. 702; A. Hardgrave, p. 949-961; L. H. Parker, p. 1470; E. C. Alvord, p. 1780-81, 1790, 1798; L. J. McWain, p. 1982-85; J. C. Cowdin, p. 2062; J. J. Forstall, p. 2231)

Allowing relief through increased credit measured by increased sales. (C. F. Hotchkiss, Jr., p. 429-443; K. T. Norris, p. 1010-17; W. M. Ringer, p. 1570-73)

Not confining relief to events occurring prior to 1940. (H. B. Fernald, p. 979; W. M. Ringer, p. 1569; E. C. Alvord, p. 1798-99; A. B. Chapman, p. 2079-80, 2086-87)

Allowing special relief for canning industry. (T. C. Hayes, p. 1017-20)

Applying relief by reference to normal earnings, not necessary those of base period. (C. W. Lewis, p. 2224-28)

EPTA
6

SEC. 722. ADJUSTMENT OF ABNORMAL BASE PERIOD NET INCOME.

. **(a) General Rule.**—In the case of a taxpayer whose first taxable year under this subchapter begins in 1940, if the taxpayer establishes—

(1) that the character of the business engaged in by the taxpayer as of January 1, 1940, is different from the character of the business engaged in during one or more of the taxable years in its base period (as defined in section 713 (b) (1)); or

(2) that in one or more of the taxable years in such base period normal production, output, or operation was interrupted or diminished because of the occurrence of events abnormal in the case of such taxpayer; and

(3) the amount that would have been its average base period net income—

(A) if the character of the business as of January 1, 1940, had been the same during each of the taxable years of such base period; and

(B) if none of the abnormal events referred to in paragraph (2) had occurred; and

(C) if in each of such taxable years none of the items of gross income had been abnormally large, and none of the items of deductions had been abnormally small; and

(4) that the amount established under paragraph (3) is greater than the average base period net income computed under section 713 (d) or section 742, as the case may be, then the amount established under paragraph (3) shall be considered as the average base period net income of the taxpayer for the purposes of this subchapter.

Committee Reports

Report—Ways and Means Committee (77th Cong., 1st Sess., H. Rept. 146).—The bill affords relief in the following situations:

* * *

5. Since the average earnings credit is based upon the amount of the taxpayer's average income during the base period, the happening of some unusual event during this period may create a grave hardship on the taxpayer. For example, the taxpayer's plant may be destroyed by fire or windstorm or its operations for any year greatly impeded by flood, strikes, or other events hampering production and greatly curtailing income for a given period. The bill would attribute to the taxpayer in such an event the earnings which it would normally have experienced had such event not occurred. Likewise, if the taxpayer can establish that the char-

acter of its business as of January 1, 1940, is different from the character of the business engaged in during one or more taxable years of the base period, the taxpayer is permitted to establish what its average base period net income would have been if the character of the business had been the same during each of the taxable years of such base period. The differences which constitute a change in the character of the business are set forth in the bill.

This general relief provision is felt by your committee to be necessary in order to protect the unanticipated cases not covered by the specific relief provisions covered by existing law and the other provisions of this bill. To be effective, the provision must be elastic and as flexible as administrative demands will allow.

Proper safeguards, however, are taken to prevent abuse. For example, the burden is upon the taxpayer to establish the abnormality of its experience during the base period. (p. 2, 3)

Your committee feel that so safeguarded and restricted this relief provision, though broad and general in nature, will satisfactorily alleviate hardships due to abnormal conditions in the base period, and at the same time prevent abuses. (p. 4)

Section 722 of the bill is designed to afford relief in the case of certain situations not covered by other sections of the bill. The relief is confined to the adjustment of the abnormal base period net income of a taxpayer electing the average earnings credit, and applies only in the case of a taxpayer whose first excess-profits tax taxable year begins in 1940.

In order to obtain any benefit under this section, the taxpayer must meet one of the following tests:

(1) The character of its business as of January 1, 1940, must have been different from the character of the business engaged in during one or more of the taxable years in its base period, or

(2) Normal production, output, or operation in one or more of the taxable years in the base period must have been interrupted or diminished because of events abnormal in the case of the taxpayer. (p. 10)

Having established that the character

of its business as of January 1, 1940, is different from the character of the business engaged in during one or more of the taxable years in its base period, the taxpayer is permitted to establish what its average base period net income would have been if the character of its business had been the same during each of the taxable years of such base period. (p. 11)

Moreover, the taxpayer in constructing its average base period net income would be required to eliminate that part of the items of gross income which were abnormally large or the deductions which were abnormally small. This net income would also have to be constructed as if the base period normal production, output, or operation had not been interrupted or diminished because of the occurrence of events abnormal in the case of such taxpayer. Such abnormal events might include a flood, a strike, or other events hampering production, output, or operation.

The amount of the average base period net income so established, if it is greater than its actual average base period net income, will be considered its average base period net income for the purposes of its excess-profits credit. (p. 11)

A taxpayer may secure relief under this section if its normal production, output, or operation was interrupted or diminished because of events abnormal in the case of the taxpayer. As in the case of taxpayers under the first category, high prices of materials, labor, capital, or any other agent of production, low selling price of the product of the taxpayer, or low physical volume of sales owing to low demand for such product or for the output of the taxpayer are not considered as abnormal. A common example of such an abnormality is where the business of the taxpayer has been interrupted or diminished due to a fire, flood, or strike. For example, if fire in 1935 had destroyed a taxpayer's plant so that the taxpayer's normal production in 1936 was diminished, the taxpayer would be permitted to establish what its normal income would have been if normal production had existed in 1936. (p. 12)

Report—Senate Finance Committee (77th Cong., 1st Sess., S. Rept. 75).— Same as Ways and Means Committee Report, except that the first sentence of the second paragraph under number 5 reads as follows:

This general relief provision is felt by your committee to be necessary in order to protect the unanticipated cases not covered by the specific relief provisions of existing law and the other provisions of this bill. To be effective, the provision must be elastic and as flexible as administrative demands will allow. (p. 3-4, 4, 10-11, 11, 12, respectively)

Congressional Discussion

Discussion—House (Cong. Rec. Vol. 87).—MR. COOPER. * * * Section 6 of this bill includes the new section 722 of the Internal Revenue Code, which is the general relief provision. First, it is provided that where a corporation is in a new type of business; second, where it is in the same type of business but has experienced very low income during the base period because of some unusual cause or some extraordinary event, such as a flood or something of that sort. It also must meet two further tests.

* * *

MR. DISNEY. I was going to ask a question in connection with the explanation. Would the gentleman consider that Government action would be a change in business or action by the Government in the changing of contracts?

MR. COOPER. It might well be; but it all depends upon the circumstances. (p. 1380)

Discussion—Senate (Cong. Rec. Vol. 87).—MR. HARRISON. * * * Section 6 of the bill permits a taxpayer whose first excess-profits tax begins in 1940, substantial relief.

If such a taxpayer can establish that the character of the business as of January 1, 1940, is different from the character of the business engaged in in one or more taxable years of the base period, the taxpayer is permitted to establish what if its average base period would have been if during the base period the character of its business had been the same as of January 1, 1940. The differences which constitute the character of the business are set out in the statute. This section also gives relief where the happening of some unusual event may create a grave hardship to the taxpayer. An ordinary example is where the business of the taxpayer has been interrupted or diminished due to a fire, flood, or strike. For example, if a fire in 1935 had destroyed a plant, so that the taxpayer's normal production in 1936 was diminished, the taxpayer would be permitted to establish what its normal production would have been if the fire had not occurred. The taxpayer in such cases is entitled to have its case reviewed by the Board of Tax Appeals. (p. 1638)

MR. VANDENBERG. * * * But I wish to point out that we are eliminating the general relief clause from the law by these amendments. I am making this statement particularly in response to an inquiry submitted to me by the able Senator from Vermont [MR. AUSTIN] who presents a telegram which he has received pointing out that there still remains certain abnormalities which are not reached by the pending corrections. The constituent of the Senator from Vermont asks that the general basket clause, the general relief clause, in the old law, section 722, should be retained in its original form. I point out that it is not retained in its original form. It is not retained at all. The general-relief section is eliminated, but it is pleaded in behalf of the elimination that the general section never did really promise any specific relief, but was much more a matter of pretense rather than a matter of substance. It is argued that this clause was so general that it really promised no relief at all, and that the limited specific relief, though admittedly inadequate, contained in the pending bill really represents a net advance.

Mr. President, I think it is true that the amendments upon which we are now about to vote do make specific progress in the direction of certain corrections of hardship cases, but I think it should be made very plain that they do not go the whole way by any manner of means. It still leaves many other abnormalities which need correction. They should be corrected as soon as possible. Taxpayers should not be left at the mercy of any of these miserably unfair levies. (p. 1639)

Committee Hearings
1941 Act

Hearings—Ways and Means Committee.—Allowing relief for new types of business in current year. (A. C. Nielsen, p. 1227-32)

Hearings—Senate Finance Committee.—Treating increase in expense because of abnormal event as basis for relief. (R. V. Fletcher, p. 271-272)

[SEC. 722. ADJUSTMENT OF ABNORMAL BASE PERIOD NET INCOME.]   EPTA
6

(b) **Rules for Application of Subsection (a).**—For the purposes of subsection (a)—

(1) High prices of materials, labor, capital, or any other agent of production, low selling price of the product of the taxpayer, or low physical volume of sales owing to low demand for such product or for the output of the taxpayer, shall not be considered as abnormal.

Committee Reports

Report—Ways and Means Committee (77th Cong., 1st Sess., H. Rept. 146).—In addition, relief is not granted in situations brought on by (a) high prices of material, labor, capital, or any other agent of production, (b) low selling price of the product of the taxpayer, or (c) low physical volume of sales due to low demand for the taxpayer's product. (p. 3)

In constructing its average base period net income, high prices of materials, labor, capital, or any other agent of production, low selling price of the product a low physical volume of sales owing to low demand for such product, or for the output of the taxpayer during the base period would not be considered as making the net income abnormal. (p. 11)

Report—Senate Finance Committee (77th Cong., 1st Sess., S. Rept. 75).—Same as Ways and Means Committee Report. (p. 4, 11-12, respectively)

[SEC. 722. ADJUSTMENT OF ABNORMAL BASE PERIOD NET INCOME.]   EPTA
6

[(b) **Rules for Application of Subsection (a).**—For the purposes of subsection (a)—]

(4) If subsection (a) (1), or both subsections (a) (1) and (a) (2) are applicable to any taxpayer, its average base period net income under subsection (a) (3) shall not exceed the excess profits net income (as computed for the purposes of subsection (a) (3)) for the last taxable year in such base period. * * *

Committee Reports

Report—Ways and Means Committee (77th Cong., 1st Sess., H. Rept. 146).—In no case, may the taxpayer's average base period net income, as established, exceed the excess-profits net income established for the last taxable year in such period. (p. 11)

This relief will, however, be limited to the amount of its excess-profits net income established for the last year of its base period. Thus, if the corporation was able to establish that if the rival newspaper had been acquired as of April 1, 1939, it would have earned for the full fiscal year 1940 an amount which would make its excess-profits net income for that year $300,000, this would be the highest amount it could substitute for its average base period net income. (p. 12)

A taxpayer with both a change in the character of business and an occurrence of an abnormal event interrupting its normal production, output, or operation in the base period is subject to the limitation that its average base period net income under this section cannot exceed the excess-profits net income established for the last taxable year of such base

period. (p. 12)

Report—Senate Finance Committee (77th Cong., 1st Sess., S. Rept. 75).— Same as Ways and Means Committee Report. (p. 12, 12, 13, respectively)

Committee Hearings

Hearings—Senate Finance Committee.—Explanation and shortcomings of

provision. (L. J. Hoban, p. 968-972, 976)

[1] SEC. 722. ADJUSTMENT OF ABNORMALITIES IN INCOME AND CAPITAL BY THE COMMISSIONER.

[*The Commissioner shall also have authority to make any adjustments which abnormally affect income or capital, and his decision shall be subject to review by the United States Board of Tax Appeals.*] FOR THE PURPOSES OF THIS SUBCHAPTER, THE COMMISSIONER SHALL ALSO HAVE AUTHORITY TO MAKE SUCH ADJUSTMENTS AS MAY BE NECESSARY TO ADJUST ABNORMALITIES AFFECTING INCOME OR CAPITAL, AND HIS DECISION SHALL BE SUBJECT TO REVIEW BY THE UNITED STATES BOARD OF TAX APPEALS.

[1] The heading is as worded by the Conference Committee. The Senate heading read "Review By United States Board Of Tax Appeals."

Committee Reports

Report—Ways and Means Subcommittee (76th Cong., 3d Sess., H. Rept. Aug. 8, 1940).—Your subcommittee believes that the need for special assessment under the plan formulated by it is much less than it was under the excess-profits tax legislation of the World War period. This is due to the following reasons:

(1) Allowing corporations to compute their excess-profits tax on the basis of the excess of their income for the taxable year over the income of a base period.

(2) The inclusion in invested capital of borrowed capital to a considerable extent.

(3) The omission of any percentage limitation upon the value of intangible property paid in for stock that may be included in invested capital.

(4) The elimination of gains or losses from the sale or exchange of assets (depreciable or nondepreciable) held over 18 months.

(5) The fixing of a minimum credit of 6 percent on the first $500,000 of invested capital, plus 4 percent of the remainder of the invested capital.

(6) Allowing new capital a return (free of excess-profits tax) of 10 percent up to a total of $500,000 invested capital and 8 percent on the balance, and recognizing that the capital of corporations coming into existence after December 31, 1939, is new capital.

(7) Allowing corporations which were in existence during only part of the base period, an invested capital for such part of the period they were not in existence, consisting of the invested capital as of the beginning of the taxable year 1940 upon which they are deemed to have earned 10 percent on the first $500,000 and 8 percent on the balance. (p. 8-9)

Report—Conference Committee (76th Cong., 3d Sess., H. Rept. 3002).—Section 721½ of the Senate amendment provides that the Commissioner shall have authority to make any adjustments which abnormally affect income or capital, and that his decision shall be subject to review by the Board of Tax Appeals.

Conference agreement.—Under the conference agreement section 721½ is renumbered section 722 and given the heading "Adjustment of Abnormalities of Income and Capital." It grants the Commissioner authority to adjust any items which abnormally affect income or capital, and provides that the Commissioner's decision shall be subject to review by the Board of Tax Appeals. It is understood that the Treasury and members of the staff of the Joint Committee on Internal Revenue Taxation will give further study to the entire problem covered by this section and will report to the appropriate committees on the subject as soon as possible. (p. 52)

Congressional Discussion

Discussion—Senate (Cong. Rec. Vol. 86).—MR. ADAMS. There can be no effective appeal from a discretionary action. If it is discretionary with the Commissioner to determine how much shall be attributed to previous years, an appeal may not be taken to the Board of Appeals on a question of discretion. (p. 12176)

MR. GEORGE. Mr. President, I will say in connection with this amendment what I said with respect to the other one. It is intended to supplement the relief provisions of section 721. * * *

MR. LA FOLLETTE. Mr. President, I understand the purpose of the Senator's amendment and his desire to have it in conference, but it seems to me that having provided a carry-over provision for the mining companies and canners, taken together with the relief section which is already in the bill this amendment would only have the result of making the excess-profits tax which is proposed to be levied by this bill less likely to yield revenue. (p. 12185)

Discussion—Senate; on Report of Conference Committee (Cong. Rec. Vol. 86).—MR. BROWN. Mr. President, I was interested, as the Senator recalls, in the consideration of the record with respect to development of a process, patents, and so forth, of the predecessor corporation, or copartnership, or other form of business organization, of a taxpayer in figuring the excess-profits tax. I understand that while the provision I introduced in the Senate was stricken out of section 721, section 722 was added, which reads as follows:

For the purposes of this subchapter, the Commissioner shall also have authority to make such adjustments as may be necessary to adjust abnormalities affecting income or capital—

With the right of appeal to the United States Board of Tax Appeals. Under that section, does the Senator think the relief could be given to corporations which had been formed out of prior corporations or partnerships substantially similar in ownership, as is given to a taxpayer who had no change in its corporate organization?

MR. HARRISON. If, as the result of such a situation, there developed an abnormality of income, it is entirely possible that section 722 would afford relief.

MR. BROWN. May I ask if section 722 is taken from the Excess-Profits Tax Act of 1918? Is it substantially the same provision that is in that act?

MR. HARRISON. No; it is substantially the provision of the Senate bill. I may say, in that respect, that in my opinion the general-relief provision is one of the most important features in this bill. Indeed, I would have liked to have seen it perfected; but the Senator will recall that when the relief provision was recommended by the Senate Finance Committee, some doubt was expressed by the drafting experts and the Treasury Department representatives as to whether or not they could draft it in perfect form, and so forth. We gave them the time to do it in the way that they insisted it be done, and brought in a draft dealing only with abnormalities in income for the taxable year. This was subject to some criticism, and on the floor the Senator from Georgia [Mr. GEORGE] offered another provision giving the Commissioner general authority to make adjustments where abnormalities existed in income or capital and giving the Board of Tax Appeals the right to review the decision of the Commissioner.

One of the hardest fights made in the conference was the attempt of the Senate conferees to get this Senate amendment or the substitute offered by the Senator from Georgia [Mr. GEORGE] adopted. The Senate amendment, with slight modifications, was finally adopted and the Treasury and the staff of the Joint Committee on Internal Revenue Taxation were instructed by the conference to study the entire problem covered by this section, and report to the appropriate committees on the subject as soon as possible.

MR. BROWN. Mr. President, the idea is that the report will be made soon enough so that the Congress may legislate upon that subject, with effect upon the tax returns for the calendar year 1940?

MR. HARRISON. The Senator is correct.

MR. BROWN. And the Senator feels that section 722, on page 14 of the bill, which is a very general relief section, may be used for the purpose of assisting corporations which have been formed out of other corporations, partnerships, or individuals with substantially the same ownership?

MR. HARRISON. The Senator is correct. Of course, the Senator is aware of the fact that the whole Finance Committee was insistent that something like the 1918 law, with some discretion vested in the Commissioner or the Board of Tax Appeals, should be written into the law.

MR. BROWN. The Senator will recall that the Finance Committee unanimously approved the general proposition that the development period and earnings, or lack of earnings, of predecessor corporations, predecessor partnerships, and predecessor individuals should be considered in the calculation of the excess-profits tax base.

MR. HARRISON. The Senator is correct. I merely wish to say that we did our best to hold that provision, so that there would be no question about the matter. (p. 12918–919)

MR. GEORGE. * * * There is one other feature of the bill to which I wish to refer. On the floor, in addition to the specific provisions for relief made in extreme hardship cases in section 721, I offered an amendment known as section 721½. That amendment, in substance—and I think as it was intended to mean at the time—is contained in the bill as section 722. Broadly, it gives authority to the Commissioner of Internal Revenue to make adjustments in the case of abnormally affected income or capital and also makes his decision reviewable by the Board of Tax Appeals. Not only, Mr. President, is that in the bill, but it is in

the bill with my express concurrence; but coupled with the statement that at the very first opportunity, on bills that must be favorably considered by the House and Senate, I propose to offer and carry through, if it is humanly possible, additional provisions to make effective, and provide the method of procedure by which it can be made effective, this broad provision in this bill, because in no other way can exceptional hardship cases be saved under this particular bill. (p. 12923)

MR. BROWN. On page 51 of the report, under the subsection in regard to the predecessor-corporation proposition, in which I have taken a good deal of interest, appears this statement:

Income resulting from activities of such a character carried on by a predecessor corporation is not entitled to the treatment provided in section 721.

Then following section 721 in the conference report—the bill as it is about to pass—is section 722, which, I understand, is the section which the Senator from Georgia drafted and which reads:

For the purposes of this subchapter the Commissioner shall also have authority to make such adjustments as may be necessary—

To take care of these abnormalities. Would the relief provided for in section 722, in his opinion, be open to a taxpayer whose predecessor, substantially identical in ownership, was the business organization that had developed the patent or process which resulted in the profit for the taxable year? I ask this in view of the fact that such relief is denied under section 721; could it be granted under section 722?

MR. GEORGE. I do not think it would specifically come within section 722, except under these circumstances: If the failure to permit the history of the predecessor to be considered resulted in an abnormality either in capital investment or in income, then that abnormality, if it resulted in exceptional hardship, would clearly come within the spirit of the section.

MR. BROWN. I am satisfied with that answer, because, as I understand, relief is not given in any case unless there is an abnormality.

MR. GEORGE. That is true.

MR. BROWN. If the abnormality existed because of the predecessor-corporation situation, it seems to me a fair interpretation of section 722 is that relief could be granted.

MR. GEORGE. I believe it should and could be, if the failure to consider the history of the predecessor had brought about circumstances and conditions which resulted in an abnormality in investment or in income for the taxable year.

MR. BROWN. I agree with the Senator. May I ask him if that opinion is concurred in by Mr. Stam, counsel for the joint committee who aided in drafting this section?

MR. GEORGE. I should think Mr. Stam would concur in that opinion, and my recollection of some discussion of it leads me to that belief. Of course, I would not speak for him otherwise.

MR. BROWN. My understanding was that he did agree.

MR. GEORGE. I think he did.

MR. KING. Mr. President, I am very

glad the Senator from Michigan brought to the attention of the Senate the matter now under discussion.

I share the views expressed by my colleague the Senator from Georgia [Mr. GEORGE]. If there should be any dubiety upon the part of the representatives of the Treasury in the interpretation of the provision, I am sure the statements made by conferees as to their interpretation would be considered as part of the res gestae, and would influence the representatives of the Treasury in arriving at an interpretation of the provision; and that is one reason why, among others, I finally yielded instead of contending to the end for the amendment offered by the Senator from Georgia. It was a just and fair amendment, and ought to have been adopted, but with the provisions now in the bill, together with the statement just made, I think the Treasury Department will place upon the provision referred to the interpretation which has just been indicated.   (p. 12923-924)

1945 Act

Discussion—Senate; on Report of Conference Committee (Cong. Rec. Vol. 91).—MR. WHERRY. * * * If they are to be denied the relief—and they are, if we adopt this report—then there is one more thing I would suggest to the Senator from Georgia, namely, that he proceed with the joint hearings to be held on section 722, because in my section of the country, where the period following the drought was fixed as the base, there has been an inequitable tax exemption. I wish to point out to the distinguished chairman of the Committee on Finance that more than 30,000 appeals which have been filed have not been passed on in Washington. Our constituents are still anxiously waiting to see what is to happen by way of a decision on those cases. In my State by taking the years 1936 to 1939, following the drought, the Government has established a period that is not equitable in arriving at excess profits, and I sincerely trust that the distinguished chairman of the Committee on Finance will hold hearings and, if it can be done, afford the relief our people must have. Let us go back and establish a fair base period for the drought States so they may be given the relief to which I think they are entitled.

MR. GEORGE. Mr. President, I can assure the Senator that that question will be looked into. The Senator is quite right in saying that section 722, the general relief provision against the hardships of the excess-profits tax, has not been administered. Whose fault it is is precisely what the committee wishes to find out. It wishes to know why that section cannot be administered. Although the excess-profits tax is repealed for the future, that is beginning with the next year, the point raised by the Senator is of extreme importance to small corporations and other corporations whatever size they may be, suffering severe hardships because they still have unclosed certainly their taxes for 1945, perhaps for 1944, many of them for 1943. If section 722 can be administered as the Finance Committee intended it to be administered, and hoped it would be administered when it was placed in the law, very great relief would come to the excess-profits taxpayers, the taxpayers, of course, who would have been benefited by the Vandenberg amendment.

MR. WHERRY. I thank the Senator from Georgia for his statement, because I know that the section of the country we call the drought States will appreciate any relief which can be obtained under a proper and sympathetic interpretation of section 722. It is significant to note that there are 30,000 appeals under that section pending in Washington.

I should like to say further that I have before me a bulletin issued in Washington which said that the district offices would permit the establishment of a satisfactory base period, and advised claimants that they could obtain relief if they would submit their appeals to Washington. After they appealed to Washington last year another bulletin was issued countermanding or contradicting the former bulletin.

So I say once again that if we are not to be given relief from the excess-profits tax retroactively for 1945, I hope that the committee will take action which will permit the claimants from the drought-stricken States to use a base period which is equitable in determining their excess-profits tax for the years following the drought, and that the law will be administered sympathetically. (Daily, p. 10421)

Committee Hearings

Hearings—Ways and Means Committee.—Allowing special relief for new companies. (E. G. Sperry, p. 245-248; W. H. Cooper, p. 318; A. S. Bowes, p. 367-368)

Need for broad special relief provisions. (J. L. Sullivan—Treas. Dept.— p. 95; J. W. Hooper, p. 107; P. E. Shorb, p. 117; A. Lowenhaupt, p. 162; H. B. Fernald, p. 285-286; E. C. Alvord, p. 313; A. B. Chapman, p. 382; E. F. Connely, p. 435)

Hearings—Senate Finance Committee.—Need for broad special relief provisions. (K. Carroad, p. 29-32, 38; W. A. Cooper, p. 45, 58; J. E. McClure, p. 85-86; C. F. Kuehnle, p. 90; J. L. Sullivan—Treas. Dept.—p. 132-133; C. F. Stam—Jt. Com. on Int. Rev. Taxn.— p. 189-190; G. R. Blodgett, p. 229-231; W. B. Stokely, Jr., p. 253-255; H. B. Fernald, p. 285; K. F. Pantzer, p. 293-298; J. Iglauer, p. 331; P. E. Shorb, p. 340-347; J. W. Hooper, p. 348-350, 352; J. D. Battle, p. 370; D. A. Callahan, p.

375; A. B. Chapman, p. 386, 391; C. W. Dudley, p. 402, 405; J. M. Haynes, p. 407-409; J. V. Toner, p. 466-467; G. Rogers, p. 469-471; H. Campbell, p. 488; J. L. Donnelly, p. 494)

Explanation of provision. (J. O'Brien, H. Legis. Counsel, p. 108-109)

Hearings—Joint Committee on Internal Revenue Taxation (Feb.-May 1946).—Difficulties in determining events of unusual and temporary character. (J. D. Nunan, Jr.—Comm'r. of Int. Rev.—p. 16-18; E. H. McDermott, p. 236; C. N. Goodwin, p. 336-337; W. G. Russell, p. 389-390)

Clarifying meaning of "immediately prior to the base period." (E. C. Alvord, p. 120-121, 126-127, 137)

Allowing additional causative factors to be taken into consideration. (E. H. McDermott, p. 243)

Recognizing different effects of drought on agricultural and non-agricultural taxpayers. (J. D. Nunan, Jr.—Comm'r. of Int. Rev.—p. 399-449, 457-458)

1918 ___ 327	[Set forth on page 338]
1918 ___ 328	[Set forth on page 342]
1917 ___ 203(d)	[Set forth on page 351]
1917 ___ 205(a)	[Set forth on page 353]

UNENACTED RELATED PROVISION

1942 Act

[Sec. 213(a) of Ways and Means Committee bill]

These provisions, stricken by the Senate Finance Committee, had to do with limitations on the extent of relief. They provided for minimum and maximum amounts of relief. Applicable legislative history references are:

Report—Ways and Means Committee (77th Cong., 2d Sess., H. Rept. 2333, July 14, 1942, p. 25-26, 148).

Report—Senate Finance Committee (77th Cong., 2d Sess., S. Rept. 1631, Oct. 2, 1942, p. 36-37, 204).

Hearings—Senate Finance Committee (p. 811-816, 1799, 2080).

Sec. 722(b)(1)

[SEC. 722.   GENERAL RELIEF—CONSTRUCTIVE AVERAGE BASE PERIOD   1942
NET INCOME.]   222(a)

(b) **Taxpayers Using Average Earnings Method.**—The tax computed under this subchapter (without the benefit of this section) shall be considered to be excessive and discriminatory in the case of a taxpayer entitled to use the excess profits credit based on income pursuant to section 713, if its average base period net income is an inadequate standard of normal earnings because—

(1) in one or more taxable years in the base period normal production, output, or operation was interrupted or diminished because of the occurrence, either immediately prior to, or during the base period, of events unusual and peculiar in the experience of such taxpayer,

Committee Reports

Report—Ways and Means Committee (77th Cong., 2d Sess., H. Rept. 2333).— If in one or more taxable years in the base period the normal production, or output, or operation was interrupted or diminished because there occurred immediately prior to or during the base period events unusual and peculiar to the experience of the taxpayer it may obtain this relief. An example of such an occurrence would be a fire, a flood, or a strike. If as a result of a fire in 1938 the earnings in 1939 were abnormally low, there might be substituted for 1939 an amount approximating what the volume of business would have been if the fire had not occurred. This relief is similar to the relief granted under section 722 of the present law. (p. 22)

To be eligible for relief, taxpayers which are entitled to use the average-earnings credit under section 713 must establish that the average base period net income is not a fair measure of normal earnings because of one or more of the following reasons:

1. Normal production, output, or operation was interrupted or diminished in one or more of the taxable years in the base period because of events unusual or peculiar in the experience of the taxpayer occurring during or immediately prior to the base period. This is an expression of the same situation for which relief is granted under existing law, and is concerned primarily with physical rather than economic events or circumstances. Fires or floods would be events hinder-

ing the operations of the business. (p. 142-143)

Report—Senate Finance Committee (77th Cong., 2d Sess., S. Rept. 1631).— To be entitled to the benefits of this provision, it must show the following:

(1) Interruption or diminution of production in the base period; (p. 36)

To be eligible for relief, taxpayers which are entitled to use the average earnings credit under section 713 must establish that the average base period net income is not a fair measure of normal earnings because of one or more of the following reasons:

1. Normal production, output, or operation (including, in the case for example of corporations rendering a service such as advertising agencies, the services rendered) was interrupted or diminished in one or more of the taxable years in the base period because of events unusual or peculiar in the experience of the taxpayer occurring during or immediately prior to the base period. This is an expression of the same situation for which relief is granted under existing law, and is concerned primarily with physical rather than economic events or circumstances. Fires or floods would be events hindering the operations of the business. (p. 198)

Congressional Discussion
1945 Act

Discussion—Senate (Cong. Rec. Vol. 91).—Mr. Wherry. * * * When Congress passed the excess-profits-tax law, it was recognized that the two methods adopted for measuring excess profits—the invested capital method and the earnings method—would be very inequitable to many corporate taxpayers. At the time when the law was up for consideration, we folks who lived in Nebraska and in the other neighboring drought States were very much disturbed over the fact that the base years under the earnings method for measuring normal profits were those of the 4-year period 1936-39. Probably not many years in all our history come the farthest from measuring normal profits in our area than these 4 years. We, in our part of the country, knew that the drought had made it impossible for most corporations to make any money at all during these years. It is believed that the large proportions of corporations were actually losing money at this time and the average earnings for Nebraska corporations for 1936-39 is a loss rather than a profit, therefore, under the earnings method, any profit that it made is defined under the excess-profits-tax law "as excess profits."

When corporations in Nebraska are forced to use the invested capital method, they are very badly treated because the average small corporation in Nebraska does not make profit from the capital invested in its business but from the personal ability and efforts of the stockholders and managers. Eight percent of the invested capital of the Nebraska corporation is almost a negligible amount; also for large numbers of corporations in our area. Under the excess-profits-tax law we are bound to use one or two of these methods in measuring normal profits and are assessed the excess-profits-tax rates on all profits earned above these amounts after subtracting the specific exemption. As stated above, those interested in sound taxation, were much opposed to the use of the years 1936-39 as the base years, but when we found that the excess-profits-tax law included section 722, we felt that this provision of the law would result in equitable treatment for the average corporate taxpayer in our area. We were sure that the drought was an event contemplated under section 722 which would permit the average corporate taxpayer in Nebraska to reconstruct his base-year earnings under the law and thus justice would be done in the last analysis.

The excess-profits-tax law left the administration of section 722 to the Treasury Department. A special bulletin has been issued by the Treasury Department instructing revenue agents quite generally to deny all claims for relief due to the drought for all nonfarming taxpayers. This bulletin admits that we had a severe drought but will not admit that the average corporation suffered any because of the drought. The Bureau will grant relief to all farmers who paid an excess-profits tax but I have yet to find a farmer who is incorporated who could have paid an excess-profits tax. Therefore, any relief due to the drought has been for the most part eliminated by the instructions to internal-revenue agents who are administering the law.

The Treasury Department has a definite thumbs-down attitude toward section 722. At the present time there is a campaign on in Nebraska to collect from corporate taxpayers excess profits that have been held back under section 722 and taxpayers are instructed by revenue agents that their cases will have to be taken to The Tax Court if they care to insist upon any relief from these high excess-profits taxes.

I am quite sure that if a study were made, it would be found that corporations in Nebraska and the other drouth States have been paying out a much larger proportion of their income in taxes than corporations doing business in other parts of the country. The reason for this is that in the other parts of the country, earnings during the base years 1936 to 1939 were fair, normal, or above normal, so that corporations doing business in all areas other than the drouth States have favorable base-year earnings and their excess-profits tax payments are greatly reduced thereby.

It is my judgment that section 722 of the Internal Revenue Code provides all the relief that we should expect, provided this law can be administered by someone with a sympathetic point of view. If the average taxpayer could sit across the table from a fair-minded administrator it is probable that relief would be granted to taxpayers if they are rightly entitled to it under section 722.

If we are going to have to look to The Tax Court for relief provided for under section 722, then most of the corporations who now need the relief will be dead and buried before the relief so sorely needed reaches them. In all other tax matters, taxpayers have a right to appeal from the decisions of The Tax Court to the Supreme Court, if that is desired. The Tax Court is the exclusive body for hearing section 722 cases and their decisions are final. It is my opinion that there should be the same privilege of appeal from the decisions of The Tax Court in section 722 cases that exists in all other tax cases.

In all other tax matters the taxpayer has the privilege of paying the tax due and suing for a refund in a local district court. As I understand, there have been more than 30,000 claims for refund filed under section 722, and under the present buck-passing procedure of the Treasury Department most of these cases will have to be tried in The Tax Court. Why not open up the district courts for consideration of these cases? I am sure that a local judge will be much more familiar with the conditions in his own territory than is possible for members of The Tax Court to understand. And there might be better administration if section 722 cases were tried in the local district courts. At least taxpayers ought to have the privilege to try their cases there if they care to. And it would make it possible to speed up the decision of section 722 cases and clear the dockets of The Tax Court, which will be full for many years to come if the present practice of the Bureau of sending everything to The Tax Court is continued.

Several years ago the desirable practice of decentralizing income-tax investigations was instituted by the Internal Revenue Bureau. The local internal-revenue agents are best equipped to examine tax returns and especially section 722 claims. At the outset the local agents settled many section 722 cases, but when the settlements reached the central office in Washington, practically all cases were returned to the field agents with instructions to disallow the claims which they had previously allowed. This very bad administrative practice has worked against the interests of the taxpayers. The result has been that the local field agents have no desire to do anything but reject all section 722 claims. They cannot be criticized from Washington when they disallow a claim as they have been for allowing claims.

It is believed that the settlement of section 722 cases can best be reached in the field. When authority from Washington is adverse to this practice, it makes it almost impossible to administer the section 722 law with speed and equity. There must be sympathetic administration of section 722 if the purposes for which it was intended are to be realized. (Daily, p. 10151-52)

[Set forth on page 146]

Sec. 722(b)(2)

[SEC. 722.   GENERAL RELIEF—CONSTRUCTIVE AVERAGE BASE PERIOD
          NET INCOME.]

[(b)   Taxpayers Using Average Earnings Method.—The tax * * * shall be considered to be excessive * * * if its average base period net income is an inadequate standard of normal earnings because—]

(2) the business of the taxpayer was depressed in the base period because of temporary economic circumstances unusual in the case of such taxpayer or because of the fact that an industry of which such taxpayer was a member was depressed by reason of temporary economic events unusual in the case of such industry,

Committee Reports

Report—Ways and Means Committee (77th Cong., 2d Sess., H. Rept. 2333).— If the business of the taxpayer, or the class of business in which it engaged, was depressed in the base period by reason of temporary economic circumstances unusual in the case of the taxpayer or the class of business in which it is engaged, it is entitled to this relief.   For example, if the business of the taxpayer was supplying a certain manufactured product to a firm in 1936, and in 1937 the second firm decided to manufacture the product for its own use, compelling the taxpayer to obtain other customers which it was successful in doing in 1939, and as a result of these circumstances the taxpayer was depressed for 2 years of its base period, it would be allowed a constructive average base period net income for the depression years. Consideration will be given to business conditions in the depression years for the class of business in which the taxpayer was engaged and the probable earnings of the taxpayer had it not been depressed by reason of losing its principal customer. (p. 22)

To be eligible for relief, taxpayers which are entitled to use the average earnings credit under section 713 must establish that the average base period net income is not a fair measure of normal earnings because of one or more of the following reasons:

*   *   *

2.   The business of the taxpayer was depressed in the base period because of temporary economic conditions peculiar to such taxpayer or because it was a member of an industry which was depressed on account of temporary economic circumstances peculiar to such industry. A declining business or industry which was depressed because of economic conditions of a permanent rather than a temporary nature does not come within this classification. As a general rule, high costs of production because of high costs of material, labor, capital, or other elements, low selling price of the finished product, low volume of sales due to a low demand for such product or the taxpayer's output, or other ordinary economic hazards to which business in general is subject are not sufficient reason to make the taxpayer eligible under this paragraph. Cases may obtain, however, where the presence of one or more of such factors is adequate reason for granting relief. For example, assume that a corporation for a long period of years conducted business with one customer which, during the base period, it lost because such customer decided to manufacture the product it heretofore bought. The corporation would be compelled to develop a new market. The average earnings of such corporation for

the period of time during which it was engaged in obtaining new customers might not be a fair reflection of the normal earnings of such corporation and might furnish an unjust measurement for the computation of excess profits. Another illustration of this paragraph would be a corporation which belonged to an industry the members of which were engaged in a price war during several base-period years. As a result of sales below cost during those years, the members of the industry sustained losses; when the price war was ended, such members resumed their normal earning level. Relief should be given to the corporation which, except for the

unusual temporary economic conditions prevailing in its industry, would have earned normal profits throughout the base period. (p. 143)

Report—Senate Finance Committee (77th Cong., 2d Sess., S. Rept. 1631).— Same as p. 143 of Ways and Means Committee Report (p. 198-199). In addition, there is the following:

* * * To be entitled to the benefits of this provision, it must show the following:

* * *

(2) Depression in the base period due to temporary economic circumstances; (p. 36)

Committee Hearings

Hearings—Joint Committee on Internal Revenue Taxation (Feb.-May 1946).—Difficulties in determining events of unusual and temporary character. (J. D. Nunan, Jr.—Comm'r. of Int. Rev. —p. 16-18; E. H. McDermott, p. 236;

C. N. Goodwin, p. 336-337; W. G. Russell, p. 389-390)

Allowing additional causative factors to be taken into consideration. (E. H. McDermott, p. 243)

Sec. 722(b)(3)

[SEC. 722. GENERAL RELIEF—CONSTRUCTIVE AVERAGE BASE PERIOD NET INCOME.]

1942
222(a)

[(b) Taxpayers Using Average Earnings Method.—The tax * * * shall be considered to be excessive * * * if its average base period net income is an inadequate standard of normal earnings because—]

(3) the business of the taxpayer was depressed in the base period by reason of conditions generally prevailing in an industry of which the taxpayer was a member, subjecting such taxpayer to
(A) a profits cycle differing materially in length and amplitude from the general business cycle, or
(B) sporadic and intermittent periods of high production and profits, and such periods are inadequately represented in the base period,

Committee Reports

Report—Ways and Means Committee (77th Cong., 2d Sess., H. Rept. 2333).— A taxpayer may obtain relief if its earnings in the base period were depressed by reason of a profits cycle differing materially in length and amplitude from

the general business cycle. An example of this would be the case of a manufacturer of heavy machinery. Such machinery is replaced infrequently. Suppose its last period of high earnings was 1926-29, that it maintained itself in the industry absorbing losses, anticipating renewed earnings, and that the earnings in 1936-39 were poor. Consideration will be given to the taxpayer's entire profits cycle in constructing an average base period net income, which might be somewhat in line with the earnings of the period 1926-29.

Due to conditions generally prevailing in an industry in which the taxpayer is engaged it may have had intermittent and sporadic periods of high production and profits but none of these was experienced in the base period. If, for example, the earnings record of a taxpayer in the canning industry indicates that ordinarily in one out of every four years the earnings were substantially above the average of the other three, and that it had no such high earnings in the base period but had poor base period earnings, in constructing an average base period net income it might be allowed average earnings of a representative period which included a good year, as shown below:

Income (in thousands of dollars)

1926	50	1933	25
1927	10	1934	48
1928	15	1935	22
1929	55	1936	15
1930	12	1937	25
1931	45	1938	18
1932	18	1939	10

In this case the taxpayer might be permitted to use the period 1930-33, since this period includes one of the years of high earnings periodically experienced by the taxpayer. (p. 22-23)

To be eligible for relief, taxpayers which are entitled to use the average-earnings credit under section 713 must establish that the average base period net income is not a fair measure of normal earnings because of one or more of the following reasons:

*   *   *

3.   The business of the taxpayer was depressed in the base period because conditions generally prevailing in an industry of which the taxpayer is a member are such that the taxpayer is subject either to a profits cycle which differs materially in length and in amplitude from the general business cycle, or to sporadic and intermittent periods of high production and profits and such periods are not adequately represented in the base period. The conditions which prevail in industries of the type described in

this paragraph are conditions extending over the entire economic history of the industries rather than in the base period alone. Although it is impossible to define, categorically, the general business cycle, it is believed that the period from 1936 through 1939 was a period of moderate prosperity for business in general. If, therefore, the profit cycle of an industry did not coincide with the general business cycle, the base period might not furnish a satisfactory period for the determination of normal average profits of such industry. Consequently the members of the industry should not be penalized by being compelled to use the base period years if such period embraced only the trough of its cycle, but should be given the opportunity to establish the normal average earnings in periods which, with respect to the industry, are comparable to the base period with respect to business in general. The machine tool industry is a possible example of this type of business with a business cycle different from the general business cycle. Machine tools remain in service for many years, and retooling orders, furnishing the opportunity for profit, do not necessarily occur with every period of business prosperity. Another type of industry, the business cycle of which may vary from the general business cycle, is the building industry.

The second type of taxpayer made eligible for relief is a member of an industry which does not have an earnings experience which can be segregated into definite cycles, but whose prosperous years occur at irregular intervals and are dependent upon fortuitous combinations of advantageous circumstances. If such years are not sufficiently reflected in the base period, the taxpayer will be compelled to use as a measurement of normal earnings a period which does not represent average earnings. An industry engaged in the preparation and canning of fruit is a possible example of this class of business. Profits are dependent upon the size of the pack and the market price obtainable. Unless the base period reflects good years as well as poor, normal earnings are not adequately portrayed.

In the class of case described in this paragraph, depression during the base period resulted solely from circumstances usual in the case of the industry involved. This fact distinguishes such cases from those described in paragraph 2 wherein the depression is the result of unusual conditions. In order to qualify for relief under this paragraph, it is of course necessary for the taxpayer to show that the conditions which made the base period an inadequate measure for the industry in general also obtained specifically with respect to the taxpayer. (p. 142, 143-144)

Report—Senate Finance Committee

(77th Cong., 2d Sess., S. Rept. 1631).— Same as Ways and Means Committee Report (p. 199-200). In addition, there is the following:

* * * To be entitled to the benefits of this provision, it must show the following:

* * *

(3) Depression due to a profits cycle differing from the general business cycle;

(4) Sporadic and intermittent periods of high production and profits; (p. 36)

Committee Hearings

Hearings—Joint Committee on Internal Revenue Taxation (Feb.-May 1946).—Difficulties in determining variant profit cycles. (J. D. Nunan, Jr.—Comm'r. of Int. Rev.—p. 18; S. B. Gambill, p. 91-93; G. Simons, p. 209-210, 216-220; E. H. McDermott, p. 236-237;

C. N. Goodwin, p. 333-336; W. K. Shaw, p. 378; A. W. Schede, p. 383-385; A. H. Paul, p. 388; H. J. Forrester, p. 457)

Modifying requirement that industry profit data be produced. (E. C. Alvord, p. 123-124, 136; J. B. Weed, p. 179-180)

Sec. 722(b)(4)

[SEC. 722. GENERAL RELIEF—CONSTRUCTIVE AVERAGE BASE PERIOD NET INCOME.]

1942
———
222(a)

[(b) **Taxpayers Using Average Earnings Method.**—The tax * * * shall be considered to be excessive * * * if its average base period net income is an inadequate standard of normal earnings because—]

(4) the taxpayer, either during or immediately prior to the base period, commenced business or changed the character of the business and the average base period net income does not reflect the normal operation for the entire base period of the business. If the business of the taxpayer did not reach, by the end of the base period, the earning level which it would have reached if the taxpayer had commenced business or made the change in the character of the business two years before it did so, it shall be deemed to have commenced the business or made the change at such earlier time. For the purposes of this subparagraph, the term "change in the character of the business" includes a change in the operation or management of the business, a difference in the products or services furnished, a difference in the capacity for production or operation, a difference in the ratio of non-borrowed capital to total capital, and the acquisition before January 1, 1940, of all or part of the assets of a competitor, with the result that the competition of such competitor was eliminated or diminished. Any change in the capacity for production or operation of the business consummated during any taxable year ending after December 31, 1939, as a result of (306)~~commitments made prior to January 1, 1940,~~

~~binding the taxpayer to make the change~~ *a course of action to which
the taxpayer was committed prior to January 1, 1940,* or any acquisition
before May 31, 1941, from a competitor engaged in the dissemination
of information through the public press, of substantially all the assets
of such competitor employed in such business with the result that competition between the taxpayer and the competitor existing before
January 1, 1940, was eliminated, shall be deemed to be a change on
December 31, 1939, in the character of the business, or

Committee Reports

Report—Ways and Means Committee
(77th Cong., 2d Sess., H. Rept. 2333).—
If a taxpayer during or immediately prior
to the base period (approximately 2
years) commenced or substantially improved the business through a change in
the character of the business, and the
average base period net income under
subchapter E does not reflect the normal
operation of the entire base period, it
may obtain this relief. If the business
did not reach by the end of the base
period the earnings level which it would
have reached if it had been begun or the
change made 2 years earlier, it will be
considered to have commenced business
or made the change at the earlier date.
By change in the character of the business is meant either a change in the operation or management, a difference in the
products or services furnished, difference
in the ratio of nonborrowed capital to
total capital, and the acquisition before
January 1, 1940, of all or part of the
assets of a competitor whereby competition of the competitor was eliminated
or diminished. The term also includes
a change in capacity for production or
operation taking place in any taxable
year ending after December 31, 1939,
as a result of commitments made prior to
January 1, 1940, binding the taxpayer to
make the change; also the acquisition
before May 31, 1941, from a competitor
engaged in dissemination of information
through the public press of substantially
all the assets of the competitor, resulting
in the elimination of competition between
the taxpayer and the competitor existing
before January 1, 1940.

For example, in 1936 a taxpayer's
directors became dissatisfied with its
management and replaced it. The new
management made changes in sales and
production policies resulting in sub-

stantial increases in the earnings in 1939,
but not reflected in earnings in 1937 and
1938. Assuming that the new management increased the earnings record by
50 percent the following adjustment
might be made:

Earnings (in thousands of dollars)

	Unadjusted earnings	Adjusted earnings
1936...............	50	75
1937...............	60	90
1938...............	60	90
1939...............	90	90
Average...........	65	86

The earnings for 1937 and 1938 are increased by 50 percent.

In another case a company commenced
the construction of new plant facilities in
1937 which it did not complete until
1941. It committed itself during the
base period to the completion of the program and would be entitled to treatment
as if the new facilities had been in operation on December 31, 1939.

Another company started a delivery
route in 1938 selling food products. In
1938 it had a net loss, in 1939 a moderate
profit. Its steady growth during 1938-
39 indicates if it had commenced the
business 2 years earlier it would have had
substantially higher earnings. Its earnings record is shown below:

1938...................................	−5
1939 (first quarter).......................	1
1939 (second quarter).....................	5
1939 (third quarter)......................	9
1939 (fourth quarter)	12

On account of the expansion in 1939
it might be awarded a constructive base
period net income.

A taxpayer during the base period was
engaged in the manufacture of a variety
of products, some of them under patents
it had developed. During the base

period it increased its plant capacity, carried on extensive research, developed new products, perfected and obtained a patent, and employed new marketing methods, enabling it to sell a leading product in new markets. A change in the character of the business occurred during the base period which makes it eligible for relief.

In April 1941 a newspaper acquired substantially all of the assets employed in publishing a competitive newspaper, with the result that competition between the taxpayer and the competitor existing prior to January 1, 1940 was eliminated. A change in the character of the business is deemed to have occurred prior to January 1, 1940, and the taxpayer is eligible for relief.

A taxpayer immediately prior to and during the base period was engaged in research for developing an American raw material for the manufacture of a product necessary to the industry of, but not theretofore practicable of manufacture in the United States. In early 1938 a process was perfected for such manufacture. It entered into sales contracts, commenced a program of building of plant and equipment, ultimately completed in 1941, and began to supply its customers in September 1939, largely on capital borrowed from them. It operated with low-invested capital and its earnings did not by the end of the base period reach the level they would have reached had taxpayer commenced business shortly before the base period. It will be deemed to have commenced business at the earlier date and would be eligible for relief. (p. 23-24)

To be eligible for relief, taxpayers which are entitled to use the average-earnings credit under section 713 must establish that the average base period net income is not a fair measure of normal earnings because of one or more of the following reasons:

*   *   *

4. The taxpayer, either during or immediately prior to the base period, commenced business or changed the character of the business, and the average base period net income does not reflect the normal operation of the business so commenced or changed for the entire base period of such business. No arbitrary temporal limitations can be set forth upon the commencement of business or change in the character of business "immediately prior to the base period". Generally, an event can be considered to have occurred "immediately prior to the base period" if under normal conditions the effect of such event would not be manifested until some time during the base period and would be directly related to such occurrence. For example, a corporation, which until 1934 manufactured snuff at a loss, in that year changed to the manufacture of cigars. Due to normal difficulties in establishing trade connections and in establishing its product, it did not realize normal earnings until 1938. Such corporation should be considered to have changed the character of its business "immediately prior to the base period." However, assume that in 1930 a manufacturer of general textiles converted its business to the manufacture of automobile upholstery. It enjoyed earnings for 8 years which were reasonable and stable. In 1938 it made a profitable connection with a large automobile manufacturer and, as a result, realized larger profits. The fact of such connection is not related to the change in the character of the business in 1930, and such change is too remote to have occurred "immediately prior to the base period."

If the business of the taxpayer, so commenced or changed, was growing so that by the end of the base period the taxpayer did not reach the earning level it would have attained had it commenced business or changed the character of its business 2 years before it did, the taxpayer shall be deemed to have commenced business or made the change at such earlier time. Opportunity is thus afforded growing taxpayers to establish within a period of normal earnings a larger earning capacity as a result of the assumption that such taxpayer commenced business or changed the character of the business 2 years earlier than such events actually occurred. In determining whether such taxpayer was growing, consideration shall be given to the business experience of the taxpayer and to its prospects at the end of the base period. Events occurring or existing after December 31, 1939, shall not be considered in ascertaining the growth of the taxpayer. For example, a concern which had formerly operated abroad commenced business in the United States in October 1939. Its known market was such that a plant capacity of X units was projected, although the concern had contracted for only half of these units as of December 31, 1939. Contracts for the remaining units were placed in 1940, and the concern was operating X units by the latter part of 1941. If such concern can prove, on the basis of facts existing prior to January 1, 1940, that it was expanding it will be deemed to have commenced business in October 1937. Another example of a growing business would be a corporation which, in 1938, started a delivery route selling food products such as peanuts, potato chips, and similar products. For 1938 it showed a loss. Its earnings for 1939 increased in each quarter-year period. With a record of steady growth such corporation might be deemed to have commenced business in 1936.

A "change in the character of the business" includes (a) a change in the operation or management of the business (b) a difference in the products or services furnished (c) a difference in the capacity for production or operation (d) a difference in the ratio of nonborrowed capital to total capital, and (e) the acquisition before January 1, 1940, of all or part of the assets of a competitor with the result that the competition of such competitor was eliminated or diminished. Classifications (b), (c), (d), and (e) are recapitulations of definitions of change in the character and nature of the business found in existing law. Classification (a) is new. It is designed to make available the relief provisions to those corporations which have substantially improved business by the introduction of new processes of manufacture, or through the stimulation of new management running such business. For example, in 1936, a corporation was reorganized and the new directors made drastic changes in the management of the enterprise. The effect of the changes in sales and production policies initiated by the new management was not reflected in the company's earnings until 1939. A "change in the character of the business" has occurred warranting relief under this section. In 1936, a company engaged in coal mining converted from a system of hand loading,

under which it lost money, to mechanized loading. As a result of decreased costs it showed profits for subsequent years. The corporation is entitled to relief under this section. In 1938, a concern which marketed its product from door to door changed such sales methods to direct sales to retailers. As a result, its earnings increased. Such concern is eligible for relief. In all of the above cases the changes were so substantial as to warrant the conclusion that a "change in the character of the business" had occurred.

If a corporation, prior to January 1, 1940, has made commitments, binding it to make changes in the capacity for production or operation, and such changes are effectuated during a taxable year ending after December 31, 1939, the changes shall be deemed to give rise to a change in the character of the business on December 31, 1939. Such change shall not be taken into effect in determining the constructive average base period net income with respect to any year prior to that in which the change was completed. Such commitments may take the form of a contract, the expenditure of money in the commencement of the desired changes, or other changes in position, unequivocally establishing the intent to make the changes. For example, in 1937 a mining company began the development of a new mine and the construction of a new plant to be used in connection with such mine. Considerable sums of money were expended upon this product during the base period. The mine and the plant were completed and entered production in November 1941. There will be considered to be a change in the character of the business on December 31, 1939, for the purposes of the constructive average base-period net income to be determined for the year in which such facilities were completed, and for subsequent years. In determining the amount of the constructive average base-period net income, the extent to which the new facilities entered into the business of the corporation for the taxable year shall be considered to be the extent to which the character of the business was changed on December 31, 1939. It is also contemplated that the constructive average base-period net income will be computed so as not to duplicate any credit inuring to the corporation on account of the treatment as new capital of such portion of the new facilities, or money or property expended in obtaining such facilities, which may have been paid into the corporation after the base period. (p. 142, 144-146)

Report—Senate Finance Committee (77th Cong., 2d Sess., S. Rept. 1631).— Same as first three paragraphs of p. 144-146 of the Ways and Means Committee Report. In addition, there is the following:

Paragraph 4 of the House bill contains a provision that if a corporation, prior to January 1, 1940, has made commitments binding it to make changes in the capacity for production or operation, and such changes are effectuated during a taxable year ending after December 31, 1939, the changes shall be deemed to give rise to a change in the character of the business December 31, 1939. Your committee has made a clarifying amendment to this provision to make it manifest that the commitments made need not take the form of legally binding contracts only. The amendment provides that any change in the capacity for production or operation of the business consummated during any taxable year ending after December 31, 1939, as a result of a course of action to which the taxpayer was committed prior to January 1, 1940, shall be deemed to be a change in the character of the business as of December 31, 1939. The change described shall not be taken into effect in determining the constructive average base period net income with respect to any year prior to that in which the change was completed. A course of action to which the taxpayer was committed may be evidenced by a contract, the expenditure of money in the commencement of the desired changes, or other changes in position unequivocally establishing the intent to make the changes. For example, in 1939 a mining company began the development of a new mine and the construction of a new plant to be used in connection with such mine. Considerable sums of money were expended upon this product during the base period. The mine and the plant were completed and entered production in November 1941. There will be considered to be a change in the character of the business on December 31, 1939, for

the purposes of the constructive average base period net income to be determined for the year in which such facilities were completed, and for subsequent years. In determining the amount of the constructive average base period net income, the extent to which the new facilities entered into the business of the corporation for the taxable year shall be considered to be the extent to which the character of the business was changed on December 31, 1939. It is also contemplated that the constructive average base period net income will be computed so as not to duplicate any credit inuring to the corporation on account of the treatment as new capital of such portion of the new facilities, or money or property expended in obtaining such facilities, which may have been paid into the corporation after the base period. (p. 201-202)

To be entitled to the benefits of this provision, it must show the following:

* * *

(5) That the business was commenced or its character changed during the base period; or   (p. 36)

Your committee has made the following changes in the House bill:

* * *

5. In the case of taxpayers commencing business or changing the character of the business during the base period, the House bill defines such changes. One such change includes a change in capacity for production, operation or services taking place in any taxable year ending after December 31, 1939, as a result of commitments made prior to January 1, 1940, binding the taxpayer to make the change. Your committee felt that it was the purpose of the provision to afford relief to taxpayers who were committed to a course of action prior to January 1, 1940, and amended the provision accordingly. Such a course of action to which taxpayer was committed may be evidenced by such factors as a contract, action by a board of directors or governing body as to a particular course of action, expenditures in the commencement of such changes or other courses of action clearly indicating the intent to make such changes even though later modified.

The following illustrates certain types of cases which your committee believes properly come within the scope of this section.

(1) A distillery organized in 1935 distilled whisky and was engaged in the base period in aging its product for sale. It had relatively little reserve stock for the market in the base period and its earnings were abnormally low and did not reflect the result of its base period operations. Relief will be extended to this taxpayer under this section.

(2) A taxpayer during the base period, in addition to its regular business of manufacturing dental equipment, in 1937 entered the field of manufacture of custom-built precision parts and instruments for the aviation industry, using surplus capacity for the purpose. Such a change would entitle it to relief, and the normal expansion, including expansion of line of products, which it would have experienced in this new field under the circumstances of the base period had it entered such field two years earlier, would be considered.

(3) A taxpayer during 1936, 1937, and 1938 experienced a severe reduction in the volume of its business due in part to economic conditions but principally to financial mismanagement, suffering a deficit in 1938. New management was provided early in 1939 and its earnings were greatly increased in that year. Suppose its net earnings were as follows:

In thousands of dollars

1936	$283
1937	150
1938	−60
1939	461

Since such a taxpayer experienced a change in operation and management in its base period, it would be eligible for this relief and the factors mentioned should be considered in determining the amount of relief to which it is entitled. (p. 36, 37-38)

Report—Conference Committee (77th Cong., 2d Sess., H. Rept. 2586).—Under the House bill a corporation may be entitled to relief if, prior to January 1, 1940, commitments were made binding it to make changes in the operation, management, etc., and such changes are effectuated during a taxable year ended after December 31, 1939. In this case the changes are deemed to result in a change in the character of the business as of December 31, 1939. The Senate has made a clarifying amendment to make it manifest that the commitments made need not take the form of legally binding contracts only. The Senate has also deleted those provisions of the House bill which provide for certain limitations to be applied in determining eligibility for relief and in computing the final tax liability after relief has been given. (p. 62)

Congressional Discussion

Discussion—Senate (Cong. Rec. Vol. 88).—MR. GURNEY. Mr. President, at the time the Finance Committee had the pending tax bill under consideration some radio stations in my section of the country sent some inquiries to me as to how the provisions of certain sections of the bill would affect their tax payments. Not being able to answer the questions, I turned them over to the chairman of the Finance Committee, the senior Senator from Georgia [Mr. GEORGE], and received in reply from the tax expert of the committee, Mr. Stam, a very prompt and clarifying statement, and later a confirmation from the Senator from Georgia himself, which completely answered the questions * * * the matter was ordered to be printed in the RECORD, as follows:

UNITED STATES SENATE,
September 10, 1942.
Hon. WALTER F. GEORGE,
Chairman, Senate Finance Committee,
Washington, D. C.

DEAR SENATOR GEORGE: I would appreciate answers to three questions as to the eligibility of taxpayers for relief under section 213 of H. R. 7378, which, as you know, completely rewrites section 722 of the existing internal-revenue law.

Paragraph 4 of subsection (b), beginning on page 209 of H. R. 7378, reads:

"The taxpayer, either during or immediately prior to the base period, commenced business or changed the character of the business, and the average base period net income does not reflect the normal operation for the entire base period of the business."

Question No. 1: During the base period radio station A increased its power, necessitating changes and expansion of the physical property of the station and thus enlarged the area it served, thereby enabling the station to increase its volume of advertising and advertising rates. Would this qualify the radio station to secure a "constructive base period net income"?

Question No. 2: Radio station B had been operated by a seed and nursery company prior to October 24, 1938, and had been used as a merchandising agency for the seed and nursery company. After October 24, 1938, the station was operated by a new owner as a strictly commercial venture. Would this change in the character of the business and change in management qualify this station for relief?

Again quoting from paragraph (4), subsection (b), at the bottom of page 210, the House bill provides:

"Any change in the capacity for production or operation of the business consummated during any taxable year ending after December 31, 1939, as a result of commitments made prior to January 1, 1940, binding the taxpayer to make the change * * * shall be deemed to be a change on December 31, 1939."

Question No. 3: Radio station C entered into a contract on July 6, 1939, and thereby committed itself to changing its basic network affiliation from a network with a low volume of business and less valuable programs to one of the greater networks with a very large volume of business and superior programs. This change in the operation of the business enabled the station to greatly increase its revenue. The contract with the new network was signed and the station committed to the change prior to January 1, 1940, but the actual broadcasting of the new network's programs could not begin until March 1940. (p. 8001)

CONGRESS OF THE UNITED STATES,
JOINT COMMITTEE ON INTERNAL
REVENUE TAXATION,
Washington, September 17, 1942.
Hon. CHAN GURNEY,
United States Senate,
Washington, D. C.

DEAR SENATOR: This is in reply to your letter to Senator GEORGE of September 10 regarding the application of section 213 of H. R. 7378, which rewrites section 722 of the Internal Revenue Code.

Each of the questions raised in your letter regarding the application of section 722 of the Internal Revenue Code as amended by the pending revenue bill can, in my opinion, be answered "yes."

As to question No. 1, it seems very clear that the substantial expansion of the physical properties of a radio station, thus enlarging the area it serves and enabling the station to increase its volume of advertising and its advertising rates, would make the taxpayer eligible to the benefits of section 722.

With regard to question No. 2, it seems clear that a radio station which had been operated by a seed and nursery company prior to October 24, 1938, and had been used as a merchandising agency for such company but after that date was operated by a new owner as a strictly commercial venture, would come under the application of section 722. (p. 8001-02)

It seems equally clear that the case covered in your third question would also be entitled to relief; and while the change did not take place until after the base period, the taxpayer was committed in 1939 to make the change, which was consummated in 1940. Incidentally, the language covering this case in the House bill has been liberalized. In the House bill the relief was limited to cases in which the taxpayer was under a binding commitment to make the change. This language connoted a legal obligation to go through with the intended change. The Finance Committee desired to more closely approximate the idea involved here, therefore, the changes, which are the result of a course of action to which the taxpayer was committed during his base period, will be allowed. In any case, the situation stated in question No. 3 would, in my opinion, be clearly covered by the pending legislation. (p. 8002)

MR. GEORGE. * * * I have carefully

considered questions No. 1, 2, and 3, and in my opinion all of them should be answered in the affirmative. I think the situations described in your letter fall clearly within the purpose and intent of section 722 of the tax bill and that radio station C, referred to in your third question, will qualify for a constructive base period net income under section 722. (p. 8002)

Discussion—House; on Report of Conference Committee (Cong. Rec. Vol. 88).—MR. KNUTSON. * * * Considerable interest has been evinced in section 722, better known as the relief section, and in order to further clarify that section, at this point I insert for the RECORD certain correspondence that has passed between several Members of the House and the chairman of the Ways and Means Committee, Mr. DOUGHTON. This is being done with the knowledge and approval of the chairman. The correspondence follows:

CONGRESS OF THE UNITED STATES,
HOUSE OF REPRESENTATIVES,
Washington, D. C., October 10, 1942.
Hon. ROBERT L. DOUGHTON,
Chairman, House Ways and Means
Committee, House Office Building,
Washington, D. C.

DEAR MR. DOUGHTON: H. R. 7378 as passed the House contained section 213 which amended section 722 (b.4) of the Internal Revenue Code, reads in part as follows:

"Any change in the capacity for production or operation of the business consummated during the taxable year ending after December 31, 1939, as a result of commitments made prior to January 1, 1940, binding the taxpayer to make the change."

This language was changed by the Senate and is contained in section 221, and reads in part as follows:

"Any change in the capacity for production or operation of the business consummated during any taxable year ending after December 31, 1939, as a result of a course of action to which the taxpayer was committed prior to January 1, 1940."

Inasmuch as the Senate version, according to the Finance Committee's report, affords relief to a taxpayer who was committed to a course of action prior to January 1, 1940, I would like you to advise me if the following course of action taken by a corporation in Minnesota would constitute "a course of action to which the taxpayer was committed prior to January 1, 1940":

"The corporation in question had been carrying on a program of expansion over a period of probably 15 years. It was the policy of the company to pay modest dividends and finance all new construction out of earnings. In 1939 the company's earnings were exceptionally high and at its last dividend meeting of that year, held December 2, 1939, the president, in a written report, requested that "before a decision is made as to the amount of the dividend to be declared for the final quarter of the year certain matters be considered by the board, namely:

"(a) The question of retaining a sufficient amount of the current year's earnings to enable the company to carry on its probable expansion and research programs, and "(b) Will such retention subject the company to a tax under section 102 of the revenue act, which is a tax on corporations for improperly accumulating surplus, in view of the recent ruling of the Commissioner of Internal Revenue to his examining agents requiring such agent to make a report of all corporations examined containing a specific recommendation as to whether or not section 102 applies to the corporation examined, particularly where the corporation has not distributed at least 70 percent of its earnings as taxable dividends, and has large investments of stocks or securities or other properties not related to its normal business activities?

"(c) If the company retains a part of its current year's earnings, and the earnings so retained are not all required in the company's program of expansion and research, and later distributed, it is possible that the stockholders would be subject to higher surtax rates, in view of the President's proposed program of defense.

"Regardless of the tax question involved, the directors should seriously consider whether or not they want to depart from the past policy of the company—which has been to keep a substantial amount of cash in the treasury and to finance its growth entirely from current earnings. This policy has made the company an outstanding success; and the record clearly demonstrates that, at no time in the company's history have earnings been retained for any purpose other than for reinvestment in the business. The company is spending large amounts for laboratories and research, and, for that reason, it is certainly sound business to keep the company in a financial position to equip itself to exploit new products."

In line with this, the president then listed a number of expansion projects, including:

(a) Addition to two factory buildings at an estimated cost of $215,000.

(b) An entirely new factory at an estimated cost of $1,250,000.

The board of directors concurred in the President's program as outlined; the dividend was increased from $1.80 per share in 1938 to $2.40 per share in 1939, despite high earnings which could have justified a much larger dividend; a sufficient sum was retained to finance the proposed projects; and this company, by this action of the board of directors, was put in a position to proceed with the expansion program as outlined.

Project (a) was started in June 1940 and completed early in 1941, in line with the reasoning and course of action at said meeting in December 1939.

Project (b) was started in 1941 and completed in 1942, and this again was in line with the reasoning and course of action at said meeting in December 1939.

It seems to me that this course of action is quite in keeping with the intent of the Senate Finance Committee when in its report (p. 37, par. 5), it says: "Such a course of action to which taxpayer was committed may be evidenced by such factors as a contract, action by the board of directors or governing body as to a particular course of action, expenditures in the commencement of such changes, or other courses of action clearly indicating the intent to make such changes, even though later modified."

Yours very truly,

RICHARD P. GALE,
Member of Congress.

CONGRESS OF THE UNITED STATES,
JOINT COMMITTEE ON INTERNAL
REVENUE TAXATION,
Washington, October 20, 1942.

Hon. ROBERT L. DOUGHTON,
Chairman, Joint Committee
on Internal Revenue Taxation,
House of Representatives,
Washington, D. C.

DEAR MR. CHAIRMAN: Reference is made to the letter to you from the Honorable RICHARD P. GALE of October 10 regarding the application of section 722 of the Internal Revenue Code, as amended by section 213 of the pending revenue bill. Mr. GALE, after a statement of facts regarding the situation of a corporate taxpayer, asks whether or not such taxpayer will be entitled to relief under section 722, as amended.

It is difficult to make a definite answer in the absence of all of the facts bearing on this case. However, upon the facts contained in Mr. GALE's letter, I am of the opinion that the taxpayer described therein is entitled to the benefits of section 722.

I am returning Mr. GALE's letter for your files.

Respectfully yours,

COLIN F. STAM,
Chief of Staff.

HOUSE OF REPRESENTATIVES,
October 12, 1942.

The Honorable ROBERT L. DOUGHTON,
Chairman, Committee on Ways and
Means, House of Representatives,
Washington, D. C.

MY DEAR MR. DOUGHTON: I would like to draw your attention to the attached page from the CONGRESSIONAL RECORD for October 9, 1942, giving correspondence between Senator GURNEY and Mr. Stam in connection with section 722 as amended by the 1942 tax bill, and a letter from Senator GEORGE, chairman of the Senate Finance Committee, to Senator GURNEY confirming the views of Mr. Stam.

I happen to have an interest in similar questions involving the same section of the bill, and I would like to know if you, as chairman of the Ways and Means Committee, concur in the interpretations given by Senator GEORGE to Senator GURNEY.

Sincerely yours,

FRANCIS CASE.

COMMITTEE ON WAYS AND MEANS,
HOUSE OF REPRESENTATIVES,
Washington, D. C., October 16, 1942.

Hon. FRANCIS CASE,
House of Representatives,
Washington, D. C.

DEAR MR. CASE: Your letter of October 12, enclosing reprint from the CONGRESSIONAL RECORD of correspondence between Senator GURNEY and Senator GEORGE and Mr. Colin F. Stam has been received.

I have read this enclosure and concur in the replies given Senator GURNEY by Senator GEORGE and Mr. Stam with respect to relief under section 213 of H. R. 7378.

Sincerely yours,

R. L. DOUGHTON.
(p. 8471-72)

Committee Hearings

Hearings—Ways and Means Committee.—Giving effect to changes after 1939. (R. Paul—Treas. Dept.—p. 121)

Allowing for commitments prior to January 1, 1940. (C. Hayden, p. 2286-88)

Hearings—Senate Finance Committee.—Treating normal growth as a change in business. (J. J. Forstall, p. 2231-32)

Hearings—Joint Committee on Internal Revenue Taxation (Feb.-May 1946).—Difficulties in determining changes in character of business. (J. D. Nunan, Jr.—Comm'r. of Int. Rev.—p. 18-22; E. H. McDermott, p. 237-239)

Difficulties in applying push-back rule. (J. D. Nunan, Jr.—Comm'r of Int. Rev. —p. 22; E. C. Alvord, p. 112-114, 137-139; M. Austin, p. 162; G. K. Gardner, p. 172-173, 379-380; P. D. Seghers, p. 175-177; F. H. Terrell, p. 268-271; E. McFarland, p. 274-275; E. Groseclose, p. 356-357; R. Magill, p. 376; W. C. Mills, p. 377)

Problem in determining reconstructed demand figures. (E. C. Alvord, p. 114)

Problems about commitments for increased capacity. (E. C. Alvord, p' 115-116, 141)

Eliminating motive as a factor in change of business. (E. C. Alvord, p. 118-120)

Recognizing change of business effected through organization of foreign subsidiary. (E. C. Alvord, p. 121)

Eliminating requirement that change be substantial. (E. C. Alvord, p. 121-123, 141-142; C. M. Edelmann, p. 220-225)

Clarifying meaning of "immediately prior to the base period." (E. C. Alvord, p. 120-121, 126-127, 137)

Allowing relief where business changed to war products. (H. Satterlee, p. 204)

Liberalizing status of commitments made prior to 1940. (G. Rogers, p. 287; E. Groseclose, p. 356; R. Magill, p. 376; W. C. Mills, p. 377)

Eliminating requirement to establish demand for new product in years prior to actual production. (J. Carlson, p. 313)

Eliminating adjustment for normal growth and competitive position. (J. Carlson, p. 313-314)

1941 Act

Hearings—Ways and Means Committee.—Allowing relief for new types of business in current year. (A. C. Nielsen, p. 1227-32)

Allowing relief for new business. (C. N. Monson, p. 1304-12)

[SEC. 722.   ADJUSTMENT OF ABNORMAL BASE PERIOD NET INCOME.]

EPTA 6

[(b)   Rules for Application of Subsection (a).—For the purposes of subsection (a)—]

(2)   The character of the business engaged in by the taxpayer as of January 1, 1940, shall be considered different from the character of the business engaged in during one or more of the taxable years in its base period only if—

(A)   there is a difference in the products or services furnished; or

(B)   there is a difference in the capacity for production or operation; or

(C)   there is a difference in the ratio of nonborrowed capital to total capital; or

(D)   the taxpayer was in existence during only part of its base period; or

(E)   the taxpayer acquired, before January 1, 1940, all or part of the assets of a competitor with the result that the competition of such competitor was eliminated or diminished.

Committee Reports

Report—Ways and Means Committee (77th Cong., 1st Sess., H. Rept. 146).—

The character of the business engaged in by the taxpayer as of January 1, 1940, is considered different from the character of the business engaged in during one or more of the taxable years in its base period only if:

(1) There is a difference in the products or services furnished. For example, if a corporation in 1 year of the base period was engaged in both the radio broadcasting and department store business and on January 1, 1940, was engaged only in the radio broadcasting business, the department store business having been discontinued, the corporation is deemed to have changed the character of its business. The same is true where a corporation was engaged in one of the base period years in both the wholesale and retail dry goods business and on January 1, 1940, was engaged only in the retail dry goods business.

(2) There is a difference in the capacity for production or operation. An illustration of such a difference would be where the corporation has enlarged its plant or increased its capital.

(3) There is a difference in the ratio of nonborrowed capital to total capital. A corporation which during the base period was operating largely on borrowed capital but as of January 1, 1940, was operating largely on equity capital is deemed to have such a difference.

(4) The taxpayer was in existence during only part of the base period. An example is where a corporation in 1938 reorganized into two or more corporations. The new corporations would have been in existence for only a part of the base period.

(5) The taxpayer acquired before January 1, 1940, all or a part of the assets of a competitor with the result that the competition of such competitor was eliminated or diminished. Assume that two newspapers were operating at a loss or with very little income during all or part of the base period. Prior to January 1, 1940, the first newspaper purchased the franchises or other assets of the second newspaper and as a result of this transaction the condition of the surviving paper was much more promising. A difference in the character of the business of the taxpayer has occurred. (p. 10-11)

Assume, for example, that a newspaper corporation, which had a fiscal year ending March 31, 1940, had acquired the franchises of a rival newspaper in December 1939. Prior to that time, both papers had operated at a loss or a small profit. After such acquisition, the surviving newspaper showed a much larger profit for the remainder of its fiscal year ending March 31, 1940. Under this section, such a newspaper, by establishing what it would have earned in the base period if the character of its business had been the same throughout its base period, will be able to secure substantial relief. (p. 12)

Report—Senate Finance Committee (77th Cong., 1st Sess., S. Rept. 75).— Same as Ways and Means Committee Report. (p. 11, 12, respectively)

EPTA 6

[Set forth on page 146]

Sec. 722(b)(5)

1942 222(a)

[SEC. 722. GENERAL RELIEF—CONSTRUCTIVE AVERAGE BASE PERIOD NET INCOME.]

[(b) Taxpayers Using Average Earnings Method.—The tax * * * shall be considered to be excessive * * * if its average base period net income is an inadequate standard of normal earnings because—]

(5) of any other factor affecting the taxpayer's business which may reasonably be considered as resulting in an inadequate standard

of normal earnings during the base period and the application of this section to the taxpayer would not be inconsistent with the principles underlying the provisions of this subsection, and with the conditions and limitations enumerated therein.

Committee Reports

Report—Ways and Means Committee (77th Cong., 2d Sess., H. Rept. 2333).— Taxpayers may obtain relief by meeting one of the specific tests contained in section 722, but the inability to meet the specific tests will not necessarily exclude the taxpayer from the benefits of the section if it can satisfy the Commissioner or the Relief Court that its claim is consistent with the principles underlying the specific tests. If these are met, the tax will be determined on the basis of a constructive base period net income in lieu of the average base period net income determined under the specific provisions of subchapter E.   (p. 21)

Relief may be obtained if any other factor affects the taxpayer's business which may be reasonably considered as resulting in an inadequate standard of normal earnings during the base period if application of the section to the taxpayer would not be inconsistent with the principles, conditions, and limitations of section 722 (b).   (p. 24)

To be eligible for relief, taxpayers which are entitled to use the average-earnings credit under section 713 must establish that the average base period net income is not a fair measure of normal earnings because of one or more of the following reasons:

*   *   *

5.   The business of the taxpayer during the base period was adversely affected by any other factor, resulting in an average base-period net income which is an inadequate standard of normal earnings, and the taxpayer's claim for relief and the application of the relief as provided in this section would not be inconsistent with the principles underlying the eligibility requirements and the conditions and limitations set forth therein. Thus, corporations which do not meet the strict eligibility requirements set forth in this section are not debarred from relief if their case is within the spirit of the statute and if its application would not be inconsistent with its principles and conditions and limitations. (p. 146)

Report—Senate Finance Committee (77th Cong., 2d Sess., S. Rept. 1631).— * * * To be entitled to the benefits of this provision, it must show the following:

*   *   *

(6)   Other factors affecting the business of the taxpayer which may be reasonably considered as resulting in an inadequate standard of normal earnings during the base period if application of the provisions to the taxpayer would not be inconsistent with the principles, conditions, and limitations of this section. (p. 36)

To be eligible for relief, taxpayers which are entitled to use the average earnings credit under section 713 must establish that the average base period net income is not a fair measure of normal earnings because of one or more of the following reasons:

*   *   *

5.   The business of the taxpayer during the base period was adversely affected by any other factor, resulting in an average base period net income which is an inadequate standard of normal earnings, and the taxpayer's claim for relief and the application of the relief as provided in this section would not be inconsistent with the principles underlying the eligibility requirements and the conditions and limitations set forth therein. Thus, corporations which do not meet the strict eligibility requirements set forth in this section are not debarred from relief if their case is within the spirit of the statute and if its application would not be inconsistent with its principles and conditions and limitations.

An example which your committee believes illustrates this paragraph would be a taxpayer which shortly before the base period undertook a business involving the manufacture of a product requiring an extensive period for preparation or manufacture, and which had no stocks of such product on hand at the commencement of such business. Since a large portion of the base period would be devoted to preparation of the product for sale, and since sales would consequently be small or nonexistent and would not serve as a measure of the normal operations of the business, the base period would represent an abnormal standard by which to compute excess profits. Although in such a case, it might be said that the business was not depressed during the base period since it was operating at full manufacturing capacity, and thus might not be entitled to relief under paragraph 2, it would seem clear that such a taxpayer is entitled to relief by way of a constructive excess profits net income based upon more normal operations. For example, assume that a taxpayer was organized in 1935 to distill and sell whisky. It had no reserve whisky stocks on hand. During 1935 and for the greater part of its base period, it was aging the whisky it had distilled. Because of a lack of a marketable product, the sales of such taxpayer, and consequently its base period net income, were abnormally low and do not reflect results of usual operations. Relief should be extended to such taxpayer, the base period net income of which would not have been distorted if it had adequate whisky stocks on hand at the beginning of the base period. (p. 198, 202-203)

Congressional Discussion

Discussion—Senate (Cong. Rec. Vol. 88).—MR. GURNEY. Mr. President, at the time the Finance Committee had the pending tax bill under consideration some radio stations in my section of the country sent some inquiries to me as to how the provisions of certain sections of the bill would affect their tax payments. Not being able to answer the questions, I turned them over to the chairman of the Finance Committee, the senior Senator from Georgia (Mr. GEORGE), and received in reply from the tax expert of the committee, Mr. Stam, a very prompt and clarifying statement, and later a confirmation from the Senator from Georgia himself, which completely answered the questions * * * the matter was ordered to be printed in the RECORD, as follows:

Question No. 3: Radio station C entered into a contract on July 6, 1939, and thereby committed itself to changing its basic network affiliation from a network with a low volume of business and less valuable programs to one of the greater networks with a very large volume of business and superior programs. This change in the operation of the business enabled the station to greatly increase its revenue. The contract with the new network was signed and the station committed to the change prior to January 1, 1940, but the actual broadcasting of the new network's programs could not begin until March 1940.

Paragraph (5) of subsection (b), page 211, line 6, reads:

"Of any other factor affecting the taxpayer's business which may reasonably be considered as resulting in an inadequate standard of normal earnings during the base period * * *."

Inasmuch as this factor affecting the taxpayer's business certainly resulted in an inadequate standard of earnings during the base period, could radio station C qualify for a "constructive base period net income?" (p. 8001)

CONGRESS OF THE UNITED STATES,
JOINT COMMITTEE ON INTERNAL
REVENUE TAXATION,
Washington, September 17, 1942.
Hon. CHAN GURNEY,
United States Senate,
Washington, D. C.

DEAR SENATOR: This is in reply to your letter to Senator GEORGE of September 10 regarding the application of section 213 of H. R. 7378, which rewrites section 722 of the Internal Revenue Code.

Each of the questions raised in your letter regarding the application of section 722 of the Internal Revenue Code as amended by the pending revenue bill can, in my opinion, be answered "yes." (p. 8001)

MR. GEORGE. * * * I have carefully considered questions No. 1, 2, and 3, and in my opinion all of them should be answered in the affirmative. I think the situations described in your letter fall clearly within the purpose and intent of section 722 of the tax bill and that radio station C, referred to in your third question, will qualify for a constructive base period net income under section 722. (p. 8002)

Committee Hearings

Hearings—Senate Finance Committee.—Allowing relief where substantial discrepancy between tax basis and cost. (H. B. Fernald, p. 978-979)

Hearings—Joint Committee on Internal Revenue Taxation (Feb.-May 1946).—Omitting requirements of consistency with conditions and limitations of other provisions. (P. W. Phillips, p. 72-73, 75; E. C. Alvord, p. 139-140; E. H. McDermott, p. 239; W. C. Mills, p. 377)

Providing for situation of incorporation prior to 1940 but commencement of business afterwards. (E. C. Alvord, p. 135; E. J. Keogh, p. 143-146, 351-353; F. C. Hedrick, Jr., p. 169-171; H. Satterlee, p. 203; D. Petty, p. 316-317; R. Magill, p. 375; A. H. Paul, p. 387; H. A. Smith, Jr., p. 390-391; J. D. Nunan, Jr. —Comm'r. of Int. Rev.—p. 398)

Allowing relief where small base period income due to mistakes of judgment. (H. Satterlee, p. 204)

Allowing relief where facilities furnished by government. (H. Satterlee, p. 203)

Problems of lessor companies in getting relief. (A. G. Kubach, p. 227-232)

Allowing for base period subnormal income because of abandonment of assets. (R. J. Welti, p. 288-289)

Allowing cash basis taxpayers reconstruction on accrual basis. (J. Carlson, p. 310-313)

Problems in determining abnormal deductions to be eliminated in reconstruction of base period earnings. (E. C. Alvord, p. 110-112)

Applying to base period any reduced depreciation rate of war years. (J. Carlson, p. 314-315)

Allowing relief where allocations under section 721 difficult. (S. A. Knisely, p. 371-372)

1941 Act

Hearings—Ways and Means Committee.—Allowing relief for new types of business in current year. (A. C. Nielsen, p. 1227-32)

Allowing relief for new business. (C. N. Monson, p. 1304-12)

Sec. 722(c)

[SEC. 722. GENERAL RELIEF—CONSTRUCTIVE AVERAGE BASE PERIOD NET INCOME.]

(c) **Invested Capital Corporations, Etc.**—The tax computed under this subchapter (without the benefit of this section) shall be considered to be excessive and discriminatory in the case of a taxpayer, not entitled to use the excess profits credit based on income pursuant to section 713, if the excess profits credit based on invested capital is an inadequate standard for determining excess profits, because—

(1) the business of the taxpayer is of a class in which intangible assets not includible in invested capital under section 718 make important contributions to income,

(2) the business of the taxpayer is of a class in which capital is not an important income-producing factor, or

(3) the invested capital of the taxpayer is abnormally low.

In such case for the purposes of this subchapter, such taxpayer shall be considered to be entitled to use the excess profits credit based on income, using the constructive average base period net income determined under subsection (a). For the purposes of section 713 (g) and section 743, the beginning of the taxpayer's first taxable year under this subchapter shall be considered to be that date after which capital additions and capital reductions were not taken into account for the purposes of this subsection.

Committee Reports

Report—Ways and Means Committee (77th Cong., 2d Sess., H. Rept. 2333).— Relief under section 722 is available to two classes of corporations.

*   *   .*

Second, to those corporations not entitled to use the excess profits credit based on income if the invested capital credit of such corporations is abnormally low. (p. 142)

In the case of a taxpayer who is not entitled to use the excess-profits credit based on income pursuant to section 713, the tax computed under subchapter E will be considered to be excessive and discriminatory and it will be allowed the constructive average base period net income of section 722 in the following cases:

(1) EARNING ASSETS NOT INCLUDED IN INVESTED CAPITAL

Where the business of the taxpayer is of a class in which intangible assets not includible in invested capital under section 718 make important contributions to income. For example, a taxpayer commenced business early in 1940. Its business was of a class which required little invested capital but required the establishment of contacts with its customers. For the first 2 years it operated at a loss but by 1942 had built up patronage and showed a profit of $50,000. If it had invested capital of only $10,000, it would be given a constructive average base period net income because one of its principal assets—goodwill—was not includible in its invested capital.

(2) CAPITAL NOT AN IMPORTANT INCOME-PRODUCING FACTOR

Where the business of the taxpayer is of a class in which capital is not an important income-producing factor. For example, a taxpayer commenced business in 1940. It requires very little capital and cannot qualify as a personal service corporation. Such a taxpayer might be given a constructive average base period net income similar to that of comparable firms in the class of business in which it was engaged.

(3) ABNORMALLY LOW CAPITAL

Where the invested capital is abnormally low. For example, a taxpayer operating a leased plant valued at $1,000,000 commenced business in 1940 with invested capital of $40,000 plus the lease. The invested capital in this case is unusually low compared to the size of its operation and the taxpayer would be allowed a constructive average base period net income. (p. 25)

Under existing law, a taxpayer not entitled to use the excess profits credit based on income is not entitled to relief. This places in a disadvantageous competitive position corporations commencing business after January 1, 1940, as well as other corporations deprived of such credit, if the business is of a type showing a high return on invested capital, or if for some reason peculiar to the corporation, the invested capital is unusually low. The privilege of using the excess profits credit based on income is therefore extended to a taxpayer presently not entitled to use such credit, if the excess profits credit based upon the invested capital of such taxpayer furnishes an inadequate standard for the computation of excess profits because of one or more of the following reasons:

1. The business of the taxpayer is of a class in which intangible assets not includible in invested capital under section 718 make important contributions to income. For example, a corporation, which was of a class requiring little invested capital but necessitating the establishment of contacts with the trade which it was its business to supply, commenced business early in 1940. It lost money during its first 2 years of operations but by 1942 began to realize sizable profits. This company would be eligible to receive a constructive average base period net income on the grounds that one of its principal assets, the goodwill of its clientele, was not reflected in invested capital.

2. The business of the taxpayer is of a class in which capital is not an important income-producing factor. An illustration would be a corporation commencing business after January 1, 1940, doing business as fashion consultants. Although the corporation operates with very little capital, it cannot qualify as a personal service corporation because it employs a large technical and professional staff. The invested capital credit

might not be an adequate credit for such a company. It would therefore be eligible for relief under this section.

3. The invested capital of the taxpayer is abnormally low. If the type of business done by the taxpayer is not one in which invested capital is small, but the invested capital of the taxpayer is unusually low because of reasons peculiar to itself such taxpayer is eligible for relief. An illustration would be a corporation which commenced business in 1941 with a leased plant valued at $1,000,000, but with invested capital paid in of only $40,000. Since the invested capital of such company is unusually low relative to the size of its operations, it would be subject to an unreasonable tax burden if required to compute its excess profits tax under the invested capital method. It would therefore be given constructive average base period net income and would be entitled to compute its credit on the average earnings method.

The constructive average base period net income computed in the case of a corporation commencing business after January 1, 1940, is likely to duplicate, in some degree, the credit based upon capital additions. It is therefore provided that, for the purposes of adjustments in the excess profits credit on account of capital changes, the beginning of the taxpayer's first taxable year under the excess profits tax law shall be the date after which capital additions and reductions are not taken into account in ascertaining the constructive average base period net income. For example, a corporation commenced business on April 1, 1940, with $10,000 of property paid in for stock. By November 1, 1940, $20,000 additional had been paid

in, and by the end of its taxable year, December 31, 1940, $10,000 additional had been paid in. It is determined that the corporation is entitled to relief under this section, and a constructive average base period net income of a business of the kind existing on November 1, 1940, is given to the taxpayer. For the purpose of adjustments to the excess-profits credit on account of capital additions or reductions, November 1, 1940, rather than May 1, 1940, will be deemed to be the beginning of the taxpayer's first excess profits tax taxable year. (p. 146-148)

Report—Senate Finance Committee (77th Cong., 2d Sess., S. Rept. 1631).—Same as p. 146-148 of Ways and Means Committee Report (p. 203-204). In addition there is the following:

This relief is granted to all taxpayers in existence during the base period, even though they computed their excess profits on the invested-capital basis. Taxpayers who did not come into existence until after the base period, are permitted to have their income constructed for the base period on a basis comparable with other taxpayers similarly situated. (p. 35)

In the case of taxpayers coming into existence after the base period an average constructive base period net income will be permitted where:

(1) The business of the taxpayer is of a class in which intangible assets not includible in invested capital make important contributions to income;

(2) Where the business of the taxpayer is of a class in which capital is not an important income-producing factor;

(3) Where the invested capital is abnormally low. (p. 36)

Committee Hearings

Hearings—Senate Finance Committee.—Allowing relief where substantial discrepancy between tax basis and cost. (H. B. Fernald, p. 978-979)

Allowing relief for abnormalities of invested capital. (J. W. Hooper, p. 1168; E. C. Alvord, p. 1798; A. B. Chapman, p. 2083-84)

Hearings—Joint Committee on Internal Revenue Taxation (Feb.-May

1946).—Allowing relief where facilities furnished by government. (H. Satterlee, p. 203)

Allowing constructive invested capital. (J. V. Lynskey, p. 320-321, 326-327)

Difficulties in determining abnormal invested capital cases. (J. D. Nunan, Jr.—Comm'r. of Int. Rev.—p. 22-23)

1941 Act

Hearings—Senate Finance Committee.—Allowing relief for abnormalities of invested capital. (H. M. Bennett, p. 116-124; R. N. Miller, p. 520-521; E. C.   Alvord, p. 640, 683-687; A. B. Chapman, p. 754, 765-766; H. B. Fernald, p. 885; G. M. Ungaro, p. 1084-86, 1088-92)

$\dfrac{1918}{327}$ [Set forth on page 338]

$\dfrac{1918}{328}$ [Set forth on page 342]

$\dfrac{1917}{205\,(a)}$ [Set forth on page 353]

Sec. 722(d)

Act 12/17/43   [SEC. 722.   GENERAL RELIEF—CONSTRUCTIVE AVERAGE BASE PERIOD NET INCOME.]

(d) **Application for Relief Under This Section.**—The taxpayer shall compute its tax, file its return, and pay the tax shown on its return under this subchapter without the application of this section, except as provided in section 710 (a) (5). The benefits of this section shall not be allowed unless the taxpayer within the period of time prescribed by section 322 and subject to the limitation as to amount of credit or refund prescribed in such section makes application therefor in accordance with regulations prescribed by the Commissioner with the approval of the Secretary. If a constructive average base period net income has been determined under the provisions of this section for any taxable year, the Commissioner may, by regulations approved by the Secretary, prescribe the extent to which the limitations prescribed by this subsection may be waived for the purpose of determining the tax under this subchapter for a subsequent taxable year.

Committee Reports

Report—Ways and Means Committee (78th Cong., 1st Sess., H. Rept. 722).— In order to obtain relief, the taxpayer must under the bill within the period of time prescribed for filing refund claims under section 322, and subject to the limitations prescribed therein, make application for relief in accordance with regulations prescribed by the Commissioner of Internal Revenue with the approval of the Secretary. In general, refund claims must be filed within 3 years from the time the return was filed, or 2 years from the time the tax was paid. * * * The provisions of section 322, which are applicable to the taxable year for which an application for relief under section 722 is filed, shall be applicable in determining the period of time within which such application must be filed for such year and the limitation upon the amount of credit or refund for such year. (p. 2)

[SEC. 722.   GENERAL RELIEF—CONSTRUCTIVE AVERAGE BASE PERIOD   **1942**
NET INCOME.]   **222(a)**

(d) **Application for Relief Under This Section.**—The taxpayer shall compute its tax, file its return, and pay its tax under this subchapter without the application of this section, * * * If the application is not filed within six months after the date prescribed by law for the filing of the return, * * * the operation of this section shall not reduce the tax otherwise determined under this subchapter by an amount in excess of the amount of the deficiency finally determined under this subchapter without the application of this section.   If a constructive average base period net income has been determined under the provisions of this section for any taxable year, the Commissioner may, by regulations approved by the Secretary, prescribe the extent to which the limitations prescribed by this subsection may be waived for the purpose of determining the tax under this subchapter for a subsequent taxable year.

Committee Reports

Report—Ways and Means Committee (77th Cong., 2d Sess., H. Rept. 2333).—The administrative procedure presently provided for in section 722 is retained. It is contemplated that the Commissioner, under the authority given to prescribe regulations providing for the extent to which the administrative limitations of the relief section may be waived for the purpose of determining excess-profits tax for subsequent taxable years, will provide that the constructive average base period net income determined under this section shall, in the absence of substantial evidence requiring a redetermination for future years, be the constructive average base period net income of the taxpayer for all such future years. (p. 148)

Report—Senate Finance Committee (77th Cong., 2d Sess., S. Rept. 1631).—Same as Ways and Means Committee Report (p. 204-205). In addition there is the following:

Your committee has made the following changes in the House bill: * * *

2. Under the existing law, as interpreted by the Commissioner of Internal Revenue, it was necessary for the taxpayer to compute his tax without regard to the relief provisions and file a claim for refund for each taxable year. Your committee does not believe that such a procedure should be followed where the taxpayer has had its constructive average base period net income finally deter-

mined for any year. Such determination should permit the taxpayer to use the base period net income so determined as a basis in computing its excess profits tax for any future year. (p. 36)

If an application for relief for such years is not timely filed, any relief will be limited, as in the case of a claim for the current year not timely filed, to the amount of the deficiency finally determined without the application of the relief section. (p. 204)

Report—Conference Committee (77th Cong., 2d Sess., H. Rept. 2586).—If an application for relief for such years is not timely filed, any relief will be limited, as in the case of a claim for the current year not timely filed, to the amount of any deficiency finally determined without the application of the relief section. (p. 62)

Under the existing law, as interpreted by the Commissioner of Internal Revenue, it was necessary for the taxpayer to compute his tax without regard to the relief provisions and file a claim for refund for each taxable year. It is believed that such a procedure should not be followed where the taxpayer has had its constructive average base period net income finally determined for any year. Such determination should permit the taxpayer to use the base period net income so determined as a basis in computing its excess profits tax for any future year. (p. 64)

Committee Hearings

Hearings—Joint Committee on Internal Revenue Taxation (Feb.-May 1946).—Treating applications for relief as claims for refund. (H. Satterlee, p. 204)

Allowing relief in reduction of deficiency though no tax paid. (E. C. Alvord, p. 125-126)

[SEC. 722. ADJUSTMENT OF ABNORMAL BASE PERIOD NET INCOME.]

(e) **Application for Relief Under This Section.**—The taxpayer shall compute its tax and file its return under this subchapter without the application of this section. The benefits of this section shall not be allowed unless the taxpayer, within six months from the date prescribed by law for the filing of its return, makes application therefor in accordance with regulations to be prescribed by the Commissioner with the approval of the Secretary, except that if the Commissioner in the case of any taxpayer with respect to the tax liability of any taxable year—

(1) issues a preliminary notice stating a deficiency in the tax imposed by this subchapter such taxpayer may, within ninety days after the date of such notice, make such application, or

(2) mails a notice of deficiency (A) without having previously issued a preliminary notice thereof or (B) within ninety days after the date of such preliminary notice, such taxpayer may claim the benefits of this section in its petition to the Board or in an amended petition in accordance with the rules of the Board. If the application is not filed within six months after the date prescribed by law for the filing of the return, the application of this section shall not reduce the tax otherwise determined under this subchapter by an amount in excess of the amount of the deficiency finally determined under this subchapter without the application of this section. If the average base period net income has been determined under subsection (a) for any taxable year, the Commissioner may, by regulations approved by the Secretary, prescribe the extent to which the limitations prescribed by this subsection may be waived for the purpose of determining the tax under this subchapter for a subsequent taxable year.

Committee Reports

Report—Ways and Means Committee (77th Cong., 1st Sess., H. Rept. 146).— The taxpayer must first compute and pay his tax without regard to this relief provision and then must petition the Commissioner for relief by way of claim for refund. (p. 4)

It is deemed advisable in the interests of good administration, in view of the nature of the problem presented by section 722, that the taxpayer should not be permitted to apply the section in the computation of the excess-profits tax lia-

bility shown upon its return and that the taxpayer should be required to conform to reasonable restrictions with respect to the time within which it may make application for the benefits of the section. Accordingly, under the provisions of subsection (d) a taxpayer is not permitted to claim the benefits of section 722 in computing its tax upon the return. A taxpayer, in order to obtain the benefits of section 722, must make an application to the Commissioner of Internal Revenue under regulations to be prescribed by the Commissioner with the approval of the Secretary of the Treasury. Generally, this application must be made within 6 months from the date prescribed by law for the filing of the return. The time prescribed by law for filing the return includes the period of any extension of time for filing the return granted by the Commissioner. If the application is not made within such period, further opportunities in the following situations are afforded the taxpayer to secure the benefits of section 722. These situations are as follows:

(1) Under established practice and with a view to disposition of tax cases without litigation, the Commissioner ordinarily issues what is termed a preliminary notice of tax liability so as to afford the taxpayer an opportunity of a hearing before the formal notice of deficiency is mailed under section 272 (a) (1) from which appeal lies only to the Board. Where such preliminary notice is issued to the taxpayer, the latter is given a period of 90 days from the date of such notice in which to make application to the Commissioner for the benefits of section 722. If in such case a formal notice of deficiency is not issued until after the expiration of such 90-day period and the taxpayer does not avail itself of the opportunity to make such application within such period, the taxpayer cannot thereafter claim the benefits of

the section.

(2) Owing to the running of the statute of limitations against the making of assessments, the Commissioner may find it necessary (a) to mail a formal notice of deficiency without having issued a preliminary notice of the tax or (b) having issued a preliminary notice, to mail a formal notice of deficiency prior to the termination of 90 days. In either (a) or (b) the taxpayer may claim the benefits of section 722 in its petition to the Board or by means of an amended petition conformable to the rules of the Board.

In cases under (1) or (2), the benefits of the section shall not reduce the tax under chapter 2E by an amount in excess of the deficiency determined under that subchapter without the application of section 722.

If for any taxable year the average base period net income has been determined under section 722, the Commissioner is authorized by regulations approved by the Secretary to prescribe the extent to which the requirement of subsection (d), with respect to filing application for the benefits of section 722, may be waived for a subsequent taxable year. (p. 13-14)

Report—Senate Finance Committee (77th Cong., 1st Sess., S. Rept. 75).— Same as Ways and Means Committee Report. (p. 4, 13-14, respectively)

Congressional Discussion

Discussion—House (Cong. Rec. Vol. 87).—Mr. Nelson. I notice at the top of page 4 of the report to which my colleague has referred what seems to be a very reasonable safeguard:

The taxpayer must first compute and pay his tax without regard to this relief provision and then must petition the Commissioner for relief by way of claim for refund.

Mr. Doughton. That is under the

general-relief provision. Under the specific provisions[1] he can take care of it in his return, and then if the Bureau does not accept his return, it can assess a deficiency against him, and if he is not satisfied or if the Government is not, either one can appeal to the Board of Tax Appeals. (p. 1375)

[1] Relating to sec. 721.

Sec. 722(e)

[SEC. 722.   GENERAL RELIEF—CONSTRUCTIVE AVERAGE BASE PERIOD   1942
NET INCOME.]   222(a)

(e) Rules for Application of Section.—For the purposes of this section— * * *

(2)   in the case of a taxpayer, the average base period net income of which is computed under Supplement A, for the period for which the income of any other person is included in the computation of the average base period net income of the taxpayer, the taxpayer shall be treated as if such other person's business were a part of the business of the taxpayer.

Committee Reports

Report—Ways and Means Committee (77th Cong., 2d Sess., H. Rept. 2333).—If the average base period net income of a corporation is computed under Supplement A such corporation shall be treated as if the business of any person, for the period for which the income of such person is included in the computation of the average base period net income of the corporation, were a part of the business of the corporation.   (p. 142)

Sec. 722(f)

1942
222(a)   [SEC. 722.   GENERAL RELIEF—CONSTRUCTIVE AVERAGE BASE PERIOD NET INCOME.]

(f) Mining Corporations.—*In the case of a taxpayer to which section 711 (a) (1) (I) or section 711 (a) (2) (K) applies, if its constructive average base period net income is established under this section, there shall also be determined a fair and just amount to be used as normal output and normal unit profit for the purposes of section 735.*

Committee Reports

Report—Senate Finance Committee (77th Cong., 2d Sess., S. Rept. 1631).—It is provided that if a corporation's constructive average base period income is established under section 722, the general relief section, there shall also be determined a fair and just amount to be used as normal output and normal unit of profit.   (p. 39)

In section 209 your committee has amended the Code by inserting section 711 (a) (1) (I), section 711 (a) (2) (K), and section 735 so as to extend relief to certain mining corporations. Such relief is accomplished by exempting from excess profits tax a certain portion of current income. This portion is determined by multiplying the normal unit profit during a defined base period by a specified portion of current production in excess of normal output during such base period, or in the case of coal and iron mines by multiplying current excess production by one-half of the current net income per unit of coal or iron. In case the taxpayer was depressed during the base period, or would otherwise be entitled to relief by way of a constructive average base period net income under the provisions of section 722 there will exist no adequate unit profit and no normal output during the base period to be used in computing the special mining relief. Your committee has therefore added a subsection to section 722 to provide that if the constructive average base period net income of a mining corporation to which section 711 (a) (1) (I) or section 711 (a) (2) (K) applies is established under this section, there shall also be determined the fair and just amount to be used as normal output and normal unit profit for the purposes of section 735.   (p. 205)

Report—Conference Committee (77th Cong., 2d Sess., H. Rept. 2587).—As a result of the provisions added by the Senate, extending relief to certain

mining corporations by exempting from
excess profits tax a certain portion of the
current income, a further amendment
was made in the general relief provisions
to provide that, if the constructive average base period net income of a taxpayer,
to which section 711 (a) (1) (I) or sec-

tion 711 (a) (2) (K) of the Code applies,
is established under section 722, there
shall also be determined a fair and just
amount to be used as normal output and
normal unit profit for the purposes of
section 735.   (p. 62)

Sec. 723(a)

SEC. 723. EQUITY INVESTED CAPITAL IN SPECIAL CASES.

Where the Commissioner determines that the equity invested capital as of the beginning of the taxpayer's first taxable year under this
subchapter cannot be determined in accordance with section 718, the
equity invested capital as of the beginning of such year shall be an
amount equal to the sum of (a) the money plus (b) the aggregate of
the adjusted basis of the assets of the taxpayer held by the taxpayer
at such time, such sum being reduced by the indebtedness outstanding
at such time.   The amount of the money, assets, and indebtedness at
such time shall be determined in accordance with rules and regulations
prescribed by the Commissioner with the approval of the Secretary.
In such case, the equity invested capital ~~for each day in the taxpayer's base period and~~ for each day after the beginning of the taxpayer's first taxable year under this subchapter shall be determined,
in accordance with rules and regulations prescribed by the Commissioner
with the approval of the Secretary, using as the basic figure the equity
invested capital as so determined.

Committee Reports

Report—Ways and Means Subcommittee (76th Cong., 3d Sess., H. Rept.
Aug. 8, 1940).—Your subcommittee has
granted special relief only in cases where
the Commissioner is unable to determine
the taxpayer's equity invested capital for
the first day of the first taxable year beginning after December 31, 1939. In
such a case, such equity invested capital
shall be an amount, determined in accordance with rules and regulations prescribed by the Commissioner, with the
approval of the Secretary, equal to the
cash on hand plus the aggregate of the
adjusted bases at such time of the assets
of the taxpayer then held minus the indebtedness outstanding at such time.
The equity invested capital for each day
in the taxpayer's base period and for
each day after the beginning of the taxpayer's first taxable year shall be deter-

mined using as the basic figure the equity
invested capital as of the beginning of
such first taxable year.   (p. 9)

*Rule for cases where equity invested
capital cannot be determined under general
rule.*—It is recommended that, in cases
where the Commissioner determines that
the equity invested capital of a corporation as of the beginning of the taxpayer's first taxable year which begins
after December 31, 1939, cannot be determined in accordance with the method
previously described, such equity invested capital be an amount, determined
in accordance with regulations prescribed
by the Commissioner with the approval
of the Secretary, equal to the cash on
hand plus the aggregate adjusted bases
at such time of the assets of the taxpayer
then held minus the indebtedness outstanding at such time.   The equity in-

vested capital for each day in the base period and for each day after the beginning of the taxpayer's first taxable year which begins after December 31, 1939, shall be computed in accordance with regulations, using as the basic figure the equity invested capital as of the beginning of such taxable year. (p. 13-14)

Report—Ways and Means Committee (76th Cong., 3d Sess., H. Rept. 2894).— Substantially as reported by the Ways and Means Subcommittee (p. 9). In addition, there is the following:

The following example will illustrate how this provision will apply. The equity invested capital as of January 1, 1940, is computed as follows:

	Adjusted basis
Assets:	
Cash	$100,000
Other assets	400,000
Total	500,000
Less: Liabilities	200,000
Equity invested capital	300,000

When the equity invested capital has been determined as of any particular date, for example, January 1, 1940, it may be computed for any other date by making adjustments for profits and losses, dividends paid, and additions or withdrawals of capital occurring during the intervening period. Thus, if between January 1, 1937, and January 1, 1940, the above corporation had profits (after taxes) of $200,000 and paid dividends of $150,000, the equity invested capital as of January 1, 1936, would have been $250,000. Similarly, if between January 1, 1940, and January 1, 1942, the corporation had profits of $100,000 and paid dividends of $60,000, its equity

invested capital as of January 1, 1942, would be $340,000. (p. 14)

The bill provides a special method of determining equity invested capital in cases where the Commissioner is unable to determine the taxpayer's equity invested capital for the first day of the first taxable year beginning after December 31, 1939, under the rules previously discussed. In such a case, the equity invested capital as of such date shall be an amount equal to the cash on hand plus the aggregate of the adjusted bases at such time of the assets of the taxpayer then held minus the indebtedness outstanding at such time. The amount of the money, assets, and indebtedness at such time shall be determined in accordance with regulations of the Commissioner with the approval of the Secretary. The equity invested capital for each day in the taxpayer's base period and for each day after the beginning of the taxpayer's first taxable year shall be determined (under such regulations) using as the basic figure the equity invested capital so determined. (p. 27)

Report—Senate Finance Committee (76th Cong., 3d Sess., S. Rept. 2114).— There have been no changes in these sections as contained in the House bill except for the elimination of a reference to the base period in section 722.[1] (p. 16)

[1] Sec. 723 of the Code.

Report—Conference Committee (76th Cong., 3d Sess., H. Rept. 3002).— In addition to changes in section numbers, a clerical change was made by the Senate amendment because of the changes made in section 714. The Senate provision is adopted * * *. (p. 52)

Committee Hearings
1942 Act

Hearings—Ways and Means Committee.— Giving taxpayer discretionary right to apply section. (J. W. Hooper, p. 498)

Hearings—Senate Finance Committee.— Giving taxpayer discretionary right to apply section. (J. W. Hooper, p. 1175)

1918
327

[Set forth on page 338]

1918
328

[Set forth on page 342]

[Set forth on page 351]

1917
203(d)

[Set forth on page 353]

1917
210

Sec. 723(b)

[SEC. 723. EQUITY INVESTED CAPITAL IN SPECIAL CASES.]

1942
205(f)

   (b) *The equity invested capital of mutual insurance companies other than life, or marine, shall be the mean of the surplus, plus 50 per centum of the mean of all reserves required by law, both surplus and reserves being determined at the beginning and end of the taxable year. The surplus shall include all of the assets of the company other than reserves required by law.*

Committee Reports

Report—Conference Committee (77th Cong., 2d Sess., H. Rept. 2586).— Amendment No. 272: This amendment would amend section 723 of the Code to provide that the equity invested capital of mutual insurance companies other than life or marine shall be the mean of the surplus, plus 50 percent of the mean of all reserves required by law. The House recedes. (p. 58)

Congressional Discussion

Discussion—Senate (Cong. Rec. Vol. 88).—MR. LA FOLLETTE. The amendment provides that the equity invested capital of a mutual insurance company, other than life or marine, shall be the surplus funds of the company which are defined to be the assets of the company other than the reserves required by law. The reserves required by the laws of the individual States in the case of mutual fire companies is the unearned premium reserve and in the case of mutual casualty companies the unearned premium reserve and the loss reserve, the loss reserve being more important. The amendment provides that 50 percent of these reserves shall be the amount to be included with the surplus of the company as the equity invested capital.

* * *

MR. TAFT. Is the Senator proposing to put the surplus into the equity capital on which is based an excess-profits credit?

MR. LA FOLLETTE. The amendment provides that 50 percent of these reserves shall be the amount to be included with the surplus of the company as the equity invested capital.

MR. TAFT. I have some doubt about it.

* * *

MR. GEORGE. As I understand, the amendment offered by the Senator from Wisconsin would relate only to the excess profits in connection with mutual insurance companies.

MR. LA FOLLETTE. That is all. (p. 8032)

Sec. 724(a)

1942
———
212(a)   * * * **section 724** (relating to invested capital in the case of foreign corporations and corporations entitled to benefits of section 251) are amended by striking out "or having an office or place of business therein", wherever occurring therein and * * *

Committee Hearings

Hearings—Senate Finance Committee.—Explanation of provision. (J.   O'Brien—H. Legis. Counsel—p. 103)

1940
———
201   **SEC. 724. FOREIGN CORPORATIONS [1] AND CORPORATIONS ENTITLED TO BENEFITS OF SECTION 251—INVESTED CAPITAL.**

Notwithstanding section 715, in the case of a foreign corporation engaged in trade or business within the United States or having an office or place of business therein, AND IN THE CASE OF A CORPORATION ENTITLED TO THE BENEFITS OF SECTION 251, the invested capital for any taxable year shall be determined in accordance with rules and regulations prescribed by the Commissioner with the approval of the Secretary, under which—

(a) General Rule.—The daily invested capital for any day of the taxable year shall be the aggregate of the adjusted basis of each United States asset held by the taxpayer on the beginning of such day. In the application of section 720 in reduction of the average invested capital (determined on the basis of such daily invested capital), the terms "admissible assets" and "inadmissible assets" shall include only United States assets; or

[1] The words "And Corporations Entitled To Benefits Of Section 251" were added by the Conference Committee.

Committee Reports

Report—**Ways and Means Subcommittee (76th Cong., 3d Sess., H. Rept. Aug. 8, 1940).**—In the case of such foreign corporations, which were not in existence during the entire base period, the tax shall be computed by reference to the invested capital, which shall be determined as follows:

The daily invested capital for any day of the taxable year shall be the aggregate of the adjusted basis of each United States asset held by the taxpayer in the United States on the beginning of such day. For the purpose of reducing the average invested capital by the ratio of inadmissible assets to total assets, the terms "admissible assets" and "inadmissible assets" shall include only United States assets.   (p. 8)

Invested capital of foreign corporations.—It is recommended that in the case of foreign corporations (in existence during the whole of the base period) in trade or business within the United States, or having an office or place of business therein, the excess-profits credit be computed under the second alternative method. For this purpose the invested capital shall be based only on the assets of the taxpayer held by it in the United States. Such assets shall be taken into account in accordance with their adjusted bases as of the day for which the computation is made. (p. 14)

Report—Ways and Means Committee (76th Cong., 3d Sess., H. Rept. 2894).— In the case of such foreign corporations which were not in existence during the entire base period, the tax is computed by reference to the invested capital, which is determined as follows:

The daily invested capital for any day of the taxable year is the aggregate of the adjusted basis of each United States asset held by the taxpayer in the United States on the beginning of such day. For the purpose of reducing the average invested capital by the ratio of inadmissible assets to total assets, the terms "admissible assets" and "inadmissible assets" include only United States assets. (p. 12)

In the case of a foreign corporation required to compute its excess-profits credit by the invested-capital method under section 714, the invested capital is based only on the assets of the taxpayer held by it in the United States. The bill provides that the daily invested capital for any day of the taxable year shall be the aggregate of the adjusted basis of each United States asset held by the taxpayer in the United States on the beginning of such day, the determination to be made in accordance with rules and regulations prescribed by the Commissioner with the approval of the Secretary. For the purpose of reducing the average invested capital by the ratio of inadmissible assets to the sum of admissible and inadmissible assets, the terms "admissible assets" and "inadmissible assets" include only United States assets. (p. 27-28)

[Set forth on page 337]

$$\frac{1918}{326(d)}$$

Sec. 724(b)

[SEC. 724. FOREIGN CORPORATIONS AND CORPORATIONS ENTITLED TO BENEFITS OF SECTION 251—INVESTED CAPITAL.]

$$\frac{1940}{201}$$

(b) Exception.—If the Commissioner determines that the United States assets of the taxpayer cannot satisfactorily be segregated from its other assets, the invested capital for the taxable year shall be an amount which is the same percentage of the aggregate of the adjusted basis of all assets held by the taxpayer as of the end of the last day of the taxable year which the net income for the taxable year from sources within the United States is of the total net income of the taxpayer for such year.

Committee Reports

Report—Ways and Means Subcommittee (76th Cong., 3d Sess., H. Rept. Aug. 8, 1940).—If the Commissioner determines that the amount of the United States assets cannot be determined, invested capital is to be an amount which is the same percentage of all the assets of the corporation as the United States income is of the total income. (p. 14)

Report—Ways and Means Committee (76th Cong., 3d Sess., H. Rept. 2894).— If the Commissioner determines that the United States assets of the taxpayer cannot satisfactorily be segregated from all its assets, section 722 (b) of the bill provides that the invested capital for the taxable year shall be an amount which is the same percentage of the aggregate of the adjusted basis of all assets held by the taxpayer as of the end of the last day of the taxable year which the net income for the taxable year from sources within the United States is of the total net income of the taxpayer for such year. (p. 28)

Sec. 724(c)

1940
201

[SEC. 724. FOREIGN CORPORATIONS AND CORPORATIONS ENTITLED
             TO BENEFITS OF SECTION 251—INVESTED CAPITAL.]

(c) **Definition of United States Asset.**—As used in this subsection,
the term "United States asset" means an asset held by the taxpayer
in the United States, determined in accordance with rules and regulations prescribed by the Commissioner with the approval of the Secretary.

Committee Reports

Report—**Ways and Means Subcommittee (76th Cong., 3d Sess., H. Rept.
Aug. 8, 1940).**—The term "United States
asset" means an asset held by the taxpayer in the United States, determined
in accordance with rules and regulations
prescribed by the Commissioner with
the approval of the Secretary. (p. 27-
28)

Sec. 725(a)

1940
201

SEC. 725. PERSONAL SERVICE CORPORATIONS.

(a) **Definition.**—As used in this subchapter, the term "personal
service corporation" means a corporation <whose> [*in which capital
is not a material income-producing factor and either*]

[*(1) Whose*] WHOSE income is to be ascribed primarily to
the activities of shareholders who are regularly engaged in the active conduct of the affairs of the corporation and are the owners at
all times during the taxable year of at least [80] 70 per centum in
value of [all the] EACH CLASS OF stock of the corporation, <and
in which capital is not a material income-producing factor:> *or*

[*(2) Whose income is to be ascribed primarily to the activities of
shareholders who are regularly engaged in the active conduct of the affairs
of the corporation, all of whose stock is owned at all times during the
taxable year by or for not more than 20 individuals.*] AND IN WHICH
CAPITAL IS NOT A MATERIAL INCOME-PRODUCING FAC-
TOR; but does not include any foreign corporation, nor any corporation 50 per centum or more of whose gross income consists of gains,
profits, or income derived from trading as a principal. For the purposes of this subsection, an individual shall be considered as owning,
at any time, the stock owned at such time by his spouse or minor
child OR BY ANY GUARDIAN OR TRUSTEE REPRESENTING
THEM.

[(b) Definitions.—*As used in this subchapter, the term "personal service corporation" means a corporation in which capital is not a material income-producing factor and either—*

(1) *At least 80 per centum in value of whose capital stock is owned at all times during the taxable year by shareholders who are regularly engaged in the active conduct of the affairs of the corporation, or*

(2) *Whose income is to be ascribed primarily to the activities of shareholders who are regularly engaged in the active conduct of the affairs of the corporation, all of whose stock is owned at all times during the taxable year by or for not more than 20 individuals but does not include any foreign corporation, nor any corporation 50 per centum or more of whose gross income consists of gains, profits or income derived from trading as a principal. For the purposes of this subsection, an individual shall be considered as owning, at any time, the stock owned at such time by his spouse or minor child or by any guardian or trustee representing them.]*

Committee Reports

Report—Ways and Means Subcommittee (76th Cong., 3d Sess., H. Rept. Aug. 8, 1940).—For this purpose it is proposed to define a personal-service corporation as any corporation whose income is to be ascribed primarily to the activities of the principal owners or shareholders who are themselves regularly engaged in the active conduct of its affairs and in which capital, whether invested or borrowed, is not a material income-producing factor, but not including any foreign corporation or any corporation 50 percent or more of the gross income of which consists of gains, profits, or income derived from trading as a principal. (p. 13)

Report—Ways and Means Committee (76th Cong., 3d Sess., H. Rept. 2894).—A personal-service corporation is defined as a corporation whose income is to be ascribed primarily to the activities of shareholders who are regularly engaged in the active conduct of the affairs of the corporation and are the owners at all times during the taxable year of at least 80 percent in value of all the stock of the corporation and in which capital is not a material income-producing factor. For this purpose an individual is considered as owning at any time the stock owned at such time by his spouse or minor child.

Thus all the shareholders, who are regularly engaged in the active conduct of the affairs of the corporation may be counted in determining whether such a corporation may be classified as a personal-service corporation, instead of merely the principal shareholders. Moreover, to determine whether such shareholders own at least 80 percent in value of the stock of the corporation, the stock owned by their spouses or minor children may be included. A personal-service corporation does not include a foreign corporation or any corporation 50 percent or more of whose gross income consists of gains, profits, or income derived from trading as a principal. (p. 11-12)

Section 723 (a)[1] defines a personal-service corporation as a corporation whose income is attributable primarily to the activities of shareholders who are regularly engaged in the active conduct of the affairs of the corporation and are the owners at all times during the taxable year of at least 80 percent in value of the stock of the corporation, and in which capital (whether invested or borrowed) is not a material income-producing factor. For the purpose of the stock-ownership requirement an individual is considered as owning, at any time, the stock owned at such time by his spouse or minor child. The term "personal-service corporation" does not include any foreign corporation, nor any corporation 50 percent or more of whose gross income consists of gains, profits, or income derived from trading as a principal. (p. 28)

¹ Sec. 725(a) of the Code

Report—Senate Finance Committee (76th Cong., 3d Sess., S. Rept. 2114).— No change is made by your committee in the provisions of the House bill relating to personal-service corporations. (p. 6)

Report—Conference Committee (76th Cong., 3d Sess., H. Rept. 3002).— *House bill.* * * * A personal service corporation was defined to mean a corporation whose income is attributable primarily to the activities of shareholders who are regularly engaged in the active conduct of the affairs of the corporation and are owners at all times during the taxable year of at least 80 percent in value of the stock of the corporation, and in which capital (whether invested or borrowed) is not a material income-producing factor. Foreign corporations and any corporation 50 percent or more of whose gross income consisted of gains, profits, or income derived from trading as a principal were excluded. For the purposes of the stock-ownership test, an individual was considered as owning stock owned by his spouse or minor child.

Senate amendment.—The Senate amendment contains, in effect, three alternative definitions of a personal service corporation. The first is that contained in the House bill. The second defines a personal service corporation as a corporation (in which capital is not an income-producing factor) at least 80 percent in value of whose stock is owned at all times during the taxable year by shareholders who are regularly engaged in the active conduct of the corporation's affairs. This definition differs from the House definition in that it does not require the corporation's income to be ascribed primarily to the activities of such shareholders. The third alternative contained in the Senate amendment defines a personal service corporation as a corporation (in which capital is not an income-producing factor) the income of which is to be ascribed primarily to the activities of shareholders who are actively engaged in the conduct of the corporation's affairs and all of the stock of which is owned at all times during the taxable year by or for not more than 20 individuals. The effect of this alternative is to include corporations which have so-called silent partners who own more than 20 percent of its stock. As to both alternatives added by the Senate amendment, it is provided that an individual shall be considered as owning stock owned not only by his spouse or minor child, but by any guardian or trustee representing them.

Conference agreement.—Under the conference agreement a personal service corporation is defined to mean a corporation whose income is attributable primarily to the activities of shareholders who are regularly engaged in the active conduct of the affairs of the corporation and are owners at all times during the taxable year of at least 70 percent in value of each class of stock of the corporation, and in which capital (whether invested or borrowed) is not a material income-producing factor. Foreign corporations and any corporation 50 percent or more of whose gross income consisted of gains, profits, or income derived from trading as a principal are excluded. For the purposes of the stock-ownership test, an individual is considered as owning stock owned by his spouse or minor child or by any guardian or trustee representing them. (p. 52-53)

Congressional Discussion

Discussion—House (Cong. Rec. Vol. 86).—Mr. Lewis of Colorado. * * * The personal holding corporation provisions do not and cannot take care of the cases where limited capital is necessary and services of other than the principal stockholders are availed of. (p. 11253)

Discussion—Senate (Cong. Rec. Vol. 86).—Mr. Brown. Mr. President, as the Senator from Mississippi [Mr. Harrison] recalls, we had considerable difficulty over the definition of personal-service corporations; and a great deal of complaint has come from that particular class of corporations about the way in which we finally drafted the amendment appearing in the bill. The principal complaint is that no corporation may be considered a personal-service corporation unless 80 percent of its stock is owned by the individuals who actually operate the corporation.

My attention has been called to the fact that there are a great many personal-service corporations, such as—if I may give an example—incorporated advertising agencies. Of course, a firm of lawyers may not incorporate, but it will serve as a good example of the situation. Attention has been called to the fact that many times a so-called silent partner puts up the money and demands more than 20 percent of the stock. That particular kind of personal-service corporation could not possibly qualify and get the benefits which we intend to give to personal-service corporations.

I may say that those benefits are these: Such corporations are not within the provisions of this proposed statute, but their income is taxed just the same, because, of course, the income of that class of corporations is largely distributed, and becomes taxable under personal income-tax statements.

The amendment which has been suggested to me is as follows, having identically the same definition as the bill in section 724, but adding this language:

Whose income is to be ascribed primarily to the activities of shareholders who are regularly engaged in the active conduct of the affairs of the corporation, all of whose stock is owned at all times during the taxable year by or for not more than 20 individuals, and whose invested capital for the taxable year is not in excess of $500,000.

If the amendment in that form had been presented to us before the Finance Committee reported the bill, I think it would have been accepted. Since that time I have discussed it with representatives of this class of corporations, and I feel that it is fair. I realize that if those who are in charge of the business of the Senate find, upon a thorough examination of the amendment, that it goes too far or does not go far enough, it may be rejected.

I will say to the Senator from Mississippi that the amendment I suggest does not change the present law at all. It uses the same language, except that it includes within personal-service corporations a corporation whose total number of members or stockholders is not more than 20, and whose capital is not in excess of $500,000; but those actively engaged need not be the owners of 80 percent of the stock.

MR. HARRISON. Mr. President, so far as I am concerned I am willing to let the amendment proposed by the Senator from Michigan go to conference. Different views have been expressed about these personal-service corporations.

* * *

MR. NORRIS. I wonder why the Senator limits his amendment to corporations having $500,000 of capital stock or less?

MR. BROWN. Because when the capital of the corporation is larger than $500,000 regardless of the statement in the statute that the capital must not be a material income-producing factor, it seemed to me—and I was the one who placed that limitation on it—that the capital is a material factor.

MR. NORRIS. I wonder why the Senator reached that conclusion. To me it would seem that the amendment is intended to apply to cases in which the capital stock, as the amendment says, is not a material factor. If a corporation has a capital stock, let us say, of $490,000, does not the Senator think that is a case, on its face at least, in which the capital stock plays a very important part, and the amendment ought not to apply to it?

MR. BROWN. Of course, it is necessary to draw the line somewhere. If the maximum were $100,000, I am fearful that it would be a little bit too small, and this particular sum was selected for that reason.

MR. NORRIS. The Senator's amendment is intended to apply to cases in which the capital stock is practically an immaterial factor.

MR. BROWN. That is true.

MR. NORRIS. I can see some reason for that. It is a personal corporation, but when that kind of a corporation has a capital stock of even $100,000 it shows on its face, it seems to me, that the capital stock is important, if not the most important thing.

MR. BROWN. The Senator did not hear the entire definition read.

MR. NORRIS. I heard the entire amendment read.

MR. BROWN. The first paragraph I did not read. It says:

As used in this subchapter the term "personal-service corporation" means a corporation in which the capital stock is not a material income-producing factor.

MR. NORRIS. I heard that read.

MR. BROWN. Therefore, a corporation could have a capital of $10,000 and still not qualify under this definition. Not only must it be a corporation having not in excess of 20 stockholders, and not only must it be a corporation having a capital stock of less than $500,000, but it must also be a corporation in which the capital is not a material income-producing factor.

MR. NORRIS. That is where I think the contradiction comes in. It seems to me that where a corporation has a capital stock let us say of $495,000, under a provision under which capital stock is supposed not to be a material factor, there is a contradiction in the face of things. That amount of capital stock, it seems to me, would be considered very large for a corporation. Here we are dealing with a corporation where we say, to begin with, that capital stock is not a material thing; it is a personal corporation. It seems to me the amendment contradicts itself.

MR. BARKLEY. Mr. President, these personal corporations are corporations where the personal services, the activities of the members, are the chief factor in the income. What really is the need for such a corporation having $500,000 capital stock? What do they do with the capital stock if it does not have any part to play in their business or profits?

MR. BROWN. I presume that in large personal corporations such as an advertising agency—and it was the advertising people who discussed the matter with me, among others—there might be considerable capital.

MR. BARKLEY. What do they do with it if it is not used in the business, and does not play some part in the activity? At the end of the year, when they distribute their earnings, do they declare a dividend on the capital, or is it all taken up in salaries; or how does it operate?

MR. BROWN. I understand that the first paragraph of the amendment, as well as the committee amendment, takes care of that by insisting that capital must not be a material factor in the production of the income. I do not mind if it is a smaller sum than that. I have no particular interest in the matter other than that it was brought before the Finance Committee, and this seemed to me, after a careful examination of the entire situation, to be about as fair an amendment as could be devised.

MR. NORRIS. Of course, I have no interest in it, either. But in dealing with corporations as to which capital stock is not a material factor, because we are dealing with personal corporations, the corporation being controlled entirely by stockholders themselves, if that kind of a corporation deserves different treatment from another, it seems to me that the capital stock is only a nominal consideration. Indeed, there should be no capital stock.

MR. BROWN. Would the Senator say we should strike out the $500,000 limitation?

MR. NORRIS. I think so.

MR. BROWN. That would suit me entirely.

MR. HARRISON. Would $100,000 be all right?

MR. NORRIS. Why have any capital stock limitation? I do not see any use of it where the personal services of the stockholders are united, where they are together, and act as one, instead of acting separately. They are not going to use their capital stock if they have any, and if they do, then the corporation loses the attribute of being a personal corporation.

MR. BROWN. I am satisfied and will modify my amendment.

MR. McKELLAR. Is it not a case where personal services are used instead of money, instead of capital?

MR. BROWN. Where it is the material income-producing factor.

MR. McKELLAR. Where personal services are the material income-providing factor.

MR. BROWN. I thought there should be some limitation. I modify my amendment in accordance with the suggestion of the Senator from Nebraska.

MR. HARRISON. Mr. President, I would suggest $100,000.

THE PRESIDING OFFICER. The clerk

will state the amendment as modified.

THE CHIEF CLERK. On page 113, line 20, in the committee amendment, it is proposed to strike out section 724 and to insert:

SEC. 724. Personal service corporations. As used in this subchapter the term "personal-service corporation" means a corporation in which the capital is not a material income-producing factor and whose income is to be ascribed primarily to the activities of stockholders who are regularly engaged in the active conduct of the affairs of the corporation, all of whose stock is owned at all times by not more than 20 individuals.

At this point it is proposed to strike out the words "and whose invested capital for the taxable year is not in excess of $500,000." (p. 12179-180)

MR. CLARK of Missouri. * * * The amendment of the Senator from Michigan was intended to obviate some ambiguities in the bill, and it appears that that has not been completely done. The purpose of the amendment which I now seek to offer is simply to remove the ambiguities. * * *

MR. CLARK of Missouri. * * * I will say to the chairman of the committee that I have discussed the matter both with the officials of the Treasury and with members of the staff of the Joint Committee on Internal Revenue Taxation, and they say there is no question that the old definition of the 1917 act, which has been adopted practically verbatim in this bill as it came over from the House, was ambiguous, and resulted in a great deal of litigation, I think to the extent of 14,000 lawsuits. What we are seeking to do is to remove the ambiguity as to what are personal-service corporations. The Treasury officials and the members of the staff of the joint committee have told me that the subject ought to be redefined, but they have frankly stated that they have been so over-pressed with the amount of work which has been put upon them by the two committees that they have not had an opportunity to do it.

* * *

MR. CLARK of Missouri. Then I will change the text of this amendment, and offer it as a new subsection to be inserted at the proper place, which I assume would be immediately after the amendment adopted the other day at the suggestion of the Senator from Michigan.

The amendment of Mr. CLARK of Missouri is as follows:

Insert at the proper place in the bill the following:
"As used in this subchapter, the term 'personal-service corporation' means a corporation in which capital is not a material income-producing factor and either * * * (p. 12350)

Discussion—Senate; on Report of Conference Committee (Cong. Rec. Vol. 86).—MR. HARRISON. The question of personal-service corporations was advanced in the debate. We were unable to get the House conferees to agree to the Senate amendments in toto. However, under the conference agreement, the definition of a personal service corporation was defined to mean a corporation where income was attributed primarily to the activities of shareholders who are regularly engaged in the active conduct of the affairs of the corporation and are the owners at all times during the taxable year of at least 70 percent in value of each class of stock of the corporation and in which capital is not a material income-producing factor. Under the House bill, the persons actively engaged in the business had to own 80 percent of the stock.

In the case of determining whether the shareholders own the requisite shares of stock the Senate provision was adopted, which permitted that the individual shall be considered as owning stock owned not only by his spouse or minor child but by any guardian or trustee representing them.

So we did the best we could in trying to work out that very delicate question. (p. 12920)

Committee Hearings

Hearings—Ways and Means Committee.—Eliminating requirement that stockholder be regularly engaged in active conduct of corporate affairs. (C. Davidson, p. 119-122, 131; J. Benson, p. 136, 141-144; A. C. Nielsen, p. 254-257)

Hearings—Senate Finance Committee.—Eliminating requirement that stockholders be regularly engaged in active conduct of corporate affairs. (J. Benson, p. 13-20; K. Carroad, p. 26, 39-40; C. Davidson, p. 72-77; E. C. Alvord, p. 273; J. W. Hooper, p. 354; L. Bush,

p. 475-477)

Explanation of provision. (J. L. Sullivan—Treas. Dept.—p. 122; C. F.

Stam—Jt. Com. on Int. Rev. Taxn.— p. 210)

1942 Act

Hearings—Ways and Means Committee.—Clarifying situation as to when income is ascribed to stockholder. (J. Benson, p. 1877-84)

Clarifying situation as to when capital is a material income producing factor. (J. Benson, p. 1878-84)

1941 Act

Hearings—Ways and Means Committee.—Distinguishing between workmen and executive heads in determining primary source of income. (J. Benson, p. 1173-74)

Eliminating provision limiting extent of trading as a principal. (J. Benson, p. 1174-75)

Clarifying situation as to when capital

is a material income producing factor. (J. Benson, p. 1175; A. C. Nielsen, p. 1232-33)

Eliminating requirement about activities of stockholder. (A. C. Nielsen, p. 1233)

Eliminating requirement about distribution to stockholder. (A. C. Nielsen, p. 1234)

$\frac{1918}{300}$ [Set forth on page 322]

$\frac{1918}{303}$ [Set forth on page 322]

$\frac{1917}{201}$ [Set forth on page 348]

$\frac{1917}{207}$ [Set forth on page 359]

$\frac{3/3/17}{204}$ [Set forth on page 375]

Sec. 725(b)

$\frac{1942}{223(b)}$

[SEC. 725. PERSONAL SERVICE CORPORATIONS.]

(b) **Election as to Taxability.**—If a personal service corporation signifies * * * it shall be exempt from such tax for such year * * * *Such corporation shall not be exempt for such year if it is a member of an affiliated group of corporations filing consolidated returns under section 141.*

Committee Reports

Report—Senate Finance Committee (77th Cong., 2d Sess., S. Rept. 1631).—It amends section 725 (relating to exemptions of personal service corporations from excess profits tax) * * * so as to provide that any corporation which would otherwise be exempt from excess profits tax and which is a member of an affiliated group of corporations which files a consolidated return under section 141 shall not be exempt from the excess profits tax. (p. 209-210)

Report—Conference Committee (77th Cong., 2d Sess., H. Rept. 2586).—Amendment No. 336: This amendment provides that a corporation which would otherwise be exempt from excess profits tax shall not be exempt if it is a member of an affiliated group of corporations which files a consolidated return under section 141 of the Code. The reason for this change is explained in connection with amendment No. 186.[1] The House recedes. (p. 64)

[1] Relating to sec. 141(a) of the Code.

Committee Hearings
1943 Act

Hearings—Ways and Means Committee.—Continuing excess profits tax exemption for corporations despite consolidated returns. (E. C. Alvord, p. 685; Controllers Institute of America, p. 1331)

Hearings—Senate Finance Committee.—Continuing excess profits tax exemption for corporations despite consolidated returns. (E. C. Alvord, p. 615-616; M. B. Carroll, p. 745-746; A. B. Chapman, p. 830)

[SEC. 725. PERSONAL SERVICE CORPORATIONS.]

(b) **Election as to Taxability.**—If a personal service corporation signifies, in its return under Chapter 1 for any taxable year, its desire not to be subject to the tax imposed under this subchapter for such taxable year, it shall be exempt from such tax for such year, and the provisions of Supplement S of Chapter 1 shall apply to the shareholders in such corporation who were such shareholders on the last day of such taxable year of the corporation.

Committee Reports

Report—Ways and Means Subcommittee (76th Cong., 3d Sess., H. Rept. Aug. 8, 1940).—A corporation whose income is to be attributed primarily to the activities of the principal owners or stockholders who are themselves regularly engaged in the active conduct of the affairs of the corporation and in which capital is not a material income-producing factor is classed as a personal service corporation. Such a corporation may signify in its return for any taxable year its desire not to be subject to the excess-profits tax and in such case it will be exempt from tax for such year. However, in order to obtain such treatment the shareholders of the corporation are required to include the undistributed income of such a corporation in their gross

income, which then is subject to normal tax and surtax. (p. 9)

It is further recommended that a personal service corporation be permitted to elect to have its income taxed in the hands of its shareholders in lieu of paying the excess-profits tax. (p. 10)

Personal-service corporations.—It is recommended that a personal-service corporation be given the privilege of electing whether to be taxed under the excess-profits tax provisions applicable to other corporations or, in lieu of paying such tax, to have its shareholders include their pro rata share of the corporation's net income in their own income as a constructive dividend subject to tax in the same manner as other dividends. * * * Whichever method of taxation is chosen by the corporation, the corporation will, of course, continue to be subject to the normal corporate income tax. (p. 13)

Report—Ways and Means Committee (76th Cong., 3d Sess., H. Rept. 2894).— A personal-service corporation, as defined in the bill, may be relieved from the excess-profits tax for any year by electing to have its income for such year taxed in the hands of the shareholders, whether or not actually distributed to them. (p. 3)

Under the bill, a personal-service corporation may signify in its return for any taxable year its desire not to be subject to the excess-profits tax, and it will be exempt from the tax for such year. However, in order for the corporation to be exempt, the shareholders are required to include the undistributed income of such a corporation in their gross income, which then is subject to normal and surtax. (p. 11)

Section 723[1] provides special treatment for personal-service corporations. Such corporations may elect not to be subject to the excess-profits tax, and in such event the undistributed income of the corporation will be taxed to its shareholders. (p. 28)

Subsection (b) of section 723[1] provides that a personal-service corporation may elect in its income-tax return under chapter 1 for any taxable year not to be subject to the excess-profits tax and in such event it will be exempt from tax for such taxable year. A new election must be made for each taxable year and may be made only in its income-tax return for such year. If the corporation so elects for any taxable year its undistributed net income is required to be included in the gross income of the persons who were shareholders of the corporation on the last day of the corporation's taxable year.

The treatment of the undistributed income of the corporation for tax purposes both with respect to the corporation and its shareholders is prescribed in the new Supplement S. This supplement is explained later in this report. (p. 28)

[1] Sec. 725 of the Code.

Report—Senate Finance Committee (76th Cong., 3d Sess., S. Rept. 2114).— No change is made by your committee in the provisions of the House bill relating to personal-service corporations. (p. 6)

Report—Conference Committee (76th Cong., 3d Sess., H. Rept. 3002).— *House bill.*—The House bill allowed a personal service corporation an election to have its income taxed in the hands of its shareholders in lieu of paying an excess-profits tax. (p. 52)

Congressional Discussion
1940 (1st) Act

Discussion—Senate (Cong. Rec. Vol. 86).—Mr. La Follette. * * * In conformity with the old law, personal-service corporations would not be subject to this tax[1] for the reason that capital is not a material income-producing factor in corporations of that type. (p. 8598)

[1] Relating to the excess profits tax.

Committee Hearings

Hearings—Ways and Means Committee.—Explanation of recommendation of Ways and Means subcommittee. (J. L. Sullivan—Treas. Dept.—p. 74, 90)

1941 Act

Hearings—Ways and Means Committee.—Eliminating stockholders' tax on profits invested in fixed assets. (A. C. Nielsen, p. 1235)

Granting personal service corporations an option to be taxed based on percent of sales. (A. C. Nielsen, p. 1236-41)

Sec. 726

SEC. 726. CORPORATIONS COMPLETING CONTRACTS UNDER MERCHANT MARINE ACT, 1936.

1940
201

(a) If the United States Maritime Commission certifies to the Commissioner that the taxpayer has completed within the taxable year any contracts or subcontracts which are subject to the provisions of section 505 (b) of the Merchant Marine Act of 1936, as amended, then the tax imposed by this subchapter for such taxable year shall be, in lieu of a tax computed under section 710, a tax computed under subsection (b) of this section, if, and only if, the tax computed under subsection (b) is less than the tax computed under section 710.

(b) The tax computed under this subsection shall be the excess of—

(1) A tentative tax computed under section 710 with the excess profits net income and the normal-tax net income increased by the amount of any payments made, or to be made, to the United States Maritime Commission with respect to such contracts or subcontracts; over

(2) The amount of such payments.

Committee Reports

Report—Ways and Means Committee (76th Cong., 3d Sess., H. Rept. 2894).—Under section 505 of the Merchant Marine Act, 1936, as amended, if any contracting party within an income taxable year completes one or more contracts or subcontracts for the construction of a vessel under such act, such party is required to pay to the United States Maritime Commission profit in excess of 10 percent of the total contract prices of such contracts and subcontracts. The excess profit so paid to the Maritime Commission, together with all other receipts of the Commission, are placed in a revolving construction fund and are available for further ship construction.

In view of the fact that such profit-limiting provisions are retained, it is believed that a taxpayer subject thereto should have some relief from the excess-profits tax.

Section 724[1] is designed to accomplish this purpose. It provides for an alternative tax which is to be paid if it is less than the tax computed under section 710.

As a general rule the amounts received by the contracting party and recaptured by the Maritime Commission would be excluded from net income in computing the excess-profits tax under section 710. In computing the alternative tax provided for by section 724[1] the taxpayer will be required to increase its excess-profit net income and its normal-tax net income by the amount of the payments to the Maritime Commission. The tax computed upon this basis is then reduced by the amount of the payments to the Maritime Commission, and the remainder constitutes the tax which is to be paid if it is less than the tax computed under section 710. (p. 29)

[1] Section 726 of the Code.

Report—Senate Finance Committee (76th Cong., 3d Sess., S. Rept. 2114).—This section is the same as section 724 of the House bill except for a clarifying change. (p. 16)

Report—Conference Committee (76th Cong., 3d Sess., H. Rept. 3002).—In addition to changing the section number, only a clarifying change was made in this section by the Senate amendment. (p. 53)

Committee Hearings

Hearings—Senate Finance Committee.—Explanation of provision. (J. L. Sullivan—Treas. Dept.—p. 129-130; C. F. Stam—Jt. Com. on Int. Rev. Taxn.— p. 211)

Applying provision to subcontractors. (E. S. Land, p. 130-131)

Sec. 727(a)

1942
223(a)

So much of section 727 as reads "The following corporations shall be exempt from the tax imposed by this subchapter" is amended to read as follows: "The following corporations, except a member of an affiliated group of corporations filing consolidated returns under section 141, shall be exempt from the tax imposed by this subchapter".

Committee Reports

Report—Senate Finance Committee (77th Cong., 2d Sess., S. Rept. 1631).— It amends section * * * 727 (relating to corporations exempt from excess profits tax) so as to provide that any corporation which would otherwise be exempt from excess profits tax and which is a member of an affiliated group of corporations which files a consolidated return under section 141 shall not be exempt from the excess profits tax. (p. 209-210)

Report—Conference Committee (77th

Cong., 2d Sess., H. Rept. 2586).— Amendment No. 336: This amendment provides that a corporation which would otherwise be exempt from excess profits tax shall not be exempt if it is a member of an affiliated group of corporations which files a consolidated return under section 141 of the Code. The reason for this change is explained in connection with amendment No. 186.[1] The House recedes. (p. 64)

[1] Relating to sec. 141(a) of the Code.

Committee Hearings
1943 Act

Hearings—Ways and Means Committee.—Continuing excess profits tax exemption for corporations despite consolidated returns. (E. C. Alvord, p. 685; Controllers Institute of America, p. 1331)

Hearings—Senate Finance Committee.—Continuing excess profits tax exemption for corporations despite consolidated returns. (E. C. Alvord, p. 615-616; M. B. Carroll, p. 745-746; A. B. Chapman, p. 830)

1918
304
[Set forth on page 325]

1917
201
[Set forth on page 348]

1917
202
[Set forth on page 349]

[Set forth on page 350] $\frac{1917}{203(c)}$

[Set forth on page 375] $\frac{3/3/17}{204}$

Sec. 727(b)
Sec. 727(e)

[SEC. 727. EXEMPT CORPORATIONS.] $\frac{1940}{201}$

[The following corporations shall be exempt from the tax imposed by this subchapter:]

(b)   Foreign personal-holding companies, as defined in section 331.

(e)   Personal-holding companies, as defined in section 501.

Congressional Discussion
1940 (1st) Act

Discussion—Senate (Cong. Rec. Vol. 86).—MR. LA FOLLETTE. * * * In conformity with the old law, personal-service corporations would not be subject to this tax for the reason that capital is not a material income-producing factor in corporations of that type. This is also true with respect to personal holding companies which are now subject to surtaxes on their undistributed profits, as high as 75 percent, in addition to the existing corporation taxes. It is also true with respect to foreign personal-holding companies, which are taxed like partnerships as far as American shareholders are concerned, in that the American shareholder is required to take up his distributive share of the net income of the corporation, whether distributed or not, and such income is therefore subject to our present surtaxes.   (p. 8598)

Hearings—Senate Finance Committee.—Explanation of provision.   (C. F. Stam—Jt. Com. on Int. Rev. Taxn.— p. 213)

Sec. 727(c)

[SEC. 727. EXEMPT CORPORATIONS.] $\frac{1942}{223(c)}$

[The following corporations shall be exempt from the tax imposed by this subchapter:]

(c)   Regulated investment companies as defined in section 361 without the application of section 361 (b) **<{3}>** *(4).*

Committee Reports

Report—Ways and Means Committee (77th Cong., 2d Sess., H. Rept. 2333).— This section amends section 727 (c) and (d) (relating to exemption of certain investment companies from excess profits tax) so as to conform with amendments made by section 151[1] of the bill, relating to the income tax applicable to regulated investment companies.   Under the amendment an investment company that is entitled to the special income tax treatment under Supplement Q for its taxable year is exempt from excess profits tax for the same taxable year. However, in order for such an investment company to be exempt from the excess profits tax, it is not required to comply with the provisions of section 361 (b) (3) which requires an amount not less than 90 percent of its net income for the taxable year, computed without regard to net long-term and net short-term capital gains, to be distributed to shareholders as taxable dividends during the taxable year. (p. 150)

[1] Sec. 170 of the Act.

In addition, this section amends section 727 (c) and (d) (relating to exemption of certain investment companies from excess profits tax) so as to conform

with amendments made by section 172[1] of the bill, relating to the income tax applicable to regulated investment companies. Under the amendment an investment company that is entitled to the special income tax treatment under supplement Q for its taxable year is exempt from excess profits tax for the same taxable year. However, in order for such an investment company to be exempt from the excess profits tax, it is not required to comply with the provisions of section 361 (b) (3) which requires an amount not less than 90 percent of its net income for the taxable year, computed without regard to net long-term and net short-term capital gains, to be distributed to shareholders as taxable dividends during the taxable year. (p. 210)

[1] Sec. 170 of the Act.

Committee Hearings

Hearings—Senate Finance Committee.—Explanation of provision. (J.

O'Brien—H. Legis. Counsel—p. 109)

$\frac{1918}{304}$	[Set forth on page 325]
$\frac{1917}{201}$	[Set forth on page 348]
$\frac{1917}{202}$	[Set forth on page 349]
$\frac{1917}{203(c)}$	[Set forth on page 350]
$\frac{3/3/17}{204}$	[Set forth on page 375]

Sec. 727(d)

$\frac{1940}{201}$

[SEC. 727. EXEMPT CORPORATIONS.]

[The following corporations shall be exempt from the tax imposed by this subchapter:]

(d) Investment companies which under the Investment Company Act of 1940 are registered as diversified companies at all times during

the taxable year.   ~~In the case of taxable years beginning in 1940 a~~
~~company shall be considered as so registered at all times during such~~
~~taxable year before the date of such registration, if such registration~~
~~is made before December 1, 1940.~~   *For the purposes of this subsection,
if a company is so registered before July 1, 1941, it shall be considered
as so registered at all times prior to the date of such registration.*

Committee Reports

Report—Senate Finance Committee
(76th Cong., 3d Sess., S. Rept. 2114).—
(1) Section 726 (d) relating to investment companies registered as diversified
companies under the Investment Company Act of 1940 is amended to allow
such companies until July 1, 1941, to so
register and thereby obtain exemption
from the excess-profits tax, instead of
December 1, 1940, as under the House
bill. (p. 16)
Report—Conference Committee (76th
Cong., 3d Sess., H. Rept. 3002).—The

Senate amendment made no change in
this section as contained in the House
bill except to change the section number
and to advance from December 1, 1940,
to July 1, 1941, the date before which an
investment company must register as a
diversified company under the Investment Company Act of 1940 in order to
qualify for exemption for the taxable
years 1940 and 1941. The Senate provision is adopted with a further change
in section number. (p. 53)

Committee Hearings

Hearings—Ways and Means Committee.—Exempting mutual investment
companies. (J. L. Sullivan—Treas.
Dept.—p. 91-92)
Exempting diversified investment
companies registered under the Investment Company Act of 1940. (A.
Jaretzki Jr., p. 234-238)

Exempting insurance companies.
(W. H. Cooper, p. 317)
Hearings—Senate Finance Commit-
tee.—Exempting management com-
panies. (F. B. Odlum, p. 481-483)
Exempting insurance companies.
(W. A. Cooper, p. 57-58)

[Set forth on page 325]

[Set forth on page 348]

[Set forth on page 349]

[Set forth on page 350]

[Set forth on page 375]

1918
304

1917
201

1917
202

1917
203(c)

3/3/17
204

Sec. 727(e)

[Set forth with sec. 727(b), page 187]

Sec. 727(f)

1942
212(b)

[SEC. 727. EXEMPT CORPORATIONS.]

[The following corporations shall be exempt from the tax imposed by this subchapter:]

[(f) Foreign corporations not engaged in trade or business within the United States and not having an office or place of business therein.]

Section 727 (f) (relating to exempt corporations) is amended by striking out "and not having an office or place of business therein".

Committee Hearings

Hearings—Senate Finance Committee.—Explanation of provision. (J. O'Brien—H. Legis. Counsel—p. 103)

Sec. 727(h)

1943
209(a)

[SEC. 727. EXEMPT CORPORATIONS.]

[The following corporations shall be exempt from the tax imposed by this subchapter:]

(h) Any corporation subject to the provisions of Title IV of the Civil Aeronautics Act of 1938 * * * [*For the purposes of this paragraph, such exclusion shall also be made in determining the unused excess profits credit for such year.*] SUCH EXCLUSION FROM GROSS INCOME FOR SUCH YEAR SHALL ALSO BE MADE IN COMPUTING THE UNUSED EXCESS PROFITS CREDIT ADJUSTMENT FOR ANY OTHER TAXABLE YEAR, BUT ONLY FOR THE PURPOSE OF DETERMINING WHETHER THE CORPORATION IS EXEMPTED BY THIS SUBSECTION FROM THE TAX IMPOSED BY THIS CHAPTER FOR SUCH OTHER TAXABLE YEAR.

Congressional Discussion

Discussion—House (Cong. Rec. Vol. 90).—Mr. Reid of N. Y. * * * Now then, what are the facts with reference to the civil air lines which he[1] claims are granted an unjustifiable extension of the tax subsidy on their airmail contracts under the terms of this bill?

Let us not so soon forget the lessons this war has taught us.

The one thing we had when war came that was ready for war on a minute's notice was the civil air-line industry.

Without the need for long delay and painfully drawn out preparation that industry afforded us transport aircraft and trained men for use throughout the world.

The reason for this is to be found in

two acts of Congress.   One was the Civil Aeronautics Act of 1938.   The other was a provision of the original Excess-Profits Tax Act.

The 1938 act provided for mail compensation fixed by the Civil Aeronautics Board so as to enable the air lines to prepare for the national defense.   This meant buying equipment, expanding organizations, extending routes, and laying the ground work for mobilization to do the wartime tasks for which the civil air lines are so peculiarly qualified.

The 1940 Excess-Profits Tax Act would, however, have resulted in defeating the purposes of the 1938 act, by simply taking away what Congress had provided for in 1938, had it not been for a provision we included therein.   That provision was that the tax would not apply to an air line in a given year unless the nonmail income alone is such as to give an air line adjusted excess-profits net income.

The amendment to this provision made in the act which the President has vetoed is only a perfecting technical amendment.   The present law subjects the air line to the tax if in a single year, due to temporary abnormal conditions, its nonmail income jumps—even though in prior and subsequent years that income is low. So, by the amendment, we would provide simply that for the purpose of figuring the excess-profits credit to be carried over or carried back in determining the air line's status in the tax year there shall also be the mail pay exclusion.   Thus the air line will be dealt with in the light of its experience over the period of the carry-over and carry-back years, which is entirely consistent with sound tax policy and, indeed, with the theory of the Excess-Profits Tax Act itself.

It was only because of the 1938 act, buttressed and protected by the provision of the act of 1940, that the air lines were ready for war.   Without that legislation we would have had an air-line industry in a hopelessly impotent state. Without that legislation we would not have had the aircraft which saved Dutch Harbor, which stopped Rommel in Egypt, which in so many ways have helped shorten this war.   The lives of hundreds of thousands of our troops have been saved by the action of Congress in 1938 and 1940.   And a Jap invasion of Alaska, which would have given it bases to bomb

our Northwest, was forestalled.

No man can say today how or when this war will end.   It, and its succeeding crises, may drag on intermittently for years.   We may be, 2 or 4 or 6 years hence, in the same desperate need for those air-line facilities that we faced on December 7, 1941.

But provision of those facilities is no simple and inexpensive matter.   The air lines today require new equipment, and lots of it—as soon as equipment is available—to enable them to resume their place as the necessary civil air auxiliary of the armed forces.

That auxiliary can be effective only if it is always ready to carry out its role on the instant.   Emergencies, in an air age, will not permit a long and leisurely period of getting ready.   We must always have the wings available to fly where it is necessary to fly in order to stamp out the flame of aggression.

The amendment to the law affecting the air lines is, as I have said, only a perfecting, technical amendment.   The provision affected is an indispensable item in our program for assuring in the future that we will be strong.   (p. 2003)

[1] Relating to veto message from the President (78th Cong., 2d Sess., H. Doc. 443, p. 2).

Discussion—Senate (Cong. Rec. Vol. 90).—MR. GEORGE.   Mr. President, the purpose of this amendment is to provide an excess-profits-credit carry-over for air transport companies for purposes of section 727 (h) of the code, computed consistently with the excess-profits-tax exemption now provided for them under that section.

Under section 727 (h), such companies are exempt from excess-profits tax if, in effect, their excess-profits credit equals or exceeds their excess-profits net income from sources other than mail revenue.   The intended effect of this provision was to exempt mail revenue from the excess-profits tax if ordinary income was less than the excess-profits credit.   However, a carry-over must be provided in those cases where ordinary income is less than the excess-profits credit in order to effectuate this policy. This amendment carries out this policy, and treats the amount of the difference between ordinary revenue and the credit as an unused excess-profits credit, to be carried over as a part of the excess-profits-credit carry-over for the purpose of determining the status of the taxpayer under section 727 (h) for any year which may be affected.

I should add, Mr. President, that I am asking the adoption of this amendment because the matter was discussed in one conference heretofore, and at the time of the discussion it was found that the bill then under consideration was not open in conference for such an amendment. At that time it was believed that an amendment could be formulated which would have Treasury approval. I should say frankly that the Treasury does not approve this amendment, but I have the feeling that it sets forth a sound public policy. I ask for its adoption by the Senate in order that it may have fuller consideration in the conference. (p. 375)

MR. GEORGE. * * * The next ground enumerated in the veto message[1] is as follows:

(e) Commercial air lines are granted an unjustifiable extension of the tax subsidy on their air-mail contracts.

When the conferees were sitting on the 1942 tax bill, I believe it was—at least, the tax bill prior to the present one—the question involved in this amendment was presented to the conference. The Treasury expressed approval of the principle; whereupon I said that the Senate conferees would abandon any effort to insert an amendment which we thought was open in conference on this particular point. In all good faith, Mr. Surrey undertook to perfect an amendment, to be offered during the committee consideration of the tax bill on this particular subject. Mr. Surrey was directed to confer with, or he elected to confer with, the Civil Aeronautics Ad-

ministration, whereupon they raised some objection to the whole method of taxing commercial air lines, and objected. Mr. Surrey very properly stated the case to me. Nevertheless, we offered the amendment, and I offered it with a full explanation of precisely what it was; and it went into the conference, and was accepted.

Under the Second Revenue Act of 1940, an airplane company was not required to pay an excess-profits tax if its excess-profits-tax net income, after excluding its air-mail subsidy, did not exceed its excess-profits-tax credit. That is in existing law. If its excess-profits-tax net income exceeded its excess-profits credit, with the air-mail subsidy excluded, it was required to pay a tax on its air-mail subsidy income as well as on its other income. The advantage of this relief was nullified to a large extent where the corporation had an unused excess-profits carry-over. This exempt air-mail income reduced the amount of the unused excess-profits credit available as an offset in reducing the excess-profits-tax net income in other taxable years. This section provides that where the air-mail subsidy exclusion prevents the taxpayer from paying an excess-profits tax for the year excluded, it shall not reduce the unused excess-profits credit to be carried over and applied to other taxable years.

That is the full effect of the amendment. It is entirely in harmony with the theory of existing law. It is just. But beyond all that it applies to only two or possibly three commercial air lines in the United States. That would not seem to be a substantial basis upon which to veto a general tax bill. (p. 1950)

[1] Relating to veto message from the President (78th Cong., 2d Sess., H. Doc. 443, p. 2).

[SEC. 727. EXEMPT CORPORATIONS.]

[The following corporations shall be exempt from the tax imposed by this subchapter:]

(h) Any corporation subject to the provisions of Title IV of the Civil Aeronautics Act of 1938, * * *

Committee Hearings

Hearings—Ways and Means Committee.—Exempting air carriers subject to Civil Aeronautics Act. (E. S. Gorrell, p. 176-190)

Hearings—Senate Finance Committee.—Explanation of provision. (C. F. Stam—Jt. Com. on Int. Rev. Taxn.— p. 210)

[Set forth on page 325]

$\dfrac{1918}{304}$

[Set forth on page 348]

$\dfrac{1917}{201}$

[Set forth on page 349]

$\dfrac{1917}{202}$

[Set forth on page 350]

$\dfrac{1917}{203(c)}$

[Set forth on page 375]

$\dfrac{3/3/17}{204}$

Sec. 728

SEC. 728. MEANING OF TERMS USED.

$\dfrac{1940}{201}$

The terms used in this subchapter shall have the same meaning as when used in Chapter 1.

[Set forth on page 322]

$\dfrac{1918}{300}$

[Set forth on page 348]

$\dfrac{1917}{200}$

[Set forth on page 370]

$\dfrac{3/3/17}{200}$

Sec. 729(a)

SEC. 729. LAWS APPLICABLE.

$\dfrac{1940}{201}$

(a) **General Rule.**—All provisions of law (including penalties) applicable in respect of the taxes imposed by Chapter 1, shall, insofar as not inconsistent with this subchapter, be applicable in respect of the tax imposed by this subchapter.

Committee Reports

Report—Ways and Means Committee (76th Cong., 3d Sess., H. Rept. 2894).— Section[1] 727 (a) makes applicable in respect of the excess-profits tax all provisions of law (including penalties) applicable in respect of the taxes imposed by chapter 1 which are not inconsistent with the provisions of the bill. Examples of such provisions are provisions relating to the assessment and collection of deficiencies, claims for refund, periods of limitation on the assessment and collection of deficiencies or the allowance of refunds, the jurisdiction, procedure, and powers of the Board of Tax Appeals, closing agreements, etc.   (p. 29)

[1] Sec. 729(a) of the Code.

1917 212	[Set forth on page 368]
1917 213	[Set forth on page 369]
3/3/17 203	[Set forth on page 374]
3/3/17 206	[Set forth on page 381]
3/3/17 207	[Set forth on page 381]

Sec. 729(c)

1940
201

[SEC. 729. LAWS APPLICABLE.]

(c) Foreign Taxes Paid.—In the application of section 131 for the purposes of this subchapter the tax paid or accrued to any country shall be deemed to be the amount of such tax reduced by the amount of the credit allowed with respect to such tax against the tax imposed by Chapter 1.

Committee Reports

Report—Ways and Means Committee (76th Cong., 3d Sess., H. Rept. 2894).— The bill allows a credit against the excess-profits tax for income and profit taxes paid or accrued during the taxable year by any domestic corporation to any foreign country or to any possession of the United States.   (p. 12)

Under existing law an American corporation which pays income tax to a foreign country or to a possession of the United States upon its income from such source is allowed (if it claims such credit on its return) a credit for such tax against its United States income tax but only to the extent of the American tax upon the income from such country or possession. Thus, if the United States effective tax rate is 20 percent, and the foreign effective tax rate is 25 percent, a part of the foreign tax is not allowed. Since the excess-profits tax proposed in this bill is a tax imposed upon, and measured by, income it is believed that the excess-profits tax should be included in the American tax burden against which is allowed the credit for income taxes paid to foreign countries or possessions of the United States by our domestic corporations. Accordingly, section 727[1] provides in effect that, where a credit for the tax paid to such foreign country or possession of the United States is allowed

under chapter 1, the portion, if any, of such tax not used as a credit against the tax imposed by chapter 1 by reason of the limitations of section 131 (b), will be available as a credit against the excess-profits tax subject to substantially the same principles of limitation as are applicable for normal tax purposes. (p. 29-30)

[1] Sec. 729 of the Code.

Report—Senate Finance Committee (76th Cong., 3d Sess., S. Rept. 2114).— No change has been made in the allowance of the credit for foreign taxes provided in the House bill. (p. 6)

Committee Hearings

Hearings—Senate Finance Committee.—Explanation of provision. (J. L. Sullivan—Treas. Dept.—p. 122)

Allowing foreign taxes on blocked income in year income is unblocked. (E. P. Thomas, p. 492)

Sec. 729(d)

[SEC. 729. LAWS APPLICABLE.]

(d) **Limitations on Amount of Foreign Tax Credit.**—The amount of the credit taken under this section shall be subject to each of the following limitations:

(1) The amount of the credit in respect of the tax paid or accrued to any country shall not exceed the same proportion of the tax against which such credit is taken, which the taxpayer's excess profits net income from sources within such country bears to its entire excess profits net income for the same taxable year; and

(2) The total amount of the credit shall not exceed the same proportion of the tax against which such credit is taken, which the taxpayer's excess profits net income from sources without the United States bears to its entire excess profits net income for the same taxable year.

Committee Reports

Report—Ways and Means Committee (76th Cong., 3d Sess., H. Rept. 2894).— The credit is subject to the same limitations which apply to the credit allowed for the purpose of the corporate normal income tax. This prevents the credit from reducing the tax on any excess-profits tax net income derived from American sources. The American tax,

by reason of the credit, will apply against the income from foreign sources only where the foreign tax rate is less than the tax rate imposed by the United States. It was believed necessary to provide such a credit to place our American corporations on an equal competitive basis with foreign corporations located abroad. (p. 12)

Sec. 730(a)

SEC. 730. CONSOLIDATED RETURNS.

(a) Privilege to File Consolidated Returns.—*An affiliated group of corporations shall, subject to the provisions of this section, have the privilege of making a consolidated return for the taxable year in lieu of separate returns. The making of a consolidated return shall be upon the condition that all the corporations which have been members of the affiliated group at any time during the taxable year for which the return is made consent to all the regulations under subsection (b) prescribed prior to the last day prescribed by law for the filing of such return; and the making of a consolidated return shall be considered as such consent. In the case of a corporation which is a member of the affiliated group for a fractional part of the year the consolidated return shall include the income of such corporation for such part of the year as it is a member of the affiliated group*

Committee Reports

Report—Ways and Means Committee (76th Cong., 3d Sess., H. Rept. 2894).—Your committee gave consideration to requiring consolidated returns in connection with the excess-profits tax. However, it was not possible to prepare a consolidated return provision without delaying the bill for a considerable length of time. (p. 15)

Report—Senate Finance Committee (76th Cong., 3d Sess., S. Rept. 2114).—Your committee has provided that an affiliated group of corporations may file a consolidated return in lieu of separate returns. This privilege is conditioned upon the consent by each of the corporations of the group to the regulations prescribed by the Commissioner with respect to such returns. (p. 8)

This section was not in the House bill. It permits consolidated returns to be filed by affiliated groups of corporations under certain circumstances, among which is the requirement that all the corporations which have been members of the affiliated group at any time during the taxable year for which the return is made must consent to regulations prescribed by the Commissioner, with the approval of the Secretary, prior to the last day prescribed by law for the filing of such return. The making of a consolidated return shall be considered as such consent. (p. 17)

Report—Conference Committee (76th Cong., 3d Sess., H. Rept. 3002).—Same, except for clerical changes, as Senate Finance Committee Report. (p. 54)

Congressional Discussion

Discussion—House (Cong. Rec. Vol. 86).—On permitting consolidated returns, in general. (p. 11264)

Discussion—Senate (Cong. Rec. Vol. 86).—On permitting consolidated returns, in general. (p. 12058)

Discussion—Senate; on Report of Conference Committee (Cong. Rec. Vol. 86).—Mr. O'Connor. I would like to inquire what prompted the committee to write into the bill a provision for consolidated returns of corporations. In other words, I would like to have the reasons

for it explained.

Mr. Cooper. There are a number of reasons. I cannot detail all of them in a minute, but one of the first reasons was that every excess-profits tax we have had, provided for that.

Mr. O'Connor. In other words, you are following precedent in that respect?

Mr. Cooper. We followed precedent.

I may say also that I think all of us were impressed with the inherent fairness of it. (p. 12968)

1940 (1st) Act

Discussion—Senate (Cong. Rec. Vol. 86).—MR. LA FOLLETTE. * * * Consolidated returns are restored for the purpose of this tax in order to prevent evasion of the tax.   (p. 8598)

Committee Hearings

Hearings—Ways and Means Committee.—Allowing or requiring consolidated returns.   (P. D. Seghers, p. 150; J. W. Hooper, p. 108, 227-228; C. H. Brook, p. 243; J. D. Battle, p. 271; H. B. Fernald, p. 284, 289-291; E. C. Alvord, p. 296-301, 313; W. H. Cooper, p. 315; C. N. Osborne, p. 337-338; R. V. Fletcher, p. 355; F. P. Byerly, p. 363-364; J. L. Connally, p. 366; A. B. Chapman, p. 380, 383-384; R. H. Miner, p. 421; D. E. Casey, p. 427-428; E. F. Connely, p. 435; Boston Chamber of Commerce, p. 439)

Hearings—Senate Finance Committee.—Allowing or requiring consolidated returns.   (K. Carroad, p. 25-26, 33-34, 40-41; W. A. Cooper, p. 45-46, 50-51; A. B. Trudgian, p. 84; J. L. Connolly, p. 103; W. S. Parks, p. 107; C. F. Stam —Jt. Com. on Int. Rev. Taxn.—p. 199; E. C. Alvord, p. 271; H. B. Fernald, p. 281, 284-285; N. Sargent, p. 305-306, 307; J. W. Hooper, p. 353; R. V. Fletcher, p. 356-357; J. C. Cowdin, p. 360; P. W. Haberman, p. 363, 365-368; A. B. Chapman, p. 388, 394; H. C. Jackson, p. 400; J. V. Toner, p. 465; California Chamber of Commerce, p. 484; H. Campbell, p. 487-488; J. L. Donnelly, p. 494)

1918 Act

Hearings—Senate Finance Committee.—Allowing consolidated returns.   (J. F. Callbreath, p. 183)

[Set forth on page 348]

$$\boxed{\text{Sec. 730(b)}}$$

[SEC. 730. CONSOLIDATED RETURNS.]

(b) **Regulations.**—*The Commissioner, with the approval of the Secretary, shall prescribe such regulations as he may deem necessary in order that the tax liability of any affiliated group of corporations making a consolidated return and of each corporation in the group, both during and after the period of affiliation, may be returned, determined, computed, assessed, collected, and adjusted, in such manner as clearly to reflect the excess profits tax liability and the various factors necessary for the determination of such liability, and in order to prevent avoidance of such tax liability.*

Committee Reports

Report—Senate Finance Committee (76th Cong., 3d Sess., S. Rept. 2114).— The regulations which the Commissioner is authorized to prescribe are such regulations as he may deem necessary in order that the tax liability of any affiliated group of corporations making a consolidated return and of each corporation in the group, both during and after the period of affiliation, may be returned, determined, computed, assessed, collected, and adjusted, in such manner as clearly to reflect the excess-profits tax liability and the various factors necessary for the determination of such liability, and in order to prevent avoidance of such tax liability in addition to the matters which, in the light of current and previous consolidated returns regulations, are expected to be covered in detail in the regulations to be issued by the Commissioner, are the extent to which and the manner in which the following items, among others, will be computed and given effect in determining the excess-profits-tax liability of an affiliated group: (a) Equity invested capital, borrowed capital, and invested capital, (b) admissible and inadmissible assets, and excluded capital, (c) net capital additions and reductions, (d) consolidated net operating losses, net operating losses incurred by members of the group in taxable years prior to that for which the consolidated return is filed, and the net operating loss deduction of members of the group in taxable years following that for which the consolidated return was filed, and (e) excess-profits net income and adjusted excess-profits net income. (p. 17)

Report—Conference Committee (76th Cong., 3d Sess., H. Rept. 3002).—Under section 141 of the Internal Revenue Code and corresponding sections of prior revenue acts, the Commissioner has prescribed by regulations the requirement that all corporations falling within the affiliated group at any time during the taxable year shall join in the consolidated return. The section provides that all the members of the group shall consent to such regulations as a condition to the privilege of filing such return. It is contemplated that the Commissioner will prescribe like requirements for the purposes of the consolidated returns authorized by this section and the section provides that such regulations shall be consented to by all of the includible corporations. (p. 55)

Sec. 730(d)

[SEC. 730. CONSOLIDATED RETURNS.]

(d) Definition of "Affiliated Group."—*As used in this section an "affiliated group" means one or more chains of* INCLUDIBLE *corporations connected through stock ownership with a common parent corporation* WHICH IS AN INCLUDIBLE CORPORATION *if—*

(1) *At least 95 per centum of each class of the stock of each of the* INCLUDIBLE *corporations (except the common parent corporation) is owned directly by one or more of the other* INCLUDIBLE *corporations; and*

(2) *The common parent corporation owns directly at least 95 per centum of each class of the stock of at least one of the other* INCLUDIBLE *corporations.* AS USED IN THIS SUBSECTION, THE TERM "STOCK" DOES NOT INCLUDE NONVOTING STOCK WHICH IS LIMITED AND PREFERRED AS TO DIVIDENDS.

Committee Reports

Report—Senate Finance Committee (76th Cong., 3d Sess., S. Rept. 2114).—The term "affiliated group" is defined to mean one or more chains of corporations connected through stock ownership with a common parent corporation if—

(1) At least 95 percent of each class of the stock of each of the corporations

(except the common parent corporation) is owned directly by one or more of the other corporations; and

(2) The common parent corporation owns directly at least 95 percent of each class of the stock of at least one of the other corporations. (p. 17)

Report—Conference Committee (76th Cong., 3d Sess., H. Rept. 3002).—The term "affiliated group" is defined to mean one or more chains of corporations connected through stock ownership with a common parent corporation if—

(1) At least 95 percent of each class of the stock of each of the corporations (except the common parent corporation) is owned directly by one or more of the other corporations; and

(2) The common parent corporation owns directly at least 95 percent of each class of the stock of at least one of the other corporations. (p. 54)

(2) The definition of the term "affiliated group" has been revised so as to speak in terms of includible corporations (all corporations not excluded from membership in an affiliated group being termed includible corporations) and to provide that the type of stock to which the 95-percent ownership test applies shall not include nonvoting stock which is limited and preferred as to dividends.

The term "affiliated group" is defined to mean one or more chains of includible corporations connected through stock ownership with a common parent cor-

poration which is itself an includible corporation if—

(a) At least 95 per centum of the stock of each of the includible corporations (except the common parent corporation) is owned directly by one or more of the other includible corporations; and

(b) The common parent corporation owns directly at least 95 per centum of the stock of at least one of the other includible corporations.

In view of the above definition consolidated returns may not be filed by subsidiary corporations as an affiliated group unless the parent corporation through which such subsidiaries are connected is a member of the group. For instance, there will not be recognized as an affiliated group two industrial corporations the common parent of which is an insurance company or a personal holding company. In addition, no corporation which is connected by stock ownership with an affiliated group of includible corporations only through a nonincludible corporation may be included in a consolidated return. If a common parent which is an includible corporation owns 95 percent of the stock of a nonincludible corporation and 95 percent of the stock of an includible corporation, it, and the other includible corporations may, of course, file a consolidated return. (p. 54-55)

| Sec. 730(e) |
| Sec. 730(f) |

[SEC. 730. CONSOLIDATED RETURNS.]

[(e) Definition of "Includible Corporation".—As used in this section, the term "includible corporation" means any corporation except—]

(6) Insurance companies subject to taxation under section 201 or 207.

Committee Reports

Report—Ways and Means Committee (77th Cong., 1st Sess., H. Rept. 146).— Section 730 of the present law dealing with consolidated returns under the

excess-profits tax does not permit an insurance company to join in a consolidated return with a noninsurance company. This restriction was inserted because of the special manner in which the income of insurance companies is computed under the income-tax laws. It is believed, however, that the differences of computation in the case of an insurance company other than life or mutual are not so significant as to prevent such a company from filing a consolidated return with an ordinary corporation with which it is affiliated. Consequently, this section amends section 730 to permit such insurance companies, i. e., those subject to taxation under section 204, to join in consolidated returns with ordinary corporations. (p. 14)

Report—Senate Finance Committee (77th Cong., 1st Sess., S. Rept. 75).— Same as Ways and Means Committee Report. (p. 14)

Congressional Discussion

Discussion—House (Cong. Rec. Vol. 87).—Mr. Cooper. * * * Page 22 of the bill, section 7, relates to consolidated returns of insurance companies, other than life or mutual insurance companies. This takes care of corporations that do their own insuring, or, as an illustration, take a corporation, and if it gets a large contract and carries its own casualty insurance, has its own insurance company, this provides for the consolidated return of the insurance company with the parent corporation. (p. 1380)

Discussion—Senate (Cong. Rec. Vol. 87).—Mr. Harrison. * * * Section 7: This section permits an insurance company which is not a life or mutual company to file a consolidated return with an ordinary corporation with which it is affiliated. The only reason insurance companies were not permitted to file consolidated returns with other corporations in the first instance was because their income was computed differently from that of the ordinary corporations. However, upon investigation, it was found that the income of a fire or casualty stock insurance company is computed in substantially the same manner as an ordinary corporation. Therefore, there was no reason to prohibit such insurance companies from filing consolidated returns with ordinary corporations with which they are affiliated. (p. 1638)

1940
201
[730(e)]
[730(f)]

[SEC. 730. CONSOLIDATED RETURNS.]

(e) Definition of "Includible Corporation".—[(e) Foreign Corporations.—*A foreign corporation shall not be deemed to be affiliated with any other corporation within the meaning of this section.*]

[(f) China Trade Act Corporations.—*A corporation organized under the China Trade Act, 1922, shall not be deemed to be affiliated with any other corporation within the meaning of this section.*]

[(g) Corporations Deriving Income From Possessions of United States.—*For the purposes of this section a corporation entitled to the benefits of section 251, by reason of receiving a large percentage of its income from possessions of the United States, shall be treated as a foreign corporation.*] As used in this section, the term "includible corporation" means any corporation except—

(1) Corporations exempt from the tax imposed by this subchapter.

(2) Foreign corporations.

(3) Corporations organized under the China Trade Act, 1922.

(4) Corporations entitled to the benefits of section 251, by reason of receiving a large percentage of their income from possessions of the United States.

(5) Personal service corporations.

(6) Insurance companies subject to taxation under section 201, 204, or 207.

(f) Includible Insurance Companies.—Despite the provisions of paragraph (6) of subsection (e), two or more domestic insurance companies each of which is subject to taxation under the same section of Chapter 1 shall be considered as includible corporations for the purpose of the application of subsection (d) to such insurance companies alone.

These subsections were added by the Conference Committee.

Committee Reports

Report—Senate Finance Committee (76th Cong., 3d Sess., S. Rept. 2114).— Foreign corporations, China Trade Act corporations, and corporations entitled to the benefits of section 251 by reason of receiving a large percentage of their income from possessions of the United States are not to be deemed to be affiliated with any other corporation within the meaning of section 729.[1] (p. 17)

[1] Sec. 730 of the Code.

Report—Conference Committee (76th Cong., 3d Sess., H. Rept. 3002).—Foreign corporations (except certain 100-percent owned foreign subsidiaries of domestic corporations), China Trade Act corporations, and certain corporations deriving income from United States possessions are not to be deemed to be affiliated with any other corporation within the meaning of this provision.

Under the conference agreement— (1) The class of corporations excluded from membership in an affiliated group is expanded to include certain other corporations in addition to those specified in the Senate amendment. As thus expanded, the class of corporations excluded from the affiliated group includes all those corporations which, by reason of the fact that they are themselves exempt from the excess-profits tax, or are taxable on a basis different from that used in the case of corporations generally (as in the case of foreign corporations), or are otherwise allowed special treatment (as in the case of China Trade Act corporations, personal service corporations, and corporations doing business in possessions of the United States), cannot appropriately be associated for tax purposes with corporations not accorded such special treatment. While insurance companies in general are not includible in an affiliated group, an insurance company may be affiliated with other insurance companies of the same taxable character. For example, an insurance company taxable under section 201 may file a consolidated return with another insurance company taxable under the same section, assuming both companies meet the stock ownership test. An insurance company taxable under section 201 may not, however, file a consolidated return with another insurance company taxable under section 204 or section 207. The conference agreement preserves the exception relative to certain 100-percent owned foreign subsidiaries of domestic corporations contained in the Senate amendment. (p. 54)

Sec. 730(g)

[SEC. 730. CONSOLIDATED RETURNS.]

(g) Subsidiary Formed to Comply With Foreign Law.—*In the case of a domestic corporation owning or controlling, directly or indirectly, 100* *per centum of the capital stock (exclusive of directors' qualifying shares) of a corporation organized under the laws of a contiguous foreign country and maintained solely for the purpose of complying with the laws of such country as to title and operation of property, such foreign corporation may, at the option of the domestic corporation, be treated for the purpose of this [section] SUBCHAPTER as a domestic corporation.*

Committee Reports

Report—Senate Finance Committee (76th Cong., 3d Sess., S. Rept. 2114).— For the purpose of this limitation, a 100-percent owned foreign subsidiary of a domestic corporation, organized under the laws of a contiguous foreign country and maintained solely for the purpose of complying with the laws of such country as to title and operation of property, may, at the option of the domestic parent corporation, be treated as a domestic corporation. (p. 17)

Sec. 730(h)

1940
201

[SEC. 730. CONSOLIDATED RETURNS.]

(h) **Suspension of Running of Statute of Limitations.**—*If a notice under section 272 (a) in respect of a deficiency for any taxable year is mailed to a corporation, the suspension of the running of the statute of limitations, provided in section 277, shall apply in the case of corporations with which such corporation made a consolidated return for such taxable year.*

Committee Reports

Report—Senate Finance Committee (76th Cong., 3d Sess., S. Rept. 2114).— It is also provided that a notice of deficiency for any taxable year mailed to a corporation shall suspend the running of the statute of limitations as to all corporations with which such corporation made a consolidated return for such taxable year. (p. 18)

Sec. 731

1943
207(a)

Section 731 (relating to corporations engaged in mining certain strategic minerals) is amended by inserting after "tungsten," the following: "fluorspar, flake graphite, vermiculite,".

Committee Reports

Report—Ways and Means Committee (78th Cong., 1st Sess., H. Rept. 871).— Fluorspar, flake graphite, and vermiculite are added to the list of strategic minerals exempt from the excess-profits tax. (p. 33)

This section amends section 731 of the code relating to the exemption from excess profits tax of the portion of the adjusted excess profits net income attributable to the mining in the United States of certain strategic minerals so as to extend the benefits of such section to corporations mining fluorspar, flake graphite, and vermiculite. (p. 58)

Report—Senate Finance Committee (78th Cong., 1st Sess., S. Rept. 627).— This section is identical with section 207 of the House bill. It amends section 731 of the code relating to the exemption from excess profits tax of the portion of the adjusted excess profits net income

attributable to the mining in the United States of certain strategic minerals so as to extend the benefits of such section to corporations mining fluorspar, flake graphite, and vermiculite. The portion of the adjusted excess profits net income attributable to strategic mining is determined according to detailed regulations as contemplated by the section. (p. 74-75)

Committee Hearings

Hearings—Senate Finance Committee.—Exempting entirely companies

mining strategic minerals. (R. Paul—Treas. Dept.—p. 66-67)

SEC. 731. CORPORATIONS ENGAGED IN MINING OF STRATEGIC MINERALS.

1942
226(a)

In the case of any domestic corporation engaged in the mining of antimony, chromite, manganese, nickel, platinum, quicksilver, sheet mica, tantalum, tin, tungsten, or vanadium, the portion of the adjusted excess profits net income attributable to such mining in the United States shall be exempt from the tax imposed by this subchapter. The tax on the remaining portion of such adjusted excess profits net income shall be an amount which bears the same ratio to the tax computed without regard to this section as such remaining portion bears to the entire adjusted excess profits net income.

Committee Reports

Report—Senate Finance Committee (77th Cong., 2d Sess., S. Rept. 1631).— In order to encourage production of minerals in connection with the war effort, certain special allowances are granted to mines. These are as follows:

*   *   *

(3) *Exemption from excess-profits tax of corporations engaged in mining of strategic metals.*

Under the Revenue Act of 1940, income from the mining of strategic materials was exempt from the excess-profits tax. These metals were tungsten, quicksilver, manganese, platinum, antimony, chromite, and tin. These minerals have been declared to be strategic metals by the War Production Board. This exemption was removed by the Revenue Act of 1941. Your committee was requested by representatives of the War Production Board to restore this exemption, as these minerals are vitally needed for the war effort. In addition to the minerals enumerated above, there has been added sheet mica, tantalum, vanadium, and nickel, at the request of the War Production Board. (p. 38, 40)

This section does not appear in the House bill. It exempts from excess profits tax that portion of the adjusted excess profits net income which is attributable to the mining by a domestic corporation in the United States of antimony, chromite, manganese, nickel, platinum, quicksilver, sheet mica, tantalum, tin, tungsten, and vanadium. The tax on the remaining portion of the adjusted excess profits net income is an amount which bears the same ratio to the tax computed on the entire adjusted excess profits net income (including the adjusted excess profits net income attributable to the entire adjusted excess profits net income). (p. 211)

Report—Conference Committee (77th Cong., 2d Sess., H. Rept. 2586).— Amendment No. 341: The Senate has added a new section 731 to the Code to exempt from excess profits tax that portion of the adjusted excess profits net income attributable to the mining by a domestic corporation in the United States of certain specified strategic metals. * * * The House recedes. (p. 64)

Congressional Discussion

Discussion—Senate (Cong. Rec. Vol. 88).—Withdrawn amendment to include flake graphite. (p. 8035-37)

1941 E.P.T.A.

Discussion—House (Cong. Rec. Vol. 87).—Including profits on mining of gold in exemption. (p. 731, 1388-92)
Discussion—Senate (Cong. Rec. Vol. 87).—Including profits on mining of gold in exemption. (p. 1635, 1640)
Objections to removal of exemption of profits on strategic materials. (Appendix 3680)

Committee Hearings

Hearings—Senate Finance Committee.—Restoring exemption of profits on strategic metals. (H. B. Fernald, p. 975-977; W. A. Nelson, p. 1929)

1941 Act

Hearings—Ways and Means Committee.—Exempting profits on mining of gold and silver. (H. B. Fernald, p. 1572)

1941
204

Section 731 of the Internal Revenue Code (exempting from excess profits tax income derived from mining certain metals) shall not apply with respect to any taxable year beginning after December 31, 1940.

This section was stricken by the Senate Finance Committee, but restored by the Conference Committee.

Committee Reports

Report—Ways and Means Committee (77th Cong., 1st Sess., H. Rept. 1040).— The existing law exempts from the excess-profits tax that portion of the adjusted excess-profits net income of a domestic corporation which is attributable to mining within the United States of tungsten, quicksilver, manganese, platinum, antimony, chromite, or tin.

Your committee has removed this exemption as it is believed that these corporations which make money out of the defense program should bear their share of the tax burden. (p. 26)

Under section 731 of the present law in the case of corporations engaged in mining certain metals, only that portion of adjusted excess-profits net income not attributable to such mining is subject to the excess-profits tax. Section 206[1] of the bill makes this provision inapplicable to taxable years beginning after December 31, 1940. (p. 50)

[1] Sec. 204 of the Act.

Corporations mining strategic metals.—

Section 206[1] of the House bill repeals section 731 of the Internal Revenue Code, a provision exempting from excess-profits tax income derived from the mining of tungsten, quicksilver, manganese, platinum, antimony, chromite, or tin. In striking out this section of the House bill your committee leaves the existing exemption unchanged.

It was felt that the discontinuance of the exemption would operate unfairly to corporations which had proceeded in the establishment and extension of the mining properties affected. These enterprises, moreover, have the character largely of emergency enterprises, and the purpose of the existing provision was mainly to encourage the discovery and production of the metals mentioned. It is conceded that the production of such metals in normal times is largely in foreign countries and that after the existing emergency is over their importation will be resumed. (p. 13-14)

[1] Sec. 204 of the Act.

Report—Conference Committee (77th Cong., 1st Sess., H. Rept. 1203).— Amendment No. 54: This amendment strikes out section 206 of the House bill, which provides that section 731 of the Internal Revenue Code (exempting from excess-profits tax income derived from mining certain metals) shall not apply with respect to any taxable year beginning after December 31, 1940. The Senate recedes. (p. 12–13)

Congressional Discussion

Discussion—House (Cong. Rec. Vol. 87).—On need for continuing exemption, in general. (p. 6710-11, 6725-27)

Discussion—Senate (Cong. Rec. Vol. 87).—On need for continuing exemption, in general. (p. 7269, 7439, 7440-41, 7442)

Committee Hearings

Hearings—Senate Finance Committee.—Need for continuing exemption. (P. McCarran, p. 567-571; R. C. Holman, p. 571; C. F. Willis, p. 899-906; D. A. Callahan, p. 960-967; M. Thorner, p. 976-979; J. C. Adkerson, p. 979-985; B. L. Bunker, p. 985, 986-988)

SEC. 731. CORPORATIONS ENGAGED IN MINING OF STRATEGIC METALS.

1940
201

[*Income derived from the mining reduction or beneficiation of tungsten, quicksilver, manganese, platinum, antimony, chromite, and tin, or the ores and material containing such metals, shall not be subject to the excess-profits tax provided for in this Act.*] IN THE CASE OF ANY DOMESTIC CORPORATION ENGAGED IN THE MINING OF TUNGSTEN, QUICKSILVER, MANGANESE, PLATINUM, ANTIMONY, CHROMITE, OR TIN, THE PORTION OF THE ADJUSTED EXCESS PROFITS NET INCOME ATTRIBUTABLE TO SUCH MINING IN THE UNITED STATES SHALL BE EXEMPT FROM THE TAX IMPOSED BY THIS SUBCHAPTER. THE TAX ON THE REMAINING PORTION OF SUCH ADJUSTED EXCESS PROFITS NET INCOME SHALL BE AN AMOUNT WHICH BEARS THE SAME RATIO TO THE TAX COMPUTED WITHOUT REGARD TO THIS SECTION AS SUCH REMAINING PORTION BEARS TO THE ENTIRE ADJUSTED EXCESS PROFITS NET INCOME.

The section heading is as worded by the Conference Committee. The Senate heading read "Income From Mining Operations".

Committee Reports

Report—Conference Committee (76th Cong., 3d Sess., H. Rept. 3002).—This section is new in the Senate amendment, no comparable provision having been contained in the House bill. It exempts from excess-profits tax income derived from mining, reduction or beneficiation of tungsten, quicksilver, manganese, platinum, antimony, chromite, and tin, or the ores and material containing such metals. These materials have been declared to be strategic materials by the War Department. The exemption provided in section 730 is intended to encourage their domestic production.

Under the conference agreement, this

section is changed to section 731 and it is given a new caption. It exempts from excess-profits tax that portion of the adjusted excess-profits net income of a domestic corporation which is attributable to mining within the United States of tungsten, quicksilver, manganese, platinum, antimony, chromite, or tin. The tax on the remaining portion of the adjusted excess-profits net income is an amount which bears the same ratio to the tax computed on all the adjusted excess-profits net income as such remaining portion bears to the entire adjusted excess-profits net income. (p. 55-56)

Congressional Discussion

Discussion—House (Cong. Rec. Vol. 86).—On exempting gold mining. (p. 11264)

Discussion—Senate (Cong. Rec. Vol. 86).—Mr. Pittman. Mr. President, I should like to make a brief statement with respect to the amendment.

This subject has not been touched in any of the amendments. The War Department has established certain metals as strategic metals. The list is as follows: Manganese, chromium, mercury, tungsten, nickel, tin, and antimony.

* * *

The position I present is merely this: These are essential war materials. It is so stated by the War Department. Our importations may be cut off. It is necessary to increase production in this country. With these new industries expanding rapidly, or attempting to expand rapidly, generally with a great loss of money for several years, it is impracticable to attempt to assess excess profits taxes against them. (p. 12347-348)

Discussion—Senate; on Report of Conference Committee (Cong. Rec. Vol. 86).—Mr. Harrison. * * * As to the Senate amendment which the senior Senator from Nevada [Mr. Pittman] offered, and which was adopted by the Senate, dealing with strategic metals, we were able to work out a compromise confining the exemption to the mining of such metals by domestic corporations within the United States. That was the very best arrangement that could be made. (p. 12919)

Mr. Pittman. Mr. President, will the Senator explain again the matter of exemption of taxation of the profits derived from the mining of strategic metals? What is his understanding with regard to the change made in the provision.

Mr. Harrison. I stated that there were some six or seven metals represented or dealt with in the Senator's amendment. We were not able to get the House conferees to agree to the exact language of the Senate amendment, but we were able to point out that the President in a message to the Congress, as I recall—I do not know that he included all of these metals—had asked us to enact legislation to preserve these strategic metals in the United States for our own defense.

Mr. Pittman. I simply wanted to see how it was worded.

* * *

Mr. Pittman. Does that mean there is no excess-profits tax charged against the profits derived from that character of industry?

Mr. Harrison. In effect, yes. (p. 12920)

Committee Hearings

Hearings—Ways and Means Committee.—Need for special provision as to mining industries. (P. D. Seghers, p. 151; M. Thorner, p. 218-224; R. H. Strange, p. 224-227)

Hearings—Senate Finance Committee.—Need for special provision as to mining industries. (K. Carroad, p. 38; W. E. Terry, p. 216-218)

Sec. 732(a)

SEC. 732. REVIEW OF ABNORMALITIES BY BOARD OF TAX APPEALS.

(a) **Petition to the Board.**—If a claim for refund of tax under this subchapter for any taxable year is disallowed in whole or in part by the Commissioner, and the disallowance relates to the application of section 711 (b) (1) (H), (I), (J), or (K), section 721, or section 722, relating to abnormalities, the Commissioner shall send notice of such disallowance to the taxpayer by registered mail. Within ninety days after such notice is mailed (not counting Sunday or a legal holiday in the District of Columbia as the ninetieth day) the taxpayer may file a petition with the Board of Tax Appeals for a redetermination of the tax under this subchapter. If such petition is so filed, such notice of disallowance shall be deemed to be a notice of deficiency for all purposes relating to the assessment and collection of taxes or the refund or credit of overpayments.

Committee Reports

Report—Ways and Means Committee (77th Cong., 1st Sess., H. Rept. 146).—Section 9 of the bill (adding sec. 732 to the Excess Profits Tax Act of 1940) extends to the Board exclusive jurisdiction to review the Commissioner's decision upon any question the determination of which is necessary solely by reason of section 711 (b) (1) (H), (I), (J), or (K), section 721 or 722. For example, an item of income of $100,000, the amount of which is not in dispute, is includible in gross income for 1940 and involves a question concededly arising under section 721 (a) (2) (A). The Commissioner determines that the item is attributable to 1939 and 1940 in the respective sums of $25,000 and $75,000. Such determination is made upon an issue arising solely under section 721 and, if the taxpayer contests such allocation, the determination of the Commissioner in such case is reviewable only by the Board. If, however, the Commissioner determines, for example, the amount of income derived by a taxpayer from a transaction falling within section 721 (a) (2) (E), relating to amounts included in gross income for the taxable year by reason of the termination of a lease of real property, and the amount so determined is contested by the taxpayer, the question as to amount of such income is not one arising solely by reason of the abnormality provisions but independently of them and hence review of the determination as to the amount in such a case is not confined to the Board.

Likewise, review is not confined to the Board if, for example, the Commissioner determines that the taxpayer realized in 1940 income of a character which, if realized in that year, would fall within section 721 (a) (2) (A) but which the taxpayer contends was realized in 1939. In such case the question whether income was so realized in 1940 may be reviewed by the courts upon appeal from the decision of the Board. Assuming in such case that it is ultimately held that the income was realized in 1940, a dispute as to the resulting question of allocation as between years of such item may not be carried beyond the Board.

Under existing law, unless a deficiency has been determined by the Commissioner, a taxpayer has no right of appeal to the Board (sec. 272 (a) (1), I. R. C.). Thus, for example, if a refund claim were filed by a taxpayer and the Commissioner disallowed the claim in whole or in part but did not determine deficiency, no right of review of the Commissioner's action by the Board would be present. Inasmuch as the taxpayer's right to relief under certain of the relief provisions provided in this bill may only be raised by a claim for refund, it is necessary that a procedure be provided whereby the Board may obtain jurisdiction to review a decision by the Commissioner disallowing such claims. Accordingly, section 732 (added to the Excess Profits Tax Act of 1940 by sec. 9 of the bill) provides that the taxpayer may file a petition with the Board of Tax Appeals within 90 days after notice of such disallowance is mailed for redetermination of the excess-profits tax. If such petition is filed such notice of disallowance is deemed to constitute a notice of deficiency for the purposes of assessment and collection of any deficiencies and the credit or refund of overpayments (including the suspension of the statute of limitations with respect thereto). If such appeal is taken, then all pertinent issues bearing upon the tax liability under chapter 2E may be raised by the taxpayer and reviewed by the Board. (p. 14-15)

Report—Senate Finance Committee (77th Cong., 1st Sess., S. Rept. 75).— Same as Ways and Means Committee Report. (p. 15-16)

Sec. 732(b)

[SEC. 732. REVIEW OF ABNORMALITIES BY BOARD OF TAX APPEALS.]

(b) Deficiency Found by Board in Case of Claim.—If the Board finds that there is no overpayment of tax in respect of any taxable year in respect of which the Commissioner has disallowed, in whole or in part, a claim for refund described in subsection (a) and the Board further finds that there is a deficiency for such year, the Board shall have jurisdiction to determine the amount of such deficiency and such amount shall, when the decision of the Board becomes final, be assessed and shall be paid upon notice and demand from the collector.

Committee Reports

Report—Ways and Means Committee (77th Cong., 1st Sess., H. Rept. 146).— If the Board does not find an overassessment but finds a deficiency in such cases, such deficiency may be assessed and collected, regardless of any statute of limitations otherwise applicable. (p. 15)

Report—Senate Finance Committee (77th Cong., 1st Sess., S. Rept. 75).— Same as Ways and Means Committee Report. (p. 16)

Sec. 732(c)

[SEC. 732. REVIEW OF ABNORMALITIES BY BOARD OF TAX APPEALS.]

(c) Finality of Determination.—If in the determination of the tax liability under this subchapter the determination of any question is necessary solely by reason of section 711 (b) (1) (H), (I), (J), or (K), section 721, or section 722, the determination of such question shall not be reviewed or redetermined by any court or agency except the Board.

Committee Reports

Report—Ways and Means Committee (77th Cong., 1st Sess., H. Rept. 146).— If a claim for refund involving an issue of abnormality is disallowed in whole or in part, and the taxpayer does not wish to appeal to the Board, it still has the right to sue in the courts upon any issue raised in such claim except the issue with respect to abnormalities.   (p. 15)

Report—Senate Finance Committee (77th Cong., 1st Sess., S. Rept. 75).— Same as Ways and Means Committee Report.   (p. 16)

Sec. 732(d)

[SEC. 732. REVIEW OF ABNORMALITIES BY BOARD OF TAX APPEALS.]   1942
                                                                                222(c)

(d) Review by Special Division of Board.—~~Special Division of Board. The determinations and redeterminations by the Board provided for in this section shall be made by a special division of the Board which shall be constituted by the Chairman and consist of not less than three members of the Board. Such determinations and redeterminations shall not be reviewable by the Board, and the decisions of such division making such determinations and redeterminations shall be deemed decisions of the Board.~~ *The determinations and redeterminations by any division of the Board involving any question arising under section 721 (a) (2) (C) or section 722 shall be reviewed by a special division of the Board which shall be constituted by the Chairman and consist of not less than three members of the Board. The decisions of such special division shall not be reviewable by the Board, and shall be deemed decisions of the Board.*

Committee Reports

Report—Ways and Means Committee (77th Cong., 2d Sess., H. Rept. 2333).— The presiding judge of the United States Tax Court designated under existing law as the United States Board of Tax Appeals is directed to set up within the court a special division of not less than three members whose sole duties will be the determination of issues arising under the relief provisions. The decisions of the division will not be reviewable by the court but will be deemed to be the decisions of the court. It is the intention that due to the nature of the issues that will arise under the relief provisions all such issues should be decided by a special body qualified for that purpose. (p. 26)

Section 732 is amended so as to provide for the establishment within the Board of Tax Appeals of a special division which will be the sole division of the Board determining and redetermining issues arising under section 711 (b) (1) (H), (I), (J), or (K) (relating to abnormal deductions within the base period), section 721 (relating to ab-

normal income in the taxable period), and section 722 (relating to general relief from discriminatory excess profits taxes). Such special division shall be constituted by the chairman and shall consist of not less than three members of the Board. The determinations and redeterminations of this division shall not be reviewable by the Board and the decisions of the division upon the issues described above shall be deemed to be decisions of the Board.

Because of the complicated nature of the issues involving relief under section 722 and abnormalities under sections 711 (b) (1) and 721, and the wide discretionary powers lodged in the Board in the determination of such issues, it is essential that all such issues be decided by one group familiar with the problems involved. Only by this method can a consistent and uniform application of the principles established be assured in all cases. At the same time there is provided flexible machinery to coordinate cases involving both relief and abnormality issues as well as other questions. (p. 149)

Report—Senate Finance Committee (77th Cong., 2d Sess., S. Rept. 1631).— The determination and redetermination of questions arising under this general relief section are reviewable by a Special Division of the Board of Tax Appeals, to be organized by the Chairman and to consist of not less than three members of the Board. The decisions of the Special Division are not reviewable by the Board of Tax Appeals and are to be the decisions of the Board. (p. 38)

The provisions appearing in subsection (c) of this section, which corresponds to section 213 (d) of the House bill, have been changed by your committee from the provisions of the House bill. The House bill amended section 732 of the Code to provide for the establishment within the Board of Tax Appeals of a special division which would be the sole division of the Board hearing and determining and redetermining issues arising under section 711 (b) (1) (H), (I), (J), or (K) (relating to abnormal deductions within the base period), section 721 (relating to abnormal income in the taxable period), and section 722 (relating to general relief from discriminatory excess-profits taxes). Your committee believes that the burden upon such division would be too great were it required to hear, as well as to determine or redetermine these relief issues, especially with the abandonment of the limitations upon applications for relief contained in the House bill. Moreover, your committee believes that the involved economic problems inherent in section 722 are not present in cases under section 711 (b) (1) (H), (I), (J), or (K), or section 721 except subsection (a) (2) (C) thereof relating to income resulting from exploration, discovery, prospecting, research, or development of tangible property, patents, formulas, or processes, or any combination of the foregoing, extending over a period of more than 12 months. It believes that although cases under section 722 and section 721 (a) (2) (C) should still be reviewed by the special division of the Board established in the House bill, such cases may be heard initially by the regular divisions of the Board. Abnormality cases under section 711 (b) (1) (H), (I), (J), or (K) or

under section 721, except section 721 (a) (2) (C), which on the whole do not involve problems of the nature of those presented by section 722, will, however, be disposed of without any review by the special division, in the same manner in which such cases are currently handled under existing law.

Your committee has therefore amended section 722 so as to provide for the establishment within the Board of Tax Appeals of a special division which shall review the determinations and redeterminations by any division of the Board involving any question arising under section 721 (a) (2) (C) or section 722. Such special division shall be constituted by the chairman and shall consist of not less than three members of the Board. The decisions of this special division shall not be reviewable by the Board, and the decisions upon issues under section 721 (a) (2) (C) and section 722 shall be deemed to be decisions of the Board.

Because of the complicated nature and the economic character of the issues involving relief under section 722, and abnormalities under section 721 (a) (2) (C), and the broad discretionary powers lodged in the Board in the determination of such issues, it is essential that all such issues be decided by one group familiar with the problems involved. Only by this method can a consistent and uniform application of the principles established be assured in all cases. At the same time there is provided flexible machinery to coordinate cases involving both relief and abnormality issues as well as other questions. (p. 206-207)

Report—Conference Committee (77th Cong., 2d Sess., H. Rept. 2586).— The House bill provided for the establishment within the Board of Tax Appeals of a special division which would be the sole division of the Board hearing and determining and redetermining issues arising under section 711 (b) (1) (H), (I), (J), or (K), (relating to abnormal deductions within the base period), section 721 (relating to abnormal income within the taxable period), and section 722 (relating to general relief from discriminatory excess profits taxes). The abnormality cases under section 711 (b) (1) (H), (I), (J), or (K), or under section 721, except section 721 (a) (2) (C), do not on the whole involve problems of the complexity of those presented by section 722. Such cases will be disposed of under the Senate amendments in the same manner in which such cases are currently handled under existing law. Determination and redetermination by any division in the Board involving any question arising under section 721 (a) (2) (C) or section 722 would be reviewed by the special division of the Board. (p. 62-63)

Congressional Discussion
1941 Act

Discussion—House (Cong. Rec. Vol. 87).—MR. DIVORSHAK. * * * It is conceded that from any practical standpoint, it is impossible to write into the tax bill all the provisions necessary to grant relief to all distress cases. The practical and equitable procedure is to grant broad relief powers either to an independent board, or to the Commissioner of Internal Revenue. The taxpayer should have the right of appeal to the Board of Tax Appeals.

It has been argued that such a provision would give the Treasury Department a serious administrative problem. This would not be true if the grant of power was to an independent board. Even, however, if the power be conferred on the Commissioner of Internal Revenue, and granting that the administration will be difficult, it is to be noted that the taxpayer in need of relief is also in a difficult position; and to refuse to grant him relief merely because the subject is difficult of administration is not only unfair, but considers the comfort of the tax gatherer as more desirable than the relief of the taxpayer from discrimination and a difficult competitive position.

Actually it will be much simpler in very many cases to determine what would be fair equitable relief, than it would be to try to determine all the facts and points of law involved in making the statutory computations for invested capital. (p. 6549)

Committee Hearings

Hearings—Ways and Means Committee.—Establishing special relief Board. (J. W. Hooper, p. 499)

Hearings—Senate Finance Committee.—Objection to special division of Board for relief cases. (J. E. Murdock —B.T.A.—p. 2306-07)

Hearings—Joint Committee on Internal Revenue Taxation (Feb.-May 1946).—Allowing Board review on basis broader than evidence presented to Commissioner. (E. C. Alvord, p. 126; H. Satterlee, p. 204-205; E. Groseclose, p. 355-356)

Allowing appeals from Board on questions of law. (H. Satterlee, p. 205)

Sec. 733(a)

SEC. 733. CAPITALIZATION OF ADVERTISING, ETC., EXPENDITURES.

EPTA
10(a)

(a) **Election to Charge to Capital Account.**—For the purpose of computing the excess profits credit, a taxpayer may elect, within six months after the date prescribed by law for filing its return for its first taxable year under this subchapter, to charge to capital account so much of the deductions for taxable years in its applicable base period on account of expenditures for advertising or the promotion of good will, as, under rules and regulations prescribed by the Commissioner with the approval of the Secretary, may be regarded as capital investments. Such election must be the same for all such taxable years, and must be for the total amount of such expenditures which may be so regarded as capital investments. In computing the excess profits credit, no amount on account of such expenditures shall be charged to capital account:

(1) For taxable years in the base period unless the election authorized in subsection (a) is exercised, or

(2) For any taxable year prior to the beginning of the base period.

Committee Reports

Report—Ways and Means Committee (77th Cong., 1st Sess., H. Rept. 146).— The bill affords relief in the following situations:

* * *

7. Under section 10 of the bill, a taxpayer in computing its excess-profits credit may elect within 6 months after the date prescribed by law for filing its first excess-profits return, to charge to capital account, so much of expenditures deducted in the base period for advertising or the promotion of good will, as under rules and regulations prescribed by the Commissioner may be regarded as capital investments. (p. 2, 4)

This section permits a taxpayer, under certain limitations, to capitalize expenditures for advertising and goodwill promotion made in the base period, which the taxpayer had previously deducted as an expense. Such a provision will prevent hardship to taxpayers who deducted such items at a time when the effect of such deduction on their excess-profits credit could not be foreseen.

Only expenditures which, under rules and regulations prescribed by the Commissioner with the approval of the Secre-

tary, may be determined to be in the nature of a capital investment are allowed to be capitalized. It is expected that such regulations will provide a method by which to differentiate normal advertising and goodwill expenditures which may properly be classified only as current expenses from those expenditures which may be considered to build up permanent business values, such as those embodied in trade-marks or trade names, and which are in effect a further investment in and a permanent asset of the taxpayer's business. (p. 16)

A taxpayer electing under this section must capitalize all such expenditures deducted for base period taxable years which may be regarded as a capital investment. It is further provided that amounts allowed as a deduction on account of such expenditures in taxable years prior to the base period may not, under any circumstances, be capitalized. (p. 16)

Report—Senate Finance Committee (77th Cong., 1st Sess., S. Rept. 75).— Same as Ways and Means Committee Report. (p. 3, 4-5, 16, 17, respectively)

Congressional Discussion

Discussion—House (Cong. Rec. Vol. 87).—MR. COOPER. * * * Section 10 on page 26 provides for capitalization of advertising and expenditures of that type. Corporations have followed the practice for many years of charging advertising as expense. Yet it is a matter well known that frequently this advertising has increased the value of the

product or the value of the business to the extent that it might well consider a part of this increase in connection with its capital structure. This allows a corporation to go back and treat this as a part of the capital increase, provided it pays the proper income tax in that connection. (p. 1380)

Sec. 733(b)

[SEC. 733. CAPITALIZATION OF ADVERTISING, ETC., EXPENDITURES.]

(b) Effect of Election.—If the taxpayer exercises the election authorized under subsection (a)—

EPTA
10(a)

(1) The net income for each taxable year in the base period shall be considered to be the net income computed with such deductions disallowed, and such deductions shall not be considered as having diminished earnings and profits. This paragraph shall be retroactively applied as if it were a part of the law applicable to each taxable year in the base period; and

(2) The treatment of such expenditures as deductions for a taxable year in the base period shall, for the purposes of section 734 (b) (2), be considered treatment which was not correct under the law applicable to such year.

Committee Reports

Report—Ways and Means Committee (77th Cong., 1st Sess., H. Rept. 146).—This will benefit the taxpayer, whether it elects the income credit or the invested capital credit in computing its excess-profits tax. Taxpayers using the income credit will have their base-period income increased by the amount of the deduction disallowed. Taxpayers using the invested-capital credit will have their invested capital increased by reason of a restoration of such expenditures to their earnings and profits account. A taxpayer who elects under this section must capitalize all such expenditures not only for the base-period years but also for taxable years subsequent to the base period. Since the deductions in such cases are retroactively disallowed, the taxpayer is required to pay any additional income tax, plus interest thereon, which is due by reason of the disallowance of the deduction. (p. 4)

If a taxpayer makes an election under this section, its normal-tax or special-class net income for each base period taxable year in which advertising and goodwill expenditures were deducted shall be recomputed as if that portion of such expenditures which is permitted to be capitalized had been capitalized in such taxable year. Hence, the net income for each such year will be increased by the amount of the deduction disallowed, and in the case of a corporation electing the invested capital credit, the increase in net income will effect an increase in earnings and profits.

Since the revenue laws applicable to each taxable year are retroactively amended by this section in order to make the election here provided govern the deductibility of advertising and goodwill expenditures in such prior taxable years, the deductions taken are deemed to have been disallowed, and the taxpayer must pay the additional income tax which would have been due if the treatment in the prior income tax taxable year had been in accordance with the election provided for in this section, plus interest thereon. This prevents a taxpayer from obtaining the benefits of both a deduction and a capitalization with respect to the same item.

If no provision or rule of law prevents correction of the effect of disallowing such deductions, any additional income tax which would have been due if such deductions had been capitalized, will be collected as a deficiency for the particular base period taxable year. If, however, correction of the effect of such treatment is barred, correction will be made by means of the adjustment provided under section 734. * * *

In order to secure a treatment of expenditures for advertising and goodwill promotion in taxable years beginning after December 31, 1939, uniform with the treatment accorded similar expenditures in base-period years, subsection (b) provides that a taxpayer which has elected to capitalize expenditures which it has shown to be properly considered

capital investments, must capitalize for income and excess-profits tax purposes any similar capital expenditures in subsequent taxable years. (p. 16-17)

Report—Senate Finance Committee (77th Cong., 1st Sess., S. Rept. 75).— Same as Ways and Means Committee Report. (p. 4-5, 16-17, respectively)

Congressional Discussion

Discussion—House (Cong. Rec. Vol. 87).—Mr. Rich. Take what the gentleman refers to as capitalization for advertising. If a corporation goes back and sets up as a part of its capital structure the amount or part of the amount it would pay for advertising, then it will have necessarily to go back for the years they took that money to make that capital, and pay the additional tax back in those years, besides the capital-stock

tax additional that they have set up for that particular purpose; will it not?

Mr. Cooper. The gentleman is correct in that they will have to make the proper adjustment of their income-tax payments back during the period for which they are now seeking relief from excess-profits taxes, but no adjustment is made in the capital-stock tax. (p. 1380)

Sec. 734(a)(4)

[SEC. 734. ADJUSTMENT IN CASE OF POSITION INCONSISTENT WITH PRIOR INCOME TAX LIABILITY.]

[(a) Definitions.—For the purposes of this section—]

   (4)   *The term "predecessor of the taxpayer" means—*

    (A)   A person which is a component corporation of the taxpayer within the meaning of section 740; and

    (B)   A person which on April 1, 1941, or at any time thereafter, controlled the taxpayer. The term "controlled" as herein used shall have the same meaning as "control" under section 112 (h), and

    (C)   Any person in an unbroken series ending with the taxpayer if subparagraph (A) or (B) would apply to the relationship between the parties.

Committee Reports

Report—Senate Finance Committee (77th Cong., 2d Sess., S. Rept. 1631).— Your committee bill makes a number of amendments to section 734 of the Internal Revenue Code of which those of major importance are as follows:

(a) The definition of "predecessor of the taxpayer" has been considerably narrowed so as to include only such predecessors as would be components of the taxpayer for the purposes of section

740 or a predecessor which, on April 1, 1941, was in control of the taxpayer. For this purpose "control" has the same meaning as when used in section 112 (h). (p. 54)

Section 734 authorizes an adjustment where the treatment for excess profits tax purposes is inconsistent with the treatment for income tax purposes either by the taxpayer or by a "predecessor." The term "predecessor" is not defined in the statute. The definition contained in the regulations finds support from the statement and example contained in the Committee Reports (Rept. No. 75, Senate Finance Committee, 77th Cong., 1st sess., pp. 18 and 20). But your committee feels that it is too broad and operates to authorize somewhat inequitable adjustments in cases in which the taxpayer could not be charged with responsibility for the inconsistency. The definition provided by your committee includes only a person which is a component corporation of the taxpayer within the meaning of section 740 and a person which on April 1, 1941 (the date of enactment of sec. 734), or at any time thereafter controlled (as defined in sec. 112 (h) of the Code) the taxpayer and any person which is a predecessor of a person which is a predecessor of the taxpayer under the definition. For the purpose of section 734 a component corporation of the taxpayer within the meaning of section 740 is a predecessor of the taxpayer even though section 740 is not applicable in the determination of the excess profits tax liability of the taxpayer. It is believed that the definition provided by your committee will include only those cases in which there is sufficient identity of interest between the parties to warrant their treatment as one

for the purpose of the section and to require an adjustment where the treatment of an item for excess profits tax purposes by the one is inconsistent with the treatment of the item by the other for income tax purposes. The definition will cover most of the cases in which the excess profits tax liability of the taxpayer is determined by reference to the base period experience of its predecessor or by reference to the basis of property in the hands of its predecessor. The limitation of the definition to the above cases, and the resulting exclusion of other cases, should not be construed to affect the established judicial doctrines commonly known as estoppel, recoupment, set-off, etc., which may be applied by the courts in appropriate cases. (p. 212-213)

Report—Conference Committee (77th Cong., 2d Sess., H. Rept. 2586).—The Senate has defined the term "predecessor" specifically to include only a person which is a component corporation of the taxpayer within the meaning of section 740 and a person which on April 1, 1941, or at any time thereafter controlled the taxpayer and any person which is a predecessor of a person which is a predecessor of the taxpayer under the definition. (p. 65)

Committee Hearings

Hearings—Ways and Means Committee.—Need for definition of predecessor. (G. R. Blodgett, p. 974)

Hearings—Senate Finance Committee.—Need for definition of predecessor. (G. R. Blodgett, p. 413-416)

```
Sec. 734(b)(1)
Sec. 734(b)(2)
```

[SEC. 734. ADJUSTMENT IN CASE OF POSITION INCONSISTENT WITH PRIOR INCOME TAX LIABILITY.]

(b) Circumstances of Adjustment.—

(1) *If—*
(A) *in determining at any time the tax of a taxpayer under this subchapter an item affecting the determination of the excess profits credit is treated in a manner inconsistent with the treatment accorded such item in the determination of the income-tax liability of such taxpayer or a predecessor for a prior taxable year or years, and * * ***

(C) on the date of such determination of the tax under this sub-chapter correction of the effect of the inconsistent treatment in any one or more of the prior taxable years is prevented (except for the provisions of section 3801) by the operation of any law or rule of law (other than section 3761, relating to compromises), then the correction shall be made by an adjustment under this section. If in a subsequent determination of the tax under this subchapter for such taxable year such inconsistent treatment is not adopted, then the correction shall not be made in connection with such subsequent determination.

(2) Such adjustment shall be made only if there is adopted in the determination a position maintained by the Commissioner (in case the net effect of the adjustment would be a decrease in the income taxes previously determined for such year or years) or by the taxpayer with respect to whom the determination is made (in case the net effect of the adjustment would be an increase in the income taxes previously determined for such year or years) which position is inconsistent with the treatment accorded such item in the prior taxable year or years which was not correct under the law applicable to such year.

Committee Reports

Report—Senate Finance Committee (77th Cong., 2d Sess., S. Rept. 1631).— In order to clarify some questions which have arisen while this bill was under consideration by your committee regarding situations in which the inconsistent position is taken inadvertently, it should be made clear that the taxpayer may withdraw or retreat from such a position at any time prior to the final determination of this tax liability for the taxable year. (p. 54)

This section of the bill reenacts section 734 of the Code with appropriate amendments proposed by your committee in the interest of equity and clarity.

Section 734, added to the Code by the excess profits tax amendments of 1941, authorizes an adjustment to the excess profits tax in certain cases in which the treatment of an item or transaction for excess profits tax purposes is inconsistent with the prior erroneous treatment of such item or transaction for income tax purposes, and correction of the error is prevented by some provision or rule of law such as the statute of limitations, res judicata, etc. Section 734 is an equitable provision designed not to prevent inconsistency but to discourage such inconsistency by depriving the guilty party of any pecuniary benefit therefrom. This purpose is evidenced by the fact that an adjustment is not authorized if the party

maintaining the inconsistent position is the party who would derive a pecuniary benefit from the adjustment.

In view of the criticisms of this section presented to your committee, a careful study of the section has been made with special attention to the following problems:

(1) The effect of a previous adjustment under section 3801.

(2) The effect of an inconsistent position in a subsequent excess profits tax taxable year.

(3) Whether consistency with the prior year treatment of an item or transaction is permitted for excess profits tax purposes, although under current rulings and decisions such treatment is erroneous.

(4) The right to withdraw from an inconsistent position.

(5) The meaning of the term "predecessor" as used in the statute.

(6) The character for tax purposes of that portion of an adjustment which represents interest.

(7) The proper treatment of the excess of an adjustment representing a decrease over the excess profits tax for the taxable year.

(8) The computation of interest in determining the amount of an adjustment.

(9) The burden of proof as to

whether an inconsistency exists.

With respect to the matters noted under (1), (2), (3), and (4) above, your committee finds that the Commissioner has, by regulations, provided appropriate rules which correctly reflect the purpose and effect of the statute. These regulations provide * * * (b) that no adjustment is authorized by reason of an inconsistent position in an excess profits tax taxable year if an adjustment under the section has been made because of a similar position with respect to the same item or transaction in a prior excess profits tax taxable year; (c) that the taxpayer is not required to take an inconsistent position for excess profits tax purposes because of the fact that under current rulings and decisions the previous income tax treatment of the item was incorrect. If the Commissioner in such case requires the correct treatment of the item for excess profits tax purposes, no adjustment is authorized unless such adjustment would result in a reduction of the excess profits tax; and (d) that a taxpayer which has taken an inconsistent position may, upon notice to the Commissioner in writing, withdraw from such position. In view of these provisions of the regulations, your committee feels that legislation with respect to these matters is unnecessary. (p. 211-212)

Report—Conference Committee (77th Cong., 2d Sess., H. Rept. 2586).—Amendment No. 342: This amendment revises section 734 of the Code, relating to adjustment in the case of an inconsistent position taken by a taxpayer with respect to a prior income tax liability. The Committee of Conference considered a number of problems arising under this section, some of which appear to be satisfactorily determined under existing regulations issued by the Commissioner. Thus, the effect of a previous adjustment under section 3801, or of an inconsistent position in a subsequent excess profits tax taxable year, or the determination whether consistency with the prior year treatment of an item or transaction is permitted for excess profits tax purposes, although under current rulings and decisions such treatment is erroneous, and whether the taxpayer has a right to withdraw from an inconsistent position, are properly treated under existing law. (p. 64-65)

Committee Hearings

Hearings—Ways and Means Committee.—Repealing provision entirely. (R. N. Miller, p. 173-175, 181; H. Satterlee, p. 2256-57; E. C. Alvord, p. 2774-77)

Explanation and shortcomings of provision. (G. R. Blodgett, p. 973-980; J. G. Jackson, p. 1317-18; P. D. Seghers, p. 1966)

Difficulties of applying phrase "maintaining a position". (G. R. Blodgett, p. 974)

Hearings—Senate Finance Committee.—Repealing provision entirely. (R. N. Miller, p. 352; H. Satterlee, p. 392-394, 397-399; G. R. Blodgett, p. 412; H. B. Fernald, p. 979; J. W. Hooper, p. 1170; E. C. Alvord, p. 1791, 1800; A. B. Chapman, p. 2087)

Explanation and shortcomings of provision. (G. R. Blodgett, p. 412-419; P. D. Seghers, p. 693-694)

[SEC. 734. ADJUSTMENT IN CASE OF POSITION INCONSISTENT WITH PRIOR INCOME TAX LIABILITY.] EPTA 11

(b) Circumstances of Adjustment.—

(1) If—

(A) in determining at any time the tax of a taxpayer under this subchapter an item affecting the determination of the excess profits credit is treated in a manner inconsistent with the treatment accorded such item in the determination of the income-tax liability of such taxpayer or a predecessor for a prior taxable year or years, and

(B)   the treatment of such item in the prior taxable year or years consistently with the determination under this subchapter would effect an increase or decrease in the amount of the income taxes previously determined for such taxable year or years, and

(C)   on the date of such determination of the tax under this subchapter correction of the effect of the inconsistent treatment in any one or more of the prior taxable years is prevented (except for the provisions of section 3801) by the operation of any law or rule of law (other than section 3761, relating to compromises), then the correction shall be made by an adjustment under this section. If in a subsequent determination of the tax under this subchapter for such taxable year such inconsistent treatment is not adopted, then the correction shall not be made in connection with such subsequent determination.

(2) Such adjustment shall be made only if there is adopted in the determination a position maintained by the Commissioner (in case the net effect of the adjustment would be a decrease in the income taxes previously determined for such year or years) or by the taxpayer with respect to whom the determination is made (in case the net effect of the adjustment would be an increase in the income taxes previously determined for such year or years) which position is inconsistent with the treatment accorded such item in the prior taxable year or years which was not correct under the law applicable to such year.

Committee Reports

Report—Ways and Means Committee (77th Cong., 1st Sess., H. Rept. 146).— Section 11 of the bill amends the Internal Revenue Code by the addition of a new section designated section 734. Section 734 provides for an equitable adjustment when a determination of the tax liability under chapter 2E treats an item or transaction affecting such tax liability in a manner inconsistent with the treatment accorded such item or transaction in the determination of the income-tax liability of the taxpayer, or a predecessor for a taxable year or years beginning prior to January 1, 1940. Adjustment is authorized only if (1) upon the date of the determination under chapter 2E correction of the effect of the inconsistent treatment of the item or transaction is prevented (except for the provisions of sec. 3801) in some one or more of such prior taxable years by the operation of a provision of law (other than the provisions of sec. 3761 relating to compromises) or a rule of law, e. g., statute of limitations, closing agreement, Board decision, or rule of res judicata, etc., and (2) the inconsistent position adopted in the determination is asserted

and maintained by the party (either the Commissioner or the taxpayer) who would be adversely affected by an adjustment under this section.

A final determination is not a prerequisite to the application of the section. Whenever the tax liability is determined under chapter 2E and the conditions prescribed in subsection (b) are satisfied, the adjustment is made as an essential part of the determination of such tax liability. If there are further proceedings in the case and the determination is overruled, the adjustment falls with the determination. If the determination becomes final, the adjustment likewise becomes final.

No adjustment under the section is authorized for any taxable year unless correction under the ordinary procedure applicable to the assessment and collection of deficiencies or the refund or credit of overpayments, as the case may be, for such taxable year is prevented. (p. 17)

If a determination under the provisions of chapter 2E adopts an inconsistent position with respect to an item and results in an adjustment under this section, similar treatment of the same item for subsequent taxable years under chapter 2E is not an inconsistency authorizing further adjustment under this section.

Inconsistent treatment within the meaning of the section may relate to the principle or rule of law applied in determining the taxable status of an item or transaction or it may relate only to the amount of the item which is to be taken into account for tax purposes. The inconsistency is to be ascertained by reference to the actual treatment of the item in the earlier year rather than to what the taxpayer or the Commissioner may have urged at that time. Moreover, the fact that the inconsistent position in the later year is based upon an authoritative judicial interpretation of the revenue law which differs from the accepted interpretation of such law in the earlier year does not remove a case from the scope of the section.

Adjustments to income specifically authorized under the provisions of chapter 2E in computing the excess-profits net income do not occasion an adjustment under this section, as the section permits adjustment only where the treatment in the prior taxable year was not correct under the law applicable to such year. This exception does not, however, extend to the disallowance of deductions for taxable years in the base period pursuant to an election under section 733 to capitalize expenditures made for advertising or the promotion of good will which were previously allowed as deductions. Section 733 specifically provides for an adjustment under this section if correction of the tax liability for the taxable year in which the deduction was previously allowed is otherwise prevented.

The term "predecessor" as used in this section means any taxpayer, other than a taxpayer subject to an adjustment under this section, whose tax liability in a prior taxable year in respect of a particular item affects the liability of a taxpayer under chapter 2E with respect to such item, and whose tax liability in such prior taxable year in respect of such item would have been different if there had been no inconsistency between the determination of the liability of the taxpayer under chapter 2E and the determination of its own liability for such prior taxable year. The term includes, among others, a member of an affiliated group as defined in section 730 or a component corporation within the meaning of section 740 (b) (or, if such component corporation is a partnership, the members of such partnership). (p. 19-20)

Report—Senate Finance Committee (77th Cong., 1st Sess., S. Rept. 75).— Same as Ways and Means Committee Report. (p. 17-18, 20 respectively)

Congressional Discussion

Discussion—House (Cong. Rec. Vol. 87).—MR. COOPER. * * * Page 28, section 11, provides for adjustment in case of inconsistent positions. This allows for adjustments during the base period as to income and amounts reported for income taxes. It will be remembered that the present law bases the credit on the amount of the normal tax net income for the corporation during the base period. It does not provide for the amount of income as reported on the corporation's income-tax report, but it provides for the income during the years of the base period. As an illustration, assume that a corporation reported on its income-tax return for one of the years of the base period $100. Now, it comes along when it wants to show as large an amount as it can during the base period for excess-profits tax purposes, and says, "My income for a certain year during the base period was not $100, as was reported, but it was $175, and, therefore, I want the advantage of $175 in that year of the base period, for excess-profits tax purposes." This provision says to the corporation, in effect, "Very well. You may go back and make that adjustment but you must pay the income tax for the difference between what you reported and what you now say you made during that year of the base period plus interest." (p. 1380-81)

Discussion—Senate (Cong. Rec. Vol. 87).—MR. HARRISON. * * * Section 11: This section provides for an equitable adjustment where either the taxpayer or the Commissioner in determining the excess-profits tax treats an item or transaction inconsistent with a prior income-tax liability. It is applicable only where the prior income-tax year is already closed. It is believed that it will add

materially to keeping those old-year determinations from being reopened. (p. 1638)

Committee Hearings
1943 Act

Hearings—Ways and Means Committee.—Making special adjustment on change by railroads from retirement to

depreciation accounting. (R. V. Fletcher, p. 569-571)

1941 Act

Hearings—Ways and Means Committee.—Inequities of provision. (Controllers Institute of America, p. 1715)

Hearings—Senate Finance Committee.—Explanation and shortcomings of provision. (G. R. Blodgett, p. 140-141, 143-147, 149-155; H. Satterlee, p. 168; A. W. Clapp, p. 559-561, 565-566; E. C.

Alvord, p. 629, 680-682; J. W. Hooper, p. 700; A. B. Chapman, p. 755, 760-761; H. B. Fernald, p. 886-887)

Difficulties of applying phrase "maintaining a position". (G. R. Blodgett, p. 141)

Need for definition of predecessor. (G. R. Blodgett, p. 141-142, 148, 150)

1940 Act

Hearings—Ways and Means Committee.—Need for special provision on mitigating effect of statute of limitations. (P. D. Seghers, p. 151)

Hearings—Senate Finance Committee.—Need for special provision on mitigating effect of statute of limitations. (K. Carroad, p. 38)

Sec. 734(b)(3)

[SEC. 734. ADJUSTMENT IN CASE OF POSITION INCONSISTENT WITH PRIOR INCOME TAX LIABILITY.]

[(b) Circumstances of Adjustment.—]

(3) **Burden of Proof.**—*In any proceeding before the Board or any court the burden of proof in establishing that an inconsistent position has been taken (A) shall be upon the Commissioner, in case the net effect of the adjustment would be an increase in the income taxes previously determined for the prior taxable year or years, or (B) shall be upon the taxpayer, in case the net effect of the adjustment would be a decrease in the income taxes previously determined for the prior taxable year or years.*

Committee Reports

Report—Senate Finance Committee (77th Cong., 2d Sess., S. Rept. 1631).— Your committee bill makes a number of amendments to section 734 of the Internal Revenue Code of which those of major importance are as follows:

*   *.   *

(b) The burden of proof in establishing that the inconsistent position has been taken is placed upon the Commissioner if the net effect of the adjustment would be to increase the taxpayer's income taxes previously determined for prior taxable years, and upon the taxpayer if the net effect of the adjustment would be to decrease such taxes for such prior years. (p. 54)

In view of the criticisms of this section presented to your committee, a careful study of the section has been made with special attention to the following problems:

* * *

(9) The burden of proof as to whether an inconsistency exists. (p. 211-212)

Section 734 (b) has been amended by the addition of paragraph (3) to provide an appropriate rule respecting the burden of proof in any case in which there may be a dispute as to whether the treatment of an item or transaction is inconsistent with the treatment of such item or transaction in a prior taxable year. The rule provided places the burden of

proof upon the Commissioner in those cases in which the net effect of the adjustments would be an increase in the income taxes previously determined for the prior taxable year or years and upon the taxpayer in those cases in which the net effect of the adjustment would be a decrease in the income taxes previously determined for the prior taxable year or years. It is not intended that this provision shall be construed to relieve the taxpayer from liability for the penalties imposed for a false or fraudulent return or for a willful failure to supply the information required by law or regulations made under authority of law. (p. 214)

Report—Conference Committee (77th Cong., 2d Sess., H. Rept. 2586).—This amendment also provides a statutory rule for the burden of proof in cases arising under section 734. The House recedes. (p. 65)

Sec. 734(c)

[SEC. 734. ADJUSTMENT IN CASE OF POSITION INCONSISTENT WITH PRIOR INCOME TAX LIABILITY.]

1942
227(a)

[(c) Method and Effect of Adjustment.—* * *]

(3) *If all the adjustments under this section, made on account of the adoption of an inconsistent position or positions with respect to one taxable year under this subchapter, result in an aggregate net increase, the tax imposed by this subchapter shall in no case be less than the amount of such aggregate net increase.*

(4) *If all the adjustments under this section, made on account of the adoption of an inconsistent position or positions with respect to a taxable year under this subchapter (hereinafter in this paragraph called the current taxable year), result in an aggregate net decrease, and the amount of such decrease exceeds the tax imposed by this subchapter (without regard to the provisions of this section) for the current taxable year, such excess shall be subtracted from the tax imposed by this subchapter for each succeeding taxable year, but the amount of the excess to be so subtracted shall be reduced by the reduction in tax for intervening taxable years which has resulted from the subtraction of such excess from the tax imposed for each such year.*

Committee Reports

Report—Senate Finance Committee (77th Cong., 2d Sess., S. Rept. 1631).— Section 734 (c) is amended by the addition of a new paragraph (4) to provide for the carry-over to exhaustion in subsequent taxable years that portion of an adjustment representing a decrease in the excess profits tax which exceeds the amount of the excess profits tax computed without regard to the adjustment. Under section 734 the amount of the adjustment is added to or subtracted from, as the case may be, the excess profits tax determined without regard to the adjustment. If the amount of such adjustment represents an increase in the tax, the statute provides that "the tax imposed by this subchapter shall in no case be less than the amount of such aggregate net increase." However, in the case of an adjustment representing a net decrease the statute made no provision respecting treatment of the excess of such decrease over the amount of the tax computed without regard to the adjustment. This distinction would appear to be inequitable and has been remedied by your committee amendment. If it should happen that such excesses result from adjustments in two or more excess profits tax taxable years, the amounts to be carried over to subsequent taxable years should be applied in the order of their occurrence. For instance, if excesses occurred in both 1942 and 1943, the excess from 1942 should be carried over to 1944 and subsequent years before applying the excess from 1943. (p. 213)

EPTA
11

[SEC. 734. ADJUSTMENT IN CASE OF POSITION INCONSISTENT WITH PRIOR INCOME TAX LIABILITY.]

(c) Method and Effect of Adjustment.—(1) The adjustment authorized by subsection (b), in the amount ascertained as provided in subsection (d), if a net increase shall be added to, and if a net decrease shall be subtracted from, the tax otherwise computed under this subchapter for the taxable year with respect to which such inconsistent position is adopted.

(2) If more than one adjustment under this section is made because more than one inconsistent position is adopted with respect to one taxable year under this subchapter, the separate adjustments, each an amount ascertained as provided in subsection (d), shall be aggregated, and the aggregate net increase or decrease shall be added to or subtracted from the tax otherwise computed under this subchapter for the taxable year with respect to which such inconsistent positions are adopted.

(3) If all the adjustments under this section, made on account of the adoption of an inconsistent position or positions with respect to one taxable year under this subchapter, result in an aggregate net increase, the tax imposed by this subchapter shall in no case be less than the amount of such aggregate net increase.

Committee Reports

Report—Ways and Means Committee (77th Cong., 1st Sess., H. Rept. 146).— The method of adjustment is prescribed in subsections (c) and (d). If the adjustment represents an increase in tax, it is added to the tax imposed by chapter 2E; if the adjustment represents a decrease in tax, it is subtracted from the tax imposed by that chapter. (p. 18)

In any case where a determination of the tax liability under chapter 2E results in the adoption of inconsistent positions with respect to several items, whether such inconsistent positions were maintained by the taxpayer or the Commissioner, or both, an independent determination under the provisions of this section shall be made in respect of each such item both for the purpose of determining the amount of the adjustment and whether such adjustment is authorized. The several adjustments authorized shall be aggregated for the purpose of determining the net addition to, or the net reduction in, the tax imposed by chapter 2E. If the adjustments result in an aggregate net increase, the tax imposed by chapter 2E shall in no case be less than the amount of such aggregate net increase. (p. 19)

Report—Senate Finance Committee (77th Cong., 1st Sess., S. Rept. 75).— Same as Ways and Means Committee Report. (p. 19, 19-20, respectively)

Sec. 734(d)

[SEC. 734. ADJUSTMENT IN CASE OF POSITION INCONSISTENT WITH PRIOR INCOME TAX LIABILITY.]   1942
227(a)

(d) Ascertainment of Amount of Adjustment.—*In computing the amount of an adjustment under this section there shall first be ascertained the amount of the income taxes previously determined for each of the prior taxable years for which correction is prevented. * * * There shall then be ascertained the increase or decrease in each such tax previously determined for each such year which results solely from the treatment of the item consistently with the treatment accorded such item in the determination of the tax liability under this subchapter. * * ***

Committee Reports

Report—Senate Finance Committee (77th Cong., 2d Sess., S. Rept. 1631).— * * * your committee finds that the Commissioner has, by regulations, provided appropriate rules which correctly reflect the purpose and effect of the statute. These regulations provide (a) that a previous adjustment under section 3801 shall be taken into account in determining the amount of the adjustment under section 734. (p. 212)

[SEC. 734. ADJUSTMENT IN CASE OF POSITION INCONSISTENT WITH PRIOR INCOME TAX LIABILITY.]   EPTA
11

(d) Ascertainment of Amount of Adjustment.—In computing the amount of an adjustment under this section there shall first be ascertained the amount of the income taxes previously determined for each of the prior taxable years for which correction is prevented. * * * There shall then be ascertained the increase or decrease in each such tax previously determined for each such year which results solely from the treatment of the item consistently with the treatment accorded such item in the determination of the tax liability under this subchapter. To the increase or decrease so ascertained for each such tax for each such year there shall be added interest thereon computed as if the increase or decrease constituted a deficiency or an overpayment, as the case may be, for such prior taxable year. There shall be ascertained the difference between the aggregate of such increases, plus the interest attributable to each, and the aggregate of such decreases, plus the interest attributable to each, and the net increase or decrease so ascertained shall be the amount of the adjustment under this section with respect to the inconsistent treatment of such item.

Committee Reports

Report—Ways and Means Committee (77th Cong., 1st Sess., H. Rept. 146).— If, however, the item or transaction; in respect of which the inconsistent position is adopted in the determination, affected the determination of the tax liability in several of the prior taxable years, the ascertainment of the amount of the adjustment will require a recomputation with respect to each such year as to which correction of the effect of the inconsistent treatment is prevented.

Example.—In December 1934 corporation X transferred depreciable property to corporation Y in exchange for stock of Y having a fair market value of $100,000. At the time of the transfer the property had an adjusted basis in the hands of X corporation of $80,000 and an estimated remaining life of 20 years. The exchange was treated as nontaxable and the gain of $20,000 realized by the X corporation was not recognized. For each of the years 1935 to 1939, inclusive, corporation Y was allowed deductions for depreciation in the amount of $4,000, computed on a basis of $80,000, the same basis the property had in the hands of the X corporation. In its excess-profits tax return for the taxable year 1940, corporation Y claimed that the property should have a basis of $100,000 for invested capital purposes, and also claimed a deduction of $5,000 for depreciation for such year. This position was based upon the contention that the 1934 exchange was taxable and the gain of $20,000 should have been recognized and added to the basis of the property in the hands of the Y corporation. Timely claims for refund based upon the allowance of additional deductions for depreciation for the taxable years 1938 and 1939 were filed. The statute of limitations prevents any adjustment either by way of refund of overpayments or assessment of deficiencies for the taxable years 1934 to 1937, inclusive. The Commissioner's determination of the excess-profits-tax liability for the taxable year 1940 adopted the inconsistent position asserted by corporation Y and, accordingly, if the computation under section 734 (d) discloses a net increase in the taxes previously determined for the taxable years for which correction is prevented an adjustment is authorized under the provisions of section 734. The ascertainment of the amount of the adjustment under subsection (d) requires a revision of the tax of X corporation previously determined for the year 1934 to reflect the recognition of gain in the amount of $20,000, and a revision of the tax of Y corporation previously determined for the years 1935, 1936, and 1937 to reflect the allowance of an additional $1,000 depreciation deduction for each of those years. If, in any of the prior taxable years, the Y corporation had been liable to the tax imposed on personal holding companies by title IA of the Revenue Acts of 1934, 1936, or 1938, it would be necessary to determine the increase or decrease in such tax for each such year plus the interest attributable to each.

Any such increases would be aggregated with the increases in the title I taxes for the prior taxable years and the decreases likewise would be aggregated with the decreases in the title I taxes. The difference between the aggregate of the increases and the aggregate of the decreases would then be ascertained and the net increase so determined would be the amount of the adjustment under the terms of the above example. If the difference between the aggregate of the increases and the aggregate of the decreases so ascertained were a net decrease, then no adjustment under this section would be authorized, since by the terms of the example the taxpayer had maintained the inconsistent position, and the section does not permit either the taxpayer or the Commissioner to obtain a tax benefit by his own inconsistency. (p. 17-18)

The recomputation prescribed in subsection (d) is merely the ascertainment of the amount of the increase or decrease in each income tax previously determined in each of the prior taxable years if the item or transaction in question had been treated consistently with the treatment accorded such item or transaction in the taxable year for which the determination under chapter 2E is made. The recomputation does not admit of revision of any other items except to the extent that the treatment of items taken into account in ascertaining the tax previously determined is affected by the change in the gross or net income. If any such items are affected, as, for instance, deductions for contributions, foreign-tax credit, etc., revision should be made in conformity with such change. If only one taxable year is involved, the increase or decrease in each of the income taxes previously determined plus interest thereon, computed as if each such increase or decrease were a deficiency or an overpayment, as the case may be, for such taxable year, shall be ascertained. The net increase or net decrease in respect of such taxes and interest for such taxable year is the amount of the adjustment. If the inconsistent treatment of the item or transaction affected more than one of the prior taxable years, it is necessary to determine the increases or decreases in each of the taxes previously determined for each such year in which correction under the ordinary procedure is prevented. To the increases or decreases so ascertained in each such tax for each such year there shall be added interest thereon computed as if each increase or decrease constituted a deficiency or an overpayment, as the case may be, for such year. The difference between the sum of the increases, including the interest computed on such increases, and the sum of the decreases, including the interest computed on such decreases, shall be ascertained and the net increase or net decrease so determined is the amount of the adjustment under this section.

In computing the tax previously determined for any prior taxable year there shall be taken into account any adjustment previously made under the provisions of section 3801.

While the amount of the adjustment under this section is to be computed by determining the difference which would have resulted in the tax previously determined in the prior taxable years in which the inconsistent treatment took place, such prior taxable years are brought into the picture only for the purpose of measuring the amount of the adjustment. The amount of the adjustment so ascertained is to be added to or subtracted from, as the case may be, the excess-profits tax for the taxable year of the determination under chapter 2E. (p. 18-19)

Report—Senate Finance Committee (77th Cong., 1st Sess., S. Rept. 75).— Same as Ways and Means Committee Report. (p. 18-19, 19, respectively)

Sec. 735(a)(1)

SEC. 735. NONTAXABLE INCOME FROM CERTAIN MINING AND TIMBER OPERATIONS, AND FROM NATURAL GAS PROPERTIES.

1943
208(b)
(1)

(a) **Definitions.—** * * *

(1) **Producer; Lessor; Natural Gas Company.**—The term "producer" means a corporation which extracts minerals from a mineral property, or which cuts logs from a timber block, in which an economic interest is owned by such corporation. The term "lessor" means a corporation which owns an economic interest in a mineral property or a timber block, and is paid in accordance with the number of mineral units or timber units recovered therefrom by the (95) ~~producer~~ *person* to which such property or block is leased (96) ~~by the lessor.~~ The term "natural gas company" means a corporation engaged in the withdrawal (97)~~, or transportation by pipe line,~~ ,OR TRANSPORTATION BY PIPE LINE, of natural gas (98) [*from a natural gas property in which it owns an economic interest and which was in operation during the base period.*]

Committee Reports

Report—Ways and Means Committee (78th Cong., 1st Sess., H. Rept. 871).— The term "lessor" has been defined to mean a corporation which owns an economic interest in a mineral property or a timber block, and is paid in accordance with the number of mineral units or timber units recovered therefrom by the producer to which such property or block is leased by the lessor. (p. 58)

Section 735 (a) (1) is amended by including the term "natural gas company" which means a corporation engaged in the withdrawal, or transportation by pipe line, of natural gas. (p. 59)

Report—Senate Finance Committee (78th Cong., 1st Sess., S. Rept. 627).— In the House bill the term "lessor" has been defined to mean a corporation which owns an economic interest in a mineral property or a timber block, and is paid in accordance with the number of mineral units or timber units recovered therefrom by the producer to which such property or block is leased by the lessor. Your committee has changed the definition of "lessor" to mean a corporation which owns an economic interest in a mineral property or a timber block, and is paid in accordance with the number of mineral units or timber units recovered therefrom by the person to which such property or block is leased. By changing the word "producer" to "person" and by deleting the words "by the lessor", it is made explicit that subleases are included within the purview of section 735 as respects lessors. (p. 75)

Section 735 (a) (1) is amended by including the term "natural gas company," which means a corporation engaged in the withdrawal of natural gas from a natural gas property in which it owns an economic interest and which was in operation during the base period; under the House bill a "natural gas company" was defined as a corporation engaged in the withdrawal, or transportation by pipe line, of natural gas. (p. 76)

Report—Conference Committee (78th Cong., 2d Sess., H. Rept. 1079).— Amendments Nos. 95 and 96: Under the House bill which included lessors within the scope of section 735 of the code, the term "lessor" was defined as a corporation which owns an economic interest in a mineral property or a timber block, and is paid in accordance with the number of mineral or timber units recovered from the mineral property or timber block by the producer to which such property or block is leased by the lessor. These amendments change the word "producer" to "person" and eliminate the requirement that such person must be the person to which the mineral property or timber block is leased by the lessor. Thus, individual lessees as well as sublessees are included within the purview of section 735 as respects lessors. The House recedes. (p. 60)

The term "natural-gas property" was defined as the property of a natural-gas company used for the withdrawal, storage, and transportation by pipe line of natural gas, excluding any part of such property which is an emergency facility under section 124. (p. 60)

* * * amendments Nos. 97 and 98 redefine the term "natural-gas company" to mean a corporation engaged in the withdrawal of natural gas from natural-gas property in which it owns an economic interest and which was in operation during the base period. (p. 61)

Committee Hearings

Hearings—Ways and Means Committee.—Extending same relief to lessors as to owners. (J. M. B. Lewis, Jr., p. 238-243; G. T. Howard, p. 243-247)

Extending relief to natural gas industry. (I. J. Underwood, p. 717-741)

Hearings—Senate Finance Committee.—Extending same relief to lessors as to owners. (R. Paul—Treas. Dept.—p. 68-69; H. B. Fernald, p. 932)

Extending relief to natural gas industry. (I. J. Underwood, p. 181-201)

Sec. 735(a)(2)

[SEC. 735. NONTAXABLE INCOME FROM CERTAIN MINING AND TIM- 1943
BER OPERATIONS, AND FROM NATURAL GAS PROPERTIES.] 208(b)

[(a) Definitions.— * * *] (1)

(2) **Mineral Unit, Natural Gas Unit, and Timber Unit.**—The
term "mineral unit" means a unit of metal, coal, or nonmetallic substance in the minerals recovered from the operation of a mineral property. The term "natural gas unit" means a unit of natural gas (99)
~~sold by a natural gas company~~ [*withdrawn from a natural gas property*] SOLD BY A NATURAL GAS COMPANY. The term "timber
unit" means a unit of timber recovered from the operation of a timber
block.

Committee Reports

Report—Ways and Means Committee
(78th Cong., 1st Sess., H. Rept. 871).—
Section 735 (a) (2) and (3) (relating to
the definition of "mineral unit" and
"timber unit") are consolidated into section 735 (a) (2) and this section is expanded to include the term "natural gas
unit" which means a unit of natural gas
sold by a natural gas company. (p. 59)
Report—Senate Finance Committee
(78th Cong., 1st Sess., S. Rept. 627).—
Section 735 (a) (2) and (3) (relating to
the definition of a "mineral unit" and
"timber unit") are consolidated into section 735 (a) (2), and this section is expanded to include the term "natural gas
unit," which means a unit of natural gas

withdrawn from a natural gas property;
under the House bill a "natural gas
unit" was a unit of natural gas sold by a
natural gas company. (p. 76)
Report—Conference Committee (78th
Cong., 2d Sess., H. Rept. 1079).—In
determining the excess output, which
meant the excess of the natural-gas units
for the taxable year over the normal output, the term "natural-gas unit" was defined as a unit of natural gas sold by a
natural-gas company, * * *. (p. 60)
For purposes of determining the excess
output the term "natural-gas unit," as
redefined by amendment No. 99, means
a unit of natural gas withdrawn from a
natural-gas property, * * *. (p. 61)

Sec. 735(a)(3)

[SEC. 735. NONTAXABLE INCOME FROM CERTAIN MINING AND TIM- 1942
BER OPERATIONS.] 209(c)

[(a) Definitions.— * * *]

(4) **Excess Output.**—*The term "excess output" means the excess
of the* MINERAL UNITS OR THE TIMBER *units* [*of metal, coal,
or nonmetallic substance in the minerals recovered from the operation of
a mineral property*] *for the taxable year over the normal output* [*from
such property*].

Committee Reports

Report—Senate Finance Committee (77th Cong., 2d Sess., S. Rept. 1631).— Excess output is defined to mean the excess of the units of metal, coal, or nonmetallic substance in the minerals re-

covered from the operation of a mineral property for the taxable year over the normal output from such property. (p. 187)

Sec. 735(a)(4)

1943
208(b)
(1)

[SEC. 735. NONTAXABLE INCOME FROM CERTAIN MINING AND TIMBER OPERATIONS, AND FROM NATURAL GAS PROPERTIES.]

[(a) Definitions.— * * *]

(4) Normal Output.—The term "normal output" means the average annual mineral units, or the average annual timber units, as the case may be, recovered in the taxable years beginning after December 31, 1935, and not beginning after December 31, 1939 (100) (hereinafter [in this section] HEREINAFTER called "base period"), of the person owning the mineral property or the timber block (whether or not the taxpayer). The term "normal output", in the case of a natural gas company, means the average annual natural gas units (101) sold [withdrawn] SOLD in the (102)* taxable years beginning after December 31, 1935, and not beginning after December 31, 1939 (hereinafter called "base period"),* base period of the person owning the natural gas property (whether or not the taxpayer). * * *

*The part between the asterisks was stricken by the Senate Finance Committee, but restored by the Conference Committee.

Committee Reports

Report—Senate Finance Committee (78th Cong., 1st Sess., S. Rept. 627).— Section 735 (a) (5) (relating to the definition of "normal output") is renumbered section "735 (a) (4)," and is amended to include the determination of normal putput in the case of a natural gas company. In such case, the term "normal output" means the average annual natural gas units withdrawn in the base period (the base period having been defined for the purposes of section 735 by a technical amendment made in section 735 (a) (4) to mean the taxable years beginning after December 31, 1935, and not beginning after December 31, 1939) of the person owning the natural gas property (whether or not the taxpayer). In the House bill the term "normal output" is defined as the aver-

age annual natural gas units sold in such base period. The remaining provisions of section 735 (a) (4), as renumbered, are amended to include, along with mineral units and timber units and mineral property and timber blocks, natural gas units and natural gas properties. (p. 76-77)

Report—Conference Committee (78th Cong., 2d Sess., H. Rept. 1079).— * * * the term "normal output" was defined as the average annual natural-gas units sold in the taxable years beginning after December 31, 1935, and not beginning after December 31, 1939, of the person owning the natural-gas property (whether or not the taxpayer). (p. 60)

* * * the term "normal output," as redefined by amendment No. 101, means the average annual natural-gas units withdrawn in the base period (taxable

years beginning after December 31, 1935, and not beginning after December 31, 1939) of the person owning the natural-gas property (whether or not the tax-payer).   (p. 61)

Amendments Nos. 100 and 102: These amendments are technical amendments simplifying the use of the term "base period" in section 735 (a) (4), as amended.   The Senate recedes.   (p. 61)

[SEC. 735.   NONTAXABLE INCOME FROM CERTAIN MINING AND TIMBER OPERATIONS.]

1942
209(c)

[(a)   Definitions.— * * *]

(5)   **Normal Output.**—*The term "normal output" means the average annual* MINERAL *units or the average annual timber units, as the case may be,* [*of metal, coal, or nonmetallic substance in the minerals*] *recovered* [*from the operation of a mineral property*] *in the taxable years beginning after December 31, 1935, and not beginning after December 31, 1939 (hereinafter called "base period"), of the person owning* [*such*] THE MINERAL *property* OR THE TIMBER BLOCK *(whether or not the taxpayer)* [*(hereinafter called "base period")*].   *The average annual* MINERAL UNITS OR TIMBER *units* [*of metal, coal, or nonmetallic substance recovered*] *shall be computed by dividing the aggregate of* [*the*] SUCH MINERAL UNITS OR TIMBER *units* [*recovered during*] FOR *the base period by the number of months for which the* MINERAL *property* OR THE TIMBER BLOCK *was in operation during the base period and by multiplying the amount so ascertained by twelve.* IN ANY CASE IN WHICH THE TAXPAYER ESTABLISHES, UNDER REGULATIONS PRESCRIBED BY THE COMMISSIONER WITH THE APPROVAL OF THE SECRETARY, THAT THE OPERATION OF ANY MINERAL PROPERTY OR ANY TIMBER BLOCK IS NORMALLY PREVENTED FOR A SPECIFIED PERIOD EACH YEAR BY PHYSICAL EVENTS OUTSIDE THE CONTROL OF THE TAXPAYER, THE NUMBER OF MONTHS DURING WHICH SUCH MINERAL PROPERTY OR TIMBER BLOCK IS REGULARLY IN OPERATION DURING A TAXABLE YEAR SHALL BE USED IN COMPUTING THE AVERAGE ANNUAL MINERAL UNITS, OR TIMBER UNITS, INSTEAD OF TWELVE. *Any* MINERAL *property* OR ANY TIMBER BLOCK, *which was in operation for less than six months during the base period shall, for the purposes of this section, be deemed not to have been in operation during the base period.*

Committee Reports

Report—Senate Finance Committee (77th Cong., 2d Sess., S. Rept. 1631).— Normal output means the average annual units of metal, coal, or nonmetallic substance in the minerals recovered from the operation of a mineral property in the base period which, for the purposes of this section, means the taxable years beginning after December 31, 1935, but not beginning after December 31, 1939, of the person owning such property, whether or not such person be the taxpayer currently owning the property. The average annual units of metal, coal, or nonmetallic substance in the minerals recovered shall be determined by dividing the aggregate of the units recovered during such base period by the number of months for which the property was in operation during such period, and by multiplying the amount so ascertained by 12. Any property which was in operation for less than 6 months during such base period shall, for the purposes of section 735, not be considered to have been in operation during the base period. (p. 187)

Report—Conference Committee (77th Cong., 2d Sess., H. Rept. 2586).— * * * "normal output" is expanded to give a discretion to the Commissioner to reduce the number of months to be used in computation, where physical events normally prevent working during certain months during the year. (p. 60)

Sec. 735(a)(5)

1943
208(b)
(1)

[SEC. 735. NONTAXABLE INCOME FROM CERTAIN MINING AND TIMBER OPERATIONS, AND FROM NATURAL GAS PROPERTIES.]

[(a) Definitions.— * * *]

(5) Natural Gas Property.—The term "natural gas property" means (103)* the property of a natural gas company used for the withdrawal, storage, and transportation by pipe line, of natural gas* [*a gas well, the development and plant necessary for the withdrawal of natural gas therefrom, and so much of the surface of the land as is necessary for such withdrawal,*] excluding any part of such property which is an emergency facility under section 124.

*The part between the asterisks was stricken by the Senate Finance Committee, but restored by the Conference Committee.

Committee Reports

Report—Ways and Means Committee (78th Cong., 1st Sess., H. Rept. 871).— A new paragraph (5) is added to section 735 (a) to define the term "natural gas property" which means the property of a natural gas company used for the withdrawal, storage, and transportation by pipe line, of natural gas, excluding any part of such property which is an emergency facility within the provisions of section 124. (p. 59)

Report—Senate Finance Committee (78th Cong., 1st Sess., S. Rept. 627).— A new paragraph (5) is added to section 735 (a) to define the term "natural gas property" which means a gas well, the development and plant necessary for the withdrawal of natural gas therefrom, and so much of the surface of the land as is necessary for such withdrawal, excluding any part of such property which is an emergency facility under section 124. In the House bill a "natural gas property" was defined as the property of a

natural gas company used for the withdrawal, storage, and transportation by pipe line, of natural gas, excluding any part of such property which is an emergency facility within the provisions of section 124. (p. 77)

Report—Conference Committee (78th Cong., 2d Sess., H. Rept. 1079).— Amendments Nos. 97, 98, 99, 101, 103, 104, 106, and 107: Under the House bill, relief under section 735 was extended to natural-gas companies which were defined as corporations engaged in the withdrawal or transportation by pipe line of natural gas. (p. 60)

As redefined by amendment No. 103, the term "natural-gas property" means a gas well, the development and plant necessary for the withdrawal of natural gas therefrom, and so much of the surface of the land as is necessary for such withdrawal, excluding any part of such property which is an emergency facility under section 124. (p. 61)

Sec. 735(a)(6)

[SEC. 735. NONTAXABLE INCOME FROM CERTAIN MINING AND TIM-
BER OPERATIONS.]

1942
209(c)

[(a) Definitions.— * * *]

(6) Mineral Property.—*The term "mineral property" means a
mineral deposit, the development and plant necessary for the extraction of
the deposit, and so much of the surface of the land as is necessary for
purposes of such extraction.*

Committee Reports

Report—Senate Finance Committee
(77th Cong., 2d Sess., S. Rept. 1631).—
A mineral property means a mineral deposit, the development and plant necessary for the extraction of the deposit, and
so much of the surface of the land as is
necessary for purposes of such extraction.
(p. 187)

Committee Hearings
1943 Act

Hearings—Senate Finance Committee.—Need for clarification of definition
of "mineral property."   (H. B. Fernald,
p. 930)

Sec. 735(a)(7)

[SEC. 735. NONTAXABLE INCOME FROM CERTAIN MINING AND TIM-
BER OPERATIONS.]

1942
209(c)

[(a) Definitions.— * * *]

(7) Minerals.—*The term "minerals" means ores of the metals,
coal, and such nonmetallic substances as abrasives, asbestos, asphaltum,
barytes, borax, building stone, cement rock, clay, crushed stone, feldspar,
fluorspar, fuller's earth, graphite, gravel, gypsum, limestone, magnesite,
marl, mica, mineral pigments, peat, potash, precious stones, refractories,
rock phosphate, salt, sand, silica, slate, soapstone, soda, sulphur, and talc.*

Committee Reports

Report—Senate Finance Committee
(77th Cong., 2d Sess., S. Rept. 1631).—
The minerals covered by the provision
are the metals, coal, and such nonmetallic substances as abrasives, asbestos,
asphaltum, barytes, borax, building
stone, cement rock, clay, crushed stone,
feldspar, fluorspar, fuller's earth, graphite, gravel, gypsum, limestone, magnesite, marl, mica, mineral pigments,
peat, potash, precious stones, refractories, rock phosphate, salt, sand, silica,
slate, soapstone, soda, sulfur, and talc.
(p. 38-39)

Minerals are ores of the metals, coal,
and such nonmetallic substances as abrasives, asbestos, asphaltum, barytes,
borax, building stone, cement rock, clay,

crushed stone, feldspar, fluorspar, fuller's earth, graphite, gravel, gypsum, limestone, magnesite, marl, mica, mineral pigments, peat, potash, precious stones, refractories, rock phosphate, salt, sand, silica, slate, soapstone, soda, sulfur, and talc. (p. 187)

Congressional Discussion

Discussion—Senate (Cong. Rec. Vol. 88).—Mr. Taft. * * * Clay, of course, includes ball and sagger clay, as well as all other clays. In taking care of the question of increased production due to the war, we have included everybody affected by the war, if there shall be an increased production, so the parties sought to be benefited are taken care of, so far as that is concerned.

Mr. McKellar. That refers only to the excess-profits tax. It is under the head of excess-profits tax.

Mr. Taft. Oh, yes; it takes care of excess profits. (p. 8027)

Sec. 735(a)(8)

1943
208(b)
(2)

[SEC. 735. NONTAXABLE INCOME FROM CERTAIN MINING AND TIMBER OPERATIONS, AND FROM NATURAL GAS PROPERTIES.]

[(a) Definitions.— * * *]

(8) Timber Block.—The term "timber block" means an operation unit which includes all the taxpayer's timber which would logically go to a single given point of manufacture.

Committee Reports

Report—Ways and Means Committee (78th Cong., 1st Sess., H. Rept. 871).—Section 735 (a) (8) (relating to the definition of "timber block") has also been amended so as to strike out the prohibition that an operation unit acquired after December 31, 1941, would not be included in the composition of a timber block. (p. 59)

Report—Senate Finance Committee (78th Cong., 1st Sess., S. Rept. 627).—Same as Ways and Means Committee report. (p. 76)

Sec. 735(a)(9)

1942
209(c)

[SEC. 735. NONTAXABLE INCOME FROM CERTAIN MINING AND TIMBER OPERATIONS.]

[(a) Definitions.— * * *]

(9) Normal Unit Profit.—*The term "normal unit profit" means the average profit for the base period per* MINERAL *unit* [*of metal, coal, or nonmetallic substance in the minerals recovered from the mineral property during*] FOR *such period, determined by dividing the net income with respect to minerals recovered from the mineral property (computed with the allowance for depletion computed in accordance with the basis*

for depletion applicable to the current taxable year) during the base period by the number of MINERAL units [of metal, coal, or nonmetallic substance in the minerals] recovered from [such] THE MINERAL property during the base period.

Committee Reports

Report—Senate Finance Committee (77th Cong., 2d Sess., S. Rept. 1631).— The term "normal unit profit" means the average profit for the base period per unit of metal, coal, or nonmetallic substance in the minerals recovered from the mineral property during such period, determined by dividing the net income computed with the allowance for depletion computed in accordance with the basis for depletion applicable to the current taxable year, with respect to minerals recovered from the mineral property during the base period by the number of units of metal, coal, or nonmetallic substance in the minerals recovered from such property during the base period. Your committee expects that the Commissioner, with the approval of the Secretary, will prescribe regulations so that in any case in which two or more metals or nonmetallic substances, or one or more metals or nonmetallic substances and coal, exist in the minerals extracted from a mining property, proper allocation will be made of the net income attributable to such minerals among the units of metal, coal, or nonmetallic substances in the minerals. (p. 188)

$$\boxed{\text{Sec. 735(a)(10)}}$$

[SEC. 735. NONTAXABLE INCOME FROM CERTAIN MINING AND TIMBER OPERATIONS.]   1942 209(c)

[(a) Definitions.— * * *]

(10) **Estimated Recoverable Units.—***The term "estimated recoverable units" means the estimated number of units of metal, coal, or nonmetallic substances in the estimated recoverable minerals from the mineral property at the end of the taxable year plus the excess output for such year. All estimates shall be subject to the approval of the Commissioner, the determinations of whom, for the purposes of this section, shall be final and conclusive.*

Committee Reports

Report—Senate Finance Committee (77th Cong., 2d Sess., S. Rept. 1631).— The estimated recoverable units are the estimated number of units of metal, coal, or nonmetallic substances in the estimated recoverable minerals from the mineral property at the end of the taxable year plus the excess output for such year. This formula should be applicable whether the estimated recoverable units at the end of the year have been computed upon the basis of the estimated number of units at the beginning of the year less the year's output, or whether a new estimate has been made as of the end of the year. In any event, all estimates shall be subject to the approval of the Commissioner, and his determinations, for the purposes of section 735, shall be final and conclusive. (p. 188)

Sec. 735(a)(11)

1942
209(c)

[SEC. 735. NONTAXABLE INCOME FROM CERTAIN MINING AND TIM-
BER OPERATIONS.]

[(a) Definitions.— * * *]

(11) **Exempt Excess Output.**—*The term "exempt excess output"
for any taxable year means a number of units equal to the following percentages of the excess output for such year:*

*100 per centum if the excess output exceeds 50 per centum of the
estimated recoverable units;*

*   *   *

*20 per centum if the excess output exceeds 5 but not 10 per centum
of the estimated recoverable units.*

Committee Reports

Report—Senate Finance Committee
(77th Cong., 2d Sess., S. Rept. 1631).—
Exempt excess output for any taxable
year is the number of units equal to
specified percentages of the excess output for such year. These percentages
vary from 100 percent if the excess output exceeds 50 percent of the estimated
recoverable units, to 20 percent if the
excess output exceeds 5 but not 10 percent of the estimated recoverable units.
They afford a sliding scale of relief de-
pending upon the rapidity with which
the mineral property is being depleted.
(p. 188)

Sec. 735(a)(12)

1943
208(b)
(3)

[SEC. 735. NONTAXABLE INCOME FROM CERTAIN MINING AND TIM-
BER OPERATIONS, AND FROM NATURAL GAS PROPERTIES.]

[(a) Definitions.— * * *]

[(12) Unit Net Income.—* * *]

In respect of a natural gas property, the term "unit net income"
means the amount ascertained by dividing the net income, computed
in accordance with regulations prescribed by the Commissioner with
the approval of the Secretary, from such property during the taxable
year by the number of natural gas units (104) sold <*withdrawn from
such property*> SOLD in such year.

Committee Reports

Report—Ways and Means Committee
(78th Cong., 1st Sess., H. Rept. 871).—
Section 735 (a) (12) (relating to the
definition of "unit net income") is
amended to provide that in respect of a
natural gas property, the term "unit net
income" means the amount ascertained
by dividing the net income, computed in
accordance with regulations prescribed
by the Commissioner with the approval

of the Secretary, from such property during the taxable year by the number of natural gas units sold in such year. It is contemplated that the Commissioner with the approval of the Secretary will issue under this section appropriate regulations providing rules for the allocation of items of income, costs, expenses, and other deductible amounts between the natural gas property and the other property (or activities) of the natural gas company, and for the elimination of any duplication of benefits which might result from the application of this section providing for nontaxable income and any other section providing for allowable deductions which are also attributable to the natural gas property or which would effect a reduction in the income from such property. (p. 59-60)

Report—Senate Finance Committee (78th Cong., 1st Sess., S. Rept. 627).— Section 735 (a) (12) (relating to the definition of "unit net income") is amended to provide that in respect of a natural gas property, the term "unit net income" means the amount ascertained by dividing the net income, computed in accordance with regulations prescribed by the Commissioner, with the approval of the Secretary, from such property during the taxable year by the number of gas units withdrawn from such property in such year. In the House bill the divisor is the number of gas units sold by the taxpayer in such year. It is contemplated that the Commissioner, with the approval of the Secretary, will issue under this section appropriate regulations providing rules for the allocation of items of income, costs, expenses, and other deductible amounts between the natural gas property and the other property (or activities) of the natural gas company, and for the elimination of any duplication of benefits which might result from the application of this section providing for nontaxable income and any other section providing for allowable deductions which are also attributable to the natural gas' property or which would effect a reduction in the income from such property. (p. 77)

Report—Conference Committee (78th Cong., 2d Sess., H. Rept. 1079).— The term "unit net income" in the case of a natural-gas property was defined to mean the amount ascertained by dividing the net income, computed in accordance with regulations prescribed by the Commissioner with the approval of the Secretary, from such property during the taxable year by the number of natural-gas units sold in such year. (p. 60)

The definition of unit net income in respect of a natural-gas company, as changed by amendment No. 104, means the amount ascertained by dividing the net income, computed in accordance with regulations prescribed by the Commissioner with the approval of the Secretary, from the natural-gas property during the taxable year by the number of natural-gas units withdrawn from such property in such year. The Senate recedes. (p. 61)

[SEC. 735. NONTAXABLE INCOME FROM CERTAIN MINING AND TIMBER OPERATIONS.]

1942
209(c)

[(a) Definitions.— * * *]

(12) **Unit Net Income.**—The term "unit net income" means the amount ascertained by dividing the net income (computed with the allowance for depletion) from the coal or iron ore or the timber recovered from the coal mining property, iron mining property, or timber block, as the case may be, during the taxable year by the number of units of coal or iron ore, or timber, recovered from such property in such year.

This paragraph was added by the Conference Committee.

Committee Reports

Report—Conference Committee (77th Cong., 2d Sess., H. Rept. 2586).—It is contemplated that the determination of income from mining and logging operations to be excluded from excess profits net income shall be made on the basis of individual mineral properties or timber blocks rather than on the basis of an aggregate of mineral properties or timber blocks owned by a taxpayer. (p. 60)

Sec. 735(b)(1)

1942
209(c)

[SEC. 735. NONTAXABLE INCOME FROM CERTAIN MINING AND TIMBER OPERATIONS.]

(b)   Nontaxable Income From Exempt Excess Output.—

(1) [1]*General Rule.*—*For any taxable year for which the excess output of mineral property which was in operation during the base period exceeds 5 per centum of the estimated recoverable units from such property, the nontaxable income from exempt excess output for such year shall be an amount equal to the exempt excess output for such year multiplied by the normal unit profit, but such amount shall not exceed the net income (computed with the allowance for depletion) attributable to the excess output for such year.*

[1] The heading was added by the Conference Committee.

Committee Reports

Report—Senate Finance Committee (77th Cong., 2d Sess., S. Rept. 1631).—In order to encourage production of minerals in connection with the war effort, certain special allowances are granted to mines. These are as follows:

     *   *   *

(2) *Excess-profits relief for accelerated production of mines.* Many mining corporations as a result of the expanding war production, may find themselves with properties substantially or fully exhausted within a relatively short period of time. Your committee, therefore, believes that mining corporations with limited reserves should be given some relief from excess-profits taxation on income arising from such accelerated output.

The bill provides a special deduction in computing the excess-profits net income where the production of the mines in excess of normal exceeds 5 percent of the estimated reserves. (p. 38)

The amount of the deduction is determined by (1) the normal profit per unit of production from the property in the base period, (2) the excess output in the taxable year and, (3) the ratio of the excess output for any taxable year to the estimated reserves at the end of the year plus the excess output for such year. (p. 39)

The following example will illustrate the method of computation as applied to a particular case:

Example

COMPANY X

Unit output:	
Normal unit output......tons....	200,000
Taxable year unit output..do......	500,000
Excess over normal.......do......	300,000
Normal unit profit, per ton........	$1
Profit on excess unit output.......	$300,000
Recoverable units: Estimated recoverable units, as defined in the bill ....tons....	2,300,000
Exempt excess output: Percent excess unit output of estimated recoverable units, as defined in the bill ....percent....	13.04

Since the excess unit output (300,000 tons) exceeds 12½ percent but not 14³/₇ percent of estimated recoverable units (2,300,000), 40 percent of such excess units output measured in terms of normal unit of profit ($300,000), or $120,000, will be allowed as a deduction in computing excess profits net income.

NOTE.—The term "estimated recoverable units" means the estimated number of units of metal, coal, or nonmetallic substances in the estimated recoverable minerals from the mineral property at the end of the taxable year plus the excess output for such year.   (p. 39)

Section 735 provides that for any taxable year for which the excess output of a mineral property which was in operation during the base period exceeds 5 percent of the estimated recoverable units from such property, nontaxable income from exempt excess output for such taxable year shall be the exempt excess output for such year multiplied by the normal unit profit. Such amount, however, shall not exceed the net income, computed with the allowance for depletion, attributable to the excess output for such year.   (p. 186-187)

1. Assume that for each of three nonferrous metal mines, the normal output during the base period was 100,000 tons, and that the net income with respect to the minerals recovered was $100,000, resulting in a normal unit profit of $1 per ton. During the taxable year, each of the mines produced 210,000 tons at a profit of $1.40 per ton, producing net income from such minerals of $294,000. At the beginning of the year, the reserves of mine A were 300,000 tons, of mine B were 1,000,000 tons, and of mine C were 2,000,000 tons. The adjusted excess profits net income for each mine would be computed as follows:

		Mine A	Mine B	Mine C
1.	Net income....................................	$294,000	$294,000	$294,000
2.	Normal output (tons)...........................	100,000	100,000	100,000
3.	Excess output (tons)...........................	110,000	110,000	110,000
4.	Estimated reserves at end of year plus excess output (tons)...................................	200,000	900,000	1,900,000
5.	(3) as a percentage of (4).....................	55.0	12.2	5.8
6.	Percentage of (3) which will constitute exempt excess output.................................	100	30	20
7.	Exempt excess output (tons)....................	110,000	33,000	22,000
8.	Nontaxable income from excess output ((7) times normal unit profit of $1)......................	$110,000	$33,000	$22,000
9.	Excess profits net income ((1) − (8))..........	$184,000	$261,000	$272,000
10.	Excess profits credit (95 percent of base period earnings) and specific exemption of $5,000............	$100,000	$100,000	$100,000
11.	Adjusted excess profits net income ((9) − (10)).....	$84,000	$161,000	$172,000

(p. 188-189)

Report—Conference Committee (77th Cong., 2d Sess., H. Rept. 2586).— Amendment No. 290: This amendment excludes, in the computation of excess profits net income of certain producers of minerals, logs, or lumber, certain income derived from the exempt excess output of mineral and timber properties, as well as bonus income received for increased production. * * *

In the case of minerals, the exclusion is computed by reference to the nontaxable income from exempt excess output, as defined in section 735 of the Code, added by this amendment, and also to the nontaxable bonus income received from an agency of the Government, with certain provisions for the elimination of duplication between nontaxable income from exempt excess output and nontaxable bonus income.

The exclusion in the case of minerals subject to this section is determined by multiplying the normal unit profit during a defined base period by a specified portion of current production in excess of normal output during such base period, or in the case of coal and iron mines by multiplying current excess production by one-half of the current net income per unit of coal or iron. (p. 59)

Congressional Discussion

Discussion—Senate; On Report of Conference Committee (Cong. Rec. Vol. 88).— Allowing credit in mining industry based on normal profit per unit of production. (Appendix 2066)

1941 Act

Discussion—House (Cong. Rec. Vol. 87).—Need for special relief for mining industry, in general. (p. 6548-49)

Discussion—Senate (Cong. Rec. Vol. 87).—Mr. JOHNSON of Colorado. * * * It must be apparent to everyone who has given the subject much thought that, so far as taxation is concerned, the mining industry must be treated on a different basis than other industries. In an effort to establish the principle of permitting a credit based upon the normal profit per unit of mine production, it was suggested by me in committee that the drafting experts should be instructed to prepare an amendment to the bill which would prevent the excess-profits tax from being unfairly applied to the normal profits of mines.

It was suggested that the draft should be based upon the following principles:

First. Where the normal profit per unit of production is determinable on the basis of past experience, the excess-profits credit should include such normal profit per unit on the production of the taxable year.

Second. In the case of new corporations or mines not operating on a commercially profitable basis during the base period, a normal profit should be determined as if the mine had been operated in a normal manner during the base-period years.

Third. The foregoing provisions should be limited solely to mining profits. No increased allowance should be made with respect to profits from other than the mining operations. The normal profit from mining operations should be added only to such credit for base-period earnings or invested capital as is properly allocable to operations or investments other than mining.

Such an amendment was offered by me in the committee and was referred to the Treasury Department. The Treasury Department said the matter was very technical, and would require considerable study; that they thought perhaps it could be brought up later, at a time when technical matters pertaining to the administration of the taxation problem would be before the Congress; and so action was postponed by the Finance Committee on the amendment I offered.

I ask unanimous consent to insert in the RECORD at this point a letter from Mr. John L. Sullivan, Assistant Secretary of the Treasury, with respect to this matter.

The PRESIDING OFFICER. Without objection, it is so ordered.

The letter is as follows:

TREASURY DEPARTMENT,
Washington, September 2, 1941.
Hon. EDWIN C. JOHNSON,
United States Senate,
Washington, D. C.
MY DEAR SENATOR: In accordance with the action adopted by the Senate Finance Committee, I have requested that a study be made in this Department of the amendment that you submitted to H. R. 5417 with reference to a credit based on the normal profit per unit of mining production. If, as a result of the study, any amendment of this character is deemed advisable, a provision will be drafted in time for insertion in the next revenue bill.
Sincerely,
JOHN L. SULLIVAN,
Assistant Secretary of the Treasury.

MR. JOHNSON of Colorado. My amendment proposes to amend section 713 by adding a new subsection reading as follows:

"(h) Corporations engaged in mining—
"(1) A corporation engaged in the mining of natural deposits shall be entitled under this section (with respect to its mining operations) to an excess-profits credit equal to the normal profit per unit of production for its entire production during the taxable year, in addition to such other excess-profits credit as may be allowable under this subchapter which is properly allocable to its operations other than mining.
"(A) In the event that the taxpayer was actually in existence at the beginning of its base period and was, during all or a part of such base period, engaged, on a commercially profitable basis, in mining operations similar, except as to the volume of production, to those carried on during the taxable year, then the taxpayer's normal profit per unit of production during the base period (excluding the year or years in which there was a deficit in excess-profits net income) shall constitute the taxpayer's normal profit per unit of production for the purposes of this subsection. In computing such normal profit per unit, the adjustments provided by section 711 (b), so far as applicable, shall be made.
"(B) If the taxpayer was not in existence at the beginning of its base period, or if it was not, during all or a part of such base period, engaged, on a commercially profitable basis, in mining operations similar, except as to volume of production, to those carried on during the taxable year, then the normal profit per unit of production shall consist of the base period profit per unit of production which the taxpayer would have realized if it had been so engaged during such base period. Such normal profit per unit shall be computed by assuming that the taxpayer had sold in each year of the base period the number of units which it could have produced and sold, with due regard to the average prices and costs of operation prevailing in each base period year, except that the number of units assumed in such computation for any base period year shall not exceed the number of units sold in the taxable year.

"(2) The term 'base period' means, for the purposes of this subsection, the base period as elsewhere defined in this subchapter, but if the base period of a taxpayer is not elsewhere so defined, in such case the term 'base period' means the calendar years 1936 to 1939, inclusive.

"(3) This subsection shall not apply if the excess-profits credit computed under section 713, without the application of this section, or under section 714, exceeds the amount of the credit computed under this subsection."

The reasons back of this amendment are, briefly stated, as follows:

First. Mining companies as a rule did not have sufficient base-period income to serve as a sufficient credit for excess-profits taxes.

Second. The prices of metals have been stabilized at a figure very little, if any, above the average prices over a period of 40 years. The industry is cooperating willingly in keeping prices of metals down during the emergency. There is no profiteering in the mining industry in the West.

Third. The defense authorities are urging increased production of metals in order to meet requirements for weapons, plant expansions, and civilian demands.

The result of this combination is that if the mining companies increase production by taking out more units during the emergency than over the base period, they will receive but little above the base period price per unit, and yet the profits, because of increased production, will be considerably greater. The mining industry must use up its capital in its production of units of metals taken out under these conditions, and the capital can never be replaced. It differs from the ordinary industrial enterprise in this respect. At the end of the emergency the mine operator, because of his willingness to comply with the request of the Government for increased production, may see his mine exhausted.

Accordingly, I have urged an amendment to H. R. 5417 which would permit a credit based upon the normal profit per unit of mine production. That is, increased profits would not be subject to excess-profits taxes unless there were an increased price per unit of production. The following example will demonstrate what I am asking for:

If the normal production of a mine was 10,000 tons of ore for a normal profit of $2 per ton the mine would have a total profit of $20,000. If because of the need for metals for defense purposes production were stepped up to 15,000 tons at the same rate of profit—namely $2 per ton—the mining company would have a profit of $30,000. Under the proposed amendment, it would be recognized that this represents only a normal profit on the units produced and that $30,000 would not be subject to excess-profits tax. If, on the other hand, the profit realized on the 15,000 tons were to be $3 per ton or $45,000, the increased profit of $1 per ton, or $15,000, would be taxed as excess profits.

The Treasury Department has promised that this very just demand upon the part of the mining industry will receive study, and that, if deemed advisable, the amendment will be drafted in time for insertion in the next revenue bill. I wish it understood that I shall urge this amendment both as a matter of justice to an industry which is essential to our national defense and as a means of increasing the production which is so sorely needed during this emergency. (p. 7308-09)

Committee Hearings

Hearings—Ways and Means Committee.—Exempting excess production of mines from tax. (H. B. Fernald, p. 3180-83, 3186-87)

Hearings—Senate Finance Committee.—Exempting excess production of mines from tax. (H. B. Fernald, p. 973-975; M. D. Harbaugh, p. 982-988; E. C. Alvord, p. 1798; W. A. Nelson, p. 1928-29)

1941 Act

Hearings—Senate Finance Committee.—Exempting excess production of mines from tax. (B. L. Bunker, p. 986)

Need for special relief for mining industry. (A. G. MacKenzie, p. 1521-24)

Sec. 735(b)(2)

1942
209(c) [SEC. 735. NONTAXABLE INCOME FROM CERTAIN MINING AND TIM-
BER OPERATIONS.]

[(b)   Nontaxable Income From Exempt Excess Output.—]

(2) ¹Coal and Iron Mines.—*For any taxable year, the nontaxable
income from exempt excess output of a coal mining or iron mining property which was in operation during the base period shall be an amount
equal to the excess output of such property for such year multiplied by
one-half of the unit net income from such property for such year,* [*and for
such purpose "unit net income" means the amount ascertained by dividing
the net income from the coal or iron recovered from the property during
the taxable year by the number of units of coal or iron recovered from such
property in such taxable year.*] OR AN AMOUNT DETERMINED
UNDER PARAGRAPH (1), WHICHEVER THE TAXPAYER
ELECTS IN ACCORDANCE WITH REGULATIONS PRE-
SCRIBED BY THE COMMISSIONER WITH THE APPROVAL
OF THE SECRETARY.

¹ The heading was added by the Conference Committee.

Committee Reports

**Report—Senate Finance Committee
(77th Cong., 2d Sess., S. Rept. 1631).**—
Your committee has provided special
relief for coal and iron mines with accelerated production. Due to the long
life of coal mines and due to the fact that
the normal production was very low,
very little relief will be afforded under
the provisions outlined above. This
amendment will permit an adjustment
to the excess-profits net income of one-
half of the excess production in the taxable year over the production in the
base period, multiplied by the profit per
unit of production for the taxable year.
The following example will show how
the plan operates:

(1)	Average base period output...tons		100,000
(2)	Taxable year output.........do		190,000
(3)	Excess output...............do		90,000
(4)	Profit per unit of production.......cents per ton		10
(5)	Product of (3) and (4)...........		$9,000
(6)	50 percent of (5)...............		$4,500

The amount allowed in this case in
adjusting the excess-profits net income
will be $4,500. This will be allowed
whether the taxpayer uses the average-
earnings basis or the invested-capital
basis. (p. 40)

In the case of a coal mining or iron
mining property which was in operation
during the base period, nontaxable income from exempt excess output for any
taxable year shall be an amount equal
to the excess output of such property for
such taxable year multiplied by one-half
of the unit net income from such property for such year. The unit net income
of a coal mining or iron mining property
means the amount ascertained by dividing the net income from the coal or iron
recovered from the property during the
taxable year by the number of units of
coal or iron recovered from such property in such year. (p. 187)

3. Assume that the normal output of
a coal mine during the base period was
100,000 tons, and the average net income
from the property was $5,000. Assume
that the output for the taxable year is
190,000 tons producing a net income, at
a profit of $0.10 per ton, of $19,000. The
excess profits tax of such mine would be
reduced by this section by $4,050, as
follows:

1. Taxable year net income......... $19,000
2. Taxable year output (tons)....... 190,000
3. Normal output (tons)............ 100,000

4.	Excess output (tons)............	90,000
5.	Profit per unit of production......	$0.10
6.	Product of (5) and (4)..........	$9,000
7.	Nontaxable income (50 percent of (6))...........................	$4,500
8.	Excess profits net income ((1) less (7))...........................	$14,500
9.	Average earnings credit (95 percent of base period average plus $5,000 exemption).............	$9,750
10.	Adjusted excess profits net income ((8) less (9))...................	$4,750
11.	Excess profits tax at 90 percent without the benefit of sec. 735..	$8,325
12.	Excess profits tax at 90 percent with the benefit of sec. 735.....	$4,275
13.	Tax reduction..................	$4,050

(p. 189)

Report—Conference Committee (77th Cong., 2d Sess., H. Rept. 2586).—An election is given in the case of coal and iron mines to compute nontaxable income from exempt excess output either under the general rule or under the special rule applicable thereto. The provisions are applicable only to producers of minerals or logs as defined in the report of the committee of conference. (p. 60)

Sec. 735(b)(3)

[SEC. 735. NONTAXABLE INCOME FROM CERTAIN MINING AND TIMBER OPERATIONS.]

1942

209(c)

[(b) Nontaxable Income From Exempt Excess Output.—]

(3) ¹Timber Properties.—[*In the case of a producer of logs, or a producer of lumber, from timber owned by him, there shall be excluded from his income for the taxable year at his option, either (1) that part thereof attributable to the excess of production of logs over a quota based upon past production to be fixed by the War Production Board, or other governmental agency, or (2) income derived from bonus payments made to him by any agency of the United States Government on account of log production.*] FOR ANY TAXABLE YEAR, THE NONTAXABLE INCOME FROM EXEMPT EXCESS OUTPUT OF A TIMBER BLOCK WHICH WAS IN OPERATION DURING THE BASE PERIOD SHALL BE AN AMOUNT EQUAL TO THE EXCESS OUTPUT OF SUCH PROPERTY FOR SUCH YEAR MULTIPLIED BY ONE-HALF OF THE UNIT NET INCOME FROM SUCH PROPERTY FOR SUCH YEAR.

¹ The heading was added by the Conference Committee.

Committee Reports

Report—Conference Committee (77th Cong., 2d Sess., H. Rept. 2586).— Amendment No. 290: This amendment excludes, in the computation of excess profits net income of certain producers of minerals, logs, or lumber, certain income derived from the exempt excess output of mineral and timber properties, as well as bonus income received for increased production. In the case of timber, the exclusion is determined by reference either (1) to a quota based upon past production (to be fixed by the War Production Board, or other governmental agency) or (2) to the amount received in bonus payments by an agency of the Government on account of log production.

* * *

The House recedes with an amendment making drafting and clarifying

changes and the following changes of
substance:

The exclusion in the case of timber is
made the same as in the case of minerals,

namely, nontaxable income from exempt
excess output, and nontaxable income
from exempt excess output of a timber
block is defined. (p. 59-60)

Congressional Discussion

Discussion—Senate (Cong. Rec. Vol.
88).—MR. McNARY. Mr. President, the
amendment I wish to propose would give
to timber the same exemptions, in the
case of the excess-profits tax, that is
given to coal and other minerals. (p.
7995)

MR. McNARY. Mr. President, in my
amendment I desire to have no advantage. I merely want timber resources to
be on a parity of equality with other
natural resources. If the Senator will
suggest any amendment or improvement, I shall be glad to accept it, and let
it be worked out in conference. I repeat, I do not want for timber resources
anything but parity with the other resources which are specified in the bill.

MR. GEORGE. I think the amendment the Senator has drafted would give
timber an advantage over other depletable resources.

MR. McNARY. I do not think so.

MR. GEORGE. I have not had time

to check it.

MR. McNARY. I may state that I
would not consciously have offered the
amendment in such a fashion. The
Senator, of course, will perform his duty
and in conference remove the advantage,
if it exists.

MR. GEORGE. I shall be glad to let
the amendment go to conference for the
purpose of ascertaining whether or not
the amendment would give timber an
advantage over other depletable resources.

MR. McNARY. I again assert that I
do not want to have any advantage.
(p. 8010)

Discussion—Senate; on Report of
Conference Committee (Cong. Rec. Vol.
88).—MR. GEORGE. * * * The Senate
amendments dealing with mining corporations and logs were agreed to, with
the exception that logs were given the
same treatment as coal and iron under
the Guffey amendment. (p. 8410)

Sec. 735(b)(4)

1943
208(c)

[SEC. 735. NONTAXABLE INCOME FROM CERTAIN MINING AND TIM-
BER OPERATIONS, AND FROM NATURAL GAS PROPERTIES.]

[(b) Nontaxable Income From Exempt Excess Output.—]

(4) Coal and Iron Mines and Timber Properties Not in Operation During Base Period.—For any taxable year, the nontaxable income from exempt excess output of a coal mining or iron mining property or a timber block, which was not in operation during the base
period, shall be an amount equal to 1/6 of the net income for such
taxable year (computed with the allowance for depletion) from the coal
mining or iron mining property or from the timber block, as the case
may be.

The figure "1/6" was changed to "1/2" by the Senate Finance Committee,
but restored by the Conference Committee.

Committee Reports

Report—Ways and Means Committee (78th Cong., 1st Sess., H. Rept. 871).— The present provisions of section 735 extend no relief to coal mining or iron mining properties or timber blocks which were not in operation during the base period. Subsection (c) of this section of the bill adds a new paragraph to section 735 (b) which provides that for any taxable year, the nontaxable income from exempt excess output of a coal mining or iron mining property or a timber block, which was not in operation during the base period, shall be an amount equal to one-sixth of the net income for such taxable year (computed with the allowance for depletion) from the coal mining or iron mining property or from the timber block, as the case may be. (p. 58)

Report—Senate Finance Committee (78th Cong., 1st Sess., S. Rept. 627).— The Senate committee agreed to the House provisions with the following exceptions: The relief granted to new coal and iron mines was extended to allow coal-mining or iron-mining property or a timber block which was not in operation during the base period an amount equal to one-half of the net income for such taxable year (computed with the allowance for depletion) from the coal-mining or iron-mining property, or from the timber block, as the case may be. The House bill only allowed an exemption of one-sixth of such net income. (p. 30)

The present provisions of section 735 extend no relief to coal mining or iron mining properties or timber blocks which were not in operation during the base

period. Subsection (c) of this section of the bill adds a new paragraph to section 735 (b) which provides that for any taxable year, the nontaxable income from exempt excess output of a coal mining or iron mining property or a timber block, which was not in operation during the base period, shall be an amount equal to one-half of the net income for such taxable year (computed with the allowance for depletion) from the coal mining or iron mining property or from the timber block, as the case may be. Under the House bill, such amount was equal to one-sixth of such net income. (p. 75-76)

Report—Conference Committee (78th Cong., 2d Sess., H. Rept. 1079).— In the case of a natural-gas company, any of the natural-gas property of which was in operation during the base period, the nontaxable income from exempt excess output for any taxable year was the amount equal to the excess output for such year multiplied by one-half of the unit net income for such year. (p. 60)

Amendment No. 105: Under the House bill nontaxable income from exempt excess output from a coal mining or iron mining property or a timber block which was not in operation during the base period was an amount equal to one-sixth of the net income for such taxable year computed with the allowance for depletion from the coal or iron mining property or from the timber block, as the case may be. This amendment changes the allowance from one-sixth to one-half of such net income for the taxable year. The Senate recedes. (p. 61)

Committee Hearings

Hearings—Ways and Means Committee.— Extending relief to properties not in operation during base period. (R. D. Campbell, p. 780-784)

Extending relief to properties not in

operation during base period. (R. Paul —Treas. Dept.—p. 68-69; G. G. Crowder, p. 785; R. D. Campbell, p. 885-900; H. B. Fernald, p. 932)

Sec. 735(b)(5)

[Set forth on following page]

[SEC. 735. NONTAXABLE INCOME FROM CERTAIN MINING AND TIM-
BER OPERATIONS, AND FROM NATURAL GAS PROPERTIES.]

[(b) Nontaxable Income From Exempt Excess Output.—]

(5)   Natural Gas Companies.—In the case of a natural gas company 【106】 *any of the natural gas property of which was in operation
during the base period,* the nontaxable income from exempt excess
output for any taxable year shall be an amount equal to the excess
output for such year 【107】 *<from natural gas properties in which it
owns an economic interest>* multiplied by one-half of the unit net income for such year.

*The part between the asterisks was stricken by the Senate Finance Com-
mittee, but restored by the Conference Committee.

Committee Reports

**Report—Ways and Means Committee
(78th Cong., 1st Sess., H. Rept. 871).—**
In addition, this section of the bill extends to natural gas companies relief
similar to the relief granted under the
present law with respect to coal mining
and iron mining properties and timber
blocks. However, in the case of natural
gas companies, the nontaxable income
from exempt excess output is to be computed with respect to net income derived from withdrawal, storage, and
transportation by pipe line, of natural
gas, but is not to include any income
attributable to the distribution of such
gas. It is understood that the transportation by pipe line of natural gas ends
at the point where the distribution system begins, for example, the city gate in
the case of natural gas brought to a city
for local distribution. Transportation
by pipe line does not include the process
of distributing the gas to the ultimate
consumer. The relief extended to a
natural gas company is available only if
the whole or any part of its natural gas
property was in operation during the
base period as defined in section 735.
(p. 59)

A new paragraph (5) has been added
to section 735 (b) to provide for the
computation of nontaxable income from
exempt excess output in the case of
natural gas property. It prescribes that
in the case of a natural gas company,
any part of the natural gas property of
which was in operation during the base
period, the nontaxable income from
exempt excess output for any taxable

year shall be an amount equal to the
excess output for such year multiplied
by one-half of the unit net income for
such year.   (p. 60)

**Report—Senate Finance Committee
(78th Cong., 1st Sess., S. Rept. 627).—**
In the case of natural-gas companies, the
relief under the committee amendment
was granted only with respect to net income derived from the withdrawal from
the natural-gas property in which the
company owned an economic interest.
Under the House bill, the relief was extended to the net income derived from
the withdrawal, storage, and transportation by pipe line of natural gas.   The
amendments made by the House were
made retroactive to taxable years beginning after December 31, 1941, only
with respect to lessors of property in
operation during the base period and
with respect to natural-gas companies.
Under the Senate bill, all of the amendments made by this section were made
applicable with respect to taxable years
beginning after December 31, 1941.
(p. 30)

In addition, this section of the bill
extends to natural gas companies relief
similar to the relief granted under the
present law with respect to coal mining
and iron mining properties and timber
blocks. Under the House bill, in the
case of natural gas companies, the nontaxable income from exempt excess output is to be computed with respect to
net income derived from the withdrawal,
storage, and transportation by pipe line,
of natural gas, but is not to include any

income attributable to the distribution of such gas. In order to make the relief extended to natural gas companies more nearly correspond to that extended to coal mining and iron mining properties and timber blocks, your committee has provided that relief shall be granted to natural gas companies only with respect to net income derived from the withdrawal of natural gas from natural gas properties in which the natural gas company owns an economic interest, and shall not be extended to any income attributable to storage, transportation, or distribution of such gas. The relief extended to a natural gas company is applicable only with respect to natural gas properties in which such company owns an economic interest during the taxable year and only if such company is engaged in the withdrawal of natural gas from a natural gas property in which it owns an economic interest and which was in operation during the base period. (p. 76)

Subsection (c) of this section adds a new paragraph (5) to section 735 (b) to provide for the computation of nontaxable income from exempt excess output in the case of natural gas companies. It prescribes that in the case of a natural gas company, the nontaxable income from exempt excess output for any taxable year shall be an amount equal to the excess output for such year from natural gas properties in which it owns an economic interest multiplied by one-half of the unit net income for such year. This computation is to be made with respect to all natural gas properties in which a natural gas company owns an economic interest, regardless of whether such properties were in operation during the base period or whether, if in operation, the natural gas company owned an economic interest in such properties during the base period, provided that the natural gas company fulfills the requirements of section 735 (a) (1). As added by the House bill, paragraph (5) provides that in the case of a natural gas company any of the natural gas property of which was in operation during the base period, the nontaxable income from excess output for any taxable year shall be an amount equal to the excess output for such year multiplied by one-half of the unit net income for such year. (p. 77)

Report—Conference Committee (78th Cong., 2d Sess., H. Rept. 1079).—The amendments added by the Senate extend relief to a natural-gas company only with respect to the income derived from the withdrawal of natural gas from natural-gas properties in which the natural-gas company owns an economic interest and do not extend such relief to any income attributable to storage, transportation, or distribution of such gas. (p. 60-61)

Amendments Nos. 106 and 107 provide that in the case of a natural-gas company the nontaxable income from exempt excess output for any taxable year shall be an amount equal to the excess output for such year from natural-gas properties in which it owns an economic interest multiplied by one-half of the unit net income for such year. (p. 61)

Congressional Discussion

Discussion—Senate (Cong. Rec. Vol. 90).—Mr. George. * * * The next ground enumerated in the message[1] is as follows:

(d) Natural gas pipe lines are exempted from the excess-profits tax without justification and in a manner which might well lead oil companies to request similar treatment for their pipe lines.

Mr. President, I may say in all frankness that the Senate committee disagreed with that provision in the bill as passed by the House. We struck out the percentage depletion allowance for pipe lines; but the House conferees insisted, and we finally agreed, as one must finally agree in connection with any complicated bill such as a general tax bill. However, there were very strong arguments made to the effect that in the case of the pipe lines serving gas wells the pipe lines are a part, themselves, of the property, and must necessarily be given some special tax treatment, or else the excess-profits taxes would destroy the income from the gas. (p. 1950)

[1] Relating to veto message from the President (78th Cong., 2d Sess., H. Doc. 443, p. 2).

Sec. 735(c)

[SEC. 735. NONTAXABLE INCOME FROM CERTAIN MINING AND TIM-
BER OPERATIONS, AND FROM NATURAL GAS PROPERTIES.]

(c) Nontaxable Bonus Income.—The term "nontaxable bonus income" means the amount of the income derived from bonus payments made by any agency of the United States Government on account of the production in excess of a specified quota of:

(1) A mineral product or timber, the exhaustion of which gives rise to an allowance for depletion under section 23 (m), but such amount shall not exceed the net income (computed with the allowance for depletion) attributable to the output in excess of such quota; or

(2) A mineral product extracted or recovered from mine tailings by a corporation which owns no economic interest in the mineral property from which the ore containing such tailings was mined, but such amount shall not exceed the net income attributable to the output in excess of such quota.

Committee Reports

Report—Ways and Means Committee (78th Cong., 1st Sess., H. Rept. 569).—The committee amendment is as follows:

On page 2, beginning with the colon in line 7, strike out the following: "; *Provided,* That the exhaustion of such mineral product would give rise to an allowance for depletion under section 23 (m) if such corporation had an economic interest in such mineral property".

With this deletion, section 735 (c) (2) of the Internal Revenue Code will read, if the bill is enacted into law, as follows:

A mineral product extracted or recovered from mine tailings by a corporation which owns no economic interest in the mineral property from which the ore containing such tailings was mined, but such amount shall not exceed the net income attributable to the output in excess of such quota.

The stricken language was originally inserted in the bill in order to set forth clearly the limitations to which the additional relief granted by this bill was to be restricted. However, it now appears that the term "mine tailings" has a definite meaning in metallurgy which does not need to be pared down by statutory language, and that the use of this term will adequately restrict the relief to those cases which are intended to be covered by this amendment.

Existing law provides that bonus payments made to a corporation which ex-

tracts minerals from a mineral property, or recovers timber from a timber block, in which an economic interest is owned by such corporation, by any agency of the United States Government on account of the production in excess of a specified quota of a mineral or of timber, the exhaustion of which gives rise to an allowance for depletion, under section 23 (m), shall be excluded from the payment of the excess-profits tax. The amount of these excluded bonus payments or "nontaxable bonus income" is limited not to exceed the net income (computed with the allowance for depletion) attributable to the output in excess of such quota.

The relief extended by existing law is limited to those producers having an "economic interest" in the mineral property or timber block from which minerals are extracted or timber is recovered. The bill would enlarge existing law so as to provide the same relief for tailing-mill operators having no economic interest in the mineral property from which the tailings were taken. (p. 1-2)

The subject matter of this legislation has been discussed with the general counsel of the Treasury and the following communications received from him which, while they are informal in their tenor, cover, and are informative on the subject matter.

THE GENERAL COUNSEL OF THE TREASURY,
Washington, June 5, 1943.
Hon. WESLEY E. DISNEY,
House of Representatives, Washington, D. C.
MY DEAR MR. DISNEY: I understand that you are interested in amendatory legislation which would extend the benefits of section 735 of the Internal Revenue Code relating to non-taxable bonus income to bonus payments made by an agency of the Government for production of mineral products extracted or recovered from mine tailings. For your convenience and assistance, I am enclosing informally the draft of an amendment to sections 735 and 711, which it is believed would accomplish your purpose.

Under the provisions of section 735 (c), non-taxable bonus income is to be excluded from the excess-profits tax only if it is received on account of the production of a mineral product "the exhaustion of which gives rise to an allowance for depletion." If such mineral product is recovered from mine tailings, the bonus payments made on account thereof are covered by the provisions of section 735 (c), provided that the producer had an economic interest in the mineral property from which the tailings originally came; this is true because in such a case the allowance for depletion is generally available. However, if the producer has no economic interest in the original mineral property from which the tailings came, the present provisions of section 735 (c) would be inapplicable, because in this case there is no allowance for depletion. The enclosed draft has been prepared to take care of this latter situation, so that bonus payments in respect of mineral products recovered from tailings will be excludible from the excess-profits tax, whether or not the producer had an economic interest in the mineral property, provided that the exhaustion of such mineral product would give rise to an allowance for depletion if such producer did have an economic interest in such property.

Any questions that you may have with regard to this amendment I shall be glad to take up with you at your convenience.

Sincerely yours,
RANDOLPH E. PAUL, *General Counsel.*

THE GENERAL COUNSEL OF THE TREASURY,
Washington, June 15, 1943.
MY DEAR MR. DISNEY: This is with reference to the draft of the bill which I enclosed in my letter to you of June 5, 1943. This bill relates to the application of the excess-profits tax to certain production bonus payments, and was introduced in the House of Representatives by you on June 7, 1943, as H. R. 2888.

After further consideration, I feel that it would be advisable to have the proviso clause in paragraph (2) of subsection (c) of section 735 deleted from the bill. This is the clause which begins on line 7 of page 2 of H. R. 2888 and reads as follows:

"*Provided,* That the exhaustion of such mineral product would give rise to an allowance for depletion under section 23 (m) if such corporation had an economic interest in such mineral property."

This proviso clause was originally inserted in the draft forwarded to you, in order to set forth clearly the limitations to which the additional relief granted by this bill was to be restricted. It now appears that this clause is actually unnecessary, for the reason that the use of the term "mine tailings" will adequately restrict the relief to those cases which are intended to be covered by this amendment. As I understand it, "mine tailings" has a definite meaning in

metallurgy which does not need to be pared down by statutory language.
*   *   *
(p. 5)

Report—Senate Finance Committee (78th Cong., 1st Sess., S. Rept. 417).— This legislation was requested by the War Production Board, and the pending bill was drawn and approved by the Treasury. (p. 1)

This bill is to correct inadvertent technical error in tax bill of 1942, in regard to exemption from excess-profits tax on premium payments by Metals Reserve Company on zinc production from tailing piles (waste material from nonferrous metal mines). Under the act this exemption applies only to premium payments on zinc produced from mining operations entitled to depletion. Under present interpretations of various revenue acts, tailing piles are not entitled to depletion (and therefore not entitled to exemption from excess-profits tax) except in cases where the tailing mill operation is conducted by the same operator who produced the tailings from mining operations, i. e., operators having an "economic interest" in the mineral property from which the minerals are extracted. A large percentage of the original mine operators who produced tailings have gone out of business, and the piles of tailings left by them are now being retreated by others than the original mine operator because of the need for zinc.

The purpose of H. R. 2888 is to put all tailing-mill operators on an equality, giving them the same exemption under the Revenue Act of 1942, whether they have an economic interest in the mineral property or not.

Tailing-mill operations in the largest zinc-production district in the country (tri-State) have been producing approximately 15 percent of the total production of that district, and it is believed the passage of this bill will result in large expansion of tailing-mill operations in that district and in all zinc-producing districts in the country, and a large increase in production of zinc, so greatly needed for war purposes.

The 1942 act includes timber in the same paragraph with minerals, and the amending bill (H. R. 2888), therefore, includes timber. (p. 1-2)

[SEC. 735.   NONTAXABLE INCOME FROM CERTAIN MINING AND TIM-
BER OPERATIONS.]

(c)   Nontaxable Bonus Income.—[1]~~There shall be excluded income
derived from bonus payments made by any agency of the United
States Government on account of the production in excess of a specified quota of a product the exhaustion of which gives rise to an
allowance for depletion under section 23 (m).~~ *The term "nontaxable
bonus income" means the amount of the income derived from bonus payments made by any agency of the United States Government on account
of the production in excess of a specified quota of a mineral product* OR
OF TIMBER *the exhaustion of which gives rise to an allowance for depletion under section 23 (m), but such amount shall not exceed the net
income* (COMPUTED WITH THE ALLOWANCE FOR DEPLE-
TION) *attributable to the output in excess of such quota.*

[1] The Ways and Means Committee bill proposed a corresponding amendment of sec. 711(a)(2) for the invested capital credit, but it was likewise
stricken by the Senate Finance Committee.

Committee Reports

Report—Ways and Means Committee
(77th Cong., 2d Sess., H. Rept. 2333).—
For industries with depletable resources,
the increase in profits during the war
may in part result from stepped-up production which would exhaust the available reserves earlier than under normal
conditions. Thus, for the same aggregate output over a period of years, the
total amount of profits taxable as excess
profits will be greater if the output is
concentrated in a few years than if it is
spread over a longer period, since the
aggregate excess-profits tax credit for the
period depends on the number of years.
The bunching of income into a shorter
period does not raise the same problem
for industries that do not have depletable resources. The increase in their
current production need not reduce future production. The War Production
Board and the Office of Price Administration are endeavoring to stimulate the
production of key metal products by
offering premium prices; i. e., prices in
excess of the ceiling price for production
in excess of specified quotas established
on the basis of the production in 1941
or some other recent period. For example, a 5-cent bonus is offered for each
pound of copper produced in excess of a
quota established on the basis of 1941
output. The excess over these quotas
may be considered especially called for

by the war effort. Your committee has,
therefore, provided that bonuses paid
for output in excess of the quotas set by
the war agencies be deductible from
excess-profits net income and be subject
solely to normal and surtaxes. (p. 27)
The War Production Board and the
Office of Price Administration are endeavoring to stimulate the production of
certain metals by offering premium
prices, in excess of the ceiling price, for
production in excess of specified established quotas. Thus, for the same total
output over a period of years, the total
amount of taxable excess profits will be
greater if the output is concentrated in a
few years than if it is spread over a
longer period, since the aggregate excess
profits tax credit for the period depends
upon the number of years included
therein. This problem does not appear
in industries which do not have depletable resources since future production is
not thereby reduced. Section 711 (a)
(1) and (2) (relating to excess profits
credit computed, respectively, under the
average earnings method and under the
invested-capital method) is therefore
amended to exclude from excess profits
tax bonus payments made by an agency
of the United States Government on account of the production in excess of a
specified quota of products, the exhaustion of which gives rise to an allow-

ance for depletion under section 23(m). (p. 149)

Report—Senate Finance Committee (77th Cong., 2d Sess., S. Rept. 1631).— Nontaxable bonus income is the amount of income derived from bonus payments made by any agency of the United States Government on account of the production in excess of a specified quota of a mineral product the exhaustion of which gives rise to an allowance for depletion under section 23 (m), but such amount shall not exceed the net income attributable to the output in excess of such quota. (p. 187)

Your committee has transferred the provisions of subsection (e) of section 213 of the House bill, relating to bonus income of industries with depletable reserves, to section 209, which relates to nontaxable income from exempt excess output of mining and from bonus income of mines. (p. 207)

Committee Hearings

Hearings—Senate Finance Committee.—Explanation of provision. (J. O'Brien—H. Legis. Counsel—p. 109)

Extending treatment of bonus income to timber products. (W. Compton, p. 1697-1706)

Limiting nontaxable bonus income to income from the particular property. (H. B. Fernald, p. 928; C. V. Burns, p. 947-949)

Sec. 735(d)

[SEC. 735. NONTAXABLE INCOME FROM CERTAIN MINING AND TIMBER OPERATIONS.]

(d) **Rule in Case Income From Excess Output Includes Bonus Payment.**—*In any case in which the income attributable to the excess output includes bonus payments (as provided in subsection (c)), the taxpayer may elect, under regulations prescribed by the Commissioner with the approval of the Secretary, to receive either the benefits of subsection (b) or subsection (c) with respect to such income as is attributable to excess output above the specified quota.*

Committee Reports

Report—Senate Finance Committee (77th Cong., 2d Sess., S. Rept. 1631).— If the income attributable to excess output includes bonus payments, the taxpayer may elect under regulations prescribed by the Commissioner with the approval of the Secretary, to receive the benefits of nontaxable income from exempt excess output or of nontaxable bonus income with respect to that portion of the excess output in excess of the taxpayer's quota. (p. 187)

2. If the previous problem,[1] a quota of 100,000 tons had been established for each mine, and the current profit had included a bonus price of $0.40 per ton, since output in excess of the quota is 110,000 tons nontaxable bonus income would amount to $44,000. Whereas mine A would elect to retain the benefits of the exclusion for nontaxable income from exempt excess output, mines B and C would elect to receive the benefits of a $44,000 exclusion for nontaxable bonus income instead of an exclusion for nontaxable income from exempt excess output which, in the case of mine B, was $33,000, and, in the case of mine C, was $22,000. (p. 189)

[1] Relating to sec. 735(b)(1).

$$\boxed{\text{Sec. 736(a)}}$$

SEC. 736. RELIEF FOR INSTALMENT BASIS TAXPAYERS ¹AND TAXPAY-
ERS WITH INCOME FROM LONG-TERM CONTRACTS.

(a) **Election to Accrue Income.**—~~In the case of any taxpayer computing income from instalment sales under the method provided by
section (a), if such taxpayer establishes that the average volume of
credit extended to purchasers on the instalment plan in the four
preceding taxable years was more than 125 per centum of the volume
of such credit extended to such purchasers in the taxable year, it
may elect, in its first return for the taxable year, for the purposes
of the tax imposed by this subchapter, to compute, pursuant to
regulations prescribed by the Commissioner with the approval of
the Secretary, its gross income from instalment sales on the basis
of the taxable period for which such income is accrued, in lieu of
the basis provided by section 44 (a). Such election shall be irrevocable when once made and shall apply also to all subsequent taxable years, and the gross income from instalment sales for each
taxable year before the first year with respect to which the election
is made but beginning after December 31, 1939, shall be adjusted
for the purposes of this subchapter to conform to such election. In
making such adjustments, no amount shall be included in computing
excess profits net income for any excess profits tax taxable year on
account of instalment sales made in taxable years beginning before
January 1, 1940.~~

*In the case of any taxpayer computing income from instalments sales
under the method provided by section 44 (a), if such taxpayer establishes,
in accordance with regulations prescribed by the Commissioner with the
approval of the Secretary, that the average volume of credit extended to
purchasers on the instalment plan in the four taxable years preceding the
first taxable year beginning after December 31, 1941, was more than 125
per centum of the volume of such credit extended to such purchasers in
the taxable year, or the average outstanding instalment accounts receivable
at the end of each of the four taxable years preceding the first taxable year
beginning after December 31, 1941, was more than 125 per centum of the*
[*average*] AMOUNT *of such accounts receivable at the end of the taxable year, or if the taxpayer was not in existence for four previous taxable
years, the taxable years during which the taxpayer was in existence, in
either case including only such years for which the income was computed
under the method provided in section 44 (a), it may elect, in its return
for the taxable year, for the purposes of the tax imposed by this subchapter,
to compute, in accordance with regulations prescribed by the Commissioner
with the approval of the Secretary, its income from instalment sales on the
basis of the taxable period for which such income is accrued, in lieu of
the basis provided by section 44 (a). Except as hereinafter provided, such
election shall be irrevocable when once made and shall apply also to all*

subsequent taxable years, and the income from instalment sales for each taxable year before the first year with respect to which the election is made but beginning after December 31, 1939, shall be adjusted for the purposes of this subchapter to conform to such election. In making such adjustments, no amount shall be included in computing excess profits net income for any excess profits tax taxable year on account of instalment sales made in taxable years beginning before January 1, 1940. If the taxpayer establishes, in accordance with regulations prescribed by the Commissioner with the approval of the Secretary, that in a taxable year subsequent to the year with respect to which an election has been made under the preceding provisions of this subsection it would not be eligible to elect such accrual method, the taxpayer may in accordance with such regulations elect in its return for such year to abandon such accrual method. Such election shall be irrevocable when once made and shall preclude any further elections under this subsection. For the taxable year for which the latter election is made and subsequent taxable years, income shall be computed in accordance with section 44 (c).

[1] The words "And Taxpayers With Income From Long-Term Contracts" were added by the Senate Finance Committee.

Committee Reports

Report—Ways and Means Committee (77th Cong., 2d Sess., H. Rept. 2333).— Your committee has amended existing law to grant relief to taxpayers reporting on the installment basis. Under the installment method of accounting, a large part of the income arising from installment sales is reported in the year in which the installment payments are received instead of in the year in which the sales are made. On the other hand, expenses relating to installment sales are deducted in the year in which the sales are made. Due to recent regulations of the Federal Reserve Board, increasing the size of down payments and shortening the payment period on installment contracts, and the shifting of certain concerns to war contracts, there is a bunching of income in the taxable year without the normal installment selling costs to reduce such income. To overcome this hardship, taxpayers who can establish that the average volume of credit extended to purchasers on the installment plan in the 4 preceding taxable years was more than 125 percent of such credit extended to such purchasers in the taxable year, are permitted to elect to report their income from installment sales on the accrual basis with respect to installment sales made after December 31, 1939. This election, which applies only for excess-profits tax purposes, is irrevocable and applies to all subsequent taxable years. (p. 26)

Under current business conditions a corporation doing business on the installment plan and reporting income under the installment method of accounting may have a current taxable income which is larger than in previous years, although the amount of current business done is smaller than in the previous years. This result is possible (1) because with declining sales income will not fall as rapidly as operating costs, (2) because Regulation W, adopted by the Board of Governors of the Federal Reserve System in August 1941, has the effect of increasing the size of down payments and of shortening the payment period on installment contracts, and (3) because concerns which have shifted production to war products will report in the current year income received from prior installment sales as well as income currently accruing on the war contracts. Section 735[1] is therefore added to the Internal Revenue Code to provide that in the case of taxpayers which report income on the installment basis and which establish that the average volume of credit extended to purchasers on the installment plan in the 4 preceding taxable years was more than 125 percent of such credit extended to such purchasers in the taxable year, such taxpayer for excess profits tax purposes may elect in its initial return for such taxable year to compute its gross income from installment sales on the accrual basis. When once made, this election is irrevocable and applies to all subsequent taxable years. The gross income from installment sales for each taxable year prior to that with respect to which the election is made, but beginning after December 31, 1939, shall also be adjusted to conform to such election. However, no amount shall be included in excess profits net income for any taxable year on account of installment sales made in taxable years beginning before January 1, 1940, and the average base period net income shall not be increased by any payments received after the base period and attributable thereto. (p. 150)

¹ Sec. 736 of the Code.

Report—Senate Finance Committee (77th Cong., 2d Sess., S. Rept. 1631).— Your committee has amended the existing law to grant relief to taxpayers reporting on the installment basis. Under the installment method of accounting a large part of the income arising from installment sales is reported in the year in which the installment payments are received instead of in the year in which the sales are made. On the other hand, expenses relating to installment sales are deducted in the year in which the sales are made.

Due to recent regulations of the Federal Reserve Board, increasing the size of the down payments and shortening the payment period on installment contracts and the shifting of certain concerns to war contracts, there is a bunching of incomes in the taxable year without the normal installment selling costs to reduce such income. To overcome this hardship, the House bill provided that taxpayers who establish that the average volume of credit extended to purchasers on the installment plan in the 4 preceding taxable years was more than 125 percent of such credit extended to such purchasers in the taxable year, may

elect to report their income from installment sales on the accrual basis with respect to installment sales made after December 31, 1939.

Your committee has changed this provision to grant eligibility for relief if the average volume of credit extended to purchasers on the installment plan during the years 1938, 1939, 1940, and 1941 exceeds 125 percent of the volume of such credit extended in 1942 or subsequent years. However, the taxpayer is given an opportunity to establish eligibility for relief in terms of outstanding accounts receivable as well as in those of the volume of credit extended to purchasers on the installment plan. This change has been made in order that taxpayers who are unable to determine the volume of installment credit extended over any given year will not be denied relief because they do not keep their accounts in a manner which makes such a determination possible.

The House bill also provided that the election to compute gross income from installment sales on the accrual basis shall be irrevocable once it has been made. However, since the effect of Government credit restrictions on the income of installment-basis taxpayers is likely to be felt for no more than a 2- or 3-year period, there appears to be no reason why such taxpayers should be compelled to compute their income on the accrual basis for a longer period of time. Hence, your committee has amended the bill to provide that if a taxpayer establishes that in a taxable year subsequent to the year with respect to which the election has been made it would not be eligible to elect such accrual method, the taxpayer may elect in its return for such year to abandon the accrual method. This latter election would be irrevocable and would preclude any further elections under this provision of the bill. The installment relief provided under this section is limited to the excess-profits tax.

The following example will show how the provision of the committee amendment will apply:

For example, a taxpayer whose outstanding installment accounts receivable averaged $50,000 at the close of the years 1938, 1939, 1940, and 1941, and whose outstanding   installment   accounts amounted to $25,000 at the close of 1942, would be eligible to compute its income from the installment sales on the accrual basis, for the purposes of the excess-profits tax, both for 1942 and for any preceding taxable years. However, if at the close of any subsequent taxable year, the outstanding installment accounts receivable should be found to exceed $40,000, this taxpayer could elect to return to the installment method of accounting. (p. 42-43)

Subsection (d) of this section corresponds with section 213 (f) of the House bill. Your committee, however, has made certain changes in the provisions relating to installment basis taxpayers * * *.

Under current business conditions a corporation doing business on the installment plan and reporting income under the installment method of accounting may have a current taxable income which is larger than in previous years. This result is possible (1) because with declining sales income will not fall as rapidly as operating costs, (2) because regulation W, adopted by the Board of Governors of the Federal Reserve System in August 1941, has the effect of increasing the size of down payments and of shortening the payment period on installment contracts, and (3) because concerns which have shifted production to war products will report in the current year income received from prior installment sales as well as income currently accruing on the war contracts.

The House bill added section 735 to the Code to provide that in the case of a taxpayer which reports income on the installment basis and which establishes that the average volume of credit extended to purchasers on the installment plan in the 4 preceding taxable years was more than 125 percent of such credit extended to such purchasers in the taxable year, such taxpayer for excess profits tax purposes may elect in its initial return for such taxable year to compute its gross income from installment sales on the accrual basis. Your committee has renumbered this section as section 736 (a) and has amended the eligibility requirements so as to provide an election to taxpayers which can establish (a) that the average volume of credit extended to purchasers on the installment plan in

the 4 taxable years preceding the first taxable year beginning after December 31, 1941, was more than 125 percent of such credit extended to such purchasers in the taxable year, or (b) that the average outstanding installment accounts receivable at the end of each of the 4 taxable years preceding the first taxable year beginning after December 31, 1941, was more than 125 percent of the average of such accounts receivable at the end of the taxable year. If in either case the taxpayer was not in existence for the 4 previous taxable years, the taxable years during which the taxpayer was in existence shall be used; in any event only those years for which the income was computed under the installment method provided in section 44 (a) shall be taken into account. Under the amendment of your committee, the election is to compute income rather than gross income. Under the House bill the election extended by this section, when once made, is irrevocable and applies to all subsequent taxable years. Your committee has amended this provision to provide taxpayers with a new election to resume the reporting of income on the installment basis when the eligibility requirements of this section are no longer satisfied. Under the House bill the gross income from installment sales for each taxable year prior to that with respect to which the election is made to report income on the accrual basis, but beginning after December 31, 1939, as well as for the taxable year in which such election is made, shall be adjusted to conform to such election. Your committee has provided for the computation of income, rather than gross income, upon the accrual basis in such years. However, no amount shall be included in excess profits net income for any excess profits tax taxable year on account of installment sales made in taxable years beginning before January 1, 1940, and the average base period net income shall not be increased by any payment received after the base period and attributable thereto.

If a taxpayer, which has elected to report income on the accrual basis under section 736 (a) establishes, in accordance with regulations prescribed by the Commissioner with the approval of the Secretary, that in a taxable year subsequent to the year with respect to which such election has been made it would not be eligible to elect the accrual method, the taxpayer may in accordance with such regulations elect in its return for such year to abandon the accrual method. When once made, such election shall be irrevocable and shall preclude any further elections under section 736 (a). For the taxable year in which the election to resume the installment method of accounting is made and for subsequent taxable years, income shall be computed in accordance with section 44 (c) of the Code. (p. 207-208)

Report—Conference Committee (77th Cong., 2d Sess., H. Rept. 2586).—The Senate also made certain changes relating to installment basis taxpayers * * *. In the case of installment basis taxpayers the eligibility requirements have been amended by the Senate to provide an election to taxpayers which can establish (a) that the average volume of credit extended to purchasers on the installment plan in the four taxable years preceding the first taxable year beginning after December 31, 1941, was more than 125 percent of such credit extended to such purchasers in the taxable year, or (b) that the average outstanding installment accounts receivable at the end of each of the four taxable years preceding the first taxable year beginning after December 31, 1941, was more than 125 percent of the average of such accounts receivable at the end of the taxable year. Under the amendment the House bill provides for an irrevocable election which the Senate has changed to provide taxpayers with a new election to resume the reporting of income on the installment basis when the eligibility requirements are no longer satisfied. When once made, such election shall be irrevocable and shall preclude any further election under section 736 (a) and for the taxable year in which the election to resume the installment method of accounting is made and for subsequent taxable years income shall be computed in accordance with section 44 (c) of the Code. (p. 63)

Congressional Discussion

Discussion—Senate (Cong. Rec. Vol. 88).—MR. GEORGE. * * * Your committee has changed the provisions of the House bill granting relief for installment taxpayers if the average volume of credit extended to purchasers on the installment plan during the years 1938, 1939, 1940, and 1941 exceeds 125 percent of the volume of such credit extended in 1942 or subsequent years. The taxpayer is also given an opportunity to establish eligibility for relief in terms of outstanding accounts receivable as well as in those of the volume of credit extended to purchasers on the installment plan. In such cases the taxpayer is permitted to file amended returns on the accrual basis. This is limited to the excess-profits tax. (p. 7796)

Committee Hearings

Hearings—Ways and Means Committee.—Need for relief for those on installment basis. (E. McFarland, p. 1676-80; H. M. Bennett, p. 1716-27)

Hearings—Senate Finance Committee.—Explanation of provision. (J. O'Brien—H. Legis. Counsel—p. 109)

Sec. 736(b)

1942
222(d)

[SEC. 736. RELIEF FOR INSTALMENT BASIS TAXPAYERS AND TAX-PAYERS WITH INCOME FROM LONG-TERM CONTRACTS.]

(b) **Election on Long-Term Contracts.**—*In the case of any taxpayer computing income from contracts the performance of which requires more* *than 12 months, if it is abnormal for the taxpayer to derive income of such class, or, if the taxpayer normally derives income of such class but the amount of such income of such class includible in the gross income of the taxable year is in excess of 125 per centum of the average amount of the gross income of the same class for the four previous taxable years, or, if the taxpayer was not in existence for four previous taxable years, the taxable years during which the taxpayer was in existence, it may elect * * * to compute, in accordance with regulations prescribed by the Commissioner with the approval of the Secretary, such income upon the percentage of completion method of accounting. Such election shall be made in accordance with such regulations and shall be irrevocable when once made and shall apply to all other contracts, past, present, or future, the performance of which required or requires more than 12 months. The net income of the taxpayer for each year prior to that with respect to which the election is made shall be adjusted for the purposes of this subchapter, including the computation of excess profits net income in each taxable year of the base period under section 711 (b), to conform to such election but for purposes of chapter 1, the tax imposed by this subchapter for any prior taxable year on account of the adjustment required by this subsection shall be considered a part of the tax imposed by this subchapter for the taxable year in which such income is, without regard to this subsection, includible in gross income. Income described in this subsection shall not be considered abnormal income under section 721.*

Committee Reports

Report—Senate Finance Committee (77th Cong., 2d Sess., S. Rept. 1631).— Many contractors under the income-tax law have elected to report their income in the year in which the contract was completed. When the excess-profits tax was enacted, it was recognized that it would be inequitable to compel the taxpayer to report all of its income from a long-term contract in one year. A provision was inserted in the law which had the effect of permitting the taxpayer for excess-profits tax purposes to exclude from its income for the taxable year that portion of the income from the long-term contract attributable to other years. However, under the existing law, if such income was attributable to years in the base period, it was held by the Treasury that such income did not increase the base-period credit used by average earnings corporations in computing their excess-profits tax.

Your committee has amended the existing law to make it clear that in such cases the net income attributable to the base-period years will increase the average earnings credit. Under the committee bill, a taxpayer may compute its income from long-term contracts upon the percentage-of-completion method of accounting under the following circumstances:

1. If it is abnormal for the taxpayer to derive income from contracts the performance of which requires more than twelve months.

2. If the taxpayer normally derives income from such contracts but the amount of such income included in gross income for the taxable year is in excess of 125% of the average amount of the gross income from such contracts for the four previous taxable years, or if the taxpayer was not in existence during all of such years for the taxable years during which the taxpayer was in existence.

The net income of the taxpayer for the

base period years is required to be adjusted to conform to this election. (p. 43)

Your committee has added a new subsection (b) to section 736 to provide relief to taxpayers reporting income from long-term contracts upon the completed contract method of accounting. Such income is bunched in the year in which it is reported and unless it is spread out over the period of the contract under which the work has been performed a distorted picture of the taxpayer's true earnings for such year is presented. Since only one excess profits credit would be allowed in computing adjusted excess profits net income for such year, whereas several excess profits credits would have been utilized if the income from the contract were returned in the years during which the work was being done, an inordinate excess profits tax would be collected from such taxpayer upon such income. Your committee has therefore provided that if it is abnormal for the taxpayer to derive income from contracts the performance of which requires more than 12 months, or if the taxpayer normally derives income from such contracts but the amount of such income included in gross income for the taxable year is in excess of 125 percent of the average amount of the gross income from such contracts for the 4 previous taxable years, or if the taxpayer was not in existence during all of such years, the taxable years during which the taxpayer was in existence, such taxpayer may elect for excess profits tax purposes, in accordance with regulations prescribed by the Commissioner with the approval of the Secretary, to compute in its return for such taxable year its income from such contracts upon the percentage of completion method of accounting. When once made this election shall be irrevocable and shall apply to all other con-

tracts, past, present, or future, the performance of which requires more than 12 months. The net income of the taxpayer for each year prior to that with respect to which such election was made, including the base period years of the taxpayer, shall be adjusted for excess profits tax purposes to conform to this election. Income from contracts the performance of which requires more than 12 months shall not be considered abnormal income under section 721. (p. 208-209)

The provisions of section 721 (a) (2) (B) of the existing law relating to abnormalities on account of long-term contracts, are no longer necessary in view of the amendments made by your committee to section 736 (b) with respect to income from contracts the performance of which requires more than 12 months, * * *. (p. 209)

Report—Conference Committee (77th Cong., 2d Sess., H. Rept. 2586).—The Senate has added a provision extending relief to taxpayers reporting income from long-term contracts upon the completed contract method of accounting, if it is abnormal for the taxpayer to derive income from contracts, the performance of which requires more than 12 months, or, if the amount of such income is abnormally great, so that such a taxpayer may elect for excess profits tax purposes to compute in its return for such taxable year its income from such contracts upon the percentage of completion method of accounting. This election when made is irrevocable and applies to all other contracts, past, present, or future, the performance of which requires more than 12 months, and the net income for prior years including the base period years of the taxpayer is to be adjusted for excess profits tax purposes in conformity with this election. (p. 63)

Congressional Discussion

Discussion—Senate (Cong. Rec. Vol. 88).—Mr. George. * * * In the case of income from long-term contracts, your committee has amended the law to make it clear that where such income is thrown back into the base period years, it will

have the effect of increasing the average earnings credit.

That was supposed to be the law, and it was so stated in the Finance Committee report on the passage of the Excess Profits Tax Act. (p. 7796)

Committee Hearings

Hearings—Senate Finance Committee.—Need for relief to long-term contractors. (M. B. Carroll, p. 208-209, 217-218; G. V. Pach, p. 367-370)

1941 Act

Hearings—Senate Finance Committee.—Permitting percentage of completion determination of base period earnings to those whose original computations were on completed contract basis. (G. V. Pach, p. 1323-24)

Sec. 736(c)

[SEC. 736. RELIEF FOR INSTALMENT BASIS TAXPAYERS AND TAXPAYERS WITH INCOME FROM LONG-TERM CONTRACTS.]

1942
222(d)

(c) **Adjustment on Account of Change.**—If an adjustment specified in subsection (a) *or subsection (b), as the case may be,* is, with respect to any taxable year, prevented, on the date of the election by the taxpayer ~~to change its method of computing income from instalment sales~~ *under subsection (a) or subsection (b), as the case may be,* or within two years from such date, by any provision or rule of law (other than this section and other than section 3761, relating to compromises), such adjustment shall nevertheless be made * * *

If at the time of the mailing of such notice of deficiency or the filing of such claim for refund, the adjustment is so prevented, then the amount of the adjustment authorized by this subsection shall be limited to the increase or decrease in the tax *imposed by Chapter 1 and this subchapter* previously determined for such taxable year which results solely from the effect of subsection (a) *or subsection (b), as the case may be,* * * *

Committee Reports

Report—Ways and Means Committee (77th Cong., 2d Sess., H. Rept. 2333).—Provision is also made for the adjustment of the excess profits net income of years prior to that with respect to which the election is made despite the fact that such adjustment might otherwise have been prevented by any provision or rule of law (other than set forth in this section and in section 3761 relating to compromises). (p. 150)

Report—Senate Finance Committee (77th Cong., 2d Sess., S. Rept. 1631).—Your committee has retained the provisions of the House bill authorizing adjustment of the excess profits net income of the years prior to that with respect to

which the elections under this section have been made despite the fact that such adjustments might otherwise have been prevented by any other provision or rule of law (other than set forth in this section and in section 3761 relating to compromises). It has, however, broadened the scope of this provision so as to include within its purview long-term contracts under subsection (b) and adjustments in the tax imposed by chapter 1 stemming from the operation of this section. (p. 209)

Report—Conference Committee (77th Cong., 2d Sess., H. Rept. 2586).—The provisions of the House bill authorizing adjustment of the excess profits income of the years prior to that with respect to which the elections under this section have been made, despite the fact that such adjustments might otherwise have been prevented by any other provision

or rule of law, have been broadened to include long-term contracts and adjustments in the tax imposed by chapter 1 stemming from the operation of this section.　(p. 63)

> ### Sec. 740-743
> ### In General

Part II—Rules in Connection with Certain Exchanges
Supplement A—Excess Profits Credit Based on Income
*　　　*　　　*

Committee Reports

Report—Ways and Means Committee (76th Cong., 3d Sess., H. Rept. 2894).— In general, this supplement has two fundamental purposes. The first is to allow a domestic corporation which was not in existence at the beginning of its base period to elect to compute its excess-profits credit under the average-earnings method provided by section 713, if it acquired, or resulted from the coalescing of, another corporation through certain tax-free exchanges, where the other corporation was in existence at the beginning of the base period or had a predecessor which was in existence at such time; and, having so elected, to use as its excess-profits net income for the taxable years in the base period prior to such acquiring or coalescing, the excess-profits net income of the other corporation. For the years in the base period subsequent to such acquiring or coalescing, it uses its own excess-profits net income for the purpose of computing the credit.

The second is to permit a domestic corporation which was in existence at the beginning of the base period and which is thereby entitled to elect to compute its excess-profits credit under section 713 by virtue of the provisions of section 712, if it does elect to compute such credit under section 713, to add to its excess-profits net income for the years in the base period the excess-profits net incomes of corporations which it absorbs by a statutory merger or by liquidation under section 112 (b) (6), where such merged or liquidated corporation was in

existence at the beginning of the base period or had predecessors in existence on such date.　(p. 30)

The factors defined in this section may be more clearly understood by reference to the following diagram:

Taxable years:

1936	A	B				P
1937	A	C	T	M		P
1938	A	C→T				S
1939	A		T←			S
1940	A		T			
1941	A		T			
1942	A———→T					
1943			T			

Corporations A, B, and P were in existence on January 1, 1936, the beginning of the taxpayer T's, base period. Corporations T and M came into existence on January 1, 1937.

In the above example:

C acquired all the assets of B in return for all the stock of C, and is an "acquiring corporation" as defined in section 740 (a) (1); and B is a "component corporation" as defined in section 740 (b) (1).

C was liquidated by T under section 112 (b) (6), and T is an acquiring corporation under section 740 (a) (2).　C is a component corporation under section 740 (b) (2) as well as an acquiring corporation as just pointed out.

S was the result of the consolidation of M and P and is an acquiring corporation under section 740 (a) (4).　M and P are component corporations under section 740 (b) (4).

S was merged into T and, therefore, becomes a component corporation under section 740 (b) (3). T (although already an acquiring corporation as above stated) also is an acquiring corporation (under section 740 (a) (3)) by reason of the merger.

A was merged into T and is a component corporation under section 740 (b) (3), and T is once more considered as an acquiring corporation by reason of the merger.

Under section 740 (c), a qualified component corporation must be in existence, either actually or constructively, on the date of the beginning of the taxpayer's base period as defined in subsection (d). Assuming, in the example given, that T, the taxpayer, is on a calendar-year basis, then all qualified component corporations of T must have been in existence, either actually or constructively, on January 1, 1936. Thus M is not a qualified component but T itself, while not in existence on January 1, 1936, is given a hypothetical existence on that date by subsection (f) because it had one or more component corporations which were themselves actually or constructively in existence on such date. (p. 30-31)

Thus under section 741, T is permitted to elect the income credit, provided by section 713, although it was not in existence actually on January 1, 1940, and although its component A was subject to excess-profits tax for 1941 and on the part of its year 1942 prior to its merger into T. If neither A, B, nor P had been in existence on January 1, 1936, T would have had no right of election.

For the purposes of ascertaining T's average base period net income, T is first given a base period, whether actual or hypothetical under section 740 (d), consisting of 4 taxable years of 12 months each, the last of which ends with the beginning of its first taxable year beginning in 1940.

Into these taxable years are placed the excess-profits net incomes (or in the case where the deductions and credit for dividends received exceed the gross income, the amount of such excess) of T's qualified component corporations for their taxable years in the base period ending with or within T's taxable years in such period. If T's actual taxable years do not coincide with its constructive taxable years during the base period, its excess-profits net income (or, in the case where the deductions and credit for dividends received exceed the gross income, such excess) goes into its hypothetical taxable year in, or with, which such actual taxable year ends.

Under subsection (f) T is denied the right to include in its aggregate excess-profits net income for the base period, its own income for the years before it became an acquiring corporation, if it was not actually in existence at the beginning of its base period. Thus, under the example given, T cannot count its income for 1937. A similar rule applies to the income of a component corporation, under which the income of M for 1937 cannot be used by T.

The excess-profits net incomes of T's component corporations attributable to periods prior to the beginning of T's base period are excluded pro rata from T's aggregate base-period net income. The same rule is applicable to T itself where its actual and constructive taxable years do not coincide at the beginning of its base period.

Assuming that the merger of A into T took place in the middle of T's taxable year 1942, under subsection (f) (4) only one-half of A's base-period income can be used by T for the purposes of computing its income credit for 1942. Thereafter, T is entitled to A's full base period experience.

Subsection (e) provides that in the computation of the base-period income of both T and its component corporations, there shall be excluded any dividends paid by T or any of its components which would otherwise go into the taxpayer's base period net income.

For example, if in the diagram given, C had received a dividend from T in 1937 such dividend is not affected by this subsection as T's income for such year is not taken into account in the computation of the taxpayer's base-period income. However, if T in 1938, after it had become an acquiring corporation, had received a dividend from S, such dividend would be excluded since both T's and S's income for such year go into the taxpayer's base-period income and if the dividend were not excluded it would be counted twice.

The following example illustrates the computation of T's excess-profits credit for 1942. In the example the amount stated as income is the net income adjusted by the adjustments specified in the bill and excluding the dividends on excluded stock. This assumes that all transactions take place at the beginning of each of the taxable years specified, except that it is assumed that A merged with T in the middle of 1942.

For 1936, A's income is $4,000; B's income is $6,000; and P has a deficit in income of $10,000. T's base-period income for 1936 is the sum of $2,000 (one-half of A's $4,000) plus $6,000, or $8,000, minus $10,000, giving a base-period income for the year of minus $2,000.

For 1937, A's income is $4,000; C's income is $8,000; T's income is $10,000; M's income is $4,000; and P's income is $6,000. A's income is included at one-half, or $2,000. C's income is included in full, or $8,000. T's income and M's income are not included, for they were not actually in existence on January 1, 1936, and had no component in existence on that date. P's income of $6,000 is included in full, so that for 1937, T's base-period income is $2,000 plus $8,000, plus $6,000 or $16,000.

For 1938, A's income is $4,000, T has a deficit in income of $6,000, and S has a deficit in income of $10,000. A's income is included at one-half, or $2,000. T's deficit is subtracted in full, or $6,000. S's deficit is subtracted in full, or $10,-000. For the year, T's base-period net income is the sum of the plus amounts, or $2,000, minus the sum of the minus amounts, or $16,000, which equals a minus $14,000.

For 1939 A's income is $4,000; T's income is $20,000; and S's income is $8,000. For the year T's base-period net income is $2,000, plus $20,000, plus $8,000, or $30,000.

Thus T has a base-period net income for each year in the base period as follows:

1936	−$2,000
1937	+16,000
1938	−14,000
1939	+30,000

Under the rule of counting the year of greatest deficit at zero, 1938 is not included, so the aggregate base-period income of T is $30,000, plus $16,000, or $46,000, minus $2,000, or $44,000, which, divided by 4, gives a base period net income of $11,000.

By the provisions of this section,[1] the taxpayer is allowed to add the net additions to capital of its component corporations accumulated after the beginning of the first taxable year under the bill and prior to the acquiring transaction. Conversely it must take the net capital reductions of such component corporations for the same period.

For example, if the merger of A into T took place in the middle of T's taxable year, assuming that A had net capital additions as of the day of the merger of $100,000, such net capital addition will be used in computing the net capital additions of T for that and subsequent days in the same manner as T's own net capital additions. The same is applicable with respect to net capital reductions. (p. 31-33)

[1] Relating to sec. 743.

Committee Hearings

Hearings—Ways and Means Committee.—Allowing successor companies to use base period experience of predecessors. (C. W. Dudley, p. 276; H. B. Fernald, p. 281-282; W. W. Schneider, p. 356-359; A. A. Miller, p. 369-371)

Hearings—Senate Finance Committee.—Allowing successor companies to use base period experience of predecessors. (C. F. Stam—Jt. Com. on Int. Rev. Taxn.—p. 196-197; E. C. Alvord, p. 274)

Explanation of provision. (C. F. Stam—Jt. Com. on Int. Rev. Taxn.—p. 211-212)

Allowing credit not less than that of any constituent company. (W. S. Mack Jr., p. 234-235, 237-238)

Shortcomings of provision. (E. C. Alvord, p. 274)

Applying provision to practical, as distinguished from technical, reorganizations. (E. C. Alvord, p. 274; W. W. Schneider, p. 434-437)

Shortcomings of provision. (R. H. Tyrrell, p. 291-293)

1941 Act

Hearings—Senate Finance Committee.—Explanation and shortcomings of provision. (E. C. Alvord, p. 687-688; H. B. Fernald, p. 885)

Including as qualified component, subsidiary organized and dissolved in base period. (L. H. Parker, p. 1470)

> Sec. 740(a)(1)
> Sec. 740(b)(5)
> Sec. 740(h)

SEC. 740. DEFINITIONS.

For the purposes of this Supplement—

(a) Acquiring Corporation.—The term "acquiring corporation" means—

(1) A corporation which has acquired—

*   *   *

(D) Substantially all the properties of a partnership in an exchange to which section 112 (b) (5), or so much of section 112 (c) or (e) as refers to section 112 (b) (5), or to which a corresponding provision of a prior revenue law, is or was applicable.

[(b) Component Corporation.—The term "component corporation" means—]

(5) In the case of a transaction specified in subsection (a) (1) (D), the partnership whose properties were acquired.

(h) Sole Proprietorship.—For the purposes of sections 740 (a) (1) (D), 740 (b) (5), and 742 (g), a business owned by a sole proprietorship shall be considered a partnership.

EPTA
8(a)
8(b)
8(c)

Committee Reports

Report—Ways and Means Committee (77th Cong., 1st Sess., H. Rept. 146).—The bill affords relief in the following situations:

*   *   *

6. Under supplement A of existing law, corporations resulting from certain tax-free exchanges or reorganizations during or after the base period are permitted the use of their predecessor's earning experience in the computation of their excess profits credit based on income. The bill extends this privilege to corporations growing out of partnerships or sole proprietorships in tax-free exchanges during this same period. The resulting corporation would thus be allowed to use the earnings history of the predecessor partnership or sole proprietorship, after first converting such earnings to a corporate basis. (p. 2, 4)

Under present provisions a corporation formed as a result of the incorporation of a partnership or sole proprietorship may not use the earnings experienced by the latter in determining its excess-profits credit based upon income. It is believed that this restriction operates inequitably with respect to such corporations. Accordingly, this section amends the present provisions of the excess-profits tax to permit the earnings of the predecessor partnership or proprietorship to be reflected in the base period credit of the resulting corporation in those instances in which the assets of the partnership or proprietorship are transferred to the corporation in a tax-free exchange. The amendments in question are made to supplement A of the excess-profits tax provisions, which deals with a comparable situation where the component taxpayer was a corporation. (p. 14)

Report—Senate Finance Committee (77th Cong., 1st Sess., S. Rept. 75).— Same as Ways and Means Committee Report. (p. 3, 4, 14-15, respectively)

Congressional Discussion

Discussion—House (Cong. Rec. Vol. 87).—MR. COOPER. * * * On page 23 of the bill, section 8, is the provision relating to partnership experience in the base period. The corporation is allowed to show the experience during the base period of the partnership or its predecessor, and, of course, must conform to the proper rules and regulations in that respect. In other words, this provision makes it possible for a corporation in the taxable year to secure the advantage of the experience that its predecessor in business may have had, even though that predecessor was not a corporation as is provided for in existing law, but was a partnership. (p. 1380)

Discussion—Senate (Cong. Rec. Vol. 87).—MR. HARRISON. * * * Section 8: This section permits corporations which were formerly partnerships or sole proprietorships to count the earnings of their predecessor partnerships or sole proprietorship in computing their average earnings credit to the same extent as corporations are now permitted to do under the excess profits tax law, where they have taken over old corporations in mergers, consolidations, and so forth. (p. 1638)

MR. BROWN. Mr. President, I should like to say to the Senator from Colorado and the Senator from Nevada that on a previous occasion they both joined me in a proposal, which was adopted by the Senate but rejected when the bill then under consideration got into conference, which would have been of great benefit to the mining industry, that is, as to the nature of the proprietorship in the period upon which the excess-profits tax is based. Heretofore the credit could not be used unless the same corporation which is now in existence was in existence during the 3- or 4-year period. By changes which have been written into the law, if the proprietorship were a partnership or an individual out of which a corporation grew, such as a mining corporation, the earnings during the base period may be used as the basis for calculation of the tax. I think the proposed amendments are very valuable for that reason. (p. 1639)

1940 Act

Discussion—House (Cong. Rec. Vol. 86).—MR. HINSHAW. I brought up a question to one of the members of the gentleman's committee a while ago concerning a partnership which had become a corporation within the year, a profitable partnership and a profitable corporation——

MR. COOPER. I get the gentleman's question. There is no provision made for that, for the obvious reason that a partnership has paid taxes throughout the years on an entirely different basis from that on which corporations pay. You just cannot fit a partnership into the same type of structure that you can fit a corporation. (p. 11247-248)

PASADENA, CALIF., *August 15, 1940.*
Hon. CARL HINSHAW,
Representative, Washington, D. C.
* * *
This paragraph[1] as written does not appear to us to give a fair break to a business which was operating during the entire base period, but operated during a portion of it as a copartnership and then transferred the partnership business to a corporation in a nontaxable reorganization without any revaluation of assets or any change whatsoever in the assets and liabilities, the only change being merely the transfer of the partnership interest to the corporation for stock. In other words the operations of the business were the same for the entire 4-year period, the only change being in the capital set-up, that is the change from a partnership form of doing business to a corporate form of doing business.

We would, therefore, suggest that the proposed excess-profits bill include in it a provision to take care of the above situation.
* * *
MARKET BASKET,
By R. W. CARLSON, *Secretary.*
(p. 11258)

[1] Relating to sec. 712 (a).

Committee Hearings
1942 Act

Hearings—Senate Finance Committee.—Including transfers under section 112 (b) (5) as acquiring corporation. (C. M. Christensen, p. 798-801)

SEC. 740. DEFINITIONS.

For the purposes of this Supplement—

(a) **Acquiring Corporation.**—The term "acquiring corporation" means—

(1) A corporation which has acquired—

(A) *substantially* all the ~~assets~~ *properties* of another corporation and the whole or a part of the consideration for the transfer of such ~~assets~~ *properties* is the transfer to such other corporation ~~or its shareholders~~ of all the stock of all classes (except qualifying shares) of the corporation which has acquired such ~~assets;~~ *properties, or*

(B) substantially all the properties of another corporation and the sole consideration for the transfer of such properties is the transfer to such other corporation of voting stock of the corporation which has acquired such properties, or

(C) before October 1, 1940, properties of another corporation solely as paid in surplus or a contribution to capital in respect of voting stock owned by such other corporation.

For the purposes of subparagraphs (B) and (C) in determining whether such voting stock or such paid in surplus or contribution to capital, is the sole consideration, the assumption by the acquiring corporation of a liability of the other, or the fact that property acquired is subject to a liability, shall be disregarded. Subparagraph (B) or (C) shall apply only if the corporation transferring such properties is forthwith completely liquidated in pursuance of the plan under which the acquisition is made, and the transaction of which the acquisition is a part has the effect of a statutory merger or consolidation.

Committee Reports

Report—Senate Finance Committee (76th Cong., 3d Sess., S. Rept. 2114).— *First method—based on income.*—The privileges allowed under the House bill to corporations resulting from statutory mergers or consolidations are extended in your committee bill to similar reorganizations in States in which mergers or consolidations are not defined by statute. (p. 7)

This section is the same as it was in the House bill except for the definition of "acquiring corporation," which has been expanded to take into account certain types of transfers not covered by the House bill. Subsection (a) (1) has been rewritten.

Subparagraph (A) is substantially the equivalent of the entire subsection (a) (1) as it appeared in the House bill.

Subparagraph (B) covers exchanges described in section 112 (g) (1) (C), that is, the acquisition by one corporation, in exchange solely for all or a part of its voting stock, of substantially all the properties of another corporation, the assumption by the acquiring corporation of a liability of the other or the fact that property acquired is subject to a liability being disregarded in the determination of whether the exchange is solely for voting stock. This makes it possible for certain types of mergers and consolidations to qualify under the bill, though they are not statutory mergers and consolidations, owing to the absence of any State laws on the subject. Your committee is informed that there are approximately 12 States which have no statutory provisions relative to corporate mergers and consolidations.

Subparagraph (C) covers transfers before October 1, 1940, by one corporation of property to another corporation solely as paid-in surplus or a contribution to capital in respect of voting stock owned by such other corporation. Since the property transferred must be received solely as paid-in surplus or a contribution to capital made solely in respect of voting stock, it is necessary that (1) the transferor corporation receive nothing upon the exchange and (2) that, at the time the transfer takes place, the transferor own no stock of the transferee other than voting stock of the transferee.

Subparagraph (B) or (C) shall apply only if the corporation transferring such properties is forthwith completely liquidated in pursuance of the plan under which the acquisition is made, and the transaction of which the acquisition is a part has in all respects the effect of a statutory merger or consolidation. (p. 18)

Report—Conference Committee (76th Cong., 3d Sess., H. Rept. 3002).—*House bill.* * * * The types of transactions in which the assets of another corporation must have been acquired to entitle the acquiring corporation to these benefits were as follows:

(1) Whereby all the assets of another corporation were acquired in whole or in part for all the stock of the acquiring corporation. *. * *

(3) Statutory mergers or consolidations.

Senate amendment.—Aside from certain technical changes the Senate amendment changed this provision of the House bill only in the following respects:

In addition to the types of transactions covered by the House bill, the Senate amendment added the type of exchange described in section 112 (g) (1) (C) of the Internal Revenue Code, that is, the acquisition by one corporation, in exchange solely for all or a part of its voting stock, of substantially all the properties of another corporation, the assumption by the acquiring corporation of a liability of the other or the fact that property acquired is subject to a liability being disregarded in the determination of whether the exchange is solely for voting stock. There were also added transfers before October 1, 1940, by one corporation of property to another corporation solely as paid-in surplus or a contribution to capital in respect of voting stock of the transferee corporation owned by the transferor corporation, assumptions of liabilities being disregarded as in the case of section 112 (g) (1) (C) reorganizations. Neither of these types of transactions are includible unless the transferor corporation is forthwith completely liquidated in pursuance of the plan under which the acquisition is made, and the transaction of which the acquisition is a part has in all respects the effect of a statutory merger or consolidation. (p. 56)

Committee Hearings
1942 Act

Hearings—Senate Finance Committee.—Broadening definition of an acquiring corporation. (E. C. Alvord, p. 1797)

1941 Act

Hearings—Ways and Means Committee.—Broadening definition of an acquiring corporation. (H. B. Fernald, p. 1572)

[Set forth on page 268]

[Set forth on page 344]

1918
330
[740(a)(1)]

[Set forth on page 347]

1918
331
[740(a)(1)]

[Set forth on page 352]

1917
204
[740(a)(1)]

> Sec. 740(a)(2)-(4)
> Sec. 740(b)(1)-(4)

[Set forth on page 268]

1940
201
[740-3]
in gen'l

> Sec. 740(b)(5)

[Set forth with sec. 740(a)(1), page 271]

> Sec. 740(c)

[SEC. 740. DEFINITIONS.]

1942
228(a)

[For the purposes of this Supplement—]

(c) **Income of Certain Component Corporations Not Included.**—For the purposes of section 712, section 741, and section 742 *742, and section 743* in the case of a corporation which is a component corporation in a transaction described in subsection (a), (346) ~~for the purposes of computing, for any taxable year beginning after December 31, 1941, the excess profits credit of such component corporation or of an acquiring corporation of which the acquiring corporation in such transaction is not a component, no account shall be taken of the net income, capital addition, or capital reduction of such component corporation before such transaction, or of the net income, capital addition or capital reduction before such transaction, of its component corporations in any transaction before such transaction.~~

(1)   *Except as provided in paragraph (2), for the purpose of computing, for any taxable year beginning after December 31, 1941, the excess profits credit of such component corporation or of an acquiring corporation of which the acquiring corporation in such transaction is not a component, except in the application of sections 713 (f) and 742 (h) (other than the limitation on the amount of average base period net income or Supplement A average base period net income, as the case may be, determined thereunder), no account shall be taken of the excess profits net income of such component corporation for any period before the day after such transaction, or of the excess profits net income for any period before the day after such transaction of its component corporations in any transaction before such transaction, and no account shall be taken of the capital addition or capital reduction of such component corporation either immediately before such transaction or for any prior period, or of the capital addition or capital reduction either immediately before such transaction or for any prior period of its component corporations in any transaction before such transaction.*

(2)   *In case such transaction occurred in a taxable year of such component corporation beginning after December 31, 1941, for the purpose of computing the excess profits credit of such component corporation for such taxable year, the amount of its average base period net income or Supplement A average base period net income, as the case may be, shall be limited to an amount which bears the same ratio to such average base period net income or Supplement A average base period net income, as the case may be (computed without regard to this paragraph but with the application of paragraph (1) in case of a prior transaction described in subsection (a) with respect to such component corporation or a component corporation thereof), as the number of days in such taxable year before the day after such transaction bears to the total number of days in such taxable year.*

For the purposes of section 742, in the case of a corporation which is a component corporation in a transaction described in subsection (a), in computing for any taxable year the Supplement A average base period net income of the acquiring corporation in such transaction or of a corporation of which such acquiring corporation becomes a component corporation, no account shall be taken of the excess profits net income of such component corporation for any period beginning with the day after such transaction.

Committee Reports

Report—Ways and Means Committee (77th Cong., 2d Sess., H. Rept. 2333).— New subsection (c) of section 740 applies only to taxable years beginning after December 31, 1941, and is designed to prevent more than one corporation from using the same base period experience and the same capital addition or reduction of a particular corporation. Thus, if a corporation is a component corporation in, say, a transaction described in section 740 (a) (1) (A), occurring within the base period, and if the existence of such corporation is not terminated in connection with such transaction, its base period experience prior to such transaction is, for the purposes of excess profits tax for taxable years beginning after December 31, 1941, given exclusively to the acquiring corporation in such transaction or to an acquiring corporation of which the first acquiring corporation is a component corporation. Consequently, assuming that such component corporation remains in existence and continues business with properties acquired after such transaction, it will not receive any benefit from its experience prior to such transaction, nor can its experience prior to such transaction be passed on to another acquiring corporation in a subsequent transaction. The same rules will be applied to each successive transaction described in section 740 (a) to which the corporation is a party as a component corporation and in connection with which its existence is not terminated. Although the provisions of section 740 (c) are primarily intended to apply to transactions in connection with which the complete liquidation of the component corporation is not specifically required, such provisions are not by their terms confined to such transactions and are, therefore, applicable to all transactions described in section 740 (a).

The application of the provisions of section 740 (c) may be illustrated by the following example:

Example: A, B, and C, corporations on the calendar year basis, were in existence on January 1, 1936, and have been in existence since that time. On January 1, 1938, B acquired the properties of A in a transaction described in section 740 (a) (1) (A). A converted into cash the stock in B which it received in such transaction, and with the proceeds of such stock acquired new properties. It operates such properties continuously down to January 1, 1943. On the latter date, C acquires such properties from A in a transaction described in section 740 (a) (1) (A). A continues in business throughout 1943, operating properties which it purchased with the proceeds of the stock in C received in the second transaction. The operation of section 740 (c) under circumstances outlined in this example is as follows:

(a) *As to B.*—In determining its average base period net income for the purposes of the excess profits taxes for 1942 and 1943, B may take into account A's base period experience for 1936 and 1937. Inasmuch as the transaction involving B occurs within the base period, there is no capital addition or reduction of A to be transferred to B. See section 742.

(b) *As to A.*—In determining its

average base period net income for the purposes of its excess profits tax for 1942, A may take into account its base period experience for 1938 and 1939, but it is denied the right to use its base period experience for 1936 and 1937. When A determines its excess profits tax for 1943, it will not be permitted to take into account any of its base period experience, nor any capital addition or reduction attributable to the period before 1943. Its base period experience for 1936 and 1937 is given to B and its base period experience for 1938 and 1939 is given to C. A will, however, be entitled to use the credit based on invested capital.

(c) *As to C.*—Section 740 (c) is first applicable to C with respect to 1943. In determining its average base period net income for the purposes of its excess profits tax for that year, C may take into account A's base period income for 1938 and 1939. Moreover, as the transaction involving C occurs after the close of the base period, A's daily capital addition and reduction for the time immediately before the transaction will be transferred to C. See sec. 742. (p. 151-152)

Report—Senate Finance Committee (77th Cong., 2d Sess., S. Rept. 1631).— New subsection (c) of section 740 is, in general, designed to prevent more than one corporation from using the same base period experience and the same capital addition or reduction of a particular corporation. The amendments to section 740 (c) made in the bill passed by the House, however, have been substantially revised in your committee bill. As revised, section 740 (c) contains three principal rules which are set forth in new paragraphs (1) and (2) of section 740 (c) and in a new sentence added at the end of such section.

Paragraph (1) of section 740 (c) corresponds to the whole of section 740 (c) as amended by the bill passed by the House, but in your committee bill is subject to the further rule of paragraph (2) of section 740 (c). Paragraph (1) applies only to taxable years beginning after December 31, 1941. Under paragraph (1), if a corporation is a component corporation in, for example, a transaction described in section 740 (a) (1) (A), occurring within the base period, and if the existence of such corporation is not terminated in connection with such transaction, its base period experience on the day of and before such transaction is, for the purposes of excess profits tax taxable years beginning after December 31, 1941, given exclusively (except for the purpose of applying the growth formula in computing the credit of such component corporation) to the acquiring corporation in such transaction or to an acquiring corporation of which the first acquiring corporation is a component corporation.

The exception in paragraph (1) just referred to, with respect to the application of the growth formula to the component corporation, has been added by your committee bill. If a component corporation continues in existence after the supplement A transaction, it is allowed to take into account its entire base period experience (except as provided in paragraph (2)) for the purpose of the growth formula under sections 713 (f) and 742 (h), except that it cannot take into account such base period experience for the purpose of determining the greatest amount of excess profits net income for any base period year to which the average base period net income or supplement A average base period net income is limited under the growth formula.

Your committee bill also has more clearly defined in section 740 (c) the allocation of base period experience and capital additions and reductions between component and acquiring corporations with respect to the time of the transaction. With the exceptions previously noted, no account is to be taken of the excess profits net income of the component corporation for any period before the day after the supplement A transaction, or of the excess profits net income for any period before the day after such transaction of its component corporations in any supplement A transaction before such transaction, and no account is to be taken of the capital addition or capital reduction of such component corporation either immediately before the supplement A transaction or for any prior period, or of the capital addition or capital reduction either immediately before such supplement A transaction or for any prior period of its component corporations in any such transaction before such transaction.

Consequently, assuming that such component corporation remains in existence and continues business with properties acquired after such transaction, except as provided in paragraph (2) of section 740 (c) and except for the purposes of the growth formula, as previously explained, it will not receive any benefit from its base period experience for any time before the day after such transaction nor from its capital additions or capital reductions immediately before such transaction and for any prior period, nor can such experience or such capital additions or reductions be passed on to another acquiring corporation in a subsequent transaction. The same rules will be applied to each successive transaction described in section 740 (a) to which the corporation is a party as a component corporation and in connection with which its existence is not terminated. Although the provisions of section 740 (c) are primarily intended to apply to transactions in connection with which the complete liquidation of the component corporation is not specifically required, such provisions are not by their terms confined to such transactions and are, therefore, applicable to all transactions described in section 740 (a).

Paragraph (2) of section 740 (c) provides that in case the supplement A transaction occurs in a taxable year of such component corporation beginning after December 31, 1941, for the purposes of computing the excess profits credit of such component corporation for such taxable year, the amount of its average base period net income or supplement A average base period net income, as the case may be, shall be limited to an amount which bears the same ratio to such average base period net income or supplement A average base period net income, as the case may be, as the number of days in such taxable year before the day after such transaction bears to the total number of days in such taxable year. For the purpose of this limitation, the average base period net income or supplement A average base period net income in the ratio, is computed without regard to paragraph (2) but with the application of paragraph (1) in case of a prior supplement A transaction with respect to such component corporation or a component corporation thereof. Paragraph (2) applies only to taxable years beginning after December 31, 1941.

A new sentence is added at the end of section 740 (c) providing that for the purpose of computing supplement A average base period net income of an acquiring corporation (or of an acquiring corporation of which such acquiring corporation becomes a component) no account shall be taken of the excess profits net income of such component corporation for the day after the supplement A transaction in which it became a component or for any period thereafter. This provision is applicable for the purpose of computing the tax for taxable years beginning after December 31, 1939.

The application of the provisions of section 740 (c) may be illustrated by the following example:

Example: A, B, and C, corporations on the calendar year basis, were in existence on January 1, 1936, and have been in existence since that time. On December 31, 1938, B acquired the properties of A in a transaction described in section 740 (a) (1) (A). A converted into cash the stock in B which it received in such transaction, and with the proceeds of such stock acquired new properties. It operates such properties continuously down to the time C acquires such properties from A on October 19, 1943, in a transaction described in section 740 (a) (1) (A). A continues in business throughout 1943, operating properties which it purchased with the proceeds of the stock in C received in the second transaction. The operation of section 740 (c) under circumstances outlined in this example is as follows:

(a) As to B.—In determining its average base period net income for the purposes of the excess profits taxes for 1942 and 1943, B may take into account A's base period experience for 1936, 1937, and 1938. Inasmuch as the transaction involving B occurs within the base period, there is no capital addition or reduction of A to be transferred to B. See section 743.

(b) As to A.—In determining its average base period net income under the general average method for the purposes of its excess profits tax for 1942, A may take into account its base period experience for 1939, but is denied the right to use its base period experience for 1936, 1937, and 1938. However, in determining its average base period net income under the growth formula, for purposes of its excess profits tax for 1942, A may take into account its base period experience for 1936, 1937, 1938, and 1939, except that such average cannot exceed its excess profits net income for 1939. When A determines its excess profits tax for 1943 it will be permitted to take into account for the purpose of its average base period net income under the general average method only four-fifths (the ratio of the number of days in January 1, 1943–October 19, 1943, inclusive (292), over the number of days in 1943 (365) of its base period experience for 1939; for the purpose of the growth formula it will be able to take into account only four-fifths of its average base period experience determined under such formula. It will not be permitted to take into account for the purpose of its tax for 1943 any of its capital addition or reduction attributable to the time immediately before the transaction. Its base period experience for 1936, 1937, and 1938 is given to B and one-fifth of its base period experience for 1939 is given to C. See section 742 (f) (2). A will, however, be entitled to use the credit based on invested capital.

(c) As to C.—Section 740 (c) is first applicable to C with respect to 1943. In determining its average base period net income for the purposes of its excess profits tax for that year C may take into account one-fifth of A's base period experience for 1939. In determining C's average base period net income for the purposes of its excess-profits tax for 1944, C may take into account all of A's base period experience for 1939. Moreover, as the transaction involving C occurs after the close of the base period, A's daily capital addition and reduction as of the time immediately before the transaction will be transferred to C. See section 743. (p. 214-217)

Report—Conference Committee (77th Cong., 2d Sess., H. Rept. 2586).— Amendment No. 346: This amendment makes several technical changes in section 740 (c) as amended in the House bill. Section 740 (c) (1) of the bill as passed by the Senate corresponds to the whole of section 740 (c) of the House bill, but is subject to the further rule of paragraph (2) of section 740 (c) as added by the Senate. Section 740 (c) (1) also allows a component corporation to take into account its entire base period experience (except as provided in section 740 (c) (2)) for the purpose of the growth formula under sections 713 (f) and 742 (h), except that it cannot take into account such base period experience for the purpose of determining the greatest amount of excess profits net income for any base period year to which the average base period net income or Supplement A base period net income is limited under the growth formula. A technical addition to section 740 (c) (1) also gives the component corporations' base period experience for the day of the Supplement A transaction as well as the prior period (with certain exceptions) and its capital addition and capital reduction as of such day immediately prior to such transaction and for all prior periods to the acquiring corporation.

Section 740 (c) (2), as added by the Senate, applies only in case of a Supplement A transaction occurring in a taxable year beginning after December 31, 1941. In such case, the base period experience of the component corporation (after the application of section 740 (c) (1) in case of a prior transaction) is allocated to such component corporation for purposes of excess profits credit for only such year in the ratio which the number of days in such year before the transaction plus such days bears to the total tax in such year.

The last sentence of section 740 (c), as added by the Senate bill, is retroactive to taxable years beginning after December 31, 1939. In general, it prevents an acquiring corporation from taking into account any experience after the Supplement A transaction of a component corporation which continues in existence thereafter. The House recedes. (p. 65-66)

Congressional Discussion

Discussion—House (Cong. Rec. Vol. 88).—Mr. Disney. * * * Supplement A of the excess-profits-tax law lays down a set of rules, necessarily complicated, under which a corporation resulting from a merger, consolidation, liquidation, or certain other tax-free exchanges is allowed to use the base-period history of its predecessors. This supplement placed in the law in the original excess-profits-tax provisions of the Second Revenue Act of 1940 has been found faulty in a number of respects.

The bill cures some of these major defects by— (p. 6379)

Committee Hearings

Hearings—Senate Finance Committee.—Explanation of provision. (J. O'Brien—H. Legis. Counsel—p. 109)

1941 Act

Hearings—Senate Finance Committee.—Allowing acquiring corporation to use allocable amount of earnings of continuing predecessor corporation. (G. M. Ungaro, p. 1105-06)

1940
201
[740-3]
in gen'l

[Set forth on page 268]

Sec. 740(d)
Sec. 740(e)

[Set forth on following page]

[SEC. 740. DEFINITIONS.]

[For the purposes of this Supplement—]

(d) <del>Base Period. In the case of a taxpayer which is an acquiring corporation the base period shall be:</del>

<del>(1) If the tax is being computed for any taxable year beginning in 1940, the forty-eight months preceding the beginning of such taxable year; or</del>

<del>(2) If the tax is being computed for any taxable year beginning after December 31, 1940, and before January 1, 1942, the forty-eight months preceding what would have been its first taxable year beginning in 1940 if it had had a taxable year beginning in 1940 on the date on which the taxable year for which the tax is being computed began; or</del>

[(3) If the tax is being computed for any taxable year beginning after December 31, 1941, the four calendar years 1936 to 1939, both inclusive.] *In the case of a taxpayer which is an acquiring corporation the base period shall be the four calendar years 1936 to 1939, both inclusive, except that, if the taxpayer became an acquiring corporation prior to September 1, 1940, the base period shall be the same as that applicable to its first taxable year ending in 1941.*

(e) **Base Period Years.**—In the case of a taxpayer which is an acquiring corporation its base period years shall be the four successive twelve-month periods beginning on the same date as the beginning of its base period.

Committee Reports

Report—Ways and Means Committee (77th Cong., 2d Sess., H. Rept. 2333).—Under existing law, the base period of an acquiring corporation computing its average base period net income under Supplement A is determined by reference to its current taxable year. So long as the corporation remains on the same taxable year basis, either calendar or fiscal, its base period remains the same; but if the corporation changes its taxable year, or if it is acquired by a corporation with a different taxable year, the base period for the entire enterprise changes accordingly. The amendment to section 740 (d) is designed to prevent this shifting in the base period. Under the amendment, for taxable years beginning after December 31, 1941, the base period is permanently anchored to the 4 calendar years 1936-39. It will not be affected by the fact that the acquiring corporation hereafter changes its taxable year or by the fact that it is acquired by another corporation having a different taxable year. (p. 152-153)

Report—Senate Finance Committee (77th Cong., 2d Sess., S. Rept. 1631).—Under existing law, the base period of an acquiring corporation computing its average base period net income under supplement A is determined by reference to its current taxable year. So long as the corporation remains on the same taxable year basis, either calendar or fiscal, its base period remains the same; but if the corporation changes its taxable year, or if it is acquired by a corporation with a different taxable year, the base period for the entire enterprise changes accordingly. The amendment to section 740 (d) is designed to prevent this shifting in the base period. Under the amendment, for taxable years beginning after December 31, 1941, the base period is permanently anchored to the 4 calendar years 1936-39. It will not be affected by the fact that the acquiring corporation hereafter changes its taxable year or by the fact that it is acquired by another corporation having a different taxable year. (p. 217)

Report—Conference Committee (77th Cong., 2d Sess., H. Rept. 2586).— Amendment No. 347: This amendment makes the change in base period for purposes of Supplement A under the excess profits tax (changed to the four calendar years 1936 through 1939 in the House bill) subject, in general, to the election to have the amendments to Supplement A made by this act apply retroactively for the purpose of computing the excess profits tax for all taxable years beginning after December 31, 1939. The only exception is in the case of any corporation which became an acquiring corporation prior to September 1, 1940. The House recedes. (p. 66)

Congressional Discussion

Discussion—House (Cong. Rec. Vol. 88).—Mr. Disney. * * * The bill cures some of these major defects by—

* * * *

(c) Fixing the base-period years permanently. Under the present law these years may shift from time to time as the resulting corporation changes its taxable year, thus requiring a recomputation of the average base-period earnings; * * *. (p. 6379)

Committee Hearings

Hearings—Senate Finance Committee.—Explanation of provision. (J. O'Brien—H. Legis. Counsel—p. 110)

1940
201
[740-3]
in gen'l

[Set forth on page 268]

Sec. 740(f)

1942
228(a)

[SEC. 740. DEFINITIONS.]

[For the purposes of this Supplement—]

(f) **Existence of Acquiring Corporation.**—For the purposes of section 712 (a), if any component corporation of the taxpayer was in existence before January 1, 1940, the taxpayer shall be considered to have been in existence before such date.

Committee Reports

Report—Ways and Means Committee (77th Cong., 2d Sess., H. Rept. 2333).— Under existing law, an acquiring corporation was not qualified to use Supplement A unless it was in existence (either actually or constructively) at the beginning of its base period. The new requirement is that, if the acquiring corporation was in existence before January 1, 1940 (either in its own right or through a component corporation), it may compute its average base period net income under Supplement A. Section 740 (f) is amended to accord with such change. (p. 153)

Report—Senate Finance Committee (77th Cong., 2d Sess., S. Rept. 1631).— Same as Ways and Means Committee Report. (p. 217)

Congressional Discussion

Discussion—House (Cong. Rec. Vol. 88).—MR. DISNEY. * * * The bill cures some of these major defects by—

* * *

(b) Permitting the resulting corpora-

tions to use the entire base-period history of its predecessors even where such predecessors were not in existence for the entire base period; * * * (p. 6379)

[Set forth on page 268]

1940
201
[740-3]
in gen'l

Sec. 740(g)

[SEC. 740. DEFINITIONS.]

1940
201

[For the purposes of this Supplement—]

(g) **Component Corporations of Component Corporations.**—If a corporation is a component corporation of an acquiring corporation, under subsection (b) or under this subsection, it shall (except for the purposes of section 742 (d) (1) and (2) and section 743 (a)) also be a component corporation of the corporation of which such acquiring corporation is a component corporation.

This subsection was added by the Conference Committee.

Report—Conference Committee (76th Cong., 3d Sess., H. Rept. 3002).—*Conference agreement.* * * * The conference agreement also makes a clarifying change, whereby section 743 (c)[1] is stricken out and section 740 (g) inserted in lieu thereof. Section 740 (g) provides

that the term "component corporation" includes a component corporation of a component corporation, except as used in section 742 (d) (1) and (2) and section 743 (a). (p. 57)

[1] Set forth under sec. 743 (b).

[Set forth on page 268]

1940
201
[740-3]
in gen'l

Sec. 740(h)

[Set forth with sec. 740(a)(1), page 271]

Sec. 741(a)

[Set forth on following page]

1942
228(b)

(b) ¹**Repeal of Section 741(a).—**

Section 741 (a) ≤*shall not apply to any taxable year beginning after December 31, 1941*≥ *is repealed.*

¹ The heading is as worded by the Senate. The Senate Finance Committee heading read "Termination of Section 741."

Committee Reports

Report—Ways and Means Committee (77th Cong., 2d Sess., H. Rept. 2333).— Section 712 of the Code applies to any domestic corporation and provides that any such corporation in existence before January 1, 1940, shall compute its excess profits credit on the basis of its average base period income or on the basis of invested capital, whichever credit results in the lesser tax. Now that Supplement A is extended to acquiring corporations in existence (actually or constructively) before January 1, 1940, all acquiring corporations entitled to use supplement A fall within the scope of section 712. Accordingly, there is no longer any necessity for a separate provision in Supplement A authorizing corporations to use the income or invested capital method of determining their excess profits credits. Hence, the provisions of section 741 (a) of the Code are eliminated in their entirety, instead of being revised to fit Supplement A as extended. The provisions of section 741 (b) of the Code are unnecessary and are repealed. (p. 153)

Report—Senate Finance Committee (77th Cong., 2d Sess., S. Rept. 1631).— Same as Ways and Means Committee Report. (p. 218)

EPTA
14

[Set forth with sec. 712(a), page 55]

1940
201

SEC. 741. ELECTION OF INCOME CREDIT.

In addition to the corporations which under section 712 (a) may elect the excess profits credit computed under section 713 or the excess profits credit computed under section 714, a taxpayer which is an acquiring corporation which was in existence on the date of the beginning of its base period shall have such election.

Committee Reports

Report—Ways and Means Committee (76th Cong., 3d Sess., H. Rept. 2894).— The choice is available to the following classes of corporations:

*   *   *

(2) A domestic corporation, which, while not in existence for the period specified under (1), is deemed to have been in existence for a period of 48 months prior to the beginning of its first taxable year beginning in 1940, because it acquired, or resulted from the coalescing of, other corporations through certain tax-free exchanges or reorganizations, where such other corporations were in existence at the beginning of such 48-month period or had predecessors who were in existence at that time. In the opinion of your committee, the denial of the privilege of election to corporations in this category would be inequitable. (p. 4)

Under the provisions of supplement A of the bill a domestic corporation which was not in existence at the beginning of its base period is allowed to compute its excess-profits credit under this method, if it acquired, or resulted from the coalescing of, another corporation through certain tax-free exchanges, where the other corporation was in existence at the beginning of the base period or had a predecessor which was in existence at such time; * * * (p.12-13)

Report—Senate Finance Committee (76th Cong., 3d Sess., S. Rept. 2114).— The provisions of the House bill extend-ing the privilege of election of the average earnings method of computing the excess-profits tax to corporations not in existence during the base period but considered to have been so in existence by reason of having acquired, or having resulted from the coalescing of, other corporations, have not been materially changed. (p. 4)

[Set forth on page 268]

1940
201
[740-3]
in gen'l

Sec. 742(a)

SEC. 742. SUPPLEMENT A AVERAGE BASE PERIOD NET INCOME.

1942
228(c)

In the case of a taxpayer which is an acquiring corporation, its average base period net income (for the purpose of the credit computed under section 713) shall be the amount computed under section 713 or the amount of its Supplement A average base period net income, whichever is the greater. The Supplement A average base period net income shall be the amount computed without regard to subsection (h) of this section or computed under subsection (h) of this section, whichever is the greater. The Supplement A average base period net income shall be computed as follows:

(a) By ascertaining with respect to each of its base period years—

(1) The amount of its and each of its component corporation's excess profits net income for each of its and such component corporation's taxable years beginning with or within such base period year; or, * * *

(2) (A) * * * If more than one taxable year of the taxpayer or such component corporation, as the case may be, begins with or within such base period year, the aggregate of the amounts of excess profits net income minus the aggregate of the excesses of deductions plus the credit for dividends received and the credit provided in section 26 (a) (relating to interest on certain obligations of the United States and its instrumentalities) over gross income, or the aggregate of such excesses minus the aggregate of the amounts of excess profits net income, as the case may be, for such taxable years shall be ~~placed on an annual basis by dividing by the aggregate of the number of days in such taxable years and multiplying by three hundred and sixty-five~~ adjusted to such extent as the Commissioner, under regulations prescribed by him with the approval of the Secretary, prescribes as necessary in order that such base period year shall reflect income for a period of twelve months.

For the purposes of this section, a taxable year of a component corporation beginning within the base period which also begins with or within the taxable year of the acquiring corporation in which the acquisition occurred, or which also begins with or within the same base period year with which or within which began such taxable year of the acquiring corporation, shall be considered a taxable year of the acquiring corporation, and such taxable year shall be considered to have begun in the base period year with which or within which such taxable year of the acquiring corporation began.

Committee Reports

Report—Ways and Means Committee (77th Cong., 2d Sess., H. Rept. 2333).—Section 741[1] eliminates the express election in the case of acquiring corporations actually in existence before January 1, 1940. Furthermore it no longer contains the mandatory provision as to corporations not actually in existence before such date to the effect that their average base-period net income must be computed under Supplement A. Under section 741,[1] any corporation entitled to the benefits of supplement A is required, for the purposes of the credit under section 713, to compute its average base-period net income under section 713 or under supplement A, whichever is the greater. (p. 153)

[1] Sec. 742 of the Code.

This section is a consolidation of paragraphs (1) and (2) of former section 742 (a). In addition, it liberalizes the former rules as to the taxable years which may be taken into account in determining the average base-period net income under Supplement A. Section 741[1] (a) (1) now provides that an acquiring corporation may take into account (a) its own base-period experience for its taxable years beginning with or within base-period years, and (b) the base-period experience of its component corporations for their taxable years beginning with or within base-period years. Under these rules, each acquiring corporation will be given the benefit of all excess profits net income which can properly be attributed to its base period. (p. 154)

[1] Sec. 742 of the Code.

Report—Senate Finance Committee (77th Cong., 2d Sess., S. Rept. 1631).—Substantially the same as p. 153, 154 Ways and Means Committee Report

(p. 248, 218-219, respectively). In addition there is the following:

Section 742 (a) (2) of your committee bill is the same as section 742 (a) (3) of existing law with certain technical amendments necessitated by the consolidation of paragraphs (1) and (2) of section 742 (a) into paragraph (1) of section 742 (a), as amended by your committee bill.

The provisions of section 742 (a), added by the House bill, for placing on an annual basis the excess profits net income for 2 or more taxable years of the taxpayer or the component corporation, as the case may be, beginning with or within a base period year, have been modified in your committee bill. Instead of the requirement that the excess profits net income (or deficit in excess profits net income) for such 2 or more taxable years in such cases be placed on an annual basis, your committee bill provides that such amounts shall be adjusted to such extent as the Commissioner, under regulations prescribed by him with the approval of the Secretary, prescribes as necessary in order that such base period year shall reflect income for a period of 12 months. The specific situations requiring adjustment are complex, requiring detailed rules for adjustment where it is necessary. Accordingly, it seems desirable to authorize the Commissioner to prescribe the manner and the cases in which adjustment is to be made. A rule for guidance has, however, been inserted by your committee to the effect that a taxable year of a component corporation (beginning within the base period) which begins with or within the taxable year of the acquiring corporation in which the acquisition occurred, or which begins with or within the same base period year with which or within which such taxable year of the acquiring corporation begins, shall be considered a taxable year of the acquiring corporation, and such taxable year shall be considered to have begun in the base period year with which or within which such taxable year of the acquiring corporation began. (p. 219)

Report—Conference Committee (77th Cong., 2d Sess., H. Rept. 2586).— Amendment No. 354: This amendment changes the treatment of two or more taxable years beginning in the same base period year under Supplement A of the excess profits tax. The House bill requires the excess profits net income for such years to be put upon an annual basis. The Senate bill provides that the excess profits net incomes for such years shall be adjusted to such extent as the Commissioner, under regulations prescribed by him with the approval of the Secretary, prescribes as necessary in order that such base period year shall reflect income for a period of twelve months. The amendment adds a rule for guidance in the application of this provision to provide that a taxable year of a component corporation (beginning within the base period) which begins with or within the taxable year of the acquiring corporation in which the acquisition occurred, or which begins with or within the same base period year with which or within which such taxable year of the acquiring corporation begins, shall be considered a taxable year of the acquiring corporation and to have begun in the base period year with which or within which such taxable year of the acquiring corporation began. The House recedes. (p. 66)

Committee Hearings

Hearings—Ways and Means Committee.—Allowing acquiring corporations not in existence before 1940 an election not to come under Supplement A. (F. C. Ward, p. 1941-45; E. C. Alvord, p. 2783)

Explanation and shortcomings of provision. (E. C. Alvord, p. 2783)

SEC. 742. AVERAGE BASE PERIOD NET INCOME.

*In the case of a taxpayer which is an acquiring corporation the excess profits credit of which is allowed under section 741, its average base period net income (for the purpose of the credit computed under section 713) if the taxpayer was actually in existence before January 1, 1940, shall, at the election of the taxpayer made in its return for the taxable year, be computed as follows, and if the taxpayer was not actually in existence before such date, shall be computed as follows, in lieu of the method provided in section 713: * * ***

Committee Reports

Report—Senate Finance Committee (77th Cong., 1st Sess., S. Rept. 75).— The amendments made by your committee retain the principle embodied in section 13 of the House bill. Under that principle corporations required under existing law to compute their tax under supplement A may, if they so elect, compute it under such supplement or under part I as do corporations not falling under supplement A. (p. 1)

Section 15 of the committee bill retains the principle of section 13 of the House bill with respect to supplement A corporations. Supplement A of the existing provisions of the excess-profits tax provides for a method of computation of the base period net income in the case of corporations which have experienced mergers, consolidations or liquidations. Such method under the present law is mandatory for such corporations. The bill amends section 742 of existing law to make such method elective in the case of corporations actually in existence prior to January 1, 1940. Such corporations may compute their average base period net income under either section 713 or supplement A. (p. 21-22)

Congressional Discussion

Discussion—Senate (Cong. Rec. Vol. 87).—MR. HARRISON. * * * These sections also permit corporations actually in existence prior to January 1, 1940, that have gone through tax-free liquidations, mergers, or consolidations, to elect whether they shall compute their credit in the ordinary way or take the experience of their predecessors as required under supplement A. Under the present law such corporations were required to compute their credit under supplement A. In some cases it may be more beneficial for such corporations to ignore the experience of their predecessors in the base period. In other cases it may not. This election will also enable such corporations, if they do not elect to come under supplement A, to get the benefit of the "growing corporation relief" granted to corporations not coming under supplement A. (p. 1639)

1940
201

SEC. 742. AVERAGE BASE PERIOD NET INCOME.

In the case of a taxpayer which is an acquiring corporation which was *actually* in existence on the date of the beginning of its base period, *or which is entitled under section 741 to elect the excess profits credit computed under section 713*, its average base period net income (for the purpose of the credit computed under section 713) shall be computed as follows, in lieu of the method provided in section 713 (b):

(a) By ascertaining with respect to each of its base period years—

(1) The amount of its excess profits net income for each of its taxable years beginning after December 31, 1935, and ending with or within such base period year; * * *

(2) With respect to each OF ITS qualified component [corporation] CORPORATIONS the amount of its excess profits net income for each of its taxable years beginning after December 31, 1935, and ending with or within such base period year of the taxpayer; * * *

Committee Reports

Report—Ways and Means Committee (76th Cong., 3d Sess., H. Rept. 2894).— A domestic corporation which was in existence at the beginning of the base period and which is thereby entitled to elect to compute its excess-profits credit under section 713 by virtue of the provision of section 712, if it does elect to compute such credit under section 713, is permitted to add to its excess-profits net income for the years in the base period the excess-profits net incomes of corporations which it absorbs by a statutory merger or by liquidation under section 112 (b) (6), where such merged or liquidated corporation was in existence at the beginning of the base period or had predecessors in existence on such date.

(p. 13)
Report—Conference Committee (76th Cong., 3d Sess., H. Rept. 3002).—*House bill.*—Supplement A of the House bill contained provisions whereby, in computing the excess-profits credit of a taxpayer on the average earnings plan, the base-period experience of corporations, the assets of which had previously been acquired by the taxpayer in certain types of transactions, could be taken into account. This provision was intended not only to enable the base-period experience of the enterprise to be more truly reflected but to enable the income credit to be available in certain cases even though the taxpayer had not been in existence during the entire base period. (p. 56)

[Set forth on page 268]   1940
                                                             ___
                                                             201
                                                             [740-3]
                                                             in gen'l

[Set forth on page 327]   1918
                                                             ___
                                                             311(d)

[Set forth on page 352]   1917
                                                             ___
                                                             204

UNENACTED RELATED PROVISION

1941 E.P.T.A.

[Sec. 13 of House bill]

~~Sec. 13. Election To Compute Average Base Period Net Income Under Supplement A.~~

~~Section 742 of the Internal Revenue Code is amended by striking out "shall be computed as follows" and inserting in lieu thereof "if the taxpayer is entitled under section 712 (a) to elect the excess profits credit computed under section 713 shall, at the election of the taxpayer made in its return for the taxable year, be computed as follows, and if the taxpayer is not so entitled, shall be computed as follows".~~

Congressional Discussion

Discussion—House (Cong. Rec. Vol. 87).—MR. COOPER. * * * Supplement A of the excess-profits tax provides for a method of computation of the base-period earnings in the case of corporations which have gone through mergers, consolidations, or liquidations in the base period. Such method under the present law is mandatory for corporations. The amendment makes such method elective in the case of corporations who are now entitled to elect an average earnings method under section 712 (a). This change will permit such corporations to obtain the benefit of the relief afforded to growing corporations in the bill in connection with the computation average base-period net income under section 713. It will also relieve corporations from the necessity of computing their average base-period net income under supplement A if they prefer to compute it under section 713, and are entitled to do so under section 712 (a) of the existing law.

In other words, if I may state it in different words, under the existing law a corporation that has gone through a merger, or liquidation, or consolidation, or something of that kind, must use the history of its predecessors in the computations necessary to establish the base-period excess-profits-tax net income. It may well develop that some corporations by doing that would find themselves in worse condition than if they had not followed that course, so this amendment provides for the alternative plan, which they may elect. They may follow that course or may go ahead and figure the average-earnings credit on the same basis as if supplement A did not exist in the law. (p. 1388)

Report—Senate Finance Committee (77th Cong., 1st Sess., S. Rept. 75).— Same as the Ways and Means Committee Report, except that the last sentence of the first paragraph reads as follows:

In giving effect to the factor of growth during the base period, equitable demands do not indicate that growth after May 31, 1940, should be taken into account. (p. 7)

Sec. 742(b)

1942
228(c)

[SEC. 742. SUPPLEMENT A AVERAGE BASE PERIOD NET INCOME.]

[In the case of a taxpayer which is an acquiring corporation * * *. The Supplement A average base period net income shall be computed as follows:]

(b) By adding the plus amounts ascertained under subsection (a) (2) for each year of the base period; and (355) by subtracting from such sum, if for two or more years of the base period there was a minus amount, the sum of the minus amounts, excluding the greatest.

> **(1)** *If the tax under this subchapter is being computed for a taxable year not beginning after December 31, 1941, by subtracting from such sum, if for two or more years of the basis period there was a minus amount, the sum of the minus amounts, excluding the greatest; or*
> **(2)** *If the tax under this subchapter is being computed for a taxable year beginning after December 31, 1941, by subtracting from such sum the sum of the minus amounts. If the amount used under the preceding sentence for the lowest year is less than 75 per centum of the sum of the plus amounts reduced by the sum of the minus amounts for the other years in the base period divided by three, the amount which shall be used for such lowest year shall be 75 per centum of the amount last ascertained.*

Committee Reports

Report—Senate Finance Committee (77th Cong., 2d Sess., S. Rept. 1631).— Section 742 (b) has been changed by your committee bill so as to apply in determining supplement A average base period net income the same rule provided in section 713 (e) (1) as amended by section 214[1] of the bill. Under this rule, if the excess profits tax is being computed for a taxable year beginning after December 31, 1941, an adjustment is to be made in the amount of the group excess profits net income (or deficit in excess profits net income) for 1 base period year which is less than 75 percent of the average for the other three years. This average is the sum of the group excess profits net income for the other base period years, reduced by the sum of the group deficit in excess profits net income for the other base period years, divided by three. The low base period year is to be increased to 75 percent of this average. (p. 219)

[1] Sec. 215 of the Act.

Report—Conference Committee (77th Cong., 2d Sess., H. Rept. 2586).— Amendment No. 355: This amendment applies the 75 percent rule for the purpose of computing the excess profits tax under Supplement A for taxable years beginning after December 31, 1941. Under this rule, the lowest base period year of group excess profits net income is to be raised to 75 percent of the average for the other three years. The House recedes. (p. 66)

[Set forth with sec. 713(b)(1), page 62] $\frac{1940}{201}$

[Set forth on page 268]   1940
201
[740-3]
in gen'l

Sec. 742(c)

[Set forth on page 268]   1940
201 ·
[740-3]
in gen'l

Sec. 742(d)

[SEC. 742. SUPPLEMENT A AVERAGE BASE PERIOD NET INCOME.]   1942
228(c)

(d)   * * * As used in this subsection, the term "qualified component corporation" means a component corporation which was in existence on the date of the beginning of the taxpayer's base period.

Committee Reports

Report—Ways and Means Committee (77th Cong., 2d Sess., H. Rept. 2333).— Under the present amendments to Supplement A of the Excess Profits Tax Act, an acquiring corporation computing its average base period net income under such supplement is given the benefit of the base period experience of any component corporation actually in existence before January 1, 1940, irrespective of whether such component was in existence (either actually or constructively through another component corporation) at the beginning of the acquiring corporation's base period. Hence, the concept of a "qualified component corporation" has been abandoned, except for the purposes of section 741 (d).[1] Accordingly, the provision defining the term "qualified component corporation" has been eliminated from the general definitions in section 740 and incorporated in section 741 (d)[1] as the last sentence thereof. (p. 151)

[1] Sec. 742(d) of the Code.

For the reasons given above in connection with section 740 (c), the definition of the term "qualified component corporation" is incorporated in section 741 (d) as the last sentence thereof. (p. 154)

Report—Senate Finance Committee (77th Cong., 2d Sess., S. Rept. 1631).— Same as Ways and Means Committee Report.   (p. 214, 220, respectively)

[SEC. 742. AVERAGE BASE PERIOD NET INCOME.]   1940
201

[In the case of a taxpayer which is an acquiring corporation * * * its average base period net income * * * shall be computed as follows, in lieu of the method provided in section 713:]

(d) * * * *In the case of a taxpayer which becomes an acquiring corporation in any taxable year beginning after December 31, 1939, if, <prior to the date of the enactment of the Second Revenue Act of 1940> on September 11, 1940, and at all times until the taxpayer became an acquiring corporation <,>—*

(1) *the taxpayer owned not less than 75 per centum of each class of stock of each of the qualified component corporations involved in the transaction in which the taxpayer became an acquiring corporation; or*

(2) *one of the qualified component corporations involved in the transaction owned not less than 75 per centum of each class of stock of the taxpayer, and of each of the other qualified component corporations involved in the transaction,*

the average base period net income of the taxpayer shall not be less than <(1)> (A) the average base period net income of that one of its qualified component corporations involved in the transaction the average base period net income of which is greatest, or <(2)> (B) the average base period net income of the taxpayer computed without regard to the base period net income of any of its qualified component corporations involved in the transaction.

Committee Reports

Report—Senate Finance Committee (76th Cong., 3d Sess., S. Rept. 2114).— This section is the same as in the House bill except for a technical change and for the addition of a new sentence to subsection (b)[1] to prevent too great a reduction of the average base period net income of an acquiring corporation in cases where such corporation became an acquiring corporation in a taxable year beginning after December 31, 1939, and the component corporations involved in the transaction were at least 75 percent owned by the acquiring corporation. Such 75 percent ownership must have existed prior to the enactment of the bill and have been present at all times thereafter until the transaction. In such cases the average base period net income of the acquiring corporation shall not be less than either (1) its average base period net income computed without reference to the base period experience of the component corporations involved in the transaction, or (2) the average base period net income of that component corporation which possesses the highest average base period net income.

(p. 18-19)

[1] Sec. 742(d) of the Code.

Report—Conference Committee (76th Cong., 3d Sess., H. Rept. 3002).—*Senate amendment.* * * * The Senate amendment also provides that in the case of a taxpayer which became an acquiring corporation in a taxable year after December 31, 1939, if, on September 11, 1940, and at all times thereafter until the taxpayer became an acquiring corporation, either the taxpayer or one of the transferor corporations involved in the transaction in which the taxpayer became an acquiring corporation owned not less than 75 percent of each class of stock of each of the other corporations involved in the transaction, then the average base period net income of the taxpayer should not be less than either (1) its average base period net income would have been if the transaction had not taken place or (2) the average base period net income of that transferor corporation whose average base period net income is the greatest. (p. 56-57)

[Set forth on page 268]

1940
201
[740-3]
in gen'l

Sec. 742(e)(1)-(3)

[SEC. 742. SUPPLEMENT A AVERAGE BASE PERIOD NET INCOME.]

1942
228(c)

[In the case of a taxpayer which is an acquiring corporation * * *. The Supplement A average base period net income shall be computed as follows:]

(e) For the purposes of subsection (a) (1) of this section—

(1) If neither the taxpayer corporation nor any of its component corporations was actually in existence on December 31, 1936, the excess profits net income of each such corporation ⟨356⟩ ~~(except a corporation which became a component corporation of an acquiring corporation before the beginning of the acquiring corporation's first taxable year which began in 1940)~~ for each base period year at no time during which any of such corporations was actually in existence, shall ⟨357⟩ *(except in the case of a corporation which became a component corporation of its acquiring corporation before the beginning of the acquiring corporation's first taxable year which began in 1940)* be an amount equal to 8 per centum of the excess of—

(A) ⟨358⟩ *in the case of any such corporation to which paragraph (2) is not applicable,* the daily invested capital of such corporation for the first day of its first taxable year under this subchapter beginning in 1940 ⟨359⟩ ~~plus, in case it became, in such first taxable year but on a day in any other such corporation's taxable year beginning in 1939, an acquiring corporation with respect to such other corporation, the daily invested capital of such other corporation for such day,~~ over

(B) an amount equal to the same percentage of such daily invested capital as would be applicable under section 720 in reduction of the average invested capital of such corporation for the last taxable year beginning in 1939 if such section had been applicable to such year (computed as if the admissible and inadmissible assets of any other such corporation with respect to which it became, in such taxable year, an acquiring corporation, had been held by it).

(2) *In case the transaction by which a corporation became a component corporation of its acquiring corporation occurred in the last taxable year of such component corporation beginning in 1939 but on a day in a taxable year of such acquiring corporation beginning in 1940, the excess profits net income of such component corporation for each base period year described in paragraph (1) shall be an amount equal to 8 per centum of the excess of—*

(A)　the daily invested capital of such component corporation for such day, over

(B)　an amount equal to the same percentage of such daily invested capital as would be applicable under section 720 in reduction of the average invested capital of such component corporation for the twelve-month period ending with the preceding day if such twelve-month period constituted a taxable year and such section had been applicable to such taxable year.

(3)　In case any corporation described in paragraph (1) owned stock in any other such corporation on the first day of such owning corporation's first taxable year under this subchapter beginning in 1940, (362) ~~its and such other corporation's excess profits net income for each base period year described in paragraph (1) shall be determined in accordance with regulations prescribed by the Commissioner with the approval of the Secretary~~ the amounts computed under subparagraphs (A) and (B) of paragraphs (1) and (2) with respect to such corporations shall be adjusted, under regulations prescribed by the Commissioner with the approval of the Secretary, to such extent as may be necessary to prevent the excess profits net income of such corporations for the base period years described in paragraph (1) from reflecting money or property having been paid in by either of such corporations to the other for stock or as paid-in surplus or as a contribution to capital, or from reflecting stock of either having been paid in for stock of the other or as paid-in surplus or as a contribution to capital. For the purposes of this paragraph, stock in either such corporation which has in the hands of the other corporation a basis determined with reference to the basis of stock previously acquired by the issuance of such other corporation's own stock shall be deemed to have been paid in for the stock of such other corporation.

Committee Reports

Report—Ways and Means Committee (77th Cong., 2d Sess., H. Rept. 2333).— This section accomplishes two purposes: (a) It provides a method for building up income for the enterprise for the part of base period during which neither the acquiring corporation nor any of the component corporations absorbed by it was in existence, comparable to the method provided in section 713 (d) (2); and (b) it eliminates the provisions of paragraph (1) of section 742 (e) of the prior law.

Section 741[1] (e) (2) authorizes the Commissioner by regulations approved by the Secretary, in certain cases in which there is cross-ownership of stock between corporations covered by section 741[1] (e) (1), to require such adjustments in the factors to be taken into account in building up income as may be necessary under the facts in each case. A primary purpose of this section is to prevent doubling upon the factor of the daily invested capital carried into the first excess profits tax taxable year. The application of this section, from the standpoint of its primary purpose, may be illustrated by the following example:

O corporation and P corporation came into existence on January 1, 1938. Both corporations have at all times been on the calendar-year basis. On January 1, 1939, O corporation purchased for cash all of the stock in P corporation from the stockholders of the latter corporation. It holds this stock continuously until January 1, 1942, at which time it acquires P corporation in a transaction described in section 740 (a) (2). In view of the fact that assets (cash) left the system in connection with the acquisition of the P corporation's stock, adjustments in the daily invested capital of the corporations for January 1, 1940, must be made in order to prevent a doubling up of such capital. Under section 741[1] (e) (2) the Commissioner has full authority to prescribe such regulations as may be necessary to eliminate duplication and properly to reflect the invested capital of the corporations as a unit. (p. 154–155)

[1] Sec. 742 of the Code.

Report—Senate Finance Committee (77th Cong., 2d Sess., S. Rept. 1631).— Section 742 (e) (1), (2), and (3) accomplishes two purposes: (a) It provides a method for building up income for the enterprise for the part of base period during which neither the acquiring corporation nor any of the component corporations absorbed by it was in existence, comparable to the method provided in section 713 (d) (2); and (b) it eliminates the provisions of paragraph (1) of section 742 (e) of the prior law.

The rule of section 742 (e) (1), as amended in the bill passed by the House, is changed into paragraphs (1) and (2) of section 742 (e) so as to provide clearly for building up of income for "vacant" base period years in the case of a component, which became such in its last taxable year beginning in 1939 but on a day in a taxable year of the acquiring corporation beginning in 1940, on the basis of the invested capital of such component.

Section 742 (e) (2) of the bill passed by the House is renumbered section 742 (e) (3) in your committee bill, and as such is changed to state more clearly the standard of adjustment under regulations prescribed by the Commissioner with the approval of the Secretary for preventing doubling up upon the factor of invested capital for the purposes of section 742 (e) (1) and (2) in cases of cross ownership of stock between corporations. The application of this section from the standpoint of its purpose may be illustrated by the following example:

O Corporation and P corporation came into existence on January 1, 1938. Both corporations have at all times been on the calendar year basis. On January 1, 1939, O corporation purchased for cash all of the stock in P corporation from the stockholders of the latter corporation. It holds this stock continuously until January 1, 1942, at which time it acquires P corporation in a transaction described in section 740 (a) (2). In view of the fact that assets (cash) left the system in connection with the acquisition of the P corporation's stock, adjustments in the daily invested capital of the corporations for January 1, 1940, must be made in order to prevent a doubling up of such capital. Under section 742 (e) (3) the Commissioner has full authority to prescribe such regulations as may be necessary to eliminate duplication and properly to reflect the invested capital of the corporations as a unit. (p. 220)

Report—Conference Committee (77th Cong., 2d Sess., H. Rept. 2586).— Amendments Nos. 356, 357, 358, 359, 360, and 363: These Senate amendments are technical, resulting primarily from changing the rule of section 742 (e) (1) as amended in the bill passed by the House. The House recedes.

Amendments Nos. 361 and 362. In the House bill, section 741 (e) (2) under Supplement A of the excess profits tax provided for an adjustment, under the Commissioner's regulations, in excess profits net income for "vacant" base period years (which are to be filled up on the basis of 8 percent of invested capital) in cases where there was cross ownership of stock between acquiring and component corporations on the first day of the owning corporation's first taxable year beginning in 1940. The amendments renumber this section, 742 (e) (3), and provide more specifically for the situations in which the adjustment is to be made. In some cases of cross ownership of stock, adjustment under section 742 (e) (3) is not necessary by reason of the provisions for adjustment in section 742 (f) (1), as amended by this bill. Thus the example given in the House and Senate Committee reports under this section is covered by section 742 (f) (1).

The primary purpose of section 742 (e) (3) is to provide for adjustment where, by reason of the acquisition by one corporation of stock in another, the invested capital of the corporation whose stock is acquired is increased without a corresponding decrease in the invested capital of the owning corporation. This may occur, for example, in the case of a purchase by A Corporation of B Corporation's stock from B on the last day of the base period. In such case, the invested capital of B for the first day of its first taxable year in 1940 will be increased by the assets received from A, while, by reason of the operation of the inadmissible asset ratio as to A, A's invested capital for such day will not be reduced correspondingly. Section 742 (e) (3) also applies regardless of the date

prior to the first taxable year in 1940 when the stock was acquired if the inadmissible asset ratio fails to eliminate duplication of the same invested capital as between the acquiring corporation and its component. Accordingly, in such cases the Commissioner is given authority to prescribe regulations with the approval of the Secretary for adjustment in the excess profits net incomes of such corporations. The House recedes. (p. 66-67)

Congressional Discussion

Discussion—House (Cong. Rec. Vol. 88).—MR. DISNEY. * * * The bill cures some of these major defects by—

* * *

(d) Allowing supplement A companies to use the "fill-up" now permitted only to nonsupplement A companies.

The years filled up with hypothetical income for the supplement A companies, however, are only those base-period years in which neither the taxpayer nor any of its predecessors were in existence. (p. 6379)

Committee Hearings

Hearings—Senate Finance Committee.—Explanation of provision. (J.

O'Brien—H. Legis. Counsel—p. 110)

1940
201
[742(e) (1)]

[SEC. 742. AVERAGE BASE PERIOD NET INCOME.]

[In the case of a taxpayer which is an acquiring corporation * * * its average base period net income * * * shall be computed as follows, in lieu of the method provided in section 713:]

(e) For the purposes of subsection (a) (1) and (2) of this section—

(1) There shall be excluded, in the various computations, any dividends paid by the taxpayer or any OF ITS qualified component [corporation] CORPORATIONS during any of the taxable years of the payor which are included in the computation of the taxpayer's average base period net income. * * *

1940
201
[740-3]
in gen'l

[Set forth on page 268]

Sec. 742(f)(1)

1942
228(c)

[SEC. 742. SUPPLEMENT A AVERAGE BASE PERIOD NET INCOME.]

(f) (1) If, after December 31, 1935—

(A) the taxpayer acquired stock in another corporation, and thereafter such other corporation became a component corporation of the taxpayer, or

(B)   a corporation (hereinafter called "first corporation") acquired stock in another corporation (hereinafter called "second corporation"), and thereafter the first and second corporations became component corporations of the taxpayer,

then to the extent that the consideration for such acquisition was not the issuance of the taxpayer's or first corporation's, as the case may be, own stock, the Supplement A average base period net income of the taxpayer shall be reduced, and the transferred capital addition and reduction adjusted, in respect of the income and capital addition and reduction of the corporation whose stock was so acquired and in respect of the income and capital addition and reduction of any other corporation which at the time of such acquisition was connected directly or indirectly through stock ownership with the corporation whose stock was so acquired and which thereafter became a component corporation of the taxpayer, in such amounts and in such manner as shall be determined in accordance with regulations prescribed by the Commissioner with the approval of the Secretary.   (364) *For the purposes of this paragraph, stock which has, in the hands of the taxpayer or first corporation, as the case may be, a basis determined with reference to the basis of stock previously acquired by the issuance of the taxpayer's or first corporation's, as the case may be, own stock, shall be considered as having been acquired in consideration of the issuance of the taxpayer's or first corporation's, as the case may be, own stock.*

Committee Reports

Report—Ways and Means Committee (77th Cong., 2d Sess., H. Rept. 2333).— Improper duplications of base period income and capital additions and reductions result in cases in which, prior to the transaction which constitutes a corporation an acquiring corporation for the purposes of supplement A and after December 31, 1935, such corporation uses its assets to acquire stock in the corporation which becomes the component corporation of such acquiring corporation. This section contemplates that, under the detailed rules of the regulations, after the absorption of the corporation whose stock was so acquired, the part of its base-period income and deficits for the base-period years before the acquisition of its stock which is attributable to such stock shall be excluded by the taxpayer (i) in determining its average base-period net income, (ii) in applying the "growth formula" provided in section 741[1] (h), and (iii) in building up income for "vacant" base-period years, and that, in determining the amount of the daily capital addition

and reduction of the corporation whose stock was acquired which is to be transferred to the corporation into which the other corporation was absorbed, such daily capital addition and reduction shall be reduced by the portion thereof attributable to the previously acquired stock. The specific situations presented are complex, requiring detailed rules for the necessary adjustments in the computations. The Commissioner is therefore authorized to prescribe in regulations approved by the Secretary the specific situations in which specified adjustments under this section are to be made. If the acquisition of such stock by the corporation is in exchange solely for its own stock, no eliminations or adjustments are necessary, and, accordingly, section 741 (f) (1)[1] is made inapplicable. In case the acquisition is in exchange partly for its own stock and partly for other property, section 741[1] (f) (1) is applicable only to the part of the acquisition attributable to such other property. (p. 155)

[1] Sec. 742 of the Code.

Report—Senate Finance Committee (77th Cong., 2d Sess., S. Rept. 1631).—Substantially the same as Ways and Means Committee Report. In addition there is the following:

Your committee bill also takes out of the operation of this provision cases in which the taxpayer acquires stock which has in the hands of the taxpayer a basis determined with reference to the basis of stock previously acquired by the issuance of the taxpayer's own stock. (p. 221)

Report—Conference Committee (77th Cong., 2d Sess., H. Rept. 2586).—Amendment No. 364. This is a technical amendment to section 742 (f) (1) under Supplement A of the excess profits tax. Such section was designed in the House bill to eliminate experience attributable to stock acquired by the transfer of assets (other than the issuance of the acquiring corporation's stock) of the acquiring corporation, which assets thereupon went out of the system. This amendment provides that stock which has in the hands of the taxpayer a basis determined with reference to the basis of stock previously acquired by the issuance of the taxpayer's own stock shall be considered as having been acquired in consideration of the issuance of the taxpayer's own stock. The House recedes. (p. 67)

Committee Hearings

Hearings—Ways and Means Committee.—Explanation and shortcomings of provision. (E. C. Alvord, p. 2783)

1943 Act

Hearings—Ways and Means Committee.—Confining adjustment only where actual credit duplication. (E. C. Alvord, p. 686; Controllers Institute of America, p. 1331-32)

Hearings—Senate Finance Committee.—Confining adjustment only where actual credit duplication. (E. C. Alvord, p. 616; A. B. Chapman, p. 830)

1940
201

[SEC. 742.   AVERAGE BASE PERIOD NET INCOME.]

(f) (1)   In the case of a taxpayer which is an acquiring corporation and which was not actually in existence on the date of the beginning of its base period, there shall be excluded from the various computations under subsection (a) (1) of this section the portion of its excess profits net income, or of the excess over gross income therein referred to, which is attributable to any period before it first became an acquiring corporation.

Committee Reports

Report—Ways and Means Committee (76th Cong., 3d Sess., H. Rept. 2894).— * * * and, having so elected, it is allowed to use as its excess-profits net income for the taxable years in the base period prior to such acquiring or coalescing the excess-profits net income of the other corporation. For the years in the base period subsequent to such acquiring or coalescing, it uses its own excess-profits net income for the purpose of computing the credit. (p. 13)

Committee Hearings
1941 Act

Hearings—Senate Finance Committee.—Explanation and shortcomings of provision. (E. C. Alvord, p. 687-688; H. B. Fernald, p. 885)

[Set forth on page 268]

1940
———
201
[740–3]
in gen'l

Sec. 742(f)(2)

[SEC. 742. AVERAGE BASE PERIOD NET INCOME.]

1940
———
201

[In the case of a taxpayer which is an acquiring corporation * * *. The Supplement A average base period net income shall be computed as follows:]

(2) In the case of a component corporation which became a qualified component corporation only by reason of section 740 (e) (f), there shall be excluded from the various computations * * *

[Set forth on page 268]

1940
———
201
[740–3]
in gen'l

Sec. 742(g)

[SEC. 742. AVERAGE BASE PERIOD NET INCOME.]

EPTA
8(d)

(g) In the case of a partnership which is a component corporation by virtue of section 740 (b) (5), the computations required by this Supplement shall be made, under rules and regulations prescribed by the Commissioner with the approval of the Secretary, as if such partnership had been a corporation. * * *

Committee Reports

Report—Ways and Means Committee (77th Cong., 1st Sess., H. Rept. 146).— In these situations the computations required by supplement A with respect to the income of the partnership or the proprietorship shall be made as if such partnership or proprietorship were a corporation; viz, the deduction on account of income taxes shall be computed in accordance with the income taxes applicable to corporations, a deduction for salaries shall be allowed, etc. (p. 14)

Report—Senate Finance Committee (77th Cong., 1st Sess., S. Rept. 75).— Same as Ways and Means Committee Report. (p. 15)

Sec. 742(h)

[Set forth on following page]

1942
228(c)

[SEC. 742. SUPPLEMENT A AVERAGE BASE PERIOD NET INCOME.]

(h) Increased Earnings in Last Half of Base Period.—

(1) General Rule.— * * *

Committee Reports

Report—Ways and Means Committee (77th Cong., 2d Sess., H. Rept. 2333).— This section provides a growth formula for acquiring corporations using Supplement A similar to the growth formula provided in section 713 (f), with such modifications as Supplement A makes necessary. (p. 155)

Report—Senate Finance Committee (77th Cong., 2d Sess., S. Rept. 1631).— Same as Ways and Means Committee Report. (p. 221)

Congressional Discussion

Discussion—House (Cong. Rec. Vol. 88).—Mr. DISNEY. * * * The bill cures some of these major defects by—
(a) Allowing supplement A companies to use the "growth formula" now permitted to be used only by companies which were themselves in existence during the base period and which do not use supplement A; * * * (p. 6379)

Committee Hearings

Hearings—Ways and Means Committee.—Applying growth provisions to Supplement A. (R. N. Miller, p. 175-181; A. B. Chapman, p. 878, 881; H. Satterlee, p. 2250-51; E. C. Alvord, p. 2783)

Hearings—Senate Finance Committee.—Explanation of provision. (J. O'Brien—H. Legis. Counsel—p. 109)

1941 Act

Hearings—Senate Finance Committee.—Applying growth provisions to Supplement A. (A. B. Chapman, p. 754, 762-763; B. S. Embry, p. 1159-1165)

Sec. 743(a)

1942
228(d)

SEC. 743. NET CAPITAL CHANGES.

(a) **Taxpayer Using This Supplement.**—For the purposes of section 713 (g), if the transaction which constitutes the taxpayer an acquiring corporation occurs in a taxable year of the taxpayer which begins after December 31, 1939, and the taxpayer's average base period net income is computed under section 741 742, the following rules shall apply in computing the daily capital addition and reduction of the taxpayer for each day after such transaction: * * *

Committee Reports

Report—Ways and Means Committee (77th Cong., 2d Sess., H. Rept. 2333).— This section corresponds to section 743 under prior law. The former section applied to each acquiring corporation in a Supplement A transaction. The present section applies to such an acquiring corporation only if it computes its average base period net income under Supplement A.

This section also clarifies the rules to be applied in determining the net capital changes resulting from a Supplement A transaction to an acquiring corporation using such supplement. (p. 155-156)

Report—Senate Finance Committee (77th Cong., 2d Sess., S. Rept. 1631).— This section corresponds to section 743

under existing law. This section of existing law applies to each acquiring corporation in a supplement A transaction. The new section applies to such an acquiring corporation only if it computes its average base period net income under supplement A.

This section also clarifies the rules to be applied in determining the net capital changes resulting from a supplement A transaction to an acquiring corporation using such supplement. (p. 221)

[Set forth on page 268]

1940
201
[740-3]
in gen'l

Sec. 743(b)

[SEC. 743. NET CAPITAL CHANGES.]

1940
201

(b) For the purposes of this section—

(1) In computing the net capital addition of each such component corporation there shall be disregarded property paid in to such corporation by the taxpayer or by any of [the] ITS component corporations [involved in the transaction referred to in the first sentence; and] * * *

[(c) *For the purposes of paragraphs (a) and (b) only, if a corporation is a component corporation of an acquiring corporation, under section 740 or under this paragraph, it shall also be a component corporation of the corporation of which such acquiring corporation is a component corporation.*]

[Set forth on page 268]

1940
201
[740-3]
in gen'l

Sec. 744

SEC. 744. FOREIGN CORPORATIONS.

1940
201

The term "corporation" as used in this Supplement does not include a foreign corporation.

Committee Reports

Report—Ways and Means Committee (76th Cong., 3d Sess., H. Rept. 2894).— Foreign corporations are not permitted the use of this supplement and are not included as acquiring, component, or qualified component corporations. (p. 33)

[Set forth on page 268]

1940
201
[740-3]
in gen'l

UNENACTED RELATED PROVISION

1942 Act

[Sec. 216 (a) of Ways and Means Committee bill]

~~Sec. 743. Foreign Corporations.~~

~~The term "corporation" as used in this Supplement does not include a foreign corporation.~~

Sec. 750(a)

1940
201

SEC. 750. DEFINITIONS.

As used in this Supplement—

(a) **Exchange.**—The term "exchange" means an exchange, ~~described in~~ *to which* section 112 (b) (4) or (5) or ~~in~~ so much of section 112 (c), (d), or (e) as refers to section 112 (b) (4) or (5), *or to which a corresponding provision of a prior revenue law, is or was applicable,* by one corporation of its property wholly or in part for stock or securities of another corporation, or a transfer of property by one corporation to another corporation *after December 31, 1917,* the basis of which in the hands of such other corporation is or was determined under section 113 (a) (8) (B), or would have been so determined had such section been in effect.

Committee Reports

Report—Ways and Means Committee (76th Cong., 3d Sess., H. Rept. 2894).— Exchanges involving several transferors are treated as a series of separate exchanges except where the exchange is one described in section 112 (b) (5) or so much of section 112 (c) and (e) as refers to section 112 (b) (5). In the latter case the acquiring corporation is given a status reflecting the status of each of the transferor corporations, except where one transferor by itself is in control of the acquiring corporation after the transfer, in which case the transaction is treated as a split-up of such corporation alone. In section 112 (b) (5) cases where the acquiring corporation is controlled after the exchange by noncorporate transferors, it is treated as a new corporation except as regards lowest invested capital and the base period percentages applicable thereto. (p. 35)

Report—Senate Finance Committee (76th Cong., 3d Sess., S. Rept. 2114).— Under the House bill the term "exchange" was defined to mean certain exchanges "described in section 112 (b) (4) or (5)" and related sections and certain transfers of property by one corporation to another corporation the basis of which in the hands of the acquiring corporation is or was determined under section 113 (a) (8) (B), or would have been so determined had such section been in effect. The type of exchanges or transfers described would therefore have been included regardless of whether they were controlled by corresponding provisions of the revenue laws in force at the time when made. This definition has been changed so as, in effect, to include only exchanges and transfers occurring after December 31, 1917. Broadly speaking the tax-free exchange provisions did not appear in the income-tax law until after such date. (p. 19)

Report—Conference Committee (76th Cong., 3d Sess., H. Rept. 3002).— * * * the term "exchange" was clarified so as to make it clear that only transactions occurring after December 31, 1917, are embraced in the definition. Broadly speaking, the tax-free exchange provisions did not appear in the income-tax law until after such date.

Conference agreement.—The conference agreement adopts the Senate provisions. (p. 57)

Committee Hearings

Hearings—Senate Finance Committee.—Explanation of provision. (C. Stam—Jt. Com. on Int. Rev. Taxn.—p. 197, 212; E. C. Alvord, p. 274-275)

1942 Act

Hearings—Senate Finance Committee.—Repealing provision. (J. L. O'Brien—H. Legis. Counsel—p. 110)

Sec. 750(d)

[SEC. 750. DEFINITIONS.]

1940
201

(d) **Control.**—The term "control" means the ownership of stock possessing at least 90 per centum of the total combined voting power of all classes of stock entitled to vote and at least 90 per centum of the total value of shares of all classes of stock of the corporation.

Committee Reports

Report—Ways and Means Committee (76th Cong., 3d Sess., H. Rept. 2894).— For this purpose "control" is defined as ownership of stock possessing at least 90 percent of the total combined voting power of all classes of stock entitled to vote and at least 90 percent of the total value of shares of all classes of stock of a corporation. (p. 35)

Sec. 751(a)

[Set forth on following page]

SEC. 751. DETERMINATION OF PROPERTY PAID IN FOR STOCK AND OF BORROWED CAPITAL IN CONNECTION WITH CERTAIN EXCHANGES.

(a) **Property Paid in For Stock.**—In the application of section 718 (a) to a transferee upon an exchange in determining the amount paid in for stock of the transferee, or as paid-in surplus or as a contribution to capital of the transferee, in connection with such exchange, only an amount shall be deemed to have been so paid in equal to the excess of the basis in the hands of the transferee of the property of the transferor received by the transferee upon the exchange (other than stock which was neither an admissible nor an inadmissible asset in the hands of the transferor) over the sum of—

(1) Any liability of the transferor assumed upon such exchange and any liability subject to which the property was received upon such exchange, plus

(2) The aggregate of the amount of money and the fair market value of any other property transferred to the transferor not permitted to be received by such transferor without the recognition of gain.

Committee Reports

Report—Ways and Means Committee (76th Cong., 3d Sess., H. Rept. 2894).—Supplement B contains provisions relative to the effect of certain tax-free exchanges upon the computation of the excess-profits credit based on income and invested capital. Such provisions are designed * * * (3) to prevent invested capital acquired in certain tax-free exchanges from being treated as new capital to any greater extent than it was so treated in the hands of the corporation from which it was acquired.

The result is that the sum of the excess-profits credits of all such corporations is exactly the same as the excess-profits credit of the parent corporation would have been if the split-up had not taken place.

Where the A corporation merely reorganizes itself into the B corporation, transferring all its assets to the B corporation for all the B corporation's stock, the B corporation acquires the status of the A corporation.

In cases where several corporations become one corporation the equity invested capital, the borrowed capital, * * * of the resulting corporation are the sum of the equity invested capitals, the borrowed capitals, * * * of the constituent companies. (p. 34)

Since corporate split-ups may sometimes be disguised as transactions whereby one corporation acquires assets of another, as, for example, where the A corporation transfers a portion of its assets to an already existing B corporation which it or its shareholders, or both, afterward control, it is necessary that such transactions be treated in the same manner as corporate split-ups. The status of the acquiring corporation before the exchange is therefore ignored except to the extent that its equity invested capital, its borrowed capital, * * * are taken into account in the computation. (p. 35)

Similarly and to the same extent, where the shareholders of an acquiring corporation immediately before the acquisition by such corporation of the assets of another corporation are also in control after such acquisition the status of the corporation whose assets are acquired is ignored in determining the future status of the acquiring corporation. An exception to the latter rule is where corporations which resulted from a previous split-up subject to the adjustments provided by Supplement B later reunite. (p. 35)

The rules provided by Supplement B relative to the computation of equity invested capital and admissible and inadmissible assets upon tax-free exchanges apply regardless of control and regardless of whether the exchange took place before, after, or during the base period. (p. 35)

Report—Senate Finance Committee (76th Cong., 3d Sess., S. Rept. 2114).— The only change made in this section of the House bill is the elimination of the matter in parentheses in subsection (a) thereof, which excluded from the computation stock received which was neither an admissible nor inadmissible asset in the hands of the transferor.   (p. 19)

Committee Hearings

Hearings—Senate Finance Committee.—Explanation of provision.   (C. Stam—Jt. Com. on Int. Rev. Taxn.— p. 197, 212; E. C. Alvord, p. 274-275)

1942 Act

Hearings—Senate Finance Committee.—Repealing provision.   (J. L. O'Brien—H. Legis. Counsel—p. 110)

[Set forth on page 344]

$$\frac{1918}{330}$$

[Set forth on page 347]

$$\frac{1918}{331}$$

[Set forth on page 352]

$$\frac{1917}{204}$$

Sec. 751(b)

[SEC. 751. DETERMINATION OF PROPERTY PAID IN FOR STOCK AND OF BORROWED CAPITAL IN CONNECTION WITH CERTAIN EXCHANGES.]

$$\frac{1940}{201}$$

(b) **Borrowed Capital.**—In the application of section 719 (a) to a transferee upon an exchange, the term "borrowed capital" shall not include indebtedness originally evidenced by securities issued by the transferee upon such exchange as consideration for the property of the transferor received by the transferee upon such exchange if (1) such securities were property permitted to be received by the person to whom such securities were issued without the recognition of gain and (2) the indebtedness originally evidenced by such securities did not arise out of indebtedness of the transferor (other than indebtedness which in the transferor's hands was subject to the limitations of this subsection) assumed by the transferee in connection with such exchange.

Committee Reports

Report—Ways and Means Committee (76th Cong., 3d Sess., H. Rept. 2894).— In addition, securities other than stock issued by the subsidiaries upon the exchange are excluded from the borrowed capital of the subsidiaries unless issued in connection with an assumption of the liabilities of the parent. The result is that the sum of the excess-profits credits of all such corporations is exactly the same as the excess-profits credit of the parent corporation would have been if the split-up had not taken place.   (p. 32)

Supplement B contains provisions relative to the effect of certain tax-free exchanges upon the computation of the excess-profits credit based on income and invested capital. Such provisions are designed * * * (5) to prevent a corporation, the proportion of whose borrowed capital which may be included in invested capital * * * has been adjusted because of previous reorganizations, from undoing the effects of such adjustments through transferring its assets, tax-free, to another corporation which is little more than a dummy. (p. 33-34)

In cases where several corporations become one corporation the equity invested capital, the borrowed capital, * * * are the sum of the equity invested capitals, the borrowed capitals, and the lowest invested capitals respectively, of the constituent companies.   (p. 34)

The rules provided by Supplement B relative to the computation of equity invested capital and admissible and inadmissible assets upon tax-free exchanges apply regardless of control and regardless of whether the exchange took place before, after, or during the base period. (p. 35)

Since corporate split-ups may sometimes be disguised as transactions whereby one corporation acquires assets of another, as, for example, where the A corporation transfers a portion of its assets to an already existing B corporation which it or its shareholders, or both, afterward control, it is necessary that such transactions be treated in the same manner as corporate split-ups. The status of the acquiring corporation before the exchange is therefore ignored except to the extent that its equity invested capital, its borrowed capital, * * * are taken into account in the computation. (p. 35)

Similarly and to the same extent, where the shareholders of an acquiring corporation immediately before the acquisition by such corporation of the assets of another corporation are also in control after such acquisition the status of the corporation whose assets are acquired is ignored in determining the future status of the acquiring corporation. An exception to the latter rule is where corporations which resulted from a previous split-up subject to the adjustments provided by Supplement B later reunite. (p. 35)

UNENACTED RELATED PROVISION

1940 Act

[Secs. 201 of Ways and Means Committee bill]

Sec. 752. Equity Invested Capital in Connection With Certain Exchanges.

(a) In the case of any transferor upon an exchange, its equity invested capital for each day subsequent to the day on which such exchange took place shall be reduced by an amount equal to the amount by which the equity invested capital of the transferee upon such exchange was increased by reason of the receipt of property from such transferor upon such exchange.

(b) Equity invested capital for each day following the disposition of stock which is neither an admissible nor an inadmissible asset shall be increased by the sum of (1) the amount of money or the fair market value of property received therefor upon such disposition which is not permitted to be received without the recognition of

~~gain, plus (2) the amount of liabilities the assumption of which, or the acquisition of property subject to which, is not considered "other property or money" under section 112 (k), and decreased by the amount of gain or increased by the amount of loss recognized upon such disposition.~~

~~Sec. 753.   Effect of Certain Exchanges Upon Certain Admissible and Inadmissible Assets.~~

~~For the purposes of section 720, stock of a transferee upon an exchange received by a transferor upon such exchange shall be treated as neither an admissible nor an inadmissible asset in the hands of such transferor and in the hands of any transferee receiving such stock upon a subsequent exchange or upon a complete liquidation described in section 112 (b) (6) from a transferor in whose hands such stock was neither an admissible nor an inadmissible asset.~~

Committee Reports

Report—Ways and Means Committee (76th Cong., 3d Sess., H. Rept. 2894).— Stock of the subsidiaries acquired by the parent is eliminated from consideration by being treated as neither an admissible nor an inadmissible asset. (p. 34)

Report—Senate Finance Committee (76th Cong., 3d Sess., S. Rept. 2114).— Section 752 of the House bill, which made such stock neither admissible nor inadmissible in the hands of the transferor, has been eliminated. (p. 19)

These sections in the House bill required computations in the determination of certain factors employed in the computation of the invested capital credit under the House bill, necessary in order to prevent tax avoidance through tax-free exchanges. Because of the change recommended by your committee in the computation of the invested capital credit, the necessity for these sections disappears and they have, therefore, been eliminated. (p. 19-20)

Sec. 760(a)(1)

SEC. 760. EXCHANGES.

(a) **Definitions, Etc.**—For the purpose of this section—

~~(1) Exchange. The term "exchange" means an exchange, to which section 112 (b) (3), (4), or (5) or so much of section 112 (c), (d), or (e) as refers to section 112 (b) (3), (4), or (5), or to which a corresponding provision of a prior revenue law, is or was applicable, by one corporation of its property wholly or in part for stock or securities of another corporation, or a transfer of property by one corporation to another corporation after December 31, 1917, the basis of which in the hands of such other corporation is or was determined under section 113 (a) (8) (B), or would have been so determined had such section been in effect.~~

(2)   Transferee Upon an Exchange.   The term "transferee
upon an exchange" means a corporation which upon an exchange
acquires property in exchange, wholly or in part, for its stock or
securities, or which acquires property from another corporation after
December 31, 1917, the basis of which in its hands is or was determined under section 113 (a) (8) (B), or would have been so
determined had such section been in effect.

(1) "Exchange", "Transferor", and "Transferee".—*The term
"exchange" means a transaction by which one corporation (hereinafter
called "transferee") receives property of another corporation (hereinafter
called "transferor") and the basis of the property received, in the hands of
the transferee, for the purposes of section 718 (a) is determined by reference
to the basis in the hands of the transferor.*

Committee Reports

**Report—Ways and Means Committee
(77th Cong., 2d Sess., H. Rept. 2333).—**
A "transferee upon an exchange" is defined in the same terms as a similar
transferee under existing law, and "exchange" is broadened to include exchanges of the type described in section
112 (b) (3). (p. 156-157)

**Report—Senate Finance Committee
(77th Cong., 2d Sess., S. Rept. 1631).—**
Your committee has revised and simplified the definition of "exchange" and
"transferee upon an exchange" and has
added the term "transferor." It has
provided that the term "exchange"
means a transaction by which one corporation, called the "transferee," receives property of another corporation,
called the transferor, and the basis of the
property so received, in the hands of the
transferee, for the purposes of section
718 (a) (relating to the definition of
equity invested capital) is determined by

reference to the basis in the hands of the
transferor. (p. 223)

**Report—Conference Committee (77th
Cong., 2d Sess., H. Rept. 2586).—**
Amendment No. 378: This amendment
revises and simplifies the definitions of
"exchange" and "transferee upon an
exchange" and adds the term "transferor" in connection with the rules
provided for determining invested capital as the result of certain tax free
exchanges and "intercorporate liquidations." It is provided that the term
"exchange" means a transaction by
which one corporation, called the "transferee," receives property of another corporation, called the "transferor," and
the basis of the property so received, in
the hands of the transferee, for the purposes of section 718 (a) (relating to the
definition of equity invested capital) is
determined by reference to the basis in
the hands of the transferor. (p. 67-68)

Committee Hearings

**Hearings—Senate Finance Commit-
tee.—**Including as an exchange any is-

suance or acquisition of stock of another
corporation. (C. W. Lewis, p. 2207-12)

1943 Act

**Hearings—Ways and Means Commit-
tee.—**Extending provision to reorganizations generally. (E. C. Alvord, p.
685; Controllers Institute of America,
p. 1332)

**Hearings—Senate Finance Commit-
tee.—**Extending provision to reorganizations generally. (E. C. Alvord, p.
615; A. B. Chapman, p. 831)

> Sec. 760(a)(2)
> Sec. 760(b)
> Sec. 760(c)

[SEC. 760.   EXCHANGES.]

[(a)   **Definitions, Etc.**—For the purposes of this section—]

(2)   **Determination of Basis of Property Received.**—*The basis, in the hands of the transferee, of the property of the transferor received by the transferee upon the exchange shall be determined in accordance with section 718 (a).*

(b)   **Rule.**—In the application of section 718 (a) to a transferee upon an exchange in determining the amount paid in for stock of the transferee, or as paid-in surplus or as a contribution to capital of the transferee, in connection with such exchange, only an amount shall be deemed to have been so paid in equal to the excess of the basis (379) (for determining loss) in the hands of the transferee of the property of the transferor received by the transferee upon the exchange over the sum of—

(1)   The amount of any liability of the transferor assumed upon the exchange and of any liability subject to which such property was so received, plus

(2)   The amount of any liability of the transferee (not arising out of any liability described in paragraph (1)) constituting consideration for the property so received, plus

(3)   The aggregate of the amount of any money and the fair market value of any other property (other than such stock and other than property described in paragraphs (1) and (2)) transferred to the transferor.

(c)   **Reduction in Daily Invested Capital.**—In the application of section 717 to a transferee upon an exchange, the daily invested capital for any day after such exchange shall be reduced by an amount equal to the amount by which the sum of the amounts specified in paragraphs (1), (2), and (3) of subsection (b) exceeds the basis (380) (for determining loss) in the hands of the transferee of the property of the transferor received upon the exchange.

Committee Reports

Report—Ways and Means Committee (77th Cong., 2d Sess., H. Rept. 2333).— Section 760 provides that in the application of section 718 (a) to a transferee upon an exchange, in determining the amount paid in for stock, or as paid-in surplus, or as a contribution to capital in connection with such exchange, such amount shall be deemed to be the excess of the basis for determining loss in the hands of the transferee of the property so received from the transferor over the sum of (1) the amount of any liability of the transferor assumed upon the exchange and of any liability subject to which the property was so received; (2) the amount of any other liability of the transferee constituting consideration for the property so received; and (3) the aggregate of the amount of any money and the fair market value of any other property transferred to the transferor. (p. 156)

The basis in the hands of the transferee of the property received upon the exchange from the transferor is to be determined in accordance with the provisions of section 718 (a) (2), namely, the basis (unadjusted) for determining loss, adjusted, with respect to the period before its receipt by the transferee upon the exchange, by an amount equal to the adjustment proper under section 115 (1) for determining earnings or profits. If the property was not disposed of before the taxable year, such unadjusted basis is that prescribed by the law applicable to the taxable year. If the property was disposed of before the taxable year, such unadjusted basis is that prescribed by the law applicable to the year of disposition. Since the aggregate of the liabilities to which the transferee was subject, or which it assumed or created, and the money and property transferred to the transferor may be in excess of the basis in the hands of the transferee of the property acquired from the transferor, it is provided that the daily invested capital of the transferee for any day after the exchange shall be reduced by an amount equal to such excess. (p. 157)

Report—Senate Finance Committee (77th Cong., 2d Sess., S. Rept. 1631).— Same as p. 156 of Ways and Means Committee Report. (p. 222-223)

Same as p. 157 of Ways and Means Committee Report, except that at the end of the third sentence, there is the phrase "without regard to March 1, 1913

value". In addition there is in the report the following:

Under section 751 of existing law, and under section 760 which has been inserted by this bill to amend section 751, for years beginning after December 31, 1941 (relating to invested capital in case of certain tax-free exchanges), invested capital of a "transferee," as defined in such sections, is computed by taking into account the adjusted basis for determining loss in the hands of the transferee of property received from the transferor. Any loss sustained by the transferor will be reflected in the invested capital of the transferee either in a reduced basis of assets received from the transferor or in a reduced amount of property which will be deemed to have been paid in for stock in case the transferor used borrowed funds to pay its losses, since such sections provide for a reduction in the amount of property deemed to be paid in for stock by the amount of indebtedness of the transferor. Thus, the so-called deficit rule is not applicable in the case of such tax-free exchanges and reorganizations. (p. 193)

Report—Conference Committee (77th Cong., 2d Sess., H. Rept. 2586).—This amendment also provides that the basis in the hands of the transferee of the property received upon the exchange from the transferor is to be determined in accordance with the provisions of section 718 (a) (2), namely, the basis (unadjusted) for determining loss, adjusted, with respect to the period before its receipt by the transferee upon the exchange, by an amount equal to the adjustment proper under section 115 (1) for determining earnings or profits. The House recedes.

Amendments Nos. 379 and 380: These amendments are technical amendments; the House recedes. (p. 68)

Committee Hearings

Hearings—Senate Finance Committee.—Confining transferee adjustments only to those needed to eliminate duplication of invested capital. (E. C. Alvord, p. 1797)

[Set forth on page 344]

[Set forth on page 347] $\frac{1918}{331}$

[Set forth on page 352] $\frac{1917}{204}$

$$\boxed{\text{Sec. 761(a)}}$$

SEC. 761. INVESTED CAPITAL ADJUSTMENT AT THE TIME OF TAX-FREE $\frac{1942}{230(a)}$
           INTERCORPORATE LIQUIDATIONS.

(a) Definition of Intercorporate Liquidation.—~~As used in this section, the term "liquidating transaction" means:~~

~~(1)   The complete liquidation of another corporation under
section 112 (b) (6) or the corresponding provision of a prior revenue
law, or~~

~~(2)   The liquidation of another corporation, or a transaction
having the effect of liquidating in whole or in part, some or all of
the stock of another corporation—~~

~~(A) if gain or loss in whole or in part is not recognized
either in a consolidated income or excess profits tax return or because of the provisions of section 112 (b) (4) or (5), or so much of
section 112 (c) to (e), inclusive, as refers to section 112 (b) (4) or
(5), or the corresponding provision of a prior revenue law, and~~

~~(B) if the property received by the taxpayer has a basis
described in section 113 (b) (2) (A).~~

*As used in this section, the term "intercorporate liquidation" means the
receipt (whether or not after December 31, 1941) by a corporation (hereinafter called the "transferee") of property in complete liquidation of another
corporation (hereinafter called the "transferor"), to which*

*(1)   the provisions of section 112 (b) (6), or the corresponding pro-
vision of a prior revenue law, is applicable or*

*(2)   a provision of law is applicable prescribing the nonrecognition
of gain or loss in whole or in part upon such receipt (including a provision
of the regulations applicable to a consolidated income or excess profits tax
return but not including section 112 (b) (7), (9), or (10) or a corresponding
provision of a prior revenue law),*

*but only if none of such property so received is a stock or a security in
a corporation the stock or securities of which are specified in the law applicable to the receipt of such property as stock or securities permitted
to be received (or which would be permitted to be received if they were the
sole consideration) without the recognition of gain.*

The section heading is as worded by the Senate Finance Committee. The
Ways and Means Committee heading read "Transactions In Liquidation".

Committee Reports

Report—Ways and Means Committee (77th Cong., 2d Sess., H. Rept. 23330).— The invested capital adjustments provided in section 761 are applicable not only to liquidations under section 112 (b) (6) but also to other liquidations or transactions having the effect of liquidations if gain or loss is not recognized for the reasons expressed and if the basis of the property received by the taxpayer is fixed by reference to the basis in the hands of the transferor. Mergers and consolidations of parent and subsidiary, including merger of parent into subsidiary, are liquidating transactions. (p. 158)

Report—Senate Finance Committee (77th Cong., 2d Sess., S. Rept. 1631).—

(1) The term "intercorporate liquidation" has been substituted for the term "liquidating transaction" and defined so as to make it clear that (*a*) only a complete liquidation which is wholly or partially tax-free is included (including a liquidation referred to in the second sentence of sec. 113 (a) (15) and not excluding a liquidation the property received in which has a basis described in sec. 113 (b) (2) (B)); (*b*) a complete liquidation to which is applicable section 112 (b) (7), (9), or (10) is excluded, as is one to which is applicable the provisions dealing with reorganization stock or securities, or the stock or securities of specified corporations. (p. 224)

Sec. 761(b)-(e)

1942
230(a)

[SEC. 761. INVESTED CAPITAL ADJUSTMENT AT THE TIME OF TAX-FREE INTERCORPORATE LIQUIDATIONS.]

(b) **Definition of Plus Adjustment and Minus Adjustment.**—*For the purposes of this section—*

(1) **Plus Adjustment.**—*The term "plus adjustment" means the amount, with respect to an intercorporate liquidation, determined to be equal to the amount by which the aggregate of the amount of money received by the transferee in such intercorporate liquidation, and of the adjusted basis at the time of such receipt of all property (other than money) so received, exceeds the sum of—*

(A) the aggregate of the adjusted basis of each share of stock with respect to which such property was received; such adjusted basis of each share to be determined immediately prior to the receipt of any property in such liquidation with respect to such share, and

(B) the aggregate of the liabilities of the transferor assumed by the transferee in connection with the receipt of such property, of the liabilities (not assumed by the transferee) to which such property so received was subject, and of any other consideration (other than the stock with respect to which such property was received) given by the transferee for such property so received.

(2) **Minus Adjustment.**—*The term "minus adjustment" means the amount, with respect to an intercorporate liquidation, determined to be equal to the amount by which the sum of—*

(A) the aggregate of the adjusted basis of each share of stock with respect to which such property was received; such adjusted basis of

each share to be determined immediately prior to the receipt of any property in such liquidation with respect to such share, and

(B) the aggregate of the liabilities of the transferor assumed by the transferee in connection with the receipt of such property, of the liabilities (not assumed by the transferee) to which such property so received was subject, and of any other consideration (other than the stock with respect to which such property was received) given by the transferee for such property so received

exceeds the aggregate of the amount of the money so received and of the adjusted basis, at the time of receipt, of all property (other than money) so received.

    (3) Rules for Application of Paragraphs (1) and (2).—*In determining the plus adjustment or minus adjustment with respect to any share, the computation shall be made in the same manner as is prescribed in paragraphs (1) and (2) of this subsection, except that there shall be brought into account only that part of each item which is determined to be attributable to such share.*

(c) Rules for the Application of This Section.—

    (1) Stock Having Cost Basis.—*The property received by a transferee in an intercorporate liquidation attributable to a share of stock having in the hands of the transferee a basis determined to be a cost basis, shall be considered to have, for the purposes of subsection (b), an adjusted basis at the time so received determined as follows:*

    (A) The aggregate of the property (other than money) held by the transferor at the time of the acquisition by the transferee of control of the transferor (or, if such share was acquired after the acquisition of such control, at the time of the acquisition of such share, or, if such control was not acquired, at the time immediately prior to the receipt of any property in the intercorporate liquidation in respect of such share) shall be deemed to have an aggregate basis equal to the amount obtained by (i) multiplying the amount of the adjusted basis at such time of such share in the hands of the transferee by the aggregate number of share units in the transferor at such time (the interest represented by such share being taken as the share unit), and (ii) adjusting for the amount of money on hand and the liabilities of the transferor at such time.

    (B) The basis which property of the transferor is deemed to have under subparagraph (A) at the time therein specified shall be used in determining the basis of property subsequently acquired by the transferor the basis of which is determined with reference to the basis of property specified in subparagraph (A).

    (C) The basis which property of the transferor is deemed to have under subparagraphs (A) and (B) at the time therein specified shall be used in determining all subsequent adjustments to the basis of such property.

    (D) The property so received by the transferee shall be deemed to have, at the time of its receipt, the same basis it is deemed to have under the foregoing provisions of this paragraph in the hands of the transferor,

or in the case of property not specified in subparagraph (A) or (B), the same basis it would have had in the hands of the transferor.

(E) Only such part of the aggregate property received by the transferee in the intercorporate liquidation as is attributable to such share shall be considered as having the adjusted basis which property is deemed to have under subparagraphs (A), (B), (C), and (D) of this paragraph.

(2) Basis of Stock Not a Cost Basis.—*The property received by a transferee in an intercorporate liquidation attributable to a share of stock having in the hands of the transferee a basis determined to be a basis other than a cost basis shall, for the purposes of subsection (b), be considered to have, at the time of its receipt, the basis it would have had had the first sentence of section 113 (a) (15) been applicable.*

(3) Definition of Control.—*As used in this subsection, the term "control" means the ownership of stock possessing at least 80 per centum of the total combined voting power of all classes of stock entitled to vote and the ownership of at least 80 per centum of the total number of shares of all other classes of stock (except nonvoting stock which is limited and preferred as to dividends), but only if in both cases such ownership continues until the completion of the intercorporate liquidation.*

(d) Adjustment of Equity Invested Capital.—If property is received by the taxpayer in a liquidating transaction, the equity invested capital for each day following the transaction shall be adjusted as follows:

(1) If the stock of the transferor which is in effect canceled upon such liquidating transaction is determined to have been acquired by the issuance of stock in transactions in which gain or loss in whole or in part was not recognized, there shall be included, in lieu of the amounts determined to be otherwise includible in the equity invested capital of the taxpayer with respect to such stock, the amount determined to be necessary to reflect the equity invested capital and the deficit in earnings and profits, if any, of the transferor with respect to such stock.

(2) If such stock of the transferor is determined not to have been acquired by the issuance of stock in transactions in which gain or loss in whole or in part was not recognized, the equity invested capital of the taxpayer shall be adjusted to the extent necessary to reflect in its accumulated earnings and profits and its earnings and profits for the taxable year the portion of the earnings and profits or the deficit in earnings and profits, as the case may be, of the transferor accumulated subsequent to the date which is determined to be the date of acquisition by the taxpayer of control (or, with respect to stock acquired subsequent to the acquisition of control, the date of acquisition of such stock) of the transferor and determined to be attributable to such stock. For the purposes of the computations under this paragraph, the basis of the property held by the transferor or its predecessor at the time of the acquisition of control (or of acquisition of the stock in the case of property

~~determined to be attributable to stock acquired since the acquisition of control) which is attributable to such stock shall be, in lieu of the basis prescribed by section 113 or the corresponding provision of a prior revenue law, an amount determined by reference to the adjusted basis for determining loss upon a sale or exchange of such stock in the hands of the taxpayer or a predecessor. The basis so assigned shall apply, in lieu of the basis otherwise prescribed in computing any amount (determined by reference to the basis of such property in the hands of the transferor) entering into the computation of the equity invested capital of the taxpayer or any other corporation computing equity invested capital by reference to the equity invested capital of the taxpayer. For the purposes of this paragraph the adjusted basis for determining loss upon a sale or exchange of such stock shall be determined without regard to any adjustment authorized by the last sentence of section 113 (a) (11) which is already reflected in the earnings and profits or deficit in earnings and profits attributable to such stock.~~

If property is received by the transferee in an intercorporate liquidation, in computing the equity invested capital of the transferee for any day following the completion of such intercorporate liquidation—

(1) with respect to any share of stock in the transferor having in the hands of the transferee, immediately prior to the receipt of any property in such intercorporate liquidation, a basis determined to be a cost basis, the earnings and profits or deficit in earnings and profits of the transferee shall be computed as if on the day following the completion of such intercorporate liquidation the transferee had realized a recognized gain equal to the amount of the plus adjustment in respect of such share, or had sustained a recognized loss equal to the amount of the minus adjustment in respect of such share;

(2) with respect to any share of stock in the transferor having in the hands of the transferee, immediately prior to the receipt of any property in such intercorporate liquidation, a basis determined to be a basis other than a cost basis, there shall be treated as an amount includible in the sum specified in section 718 (a) the amount of the plus adjustment with respect to such share, or as an amount includible in the sum specified in section 718 (b) the amount of the minus adjustment with respect to such share.

(e) **Invested Capital Basis.**—*The adjusted basis which property received by the transferee in an intercorporate liquidation is considered to have under the provisions of subsection (c) at the time of its receipt shall be thereafter treated as the adjusted basis, in lieu of the adjusted basis otherwise prescribed, in computing any amount, determined by reference to the basis of such property in the hands of the transferee, entering into the computation of the invested capital of the transferee, or of any other corporation the computation of the invested capital of which is determined by reference to the basis of such property in the hands of the transferee.*

Committee Reports

Report—Ways and Means Committee (77th Cong., 2d Sess., H. Rept. 2333).— Under subsection (b) (2) of section 761, there is included in the invested capital of a taxpayer the amount of its investment in the stock of a subsidiary which has been liquidated under section 112 (b) (6), together with the earnings and profits or deficit in earnings and profits accumulated by the subsidiary after the acquisition of control of its stock by the taxpayer and attributable to such stock. The current rule which increases or decreases the investment of the parent to accord with the invested capital of the subsidiary is abandoned. However, where the invested capital of the parent is not an adequate representation of such investment, subsection (b) (1) provides for the adjustment of the invested capital of the parent to reflect the invested capital of the subsidiary. Although the latter situation will generally occur where the stock of the liquidated subsidiary has been acquired, with a substituted basis, by the issuance of stock in transactions in which gain or loss was not recognized, not every such case will invoke the application of subsection (b) (1). (p. 158)

These adjustments are expressions of principles applicable in the computation of consolidated invested capital where the identical problem of retaining in the invested capital of the parent the investment in the stock of subsidiary versus the inclusion of the invested capital of the subsidiary is posed. Rules are prescribed respecting comparable situations in Consolidated Returns Regulations 110 and it is contemplated that the Commissioner will use a similar approach in the regulations to be prescribed under section 761. (p. 158)

Report—Senate Finance Committee (77th Cong., 2d Sess., S. Rept. 1631).— The amendment made by your committee in section 761 makes numerous technical changes in section 761 of the House bill, and provides certain basic rules for the computation of the adjustment to invested capital.

Under section 718 (a) (5) and (b) (4) of existing law, an adjustment is made in equity invested capital in the case of property received by a taxpayer in a complete liquidation under section 112

(b) (6) (other than one to which the provisions of the second sentence of sec. 113 (a) (15) are applicable) in order to reflect in the invested capital the adjusted basis of the property so received. Section 761 of the House bill makes (in terms of equity invested capital) substantially the same adjustment, but only in certain cases. Typical of such cases is the case of property so received with respect to stock of the liquidated corporation having a substituted basis in the hands of the taxpayer by reason of having been acquired by the taxpayer from individual shareholders in exchange for its own stock in a transaction described in section 112 (g) (1) (B) or the corresponding provision of the prior law. Section 761, as amended by your committee, makes (in terms of adjusted basis) substantially the same adjustment in such cases as is made under existing law.

In other cases (typical of which is the case of property so received with respect to stock acquired by the taxpayer in a cash purchase) section 761 of the House bill changes existing law by providing that a very different adjustment in equity invested capital is to be made; namely, (1) the adjusted basis of the property of the liquidated corporation is to be changed as of the time of the acquisition of control of such corporation by the taxpayer so as to reflect in the adjusted basis of such property at such time the price paid for the stock, (2) a recomputation is to be made (using such changed adjusted basis) of the earnings or profits (or deficit in earnings or profits) of the liquidated corporation attributable to such stock, for the period beginning with the acquisition of control by the taxpayer and ending with the liquidation, and (3) after certain technical adjustments, the amount resulting from the recomputation under (2) is to be treated as an increase or decrease in the earnings and profits of the taxpayer. Section 761, as amended by your committee, makes (in terms of adjusted basis) substantially the same adjustment in such cases. (p. 223-224)

(2) The basic computation to be used in ascertaining the amount of the adjustment is set forth in subsection (b) in terms of adjusted basis.

(3) Certain basic rules are specified

in subsection (c) to be used in determining the adjusted basis which the property of the liquidated corporation is considered to have; and "control" is defined.   The term "cost basis" is used in order that it may be clear that all cases of a basis determined under the initial clause of section 113 (a) are included. (p. 224)

Examples illustrating provisions of section 761 (b), (c), and (d)

I

Corporation P buys all the stock, consisting of 100 shares, of corporation S paying $11,000 cash therefor. Corporations P and S file consolidated returns for 3 years, during which time the parent operated at a gain but the subsidiary had a loss totaling $300 for 2 years and a gain of $400 for 1 year. At the time corporation P bought the stock of S, the latter corporation had assets and liabilities as follows:

Cash	$500
Operating assets	10,600
Total	$11,100

Liabilities	$1,000
Capital stock and earnings and profits	10,100
Total	11,100

At the end of the 3-year period corporation S is liquidated under the provisions of section 112 (b) (6) of the Code. The assets and liabilities of corporation S were as follows on the date of the liquidation:

Cash	$800
Operating assets	10,400
	$11,200

Liabilities	$1.000
Capital stock equity	10,200
	11,200

The adjustment to the earnings and profits account of the parent at the time of the liquidation is equal to the "plus adjustment" computed under section 761 (b) (1)—(sec. 761 (d) (1). If it is assumed that the excess ($900) paid by corporation P for the stock of S over the book value represented goodwill, not shown on the books of corporation S, the "plus adjustment" is computed as follows:

Money and other property ($11,200 plus $900)	$12,100
Deduct:	
Cost basis of stock[1]	$11,000
Liabilities assumed	1,000
	12,000
Plus adjustment, sec. 761 (b) (1)	100

[1] The basis of the stock should not be reduced on account of losses of the subsidiary reported on the consolidated return.

II

Corporation P, which owns 5 shares of $100 par value of stock of corporation S acquired at a cost of $600 in cash, exchanges shares of its own stock for the remaining 95 shares of stock of corporation S. The latter stock takes a substituted basis (a basis other than a cost basis) of $110 per share in the hands of corporation P. The book of S at the time of the acquisition of control by corporation P showed the following:

Cash	$ 500
Depletable assets (net)	6,000
Other assets	4,600
Total	$11,100

Liabilities	$1,000
Capital stock	10,000
Surplus	100
Total	$11,100

One year later the assets and liabilities of corporation S were as follows:

Cash	$ 800
Net depletable assets	5,400
Other assets	5,000
Total	$11,200

Liabilities	$1,000
Capital stock	10,000
Surplus	200
Total	11,200

In computing profit and loss, corporation S had depleted its depletable assets at 10 percent.

Corporation P liquidates corporation S under the provisions of section 112 (b) (6) of the Internal Revenue Code (an intercorporate liquidation under sec. 761 (a) (1).

In determining the plus or minus adjustment to the invested capital of corporation P, it is necessary to make two computations, in view of the special rule contained in section 761 (c), for determining the adjusted basis of property applicable to the shares of stock having a "cost basis."

(a) The first computation (pertaining to those shares having a "basis other than a cost basis") (see sec. 761 (b) (2) and (3)) follows:

Aggregate adjusted basis of 95 shares stock	$10,450	
Liabilities assumed ($1,000 × 95/100)	950	
		$11,400
Deduct: Basis of property ($11,200 × 95/100)		10,640
Difference "minus adjustment" (sec. 761 (b) (2) and (3))		760

(Pertaining to 95 shares having a basis other than cost.)

(b) The second computation (pertaining to those shares having a "cost basis" of $120 per share) involves the ascertainment of the property, other than money, held by the transferor applicable to those 5 shares of stock. Under the formula provided by section 761 (c) (1) (A) the property applicable to those 5 shares is computed as follows:

Cost per share	$120.00
Multiply by share units	100
Product	12,000
Deduct: Cash	500
Balance	11,500
Add: Liabilities	1,000
Total	12,500
$12,500 ÷ 100 (property applicable 1 share)	125
$125 × 5 (property applicable 5 shares)	625

Assuming that the excess paid for the stock of corporation S over the book value thereof ($95) was applicable to the depletable assets, the assets on hand at the time control was acquired had values attributable to the cost of the stock as follows:

Cash (5/100 of $500)	$25
Depletable assets[2] (5/100 of $6,000) + $95)	395
Other assets	230
Total (reflecting basis of stock plus allocable portion of liabilities)	650

[2] Proportionate basis of asset plus excess paid for stock.

Upon the liquidation of corporation S the assets applicable to the 5 shares of stock (having a cost basis) were as follows (sec. 761 (c) (1) (C)):

Cash (5/100 × 800)	$ 40.00
Depletable assets[3] ($395.00 − $39.50)	355.50
Other assets ($5,000 × 5/100)	250.00
Total money and other property	645.50

[3] Adjusted basis minus 1 year depletion at 10 percent.

Computation of adjustment pertaining to 5-shares (sec. 761 (b)):

Basis of stock (5 shares at $120 per share)	$600.00
Liabilities ($1,000 × 5/100)	50.00
Total	650.00
Total money and other property (see above)	645.50
Minus adjustment (sec. 761 (b) (2) and (d) (1))	4.50

Under the provisions of section 761 (d) (1) the above "minus adjustment" of $4.50, applicable to stock having a cost basis constitutes a reduction of the earnings and profits account of the parent upon liquidation of the subsidiary—whereas the "minus adjustment" ($760) pertaining to those shares having a substituted basis constitutes an amount "includible in the sum specified in 718 (b)" (sec. 761 (d) (2)).

If Corporation S had earned $3 per share the adjustment to the parents earnings account attributable to the 5 shares of stock would have been a "plus adjustment" of $5.50. In such case the assets would have been increased to $655.50, or the liabilities would have been decreased to $45.50, thus changing the figures entering into the foregoing computation. (p. 226-228)

Report—Conference Committee (77th Cong., 2d Sess., H. Rept. 2586).—Amendment No. 381 rewrites, with numerous technical and clarifying changes, the provisions of section 761 of the House bill, providing for an invested capital adjustment at the time of a tax-free intercorporate liquidation. (p. 68)

Committee Hearings

Hearings—Senate Finance Committee.—Need for clarification of provision. (W. A. M. Cooper, p. 1609-11; E. C. Alvord, p. 1796; A. B. Chapman, p. 2078-79, 2084-85; C. W. Lewis, p. 2207-12; R. B. Ralls, p. 2350-51)

Confining transferee adjustments only to those needed to eliminate duplication of invested capital. (E. C. Alvord, p. 1797)

1943 Act

Hearings—Ways and Means Committee.—Applying same adjustments in section 761 as section 718. (E. C. Alvord, p. 686; Controllers Institute of America, p. 1332)

Hearings—Senate Finance Committee.—Applying same adjustments in section 761 as section 718. (E. C. Alvord, p. 616; A. B. Chapman, p. 831)

1918
330
                   [Set forth on page 344]

1918
331
                   [Set forth on page 347]

1917
204
                   [Set forth on page 352]

Sec. 761(f)

1942
230(a)

[SEC. 761. INVESTED CAPITAL ADJUSTMENT AT THE TIME OF TAX-FREE INTERCORPORATE LIQUIDATIONS.]

(f) Statutory[1] Mergers and Consolidations.—~~In determining the amount of the adjustments under subsections (a) and (b), if a corporation owned stock in another corporation, and~~

(1) such corporations are merged or consolidated in a statutory merger or consolidation, or

(2) such corporations are parties to a liquidating transaction which results in the liquidation of such stock in a manner similar to that resulting from a statutory merger or consolidation, for the purposes of this section such stock shall be considered to have been acquired by the corporation resulting from the merger, consolidation, or transaction, and the properties attributable thereto received by it in liquidation of such stock. *If a corporation owns stock in another corporation and such corporations are merged or consolidated in a statutory merger or consolidation, then for the purposes of this section and section 718 such stock shall be considered to have been acquired (in such statutory merger or consolidation) by the corporation resulting from the statutory merger or consolidation, and the properties of such other corporation attributable to such stock to have been received by such resulting corporation as a transferee from such other corporation as a transferor in an intercorporate liquidation.*

¹ The word "Statutory" was added by the Senate Finance Committee.

[Set forth on page 344]   1918
                                       330

[Set forth on page 347]   1918
                                       331

[Set forth on page 352]   1917
                                       204

Sec. 761(g)

[SEC. 761. INVESTED CAPITAL ADJUSTMENT AT THE TIME OF TAX-   1942
FREE INTERCORPORATE LIQUIDATIONS.]   230(a)

(g) Determinations.—

(1) Regulations.—Any determination which is required to be made under this section shall be made in accordance with regulations which shall be prescribed by the Commissioner with the approval of the Secretary. *Any determination which is required to be made under this section (including determinations in applying this section in cases where there is a series of transferees of the property and cases where the stock of the transferor is acquired by the transferee from another corporation, and the determinations of the basis and adjusted basis which property or items thereof have or are considered to have) shall be made in accordance with regulations which shall be prescribed by the Commissioner with the approval of the Secretary. If*

the transferor or the transferee is a foreign corporation, the provisions of this section shall apply to such extent and under such conditions and limitations as may be provided in such regulations.

    (2) Application to Liquidation Extending Over Long Period.— *The Commissioner is authorized to prescribe rules similar to those provided in this section with respect to the days within the period beginning with the date on which the first property is received in the intercorporate liquidation and ending with the day of its completion; and the extent to which, and the conditions and limitations under which, such rules are to be applicable.*

Committee Reports

Report—Ways and Means Committee (77th Cong., 2d Sess., H. Rept. 2333).— The Commissioner is therefore authorized to prescribe, in regulations approved by the Secretary, and under the general principles enunciated in section 761, the specific situations to which the adjustments provided in such section are applicable. Such regulations shall also prescribe the method of ascertaining (a) the amount of equity invested capital, of accumulated earnings and profits or deficit in earnings and profits attributable to the stock of the liquidated subsidiary, (b) the date of the acquisition of control of such subsidiary and the character of such control (which may vary in different cases), (c) the allocation of the adjusted basis of the stock of the subsidiary to the assets of such subsidiary (in order to avoid duplication of the invested capital of the parent through its earnings and profits account when the assets received upon the liquidation are sold or when deductions for depletion or depreciation are taken with respect thereto), and (d) of all other factors which are required to be determined under section 761. (p. 158)

    Rules are prescribed respecting comparable situations in Consolidated Returns Regulations 110 and it is contemplated that the Commissioner will use a similar approach in the regulations to be prescribed under section 761. It is contemplated that the regulations under section 761 will provide appropriate rules for all the situations to which rules prescribed by sections 718 (a) (5), 718 (b) (4), and 718 (c) (4) of existing law are now applicable. Accordingly, these statutory rules are not applicable to taxable years beginning after December 31, 1941. (p. 158)

Report—Senate Finance Committee (77th Cong., 2d Sess., S. Rept. 1631).— (4) Authority is given the Commissioner in his discretion to make an adjustment prior to the completion of the liquidation, in order to provide a rule for cases in which circumstances beyond the control of the taxpayer cause the liquidation to extend over a long period, or cases in which the period is prolonged for the avoidance of tax, and (p. 224)

    Subsection (f) (as did the House bill) makes provision for the case of a statutory merger or consolidation in which one of the corporations merged or consolidated owns stock in the other corporation merged or consolidated. In such case, a rule is necessary in order to determine whether such stock, or the properties of the other corporation attributable to such stock, have been acquired by the corporation resulting from the merger or consolidation. If such stock represents a cash investment by its owner, it seems inappropriate that the corporation resulting from the statutory merger or consolidation should be deprived of that part of the equity invested capital represented in the purchase price of such stock which is not reflected in the adjusted basis of the property of the other corporation. Subsection (f) therefore provides that the corporation resulting from the statutory merger or consolidation shall be considered to have acquired such stock in such statutory merger or consolidation with a basis in its hands of such stock determined under section 113 (a) (7), with the result that, to the extent to which under sections 718 and 760 such stock is considered to have been paid in for stock of the resulting corporation, the cash investment will be reflected in the equity invested capital of the resulting corporation. The subsection further provides that the properties attributable to such stock shall be considered as having been received by such resulting corporation as a transferee from such other corporation as a transferor in an intercorporate liquidation, with the result that the adjustments prescribed by subsection (d) become applicable.

The section, as amended by your committee, contemplates (as did the House bill) the application of the section under regulations which the Commissioner is directed to prescribe. Because of the variety of situations in which stock or property may be acquired, to which must be applied the general rules of the section, the provisions of subsection (g) have been somewhat expanded in order to make it clear that the subsection contemplates rules on the following matters:

(1) 'A series of transferees of the property": The extent to which, if the transferor is in a prior transaction a transferee, such transferor is to stand in the shoes of his transferor in the preceding transaction in determining acquisition of control, adjusted basis, etc.; the application of subsections (c) and (e) in such cases.

(2) "The stock of the transferor is acquired by the transferee from another corporation": The extent to which the transferee is to be regarded as standing in the shoes of such other corporation, in determining cost basis, acquisition of control, adjusted basis, etc.; the application of subsections (c) and (e) in such cases.

(3) "Basis and adjusted basis": The application of the terms "cost basis" and "basis other than a cost basis"; the application of the rules prescribed in the last two sentences of section 718 (a) (2) as amended by the bill; the application of the excess profits tax basis if it be different from the income tax basis; the nonapplication of adjustments authorized in section 113 (a) (11), or other adjustments inappropriate in the computation of equity invested capital; the application of other adjustments necessary to reflect invested capital, or prevent duplication or distortion; the basis to be used under section 720; the assignment to specific property of the aggregate adjusted basis under subsection (c), adjustments to be made, and the accounting principles to be used in such assignment, or adjustment. (p. 225-226)

REVENUE ACT OF 1918

Sec. 300. That when used in this title the terms "taxable year," "fiscal year," ~~(224)~~ *"personal service corporation," "paid or accrued,"* and "dividends" shall have the same meaning as provided for the purposes of income tax in ~~(225)~~ ~~section 200~~ *sections 200 and 201.* * * *

Committee Reports

Report—Ways and Means Committee (65th Cong., 2d Sess., H. Rept. 767).— In this part it is provided that the terms "taxable year," "fiscal year," and "dividends" shall have the same meaning for the purpose of the excess profits tax and war profits tax title as is provided for the purpose of the income tax in section 200, * * * (p. 16)

Report—Conference Committee (65th Cong., 3d Sess., H. Rept. 1037).— Amendments Nos. 224, 225, and 226: These amendments are clerical changes; and the House recedes. (p. 64)

Sec. 303. ~~That in the case of a corporation the earnings of which are to be ascribed primarily to the activities of the principal owners or stockholders who are themselves regularly engaged in the active conduct of the affairs of the corporation, and in which capital (whether invested, borrowed, rented, or otherwise secured) is not directly or indirectly a material income-producing factor, there shall be levied, collected, and paid for each taxable year upon its net income * * *~~

~~A corporation 50 per centum or more of whose gross income (as defined in section 213 for income tax purposes) consists of gains or profits derived from purchase and sale, or of gains, profits, or commissions derived from Government contracts, or whose invested capital is more than $100,000, shall not be subject to the tax imposed by this section, but shall be subject to the tax imposed by section 301.~~

~~Wherever in this Act reference is made to "war profits" or "excess profits" taxes, and the context shows that taxes imposed by Act of Congress are referred to, such reference shall include the tax imposed by this section.~~

*That if part of the net income of a corporation is derived (1) from a trade or business (or a branch of a trade or business) in which the employment of capital is necessary, and (2) a part (constituting not less than 30 per centum of its total net income) is derived from a separate trade or business (or a distinctly separate branch of the trade or business) which if constituting the sole trade or business would bring it within the class of "personal service corporations," then (under regulations prescribed by the Commissioner with the approval of the Secretary) the tax * * **

322

Committee Reports

Report—Ways and Means Committee (65th Cong., 2d Sess., H. Rept. 767).— In certain instances the experience under the existing excess-profits tax law has been that there are certain classes of corporations the earnings of which are to be ascribed primarily to the activities of the principal owners or stockholders and in which capital is not directly or indirectly a material income-producing factor. In such cases the excess-profits tax would bear too heavily upon such corporation, as practically all or by far the greater portion of the income would be subject to the rate provided in the highest excess-profits bracket. In order to equalize this situation the bill provides in section 303 that in the case of such a corporation, * * *. It is provided, however, that no corporation shall be taxable under this provision if 50 per cent or more of its gross income consists of gains or profits derived from purchase or sale, or of gains, profits, or commissions derived from Government contracts, or if the invested capital of such corporation is more than $100,000. Such corporations will be taxable under section 301 under the excess-profits method or the war-profits method, whichever will yield the higher tax. (p. 16-17)

Report—Senate Finance Committee (65th Cong., 3d Sess., S. Rept. 617).— The committee proposes that personal-service corporations (those whose earnings are to be ascribed primarily to the activities of the principal owners or stockholders) be exempted from the profits tax and be treated as partnerships; i. e., that the stockholders, like partners, be subject both to normal tax and surtaxes upon the entire earnings of the corporation, whether distributed or not. When the undivided shares of such earnings are large the additional surtaxes will more than make up for the loss of the profits tax. The war excess-profits tax, moreover, can not be applied to personal-service corporations, because such corporations have, as a rule, very little invested capital, and the tax, if computed in the ordinary way, would be excessive. The committee thus solves the old problem of dealing with the close corporation, which is used as a medium of avoiding payment of surtaxes. (p. 11)

Report—Conference Committee (65th Cong., 3d Sess., H. Rept. 1037).— Amendment No. 233: The House bill (in section 303) provided a special rate * * * the case of a corporation, the earnings of which are to be ascribed primarily to the activities of the principal owners or stockholders who are themselves regularly engaged in the active conduct of the affairs of the corporation. The Senate amendment strikes out this provision, having defined (by amendment 11),[1] the above class of corporations as "personal-service corporations" and having provided (by amendments[2] 92 and 132) that they should be exempt from income, war-profits, and excess-profits taxes, and be treated as partnerships. The Senate amendment also inserted, as section 303, an amendment providing for the taxation of a corporation, the net income of which is derived in part (1) from a trade or business in which the employment of capital is necessary, and in part (2) from a separate trade or business, which if constituting the sole trade or business, would bring it within the class of "personal-service corporations." The House recedes with amendments making clerical changes. (p. 65)

[1] Relating to sec. 200.
[2] Relating to secs. 218(e) and 231(14), respectively.

Congressional Discussion

Discussion—House (Cong. Rec. Vol. 56).—MR. STAFFORD. * * * Will the chairman of the committee be kind enough to give an instance of the character of corporations that would be qualified as stated in section 303?

MR. KITCHIN. An insurance agency that writes insurance on commissions and requires no capital; a corporation of architects, which require no capital; a lawyers' guaranty title company that looks up titles and requires no capital; any company where the earnings may be ascribed primarily to personal services and in which capital is not a material income-producing factor.

MR. STAFFORD. Where the capital is nominal?

MR. KITCHIN. Where it is not actually required—where the business does not require them to have capital. (p. 10449)

MR. SCOTT of Michigan. * * * Mr. Chairman, I rise for the purpose of asking the chairman of the committee with reference to the word "corporation," in line 6, whether it would include a partnership or a joint association?

MR. KITCHIN. The excess-profits and war-profits tax does not apply to partnerships or individuals.

MR. SCOTT of Michigan. My sole purpose was in making a beneficial correction of this section, and this thought presents itself: Here is a corporation, the membership of which are devoting their entire time to the activities of the corporation. Now, under the provisions of the bill as it now stands they are taxed, but if the same concern were operated not as a corporation, but as a partnership or a joint company, they would not be taxed.

MR. KITCHIN. The stockholders who are carrying on a business as managers and giving their personal services are entitled to a reasonable compensation for their personal services, while in a corporation, a copartnership, they are not; so they even up from that angle. (p. 10449)

Discussion—Senate (Cong. Rec. Vol. 57).—MR. SMOOT. * * * The reason for this remedial provision arises from the following fact: Personal service corporations many times have very little capital invested, yet there are exceedingly large profits produced by the personal efforts of the members of the corporation. If only the exemptions were allowed under the corporation provisions of the pending measure they would be very small, and in every case which was brought to the attention of the committee, at least, their gains would fall under the highest percentage bracket, and there would be imposed upon them a tax which would be very unjust. After the distribution was made they would also be taxed on the income, or on that portion that was left after paying taxes on the net profits of the corporation. (p. 501)

Discussion—House; on Report of Conference Committee (Cong. Rec. Vol.

57).—MR. KITCHIN. * * * There is one very ingenious provision that the Senate put in, which is a very wise one. It accomplishes what the House intended to accomplish and what its provision substantially would accomplish, but it would not do it in such a skillful and scientific way as will the Senate provision, which the House conferees agreed to, with an amendment excepting from its application the war-contract corporation. The House bill provided that in the case of a corporation the earnings of which are to be ascribed primarily to the activities of the stockholders of the corporation and not to the capital invested, where capital is not a material income-producing factor, the excess-profit tax should not exceed 20 per cent. That would take care of corporations doing the business of architecture, corporations doing the business of insurance agencies, or that had no capital invested, or where whatever little capital was invested was not a material factor that produced the income. (p. 3008)

Discussion—Senate; on Report of Conference Committee (Cong. Rec. Vol. 57).—MR. SIMMONS. * * * Mr. President, the Senate made a very striking amendment to the House bill in its amendment permitting a corporation whose principal income is derived from the personal activities of the principal stockholders to be taxed as a partnership instead of as a corporation. The fundamental reason for that change is found in the fact that the excess-profits taxes and the war-profits taxes for 1918 would be extremely oppressive—I might use a harsher term than that—would be almost destructive if they were imposed without allowing a reasonable exemption or deduction.

This exemption or deduction is based very largely upon the invested capital. With a deduction which for excess-profits tax can not be less than 8 per cent of the invested capital, and for war-profits tax can not be less than 10 per cent of the invested capital—with this allowance entirely exempt from taxation—a capitalistic corporation is by the very letter of the law guaranteed a reasonable profit, however high the tax may be upon that part of their profits in excess of this allowance, so that no concern whose business is based upon capital, whose profits are the returns of capital, can be bankrupted or can be deprived of what in the business world is regarded as a fair return upon the capital invested in the business. But where the income is not derived from capital, but is derived from the personal exertions of the principal owners of the corporation, there can be no exemption based upon invested capital. If these excess-profits and war-profits taxes were imposed, therefore, upon a corporation that had no capital or very little capital, they would constitute a flat tax upon the entire earnings, without any deductions except for the actual expenses incurred in the conduct of the business. That would be a great hardship. We sought in the present law to remedy that by imposing a flat 8 per cent tax in such cases. That was an unsatisfactory solution. The House sought in this bill to solve the problem by imposing a flat tax of 20 per cent upon the net income in lieu of the profits tax. That was not a satisfactory solution. But when we permit such concerns to be taxed as a partnership we exempt them under the present law from excess-profits taxes and from war-profits taxes, and put

them upon a parity with the individual and the partnership paying taxes only upon their income.

The Senate made that amendment, and I think it was one of the wisest amendments made to the bill. The House conferees accepted that amendment, but after reflection the House conferees and the Senate conferees concluded that there was a class of profits made largely by corporations with no capital invested, but which rely only on their personal services, that would escape just taxation under the Senate amendment. So, by mutual consent, we added a provision to the bill exempting from this privilege accorded personal-service corporations 50 per cent or more of whose gross incomes consists of—

Gains, profits, commissions, or other income derived from a Government contract or contracts made between April 6, 1917, and November 11, 1918, both dates inclusive.

We also provided that this provision should not include corporations "50 per cent or more of whose gross income consists of gains, profits, or income derived from trading as a principal." (p. 3135-36)

Sec. 304.   (a) That the corporations enumerated in section 231 shall, to the extent that they are exempt from income tax under Title II, be exempt from taxation under this title.

    (b)   (234) ~~The taxes imposed by this title shall not be imposed in the case of a foreign corporation the net income of which during the taxable year is less than $3,000.~~ [*Life insurance companies, mutual insurance companies, and insurance companies taxable under section 504 shall be exempt from taxation under this title.*] * * *

Secs.
304(a)
304(b)

Committee Reports

Report—Ways and Means Committee (65th Cong., 2d Sess., H. Rept. 767).— All corporations exempt under the income-tax title will be exempt from the excess-profits or war-profits tax. A list of these corporations will be found in section 231. (p. 17)

Report—Conference Committee (65th Cong., 3d Sess., H. Rept. 1037).— Amendments Nos. 234 and 235: Amendment 234 provided—as part of the Senate plan of insurance taxation—that certain insurance companies should be exempted from war tax and excess profits taxes. The House recedes. * * * (p. 65)

    (c)   *In the case of any corporation engaged in the mining of gold, the portion of the net income derived from the mining of gold shall be exempt from the tax imposed by this title, and the tax on the remaining portion of the net income shall be* [*computed upon the basis of an invested capital which bears the same ratio to the full invested capital as*] THE PRO-

Sec.
304(c)

PORTION OF A TAX COMPUTED WITHOUT THE BENEFIT
OF THIS SUBDIVISION WHICH *such remaining portion of the net
income bears to the entire net income.*

Committee Reports

Report—Conference Committee (65th Cong., 3d Sess., H. Rept. 1037).— Amendment No. 236: This amendment provides that in the case of any corporation engaged in the mining of gold the portion of the net income derived from the mining of gold shall be exempt from the war profits and excess profits tax; and the House recedes with an amendment providing that the tax on the remaining portion of the net income shall be the proportion of a tax computed without the benefit of this exemption which such remaining portion of the net income bears to the entire net income. (p. 65)

Sec. 305

Sec. 305. That if a tax is computed under this title for a period of less than twelve months, the specific exemption of $3,000, wherever referred to in this title, shall be reduced to an amount which is the same proportion of $3,000 as the number of months in the period is of twelve months.

Sec. 310

Sec. 310. That as used in this title the term "prewar period" means the calendar years 1911, 1912, and 1913, or, if a corporation was not in existence during the whole of such period, then as many of such years during the whole of which the corporation was in existence.

Committee Reports

Report—Ways and Means Committee (65th Cong., 2d Sess., H. Rept. 767).— This part fixes the prewar period as the calendar years 1911, 1912, and 1913, or, if a corporation was not in existence during the whole of such period, then as many of such years during the whole of which the corporation was in existence. (p. 17)

Sec. 311(a)

Sec. 311. (a) That the war-profits credit shall consist of the sum of:

*   *   *

(2) An amount equal to the average net income of the corporation for the prewar period, plus or minus, as the case may be, 10 per centum of the (240) ~~invested capital added or withdrawn since the close of the prewar period; but~~ *if* difference between the average invested capital for the prewar period and the invested capital for the taxable year. *If* the tax is computed for a period of less than twelve months such amount shall be reduced to the same proportion thereof as the number of months in the period is of twelve months.

Committee Reports

Report—Ways and Means Committee (65th Cong., 2d Sess., H. Rept. 767).— The bill provides a tax of 80 per cent upon the amount of the net income in excess of the war-profits credit. The war-profits credit will be determined in the following way: Every corporation will be allowed a specific exemption of $3,000 and in addition its average prewar earnings for the prewar period 1911, 1912, and 1913. In the case of corporations who have increased their capital since the prewar period, the bill provides that an additional amount be allowed equal to 10 per cent of the additional invested capital employed during the taxable year. If the corporation has reduced its capital since the prewar period, the allowance must be decreased by an amount equal to 10 per cent of the invested capital withdrawn. If a corporation was not in existence during the whole of any one calendar year during the prewar period, or if it had no net income for the prewar period, or if its prewar earnings were less than 10 per cent of its invested capital for the taxable year, it will be entitled to a specific exemption of $3,000 and an additional amount equal to 10 per cent of the invested capital for the taxable year. (p. 17)

In view of the high rate of tax imposed by this method and in view of the fact that owing to a serious depression in many industries, many corporations were making very small profits during the prewar period, your committee believes that it is only equitable and fair to allow such corporations a minimum exemption of 10 per cent and that such an exemption is necessary to allow such corporations a sufficient return upon their investment in order to assure them a reasonable profit and at the same time to enable them to maintain their plants as going concerns. (p. 17-18)

Report—Senate Finance Committee (65th Cong., 3d Sess., S. Rept. 617).— The House bill defines the war-profits credit for the new corporation—i. e., the corporation organized since the prewar period—as the sum of $3,000 plus 10 per cent of the invested capital for the taxable year. This places the new corporation in a trade or business whose normal profits for the prewar period were above 10 per cent at a great disadvantage as compared with corporations which happened to be in existence during the prewar period. A majority of the older corporations might enjoy a deduction of from 12 to 15 per cent, because their

profits in the prewar period were that high, but the new corporation under the House bill would be restricted to a deduction of 10 per cent.

The committee accordingly recommends that the new corporation be placed on an equality with the old corporation in this respect by granting to the new corporation a percentage deduction equal to same per cent of its invested capital as was earned on the average, during the prewar period, by representative corporations engaged in a trade or business of the same general class as that conducted by the new corporation in question. (p. 13)

Report—Conference Committee (65th Cong., 3d Sess., H. Rept. 1037).— Amendment No. 240: In computing the war-profits credit, the House bill provided that the average net income for the prewar period should be increased or diminished by 10 per cent of the "invested capital added or withdrawn since the close of the prewar period." The Senate amendment bases this allowance on the "difference between the average invested capital for the prewar period and the invested capital for the taxable year"; and the House recedes. (p. 65-66)

Amendment No. 241: This amendment is a clerical change necessitated by amendment 242,[1] and the House recedes. (p. 66)

[1] Relating to sec. 311(c).

Amendment No. 242: This amendment provides that if a corporation was not in existence during the whole of at least one calendar year during the prewar period, its war-profits credit shall be * * * an amount equal to the same percentage of the invested capital, for the prewar period, of corporations engaged in a trade or business of the same general class as that conducted by the taxpayer; but such amount shall in no case be less than 10 per cent of the invested capital of the taxpayer for the taxable year. (p. 66)

(b) If the corporation **(241)** ~~was not in existence during the whole of any one calendar year during the prewar period, or if it~~ had no net income for the prewar period, or if the amount computed under paragraph (2) of subdivision (a) is less than 10 per centum of its invested capital for the taxable year, then the war-profits credit shall be the sum of:

Secs.
311(b)
311(c)
311(d)

* * *

(2) An amount equal to 10 per centum of the invested capital for the taxable year.

(c) *If the corporation was not in existence during the whole of at least one calendar year during the prewar period, then,* EXCEPT AS PROVIDED IN SUBDIVISION (D), *the war-profits credit shall be the sum of:*

* * *

(2) *An amount equal to the same percentage of the invested capital of the taxpayer for the taxable year as the average percentage of net income to invested capital, for the prewar period, of corporations engaged in a trade or business of the same general class as that conducted by the taxpayer; but such amount shall in no case be less than 10 per centum of the invested capital of the taxpayer for the taxable year. Such average percentage shall be determined by the Commissioner on the basis of data contained in returns made under Title II of the Revenue Act of 1917, and the average known as the median shall be used.* * * *

(d)[1] The war-profits credit shall be determined in the manner provided in subdivision (b) instead of in the manner provided in subdivision (c), in the case of any corporation which was not in existence during the whole of at least one calendar year during the prewar period, if (1) a majority of its stock at any time during the taxable year is owned or controlled, directly or indirectly, by a corporation which was in existence during the whole of at least one calendar year during the prewar period, or if (2) 50 per centum or more of its gross income (as computed under section 233 for income tax purposes) consists of gains, profits, commissions, or other income, derived from a government contract or contracts made between April 6, 1917, and November 11, 1918, both dates inclusive.

[1] This subsection was added by the Conference Committee.

Committee Reports

Report—Conference Committee (65th Cong., 3d Sess., H. Rept. 1037).—The House recedes with an amendment providing that the ordinary war profits credit (i. e., $3,000 plus 10 per cent of the invested capital for the taxable year) shall apply in the case of any "new" corporation if (1) a majority of its stock at any time during the taxable year is owned or controlled, directly or indirectly, by a corporation which was in existence during the whole of at least one calendar year during the prewar period, or if (2) 50 per cent or more of its gross income consists of gains, profits, commissions, or other income derived from a Government contract or contracts made between April 6, 1917, and November 11, 1918, both dates inclusive. (p. 66)

Congressional Discussion

Discussion—Senate; on Report of Conference Committee (Cong. Rec. Vol. 57).—Mr. PENROSE. * * * A similar change was made in the conference in connection with the war-profits credit or deduction for new corporations; that is, corporations organized after January 1, 1913. The House gave new corporations a deduction of 10 per cent of their invested capital for the taxable year. The Senate liberalized this and made the deduction of new corporations the same percentage of their invested capital for the taxable year as was earned by corporations in the same general class of trade or business during the prewar period. The conferees adopted the Senate method, but excepted newly organized subsidiaries and corporations whose principal income is derived from war contracts. (p. 3182)

Sec. 320. (a) That for the purpose of this title the net income of a corporation shall be ascertained and returned—

(1) For the calendar years 1911 and 1912 upon the same basis and in the same manner as provided in section 38 of the Act entitled "An Act to provide revenue, equalize duties, and encourage the industries of the United States, and for other purposes," approved August 5, 1909, except that taxes imposed by such section and paid by the corporation within the year shall be included;

(2) For the calendar year 1913 upon the same basis and in the same manner as provided in Section II of the Act entitled "An Act to reduce tariff duties and to provide revenue for the Government, and for other purposes," approved October 3, 1913, except that taxes imposed by section 38 of such Act of August 5, 1909, and paid by the corporation within the year shall be included, and except that the amounts received by it as dividends upon the stock or from the net earnings of other corporations subject to the tax imposed by Section II of such Act of October 3, 1913, shall be deducted; and

(3) For the taxable year upon the same basis and in the same manner as provided for income tax purposes in Title II of this Act (247), except that in the case of oil and gas wells there shall be deducted (in lieu of the deduction provided in clause (a) of paragraph (9) of subdivision (a) of section 234) a reasonable allowance for depletion (including in the case of producers or prospectors a reasonable allowance for hazard not to exceed 10 per centum of the value in the ground of the oil withdrawn during the taxable year) such deduction to be made under rules and regulations to be prescribed by the Commissioner with the approval of the Secretary.

Committee Reports

Report—Ways and Means Committee (65th Cong., 2d Sess., H. Rept. 767).— The net income of corporations for the prewar period 1911, 1912, and 1913 will be computed exactly as under the existing excess-profits .tax law and will be comparatively easy to ascertain, since the returns are already on file in the Treasury Department. The net income for the taxable year will be computed upon the same basis and in the same manner as is provided for computing the corporate income under Title II of the proposed bill. (p. 18)

Report—Conference Committee (65th Cong., 3d Sess., H. Rept. 1037).— Amendment No. 247: The Senate amendment as a consequence of the adoption of amendment[1] 159 struck out the allowance for hazard provided for producers or prospectors of oil in the House bill at this point; and the House recedes. (p. 66)

[1] Relating to sec. 234(a)(9).

Committee Hearings

Hearings—Ways and Means Committee.—Allowing credit for payment of debts. (J. H. Stewart, p. 635-637)

Sec. 320(b)

(b)   The average net income for the prewar period shall be determined by dividing the number of years within that period during the whole of which the corporation was in existence into the sum of the net income for such years, even though there may have been no net income for one or more of such years.

Committee Reports

Report—Ways and Means Committee (65th Cong., 2d Sess., H. Rept. 767).— The average net income for the prewar period will be determined by dividing the number of years within that period during the whole of which the corporation was in existence into the sum of the net income for such years, even though there may have been no net income for one or more of such years.   (p. 18)

Sec. 325(a)

Sec. 325.   (a)   That as used in this title—

The term "intangible property" means patents, copyrights, secret processes and formulæ, good will, trade-marks, trade-brands, franchises, and other like property;

The term "tangible property" means stocks, bonds, notes, and other evidences of indebtedness, bills and accounts receivable, leaseholds, and other property other than intangible property;

The term "borrowed capital" means money or other property borrowed, whether represented by bonds, notes, open accounts, or otherwise;

The term "inadmissible assets" means stocks, bonds, and other obligations (other than obligations of the United States), the dividends or interest from which is not included in computing net income, but where the income derived from such assets consists in part of gain or profit derived from the sale or other disposition thereof, 【249】 *or where all or part of the interest derived from such assets is in effect included in the net income because of the limitation on the deduction of interest under paragraph (2) of subdivision (a) of section 234,* a corresponding part of the capital invested in such assets shall not be deemed to be inadmissible 【250】 ~~assets.~~ *assets;* 【251】 *The term "admissible assets" means all assets other than inadmissible assets,* **◁***but only to the extent that they are allowed to be included in invested capital under the provisions of section 326***▷** *valued in accordance with the provisions of subdivision (a) of section 326, section 330, and section 331.*

Committee Reports

Report—Ways and Means Committee (65th Cong., 2d Sess., H. Rept. 767).— The definition of invested capital in the existing law, while rewritten in the proposed bill in the interest of clearness and while changed slightly in order to apply a more liberal rule in a few cases where the existing law has in operation been found to produce certain inequalities, has not been changed in any important particular.

In order to simplify the definition of

invested capital it has been deemed advisable to define certain terms, such as "intangible property," "tangible property," "borrowed capital," and "inadmissible assets." These definitions will be found in section 325 of the bill.

In the case of certain investment banking houses whose business is almost entirely confined to tax-exempt securities, such as municipal and State bonds, a very difficult question arises as to what should be the invested capital of such corporation. Although the definition of invested capital in existing law specifically states that the amount invested in such securities shall not be included in invested capital if the interest income from the same is not subject to income, excess and war profits taxes, the income from the gain upon the sale of these bonds, however, is subject to all the aforementioned taxes. The bill therefore allows such a corporation to add to its invested capital an amount equal to the same proportion of the amount invested in such tax-free securities as the profit from the sale of such securities

bears to the total net income derived from the sale thereof and the interest thereon. (p. 18-19)

Report—Conference Committee (65th Cong., 3d Sess., H. Rept. 1037).— Amendment No. 249: This amendment provides that a corresponding part of the capital invested in "inadmissible assets" shall not be deemed to be inadmissible assets "where all or part of the interest derived from such assets is in effect included in the net income because of the limitation on the deduction of the interest under paragraph (2) of subdivision (a) of section 234"; and the House recedes.

Amendment No. 250: This amendment is a clerical change; and the House recedes.

Amendment No. 251: The term "admissible assets" is by this amendment defined to mean "all assets other than inadmissible assets, valued in accordance with the provisions of subdivision (a) of section 326, section 330 and section 331"; and the House recedes. (p. 66)

(b) For the purposes of this title, the par value of stock or shares shall, in the case of stock or shares (252) *issued at a nominal value or* having no par value, be deemed to be the fair market value as of the date or dates of issue of such stock or shares.

Sec. 325(b)

Committee Reports

Report—Conference Committee (65th Cong., 3d Sess., H. Rept. 1037).— Amendment No. 252: This amendment provides that the par value of stock or shares shall, in the case of stock or shares

issued at a nominal value, be deemed to be the fair market value as of the date or dates of issue of such stock or shares; and the House recedes. (p. 66)

Sec. 326.   **(a)**   That as used in this title the term "invested capital" (253) *for any year* means (except as provided in subdivisions (b) and (c) of this section):

Sec. 326(a)

(1) Actual cash bona fide paid in for stock or shares;
(2) Actual cash value of tangible property, other than cash, bona fide paid in for stock or shares, at the time of such payment, but in no case to exceed the par value of the original stock or shares specifically issued (254) ~~therefor~~ *therefor, unless the actual cash value of such tangible property at the time paid in is shown to the satisfaction of the Commissioner to have been clearly and substantially in excess of such par value, in which case such excess shall be treated as paid-in surplus:* * * *

(3)   Paid-in or earned surplus and undivided profits; not including surplus and undivided profits earned during the (255)
<taxable> year (256), and not including the increase in the value of
any asset above the original cost until such increase is actually
realized by sale;

(4)   Intangible property bona fide paid in for stock or shares
prior to March 3, 1917, in an amount not exceeding (a) the actual
cash value of such property at the time paid in, (b) the par value of
the stock or shares issued therefor, or (c) in the aggregate (257) 20
[*30*] 25 per centum of the par value of the total stock or shares of the
corporation outstanding on March 3, 1917, whichever is lowest;

(5)   (258) Patents and copyrights *Intangible property* bona
fide paid in for stock or shares on or after March 3, 1917, in an amount
not exceeding (a) the actual cash value of such property at the time
paid in, (b) the par value of the stock or shares issued therefor, or (c)
in the aggregate (259) 20 [*30*] 25 per centum of the par value of the
total stock or shares of the corporation outstanding at the beginning of
the taxable year, whichever is lowest: PROVIDED, THAT IN NO
CASE SHALL THE TOTAL AMOUNT INCLUDED UNDER
PARAGRAPHS (4) AND (5) EXCEED IN THE AGGREGATE
25 PER CENTUM OF THE PAR VALUE OF THE TOTAL
STOCK OR SHARES OF THE CORPORATION OUTSTANDING
AT THE BEGINNING OF THE TAXABLE YEAR; but

Committee Reports

Report—Ways and Means Committee
(65th Cong., 2d Sess., H. Rept. 767).—
It also has been the experience of the
Treasury Department that the excess
profits tax places a very heavy burden
upon investment houses and similar corporations whose business is largely confined to dealing in tax-free securities,
because such corporations cannot include in invested capital either such
securities or borrowed money.   In order
more nearly to equalize this burden, the
bill provides that in such cases a corporation shall be entitled to include in invested capital an amount invested in
such tax-free securities not in excess of
the borrowed capital of such corporation (other than indebtedness maturing
within one year of its creation, all accounts payable and current liabilities)
for such year, if it includes in its net income for excess profits tax purpose the
interest and dividends from the bonds
and stocks included in computing invested capital.   (p. 19)
Report—Senate Finance Committee
(65th Cong., 3d Sess., S. Rept. 617).—

In its definition of invested capital the
House bill provides that tangible property paid in for stock or shares may in
no case exceed the par value of the original stock or shares specifically issued
therefor.   Such a limitation would work
grave injustice in case of highly conservative corporations which have acquired property for stock or shares, the
par value of which was (at the date of
acquisition) materially less than the
actual value of the tangible property
acquired.   The committee recommends,
therefore, that where the actual cash
value of such tangible property is shown
to the satisfaction of the Commissioner
of Internal Revenue to have been clearly
and substantially in excess of the par
value of the stock or shares paid therefor, such excess shall be treated as paid-
in surplus.
This amendment seeks to enact into
law the substance of a regulation of the
Treasury Department, which has worked
well and which has not led either to abuse
or the filing of an excessive number of
claims.   It is highly important that this

regulation be placed on a statutory basis and continued.

The existing law and the House bill as well provide that intangible property paid in for stock or shares prior to March 3, 1917, may not be included in invested capital at a value in excess of 20 per cent of the par value of the total stock or shares of the corporation outstanding on March 3, 1917. While this figure—20 per cent—has not been changed, the definition of intangible property has been greatly enlarged. Under the existing law, however, patents and copyrights are not defined as "intangible property," and they are not subject to the 20 per cent limitation; while under the proposed bill the definition of intangible property has been extended to include patents and copyrights. Because of this increase in the scope and content of the term "intangible property," the 20 per cent limit impresses the committee as obviously too low, and we recommend accordingly that it be increased to 30 per cent.

The House bill provides flatly that intangible property (other than patents and copyrights) paid in for stock or shares on or after March 3, 1917, shall not be included in invested capital; but that patents and copyrights paid in after that date may be included in invested capital under certain specified conditions. This discrimination between patents or copyrights and other intangible property impresses the committee as unwarranted. Patents and copyrights give rise to as much abuse in connection with overcapitalization as other forms of intangible property. Moreover, sufficient protection against abuse would seem to be provided in the provision that intangible property can not be included in invested capital at an amount in excess of the actual cash value of such property at the time paid in. It is recommended therefore that all intangible property acquired for stock on or after March 3, 1917, be permitted to count as invested capital, under the conditions and safeguards applicable to patents and copyrights. (p. 13-14)

Report—Conference Committee (65th Cong., 3d Sess., H. Rept. 1037).— Amendment No. 253: This amendment is a clerical change; and the House recedes.

Amendment No. 254: The House bill provided that tangible property should be included in invested capital in an amount not to exceed the par value of the original stock or shares specifically issued therefor. The Senate amendment adds the following qualification: "Unless the actual cash value of such tangible property at the time paid in is shown to the satisfaction of the commissioner to have been clearly and substantially in excess of such par value, in which case such excess shall be treated as paid-in surplus." The House recedes with an amendment providing that the commissioner shall keep a detailed record of all cases in which tangible property is included in invested capital at a value in excess of the stock or shares issued therefor, which record shall be furnished when required by resolution of either House of Congress, without regard to the restrictions contained in section 257.

Amendment No. 255: This amendment is a clerical change; and the House recedes.

Amendment No. 256: The House bill specifically provided that "paid-in or earned surplus and undivided profits" should not include the increase in the value of any asset above the original cost until such increase is actually realized by sale. This was stricken out by the Senate amendment as surplusage and merely declaratory of an accepted general principle controlling the whole computation of invested capital; and the House recedes.

Amendment No. 257: The House bill limited to 20 per cent of the par value of the total stock or shares of the corporations outstanding on March 3, 1917, the aggregate allowance which may be made for intangible property paid in for stock or shares prior to March 3, 1917. The Senate amendment increased this limit to 30 per cent; and the House recedes with an amendment changing the 30 per cent to 25 per cent.

Amendment No. 258: The House bill excluded from "invested capital" intangible property (other than patents and copyrights) paid in for stock or shares on or after March 3, 1917. The Senate amendment permits all intangible property bona fide paid in for stock on or after March 3, 1917 (subject to the limitation noted in amendment 259), to be included in invested capital; and the

House recedes.

Amendment No. 259: The House bill limited to 20 per cent of the par value of the total stock or shares outstanding at the beginning of the taxable year the aggregate allowance which may be made (in computing invested capital) for patents and copyrights paid in for stock or shares on or after March 3, 1917. The Senate amendment increased this limit to 30 per cent (having by amendment 258 also allowed other intangible property to be included); and the House recedes with amendments changing the 30 per cent to 25 per cent, and providing that in no case shall the total allowance for intangible property paid in for stock or shares before, on, or after March 3, 1917, exceed in the aggregate 25 per cent of the par value of the total stock or shares outstanding at the beginning of the taxable year. (p. 67)

Congressional Discussion

Discussion—House (Cong. Rec. Vol. 56).—MR. DENISON. In taking care of the war-profit tax there is a 10 per cent deduction on the capital stock?

MR. KITCHIN. Invested capital.

MR. DENISON. What does that mean?

MR. KITCHIN. Invested capital in the bill is practically what it is under the present law, cash paid in, earned and paid-in surplus and undivided profits, not including surplus and undivided profits earned during the taxable year, and the value of tangible property turned over for stock or shares. (Appendix, p. 683-684)

MR. BANKHEAD. On the proposition of the allowance made on invested capital I desire to submit this question to the chairman. Take a corporation organized prior to 1911 with a capital stock of $100,000. Suppose during the three prewar years it has made less than 10 per cent. Subsequent to this time it has out of its accumulations invested in other property to the extent of, say, $50,000, say, in a mine. Would it be entitled to credit to the value of that $50,000 as a new investment plus the original capital stock of $100,000?

MR. KITCHIN. Yes. If they put in the original capital stock $100,000, and earned and accumulated a surplus of $50,000, and put it in a mine, the invested capital would be $150,000. But if they took this $100,000 and put it in a mine or timber, and in four or five years it increased in value $50,000, we would not allow them to include that $50,000 of unearned increment as capital invested.

MR. BANKHEAD. The actual value of the $50,000 additional property at the time of the investment would be included as part of the net investment?

MR. KITCHIN. What they actually put in the mine—not the unearned increment in the mine. If you bought a mine for $50,000 and held it for four or five years without doing anything to or with it, and it was then worth $100,000, there would be an unearned increment of $50,000. That is not put in as invested capital, and it should not be, for the reason that if it be put in as invested capital the company ought to pay the income tax and excess-profits tax on that $50,-000. If such unearned profit or increment should be regarded as surplus or capital for the purpose of the deduction in reducing the tax, then that $50,000 ought to be subject to tax, the same as other profits and income. But corporations that hold that they should be allowed to treat such unearned increment or profit as capital or surplus for the purpose of deduction are opposed to any law that would make such increment or profit subject to the income or excess-profits tax until the profit is realized by sale. It is never allowed as part of invested capital nor made subject to tax until realized by sale. (p. 685)

MR. CANNON. Is it the actual capital or is it what is termed "capital"?

MR. HAWLEY. It is not what the economists call capital, but it is capital under a certain plan defined in the bill, certain things being included and certain things excluded. It is a statement of what may be considered as invested capital for the purposes of the bill.

MR. CANNON. It does not make any difference what you call it, if there is that amount invested in the business, whether you call it surplus or undivided profits or capital. You take the actual amount that is invested in the business in the calendar year—for instance, 1918 —after this act is passed, because that gives you the basis to compute the taxes. Am I correct?

Mr. Hawley. If I understand the gentleman's question, I think that is correct. (p. 10241)

Discussion—Senate (Cong. Rec. Vol. 57).—Mr. Smoot. * * * As to invested capital I call attention to the fact that tangible property under the relief provisions is allowed to its full value if clearly in excess of the par value of stock paid therefor.

* * *

Then, again, in that same section, as to intangible property paid in prior to March 3, 1917, the House provided an aggregate of 20 per cent of the par value of the total stock or shares of the corporation outstanding on March 3, 1917. That was changed by an amendment in the Senate committee allowing 30 per cent.

* * *

Again, as to intangible property paid in for stock since March 3, 1917, there is the same change; that is, an allowance of 30 per cent instead of 20 per cent, as limited by the House. I ask that the following also be incorporated in the Record. (p. 505)

Discussion—House; on Report of Conference Committee (Cong. Rec. Vol. 57).—Mr. Kitchin. Now, as to the definition of "invested capital," it is practically the same as the definition in the House bill, with but one exception. The House bill provided that invested capital meant, in the case of tangible property, bona fide paid in for stock or shares, the actual cash value of such property, but in no case to exceed the par value of the original stock or shares specifically issued therefor. The Senate put in a provision, to which the House conferees finally agreed, some of us very reluctantly, that where the taxpayer can show to the satisfaction of the commissioner that the actual cash value of the tangible property at the time it was paid in was clearly and substantially in excess of the par value of the stock issued for it, the real value of the tangible property at the time it was turned over for the shares of stock could be counted as part of the invested capital.

The House bill also specifically provided that "paid-in or earned surplus and undivided profits" should not include the increase in the value of any asset above the original cost until such increase is actually realized by sale. This provision was stricken out by the Senate, and the conferees accepted the amendment, because it was surplusage and merely declaratory of an accepted general principle controlling the whole computation of invested capital. (p. 3008)

Committee Hearings

Hearings—Ways and Means Committee.—Difficulties in determining invested capital. (L. Berenson, p. 344-347, 357-358)

Allowing intangibles at full value. (R. W. Babson, p. 375-382; W. P. White, p. 382-387)

Determining invested capital by reference to current value of assets. (J. J. Shea, p. 473, 474, 477-478; F. A. Blair, p. 712-715)

Allowing discovery value in invested capital. (J. J. Shea, p. 474-475; O. West, p. 497-498)

Allowing cost of drilling dry hole in invested capital. (O. West, p. 497)

Allowing March 1, 1913 values in determining invested capital. (B. Mohun, p. 530-541; A. C. Dustin, p. 551-552, 555-556, 567-571; M. Holmes, p. 620; J. R. Van Derlip, p. 920-922)

Including legal reserves of insurance companies in invested capital. (J. E. Hedges, p. 799-813; C. P. Peterson, p. 832-833)

Hearings—Senate Finance Committee.—Determining invested capital by reference to current value of assets. (R. P. M. Davis, p. 167-171; R. R. Reed, p. 118, 120; B. G. Watson, p. 291; R. R. Wilson, p. 310; J. J. Shea, p. 377, 392-393; E. C. Lindley, p. 577-579; J. R. Vanderlip, p. 585-587; F. S. Salmon, p. 587; S. Browne, p. 589-591; R. C. Butler, p. 624)

Allowing discovery value in invested capital. (J. F. Callbreath, p. 172-183)

Allowing March 1, 1913 values in determining invested capital. (M. Holmes, p. 567-568; J. W. Fordney, p. 611-620)

Deducting deficits from invested capital. (J. R. Vanderlip, p. 584)

Sec. 326(b)

(b) As used in this title the term "invested capital" does not include (260):

~~(1) Borrowed capital; or~~

~~(2) Intangible property (other than patents and copyrights) paid in for stock or shares on or after March 3, 1917~~ *borrowed capital.*

Committee Reports

Report—Conference Committee (65th Cong., 3d Sess., H. Rept. 1037).— Amendment No. 260: This amendment strikes out the House provision excluding from "invested capital" intangible

property (other than patents and copyrights) paid in for stock or shares on or after March 3, 1917; and the House recedes. (p. 67-68)

Committee Hearings

Hearings—Ways and Means Committee.—Including borrowed capital in invested capital. (J. J. Shea, p. 477; A. C. Dustin, p. 553)

Hearings—Senate Finance Committee.—Including borrowed capital in invested capital. (F. S. Salmon, p. 587-589; R. C. Butler, p. 623, 624)

Sec. 326(c)

(c) There shall be deducted from invested capital as above defined (261) ~~an amount equal to the average amount of capital invested in inadmissible assets held by the corporation during the year: Provided, That at the option of the corporation the amount to be so deducted shall be reduced to the amount by which such average amount invested in inadmissible assets exceeds the average amount of borrowed capital of the corporation (other than indebtedness maturing within one year of its creation, all accounts payable and current liabilities) for such year; but in such case in computing the tax under this title there shall be included in the net income for such year the same proportion of the total amount of interest and dividends received during such year from such inadmissible assets as the amount of such capital invested in inadmissible assets not deducted from invested capital bears to the total amount of such inadmissible assets~~ *a percentage thereof equal to the percentage which the amount of inadmissible assets is of the amount of admissible and inadmissible assets held during the taxable year* [*: Provided, That no such deduction shall be made in the case of any dealer in securities, insurance company, bank, banking association, loan or trust company which elects to include in its net income for the purposes of this title and of Title II all income derived from inadmissible assets; but where such election is made there shall be deducted from* <the> *such net income any interest paid or accrued during the taxable year which has not been deducted under paragraph (2) of subdivision (a) of section 234: Provided further, That such election once made shall be adhered to in subsequent taxable years unless permission to change is granted by the Commissioner*].

Committee Reports

Report—Senate Finance Committee   (65th Cong., 3d Sess., S. Rept. 617).—

The committee refrains also from recommending any radical change in the method of computing invested capital, although a number of important improvements are suggested in this connection. Speaking generally, assets are valued, for the purpose of determining invested capital, at the price paid in acquiring them without recognition of subsequent appreciation. Weighty arguments have been presented in favor of abandoning this rule and valuing property acquired before March 1, 1913, as of that date. But the committee believes that such a method would be impracticable; that it would impose upon the Treasury Department the impossible task of valuing nearly all of the durable property of the country as of a date nearly six years in the past. The present statutory rule works well in a large majority of cases. The remaining cases, in which it works injustice, can and should be cared for by adequate relief provisions which the committee has carefully formulated and recommends. The committee therefore indorses the general rule expressed by the House bill in paragraph (3) of subdivision (a) of section 326, but believes that in certain exceptional cases inability to recognize appreciation furnishes just ground for relief, and in order that such relief may not be imperiled by overemphasis upon the general principle recommends that the explicit denial of the right to include any increase in the value of assets above original cost be stricken from section 326. (p. 11-12)

Report—Conference Committee (65th Cong., 3d Sess., H. Rept. 1037).— Amendment No. 261: This amendment provides that there shall be deducted from invested capital as defined in section 326 a percentage equal thereof to the percentage which the amount of inadmissible assets is of the amount of the admissible and inadmissible assets held during the taxable year, except in the case of certain dealers in securities, insurance companies, banks, banking associations, loan or trust companies; and the House recedes with an amendment striking out the exception. (p. 68)

Congressional Discussion

Discussion—House (Cong. Rec. Vol. 56).—MR. KITCHIN. * * * To illustrate: If a corporation has borrowed money to the amount, say, of $50,000, and it has what we call in the bill for the sake of simplification "inadmissible assets," which are assets whose income or interest is not subject to the tax, tax-exempt securities, to an amount of $75,000, instead of having the $75,000 deducted from capital invested there will be deducted only $25,000, being the excess of the inadmissible assets over the amount of borrowed capital. In such cases borrowed capital not in excess of the amount of such assets is practically counted as part of invested capital. (Appendix p. 684)

(d) [262] ~~In the case of a foreign corporation the term "invested capital" includes only its invested capital used or employed within the United States.~~

~~(e) The invested capital for any year shall be the average invested capital for such year, as above defined, but in the case of a corporation making a return for a fractional part of the year a corresponding reduction shall be made in the invested capital.~~ *The invested capital for any period shall be the average invested capital for such period, but in the case of a corporation making a return for a fractional part of a year, it shall (except for the purpose of paragraph (2) of subdivision (a) of section 311) be the same fractional part of such average invested capital.*

The average invested capital for the prewar period shall be determined by dividing the number of years within that period during the whole of which the corporation was in existence into the sum of the average invested capital for such years.

Sec. 326(d)

Committee Reports

Report—Conference Committee (65th Cong., 3d Sess., H. Rept. 1037).— Amendment No. 262: This amendment strikes out the definition provided in the House bill of the invested capital of a foreign corporation (see amendment[1] No. 263), makes clerical changes in the method of computing the invested capital for a fractional part of a year, and defines the average invested capital for the prewar period; and the House recedes. (p. 68)

[1] Relating to sec. 327.

Congressional Discussion

Discussion—House (Cong. Rec. Vol. 56).—MR. DENISON. In figuring the 10 per cent deduction that is levied, of course there is no allowance made for the money that is borrowed and used as capital? (Appendix p. 684)

Sec.
327

Sec. 327. ~~(a)~~ ~~That in the following cases the invested capital shall be determined as provided in subdivision (b) of this section: (1) where the Commissioner is unable satisfactorily to determine the invested capital as provided in section 326; or (2) where a mixed aggregate of tangible property and intangible property has been paid in for stock or for stock and bonds and the Commissioner is unable satisfactorily to determine the respective values of the several classes of property at the time of payment, or to distinguish the classes of property paid in for stock and for bonds, respectively; or (3) where capital is a material income-producing factor, but where, because of the fact that the capital employed is in large part borrowed, there is no invested capital or the invested capital is materially disproportionate to the net income as compared with representative corporations engaged in a like or similar trade or business. This section shall not apply in the case of a corporation 50 per centum or more of whose gross income (as defined in section 213 for income tax purposes) consists of gain, profits or commissions derived from Government contracts, unless the Commissioner is satisfied that such corporation is overcapitalized.~~

~~(b) In the cases specified in subdivision (a) the invested capital shall be the amount which bears the same ratio to the net income of the corporation for the taxable year as the average invested capital for the taxable year of representative corporations engaged in a like or similar trade or business bears to their average net income for such year.~~

~~Sec. 328. (a) That in cases where invested capital is to be determined in the manner provided in section 327,~~

That in the following cases the tax shall be determined as provided in section 328:

(a) Where the Commissioner is unable **[**satisfactorily**]** to determine the invested capital as provided in section 326;

(b) In the case of a foreign corporation;

(c) Where a mixed aggregate of tangible property and intangible property has been paid in for stock or for stock and bonds and the Com-

missioner is unable satisfactorily to determine the respective values of the several classes of property at the time of payment, or to distinguish the classes of property paid in for stock and for bonds, respectively;

[(d) *Where, as compared with representative corporations, engaged in a like or similar trade or business, the taxpayer would (under section 326) be placed in a position of substantial inequality, because of the time or manner of organization, or because the actual value of the assets on March 1, 1913, was substantially in excess of the amount at which such assets would be valued for the purpose of computing invested capital under the provisions of section 326;*

(e) *Where the invested capital is materially disproportionate to the net income as compared with representative corporations engaged in a like or similar trade or business because:*

1. *The capital employed, although a material income-producing factor, is very small or is in large part borrowed;*

2. *There are excluded from the invested capital as computed under the provisions of section 326, intangible assets of recognized and substantial value built up or developed by the taxpayer;*

3. *The net income for the taxable year is abnormally high due to the realization in one year of (a) gains, profits, or income earned or accrued during a period of years or (b) extraordinary gains or profit derived from the sale of property the principal value of which has been demonstrated by prospecting or exploration and discovery work done by the taxpayer. When the tax is determined under this paragraph proper allowance shall be made for the taxes which would have been payable in prior years if the gains, profits, or income earned or accrued in such years had been taxed at the rates then applicable;*

4. *Proper recognition or allowance can not be made for amortization, obsolescence, or exceptional depletion due to the present war, or to the necessity in connection with the present war of providing plant which will not be wanted for the purpose of the trade or business after the termination of the war.***]**

(d)[1] Where upon application by the corporation the Commissioner finds and so declares of record that the tax if determined without benefit of this section would, owing to abnormal conditions affecting the capital or income of the corporation, work upon the corporation an exceptional hardship evidenced by gross disproportion between the tax computed without benefit of this section and the tax computed by reference to the representative corporations specified in section 328. This subdivision shall not apply to any case (1) in which the tax (computed without benefit of this section) is high merely because the corporation earned within the taxable year a high rate of profits upon a normal invested capital nor (2) in which 50 per centum or more of the gross income of the corporation for the taxable year (computed under section 233 of Title II) consists of gains, profits, commissions, or other income, derived on a cost-plus basis from a Government contract or contracts made between April 6, 1917, and November 11, 1918, both dates inclusive.

¹ This subsection was added by the Conference Committee.

Committee Reports

Report—Ways and Means Committee (65th Cong., 2d Sess., H. Rept. 767).— The existing excess profits act provides that in cases where the Secretary of the Treasury is unable to determine satisfactorily the invested capital of a corporation he may construct the same upon the basis of representative concerns. The bill provides that the Commissioner of Internal Revenue be given this same discretion under the proposed excess profits tax method and adds a provision in section 327 for the construction of capital in two additional specified cases: (1) Where the mixed aggregate of tangible property and intangible property has been paid in for stock or for stock and bonds and the commissioner is unable satisfactorily to determine the representative values of the several classes of property at the time of payment or to distinguish the classes of property paid in for stock and for bonds, respectively, or (2) where capital is a material income producing factor but where, because of the fact that the capital employed is in large part borrowed, there is no invested capital, or the invested capital is materially disproportionate to the net income as compared with representative concerns engaged in a like or similar trade or business. This section is not, however, to apply to any corporation 50 per cent or more of whose gross income is derived from Government contracts. (p. 19-20)

Report—Senate Finance Committee (65th Cong., 3d Sess., S. Rept. 617).— * * * The present statutory rule works well in a large majority of cases. The remaining cases, in which it works injustice, can and should be cared for by adequate relief provisions which the committee has carefully formulated and recommends. The committee therefore indorses the general rule expressed by the House bill in paragraph (3) of subdivision (a) of section 326, but believes that in certain exceptional cases inability to recognize appreciation furnishes just

ground for relief, and in order that such relief may not be imperiled by overemphasis upon the general principle recommends that the explicit denial of the right to include any increase in the value of assets above original cost be stricken from section 326. (p. 11-12)

No part of Title III is as important as the so-called relief provisions. The business world is apprehensive about the operation of the war excess-profits tax, and it is true that the ordinary method of computing invested capital would in certain exceptional cases work great hardship. There is a measure of truth, for instance, in the current criticism that the war excess-profits tax places a heavy penalty on conservative financing and a corresponding premium on overcapitalization.

The committee therefore believes it necessary to provide a special method of determining the tax for those cases in which the ordinary method of assessment would result in grave hardship or serious inequality. To do this is not to confer an arbitrary discretion upon the administrative authorities; it is merely an exercise of the legislative power of reasonable classification. Indeed without such classification the constitutionality of the whole tax might, because of its unequal operation, be open to serious question.

The committee has materially increased the number of cases for which the House bill grants relief. It is not necessary here to enumerate these cases. It is sufficient to say that they represent the principal classes of cases which a year's experience with the excess-profits tax prove to be in need of special treatment. The committee moreover believes that these relief powers should not be hidden under vague and general phraseology. The business world is apprehensive of the operation of a war excess-profits tax at the high rates which war exigencies make necessary. It is entitled to be reassured, explicitly and frankly, by the enactment of carefully safeguarded provisions for the relief or prevention of injustice and inequality. (p. 14-15)

Report—Conference Committee (65th Cong., 3d Sess., H. Rept. 1037).—The House recedes with amendments:

(1) Making clerical changes;

(2) Consolidating a number of separate classes or cases differentiated in the Senate amendment into a single class of cases in which "upon application by the corporation the commissioner finds and so declares of record that the tax if determined without benefit of this section would, owing to abnormal conditions affecting the capital or income of the corporation, work upon the corporation an exceptional hardship evidenced by gross disproportion between the tax

computed without benefit of this section and the tax computed by reference to the representative corporations specified in section 328. This subdivision shall not apply to any case in which the tax (computed without benefit of this section) is high merely because the corporation earned within the taxable year a high rate of profits upon a normal invested capital, nor in which 50 per centum or more of the gross income of the corporation for the taxable year (computed under sec. 233 of Title II) consists of gains, profits, commissions, or other income, derived on a cost-plus basis from a Government contract or contracts made between April 6, 1917, and November 11, 1918, both dates inclusive;" and (p. 68)

Congressional Discussion

Discussion—Senate (Cong. Rec. Vol. 57).—Mr. Gore. * * * Now, take a case. Take a corporation that was doing business during the prewar period, making an average profit of 20 per cent, and let us assume that the average profit for like industries is also 20 per cent. Now, a new corporation organized since the prewar period would be entitled to an exemption of 20 per cent, based on the average profits of like industries; but a concern, we will say, that was capitalized at $50,000, operating during the prewar period, and realizing a profit of 20 per cent, has added $450,000 of new capital to its business. Upon this $450,000 of capital newly invested it is entitled to an exemption of only 10 per cent, or $45,000. Take an entirely new concern which has been organized since the prewar period, capitalized at $500,-000. It will be allowed an exemption of $100,000, because the average net earnings of like industries are 20 per cent. Now, there is a serious discrepancy between like industries.

They may be competitors; their plants may be just across the street from each other; and yet the one, simply because it existed during the prewar period, is penalized to the extent of $55,000, and the new concern is rewarded to the extent of $55,000.

Now, that is a disparity, a disproportion of burden, that ought not to be imposed upon competing concerns. It

would have been much better for the old concern, instead of adding to its invested capital, to have organized a new corporation and capitalized it, using the new capital in that way, because upon this new concern it would have been entitled to a much more generous exemption.

I can see how this would work serious injury to an old concern simply for being old. The amendment which I have offered proposes to give the old concern which has added to its capital the same exemption upon its new capital that we give to a corporation which has been organized since the prewar period. In other words, it is to give to the old corporation an exemption upon its new capital equivalent to the average net profits of like businesses. That will place them on an equal footing. (p. 798)

Discussion—House; on Report of Conference Committee (Cong. Rec. Vol. 57).—Mr. Kitchin. * * * There were in the Senate amendment several specific relief provisions other than those to which I have heretofore referred, and one section in the House bill, which included several general relief provisions, which we thought was very liberal. The conferees finally agreed that it would be safer and better and do no injustice to the honest taxpayers to strike out all these specific and general relief provisions and have just one general relief provision, which is section 327, paragraph (d), and begins on page 134. * * *

The conferees, as I said awhile ago, as a matter of safety to the Government, without doing any injustice to the taxpayer, in case he is actually entitled to relief, provide that the taxpayer, in order to get relief under this representative corporation section, must apply to the commissioner and must show to the commissioner that it is an exceptional hardship; not that he is making an exceedingly large profit on invested capital and therefore his tax is exceedingly large, but it must be an exceptional hardship owing to the peculiar and exceptional conditions surrounding the taxpayer's business, income, invested capital, and so forth; and the commissioner

must find, and so declare of record, that the case is one of exceptional hardship before it can be considered under section 327.

This provision gives a taxpayer only that to which he is entitled, because he ought not to have relief unless, owing to the peculiar situation of his business or capital or income or something, the payment of the tax would be an exceptional hardship upon him without the benefit of the relief provision. * * * I do not think the House or the Senate will object for one moment to that relief provision taking the place of the others, because it is a safeguard to the Government; and I believe it will save millions and millions of dollars by substituting it for the provisions which the Senate had. (p. 3008)

Committee Hearings

Hearings—Ways and Means Committee.—Need for broad relief provision. (T. S. Adams, p. 118-119)

Hearings—Senate Finance Committee.—Allowing relief to mortgage investment banking companies. (O. B. Taft, p. 639)

Secs. 328(a) 328(b)

Sec. 328. (a) *In the cases specified in section 327 the tax shall be the amount which bears the same ratio to the net income of the taxpayer (in excess of the specific exemption of $3,000) for the taxable year, as the average tax of representative corporations engaged in a like or similar trade or business, bears to their average net income (in excess of the specific exemption of $3,000) for such year.* [*In such cases*] IN THE CASE OF A FOREIGN CORPORATION THE TAX SHALL BE COMPUTED WITHOUT DEDUCTING THE SPECIFIC EXEMPTION OF $3,000 EITHER FOR THE TAXPAYER OR THE REPRESENTATIVE CORPORATIONS.

IN COMPUTING THE TAX UNDER THIS SECTION the Commissioner shall compare the taxpayer only with representative corporations whose invested capital can be satisfactorily determined under section 326 and which are, as nearly as may be, similarly circumstanced with respect to gross income, net income, profits per unit of business transacted and capital employed, the amount and rate of war (264) *profits* or excess profits, and all other relevant facts and circumstances.

(b) For the purposes of (265) section 327 *subdivision (a)* the ratios between the average (266) invested capital *tax* and the average net income of representative corporations shall be determined (267) for each calendar year by the Commissioner in accordance with regulations prescribed by him with the approval of the Secretary.

(268) In the case of a corporation making a return on the basis of a fiscal year the ratios determined for the calendar year ending during such fiscal year shall be used, except that in the case

~~of a fiscal year ending during the calendar year 1918 the ratios based upon returns made under Title II of the Revenue Act of 1917 shall be used.~~ * * *

Committee Reports

Report—Ways and Means Committee (65th Cong., 2d Sess., H. Rept. 767).— The bill provides in section 328 that in determining invested capital in the above cases the commissioner shall compare the taxpayer only with representative corporations whose invested capital can be satisfactorily determined and which are as nearly as may be similarly circumstanced with respect to gross income, net income, profits per unit of business transacted and capital employed, the amount and rate of war or excess profits, and all other relevant facts and circumstances. (p. 20)

Report—Conference Committee (65th Cong., 3d Sess., H. Rept. 1037).— Amendment No. 263: The House bill in the so-called "relief provisions" provided that in certain specified cases the invested capital of a corporation shall be the amount which bears the same ratio to the net income of the corporation for the taxable year as the average invested capital for the taxable year of representative corporations engaged in a like or similar trade or business bears to their average net income for such year.

The Senate amendment increases the classes of cases in which the tax is to be fixed by reference to the experience of representative corporations; includes therein all foreign corporations (see amendment[1] 262), and provides that in such cases the tax shall be the amount which bears the same ratio to the net income of the taxpayer (in excess of the specific exemption of $3,000) for the taxable year as the average tax of representative corporations engaged in a like or similar trade or business bears to their average net income (in excess of the specific exemption of $3,000) for such year. (p. 68)

[1] Relating to sec. 326(d).

Amendments Nos. 264, 265, 266, and 267: These amendments are clerical changes; and the House recedes.

Amendment No. 268: The Senate amendment strikes out the House provision that in the case of a corporation making a return on the basis of a fiscal year, the ratio (between the average invested capital and the average net income of representative corporations) for the calendar year ending during such fiscal year shall be used; and the House recedes.

Amendment No. 269: This amendment is a clerical change necessitated by Amendment 263; and the House recedes.

Amendment No. 270: This amendment is a clerical change; and the House recedes with an amendment making another clerical change. (p. 69)

Congressional Discussion

Discussion—Senate (Cong. Rec. Vol. 57).—MR. LAFOLLETTE. * * * However, the bill can not be correctly understood by merely applying these rates. There are other provisions which open the door wide for corporations to escape their just taxes. In the case of this corporation, it would claim exemption under paragraph (e) of section 327 and would be taxed under the provisions of section 328.

Paragraph (e), section 327, provides, where the invested capital is materially disproportionate to the net income of representative corporations engaged in like or similar trade or business, because—

(1) The capital employed, although a material factor, is very small or is in large part borrowed.

The tax is to be determined as provided in section 328 and shall be—

The amount which bears the same ratio to the net income of the taxpayer * * * for the taxable year as the average tax of representative corporations engaged in a like or similar trade or business bears to the average net income * * * for such year.

In this typical case the profits of $150,000 amount to 150 per cent of the capital, while it is assumed the net income of representative corporations engaged in a like or similar business is only 30 per cent.

Then this "cushion" provision would be applied as follows under section 328:

Corporations with a present and prewar capital of $100,000, prewar average annual net income $10,000; net income for the taxable year $150,000.

War excess-profits tax under section 301, $109,600, or 73⅔ per cent.

War excess-profits tax of corporations engaged in like or similar business as computed by the Treasury actuary, 45½ per cent.

This latter percentage would apply, so instead of paying a war excess-profits tax of 73⅔ per cent it would pay 45½ per cent. Instead of paying out of its profits of $150,000 $109,600 war excess-profits taxes it would pay $68,000 and would thus save $41,600, a saving of 41.6 per cent on the capital.

In addition, the corporation would pay taxes under section 230. If taxed on war excess profits under section 328, the taxes assessed under section 230 would be a different amount than if the war excess-profits tax was assessed under section 301. With war excess profits taxed under section 328 the tax under section 230 would be computed as follows:

Taxable profits $150,000 less the taxes assessed under section 328, $68,000, less specific exemption of paragraph (e) section 236, $2,000, a total deduction of $70,000, leaving $80,000 to be taxed at 12 per cent, which would yield revenue of $9,600.

So this corporation would pay under section 328, $68,000, and under section 230, $9,600, a total tax of $77,600.

The tax if levied under sections 301 and 230 would be $114,208.

With the "cushion" operating it would mean a saving on the total tax of $36,608, or 36.6 per cent of the capital.

Under these "cushion" provisions out of its $150,000 of profits this corporation would have left after paying its taxes $72,400, or in excess of seven times its peace-time profits.

The total tax assessed under sections 301 and 230 would be 76.14 per cent of the profits, but after applying the cushions under sections 328 and 230 would be only 51.7 per cent of the profits. (p. 828)

Discussion—House; on Report of Conference Committee (Cong. Rec. Vol. 57).—MR. KITCHIN. * * * The bill provides that in the cases specified in section 327 the tax shall be an amount which bears the same proportion to the net income of the taxpayer, in excess of the specific exemption of $3,000, for the taxable year as the average tax of representative corporations engaged in a like or similar trade or business bears to their average net income, in excess of the specific exemption of $3,000, for such year. Under the specific provisions no official had any particular responsibility, and one could take any case he desired, whether it was an exceptional hardship or not, and make application that the tax should be computed on the basis of representative corporations. (p. 3008)

Discussion—Senate; on Report of Conference Committee (Cong. Rec. Vol. 57).—MR. PENROSE. * * * Similar action was taken with respect to the so-called relief provisions, which permit the profits tax in any case of exceptional hardship to be fixed by reference to the experience of representative concerns. This amendment, to my mind, is a most admirable one. The Senate greatly increased the classes of cases entitled to this relief. The conferees amalgamated all these classes into a single, general class, but denied the relief to corporations whose principal income consists of profits derived on a cost-plus basis from war contracts. (p. 3182)

Committee Hearings

Hearings—Senate Finance Committee.—Allowing relief on basis of normal profit per unit of sale. (R. R. Reed, p. 124)

Sec. 330

Sec. 330. That in the case of the reorganization, consolidation, or change of ownership after January 1, 1911, of a trade or business now carried on by (272) a corporation, the corporation [the taxpayer, the *taxpayer*] A CORPORATION, THE CORPORATION shall for the purposes of this title be deemed to have been (273) in existence [*engaged in such trade or business*] IN EXISTENCE prior to that date, and the net income and invested capital of such predecessor trade or business for all or any part of the prewar period prior to (274) the organization of the corporation now carrying on such trade or business [*such reorganization, consolidation, or change of ownership*] THE ORGANIZATION OF THE CORPORATION NOW CARRYING ON SUCH TRADE OR BUSINESS shall be deemed to have been the net income and invested capital of [275] such corporation [*the taxpayer*] SUCH CORPORATION [(276): *Provided, That nothing herein contained shall be so construed as to conflict with the provisions of section 326*]. (277) If such predecessor trade or business was carried on by a partnership or individual the net income for the prewar period shall be ascertained and returned upon the same basis and in the same manner as provided for income tax purposes in Title II, except that the credits provided in subdivisions (a) and (b) <and (c)> of section 216 shall be deducted. *If such predecessor trade or business was carried on by a partnership or individual the net income for the prewar period shall, under regulations prescribed by the Commissioner with the approval of the Secretary, be ascertained and returned as nearly as may be upon the same basis and in the same manner as provided for corporations in Title II, including a reasonable deduction for salary or compensation to each partner or the individual for personal services actually rendered.*

[1]In the case of the organization as a corporation before July 1, 1919, of any trade or business in which capital is a material income-producing factor and which was previously owned by a partnership or individual, the net income of such trade or business from January 1, 1918, to the date of such reorganization may at the option of the individual or partnership be taxed as the net income of a corporation is taxed under Titles II and III; in which event the net income and invested capital of such trade or business shall be computed as if such corporation had been in existence on and after January 1, 1918, and the undistributed profits or earnings of such trade or business shall not be subject to the surtax imposed in section 211, but amounts distributed on or after January 1, 1918, from the earnings of such trade or business shall be taxed to the recipients as dividends, and all the provisions of Titles II and III relating to corporations shall, so far as practicable, apply to such trade or business: * * *

If any asset of the trade or business in existence both during the taxable year and any prewar year is included in the invested capital for the taxable year but is not included in the invested capital for such prewar year, or is valued on a different basis in computing the invested capital for the taxable year and such prewar year, respectively, then under rules and regulations to be prescribed by the Commissioner with the approval of the Secretary such readjustments shall be made as are necessary to place the computation of the invested capital for such prewar year on the basis employed in determining the invested capital for the taxable year.

[1] This paragraph was added by the Conference Committee.

Committee Reports

Report—Ways and Means Committee (65th Cong., 2d Sess., H. Rept. 767).— In the case of the reorganization, consolidation, or change of ownership after January 1, 1911, of a trade or business now carried on by a corporation, for the purpose of determining the net income and invested capital for the prewar period, the corporation shall be deemed to have been in existence prior to that date, and the net income and invested capital of the predecessor trade or business for all or any part of the prewar period prior to the organization of the corporation shall be deemed to have been the net income and invested capital of the corporation. (p. 20)

Report—Conference Committee (65th Cong., 3d Sess., H. Rept. 1037).— Amendments Nos. 272, 273, 274, and 275: These amendments are clerical changes; and the Senate recedes.

Amendment No. 276: This amendment provided that nothing contained in section 330 relating to the reorganization, consolidation, or change of ownership after January 1, 1911, of a trade or business now carried on by a corporation should be so construed as to conflict with the provisions of section 326; and the Senate recedes.

Amendment No. 277: The House bill provided that in the case of reorgani-

zations, etc., if the predecessor trade or business was carried on by a partnership or individual the net income for the prewar period should be ascertained and returned upon the same basis as provided for partnerships and individuals in Title II. The Senate amendment provides that in such cases the net income for the prewar period shall be ascertained and returned upon the basis provided for corporations in Title II, including a reasonable deduction for salary or compensation to each partner or the individual.

The House recedes with an amendment providing that in the case of the reorganization as a corporation before July 1, 1919, of certain trades or businesses previously owned by a partnership or individual, the net income of such trade or business from January 1, 1918, to the date of such reorganization may, at the option of the individual or partnership, be taxed as the net income of a corporation is taxed under Titles II and III; in which event the undistributed profits of such trade or business shall not be subject to surtaxes, but amounts distributed on or after January 1, 1918, from the earnings of such trade or business shall be taxed to the recipients as dividends. * * * (p. 69)

Congressional Discussion

Discussion—House (Cong. Rec. Vol. 56).—Mr. Kitchin. Mr. Chairman, I offer an amendment to make a typographical correction of the text.

The Chairman. The Clerk will report the amendment offered by the gentleman from North Carolina.

The Clerk read as follows:

Page 66, line 13, strike out the words and letter "(b) and (c)" and insert "(a) and (b)."
(Appendix p. 10451)

Discussion—Senate (Cong. Rec. Vol. 57).—The Secretary. On page 103, line 7, after the word "taxpayer," it is proposed to insert the following proviso:

Provided, That nothing herein contained shall be so construed as to conflict with the provisions of section 326.

Mr. Pomerene. Mr. President, if I may have the attention of the chairman, of the committee, the reason for that amendment is this: This section provides as to what shall be done with reorganized companies and goes to the question as to what shall be considered invested capital. The section reads: * * *

In section 326 "invested capital" is defined and includes cash. When the two sections are construed together I do not think that there can be very much difficulty about the construction, but a question has been raised by some of my constituents, and, if I may give the example which was presented to me, it is this: A certain corporation, with assets aggregating about $300,000, was sold out to a reorganized corporation for $200,000. They added to its capital approximately $800,000 of new capital. Under this section, as it now reads, it would seem as if the invested capital would be the same as that of the original company. I wish to make it perfectly clear that the invested capital shall be as defined in section 330 plus any newly invested capital that may be put into it. In other words, the amendment simply goes to the clarity of the provision; it in no sense, I think, changes the thought that the committee had in mind. (p. 566)

Sec. 331. In the case of the reorganization, consolidation, or change of ownership of a trade or (278) ~~business~~ *business, or change of ownership of property*, after March 3, 1917, if an interest or control in such trade or business (279) *or property* of 50 per centum or more remains in the same persons, or any of them, then no asset transferred or received from the (280) ~~predecessor trade or business~~ *previous owner* shall, for the purpose of determining invested capital, be allowed a greater value than would have been allowed under this title in computing the invested capital of such (281) ~~prior trade or business~~ *previous owner* if such asset had not been so transferred or received (282): *Provided, That if such previous owner was not a corporation, then the value of any asset so transferred or received shall be taken at its cost of acquisition (at the date when acquired by such previous owner) with proper allowance for depreciation, impairment, betterment or development, but no addition to the original cost shall be made for any charge or expenditure deducted as expense or otherwise* [since] ON OR AFTER *March 1, 1913, in computing the net income of such previous owner for purposes of taxation.*

Committee Reports

Report—Ways and Means Committee (65th Cong., 2d Sess., H. Rept. 767).— In the case of the reorganization, consolidation, or change of ownership of a trade or business after March 3, 1917, if an interest or control in such trade or business of 50 per cent or more remains in the same persons or any of them, in such case no asset transferred or received from the predecessor trade or business shall, in computing invested capital, be allowed a greater value than would have been allowed in computing the invested capital of the prior trade or business if such asset had not been so transferred or received. (p. 20)

Report—Conference Committee (65th Cong., 3d Sess., H. Rept. 1037).— Amendment No. 278: This amendment extends certain House provisions relating to the reorganization, consolidation, or change of ownership of a trade or business, to include "change of ownership of property"; and the House recedes.

Amendments Nos. 279, 280, and 281: These amendments are clerical changes dependent upon amendment 278; and the House recedes.

Amendment No. 282: This amendment provides that in cases of reorganization, etc., if the previous owner was not a corporation then the value of any asset transferred or received shall be taken at its cost of acquisition at the date when acquired by such previous owner; and the House recedes with an amendment making a clerical change. (p. 69-70)

WAR REVENUE ACT OF 1917

Sec. 200. That when used in this title—

The term "corporation" includes joint-stock companies or associations and insurance companies;

The term "domestic" means created under the [laws] LAW *of the United States, or of any State, Territory, or District thereof, and the term "foreign" means created under the* [laws] LAW *of any other possession of the United States or of any foreign country or government;*

The term "United States" means only the States, the Territories of Alaska and Hawaii, and the District of Columbia;

The term "taxable year" means the twelve months ending December thirty-first, excepting in the case of a corporation or partnership ~~allowed to fix~~ *which has fixed its own fiscal year, in which case it means such fiscal year.* * * * The term "prewar period" means the calendar years nineteen hundred and eleven, nineteen hundred and twelve, and nineteen hundred and thirteen, or, if a corporation or partnership was not in existence or an individual was not engaged in a trade or business during the whole of such period, then as many of such years during the whole of which the corporation or partnership was in existence or the individual was engaged in the trade or business. THE TERMS "TRADE" AND "BUSINESS" INCLUDE PROFESSIONS AND OCCUPATIONS.

THE TERM "NET INCOME" MEANS IN THE CASE OF A FOREIGN CORPORATION OR PARTNERSHIP OR A NONRESIDENT ALIEN INDIVIDUAL, THE NET INCOME RECEIVED FROM SOURCES WITHIN THE UNITED STATES.

Sec. 201. *That in addition to the taxes under existing law and under this Act there shall be levied, assessed, collected, and paid for each taxable year upon the income of every corporation, partnership, or individual a tax (hereinafter in this title referred to as the tax) equal to the following percentages of the* [war profits (determined as hereinafter provided)] NET INCOME:

* * *

For the [purposes] PURPOSE *of this title* [all the trades and businesses in which a] EVERY *corporation or partnership* [is engaged] NOT EXEMPT UNDER THE PROVISIONS OF THIS SECTION *shall be deemed to be* [a single trade or] ENGAGED IN *business,* AND ALL THE TRADES AND BUSINESSES IN WHICH IT IS ENGAGED SHALL BE TREATED AS A SINGLE TRADE OR BUSINESS, *and all its income from whatever source derived shall be deemed to be received from such trade or business.*

348

This title shall apply to all trades or businesses of whatever description [*(whether continuously carried on or not)*], [*including the business of rendering any services for a commission or of acting as an agent of any description,*] *except—*

(a)   [*An office or employment, including that of a commercial traveler or agent whose remuneration consists wholly of a fixed and definite sum irrespective of the amount of business done or any other contingency;*] IN THE CASE OF OFFICERS AND EMPLOYEES UNDER THE UNITED STATES, OR ANY STATE, TERRITORY, OR THE DISTRICT OF COLUMBIA, OR ANY LOCAL SUBDIVISION THEREOF, THE COMPENSATION OR FEES RECEIVED BY THEM AS SUCH OFFICERS OR EMPLOYEES;

(b)   ~~In the case of professional partnerships having no substantial capital, the income derived from the professional services of the partners shall be exempt from the provisions of this title.~~

[*A profession or occupation, the profits of which depend mainly on the personal qualifications of the individuals by whom such profession or occupation is carried on and in which there is not required the investment of more than a nominal capital.*] Corporations exempt from tax under the provisions of section eleven of Title I of such Act of September eighth, nineteen hundred and sixteen, *as amended by this Act,* and partnerships *and individuals* carrying on or doing the same business, *or coming within the same description;*

(c)   *Incomes derived from the* [*business*] BUSINESSES *of life, health, and accident insurance combined in one policy issued on the weekly premium payment plan.*

Committee Hearings

Hearings—Senate Finance Committee.—Clarifying personal service criteria.   (Servan & Joyce, p. 67-68)

Sec. 202.   *That the tax shall not be imposed in the case of* [*a*] THE *trade or business of a* [*domestic corporation or partnership or a citizen or resident of the United States the net income of which trade or business during the taxable year is less than $5,000, or in the case of a trade or business of a*] *foreign corporation or partnership or a nonresident alien individual, the net income of which trade or business during* [*such*] THE TAXABLE *year* [*from sources within the United States*] *is less than* [*the proportion of $5,000 which such net income from sources within the United States bears to the entire net income, but no exemption shall be allowed to a foreign corporation or partnership or a nonresident alien individual unless a true and accurate return of the entire net income from the trade or business is filed with the collector of internal revenue. There shall be deducted from the war profits, determined as hereinafter provided, of each citizen or resident of the United States, the sum of $5,000*] $3,000.

Secs.
203(a)
203(b)

Sec. 203.   *That for the purposes of this title the* [*amount of war profits*] DEDUCTION *shall be* [*determined*] AS FOLLOWS, *except as otherwise in this title provided*—

(a)   *In the case of a domestic* [*corporation or partnership or of a citizen or resident of the United States by deducting from the net income of the trade or business received during the taxable year the average amount of the annual net income of the trade or business during the prewar period; but such deduction shall not be an amount less than six or more than ten per centum of the actual invested capital for the taxable year.*] COR-PORATION, THE SUM OF (1) AN AMOUNT EQUAL TO THE SAME PERCENTAGE OF THE INVESTED CAPITAL FOR THE TAXABLE YEAR WHICH THE AVERAGE AMOUNT OF THE ANNUAL NET INCOME OF THE TRADE OR BUSI-NESS DURING THE PREWAR PERIOD WAS OF THE IN-VESTED CAPITAL FOR THE PREWAR PERIOD (BUT NOT LESS THAN SEVEN OR MORE THAN NINE PER CENTUM OF THE INVESTED CAPITAL FOR THE TAXABLE YEAR), AND (2) $3,000;

(b)   [1]In the case of a domestic partnership or of a citizen or resident of the United States, the sum of (1) an amount equal to the same percentage of the invested capital for the taxable year which the average amount of the annual net income of the trade or business during the prewar period was of the invested capital for the prewar period (but not less than seven or more than nine per centum of the invested capital for the taxable year), and (2) $6,000;

[1] This subsection was added by the Conference Committee.

Sec.
203(c)

(c)   *In the case of a foreign corporation or partnership or of a nonresident alien individual,* [*by deducting from the net income of the trade or business received from sources within the United States during the taxable year the average amount of the annual net income of the trade or business from sources within the United States during the prewar period; but such deduction shall not be an amount less than six or more than ten per centum of that proportion of the actual invested capital for the taxable year which the net income of the trade or business from sources within the United States bears to the entire net income.*] AN AMOUNT ASCERTAINED IN THE SAME MANNER AS PROVIDED IN SUBDIVISIONS (A) AND (B) WITHOUT ANY EXEMPTION OF $3,000 OR $6,000.

Committee Hearings

Hearings—Senate Finance Commit-tee.—Eliminating income of foreign in-surance companies on capital not used in U. S.   (A. G. Thacher, p. 39-42)

UNENACTED RELATED PROVISION

1917 Act

[Sec. 203(c) of Senate Finance Committee bill]

〔(c) *If the* <average> *capital (or, in the case of a foreign corporation or partnership or of a nonresident alien individual, that proportion thereof which the net income of the trade or business from sources within the United States bears to the entire net income)* <employed in the trade or business> *during the taxable year is greater or less than the average capital* <or proportion thereof so employed> computed upon the same basis, *during the prewar period, the war profits shall be determined by deducting from the total net income for the taxable year an amount which bears the same proportion to the average annual net income for the prewar period which* <the average capital or proportion thereof employed> such capital *during the taxable year bears to* <the> such average capital <or proportion thereof employed> *during the prewar period; but such deduction shall not be an amount less than six or more than ten per centum of the actual invested capital for the taxable year (or, in the case of a foreign corporation or partnership or of a nonresident alien individual, of that proportion of the actual invested capital for the taxable year which the net income of the trade or business from sources within the United States bears to the entire net income).*〕

(d) *If* <a taxpayer fails to present satisfactory evidence as> the Secretary of the Treasury is unable satisfactorily to determine *the average amount of the annual net income of the trade or business during the prewar period* 〔or the actual invested capital for the taxable year〕, *the* 〔war profits〕 DEDUCTION *shall be determined* IN THE SAME MANNER *as provided in* 〔subdivision (a) of〕 *section two hundred and* 〔four〕 FIVE.

Sec. 203(d)

Congressional Discussion

Discussion—Senate (Cong. Rec. Vol. 55).—MR. LA FOLLETTE. I understood the Senator in his report and in his opening address upon the bill to criticize quite severely those provisions of the House bill as involving the Treasury Department in very serious embarrassments and complications in endeavoring to ascertain what was real capital.

MR. SIMMONS. The Senator is right about that. I did. I will state to the Senator that to avoid as far as practicable the dangers that I then brought to the attention of the Senate, which grew out of a situation very common in this country, where a corporation has so-called watered stock as the result of probably a fictitious valuation of its good will, trade-mark, and so forth, the House provision attempts in very specific language to provide against that. I do not know whether the House provision has succeeded or not; but we have added— I am glad the Senator calls my attention to the matter—an additional provision to the definition of the House bill, which we hope will take care to a large extent, if not altogether, of that situation. It is this—it follows immediately after the definition:

(b) If the Secretary of the Treasury is unable satisfactorily to determine the average amount of the annual net income of the trade or business during the prewar period, or the actual invested capital as of January 1 of the taxable year, the war profits shall be determined as provided in subdivision (a) of section 204.

That is, by determining or ascertaining what were the average profits of representative concerns engaged in like business. We have attempted to leave this matter largely with the Secretary of the Treasury.

MR. LA FOLLETTE. If I might inquire, then, how is it expected that the Secretary of the Treasury could ascertain the capitalization and the amount of water in the representative concerns that are to be taken as the standard with which the business in question is to be measured?

MR. SIMMONS. When we come to determine the profits of representative concerns for this purpose, we do not deal with capitalization at all, as the Senator will discover if he will turn to that section of the amendment. We simply take the net profits as determined by their return.

MR. LA FOLLETTE. You take the average profits of representative concerns?

MR. SIMMONS. As determined by their return of net profits.

MR. LA FOLLETTE. Yes; but are you not involved in the same difficulty there, because their net profits are ascertained upon a capitalization that may be half water?

MR. SIMMONS. Yes; but the Senator, I think, does not catch the whole proposition. We first take the net profits of these representative concerns during the prewar period. Then we take their net profits during the taxable year, and we find the ratio that the one bears to the other, and find what per cent that is, and then we allow the concern whose capital stock the Secretary has been unable to ascertain accurately the same percentage.

MR. LA FOLLETTE. Yes; I followed the Senator. I understood that.

MR. SIMMONS. So that the matter of capitalization does not seem to me to be involved there.

MR. LA FOLLETTE. You allow the corporation about which the Secretary of the Treasury is in doubt the same percentage as was made by certain selected corporations, called representative corporations; and the average profits of these concerns will be based upon the book values of their respective businesses as a basis of ascertaining the average of their profits.

MR. SIMMONS. Not at all. I do not understand that the net profits of a concern are based at all upon capitalization under section 204. They are not based upon capitalization at all. They return to the Secretary of the Treasury their net profits—that is, the net profits of their operations—without regard to their capitalization, just as the net income of a person is returned without reference to his capitalization. We accept their returns for the purposes of the income tax, and we accept their returns for the purposes of this tax. It is not a return based upon capital. It is a return based upon the net income growing out of the operations of that business, whether the capital be large or be small.

MR. LA FOLLETTE. Yes; but that net income is determined after they have paid dividends upon watered stock, and so would be affected by whether the capitalization is fictitious or not.

MR. SIMMONS. I do not think that is after they have paid any dividends. Dividends are not allowed to be deducted from net incomes. Expenses of operation are deducted; taxes are deducted; insurance is deducted; any of those elements of expense are deducted, but they are not permitted to deduct dividends.

MR. LA FOLLETTE. I misstated myself in that respect.

MR. SIMMONS. Yes. (p. 6435)

Sec. 204

Sec. 204. *That [(a) if a corporation, partnership, or individual had no net income from the trade or business during the prewar period, or] if a corporation or partnership was not in existence or an individual was not engaged in the trade or business, during the whole of any one calendar year during the prewar period, the [amount of the war profits shall be*

*the same proportion of the net income of the trade or business received
during the taxable year as the proportion which the war profits for the
same calendar year of representative corporations, partnerships, and individuals, engaged in a like or similar trade or business and whose war
profits are determined as provided in section two hundred and three, bears
to the total net income of the trade or business received by such corporations, partnerships, and individuals.   In the case of a foreign corporation
or partnership or of a nonresident alien individual the net income received
from sources within the United States during the taxable year shall be
used as the basis of computation.   In no case shall the difference between
the net income for the taxable year and the war profits determined as provided in this section be an amount less than six or more than ten per
centum of the actual invested capital for the taxable year (or, in the case
of a foreign corporation or partnership, or of a nonresident alien individual, of that proportion of the actual invested capital for the taxable
year which the net income of the trade or business from sources within
the United States bears to the entire net income); but this limitation shall
not apply in the case of a tax required by subdivision (d) of section two
hundred and three to be computed under this section on account of the
inability of the Secretary of the Treasury satisfactorily to determine the
actual invested capital for the taxable year.]* DEDUCTION SHALL
BE AN AMOUNT EQUAL TO EIGHT PER CENTUM OF THE
INVESTED CAPITAL FOR THE TAXABLE YEAR, PLUS IN
THE CASE OF A DOMESTIC CORPORATION $3,000, AND IN
THE CASE OF A DOMESTIC PARTNERSHIP OR A CITIZEN
OR RESIDENT OF THE UNITED STATES $6,000.

[*The proportion between the war profits and the net income in each
trade or business shall be determined by the Commissioner of Internal
Revenue in accordance with regulations prescribed by him with the approval of the Secretary of the Treasury.   In the case of a corporation or
partnership which has fixed its own fiscal year, the proportion determined
for the calendar year ending during such fiscal year shall be used.]*

*A trade or business carried on by a corporation, partnership, or indi-
vidual, although formally organized or reorganized on or after January
second, nineteen hundred and thirteen, which is substantially a continua-
tion of a trade or business carried on prior to that date, shall, for the purposes of this title, be deemed to have been in existence prior to that date,
and the net income* AND INVESTED CAPITAL *of its predecessor prior
to that date shall be deemed to have been its net income* AND INVESTED
CAPITAL.

Sec. 205. (a) *That if the Secretary of the Treasury, upon complaint
finds either (1) that during the prewar period [the net return of any]* A
*domestic corporation or partnership, or a citizen or resident of the United
States, [from a trade or business was low as compared with the net return
during such period of representative corporations, partnerships, and in-*

dividuals engaged in a like or similar] HAD NO NET INCOME FROM THE *trade or business, or (2) that during the prewar period the [ratio between the net and gross income from such trade or business was substantially less than the like ratio in case]* PERCENTAGE, WHICH THE NET INCOME WAS OF THE INVESTED CAPITAL, WAS LOW AS COMPARED WITH THE PERCENTAGE, WHICH THE NET INCOME DURING SUCH PERIOD *of representative corporations, partnerships, and individuals, engaged in a like or similar trade or business, [then the war profits shall be determined in the same manner as provided in subdivision (a) of section two hundred and four.]* WAS OF THEIR INVESTED CAPITAL, THEN THE DEDUCTION SHALL BE THE SUM OF (1) AN AMOUNT EQUAL TO THE SAME PERCENTAGE OF ITS INVESTED CAPITAL FOR THE TAXABLE YEAR WHICH THE AVERAGE DEDUCTION (DETERMINED IN THE SAME MANNER AS PROVIDED IN SECTION TWO HUNDRED AND THREE, WITHOUT INCLUDING THE $3,000 OR $6,000 THEREIN REFERRED TO) FOR SUCH YEAR OF REPRESENTATIVE CORPORATIONS, PARTNERSHIPS, OR INDIVIDUALS, ENGAGED IN A LIKE OR SIMILAR TRADE OR BUSINESS, IS OF THEIR AVERAGE INVESTED CAPITAL FOR SUCH YEAR PLUS (2) IN THE CASE OF A DOMESTIC CORPORATION $3,000, AND IN THE CASE OF A DOMESTIC PARTNERSHIP OR A CITIZEN OR RESIDENT OF THE UNITED STATES $6,000.

THE PERCENTAGE WHICH THE NET INCOME WAS OF THE INVESTED CAPITAL IN EACH TRADE OR BUSINESS SHALL BE DETERMINED BY THE COMMISSIONER OF INTERNAL REVENUE, IN ACCORDANCE WITH REGULATIONS PRESCRIBED BY HIM, WITH THE APPROVAL OF THE SECRETARY OF THE TREASURY. IN THE CASE OF A CORPORATION OR PARTNERSHIP WHICH HAS FIXED ITS OWN FISCAL YEAR, THE PERCENTAGE DETERMINED BY THE CALENDAR YEAR ENDING DURING SUCH FISCAL YEAR SHALL BE USED.

[(b) If the net income of the trade or business for the taxable year, in the case of a corporation or partnership which was not in existence or of an individual who was not engaged in the trade or business during the whole of any one calendar year during the prewar period, is less than six per centum per annum <on> of the <average capital actually employed in such trade or business> actual invested capital for the taxable year (or in case of a foreign corporation or partnership or a nonresident alien individual is less than six per centum per annum on <the average capital actually employed in such trade or business within the United States> that proportion of the actual invested capital for the taxable year which the net income of the trade or business from sources within the United States bears to the entire net income), there shall be deemed to be no war profits.]

Sec. 209. [1]That in the case of a trade or business having no invested capital or not more than a nominal capital there shall be levied, assessed, collected and paid, in addition to the taxes under existing law and under this act, in lieu of the tax imposed by section two hundred and one, a tax equivalent to eight per centum of the net income of such trade or business in excess of the following deductions: In the case of a domestic corporation $3,000, and in the case of a domestic partnership or a citizen or resident of the United States $6,000; in the case of all other trades or business, no deduction.

Sec. 210. [1]That if the Secretary of the Treasury is unable in any case satisfactorily to determine the invested capital, the amount of the deduction shall be the sum of (1) an amount equal to the same proportion of the net income of the trade or business received during the taxable year as the proportion which the average deduction (determined in the same manner as provided in section two hundred and three, without including the $3,000 or $6,000 therein referred to) for the same calendar year of representative corporations, partnerships, and individuals, engaged in a like or similar trade or business, bears to the total net income of the trade or business received by such corporations, partnerships, and individuals, plus (2) in the case of a domestic corporation $3,000, and in the case of a domestic partnership or a citizen or resident of the United States $6,000.

For the purpose of this section the proportion between the deduction and the net income in each trade or business shall be determined by the Commissioner of Internal Revenue in accordance with regulations prescribed by him, with the approval of the Secretary of the Treasury. In the case of a corporation or partnership which has fixed its own fiscal year, the proportion determined for the calendar year ending during such fiscal year shall be used.

[1] This section was added by the Conference Committee.

Committee Reports

Report—Senate Finance Committee (65th Cong., 1st Sess., S. Rept. 103).— Under any system, however, there will remain some cases in which the war-profits principle can not be strictly applied. The above basic plan must be somewhat modified as regards two classes of concerns, and can not be applied at all to another class. These cases are: (1) Where the capital used in the business is different for the taxable year from the average capital for the prewar period; (2) where the average net income of the concern for the prewar period was below a normal return upon its investment; and (3) where the concern was not in existence for a full calendar year during the prewar period—that is, the business is so new that it did not have a full year's net income during the prewar period. Special provision is made for these classes, as follows:

(1) Where the capital has been increased or decreased for the taxable year above or below the average of the prewar period, the average net income for the prewar period, for the purpose of ascertaining the war profits, is assumed to be increased or decreased in this same proportion.

(2) Where the Secretary finds either (1) that the net returns of a trade or business for the prewar period was low as compared with the net returns during such period of representative concerns engaged in a like or similar business, or

(2) that during such period, the ratio between the net and gross income from such trade or business was substantially less than the like ratio in case of representative trades or businesses then the war profits of such trade or business shall be determined as in the case of a new concern.

(3) Where the concern was not in existence for one calendar year during the prewar period, or had no net income for the prewar period, the amount of the war profits shall be the same proportion of the net income for the taxable year which the war profits for the same calendar year of representative concerns engaged in a like or similar business, and whose war profits are computed in accordance with the general plan, bears to the net income for that year.

Under this scheme it is not necessary to take into consideration the capital of the trade or business. (p. 6-7)

Report—Conference Committee (65th Cong., 1st Sess., H. Rept. 172).—The Senate provision also provided that if the exemption on the basis of the prewar period (the average income for the years 1911, 1912, and 1913) allowed corporations, partnerships, and individuals in any individual case did not represent the deductions allowed representative concerns engaged in similar businesses, that the Secretary of the Treasury could allow an exemption in such cases equal to the same proportion of their net income for the taxable year that the deduction granted representative concerns was of the net income for the taxable year of such concerns, provided that the exemption granted should not be less than 6 nor more than 10 per cent of the actual capital invested. (p. 32)

Congressional Discussion

Discussion—Senate (Cong. Rec. Vol. 55).—Mr. Simmons. * * * We make provision for exceptional cases where, by reason of misfortune, or of circumstances, a man was not making a normal profit during that period but was making an abnormally low profit compared with the profits of like business. Under the bill now before you, if the Secretary of the Treasury shall find that a man's profit was abnormally low during the three last years, he must permit him to have an exemption equal to the average profits made by representative concerns in like business during those three prewar years. (p. 5967)

Mr. Simmons. Yes; and under another provision of this bill, if any individual or corporation, or copartnership, made during those test years a profit that was low as compared with the profits in like business, and the Secretary of the Treasury, upon complaint, should find that to be a fact, this bill will permit that unfortunate individual, whether a farmer or a merchant or a manufacturer, to have an exemption equal practically to the average profits during those years of representative concerns engaged in the same line of business.

Mr. Fletcher. I see. That is intended to cover any case of accident or misfortune that may have happened during those years?

Mr. Simmons. Yes; so that the Senator will readily see that the man who made a subnormal profit while his neighbor was making a normal profit during these prewar years, through the operations and application of this provision of the bill, will be enabled, in the average that he will be allowed, to get the benefit of the standard earnings of others engaged in like business. I thank the Senator for interrupting me, because it has enabled me to make a statement with reference to the section of the bill relating to subnormal profits that I had omitted to make, and which I think ought to have been made. (p. 5975)

Mr. Penrose. * * * Now, in relation to what the Senator from Ohio [Mr. Pomerene] said about these concerns which make subnormal profits in a further effort to extend every relief possible to the taxpayer, the committee has made careful provisions for the cases where the capital used in the business is different for the taxable year from the average capital for the prewar period; where the average net income of the concern for the prewar period was below a normal return upon its investment; and where the concern was not in existence for a full calendar year during the prewar period. Special provision is made for these classes as follows:

First. Where the capital has been increased or decreased for the taxable year above or below the average of the prewar period, the average net income for the prewar period, for the purpose of ascertaining the war profits, is assumed to be increased or decreased in this same proportion.

Second. Where the Secretary of the Treasury finds either, first, that the net returns of a trade or business for the prewar period was low as compared with the net returns during such period of representative concerns engaged in a like or similar business, or, second, that during such period, the ratio between the net and gross income from such trade or business was substantially less than the like ratio in the case of representative trades or businesses, then the war profits of such trade or business shall be determined as in the case of a new concern.

Third. Where the concern was not in existence for one calendar year during the prewar period, or had no net income for the prewar period, the amount of the war profits shall be the same proportion of the net income for the taxable year which the war profits for the same calendar year of representative concerns engaged in a like or similar business, and whose war profits are computed in accordance with a general plan, bears to the net income for that year. (p. 6003)

MR. GERRY. * * * Now, Mr. President, while the excess profits of normal corporations are determined as every other private interest. There are certain corporations that it was necessary to make exceptions for, where the capital used in the business is different from the average capital of the prewar period. In other words, if a corporation has increased or decreased the amount of its capital since the prewar period, then the average net income of the prewar period for the purpose of ascertaining the excess profits is assumed to be increased or decreased in the same proportion. In that case we have to consider capital, but we can accept the corporations' statement as to their capital before the war, and on that basis consider the average of the increase or the decrease. We would not have to go into a very detailed consideration of what the capital of the corporation was.

Where the average of the net income of a concern for the prewar period was below a normal return upon its investment the Secretary of the Treasury has the right to find, if such is the case, and if he does find that the ratio between the net and the gross income is such that the business was substantially less than the like ratio in the case of representative trades or business, the war profits of such trades or business shall be determined as in the case of a new corporation.

A new corporation or an individual who was not in the business during the prewar period is allowed to take the same average as similar trades or business. In other words, if other corporations engaged in similar trades or business have been earning a stated average it is allowed to deduct that from the amount of its earnings for the taxable year, and if it is also found that it has not earned 6 per cent in the taxable year then it is exempt from the tax. (p. 6047)

MR. SIMMONS. * * * There is also another provision in the bill which is of great importance to the man whose profits during the prewar period were subnormal. It is that provision of the bill which relates to the profits of representative concerns in like business.

If it shall be made to appear by a taxpayer that his profits were subnormal during these three years as compared with the profits of like business, he is then permitted to have the average earnings during these prewar years of representative concerns engaged in like business up to the full maximum, 10 per cent.

* * *

We have sought to be fair, Mr. President, to the man whose profits were low during these years, to the man whose profits were subnormal during these three years, and we have sought not to permit the concern or the individual that happened to be making a very large profit before the war to escape taxation in excess of the 10 per cent exemption which we have allowed. (p. 6435)

MR. SIMMONS. * * * The Senator will see that that is intended to take care of the unfortunate man who was making an income upon his investment substantially lower than others who were engaged in the same line of business, as the result, we will say, of some misfortune, or some visitation of Providence, as in my case, when we had the floods down in my State. By reason of the enormous losses, the profits were practically nothing during those years. (p. 6435-36)

Discussion—House; on Report of Conference Committee (Cong. Rec. Vol. 55).—MR. KITCHIN. * * * In case the income of a trade or business during 1911, 1912, and 1913 was not representative of like concerns engaged in similar business the Secretary of the Treasury may grant a deduction equivalent to the deduction granted such concerns. (p. 7581)

MR. DALLINGER. Section 209 uses the words "nominal capital." Suppose a family is incorporated for a small amount

of capital, and all they have is a trademark or the good will of a certain article. Suppose they could sell to-day that trade-mark for half a million dollars and they are only incorporated for $5,000. Would that come under that section?

MR. KITCHIN. How much are they making?

MR. DALLINGER. Suppose they are making net $100,000 and are only capitalized for $5,000.

MR. KITCHIN. I would say that that was not more than a nominal capital in the case the gentleman puts and the corporation would pay under section 209. (p. 7585)

Sec. 206

Sec. 206. *That for the purposes of this title* THE *net income of a corporation shall be ascertained and returned (a) for the calendar years nineteen hundred and eleven and nineteen hundred and twelve upon the same basis and in the same manner as provided in section thirty-eight of the Act entitled "An Act to provide revenue, equalize duties, and encourage the industries of the United States, and for other purposes," approved August fifth, nineteen hundred and nine* EXCEPT THAT INCOME TAXES PAID BY IT WITHIN THE YEAR IMPOSED BY THE AUTHORITY OF THE UNITED STATES SHALL BE INCLUDED; *(b) for the calendar year nineteen hundred and thirteen upon the same basis and in the same manner as provided in section II of the Act entitled "An Act to reduce tariff duties and to provide revenue for the Government, and for other purposes," approved October third, nineteen hundred and thirteen, except that* INCOME TAXES PAID BY IT WITHIN THE YEAR IMPOSED BY THE AUTHORITY OF THE UNITED STATES SHALL BE INCLUDED, AND EXCEPT THAT *the amounts received by it as dividends upon the stock or from the net earnings of other corporations, joint-stock companies or associations, or insurance companies, subject to the tax imposed by section II of such Act of October third, nineteen hundred and thirteen, shall also be deducted; and (c)* Income derived from dividends upon stock of other corporations or partnerships which are subject to the tax imposed by this title shall be exempt from the provisions of this title. *for the taxable year upon the same basis and in the same manner as provided in Title I of the Act entitled "An Act to increase the revenue, and for other purposes," approved September eighth, nineteen hundred and sixteen, as amended* by this Act, *except that the amounts received by it as dividends upon the stock or from the net earnings of other corporations, joint-stock companies or associations, or insurance companies, subject to the tax imposed by Title I of such Act of September eighth, nineteen hundred and sixteen, shall* [also] *be deducted.* * * *

[*Premiums paid on life insurance policies covering the lives of officers, employees, or those financially interested in the company or copartnership for the benefit of said company or copartnership shall not be deducted in computing the net income or profits in determining the amount of taxes to be paid under this Act or under the Act entitled "An Act to increase the revenue, and for other purposes," approved September eighth, nineteen hundred and sixteen.*]

Committee Reports

Report—Senate Finance Committee (65th Cong., 1st Sess., S. Rept. 103).—A comparison of their net incomes during the taxable year—that is, a warperiod year—with their recorded net incomes of the prewar period, establishes once and for all the basis upon which the tax should be collected. It avoids, for all such corporations, inquiry concerning their capitalization, and enters into no inquiries concerning the extent or justification of their profits in earlier years, or the extent to which their capital merely represented water or was actually invested. (p. 6)

Congressional Discussion

Discussion—House (Cong. Rec. Vol. 55).—Rejected amendment to allow credit for payment of debts. (p. 2546-47)

Discussion—Senate (Cong. Rec. Vol. 55).—Mr. SIMMONS. * * * Under the House bill page 10, lines 19-23, incomes derived by corporations from dividends in other corporations subject to the excess-profits tax are exempted to the extent of that tax.

The Senate committee amendments extend this provision so as to give like exemption to the tax on corporate incomes.

The effect of the House bill is that if a distributing corporation has paid the war excess profits tax, the receiving corporation does not pay it again, but under the House bill if the distributing corporation has paid the corporate income tax on dividends the receiving corporation also must pay it.

Under the Senate bill the receiving corporation will not have to pay the tax again in either case.

Under these circumstances, the criticism of the action of your committee in this regard made by certain members of the Ways and Means Committee is unwarranted.

But your committee had another reason for this amendment.

Under the present law and in the House bill an individual who receives dividends on stock in a corporation is allowed an exemption in his normal income tax of the tax paid by the corporation. The tax having been paid once he does not have to pay it again.

Why then should a corporation holding stock in another corporation not be entitled to the same exemption?

Your committee thought that there was no reason why individuals and corporations in this matter should not be treated alike, and that there was no reason why either should pay again a tax which has already been paid.

The Senate bill, however, differs from the House bill in this respect:

While the House bill allows each intermediate subsidiary corporation to make the deduction, the Senate bill allows only one deduction. (p. 5967)

Committee Hearings

Hearings—Senate Finance Committee.—Eliminating dividends from taxable income. (J. S. Auerbach, p. 32)

Sec. 207. THAT AS USED IN THIS TITLE, THE TERM "INVESTED CAPITAL" FOR ANY YEAR MEANS THE AVERAGE INVESTED CAPITAL FOR THE YEAR, AS DEFINED

AND LIMITED IN THIS TITLE, AVERAGED MONTHLY.

~~That for the purpose of this title, actual capital invested means (1) actual cash paid in, (2) the actual cash value of property paid in other than cash, for stock or shares in such corporation or partnership, at the time of such payment, and (3) paid in or earned surplus and undivided profits used or employed in the business: Provided, That the good will, including trade-marks and trade brands, or the franchise of a corporation or partnership, is not to be included in the actual capital invested, unless the corporation or partnership made payment therefor specifically as such in cash or tangible property, the value of such good will, trade-marks, trade brands, or franchise, not to exceed the actual cash or actual value of the tangible property paid therefor at the time of such payment.~~

As used [*in section two hundred and three and in section two hundred and four, the term "capital"*] IN THIS TITLE "INVESTED CAPITAL" *does not include* [*money or other property borrowed, nor*] *stocks, bonds* (OTHER THAN OBLIGATIONS OF THE UNITED STATES), *or other assets, the income from which is not subject to the tax imposed by this title,* NOR MONEY OR OTHER PROPERTY BORROWED, *and* [*in case of a corporation or partnership*] *means, subject to the above* [*limitation*] LIMITATIONS:

(a) IN THE CASE OF A CORPORATION OR PARTNERSHIP:

(1) [*actual*] ACTUAL *cash paid in, (2) the actual cash value of* TANGIBLE *property paid in other than cash, for* [*stock*] STOCK *or shares in such corporation or partnership, at the time of such payment,* (BUT IN CASE SUCH TANGIBLE PROPERTY WAS PAID IN PRIOR TO JANUARY FIRST, NINETEEN HUNDRED AND FOURTEEN, THE ACTUAL CASH VALUE OF SUCH PROPERTY AS OF JANUARY FIRST, NINETEEN HUNDRED AND FOURTEEN, BUT IN NO CASE TO EXCEED THE PAR VALUE OF THE ORIGINAL STOCK OR SHARES SPECIFICALLY ISSUED THEREFOR) *and (3) paid in or earned surplus and undivided profits used or employed in the business,* EXCLUSIVE OF UNDIVIDED PROFITS EARNED DURING THE TAXABLE YEAR: *Provided, That* (A) THE ACTUAL CASH VALUE OF PATENTS AND COPYRIGHTS PAID IN FOR STOCK OR SHARES IN SUCH CORPORATION OR PARTNERSHIP, AT THE TIME OF SUCH PAYMENT, SHALL BE INCLUDED AS INVESTED CAPITAL, BUT NOT TO EXCEED THE PAR VALUE OF SUCH STOCK OR SHARES AT THE TIME OF SUCH PAYMENT, AND (B) *the good will,* [*including*] *trade-marks* [*and*] *trade brands,* [*or*] *the franchise of a corporation or partnership,* OR OTHER INTANGIBLE PROPERTY, [*is not to*] SHALL *be included* AS INVESTED CAPITAL IF [*unless*] *the corporation or partnership made*

payment BONA FIDE *therefor specifically as such in cash or tangible property, the value of such good will,* [*trade-marks*] TRADE-MARK, *trade* [*brands*] BRAND, [*or*] *franchise,* OR INTANGIBLE PROPERTY, *not to exceed the actual cash or actual* CASH *value of the tangible property paid therefor at the time of such payment.* BUT GOOD WILL, TRADE-MARKS, TRADE BRANDS, FRANCHISE OF A CORPORATION OR PARTNERSHIP, OR OTHER INTANGIBLE PROPERTY, BONA FIDE PURCHASED, PRIOR TO MARCH THIRD, NINETEEN HUNDRED AND SEVENTEEN, FOR AND WITH INTERESTS OR SHARES IN A PARTNERSHIP OR FOR AND WITH SHARES IN THE CAPITAL STOCK OF A CORPORATION (ISSUED PRIOR TO MARCH THIRD, NINETEEN HUNDRED AND SEVENTEEN), IN AN AMOUNT NOT TO EXCEED, ON MARCH THIRD, NINETEEN HUNDRED AND SEVENTEEN, TWENTY PER CENTUM OF THE TOTAL INTERESTS OR SHARES IN THE PARTNERSHIP OR OF THE TOTAL SHARES OF THE CAPITAL STOCK OF THE CORPORATION, SHALL BE INCLUDED IN INVESTED CAPITAL AT A VALUE NOT TO EXCEED THE ACTUAL CASH VALUE AT THE TIME OF SUCH PURCHASE, AND IN CASE OF ISSUE OF STOCK THEREFOR NOT TO EXCEED THE PAR VALUE OF SUCH STOCK;

(B) * * * IN THE CASE OF A FOREIGN CORPORATION OR PARTNERSHIP OR OF A NON-RESIDENT ALIEN INDIVIDUAL THE TERM "INVESTED CAPITAL" MEANS THAT PROPORTION OF THE ENTIRE INVESTED CAPITAL, AS DEFINED AND LIMITED IN THIS TITLE, WHICH THE NET INCOME FROM SOURCES WITHIN THE UNITED STATES BEARS TO THE ENTIRE NET INCOME.

[*As used in such sections the term "capital for the taxable year" means the capital as of the first day of the second half of such year, except that if a corporation or partnership is not then in existence or an individual is not then engaged in the trade or business, it means the capital as of the day of commencing business.*

The limitation in sections two hundred and three and two hundred and four as to the percentage of capital allowed as a deduction shall not apply in the case of a trade or business which is chiefly carried on by means of personal services and in which the captial is only nominal as compared with the gross income.]

Committee Reports

Report—Senate Finance Committee (65th Cong., 1st Sess., S. Rept. 103).— Actual capital invested is defined by the act of March 3, 1917, to mean (1) actual cash paid in, (2) cash value of other property as valued at the time of payment, and (3) surplus paid in or earned. The House bill amended this so as to provide further that good will and the like shall not be included in actual capital invested, unless specifically paid for as such in cash or tangible property.

The fundamental difficulty in assessing a tax on these lines arises from the difficulty of establishing a standard or measure of the amount of actual capital invested. The House bill endeavors to overcome this difficulty by a proviso designed to prevent inflated valuation of good will and the like intangible assets. To be reckoned as actual capital, the House bill requires that their value must be established or accredited through their being paid for "in cash." But provisions of this kind, designed to prevent inflation of capitalization, are usually of little real effect. Indeed, it is doubtful whether they can in any way be framed so as to be effective. Payments for good will and other intangible assets can easily be made to appear on the books of a corporation to have been made in cash. Almost always they are made so to appear. This familiar way of watering the stocks of corporations is impossible to detect and counteract without a specific examination of the precise facts in each case. Such an examination, if made for all concerns of every size and kind, as the House bill contemplates, must necessarily extend over a long period of time; it must be made in an enormous number of cases; it must lead to dispute and contest, and must be productive of unlimited litigation.

This method of procedure, however, does not merely open the way to litigation and to evasion; it also fails to safeguard legitimate interests. Many concerns of long and honorable standing have patents, trade-marks, brands, and the like assets, which are intrinsically and substantially valuable. They have real good will, honestly developed through long years of successful business, for which no payment in cash appears upon their books, or indeed has ever been made. Such assets, even though intangible, are honest and substantial property, and should not fail of consideration because of the circumstance that the concern has itself developed them, instead of purchasing them in cash from another party. (p. 5)

Congressional Discussion

Discussion—House (Cong. Rec. Vol. 55).—On computing invested capital by reference to current value of assets, in general. (p. 2129-30, 2131, 2417, 2545-46, 2550-51, 7584)

On the income versus the invested capital credit, in general. (p. 2547-52, 7581)

MR. BATHRICK. Let me ask the opinion as to the effect of this law in this illustration: Suppose a corporation buys a piece of land for $10,000 and erects a building on it—although the value of the building is not necessary to my illustration—and after a term of years the land itself increased in value so it is worth $100,000 more, would this bill as it stands require his exemption to rest upon the $10,000 and not consider the $100,000 at all?

MR. FORDNEY. Absolutely. The original capital invested, not its value to-day or during the taxable year.

*   *   *

MR. STAFFORD. I desire to ascertain the gentleman's construction of the section as to what is capital, on this state of facts: Suppose a corporation invests some of its surplus in buildings and purchase of equipment, would that be considered capital on which they would be entitled to deduct the 8 per cent exemption?

MR. FORDNEY. My friend, if you put in your undivided profits and put that addition into the business it is considered capital. For instance, we will say a bank organizes with a capital of $100,000. It runs along until it has a surplus of $100,000 and undivided profits of $100,000. The capital of that bank is $300,000, and on that 8 per cent can be deducted before excess profits begin. But it is only in the case of a bank and not with an industrial institution.

MR. STAFFORD. Mr. Chairman, if the gentleman will permit, the gentleman from North Carolina—and I would like to have the attention of the gentleman from North Carolina—when I put that concrete case to him yesterday he stated it would be considered as capital and would be considered as the basis for the 8 per cent deduction.

MR. FORDNEY. Yes; only in the case of a bank.

MR. STAFFORD. My instance yesterday was in the case of an industrial corporation that uses some of its profits in the purchase of equipment, of machinery, or buildings, and the like, which is really capital, and I asked the gentleman from North Carolina the question whether that would be the basis of the 8 per cent deduction, and he said under his construction it would be.

MR. KITCHIN. In the case the gentleman put yesterday and to-day it would be considered capital and would have the deduction. It distinguishes the part of profit from wear and tear or depreciation.

MR. STAFFORD. I am not talking about the question of depreciation. I am talking about the diversion of part of its capital in the purchase of equipment, of machinery, of stock, or of buildings, and whether under the new phraseology that would be the basis of the 8 per cent deduction?

MR. FORDNEY. As I understand the gentleman's question, if the surplus is put into the buildings it is capital, but increased values are not capital under the provisions of this bill.

*   *   *

MR. SNYDER. Take the case of a corporation that was originally capitalized at $50,000, and where at several periods since that time, out of the surplus earnings, additional capital has been created. Now, of course, that, under this law, stands as capital as well as surplus and undivided profits on which the 8 per cent can be deducted. Is that right?

MR. FORDNEY. Any money paid in as capital or any money put aside as surplus account and used as capital is considered capital under the terms of this bill.

MR. SNYDER. Whether earned or paid in?

MR. FORDNEY. No; not whether earned. You have got to put it to surplus.

MR. SNYDER. And then be declared into capital stock?

MR. FORDNEY. Yes; and put into actual use.

*   *   *

MR. BRITTEN. Under a condition of that kind, where the surplus is created and put into capital stock and distributed, the tax is levied upon that distribu-

tion, the same as any other dividend, is it not?

MR. FORDNEY. Whenever a profit is about to be distributed in dividends, if it is distributed as a stock dividend, it does not come in as capital. (p. 2130)

MR. KITCHIN. * * * Suppose we have a company of $100,000 capital, a cotton mill, say, and we have a surplus of $50,-000 and undivided profits of $50,000. We want to expand our plant by putting in new machinery and enlarging our buildings. We could either do it out of the surplus or from the undivided profits, or we could enlarge our capital and issue and sell stock and with the money make the enlargement. If we did the latter, then it is clear it would be counted as capital invested.

MR. STAFFORD. Yes.

MR. KITCHIN. Instead of issuing and selling stock, suppose we take $50,000 of that surplus or undivided profits and with it expand the plant. We would still have that deduction and it would still be surplus and carried as such, to be included in the basis of deduction of 8 per cent, for the act and the bill provide that surplus and undivided profits should be included in capital invested.

MR. STAFFORD. Why, no.

MR. KITCHIN. Oh, yes. Suppose the surplus was in money and we had it in bank and our balance sheet showed $50,000 surplus. We would take that $50,000 out of the bank, and instead of having it in money in the bank we would put it into the extension of the building, and our assets would still show the $50,000. In one case it is surplus in the shape of money on deposit in the bank and in the other it is surplus in the shape of enhanced value of the buildings, because you have extended them. You would have the same deduction as to the $50,000 in each case.

MR. STAFFORD. Then the gentleman believes that under the third division, on page 8, the invested profits in the way of the purchase of equipment, stock and the like, used in connection with the business of the corporation, which is the real capital, would be considered as paid in or undivided surplus used or employed in the business?

MR. KITCHIN. Yes.

MR. STAFFORD. It would not be listed on the books of the company any longer as surplus. There is nothing to show on the books of the company that it is surplus, because it shows on the books of the company that it is capital in the way of equipment or construction.

Mr. KITCHIN. Yes; it would in the balance sheet be carried as surplus, and that surplus would exist in the shape of enhanced value of the plant by reason of its enlargement. But that is distinct, I will say to the gentleman, from the ordinary wear and tear expense, which is deducted in the income tax. Suppose a machine breaks down. You repair it or order another in its place. You have to keep it in repair, as you do your building. You have that deduction in the ordinary wear and tear as part of the running expenses. Now, when you take money from surplus or profits and actually expand your plant, then it goes in as capital invested, and it will still be counted the same as surplus.

Mr. STAFFORD. I will say to the gentleman that the accounting methods of the best accountants when the money has been transferred and used in the way of equipment and stock no longer classifies it as surplus. It is classified under the head of capital.

Mr. KITCHIN. Let me repeat the example I gave to the gentleman a moment ago. If you had a $100,000 plant, and you were going to expand it to a $200,000 plant, with larger buildings and more machinery, you would not charge that as operating expenses, current expenses, I do not care where you got the money, whether from sale of new stock or from your surplus or profits. Your plant would be increased in value to the extent of $100,000, whether you call it capital, surplus, or profit. That would be $200,-000 that you would have invested there. Suppose, instead of going out and issuing stock for that $100,000 to expand the plant, which you concede would be counted as capital, you had a surplus in the bank or in products of the company which you could convert into money, of $100,000, which you carried as surplus, and you take this surplus and with it enlarge your plant, your books would show still $100,000 surplus, but the surplus would be in the form of enhanced value of your plant instead of deposit in bank or value of products on hand, and you would be entitled to an 8 per cent deduction on that amount.

Mr. STAFFORD. I am only questioning whether the phraseology as carried in the bill provides for that character of transfer of surplus into real capital?

Mr. KITCHIN. Yes; that would still remain the same as surplus and be deducted.

Mr. STAFFORD. I was questioning whether your phraseology would include it. I recognize that it is the same financial operation, whether you vote the money as stock dividends or as a money dividend and then have stock issued in turn. I wanted to make certain that that was covered in this third subdivision.

Mr. KITCHIN. There is absolutely no doubt about that. (Appendix p. 504)

Mr. MADDEN. * * * Let us assume that two men start in business with $100,000 capital each. They remain in business for 25 years, say. One man keeps his books systematically and charges off all depreciation from the very beginning until the end of the 25-year period, so that at the end of the 25 years his capital shows what it was originally when he went into business, as it ought. The other man instead of charging off depreciation allows the depreciation to accumulate as part of his assets and carries it along as part of his surplus. The surplus in the course of 25 years amounts to $900,000, so at the end of the 25 years one man would have $1,000,000 capital against which he would be allowed to charge 8 per cent profit, and the other man only a hundred thousand dollars capital. In one case the man who kept his books systematically and was on the square in the conduct of his business would be allowed under this law to collect $8,000 as 8 per cent profit and the other man would be allowed to collect $80,000 as his 8 per cent profit, and after the collection of $80,000 in the one case and the $8,000 in the other case the excess profits would begin to lie. Did the gentleman or the committee take into consideration in the excess-profits tax a condition such as I have described?

Mr. KITCHIN. Well, yes; we have, but, of course, if the Government will permit one to do that and can not find out the facts and if it can be covered up in the books, the result would be as you stated. The Treasury Department will have to find out whether that million dollars was a real bona fide surplus or not. I imagine the department will not take the books and accounts of a partnership or corporation without examining them to see what the real facts are. I can see how one could keep books so as to have his books show that there is a million dollars of working capital when there would not be but $100,000.

MR. MADDEN. He would not be paying the same amount of taxes in the one case as in the other. One man would be paying nine times more taxes in excess profits than the other.

MR. KITCHIN. If they took it on what the books showed and not what the facts really were. I could take my books and fool my creditors if they would simply take the books showing what my balance was.

MR. MADDEN. He would have the property in one case and charge it off in the other case and——

MR. KITCHIN. I will tell you how that can not be done. If the partnership or corporation actually did not charge it off, which ought to be done and which always will be done because of the income tax it has to pay—I have never known anyone to pay an income tax without getting all the deductions which the law permits him to have. He deducts everything to which he can be possibly entitled so as to make his income tax less. (Appendix p. 505)

Discussion—Senate (Cong. Rec. Vol. 55).—On the income versus the invested capital credit, in general. (p. 6001-03, 6067-79, 6193-95, 6440-43, 6444-50, 6460-62, 6531-32, 6550-60)

On computing invested capital by reference to current value of assets, in general. (p. 6444, 6453-57, 6504-06)

MR. SIMMONS. No. Then, Mr. President, the next substantial change is in section 207, which is a new section, made necessary by the maximum and minimum rate based upon capital. That section is simply a reprint of the House bill definition of capital invested, with a slight emendation which related to borrowed money, which is not employed in their definition. (p. 6434)

MR. OVERMAN. What I want to get at is who is to determine what actual cash value is? The amendment of the Senator's colleague which the Senator has just read states the "actual cash value," and in addition to that "the actual value of all assets other than

cash." Take one of the great monopolies—it is as to those I desire to hear the Senator—in determining the actual cash value the Government is limited in placing a value on it by the words "First, actual cash," and second, "the actual value of all assets other than cash." Take the Harvester Trust, about which I have talked with the Senator. I should like to hear him in reference to that matter, since he has thought about it. In order to become a great monopoly that trust has bought up all of its competitors. For example, the Harvester Trust was competing with the Deering Co., the Aultman Co., and other great companies; but in order to destroy them to become a monopoly, it bought them out, until now we have only one company in this country which is furnishing supplies of that character to the farmers. In ascertaining their capital the Government has got not only to take the cash value, but it has got to take the part of all its assets in the way of other property paid-in.

MR. UNDERWOOD. Surely.

MR. OVERMAN. If that is so, would such a company pay any taxes at all?

MR. UNDERWOOD. The Senator is right in his theory, but why discuss it? Does the Senator think that the Secretary of the Treasury of the United States is going to put value on wind such as he describes? Is he going to put value on water?.

MR. OVERMAN. What I am afraid of is we may limit the Secretary of the Treasury by providing that, besides cash, he shall ascertain the value of other assets paid into the corporation.

MR. UNDERWOOD. Mr. President, there may have been proposals here that have sought to provide an exemption on watered stock, but there is nothing of that kind in the amendment of my colleague, and, so far as that is concerned, I do not see that there is in the Senate amendment. The Senate amendment fixes the valuation of the exemption on the actual invested capital as of January 1 of the taxable year. Actual invested capital does not mean wind nor watered stock. The Bankhead amendment says:

For the purpose of this title, actual capital invested means, first, actual cash.

Is there any watered stock or wind in actual cash that belongs to the company?

MR. OVERMAN. Not in that.

MR. UNDERWOOD. The amendment proceeds:

And, second, the actual value of all assets other than cash.

Can there be any wind in "actual value?" If it is "actual value," how can it include watered stock? Does not that tell the Secretary of the Treasury that he must consider only "actual value?" We can not go out and assess it. We can not go and say, "You shall discard this item or take that item;" but when we say to the Secretary of the Treasury that in ascertaining the amount of this exemption it shall be allowed on "actual value" that means assets that are of a market value that can be sold. (p. 6443)

MR. LA FOLLETTE. * * * Mr. President, in the first place it would be utterly impossible for the Secretary of the Treasury or any body of experts employed by him to determine what has been paid in in cash, excepting as the books show it. If he undertook to examine as to the invested capital all the corporations in this country upon that subject, he would not complete the work in 5 years or 10 years.

Now, sir, in the second place, that part of the definition which makes "paid in or earned surplus and undivided profits used or employed in the business" a part of the capital, introduces an entirely new element. (p. 6529)

MR. SIMMONS. * * * Making no difference as to whether that capital was covered by an issuance of stock or represented by undistributed profits or surplus accumulated. This provision was to the effect that if the money was actually invested in the business, employed in the business, it should be considered as capital employed in the business in determining whether there had been an increase or decrease in capital. Under no possible construction of that language could it mean anything but exactly the same as the provision in the definition of capital about which the Senator was complaining. He said this would disturb the whole scheme and introduce an element of uncertainty and confusion. It means that capital, for the purposes of this bill, should consist of cash, or property taken in the place of cash, and of

surplus and undivided profits actually used and employed in the business.

That is an ordinary and a common definition of capital. Any definition of capital invested in business which leaves out surplus and undivided profits would be a false and misleading definition. That is the definition which the House put in its bill when it attempted to apply the 8 per cent flat exemption rule. That is the definition which we adopted when we decided upon the maximum and minimum. That is in substance the definition that we adopted when we were making allowances for the increase and decrease in capital between the prewar and the taxable year. In different language, but in legal intendment and meaning, it was identically the same in each case. But the Senator seems to think it is a device injected in this bill to allow somebody to escape taxation and cheat the Government of its revenues.

The Senate will remember how he inveighed against that definition. The Senate will remember he claimed that it would disturb the equilibrium and produce disastrous results with respect to the revenue to be realized from this bill. (p. 6536)

Discussion—House; on Report of Conference Committee (Cong. Rec. Vol. 55).—MR. KITCHIN. We have agreed on a definition as to invested capital substantially as the House had it, with some modification as to good will and other intangible assets. We also provide that property turned over for shares and stock in a corporation or partnership prior to January 1, 1914, to be valued at its cash value not as of the time it was turned over, but as of January 1, 1914. All property turned over since January 1, 1914, is valued at its cash value at the time so turned over. We make another provision that I am not specially impressed with. We have modified the meaning of "capital invested" by permitting stock issued in good faith for good will, franchise, trade-marks, and trade brands prior to March 3, 1917— the date of the passage of the excess-profits act of March 3, 1917, which gave corporations notice that they could not do so any more—up to 20 per cent of the total amount of the capital stock to be counted as part of the invested capital. (p. 7583)

Discussion—Senate; on Report of Conference Committee (Cong. Rec. Vol. 55).—MR. SIMMONS. * * * That definition, as you will recall, provided in substance that tangible property paid in in the place of cash for stock or shares in a corporation should be valued as at the time of payment. This part of the definition was qualified so as to provide that in case such tangible property was paid in before January 1, 1914, it should be valued at its actual cash value as of January 1, 1914, not to exceed the par value of the stock or shares specifically issued therefor.

The provision in the definition relating to good will, trade-marks, and so forth, did not include good will paid for in stock or shares, but only when paid for in cash or tangible property. This provision was modified so as to provide that good will, and so forth, bona fide purchases prior to March 3, 1917, for stock or shares in an amount not to exceed 20 per cent of the total stock or shares of the corporation or partnership shall be included as invested capital at its value at the time of purchase, and in no case to exceed the par value of the stock.

It also provided that patents and copyrights shall be treated as material assets and allowances made to the extent of the actual value at the time of the purchase, not to exceed par value of stock or shares issued therefor. (p. 7618)

Committee Hearings

Hearings—Senate Finance Committee.—Allowing for intangibles in invested capital though not paid for in cash. (J. S. Auerbach, p. 33-36; Cullen & Dykman, p. 59; J. A. Kratz, p. 65; W. L. Sweet, p. 76-78)

Determining invested capital by reference to current value of assets. (J. S. Auerbach, p. 36-38)

Clarifying term "actual capital invested." (J. A. Kratz, p. 63)

Sec. 208. [1]That in case of the reorganization, consolidation or change of ownership of a trade or business after March third, nineteen hundred and seventeen, if an interest or control in such trade or business of fifty per centum or more remains in control of the same persons, corporations, associations, partnerships, or any of them, then in ascertaining the invested capital of the trade or business no asset transferred or received from the prior trade or business shall be allowed a greater value than would have been allowed under this title in computing the invested capital of such prior trade or business if such asset had not been so transferred or received, unless such asset was paid for specifically as such, in cash or tangible property, and then not to exceed the actual cash or actual cash value of the tangible property paid therefor at the time of such payment.

Sec. 208

[1] This section was added by the Conference Committee.

Congressional Discussion

Discussion—Senate (Cong. Rec. Vol. 55).—MR. LAFOLLETTE. Now, subdivision (a) of section 204 merely provides for determining the amount of the war profits in those exceptional cases where the person or corporation in question had no net income from the trade or business during the prewar period or where the corporation was not in existence during that period, and in such case the experience of representative corporations and individuals engaged in a like or similar business is resorted to; but the war profits of these representative corporations or individuals are determined as provided in section 203. By this process you are simply led back to the starting point.

Section 204 (a) furnishes a rule merely to determine the war profits of those persons or concerns who were not engaged in business or had no profits during the prewar period, but it presupposes the ability to determine the war profits of the representative concerns whose experience is to be adopted as the means of determining the war profits of those persons and concerns who were not engaged in business or made no profits during the prewar period. Section 204 (a) does not involve the question of capitalization at all. The point against this amendment is the same as that against the House bill, namely, that where you are dealing with individuals and concerns that were in business during the prewar period and had profits during the prewar period it must lead to endless dispute and protracted litigation to determine the amount of capital invested as of January 1 of the taxable year. (p. 6505)

Discussion—House; on Report of Conference Committee (Cong. Rec. Vol. 55).—Mr. KITCHIN. There is a provision in the bill to take care of that. Where a corporation is reorganized with practically the same owners it is considered, so far as the percentage of deduction is concerned, a continuance of the business.

Mr. COOPER of Wisconsin. But there are new owners in it.

Mr. KITCHIN. I know, but there are also the old owners in it. If the old owners succeed to the new business, then they take the percentage that they had before the war, but if it is discontinued altogether, if the old owners gave up their business and got out, and an entirely new corporation was organized since the prewar period, then it would take an 8 per cent deduction, as provided in the bill for new companies or business.

Mr. GREEN of Iowa. The prewar income is no longer the basis of taxation.

Mr. KITCHIN. It is no longer the basis of taxation, but it is still the basis of the deduction in a much more limited extent than was in the Senate amend-

ments. There still exists a differential of 7 and 9 per cent. I am going to get to that and explain it as best I can.

Mr. COOPER of Wisconsin. It is exceedingly important in the case of this particular corporation, because for this $75,000 of new capital invested they gave notes payable monthly, and it requires a profit in order to meet those notes and amortize the debt.

Mr. KITCHIN. I will say to the gentleman that if there is a change of corporation, company, business, or ownership altogether, then it is a new company that was not in existence during the prewar period, and it would take the 8 per cent deduction for the new business. That is, it would have an 8 per cent deduction upon the capital invested by the new company plus a further deduction of $3,000. Then the rate of taxation would apply on the income in excess of the deduction. (p. 7580)

Discussion—Senate; on Report of Conference Committee (Cong. Rec. Vol. 55).—Mr. SIMMONS. * * * In this connection attention is called to another important amendment adopted in conference at the instance of the Senate conferees to protect the revenues against frauds and evasions through reorganization and recapitalization. It provides in general terms that in case of a reorganization, consolidation, or change in ownership of a trade or business after March 3, 1917, if the interest or control of such trade or business remains practically the same the assets transferred or received from the prior trade or business shall have no greater value than in computing the invested capital of such prior trade or business if such assets had not been transferred, unless such assets were paid for specifically in cash or tangible property, and then not to exceed the actual cash or cash value of such tangible property paid therefor at the time of payment. (p. 7618)

Secs.
209
210

[Set forth with sec. 205(a), page 353]

Sec.
212

Sec. 212. *That all administrative, special, and general provisions of law, including the laws in relation to the assessment, remission, collection, and refund of internal-revenue taxes not heretofore specifically repealed and not inconsistent with the provisions of this title are hereby extended and made applicable to all the provisions of this title and to the tax herein imposed, and all provisions of Title I of such Act of September eighth, nineteen hundred and sixteen, as amended by this Act, relating to returns and payment of the tax therein imposed, including penalties, are hereby made applicable to the tax imposed by this title.*

Sec. 213. *That the Commissioner of Internal Revenue, with the approval of the Secretary of the Treasury, shall make all necessary regulations for carrying out the provisions of this title, and may require any corporation, partnership or individual, subject to the provisions of this title, to furnish him with such facts, data, and information as in his judgment are necessary to collect the tax imposed by this title.*

Sec.
213

ACT OF MARCH 3, 1917

Sec. 200. That when used in this title—

The term "corporation" includes **<*also*>** joint-stock companies or associations, and insurance companies;

The term "United States" means only the States, the Territories of Alaska and Hawaii, and the District of Columbia; and

The term "taxable year" means the twelve months ending December thirty-first, except in the case of a corporation or partnership allowed to fix its own fiscal year, in which case it means such fiscal year. The first taxable year shall be the year ending December thirty-first, nineteen hundred and seventeen.

Congressional Discussion

Discussion—House (Cong. Rec. Vol. 54).—Rejected amendment to exempt insurance companies from tax. (p. 2418-22, 2427-29)

Discussion—Senate (Cong. Rec. Vol. 54).—Rejected amendment to exempt insurance companies from tax. (p. 3681-85, 3884-87, 4508-15)

Sec. 201. That in addition to the taxes under existing laws there shall be levied, assessed, collected, and paid for each taxable year upon the net income of every corporation and partnership organized, authorized, or existing under the laws of the United States, or of any State, Territory, or District thereof, no matter how created or organized, ~~excepting income derived from the business of life, health, and accident insurance combined in one policy issued on the weekly premium payment plan,~~ excepting income derived from the business of life, health, and accident insurance combined in one policy issued on the weekly premium payment plan, a tax of eight per centum of the amount by which such net income exceeds the sum of (a) $5,000 ~~and~~ **<*plus*>** *and* (b) eight per centum of the actual capital invested.

Every foreign corporation and partnership, including corporations and partnerships of the Philippine Islands and Porto Rico, shall pay for each taxable year a like tax upon the amount by which its net income received from all sources within the United States exceeds the sum of (a) eight per centum of the actual capital invested and used or employed in the business in the United States, ~~and~~ **<*plus*>** *and* (b) that proportion of $5,000 which the entire actual capital invested and used or employed in the business in the United States bears to the entire actual capital invested; and in case no such capital is used or employed in the business in the United States the tax shall be imposed upon that portion of such net income which is in excess of the sum of

370

(a) eight per centum of that proportion of the entire actual capital invested and used or employed in the business which the net income from sources within the United States bears to the entire net income, ~~and~~ <*plus*> <u>and</u> (b) that proportion of $5,000 which the net income from sources within the United States bears to the entire net income.

Committee Reports

Report—Senate Finance Committee (64th Cong., 2d Sess., S. Rept. 1039).— (1) The House bill exempts the income of certain insurance companies from the provisions of this title. Your committee recommend that this provision be stricken out so that the income of all insurance companies will be treated alike and upon the same basis. (p. 6)

Sec. 202. That for the purpose of this title, actual capital invested means (1) actual cash paid in, (2) the actual cash value~~, at the time of payment,~~ <u>at the time of payment,</u> of assets other than cash ~~paid in,~~ <*at the time such assets were transferred to the corporation or partnership,*> <u>paid in</u> and (3) paid in or earned surplus and undivided profits used or employed in the business; but does not include money or other property borrowed by the corporation or partnership <*,whether evidenced by bonds or otherwise*>.

Sec. 202 (margin)

Committee Reports

Report—Ways and Means Committee (64th Cong., 2d Sess., H. Rept. 1366).— Section 202 of this title defines "actual capital invested" to mean (1) actual cash paid in, (2) the actual cash value, at the time of payment, of assets other than cash paid in, and (3) paid in or earned surplus and undivided profits used or employed in the business. Money borrowed through bonds or otherwise is not included in the actual capital invested. (p. 4)

Congressional Discussion

Discussion—House (Cong. Rec. Vol. 54).—Mr. Kitchin. * * * Capital does not include borrowed money. On borrowed money they have a deduction for interest. "Actual capital invested" means and includes (1) actual cash paid in, (2) the actual cash value at the time of payment of assets or property paid in other than cash, and (3) paid in or earned surplus and undivided profits employed in the business. (p. 2268)

Mr. Mann. * * * How do you arrive at the amount of capital invested? Here is the New York Central Railroad, for instance, which has a capital stock and a bonded indebtedness. I forget what it pays in the way of dividends, but I think 5 per cent now. It may earn as a profit as much as 8 per cent a year, deducting a portion of it for depreciation and betterment, which I suppose is done under the rules of the Interstate Commerce Commission, carrying the same as surplus. Will you take the capital stock of the New York Central Railroad as the amount invested; or, if the Interstate Commerce Commission had valued the New York Central Railroad—which it has not yet—will you take their valuation as the amount of capital invested?

Mr. Kitchin. No. The bill itself explains what is capital actually invested. It is cash actually paid in, the actual value of assets, at the time of payment, paid in other than cash—paid in or earned surplus and undivided profits.

Mr. Mann. I venture to say in the case of the New York Central Railroad that it is impossible to arrive at those figures.

MR. KITCHIN. Then, in the case of bonds, the bill provides that it does not include borrowed money—which of course covers bonds—by the corporation and partnership, but they deduct their 6 per cent or 4 per cent, or whatever it is, which they pay on the bonds, and thus they get the benefit of that. (p. 2269)

MR. FORDNEY. * * * Suppose that a firm several years ago was organized with a capital of $1,000,000, a sawmill and timber proposition, for instance. Since that time they have paid no dividends, but have added profits to the original capital to the extent of half a million dollars, while in the meantime the value of their property has enhanced another half a million dollars. The question is whether you are going to permit them to deduct a profit upon the million and a half or two millions, or what sums, or are you going to fix a date upon which time that value shall be based?

MR. KITCHIN. Mr. Chairman, I want to say to the gentleman that in the case he cites, the 8 per cent deduction would be upon a million and a half dollars. In other words, you paid in first $1,000,000. Then, instead of taking the dividends and putting them into your pocket you put them back into the company, say, a timber company, to the amount of $500,000. That is your surplus or undivided profits. So your deduction would not be 8 per cent upon a million dollars, but would be 8 per cent upon the million and a half dollars. The bill provides that it is actual cash or assets paid in, and the surplus and undivided profits upon which the 8 per cent deduction is calculated. Now, then, in that case you would have, instead of a deduction or exemption of $80,000, a deduction of $120,000, plus the $5,000 exemption. Let me ask you, between you and me, do you not think a concern that put in a few years ago a million dollars and then has $500,000 of surplus and undivided profits and makes up on that $125,000 clear money every year, is able and ought it not to help pay a little upon excess profits for the country's "preparedness"?

MR. FORDNEY. I agree that that

suggestion is right. But suppose the $1,000,000 were invested 20 years ago and no dividends paid since that time, but the profits returned to the extent of half a million dollars?

MR. KITCHIN. I understand that. A deduction, as I explained, of 8 per cent would be allowed on the half million dollars as well as on the original capital of $1,000,000.

MR. FORDNEY. But as the gentleman suggested to me, does he not believe that a fair valuation of that property should be had and that it should be permitted to earn a profit upon the valuation as of the date of the enactment of the law or certainly on March 1, 1913, the time when the income-tax amendment to the Constitution became effective?

MR. KITCHIN. Mr. Chairman, that has somewhat disturbed me, to be perfectly candid, as I told the gentleman, in thinking the matter over in my own mind. I must confess that I have not yet arrived at a definite conclusion, but rather think the proper way is as the bill has it. We say in the bill cash paid in, and assets turned over or "paid in," the value of the assets taken at the time when turned over or paid in. It has occurred to me, and I want to say it to the members of the Committee on Ways and Means, and I have been somewhat worried over it, that it may be the proper thing to fix the date of the valuation of the assets turned over instead of cash as of March 1, 1913, the date of the income-tax amendment proclamation. However, I am inclined to the opinion that under all the circumstances, considering the administration difficulties involved, it is best to leave it as we present it in the bill. (p. 2269)

MR. ROBINSON. * * *

HARTFORD, CONN., *January 29, 1917.*
Hon. P. DAVIS OAKEY,
House of Representatives,
Washington, D. C.
MY DEAR MR. OAKEY: I understand that the Federal emergency revenue measure has been agreed upon in committee and is to be reported into the House to-morrow. We are warned that as drawn the bill would compel mutual life insurance companies to pay the so-called excess-profits tax. It does not seem as if this could be possible in view of the admitted intent of the measure, to wit, to impose a tax upon concerns which are making more than what Congress assumes to fix as a reasonable return on invested capital. The necessary factors ap-

pear to be entirely lacking in the case of a mutual company. There is no invested capital in the ordinary sense and our fear is that for the purposes of the tax the book surplus would be assumed to be the so-called capital. This surplus is a relatively small amount representing a margin of safety in the value of assets over estimated liabilities. The net income of these companies under the income-tax act may be very small in a given year or it may be an amount which would represent a very large percentage of the previous small book surplus. In the latter case a tax based on the excess of the so-called net income over 8 per cent of the book surplus would mean a heavy tax. Such a result is wholly inconsistent with the intent to tax excess profits and to my mind is preposterous. If the bill does apply to mutual insurance and works in the way which I have indicated we wish to make every possible effort to remedy it.

Yours, very truly,

Lucius F. Robinson.

(p. 2322-23)

Mr. Longworth. * * * Let me call the attention of gentlemen to one class of corporations which will be particularly injuriously affected by this excess-profit tax. I refer to those corporations which desseminate throughout the country information for the use of the people. Newspapers above all other corporations will be called upon to pay this tax. Why? Because under the terms of this bill no corporation engaged in publishing a newspaper can take into consideration the value of its good will; in other words, that which makes a newspaper a success —enterprise, economy of management, and ability of management—is taxed in this bill. The plant of a newspaper is relatively of small significance. Probably in the average newspaper of this country its actual plant is not 20 per cent of its value as a going institution. And yet, under this bill no newspaper can consider as a part of the capital upon which these excess taxes are imposed anything except cash value of the plant and of its assets. (p. 2434)

Discussion—Senate (Cong. Rec. Vol. 54).—On computing invested capital by reference to current values of assets, in general. (p. 4119-23, 4493-94, 4505)

Mr. Simmons. * * * The chief controversy made by the representatives of the corporations who appeared before your committee in opposition to this tax was with reference to the language in subdivision 2 of section 202. Some of them insisted that the correct rule would be the cash value of the property at the time of the return of income for taxation, instead of at the time the property was turned over as a part of the assets of the corporation. Of course, it is to their interest to increase the amount of the exemption, and they insisted that the basis of such exemption should be the value at the time of the return, the effect of which clearly would be to give them the benefit of the unearned increment, of good will, and so forth.

Your committee adopted the basis recommended by it because they thought it would place every taxpayer upon the same basis. That is, it would allow to each taxpayer an amount estimated in cash equal to the actual investment in the business. This puts every taxpayer upon a standard of parity in estimating the invested capital.

*   *   *

If we should adopt the other basis and take the valuation at the time of the return, the unearned increment of property, and the earning capacity of the concern would be capitalized annually and be reflected in each return for taxation.

The unearned increment of real property would be very great in a place like New York, while it would be very small in many prosperous but smaller places.

The earning capacity, which is reflected in the market value of the property, depends largely upon the nature of the business, upon good will, trademarks, patents, and so forth. At the present time the earning capacity of certain concerns, like the powder factories, is very great, while for other concerns it is very small.

Under the basis as recommended, the standard for measuring the capital invested is a fixed and unchangeable one; under the basis as suggested, the standard would be a varying one, changing with every season and with every change in conditions.

Your committee believes that with the amendment proposed to section 202 of the House bill the definition therein made of actual capital invested will furnish a just and equitable basis of computation as between the taxpayer, and will secure to the Government the income sought to be derived from this source without making it necessary to increase the tax beyond 8 per cent upon net profits. (p. 3677)

Committee Hearings

Hearings—Senate Finance Subcommittee.—Clarifying meaning of "paid in or earned surplus and undivided profits." (S. C. Neale, p. 102)

Determining invested capital by reference to current value of assets. (W. C. Osborn, p. 105; C. H. Butler, p. 123-124; C. D. Joslyn, p. 125-132; J. A. Emery, p. 139, 142-143; P. Armitage, p. 151-158; A. Douglas, p. 159)

Sec. 203

Sec. 203. That the tax herein imposed upon corporations and partnerships shall be computed upon the basis of the net income shown by their income tax returns under Title I of the Act entitled "An Act to increase the revenue, and for other purposes," approved September eighth, nineteen hundred and sixteen, or under this title, and shall be assessed and collected at the same time and in the same manner as the income tax due under Title I of such Act of September eighth, nineteen hundred and sixteen. * * *

Committee Reports

Report—Ways and Means Committee (64th Cong., 2d Sess., H. Rept. 1366).—This title also provides that the excess tax upon corporations shall be computed upon the corporation returns made in accordance with the corporations' income tax returns. (p. 4)

Congressional Discussion

Discussion—House (Cong. Rec. Vol. 54).—Mr. KITCHIN. * * * Such net incomes or profits of a corporation is its next income shown by its income-tax returns, under the present income-tax law—that is, we take the net income of a corporation according to such income-tax returns as the starting point or basis of calculation for the exemption or deduction and for the tax. (p. 2268)

Discussion—Senate (Cong. Rec. Vol. 54).—The SECRETARY. Section 203 begins at the foot of page 4 of the printed bill. It is proposed to strike out, after the numeral "203," the following words:

That the tax herein imposed upon corporations and partnerships shall be computed upon the basis of the net income shown by their income-tax returns under Title I of the act entitled "An act to increase the revenue, and for other purposes," approved September 8, 1916, or under this title.

And to insert the following words:

That the tax herein imposed upon corporations and partnerships shall be computed upon the basis of the income subject to the normal tax as shown by their income-tax returns under title 1 of the act entitled "An act to increase the revenue, and for other purposes," approved September 8, 1916, or under this title, and that for the purpose of computing said tax corporations and partnerships shall be allowed a credit as provided by section 5, subdivision 3, title 1, for their profit derived from dividends.

Mr. LODGE. I will ask the Secretary to read the second amendment in a moment. Of that amendment I wish briefly to explain the purpose. The section as it stands provides that the tax imposed upon corporations and partnerships shall be computed upon the basis of the net income shown by their income-tax returns. If we look at the income-tax law of September 8, 1916, we find that the term "net income" in the case of individuals means gross income less the eight deductions allowed in section 5a, but before deducting credits allowed in section 5b and 5c. Subdivision b allows, for the purpose of the normal tax, a credit for dividends received by the individual from corporations which are themselves subject to the normal tax. The original income-tax law of 1913 was so construed by the Treasury Department that members of a partnership were deprived of any credit for dividends received by the partnership. This injustice was cured by the law of 1916 by an express provision contained in section 18, allowing individual partners a credit for their proportionate share of the profits derived from such dividends.

What I ask by this amendment is that Congress should not reject the principle in the case of the excess profits tax which it has adopted in the case of the income tax, and that is why I have proposed that the words "net income," which are included in the bill, be amended so as to read "income subject to the normal tax." The effect of this would be to allow partnerships for the purpose of this act the same credit for dividends that they are allowed under the income-tax law.

This amendment, however, goes somewhat further. I have only described a part of it. It provides also to allow corporations as well as partnerships a credit for dividends received.

I think, Mr. President, that this is certainly just in principle, as it would be an undue hardship upon so-called holding corporations to impose an excess profits tax of 8 per cent upon earnings which have already been subjected to that tax in the hands of the subsidiary corporation.   (p. 4478)

Committee Hearings

Hearings—Senate Finance Subcommittee.—Eliminating dividends from excess profits tax income.   (W. Motley, p. 136-137, 138-139)

Sec. 204.

That corporations exempt from tax under the provisions of section eleven of Title I of ~~the~~ <such> *the* Act approved September eighth, nineteen hundred and sixteen, and partnerships carrying on or doing the same business shall be exempt from the provisions of this title, and the tax imposed by this title shall not attach to incomes of partnerships <*or corporations*> derived <*exclusively*> from ~~agriculture or from~~ *agricultural or from* personal services.

Committee Reports

Report—Ways and Means Committee (64th Cong., 2d Sess., H. Rept. 1366).—Corporations, joint-stock companies, or associations, and insurance companies exempt under section 11 of the income tax, and partnerships carrying on or doing the same business, and the income of partnerships derived from agriculture or from professional services, are exempt from the excess-profits tax.   (p. 4)

Report—Senate Finance Committee (64th Cong., 2d Sess., S. Rept. 1039).—(2)   The House bill exempts the income of partnerships derived from agriculture or from personal services. Your committee recommend an amendment confining this exemption to the income of corporations or partnerships derived exclusively from personal services.   (p. 6)

Congressional Discussion

Discussion—House (Cong. Rec. Vol. 54).—Rejected amendment to exempt insurance companies from tax. (p. 2418-22, 2427-29)

MR. FESS. I would like to ask three questions. First, what was the theory of the exemption of agricultural associations?

MR. KITCHIN. The gentleman means, of course, the income of partnership derived from agriculture. I will say to the gentleman from Ohio that that question has been asked a considerable number of times. There is one very serious objection to including it, namely, the difficulty in its administration. Who knows what is invested in land and farming? If you use fertilizer this year, how much of that fertilizer is consumed by the profit making growing crop and how much goes over to next year in improvement of the soil, and next year, and so on. If you ditch it, if you put 10,000 yards of ditching on a farm, how much of that ditching can you charge up to the current year's crop or operating expenses, and how much as permanent improvement?

There are a thousand and one things that enter into farming operations that would be most difficult to say whether it is operating current expenses or is new capital put in, or should go to surplus. (p. 2270)

Mr. Fess. What is included under this exemption "personal services"?

Mr. Green of Iowa. I was just coming to that and was going on to show the injustice of this bill. The exemptions allowed to a partnership are specified very particularly in section 205 of the bill, and it will be found that they are exactly the same as the exemptions allowed an individual under the income-tax law. It is plain, therefore, that no allowance can be made for personal services in a partnership unless the income results entirely from personal services, so that the partnership is entirely exempted from the provisions of the bill as provided in another section.

Let us take some concrete examples and the injustice and wrong of this bill becomes very plain. For example, take a law partnership. Here the profits are derived entirely from personal services and consequently are exempted in this bill. They may make $50,000 or $100,-000 a year and they will pay nothing, but across the street from them is a small commercial partnership making perhaps $10,000 or $20,000 a year, a great portion of which is derived from the personal services of the partners. (p. 2323)

Mr. Fess. Would a stock brokerage company fall under the head of personal services? Is not that all personal?

Mr. Green of Iowa. Unless capital was employed in the business the profits of a brokerage firm would fall under the head of personal services and even if it made $100,000 a month it would not be taxed. (p. 2323)

Discussion—Senate (Cong. Rec. Vol. 54).—Rejected amendment to exempt insurance companies from tax. (p. 3681-85, 3884-87, 4508-15)

Mr. Simmons. The Senator is taking a corporation and segregating a part of the income that is derived from personal services from the income derived from other sources, and exempting that part of the income which is derived from personal services from the operation of this tax.

Mr. Bryan. And that part derived from agriculture.

Mr. Simmons. Yes; and that part derived from agriculture. The committee made this exemption and put it in such language, or attempted to put it in such language, as to make it certain that it would inure only to the benefit of a copartnership or a corporation that had no income that was not derived from personal services.

Mr. Oliver. Mr. President, it seems to me that a corporation may have income from one source which would be taxed under this bill and also have a large income from agriculture. A firm of merchants, for example, in a country town may have some farms out in the country; and what I aim at is to except from the operation of this tax that portion of their income which is derived from the farms, not excepting that derived from other business. (p. 3901)

Mr. Cummins. * * * How can a corporation render a personal service? Undoubtedly there must have been in the minds of the members of the committee some instances in which corporations, which are artificial beings or entities, can render personal service, but those instances do not occur to me. I should like to know what has been or is in the minds of the members of the committee with regard to that matter. (p. 3904)

Mr. Simmons. The Senator will observe the language is "the tax imposed by this title shall not attach to incomes of partnerships or corporations derived exclusively from personal services." The committee conceived a possible case where a corporation will have no income except such as is derived from the personal services of the members of the corporation. I think for a concrete example it was suggested to the committee that there is now in this country a very large corporation composed exclusively of civil engineers. The sole income of that corporation is from the professional services of the engineers who are members of the corporation. It does no business outside of obtaining contracts to do engineering work, and that work is performed by members of the corporation. The result is that the total income of the corporation is derived from personal services.

Another illustration which was in the mind of the committee and discussed was that of a law firm. Of course law firms are generally partnerships, but they are sometimes corporations. A number of lawyers can associate themselves together in a corporation, issuing, if you please, no stock, the total income of the corporation of lawyers being the fees that are earned by them, and they are divided under some rule agreed upon among themselves.

Another illustration was that of physicians. To state that would be a mere repetition of what I said about lawyers. The idea of the committee was that if there was such a corporation to do the work and they had no other income except that derived from the personal services of the members or experts in the line of the work of the corporation whom they employed, their income would be an instance where the corporation derived its sole income from personal services.

MR. CUMMINS. Mr. President, my first observation is that if it was intended by the committee to reach any such cases as have been suggested by the Senator from North Carolina, this language would not do it. If three lawyers were to incorporate it would not be the corporation that rendered the service, for no corporation has the right to practice law. It can perform no act in a professional capacity. If three physicians were to incorporate the reasoning would be exactly the same. If, however, it was intended, as I suspect it was, to release all corporations or some corporations rather without capital, then I insist it should be made so general that either the presence of capital or the absence of capital should be the test and not the rendition of a service by the corporation.

I do not believe in the distinction at all based upon any such discrimination or division as has been stated by the Senator from North Carolina. Evidently the House did not believe in any such thing, because the House very properly limited the exception to personal service rendered by a partnership, which is simply a collection of individuals without the legal characteristic which follows a corporation.

I think we ought to pause a moment before we make any such distinction as is here suggested. I am sure that the three cases cited by the Senator from North Carolina are not provided for in the act under this language, for these personal services would be rendered by

individuals and not by a corporation. I think the very character of the service is such that it can not be rendered by a corporation.

I am afraid that there are other instances which I am not able myself to mention or to describe through which some very large incomes would entirely escape taxation. There is no such discrimination in the income-tax law as I remember. This is based on the same general idea. If a corporation such as is here mentioned can be required to pay an income tax, why should not the corporation be required to pay the additional tax that is here imposed?

If I knew just who would be caught or just who would be exempted by this language I would have a more intelligent judgment, but I confess I do not know. However, I will put to the Senator from North Carolina an illustration. I do it because I have received some communications upon that subject. Suppose two or three gentlemen who are engaged in promoting Chautauqua lectures incorporate, as they have done. They have no capital substantially. They employ eminent personages to go about the country and deliver lectures and from that business acquire a considerable income. I think they ought to be excepted from the operation of this additional tax, but does the Senator from North Carolina think that these words will embrace such an instance as I have just given?

MR. SIMMONS. Mr. President, I will say to the Senator that I am inclined to think they would. I do not myself see the distinction which the Senator makes. I understand the Senator contends that a corporation which is an artificial entity can not render any personal service, and that therefore that corporation can not derive any income from the personal service of those who may render service in behalf of the corporation.

MR. CUMMINS. In the case cited by the Senator from North Carolina I thought that was true.

MR. SIMMONS. In the case the Senator put you have a number of gentlemen who are associated together as a corporation to deliver lectures. I am not quite clear as to whether that might be personal service.

MR. CUMMINS. The corporation does

not deliver the lectures.

MR. SIMMONS. They are associated together in a corporation. That is what I said. They are associated together in a corporation, and the purpose of the association is that the members of the corporation shall do a certain line of professional work.

MR. SMOOT. They may employ others.

MR. SIMMONS. They may employ others, but, as a rule, they do the personal work themselves. They are to do a certain line of personal work. In doing that personal work they receive a certain compensation. That compensation, according to the terms of the incorporation, is to be turned into the treasury of the corporation and divided between the members of the corporation according to some rule they fix among themselves. Now, that is not the corporation rendering the service, but it is an income which comes to the corporation through personal service rendered, and it only comes through the personal service.

MR. CUMMINS. Will the Senator be willing to amend this paragraph so that it will read—I will not attempt to quote it literally—but so that it will except the income of corporations derived from the personal labor or service of the members of the corporation? (p. 3904)

MR. SMOOT. I know of corporations in which there is not a single, solitary person employed except those who are members of the corporation. I know of large corporations that will not allow an employee to work for them unless they become members of the corporation and render personal service.

MR. HUGHES. The Senator will remember, however, that I insisted upon the retention of the word "exclusively."

MR. SIMMONS. Of course.

MR. SMOOT. They do not employ a single person who is not a member of the corporation.

MR. HUGHES. I do not think the Senator from Utah has in mind the case of a corporation where they derive their incomes from nothing but the personal services of their employees. If they are manufacturing corporations, they sell goods.

MR. SMOOT. But I am speaking of merchants——

MR. HUGHES. Merchants, of course,

would not fall within that class. They derive an income from the sale of goods.

MR. SMOOT. But the sale of goods comes through their personal services.

MR. HUGHES. They are not within this language.

MR. CUMMINS. I think the Senator from New Jersey is right about that and I will point it out in a moment to the Senator from Utah.

*   *   *

In the case of a merchant, his profits, or, if it is a corporation, their profits are partly derived from the capital invested, and therefore they would not come within the meaning of this language.

MR. SIMMONS. We intended to exclude them by the use of the word "exclusively."

MR. SMOOT. That would be, of course, where they had capital stock, but they do have capital stock in such cases.

MR. BRANDEGEE. What corporation does not have capital stock?

MR. SMOOT. Let me ask the Senator having the bill in charge if this was not the way this matter came about: The House provision only referred to incomes of partnerships, and, of course, that could apply to personal services; and the Senate committee put in the words "or corporations," and made no change whatever in the words "personal services"?

MR. HUGHES. I will say to the Senator that there is a species of corporations in this country which are practically partnerships; two or three civil engineers, for instance, form a corporation, and operate as a corporation. They render their services to various individuals, and the corporation sends those individuals the bills. The money goes into the treasury of the corporation and the profits are divided. They are practically a partnership.

The question with the committee was whether or not we wanted to lay an excess profits tax upon the earnings of men who had a very small capitalization, just sufficient to come within the laws of the State.

MR. SMOOT. They have incorporated for the reason that they think there is an advantage in being incorporated.

MR. HUGHES. Yes.

MR. SMOOT. And therefore they should pay the tax.

MR. HUGHES. I will say to the Senator that we discussed that phase of the matter. I have personal knowledge of a number of such cases. We went into the proposition rather fully, and considered it from every viewpoint. I have no quarrel with the Senator if he does not take the view that the committee took of the subject. But we came to the conclusion that such a corporation would not be properly subject to this excess profits tax as would be a corporation with a tremendous capitalization which would be permitted to earn a rate of profit upon its great capitalization before the excess profits tax would apply.

MR. SMOOT. Such individuals take contracts in the name of the corporation, do they not?

MR. HUGHES. I am not speaking of their taking contracts.

MR. SMOOT. They do work in the name of the corporation?

MR. HUGHES. They do work in the name of the corporation.

MR. SMOOT. Just the same practically as any other corporation does work for the corporation and in the name of the corporation?

MR. HUGHES. Exactly; yes.

MR. SMOOT. Then I do not see why they should not be taxed.

MR. HUGHES. There are a number of doctors and surgeons throughout the country who have formed partnerships and formed corporations, who run hospitals and sanitariums in connection with their practice.

MR. SMOOT. If they run hospitals they have money invested.

MR. HUGHES. Then they would pay this tax, but if their income is derived exclusively from their professional practice they would not. Take the Mayo Bros., merely for illustration. If they have a great hospital for operating and practicing medicine, and so on, in the city of Washington, and there should be three partners who decide, for the purpose of convenience, that they will incorporate themselves, which is frequently done, and they derive no income except from the surgical operations which they perform, they would not properly come within the provisions of this proposed law; at least we thought they would not, and our language is intended to exclude them.

MR. SMOOT. I think, perhaps, as a hospital is equipped with surgical instruments and apparatus of every description necessary to carve people up——

MR. HUGHES. Or to cut them down.

MR. SMOOT. And to make them whole if they are broken in two, and so forth, many times they have just as much capital invested in their business as have other corporations in their business, and it seems to me they should pay the tax.

MR. HUGHES. The Senator has the right to vote that way.

MR. CUMMINS. There is a very great hospital at Rochester, Minn.—the greatest, I suppose, in the world. I do not know whether the Mayo Bros. are incorporated or not. They have a very large income, and they deserve it. Does the committee intend that if they incorporate their hospital, to relieve their income of this tax?

MR. SMITH of Georgia. Mr. President, answering and giving my own opinion to the Senator from Iowa, I will say that their income must be derived exclusively from personal services or they would not be relieved. I do not know a corporation anywhere that has not any money invested and which derives its income exclusively from personal services. If there are any such, I do not object to it, but I myself do not know any that it would relieve.

MR. CUMMINS. There are many corporations, of course, which have no capital stock at all; but I do not believe that those corporations were intended to be relieved, for few of them could be said to derive their income exclusively from personal services. Take the case of an insurance company without capital stock. It does not derive its income exclusively from personal services, I presume, although it always begins in that way.

MR. SMITH of Georgia. No, Mr. President, it does not begin in that way.

* * *

MR. SMITH of Georgia. It does not begin in that way, because the promoters had to put up money to start it; it could not start just by personal services. It takes some money to start with.

MR. CUMMINS. So it does with a corporation of lawyers or of physicians. They must have enough money, at least, to pay the fees of incorporation and whatever costs are incidental to organization. I am very anxious that the whole of the class that was intended to be covered by this exemption shall be clearly embraced in it. If corporations of lawyers and doctors are to be exempted from the tax, then I want other corporations, altruistic in their character, also to be exempted.

MR. SIMMONS. Will the Senator from Iowa let me inquire of him whether his view about this matter would be met if, after the words "personal services," the words "rendered by the members of the corporation," were added, so that it would read "to incomes of partnerships or corporations derived exclusively from the personal services rendered by the members of the corporation."

MR. CUMMINS. I think that would be entirely satisfactory, if there was provision for a small maximum of capital; that is, the capital that is required to incorporate. It would not be substantially an earning capital, but every such corporation must, as the Senator from Georgia has said, spend a little money in preparing for its work.

MR. SMITH of Georgia. I meant to go further than that. The insurance company promoters, for instance, are compelled to put up some money to meet losses for a while until they build up a reserve. They can not start the company without having some capital, whether it is called a subscription to stock or voluntary contribution by promoters. It requires money to promote and start the company and to take care of the losses for a while.

MR. CUMMINS. But, nevertheless, Mr. President, the income at any given time might be derived entirely from personal services, even though they had invested some capital in the beginning.

Mr. President, I feel this way about it: I could not clearly see the cases that were intended to be exempted, and so I asked the question of the Senator from North Carolina, and this debate has opened up rather a pretty wide inquiry, and I hope that the amendment will not be finally disposed of to-night. It is growing late. (p. 3905-06)

MR. SMITH of South Carolina. * * * There is a sanitarium there that was organized with $100,000 capital. The income derived is from the personal services of the physicians and those who are employed to render service to those who are afflicted and brought there for treatment. Under the terms of this bill are they exempt from the operation of this tax? As I have said, their income is derived from their personal services; but suppose a dividend were to be paid to certain stockholders, would the infirmary corporation be subject to this tax?

MR. SMITH of Georgia. If the dividend was over 8 per cent it would be subject to an 8 per cent tax on all in excess of 8 per cent.

MR. HUGHES. I will say to the Senator that my recollection is that this language follows the language of the English act, and the word "exclusively" there would prevent the corporation named by the Senator from South Carolina being exempted.

MR. SMITH of South Carolina. My interpretation of that language was, that so long as their earnings were from personal services and not from the barter and sale or exchange of goods, they would be exempt, no matter what their earnings were. That was my understanding of it. (p. 3906)

The SECRETARY. The second amendment proposed to section 204, is, on page 5, line 25, after the word "title," to strike out the words "and the tax imposed by this title shall not attach to incomes of partnerships or corporations derived exclusively from agriculture or from personal services" and in lieu insert "and the tax imposed by this title shall not attach to such part of the income of any partnership or corporation as is derived from agriculture or from personal or professional services."

MR. LODGE. The main difference, Mr. President, is that I have included in the exemption professional as well as personal service and income derived from agriculture. There are many small partnerships and corporations where the business is built up by the professional exertions of the persons forming the partnership or corporation. A large part of the income, for instance, in engineering affairs comes from the ability and professional attainments of the partners. I do not think that those services ought to be taxed any more than personal services. It seems to me professional serv-

ices ought also to be exempt as much as　4478-79)
agriculture and personal services.　(p.

Committee Hearings

Hearings—Senate Finance Subcommittee.—Exempting personal service corporations.　(W. Motley, p. 133-135, 137)

Sec. 206. That all administrative, special, and general provisions of law, including the laws in relation to the assessment, remission, collection, and refund of internal-revenue taxes not heretofore specifically repealed and not inconsistent with the provisions of this title are hereby extended and made applicable to all the provisions of this title and to the tax herein imposed, and all provisions of Title I of such Act of September eighth, nineteen hundred and sixteen, relating to returns and payment of the tax therein imposed, including penalties, are hereby made applicable to the tax required by this title.

Sec.
206

Committee Reports

Report—Ways and Means Committee (64th Cong., 2d Sess., H. Rept. 1366).— The tax imposed upon corporations and partnerships is to be computed upon the basis of the net income shown by their income-tax returns made under the income-tax law, and is to be assessed and collected at the same time and in the same manner as the income tax.　(p. 4)

Sec. 207. That the Commissioner of Internal Revenue, with the approval of the Secretary of the Treasury, shall make all necessary regulations for carrying out the provisions of this title, and may require any corporation or partnership subject to the provisions of this title to furnish him with such facts, data, and information as in his judgment are necessary to collect the tax provided for in this title.

Sec.
207

ACT SECTION INDEX

EXPLANATION OF ACT SECTION INDEX

Order of arrangement.—This index lists provisions by act sections, that is, sections of the Revenue Act of 1945, Revenue Act of 1943, etc., as distinguished from Code sections. In each instance, however, the related Code section is set forth. Thus, sec. 734(a)(1) was brought into the Code by sec. 11 of the Excess Profits Tax Amendments of 1941. Accordingly, under the heading of the Excess Profits Tax Amendments of 1941, in numerical order, is listed sec. 11 and alongside of it is shown the related Code sec. 734(a)(1). As the book also contains an index by Code sections, it is always possible to get promptly to the legislative history of any provision, whether the initial point of reference be the act section or Code section.

Provisions not listed.—The index does not account for all sections and subdivisions. Those not listed have been omitted because of their insignificance from the viewpoint of this book, as explained under "Guides to the Use of This Book." That explains why, for example, sec. 16 of the Excess Profits Tax Amendments of 1941 is not listed in the index.

Listed provisions without page numbers.—Provisions without page numbers have no legislative history in the particular act and therefore have not been set forth in the book. An example of this is sec. 202 of the Revenue Act of 1942 in relation to sec. 710(a)(1)(B) of the Code.

Changes in section numbers by later amendment.—Sometimes a Code section number has been changed by amendment in a later act. Thus, Code sec. 713(c) in the 1940 Act was changed to sec. 713(g) by the Excess Profits Tax Amendments of 1941. In the section index of the 1940 Act the original number, namely, sec. 713(c) is set forth. Immediately thereafter is listed in brackets the reference to sec. 713(g), which is the number under which the material is set forth in the text of the book and in the Code section index.

Difference between unit of subdivision in the index and the one in the book.—Reference in the index may be to a subdivision such as sec. 206(a)(2). In the material, that subdivision may not be set forth as such. Instead, sec. 206(a) or sec. 206 may be treated because the legislative history material in the particular instance does not lend itself to a smaller breakdown. Sec. 206(a)(2) is, of course, to be considered as part of sec. 206(a) or sec. 206, as the case may be.

Page numbers on cross-references.—While the general arrangement of the text of the book is by Code sections in their numerical order, a particular Code section may be set forth out of numerical order because its legislative history can be more conveniently treated jointly with another Code section. As explained under "Guides to the Use of

This Book," where this is the case, a cross-reference appears at the point of numerical order. In the index, the page reference is to the place where the section is actually treated, and not where the cross-reference appears. Thus, Code sec. 711(a)(2)(C) is treated jointly with sec. 711(a)(1)(A) starting at page 17. A cross-reference to this effect is set forth on page 38 where sec. 711(a)(2)(C) comes up in numerical order. The page references in the index to sec. 711(a)(2)(C) are the same as for sec. 711(a)(1)(A).

ACT SECTION INDEX

REVENUE ACT OF 1945

[November 8, 1945, H. R. 4309, Public No. 214, 79th Cong.,
1st Sess., ch. 453, 59 Stat. 556]

PAGE	Act Sec.	CODE SEC.	PAGE	Act Sec.	CODE SEC.
7	122(b)	710(c)(3)	7	122(d)	710(c)(3)

REVENUE ACT OF 1943

[February 25, 1944, H. R. 3687, Public No. 235, 78th Cong.,
2d Sess., ch. 63, 58 Stat. 26]

PAGE	Act Sec.	CODE SEC.	PAGE	Act Sec.	CODE SEC.
93	121(d)(6)	718(a)(6)(A)	240	208(b)(1)	735(a)(5)
1	202(b)	710(a)(1)(B)	242	208(b)(2)	735(a)(8)
2	203(b)	710(a)(3)	244	208(b)(3)	735(a)(12)
212	207(a)	731	252	208(c)	735(b)(4)
—	208(a)	735(a)(1)	254	208(c)	735(b)(5)
235	208(b)(1)	735(a)(1)	33	208(d)	711(a)(1)(I)
237	208(b)(1)	735(a)(2)	33	208(e)	711(a)(2)(K)
—	208(b)(1)	735(a)(3)	200	209(a)	727(h)
238	208(b)(1)	735(a)(4)			

REVENUE ACT OF 1942

[October 21, 1942, H. R. 7378, Public No. 753, 77th Cong.,
2d Sess., ch. 619, 56 Stat. 798]

PAGE	Act Sec.	CODE SEC.	PAGE	Act Sec.	CODE SEC.
—	202	710(a)(1)(B)	31	206(b)(2)	711(a)(2)(I)
—	203(a)	710(a)(3)	20	207(a)	711(a)(1)(B)
—	204(a)	710(b)(3)	—	207(b)	711(a)(1)(C)
4	204(b)	710(c)(1)	20	207(c)	711(a)(2)(D)
5	204(b)	710(c)(2)	—	207(d)	711(a)(2)(E)
10	204(b)	710(c)(3)	20	207(e)	711(b)(1)(B)
—	204(b)	710(c)(4)	—	207(f)	711(b)(1)(C)
32	205(b)	711(a)(1)(H)	53	207(g)	711(b)(2)
40	205(c)	711(a)(2)(J)	—	207(h)	720(c)
108	205(d)	718(f)	21	208	711(a)(1)(B)
112	205(e)	719(a)(3)	21	208	711(a)(2)(D)
112	205(e)	719(a)(4)	21	208	711(b)(1)(B)
183	205(f)	723(b)	35	209(a)	711(a)(1)(I)
17	206(a)(1)	711(a)(1)(A)	35	209(b)	711(a)(2)(K)
17	206(a)(2)	711(a)(2)(C)	—	209(c)	735(a)(1)
31	206(b)(1)	711(a)(1)(G)	—	209(c)	735(a)(2)

[Code Section Index immediately follows Act Section Index]

REVENUE ACT OF 1942 (*Cont.*)

[*Code Section Index immediately follows Act Section Index*]

REVENUE ACT OF 1942 *(Cont.)*

PAGE	Act Sec.	CODE SEC.	PAGE	Act Sec.	CODE SEC.
300	228(d)	743(a)(5)	312	230(a)	761(b)(2)
300	228(d)	743(a)(6)	312	230(a)	761(b)(3)
300	228(d)	743(a)(7)	312	230(a)	761(c)(1)
300	228(d)	743(a)(8)	312	230(a)	761(c)(2)
—	228(d)	743(b)	312	230(a)	761(c)(3)
—	229(a)(1)	752(a)	312	230(a)	761(d)(1)
307	230(a)	760(a)(1)	312	230(a)	761(d)(2)
309	230(a)	760(a)(2)	312	230(a)	761(e)
309	230(a)	760(b)	318	230(a)	761(f)
309	230(a)	760(c)	319	230(a)	761(g)(1)
311	230(a)	761(a)	319	230(a)	761(g)(2)
312	230(a)	761(b)(1)	109	230(b)(2)	719(a)(1)

REVENUE ACT OF 1941

[September 20, 1941, H. R. 5417, Public No. 250, 77th Cong., 1st Sess., ch. 412, 55 Stat. 687]

PAGE	Act Sec.	CODE SEC.	PAGE	Act Sec.	CODE SEC.
18	202(c)(1)	711(a)(1)(A)	93	203	718(a)(6)(A)
18	202(c)(1)	711(a)(2)(C)	95	203	718(a)(6)(B)
18	202(c)(2)	711(b)(1)(A)	96	203	718(a)(6)(C)
32	202(d)(1)	711(a)(1)(G)	96	203	718(a)(6)(D)
32	202(d)(2)	711(a)(2)(I)	97	203	718(a)(6)(E)
6	202(e)	710(c)(2)	99	203	718(a)(6)(F)
104	202(f)	718(c)(3)	214	204	731

EXCESS PROFITS TAX AMENDMENTS OF 1941

[March 7, 1941, H. R. 3531, Public No. 10, 77th Cong., 1st Sess., ch. 10, 55 Stat. 17]

PAGE	Act Sec.	CODE SEC.	PAGE	Act Sec.	CODE SEC.
—	2(a)	710(b)(3)	—	4(b)	713(e)(1)
—	2(b)	710(c)(1)	—	4(b)	713(e)(2)
13	2(b)	710(c)(2)	—	4(b)	713(e)(3)
		[710(c)(3)]	70	4(b)	713(f)(1)
—	3	711(b)(1)(G)	70	4(b)	713(f)(2)
47	3	711(b)(1)(H)	70	4(b)	713(f)(3)
48	3	711(b)(1)(I)	70	4(b)	713(f)(4)
50	3	711(b)(1)(J)	70	4(b)	713(f)(5)
52	3	711(b)(1)(K)	70	4(b)	713(f)(6)
—	4(a)	713(a)(1)	74	4(b)	713(f)(7)
—	4(b)	713(b)(1)	—	4(c)	713(g)
—	4(b)	713(b)(2)	—	4(d)	743(a)
—	4(b)	713(c)	119	5	721(a)(1)
—	4(b)	713(d)(1)	119	5	721(a)(2)
—	4(b)	713(d)(2)	135	5	721(a)(3)
—	4(b)	713(d)(3)	—	5	721(b)

[*Code Section Index immediately follows Act Section Index*]

EXCESS PROFITS TAX AMENDMENTS OF 1941 *(Cont.)*

[Code Section Index immediately follows Act Section Index]

SECOND REVENUE ACT OF 1940 *(Cont.)*

PAGE	Act Sec.	CODE SEC.	PAGE	Act Sec.	CODE SEC.
77	201	713(c)(3)	207	201	730(b)
		[713(g)(3)]	—	201	730(c)
79	201	713(c)(4)	208	201	730(d)
		[713(g)(4)]	210	201	730(e)(1)
80	201	715	210	201	730(e)(2)
82	201	716	210	201	730(e)(3)
82	201	717	210	201	730(e)(4)
83	201	718(a)(1)	210	201	730(e)(5)
86	201	718(a)(2)	210	201	730(e)(6)
87	201	718(a)(3)	210	201	730(f)
88	201	718(a)(4)	211	201	730(g)
91	201	718(a)(5)	212	201	730(h)
100	201	718(b)(1)	215	201	731
101	201	718(b)(2)	268	201	740(a)(1)
101	201	718(b)(3)	273	201	740(a)(1)
91	201	718(b)(4)	268	201	740(a)(2)
—	201	718(c)(1)	268	201	740(a)(3)
103	201	718(c)(2)	268	201	740(a)(4)
104	201	718(c)(3)	268	201	740(b)(1)
105	201	718(c)(4)	268	201	740(b)(2)
109	201	719(a)(1)	268	201	740(b)(3)
110	201	719(a)(2)	—	201	740(b)(4)
—	201	719(b)	268	201	740(c)
114	201	720(a)(1)	268	201	740(d)(1)
114	201	720(a)(2)	268	201	740(d)(2)
117	201	720(b)	268	201	740(e)
118	201	720(c)	268	201	740(f)
114	201	720(d)	283	201	740(g)
122	201	721	284	201	741
150	201	722	288	201	742(a)(1)
181	201	723	288	201	742(a)(2)
184	201	724(a)	—	201	742(a)(3)
185	201	724(b)	64	201	742(b)
186	201	724(c)	268	201	742(c)
186	201	725(a)	291	201	742(d)
193	201	725(b)	296	201	742(e)(1)
195	201	726(a)	268	201	742(e)(2)
195	201	726(b)	298	201	742(f)(1)
—	201	727(a)	299	201	742(f)(2)
197	201	727(b)	268	201	742(f)(3)
—	201	727(c)	268	201	742(f)(4)
198	201	727(d)	268	201	743(a)
197	201	727(e)	301	201	743(b)(1)
—	201	727(f)	301	201	743(b)(2)
—	201	727(g)	301	201	744
202	201	727(h)	302	201	750(a)
203	201	728	—	201	750(b)
203	201	729(a)	—	201	750(c)
204	201	729(c)	303	201	750(d)
205	201	729(d)(1)	304	201	751(a)
205	201	729(d)(2)	305	201	751(b)
206	201	730(a)	—	201	752(a)

[Code Section Index immediately follows Act Section Index]

REVENUE ACT OF 1918

[February 24, 1919, H. R. 12863, Public No. 254, 65th Cong.,
3d Sess., ch. 18, 40 Stat. 1057]

SEC.	PAGE	SEC.	PAGE
300	322	320(b)	330
303	322	325(a)	330
304(a)	325	325(b)	331
304(b)	325	326(a)	331
304(c)	325	326(b)	336
305	326	326(c)	336
310	326	326(d)	337
311(a)	326	327	338
311(b)	327	328(a)	342
311(c)	327	328(b)	342
311(d)	327	330	344
320(a)	329	331	347

WAR REVENUE ACT OF 1917

[October 3, 1917, H. R. 4280, Public No. 50, 65th Cong.,
1st Sess., ch. 63, 40 Stat. 300]

SEC.	PAGE	SEC.	PAGE
200	348	205(a)	353
201	348	206	358
202	349	207	359
203(a)	350	208	367
203(b)	350	209	353
203(c)	350	210	353
203(d)	351	212	368
204	352	213	369

ACT OF MARCH 3, 1917

[H. R. 2573, Public No. 377, 64th Cong., 2d Sess.,
ch. 159, 39 Stat. 1]

SEC.	PAGE	SEC.	PAGE
200	370	204	375
202	371	206	381
203	374	207	381

MISCELLANEOUS ACTS

Act of December 17, 1943

[H. R. 3363, Public No. 201, 78th Cong., 1st Sess.,
ch. 346, 57 Stat. 601]

CODE SEC.	PAGE
722(d)	176

[Code Section Index immediately follows Act Section Index]

MISCELLANEOUS ACTS *(Cont.)*

Act of October 26, 1943

[H. R. 2888, Public No. 172, 78th Cong., 1st Sess.,
ch. 279, 57 Stat. 575]

UNENACTED PROVISIONS

[The references in brackets are to code-sections under which the related
unenacted provisions are set forth.]

[*Code Section Index immediately follows Act Section Index*]

CODE SECTION INDEX

EXPLANATION OF CODE SECTION INDEX

Order of arrangement.—This index lists provisions by Code sections, and shows at a glance the derivation of any Code provision through the various acts as far back as 1917 when excess profits taxes first began. In each instance, under each Code section the related act section is set forth. As the book also contains an index by act sections, it is always possible to get promptly to the legislative history of any provision, whether the initial point of reference be the act section or Code section.

Provisions not listed.—The index does not account for all sections and subdivisions. Those not listed have been omitted because of their insignificance from the viewpoint of this book, as explained under "Guides to the Use of This Book." That explains why, for example, sec. 710(a)(1) or sec. 710(a)(2) of the Code is not listed in the index.

Listed provisions without page numbers.—Provisions without page numbers have no legislative history in the particular act and therefore have not been set forth in the book. An example of this is sec. 202 of the Revenue Act of 1942 in relation to sec. 710(a)(1)(B) of the Code.

Changes in section numbers by later amendment.—Sometimes a Code section number has been changed by amendment in a later act. Thus, Code sec. 713(c) in the 1940 Act was changed to sec. 713(g) by the Excess Profits Tax Amendments of 1941. The index is on the basis of the latest numbering, hence sec. 713(g), but in showing the derivation of sec. 713(g), the provision in the 1940 Act is listed by its original number, namely, sec. 713(c).

Difference between unit of subdivision in the index and the one in the book.—Reference in the index may be to a subdivision such as sec. 713(a)(2). In the material, that subdivision may not be set forth as such. Instead, sec. 713(a) or sec. 713 may be treated because the legislative history material in the particular instance does not lend itself to a smaller breakdown. Sec. 713(a)(2) is, of course, to be considered as part of sec. 713(a) or sec. 713, as the case may be.

Page numbers on cross-references.—While the general arrangement of the text of the book is by Code sections in their numerical order, a particular Code section may be set forth out of numerical order because its legislative history can be more conveniently treated jointly with another Code section. As explained under "Guides to the Use of This Book," where this is the case, a cross-reference appears at the point of numerical order. In the index, the page reference is to the place where the section is actually treated, and not where the cross-reference appears. Thus, Code sec. 711(a)(2)(C) is treated jointly with sec. 711(a)(1)(A) starting at page 17. A cross-reference to this effect is set forth on page 38 where sec. 711(a)(2)(C) comes up in numerical order. The page references in the index to sec. 711(a)(2)(C) are the same as for sec. 711(a)(1)(A).

CODE SECTION INDEX

ACT	SECTION	PAGE	ACT	SECTION	PAGE
	710(a)(1)(B)			**711(a)(1)(G)**	
1943	202(b)	1	1942	206(b)(1)	31
1942	202	—	1941	202(d)(1)	32
	710(a)(3)			**711(a)(1)(H)**	
1943	203(b)	2	1942	205(b)	32
1942	203(a)	—		**711(a)(1)(I)**	
	710(b)(3)		10/26/43		—
1942	204(a)	—	1943	208(d)	33
EPTA	2(b)	—	1942	209(a)	35
1940	201	4		**711(a)(1)(J)**	
	710(c)(1)		1942	210(a)	35
1942	204(b)	4		**711(a)(2)(A)**	
EPTA	2(b)	—	1942	211(a)	28
	710(c)(2)		EPTA	12(b)	29
1942	204(b)	5	1940	201	29
1941	202(e)	6	1917	206	358
	710(c)(3)		3/3/17	203	374
1945	122(b)	7		**711(a)(2)(B)**	
1945	122(d)	7	1940	201	37
1942	204(b)	10		**711(a)(2)(C)**	
EPTA	2(b)	13	1942	206(a)(2)	17
	710(c)(4)		1941	202(c)(1)	18
1942	204(b)	—	1940	201	19
	711(a)(1)(A)		1918	320	329
1942	206(a)(1)	17	1917	206	358
1941	202(c)(1)	18	3/3/17	200	370
1940	201	19		**711(a)(2)(D)**	
1918	320(a)	329	1942	207(c)	20
1918	320(b)	330	1942	208	21
1917	206	358	1940	201	22
3/3/17	200	370		**711(a)(2)(E)**	
	711(a)(1)(B)		1942	207(d)	—
1942	207(a)	20	1940	201	24
1942	208	21		**711(a)(2)(F)**	
1940	201	22	1940	201	26
	711(a)(1)(C)			**711(a)(2)(G)**	
1942	207(b)	—	1940	201	38
1940	201	24		**711(a)(2)(H)**	
	711(a)(1)(D)		1940	201	27
1940	201	26	1918	320(a)	329
	711(a)(1)(E)		1917	206	358
1940	201	27		**711(a)(2)(I)**	
1918	320(a)	329	1942	206(b)(2)	31
1917	206	358	1941	202(d)(2)	32
	711(a)(1)(F)			**711(a)(2)(J)**	
1940	201	29	1942	205(c)	40
1917	206	358			
3/3/17	203	374			

[Act Section Index immediately precedes Code Section Index]

[Act Section Index immediately precedes Code Section Index]

ACT	SECTION	PAGE	ACT	SECTION	PAGE
	713(f)(2)			**718(a)(2)** (*Cont.*)	
EPTA	4(b)	70	1918	326(a)	331
1918	311(b)-(d)	327	1917	207	359
	713(f)(3)		3/3/17	202	371
EPTA	4(b)	70		**718(a)(3)**	
1918	311(b)-(d)	327	1940	201	87
	713(f)(4)			**718(a)(4)**	
EPTA	4(b)	70	1940	201	88
1918	311(b)-(d)	327		**718(a)(5)**	
	713(f)(5)		1940	201	91
EPTA	4(b)	70		**718(a)(6)(A)**	
1918	311(b)-(d)	327	1943	121(d)(6)	93
	713(f)(6)		1941	203	93
EPTA	4(b)	70	1941	203	92
1918	311(b)-(d)	327		**718(a)(6)(B)**	
	713(f)(7)		1941	203	95
EPTA	4(b)	74	1941	203	92
	713(g)(1)			**718(a)(6)(C)**	
EPTA	4(c)	—	1941	203	96
1940	201	76	1941	203	92
	713(g)(2)			**718(a)(6)(D)**	
EPTA	4(c)	—	1941	203	96
1940	201	76	1941	203	92
	713(g)(3)			**718(a)(6)(E)**	
EPTA	4(c)	—	1941	203	97
1940	201	77	1941	203	92
	713(g)(4)			**718(a)(6)(F)**	
EPTA	4(c)	—	1941	203	99
1940	201	79	1941	203	92
	713(g)(5)			**718(a)(7)**	
1942	216	79	1942	219(a)	—
	715			**718(b)(1)**	
1940	201	80	1940	201	100
1918	325(a)	330		**718(b)(2)**	
1918	325(b)	331	1940	201	101
1917	207	359		**718(b)(3)**	
3/3/17	202	371	1940	201	101
	716			**718(b)(4)**	
1940	201	82	1940	201	91
1918	326(d)	337		**718(b)(5)**	
	717		1942	219(b)	—
1940	201	82		**718(c)(1)**	
	718(a)(1)		1940	201	—
1940	201	83		**718(c)(2)**	
1918	325(b)	331	1940	201	103
1918	326(a)	331		**718(c)(3)**	
1917	207	359	1941	202(f)	104
3/3/17	202	371	1940	201	104
	718(a)(2)			**718(c)(4)**	
1942	218	84	1940	201	105
1940	201	86	1918	330	344
1918	325(b)	331			

[Act Section Index immediately precedes Code Section Index]

[*Act Section Index immediately precedes Code Section Index*]

[Act Section Index immediately precedes Code Section Index]

[Act Section Index immediately precedes Code Section Index]

ACT	SECTION	PAGE	ACT	SECTION	PAGE
	735(a)(8) *(Cont.)*			**740(a)(4)** *(Cont.)*	
1942	209(c)	—	1940	201	268
	735(a)(9)			**740(b)(1)**	
1942	209(c)	242	1942	228(a)	—
			1940	201	268
	735(a)(10)			**740(b)(2)**	
1942	209(c)	243	1942	228(a)	—
	735(a)(11)		1940	201	268
1942	209(c)	244		**740(b)(3)**	
	735(a)(12)		1942	228(a)	—
1943	208(b)(3)	244	1940	201	268
1942	209(c)	245		**740(b)(4)**	
	735(b)(1)		1942	228(a)	—
1942	209(c)	246	1940	201	268
	735(b)(2)			**740(b)(5)**	
1942	209(c)	250	1942	228(a)	—
	735(b)(3)		EPTA	8(b)	271
1942	209(c)	251	1940	201	268
	735(b)(4)			**740(c)**	
1943	208(c)	252	1942	228(a)	275
	735(b)(5)		1940	201	268
1943	208(c)	254		**740(d)**	
	735(c)(1)		1942	228(a)	281
10/26/43		256	1940	201	268
1942	209(c)	258		**740(e)**	
	735(c)(2)		1942	228(a)	281
10/26/43		256	1940	201	268
1942	209(c)	258		**740(f)**	
	735(d)		1942	228(a)	282
1942	209(c)	259	1940	201	268
	736(a)			**740(g)**	
1942	222(d)	260	1942	228(a)	—
	736(b)		1940	201	283
1942	222(d)	264	1940	201	268
	736(c)			**740(h)**	
1942	222(d)	267	1942	228(a)	—
	740(a)(1)		EPTA	8(c)	271
1942	228(a)	—	1940	201	268
EPTA	8(a)	271		**741(a)**	
1940	201	273	1942	228(b)	284
1940	201	268	EPTA	14	55
1918	330	344	1940	201	284
1918	331	347	1940	201	268
1917	204	352	1917	203	58
	740(a)(2)			**742(a)**	
1942	228(a)	—	1942	228(c)	285
1940	201	268	EPTA	15	287
	740(a)(3)		1940	201	288
1942	228(a)	—	1940	201	268
1940	201	268	1918	311(d)	327
	740(a)(4)		1917	204	352
1942	228(a)	—		**742(b)(1)**	
			1942	228(c)	290

[Act Section Index immediately precedes Code Section Index]

ACT	SECTION	PAGE	ACT	SECTION	PAGE
	742(b)(1) *(Cont.)*			**743(a)(4)**	
1940	201	64	1942	228(d)	300
1940	201	268	1940	201	268
	742(b)(2)			**743(a)(5)**	
1942	228(c)	290	1942	228(d)	300
1940	201	64	1940	201	268
1940	201	268		**743(a)(6)**	
	742(c)		1942	228(d)	300
1942	228(c)	—	1940	201	268
1940	201	268		**743(a)(7)**	
	742(d)		1942	228(d)	300
1942	228(c)	291	1940	201	268
1940	201	291		**743(a)(8)**	
1940	201	268	1942	228(d)	300
	742(e)(1)		1940	201	268
1942	228(c)	293		**743(b)(1)**	
1940	201	296	1942	228(d)	—
1940	201	268	1940	201	301
	742(e)(2)		1940	201	268
1942	228(c)	293		**743(b)(2)**	
1940	201	268	1940	201	301
	742(e)(3)		1940	201	268
1942	228(c)	293		**744**	
1940	201	268	1940	201	301
	742(e)(4)		1940	201	268
1942	228(c)	—		**750(a)**	
1940	201	268	1940	201	302
	742(f)(1)			**750(b)**	
1942	228(c)	296	1940	201	—
1940	201	298		**750(c)**	
1940	201	268	1940	201	—
	742(f)(2)			**750(d)**	
1942	228(c)	—	1940	201	303
1940	201	299		**751(a)**	
1940	201	268	1940	201	304
	742(g)		1918	330	344
1942	228(c)	—	1918	331	347
EPTA	8(d)	299	1917	204	352
	742(h)(1)			**751(b)**	
1942	228(c)	300	1940	201	305
	742(h)(2)			**752(a)**	
1942	228(c)	300	1942	229(a)(1)	—
	743(a)(1)		1940	201	—
1942	228(d)	300		**760(a)(1)**	
EPTA	4(d)	—	1942	230(a)	307
1940	201	268		**760(a)(2)**	
	743(a)(2)		1942	230(a)	309
1942	228(d)	300	1918	330	344
1940	201	268	1918	331	347
	743(a)(3)		1917	204	352
1942	228(d)	300		**760(b)**	
1940	201	268	1942	230(a)	309

[Act Section Index immediately precedes Code Section Index]

ACT	SECTION	PAGE	ACT	SECTION	PAGE
	760(b) *(Cont.)*			761(c)(2)	
1918	330	344	1942	230(a)	312
1918	331	347	1918	330	344
1917	204	352	1918	331	347
	760(c)		1917	204	352
1942	230(a)	309		761(c)(3)	
1918	330	344	1942	230(a)	312
1918	331	347	1918	330	344
1917	204	352	1918	331	347
	761(a)		1917	204	352
1942	230(a)	311		761(d)(1)	
	761(b)(1)		1942	230(a)	312
1942	230(a)	312	1918	330	344
1918	330	344	1918	331	347
1918	331	347	1917	204	352
1917	204	352		761(d)(2)	
	761(b)(2)		1942	230(a)	312
1942	230(a)	312		761(e)	
1918	330	344	1942	230(a)	312
1918	331	347	1918	330	344
1917	204	352	1918	331	347
	761(b)(3)		1917	204	352
1942	230(a)	312		761(f)	
1918	330	344	1942	230(a)	318
1918	331	347	1918	330	344
1917	204	352	1918	331	347
	761(c)(1)		1917	204	352
1942	230(a)	312		761(g)(1)	
1918	330	344	1942	230(a)	319
1918	331	347		761(g)(2)	
1917	204	352	1942	230(a)	319

UNENACTED PROVISIONS

		PAGE
Sec. 710(c)(3)(C)	— sec. 120½ of 1943 Senate bill	15
Sec. 711(a)(1)(G)	— sec. 201 of 1940 Senate bill	49
Sec. 711(a)(1)(I)	— sec. 201 of 1940 Senate bill	133
Sec. 711(b)(1)(H)	— sec. 201 of 1940 Senate bill	49
Sec. 711(b)(1)(J)	— sec. 201 of 1940 Senate bill	43
Sec. 718(d)	— sec. 201 of 1940 Ways and Means Committee bill	90
Sec. 721(a)(1)	— sec. 213(c) of 1942 Ways and Means Committee bill	133
Sec. 721(b)	— sec. 201 of 1940 Senate Finance Committee bill	16
Sec. 721(c)(1)	— sec. 201 of 1940 Senate Finance Committee bill	7
Sec. 721(c)(2)	— sec. 201 of 1940 Senate Finance Committee bill	16
Sec. 722(d)	— sec. 213(a) of 1942 Ways and Means Committee bill	155
Sec. 722(e)	— sec. 213(a) of 1942 Ways and Means Committee bill	155
Sec. 742(a)	— sec. 13 of 1941 E.P.T.A. House bill	289
Sec. 743	— sec. 216(a) of 1942 Ways and Means Committee bill	302
Sec. 752	— sec. 201 of 1940 Ways and Means Committee bill	306
Sec. 753	— sec. 201 of 1940 Ways and Means Committee bill	306

[Act Section Index immediately precedes Code Section Index]

SUBJECT INDEX

SUBJECT INDEX

A

B

C

[Code Section Index immediately precedes Subject Index]

[Code Section Index immediately precedes Subject Index]

CODE SEC.

[Code Section Index immediately precedes Subject Index]

[*Code Section Index immediately precedes Subject Index*]

[Code Section Index immediately precedes Subject Index]

[*Code Section Index immediately precedes Subject Index*]